Songs of the Troubadours and Trouvères

GARLAND REFERENCE LIBRARY OF THE HUMANITIES
VOLUME 1740

Songs of the Troubadours and Trouvères

An Anthology of Poems and Melodies

Edited by
Samuel N. Rosenberg
Margaret Switten
Gérard Le Vot

Garland Publishing, Inc.
A member of the Taylor & Francis Group
New York and London
1998

Library of Congress Cataloging-in-Publication Data

Songs of the troubadours and trouvères : an anthology of poems and melodies /
    edited by Samuel N. Rosenberg, Margaret Switten, and Gérard Le Vot.
        p.   cm. — (Garland reference library of the humanities ; vol.
1740)
    Texts in Old French, with critical matter in English.
    Includes bibliographical references and index.
    ISBN 0-8153-1341-1 (alk. paper)
    1. French poetry—To 1500.   2. Songs, Old French.   I. Rosenberg,
Samuel N.   II. Switten, Margaret Louise.   III. Le Vot, Gérard.   IV. Series.
PQ1322.S66   1998
841'.108—dc21   97–14045
                                      CIP

Cover art: Thibaut de Champagne, "Dame, ciz votre fins amis" (Cliché,
    Bibliothèque Nationale de France, Paris, fr. 846, folio 32 verso detail).

Printed on acid-free, 250-year-life paper
Manufactured in the United States of America

CONTENTS

TROUBADOURS

---

* Incipits that are shown in italics are either refrains or, in the case of Marcabru, in Latin. Occitan incipits are followed by their Pillet-Carstens number and French by their number in Linker (see References). A black dot (•) indicates that the text is printed with music. The abbreviation CD means that the song is performed on the compact disc that accompanies the Anthology.

TROUVÈRES

Anonymous Songs

Ascribed Songs

LIST OF ILLUSTRATIONS*

---

* Incipits are cited here as they occur in the edited texts and not necessarily as they appear in the captions accompanying the illustrations. In the latter case, all incipits visible in the manuscript illustrations are cited as they appear in those illustrations.

ACKNOWLEDGMENTS

Our undertaking had the benefit of help from numerous sources.

We are pleased to express our gratitude to Mount Holyoke College for research funds in support of the preparation of troubadour materials and the compact disc recording that accompanies our book; to Claire Benoit, typist-formatter, and Teena Johnson-Smith, Mount Holyoke Academic Computing Consultant, for their work on the troubadour texts; and to Zsofia Zvolensky, MHC '97, for assistance in preparing the final copy of the troubadour melodies.

We are grateful as well to Indiana University for ongoing material and moral support; and to Jeannette Brown, who turned typing into the pages of a book.

Deep appreciation goes, too, to Jeffrey S. Ankrom for all his patient encouragement and advice.

We express our thanks to Peter Becker, baritone, and to Robert Eisenstein, medieval fiddle, for bringing their expertise to the production of the Compact Disc, and to the Folger Shakespeare Library, Washington, D.C.

Manuscript illustrations are reproduced with the permission of the Bibliothèque Nationale de France, Paris; the Biblioteca Ambrosiana, Milan; and the Pierpont Morgan Library, New York; we are indebted to these libraries for their cooperation.

Credit is given for troubadour texts reprinted from the following recent editions: Gerald A. Bond, *The Poetry of William VII, Count of Poitiers, IX Duke of Aquitaine,* New York: Garland, ©1982; *The Songs of Jaufré Rudel,* ed. Rupert T. Pickens, pp. 100-102, by permission of the publisher, ©1978 by the Pontifical Institute of Mediaeval Studies, Toronto; *The Life and Works of the Troubadour Raimbaut d'Orange* by Walter D. Pattison, ©1952 by The University of Minnesota, renewed 1980; *Peire d'Alvernha: Liriche; testo, traduzione, e note,* a cura di Alberto del Monte, © 1955 by Loescher-Chiantore; *Arnaut Daniel: Canzoni,* ed. Gianluigi Toja, ©1960 by G.C. Sansoni; *Peire Vidal. Poesie,* ed. D'Arco Silvio Avalle, ©1960 by Riccardo Ricciardi, Editore; Margaret Switten, *The* Cansos *of Raimon de Miraval,* ©1985 by The Medieval Academy of America; *Les Poèmes de Gaucelm Faidit* par Jean Mouzat, ©1965 by Librairie A.G. Nizet; Peirol, *Troubadour of Auvergne,* ed. S.C. Aston, ©1953 by Cambridge University Press; *Introduction à l'étude de l'ancien provençal,* ed. Frank Hamlin, Peter Ricketts, and John Hathaway, ©1967 by Librairie Droz S.A.; *The Poems of the Troubadour Raimbaut de Vaqueiras,* ed. Joseph Linskill, ©1964 by Mouton de Gruyter; *Poésies complètes du Troubadour Peire Cardenal,* ed. René Lavaud, ©1957 by Editions Privat; *Guiraut Riquier, Las Cansos* by Ulrich Mölk, ©1962 by Universitätsverlag C. Winter.

INTRODUCTION

Samuel N. Rosenberg

Two linked repertories constitute the vernacular lyric heritage of medieval France: the work of the *troubadours* and that of the *trouvères*. These creators had in common, above all, an idea of lyric that necessarily brought words and melody together in a single vocal construct. For them, the modern notion of lyricism as a type of affective personal expression, probing the inner life and meditating on one's private response to the world, whose "music" is verbal and whose essence may be experienced as readily in silent reading as in declamation was probably not conceivable; it is in any case a creative principle that was profoundly foreign to their art. They produced *songs,* stanzaic compositions set to melodies for solo voice and intended for performance. Their works were remarkably varied in substance, in diction, in prosodic and musical style, even if their range of topic and reference was more limited than that of today's poets.

The activity of the troubadours and trouvères spanned the 12th and 13th centuries, after which that of the troubadours, for reasons political and cultural, lost its vitality, while, for the others, lyricism took on new forms and tended in different directions. Two great movements, first discernible in the last third or so of the 13th century, assumed resounding importance thereafter. One was the development of vernacular polyphony—its foremost expression being the motet—alongside traditionally monophonic composition. The other was the rise of poets exercising their craft in language alone, showing no inevitable concern with music. Such changes and others brought the period of the troubadours and trouvères to an end at the dawn of the 14th century.

If the two repertories are alike in their understanding of lyric, they are most obviously dissimilar in their choice of language. France in the Middle Ages did not yet have a standard, codified language. The country was by and large divided linguistically into a northern region which spoke a range of neo-Latin dialects collectively known as *langue d'oïl,* or Old French, and a southern region whose dialects, also stemming from Latin, formed a cluster called *langue d'oc,* normally referred to today as Old Provençal or, increasingly, Old Occitan. Since the time of the troubadours, Occitan has gradually been eclipsed by French as the tongue of the south, a change of fortune which makes the poetry today a displaced artifact on its native soil. Arising earlier than the lyric of the trouvères and rapidly establishing itself as a potent cultural phenomenon, however, the art of the troubadours served for a long while as a model for the north, and thus incorporated itself into the body of French lyric poetry with vital consequences outlasting the language itself.

The trouvères, at least insofar as we know them, did not appear until some six or seven decades after the activity of William (Guilhem) IX, duke of Aquitaine, the first known troubadour. In the intervening years, the artists of the south had time to make considerable progress in developing—partly from contemporary Latin inspiration, whether liturgical, secular, or both, and partly from Hispano-Arabic; partly, too, under the influence of the feudal social and political realities of their lives—a musical syntax, techniques of versification, and poetic motifs and registers that would eventually prove alluring and instructive to their counterparts in the north. Their example reached into other lands as well, both influencing the course of poetry in German, Italian, and other languages, and leading a number of foreign poet-composers, especially Italian and Catalan, to become Occitan-writing troubadours themselves. For Dante, notably in his *De vulgari eloquentia,* troubadour lyric was a very model of poetic achievement.

Of the various lyric genres that they developed, the troubadours gave overriding emphasis to one in particular, the *canso,* closely related to the earlier but enduring *vers.* This was defined, loosely, both by its form and by its exploration of the remarkable conceptual edifice known as *fin'amor,* "perfect" or "refined" love, which would largely structure the thematics of west European poetry for centuries to come. The ripening of troubadour traditions was hardly complete, of course, at the advent of the trouvères, and the maturation continued, with influences that were not exclusively northward bound, through the subsequent years.

The art of the troubadours bespoke above all an aristocratic culture bent upon the heightening of sentiment and taste, with an especial interest in the poetic contemplation, sometimes highly eroticized, of amorous desire. It was anchored in courtliness and tended toward the virtuosic; it was also thoroughly male in point of view, but in a way that, allowing hierarchical position primacy over gender, could accommodate the presence of some women among the creators. The art of the troubadours constituted itself in the service of an ideal of refinement, enthusiasm for which was signaled as much by broadly ranging experimentation with form as it was by the celebration of disciplined exuberance and joy.

All the poetry was not love poetry by any means. There were political songs and *pastorelas,* debate songs, dance tunes, and death laments, religious pieces and invective as well, lyrics that contained narrative and others that veered toward dramatic dialogue—an array of types variously identified by structure or substance or both, and marked off from one another by porous partitions. Lyric genres came to be established and recognized only gradually, and they never did harden into mutually exclusive categories. There was room for an abundance of poetic concerns, expressed in a flow of diverse forms.

But the heart of the corpus throbbed with love longing and the cultivation of the loving self. So central to the esthetic enterprise was this subject that love and song, loving and singing, came to be seen as inseparable, each being the necessary condition of the other. Self-consciousness marked the poetry no less than the poets, and both functioned in an essentially public realm, so that texts and even melodies could refer to themselves and engage with others in a discourse of intertextuality, and the subjectivity of the writer, for all its irreducible centrality, was significantly abstracted from the intimacies of individual experience. (If such generic subjectivity sounds foreign to us, it is only because, tricked by conventional vocabulary, we tend unwittingly to associate the lyric poetry of the troubadours with the lyric poetry of modern times—and to forget that even in the latter there is a difference between writer and poetic persona. It is more enlightening to think in terms of today's ordinary popular love songs, in whose first-person texts there is of course little question of expecting to hear the particular feelings or experiences or biographical details of either the lyricist or the singer.)

This is the repertory that captivated the first trouvères and that, through a century and a half of co-existence with the troubadours, with whatever reshaping and evolving took place, set the principal tone for the songs produced in the north. From their southern predecessors and contemporaries, the trouvères borrowed their noblest form, the *grand chant courtois,* or *chanson d'amour* —the *canso* in French garb—along with the network of motifs that undergirt it: love "service," morally uplifting and socially beneficial, rendered in hope of the "reward" of "joy" conferred by the finally "merciful" belovèd, who might well be, but not necessarily, a social superior and in either case, whether (tacitly) reciprocating the poet-lover's feelings or not, found herself, for all her anonymity, as vulnerable as he to the machinations of insincere rival lovers, "flatterers," or malicious gossips. The troubadours gave rather more attention to the "jealous" authority figure than the trouvères did, and their delight in the sensual, even in carnality, like their devotion to "youth" as a generosity of spirit informing true courtliness, found only faint echo in the somewhat more staid *chansons* of the north; similarly, though the trouvères were keenly interested in the intricacies of formal variation, they did not attempt to emulate the troubadours' extraordinary technical achievements. The compositions of both groups were elaborated within conventions of form and content, but the boundaries, soft and yielding, permit-

ted to a remarkable degree rhetorical originality, distinctiveness in style, and even occasional glimpses of an individual life. There was, in fact, one frequent feature of the *canso* that invited a touch that was personal: the *tornada,* an abridged stanza sealing the piece with a final reprise and despatching it to its audience; the French turned this into their *envoi.*

Along with the *canso,* the trouvères adopted other Occitan genres—the *descort,* for example, the *sirventes,* the *pastorela,* several debate types. Still others they mainly left behind, such as the *alba* and the *planh* (even if we do find a few striking examples of similar compositions by trouvères). In two instances, genres created in the south came to be more widely cultivated in the north: the model of the *pastorela* thus led to a profusion of *pastourelles* and the *joc-partit* became, as the *jeu-parti,* a favorite game of 13th-century French urban poets. The *sotte chanson* was invented as a parodic counterpoint to the courtly *grand chant.*

The people of the langue d'oc must have known songs of a more folkloric variety than the aristocratic types which chiefly fill the troubadour repertory. The evidence of their existence is poor, however, in the surviving sources, and it is notable that the few dozen works attributable to female composers, the *trobairitz,* belong far more, in the poetic conventions that they observe, to the largely male-focused seignorial court than to a humbler world that so often, elsewhere in western Europe, provides the traditional locus of women's songs. For whatever reason, large segments of what was surely the broad gamut of Occitan song were not selected by medieval copyists for written transmission or were afforded only scanty representation.

The trouvère repertory is much more extensive in this regard, encompassing not only the various genres adopted from the troubadours but non-aristocratic lyric types deriving from the region of the langue d'oïl itself. Indeed, these indigenous genres—defined, like the others, at least as much by content as by form—give the northern corpus a seemingly folkloric cast, not only by the relative abundance of their representation in the manuscript sources but also through their impact on the poetry of troubadour inspiration. Refrains, for example, the one- or two-line ditties with which trouvères recurrently punctuated countless pieces of the indigenous variety, came to be integrated into many of their derivatives of the *canso.* This is one index among others of a readiness on the part of the trouvères— increasing as time went on—to blend genres, to juxtapose different stylistic or lexical registers within a given composition, to bring elements of the courtly into works of native provenance and elements of folksong into the high style of the *grand chant.* Similar generic mixing occurred among the troubadours, though without the same combinations of elements.

Local traditions in the north contributed such genres as the ballad-like *chanson de toile,* dance songs ranging from the *ballette* to the early rondeau, the *reverdie,* and so on. What is particularly striking about most of these indigenous categories is the prominent position that they give to the female voice. If the troubadour corpus contains a score or two of pieces traceable to real women poets (and these, singing in a voice of aristocratic strength) while the trouvère materials include very few that may be so identified with a reasonable level of certainty, the countervailing fact is that the French repertory, mainly in that part of it which derives from northern, non-courtly sources, gives a resonant role to women. The motif—and point of view—of the *mal mariée* is appreciably well represented, which is true too of the maiden eager for love, the woman unhappily parted, perhaps by the exigencies of a crusade, from her lover, or the now-forgotten woman who regrets her past resistance to a suitor. The *chanson de toile* offers, moreover, a whole genre, neatly defined both by verse form and by a content mixing narrative and dialogue, that centers desire in the female and objectifies the male belovèd. There is no way of knowing whether any woman actually composed these songs, but their existence gives to trouvère lyric a kind of breadth not readily discerned in the Occitan repertory.

It is interesting that the northern compositions created within native traditions tend to be anonymous, while those that emulate the more aristocratic patterns of the troubadours are more likely to be ascribed to named persons. Works deemed to belong to a high style no doubt traveled more easily with authorial tags than those judged to be of a more popular order. It comes as no surprise, then, that for poetic repertories roughly equal in size we know the names of some 450 troubadours but scarcely more than half that number of trouvères. Many of the troubadours are, furthermore, clearly individuated in their manuscripts by iconographic portraits and, more tellingly, by biographical sketches in prose, the so-called *vidas,* and by commentaries on specific poems, the so-called *razos.* It is true that the portraits hardly offer photographic likenesses and that there is a good measure of fantasy in the prose passages, but historical facts can still be gleaned from them and, above all, they ringingly affirm the reality of the individual troubadour. Such interest in the trouvères was almost nonexistent.

From various historical sources, however, it is possible to piece together a picture of the poet-composers of langue d'oïl as well as those of langue d'oc. It is, to be sure, a picture that is extremely uneven, since there are many names to which no biographical data can be attached and there are countless facts that are either questionable or altogether missing. It is clear that throughout the 12th and 13th centuries, men of the highest nobility participated in the lyric endeavor, from William IX in the south through Thibaut, count of Champagne and king of Navarre, to Henri III, duke of Brabant, among the trouvères. They were flanked by many others well situated in courtly society, from such troubadours as Jaufre Rudel, prince of Blaye, and Raimbaut, lord of Orange (Aurenga), to the great baron Conon de Béthune and the Châtelain de Coucy in the north; and the aristocratic stamp they gave to the poetry of their age was evident—sometimes in a spirit of rejection, as in Marcabru—even in the work of the numerous troubadours and trouvères who came from humbler stations in life. Indeed, the troubadour Cercamon was an itinerant entertainer, as was, at a later date, the jongleur-trouvère Colin Muset; Bernart de Ventadorn, perhaps the greatest and most refined of the troubadours, seems to have been born to a castle servant. In both languages, there were clerics who composed—the Monk (Monge) of Montaudon in Occitan, for example, and Moniot d'Arras in French. Unlike the troubadours, the ranks of the trouvères included some who were important writers in areas other than lyric poetry. The first known French lyrics, in fact, are attributed to Chrétien de Troyes, the towering figure of Old French romance; Guiot de Provins, Philippe de Remy, and the dramatist Adam de la Halle are others better known for their non-lyric writings than for their songs.

The activity of the troubadours moved through the greater and lesser courts of the entire south, from Poitiers and Aquitaine through the Limousin and Auvergne, across to Toulouse and Carcassonne, then along the Mediterranean coast and everywhere in Provence, down to Marseille and well beyond. Overs the years, the troubadours demonstrated, both in explicit pronouncements and in creative application, a deep concern with level of poetic style. They came to distinguish three manners in particular: *trobar clus,* a "closed," hermetic kind of writing, accessible only to a limited audience; *trobar leu,* a "light" and easy style, readily understood by a broad public; and *trobar ric,* which emphasized "rich" verbal play and delighted in the challenges of rhyme. *Trobar clus,* developed by Marcabru, did not outlive Raimbaut d'Aurenga, so that from the end of the 12th century, *trobar leu* was the undisputed norm, while *trobar ric,* whose greatest exponent had been Arnaut Daniel (d. 1200), endured as a secondary style.

The first generation of trouvères sprang up in Champagne, encouraged by the feudal powers of that region. They were court-centered, like their southern models, and they wrote almost entirely in the Occitan manner. With the turn of the century, however, came the introduction of indigenous elements into their work. This generic enlargement was accompanied both by a move outward from Champagne and by a social spread from castles to urban settings, notably in Picardy and the Artois. While it is clear that the trouvères, like the troubadours, had from the first maintained ties among themselves—indeed, artistically significant reciprocal relations—it was only with the development of their creativity in Arras and similar towns that the organization of musico-literary confraternities, the so-called *puys,* took place; thus, to the patronage of aristocrats and local gentry, some of whom were trouvères themselves, was added the sponsorship of collegial groups, along with the perhaps inevitable growth of artistic competitions. The ranks of the trouvères underwent a certain embourgeoisement; the ground was right for the flourishing of such a genre as the *jeu-parti*; and the courtly spirit of the *grand chant* was bound to start drifting from present reality toward remembrance. This evolution was helped along by the growing piety of the age, which found expression in the abundant production of non-liturgical religious lyrics, *chansons pieuses,* chiefly devoted to extolling the virtues of the Virgin Mary, often in terms—and usually with melodies—borrowed from courtly song. In the latter part of the 13th century, polyphony began to expand into the realm of vernacular composition, notably with the *rondeaux* of Adam de la Halle, and with the first secular *motets.*

Only a small portion—but how small, we shall never know—of the lyric production of the troubadours and trouvères has come down to us from the Middle Ages, most of it in the form of extensive handwritten songbooks, or *chansonniers,* and some in various other manuscripts. There are some fifty *chansonniers,* divided fairly evenly between the two traditions, with two that contain both Occitan and French compositions. They vary considerably in material quality, as they do in content, arrangement of content, matching of texts with melodies, acknowledgment of authorship, geographic provenance, and date of compilation. Only four of the troubadour anthologies transmit their texts with music, and then not consistently, while music is far more present than absent in the trouvère songbooks. Thus, while we have a troubadour repertory of over 2500 texts but hardly more than 250 complete songs, we find a trouvère repertory of about 2200 poems, about two-thirds of which are accompanied by music.

In both cases, there is a significant gap between the opening of the era of lyric composition—end of the 11th century for the troubadours, last third of the 12th century for their French counterparts—and the beginning of the period to which we trace the manuscripts that bring us the songs in written form. The trouvère *chansonniers* stem largely from the years between the late 13th century and the mid-to-late 14th. The Occitan anthologies show an even greater distance between composition and writing down, for their production started not much earlier than the others and continued beyond them. In other words, an immense part of the lyric repertory, especially that of the troubadours, is known to us in a form separated by many decades from the time of its creation and no doubt reshaped, rearranged, recomposed to a greater or lesser extent in the course of time through the interventions of successive performers and copyists.

That songs were composed and performed outside the framework of the troubadour/trouvère repertory as preserved in the various *chansonniers* is beyond question. The very fact that a whole strain of indigenous lyric material in the north has only the faintest counterpart in the south points persuasively to the selectivity of late medieval songbook compilers. Some pieces, moreover, we find quoted or alluded to in 13th-century verse romances that were obviously songs, yet were not included in the great anthologies; some others, particularly of Anglo-Norman origin, came to be recorded in writing, but outside of a cohesive lyric context. Most striking, however, is the case of the Arthurian *lais,* occurring as lyric moments in the narrative action of, most notably, the *Prose Tristan*; these pieces actually constitute a whole genre unrepresented in the *chansonniers.* It should be understood, then, that the boundaries of the Occitan and French lyric corpora are somewhat indistinct and subject to differences of perception.

Instability of text and melody was an inevitable result of the vagaries of song circulation, the unpredictabilities of oral and written transmission in an age largely illiterate and utterly ignorant of sound-recording possibilities, and the deliberate or accidental revisions of jongleurs and scribes. It shows up continually in the innumerable instances of multiple redactions of a given song, where variation is to some degree always present and often so considerable as to entail completely different melodies or the substitution of entire stanzas. Such *mouvance,* to use the evocative term coined by Paul Zumthor (1972), means that the compositions we find in our manuscript sources can never be regarded as wholly authentic, in the sense of flowing directly from their putative originators, or reflective of their full authorial intentions. A given manuscript version of a particular song represents not an original, not a standard, but one moment in the evolving life of the piece, a stage which may be close to the creator's design or quite far from it. Once again, it is helpful to recall the case of modern popular songs, which despite the brakes of a system of reproduction and distribution promoting authenticity, come to audiences in numerous "arrangements." Even closer to the medieval reality is the state of folksongs, whose written or performed versions show wide variation.

If the chronological gap between composition and manuscript recording is greater for the troubadours than for the trouvères, another divide distinguishes the two groups even more strikingly. This is geographic, which is also to say linguistic. The French songbooks, despite certain dialectal differences, were compiled in the land where French was spoken, by scribes who shared the language of their texts. Only a small number of the Occitan collections, on the other hand, and none of the early ones, were assembled in the land of the troubadours; by and large, they are of Italian origin and, to some extent, Catalan and French. It is true that Occitan served as a poetic medium for a number of Italian and other non-Occitan lyricists in the troubadour tradition—a crossing of language borders that had no parallel among the trouvères—but the extent of the foreign role in the manuscript transmission of the corpus in general is still remarkable. (The absence of troubadour-like lyric in Italy, whose native poetic tradition was essentially verbal, no doubt helps to explain why Italian manuscripts of Occitan compositions tend to exclude music.) In space as in time, the songs we have may be far removed from those brought forth by their creators.

It follows from these considerations that, in presenting a particular composition that has been preserved in more than one redaction, it is reasonable, and respectful of the medieval sources, to select as satisfactory a version as we can find and print it with only a minimum of emendations. These should normally be limited to the correction of obvious scribal errors or omissions, with the help of variants in other manuscripts, and should not attempt to "restore" some elusive "original" text through the patching together of divergent readings. Similarly, there should normally be no attempt to bring the often inconsistent spellings of Old Occitan or Old French into line with a modern idea of orthography.

The compositions included in our Anthology are presented as the foregoing considerations dictate. The troubadour and trouvère melodies were all newly edited from the manuscripts by Gérard Le Vot, with final copy of the troubadour transcriptions prepared by Margaret Switten; the trouvère texts were prepared by Samuel N. Rosenberg, and the troubadour texts were assembled by Margaret Switten from standard printed editions as indicated for each text.

The source manuscripts, located above all in French and Italian libraries, are usually referred to by conventional sigla; the sigla used in the pages of this Anthology are furnished in the References. Complete lists of the manuscripts appear in a number of published works; see *New Grove* 1980 (s.v. "Sources" III and V) or, for the troubadours, Pillet-Carstens 1933; for the trouvères, Spanke 1955, Linker 1979, or Rosenberg-Tischler 1981 or 1995. Description and discussion of the manuscripts may be found above all, for the troubadours, in Marshall 1975, van der Werf 1984, Paden *Handbook* 1995, Aubrey 1996; for the trouvères, in Schwan 1886, Karp 1964, Parker 1978, Huot 1987; a number of sources are also described and illustrated in Wilkins 1988.

The Anthology offers a broad view of the lyric heritage described in the preceding pages. It is intended for readers and singers interested in a thorough initiation into a world of poetry and music that is increasingly attractive to our historically minded contemporaries but difficult to explore without guidance. As our introductory essays and bibliography make clear, there is no dearth of published editions of troubadour and trouvère materials and no lack of scholarly studies. These works are widely scattered, however, of uneven scope, and often highly specialized philologically or musicologically. We believe that our presentation strikes a suitable balance between the two components of medieval lyric and offers a picture of that

unitary art that takes full account of ongoing scholarly research. We hope that *Songs of the Troubadours and Trouvères* offers its basic repertory in a manner illuminating to users in a broad range of disciplines. It is meant to be self-contained yet at the same time encouraging of further study.

The compact disc that comes as an adjunct to the book is intended to give an immediate sonic reality to the repeated claim that we are concerned in this Anthology with a vocal experience as well as a visual one. It offers a number of troubadour and trouvère compositions performed—some with and some without instruments—in the versions printed here. (See Discography for relevant data.)

Two essays follow this general orientation to the subject. The first, by Gérard Le Vot, treats the problems of transmission and interpretation of the music. It is a discussion colored by the belief that, apart from largely formal convergences, the melodies are independent of the texts that they support. The other, by Margaret Switten, takes a different, integrative point of view, explaining, with model analyses of particular pieces, the ways in which words and melody may work together in the construction of song. It is clear that the several parts of this joint introduction will be seen as occasionally overlapping or at variance with one another in interpretation of the material. This is only to be expected in an area where there are still more questions than answers and it nicely suggests the reality of scholarly debate.

The division of the Anthology into troubadour and trouvère sections roughly reflects the dimensions and the formal and thematic variety of the two repertories. The half devoted to Occitan is, thanks to the manuscripts' generosity of attribution, organized entirely according to authorship. The French songs, on the other hand, are divided into a series of anonymous pieces grouped by genre and then a series of ascribed compositions grouped by trouvère. The Occitan and French poet-composers are presented in a sequence approximately chronological. In both instances, music is more prominent in this collection than it is in the manuscript sources, especially in the case of the troubadours.

Each subsection opens with a brief introduction to its subject, whether troubadour/trouvère or lyric genre; the Occitan material was prepared by Margaret Switten, the French by Samuel N. Rosenberg. In the case of the troubadours, it may include a *vida* or *razo,* and in all instances the introductory statement concludes with basic bibliographical references: major critical editions and/or studies. What follows is a set of remarks on the individual pieces belonging to the subsection. Each set begins with the incipit of the song and the song's identification number in the standard lyric bibliographies. The Occitan pieces are identified by PC number (for Pillet-Carstens 1933), the French pieces, as applicable, by L number (for Linker 1979), RS (Spanke 1955), MW (Mölk-Wolfzettel 1972), and/or, in the case of refrains or rondeaux, B (for Boogaard 1969); the Arthurian lais, not normally associated with the trouvère repertory, are not listed in these bibliographies.

The identifying paragraph goes on to indicate sources. In the case of an Occitan composition, we identify the manuscripts (together with folio numbers) and the provenance of the melody if there is one, and name the printed source of our text.

In the case of a French work, we give, first, the manuscript providing the base of our text; then, as applicable, the sigla of manuscripts containing other redactions. This is followed by an indication of the presence or absence of music in the sources. In almost every instance, a quite similar text occurs in Rosenberg-Tischler 1981 and 1995, where it is accompanied by a full critical apparatus; the page references are signaled by the abbreviation RT. Finally, there is a list of other principal editions of the text and/or melody.

In both cases, Occitan and French, the phrase "Performed on Anthology CD" indicates the inclusion of the work on the compact disc that accompanies the Anthology.

The paragraphs that follow include, as appropriate, comments on dialectal features of the poem, historical or literary background, individual lines requiring elucidation, musical matters, and so on. Troubadour commentary was prepared by Margaret Switten, taking into account the musicological observations of Gérard Le Vot; trouvère commentary, written by Samuel N. Rosenberg, concludes with Gérard Le Vot's musicological remarks. The clearly different approaches to words and music taken in the two sets of commentary reflect, of course, the differences expressed in the two essays that follow this Introduction.

After the preliminary material, we present the work or works that the subsection comprises. If there is music, it comes first, with the initial stanza of the poem underlaid. When a song has been preserved with more than one melody, we normally furnish only one. On occasion, however, for the purpose of useful comparison, we offer two or more.

Following is the entire poem, with initial stanza repeated, facing a line-by-line English translation. In both languages, refrains are printed in italics. Translations from the Occitan were prepared by Margaret Switten and those from the French, by Samuel N. Rosenberg. All English versions are intended essentially as guides to the comprehension of the original texts, though it will be clear that the approaches of the two translators do not yield equally literal results.

Stanza and verse numbers are aligned between the facing texts, stanza number to the left of the dot and verse to the right. When a troubadour text concludes with a *tornada,* it is signaled to the left of the dot by the letter T, or, if there is more than one, by T1, T2, etc. In an analogous trouvère text, we use the letter E for *envoi.* To the right of the dot is printed the appropriate line number of the *tornada* or *envoi,* and in parentheses next to it we indicate the line number which is its equivalent from the point of view of meter, rhyme, and melody.

The introductory essays are followed by a guide to the pronunciation of Old Occitan and Old French, and the volume concludes with lists of incipits, bibliographical references, and an index of names and key terms.

We might present our book as Conon de Béthune introduced his song:

Chançon legiere a entendre
Ferai, que bien m'est mestiers
Ke chascuns le puist aprendre
Et c'on le chant volentiers.

THE MUSIC OF THE TROUBADOURS AND TROUVÈRES

Gérard Le Vot

The music of the troubadours and trouvères presents delicate problems of interpretation stemming first from the fragmentary state of the manuscript sources and then from the often different ways in which modern musicians and musicologists approach the task of reconstruction. Despite their interpretative variations, however, both the tradition of medieval song and that of early-music performance today reveal the same constant. Behind the music written down by the medieval scribe and studied by the modern musicologist, a voice can be heard which unites melody and poetry in the act of singing, thereby expressing above all else the pulsation of love's desire. The poet-singer's desire, as Paul Zumthor wrote of the *canso,* "narrativizes itself in the poem"[1] and designates only allusively its distant and emblematic goal: the lady, or *domna.* To be blunt, to provide a name, would be going too far, betraying a personal reality and private imaginings.

Introducing these songs means speaking especially of the troubadours' *canso* and the trouvères' *grand chant,* the love songs that constituted the heart of their repertory and the highest achievement of their art. Now, one point needs to be clear from the start: it is not possible (though musicologists have often sought to do it) to historicize this music completely. Without the heartfelt desire of *fin'amor,* the perfection of Pure Love, one is incapable of true understanding or successful performance. As Bernart de Ventadorn puts it:

> *Chantars no pot gaire valer*
> *si d'ins dal cor no mou lo chans,*
> *ni chans no pot dal cor mover*
> *si no i es fin'amors coraus.*

> Singing can hardly have any value
> if the song does not come from the heart,
> nor can a song come from the heart
> if there is no heartfelt true love there.

For some, the significance of this passage may pale alongside the often arduous technical problems of historical musicology. No, indeed. This art of loving, *fin'amor,* is ruled by multiple prescriptions; it is an art of writing and singing that gives rise to a highly elaborate set of "appropriate" technical requirements. But the first and most challenging requirement is to be a "true lover"—which forces us to wonder how one can be both a good singer and a good *amador,* respecting the rhetorical and technical conventions of both performance and true love. The two are not readily reconciled.

Songbooks: Notation and musical transcription

The melodies of the poet-musicians of the 12th and 13th centuries are preserved in various *chansonniers,* or manuscript song anthologies, the compilation of which began toward the end of the troubadour-trouvère period and continued through the 14th century. Their enumeration and description are provided elsewhere in the present volume.

By and large, the musical transcription of a medieval song confronts editors with problems not unlike those faced by translators. They need to consider whether to accommodate their musical "text" to modern conventions by modifying the old source—notably in terms of melodic variants, the addition of rhythmic indications, instrumental accompaniment, and *musica ficta*[2]—wherever the manuscript material is imprecise or presents multiple versions. The opposite approach, a refusal to intervene, means transmitting the manuscript data uncompromisingly, with all the risks of misunderstanding that the resultant strangeness may entail. An attempt to steer a middle course between the two procedures exposes editors to the danger of producing a bastard transcription.

Actually, a transcription is always to some extent an interpretation. The assumptions underlying it need to be spelled out, together with the limits on transmissibility of the musical source. Let us, then, review the principal criteria and procedures of our musical edition.

The medieval scribes used two clefs in particular: C and F. In this way, they could usually avoid adding extra lines to their staves, which was a costly matter with parchment manuscripts. The tessitura of the melodies is generally that of a high baritone. Medieval pitch values having nothing absolute about them, we have chosen, for simplicity's sake, to use the G-clef. Our modern transcription is thus one octave higher than the original. Likewise, in the polyphonic rondeaux of Adam de la Halle and in the anonymous motets, we have given the clefs of the various parts with reference to this change of octave. Tessitura relationships between voices have, of course, been maintained.

Manuscript accidentals are indicated in the transcription just before the note to which in all likelihood they apply. Whenever, according to the medieval theory of *musica ficta,* accidentals are expected but do not occur in the source, we have added them, but in parentheses or above the staff.

Although both music and poetic text are almost always written in the songbooks in run-on lines, our transcription of the music, like that of the text, displays the songs' verse structure. The poem thus governs the arrangement on the page, and the melodies are presented in accordance with the basic prosodic units of syllable and verse. Such segmentation, normal in melodic analysis, allows us to show the compatibility of poem and music.

Imprecision in the musical sources

Reading medieval notation is not without its problems for music historians. There are at least three areas of uncertainty.

The first question concerns the exact composition of a particular piece preserved in more than one manuscript, given that its several sources will inevitably show some degree of melodic divergence. The troubadours and trouvères no doubt did not write down their melodies as they composed; sometimes they were themselves performers and reshaped their own work; at other times, they conveyed their musical inventions orally to a performer, a *jongleur,* who would then go repeating them, often consciously or unconsciously deforming, even re-inventing, them in the process. At some point, a music notator would be called on to set the music down in writing, an act requiring a technical skill that the poet-musician or performer did not necessarily have. Here again, melodies were readily revised, for notators did not feel obliged to adhere strictly to their models. In brief, then, the songbooks that have come down to us reveal both oral variants arising in the years between creation and recording, and the divers changes and errors introduced into the manuscripts by the copyists themselves.

Another problematic issue is the absence of any indication of instrumental accompaniment in the manuscript sources, an absence partly contradicted by iconographic and literary evidence. The evidence at times shows poet-musicians or their jongleurs singing or declaiming without any instrumental support, but there is also evidence showing accompaniment on a fiddle or a small harp. This matter has been the focus of considerable scrutiny in recent years.[3]

The last difficulty concerns the contradictory nature of the indications of rhythm in the square-chant notation found in our manuscripts. Indeed, apart from traces of rhythmic mode in the Occitan R (as in Marcabru's pastorela "L'autrier jost'una sebissa"), and a few late additions to W, and apart from the French manuscripts O (Cangé) and W (La Vallière), which often provide measured pieces, the principal sources offer no mensural notation, suggesting that their songs might well correspond to the *musica immensurata* defined by Johannes de Grocheio.[4] The system of rhythmic modes applied to medieval secular lyric by Ludwig, Aubry, and Beck attempted to compensate for a perceived lack of guidance; since its origins, however, it has been under attack for its rigidity.[5] The system produced mensural transcriptions based directly or

indirectly on the meter of the individual poems (or on what the transcribers perceived as that meter) and reflective of the conceptions of tempo and musical rhythm in effect in the early twentieth century. Today, the tendency of musicologists and performers, such as Hendrik van der Werf, is toward a declamatory style that takes into account the configuration of the poetic line, tense at the start, then slackening, particularly at the cadence, or rhyme, where the melody is at its most ornate.

Modal interpretation has not been totally rejected in our transcriptions. Indeed, it provides an appropriate way to sing syllabic pieces that are meant for dancing. Long, ornamented melodies, however, unless preserved with some indication of modes in the sources, are noted here in the rhythmically most neutral manner possible: as a series of large black dots on the staff. The *plicae* that occur in French-type square notation are represented for the troubadours by a small black dot and for the trouvères in the style of Hendrik van der Werf,[6] in order to underline their ornamental role. In certain cases, we have ventured into a mensural interpretation, either because it was indicated in the manuscript (as in one of the versions of Conon de Béthune's "Ce fut l'autrier en un autre païs") or because a particular trait of the song seemed to justify a somewhat subjective approach (as in the aube, "Gaite de la tor"). In all instances, we recommend that modern singers be flexible, all the while bearing in mind the sense of the poetic text.

The choice of one melody out of two or more readings

The melodic version that we present does not always come from the source of the text; that is, there are instances where we have selected melody and poem from different manuscripts. To some extent, we simply wished to offer as broad a sampling as possible of the various musical sources. In addition, however, there are three distinct considerations accounting for such choices.

First, the troubadour and trouvère traditions are quite different. The principal Occitan songbooks are, with one exception, of foreign origin: R was copied in the land of the troubadours, but G is Italian, and W and X are French. In three of the four sources, the Occitan texts are either linguistically corrupt or adapted to the dialect of the foreign scribe. Unless they restrict themselves to the "native" ms. R (and even there, the texts are hardly free of problems), music editors are necessarily forced into creating a heterogeneous composition with no true medieval antecedent.[7]

In the case of the trouvères, the problem is a little different. The songbooks are generally of French origin, and their dialectal range does not extend beyond the usual literary limits of the *langue d'oïl.* Nevertheless, there too the transcriber frequently confronts patent errors and lacunae, and these necessarily influence the choice of manuscript version. (In our edition, such instances are flagged by brackets in the transcription and acknowledged in the commentary.)

A second point is that text and melody in a song do not function in quite the same way. Essentially, the melody is contained within the metrical framework of the stanza. Inside this rigid framework, the melodic movement, somewhat paradoxically, enjoys considerable, but directed, freedom. This is manifest in the organization of ornaments at line-end or in the second half of the stanza, in the usually syllabic treatment of line openings, in the only slight correlation of functional intervals with word-meanings, and so forth.

In the case of the trouvères, even more than the troubadours, the editor cannot adopt a rigid stance but must consider the entire manuscript tradition of a given piece along with the relation between orality and writing that emerges from that tradition. Let us illustrate with two courtly songs.

1. The musical manuscript tradition of Conon de Béthune's song "Ahi, Amours! com dure departie" is abundant, with no fewer than five basically different melodies distributed through the ten manuscripts that transmit music with the poem.[8] They are grouped by manuscript as follows:

OMT/KNPX/R/V/a

Note that in light of such multiplicity, it is impossible to identify any particular melody, in contrast to the others, as the invention of Conon himself. We see here support for Hendrik van der Werf's hypothesis of an oral tradition in which singers were responsible for the development of their musical material.[9] Note, too, that, with its unequaled flexibility and capacity for replacement, the musical material functions differently from the textual material. The poetic text is, in comparison, stable and attributable to a particular creator.

2. The musical manuscript tradition of the Châtelain de Coucy's famous song "A vous, amant, plus qu'a nulle autre gent" is very different from the preceding one. The variants in mss. AKMPORTUVX occur chiefly in the ornamentation of individual notes in the second half of the stanza and make it clear that the melody is really the same in all readings. The music is thus as fully of the essence of the song as is the verbal text, and we may well risk the hypothesis—it can only, of course, be a hypothesis—that the melody, no less than the poem, was the work of the Châtelain himself. Outside support, as it happens, comes in an anonymous song that pays homage to the Châtelain ("Li chastelains de Couci ama tant") and uses the very same melody.

Third and last, we have at our disposal today a concept that proves very useful for understanding the several manuscript variants of a given song. This is the notion of *mouvance,* or the shifting nature, of the medieval poetic text, which Paul Zumthor formulated, along with its theoretical implications, in his *Essai de poétique médiévale [Toward a Medieval Poetics]* and then in *La Lettre et la voix.*[10] This concept allows us to consider the text no longer as a single, immutable object, but as a living, moving work comprising all the manuscript versions preserved. It clearly brings into question our very definition of literature and asks whether the term "literature" is in fact applicable to medieval texts. After all, these texts acquired that status only once they had been given written form, and it is too easy to forget that the works they *re-present* were created, often long before, for oral delivery and aural reception. The edition of a medieval poem consequently becomes "a working hypothesis, necessitated by a cultural difference that prevents us from perceiving the text as it was perceived in its own time."[11]

For the editor and music transcriber, the practical consequences of this idea of the poem are considerable. It demands greater flexibility in one's approach to establishing the text and to understanding its relation to melodic variants. Though it is no doubt impossible to make a wholly objective choice among the textual and musical variants of a given composition, it is nevertheless possible to revise our conception of the song, seeing it henceforth as a heterogeneous creation rather than a single work, with various realizations. The revision reflects our recognition of a change in sensorial values since the Middle Ages.

Transformation, transposition, and melodic analysis

In view of the variousness and variability of the courtly melodies, we have to ask ourselves how it is possible to analyze them. Hendrik van der Werf, in a work devoted to Gregorian chant, judiciously describes melodic transformations in monody:

Individual passages of a melody could be shifted up or down, sometimes without any apparent regard for the tonal arrangement of the surrounding passages. Similarly, the underlying structure of any passage could be converted, while that of neighboring ones remained unaltered. Finally, the structural tones of either tertial or quartal chains rarely comprise an octave. All these phenomena imply very clearly that neither the composers of the parent melodies, nor the singers of subsequent generations experienced the melodies as based on a certain scale, or as using a certain octave species. Instead, a melody consisted of quartal and later also tertial modules. Any modules could be converted, or shifted to a different position.[12]

Two trouvère melodies will provide concrete exemplification of the writer's observations. The first is Richard de Fournival's "Quant chante oisiauz tant seri," which displays the tonal indeterminacy so characteristic of many lyric pieces. In the reading in ms. M (which we present), there is no defined scale; the melodic material is composite, as shown in the four cadential tones: *c, a, g, f.* In contrast, the version in T (not presented here) reveals partial transpositions, relative to M, of the melodic material in lines 1, 3, 4, and 5.

The second melody—the ms. X version of Thibaut de Champagne's "L'autrier par la matinee"—is made up of quartal modules. In the first half of the stanza, the simple, syllabic melody is constructed on the alternation of two formulas of fourths: the *b-e* formula of lines 1 and 3 ending on *d,* and the *g-c* of lines 2 and 4 (and 9 as well) ending on *g.* Lines 7 and 8 lead the melody toward *f,* and the refrain concludes on *a.* The whole piece thus shows great tonal instability despite a compositional scheme that is classic in its regularity: ABA′B CDEFG/refrain D′.

Still, we cannot entirely go along with Hendrik van der Werf when he attempts to apply to medieval lyric the theory of chains of fourths and thirds developed by Curt Sachs.[13] At the time of the troubadours and trouvères, the theory of the eight Gregorian modes was still very much part of the frame of reference even of secular musicians, so that many of their songs are melodically homogeneous and understandable in terms of liturgical modality. To a considerable extent, however, while underlying modality is always discernible, modulations and melodic complexities are such that neither the theory of chains of fourths nor the medieval theory of the eight modes is quite enough to account for the various melodic phenomena observed.

The fact is that the transformations stemming from melodic *mouvance* are hard to describe with our modern concepts and analytic vocabulary. To understand them, the simple and common notion of transposition is likewise insufficient. Indeed, we cannot "transpose" or "transform" Gregorian monody, secular song, and vocal polyphony all in the same way, given how unstable the meaning of these terms was in the Middle Ages.[14] Moreover, the lack of tonal differentiation in the songs of the troubadours and trouvères is similar to what we often observe in songs of an oral tradition, whereas we can well imagine that the cantors of the Gregorian school or those who sang the Mass by Guillaume de Machaut were more attentive to precise transpositions of pitch.

We therefore need a certain intellectual retooling to deal with these disparate melodic "transfers" or "translations,"[15] acknowledging both the manner in which the Middle Ages understood musical ordering and the manner in which we today can imagine the musical dimensions of that period. Ian Parker,[16] for example, speaking of the composite and complex courtly songs, takes into account the modal substratum of these compositions and chooses the expression "home" mode as a useful way— particularly in the case of the troubadours—of dealing with the phenomenon of modal stability within a notably erratic fund of melody.

The example of Raimon de Miraval's *canso* "Bel m'es q'ieu chant e coindei" will help explain Parker's concept. The melody, not quite through-composed—the scheme ABCDEFFGH makes the 7th line an exact duplication of the 6th—acts as a kind of modal kaleidoscope produced by the juxtaposition of two modal sensibilities: a tonal center on *f* and the scale of *d.* Here, the tonal focus on *f,* built on the pivotal notes *c, d, f,* and *a,* appears in lines 2, 3, 6, 7, and 8. The *d* scale (authentic and plagal) serves, in its turn, to mark the major poetic articulations: the beginning and end of the stanza, and the mid-stanza break, or *diesis,* that separates the end of line 4 and the opening of line 5. In these circumstances, *d* is to be considered the "home" mode of the Raimon's *canso.*

Let us conclude this discussion of our means of musical analysis by emphasizing how central the delicate notions of transposition and transformation are to musical invention in the Middle Ages—somewhere between vocal variation and manuscript variant—and how much better understood they can be through such broad and inclusive concepts as the chain of fourths, "home" mode, and melodic transformations or metamorphoses than through an overly rigid concept of transposition. In any case, it does not seem especially desirable to systematize the melodic analysis of our songs, for the drive to clarify can too readily disturb our grasp of variable and heterogeneous phenomena.

Melodic patterns

According to Friedrich Gennrich,[17] the melodies of medieval monophony fall into four broad types: **litany**, **sequence**, **rondel**, and **hymn**. In our view, these types represent compositional techniques rather than fully developed forms. They are the processes that constituted the field of poetic and musical invention in the Middle Ages, and it is by means of these processes that musicians produced their melodic forms, exploring the system as far as it would let them go.

The four processes (which also apply to the paraliturgical compositions of the period, such as tropes and sequences) are distributed unequally in the Occitan and French repertories and among the various poetic genres. The hymn-type, for example, occurs chiefly in the troubadours' *canso* and the trouvères' *chanson d'amour.* There is, however, considerably greater diversity in the Northern corpus, for even aside from the motet, in which the original framework of the *canso* is maximally split apart, almost beyond recognition, the trouvère pieces show concurrently all four of Gennrich's melodic patterns.

1. The **litany** type, arising from the techniques of declamation that obtained for the *chansons de geste,* is defined principally by the repetition of a single melodic phrase set to assonanced or monorhymed verses. The *chansons de toile* are examples, sometimes quite old, of this style (see "Bele Doette as fenestres se siet" and "Bele Yolanz en ses chambres seoit").

2. The **sequence** type, stemming from the liturgical *sequentia,* is built on the device of melodic coupling, which

calls for a single repetition of each melodic unit. In addition to the simple *lais* built on pairs of equal lines (AABBCCDD . . .), the type gave rise to more complex monophonic forms such as the *lai-descort* (discordant), composed of lines and stanzas of unequal length (see Gautier de Dargies's "La douce pensee"), and the *estampie*, which was originally a dance involving rhythmic stamping accompanied by singing and then evolved, in the 14th century, into an instrumental dance still based on melodic coupling.

3. The **rondel** type derives from responsorial chant and the use of the antiphon as a refrain. Johannes de Grocheio called it a *cantilena rotunda* (literally, round song). It served to mark the rhythm of the open- or closed-chain dance known as the *carole,* which was performed to songs accompanied by tambourine or fiddle. Generally, the dancers themselves provided their own music, with a vocal soloist taking the lead and a chorus responding. Three fixed-form genres belong to the rondel type: the *rondeau, ballade,* and *virelai.*

Of clerical origin but spirited and secular, the *rondeau,* or *rondet de carole,* was attractive to the trouvères. The song about "Belle Aeliz" shows, with its many medieval redactions, how popular the genre was in Northern France. The form of the rondeau is relatively complex, interweaving three different elements: the poetic structure, the melodic scheme (which comprises only two units) and the alternation between soloist and chorus of dancers. In the 13th century, the genre began to evolve toward the polyphonic *rondeau-conductus* (see the rondeaux of Adam de la Halle), but then lost its original dance function in the following century.

The *balada,* or *dansa,* accompanied the round dances celebrating the advent of spring. Although originally Occitan, it is found in Northern France as well, where it bears the name *ballette.* The well-known *dansa* about the queen of April, "A l'entrada del temps clar," is constructed on a five-line stanza, the first three lines of which are each punctuated by the interjection *eya,* and the last of which is followed by a refrain that was no doubt chanted by all the dancers. This type of composition, of quite early development, is not to be confused with the later French *ballade,* comprising four melodic units and usually polyphonic.

With a name derived from the verb *virer* ("to turn"), the *virelai* perhaps brings to mind the onomatopoeic refrains, e.g., "vireli, virela," that at times characterize this dance song. In form, the *virelai* is halfway between the *rondeau* and the *balada.* The refrain, composed of two melodic units, forms part of the stanza itself, which makes use of a third melodic unit. As for the textual structure of the *virelai,* it is of the zadjalesque type and is hard to distinguish from that of the *balada.*

4. Finally, the **hymn** type occurs within a particular metrical and stanzaic framework: it is thus strophic, and by the repetition of stanzas identical in meter and melody it is

distinguished from the other types. Considerable freedom was demonstrated by the early troubadours in the composition of melodies for the stanza: many melodies were without internal repetition ("through-composed" within the stanza); others were built on repetitions of various sorts. Gradually, more structured stanzaic forms emerged. By the 14th century, in his treatise *De vulgari eloquentia,*[18] Dante was able to identify four melodic schemes that he considered basic to the *canso* or grand chant courtois. These will be adumbrated here and discussed more fully in the essay on words and music.

The first is the *oda continua sine iteratione,* or through-composed song, which takes the form of a continuous melody with no repetition of lines and with no internal stanza break (*diesis*): ABCDEFG . . . (This type is widely represented in the troubadour pieces or, among the trouvère songs, Guillaume le Vinier's "Bien doit chanter la qui chançon set plaire" in the ms. M version).

To the second, Dante gives the name *pedes cum versibus.* This scheme, ABAB/CDCD, contrasts with the first in that it breaks the stanza into two halves, each involving repetition of melody: two *pedes* ("feet") followed by two "verses" (see Conon de Béthune's "Ahi, Amours! com dure departie").

The other two schemes are simply variants of the previous ones. In the third one, called *pedes cum cauda* ("feet with a tail"), repetition occurs in the first part of the stanza, while the second shows line-to-line change: ABAB/CDEF . . . This scheme is the one found in most of the French courtly songs. The final type, called *frons cum versibus* ("head with verses"), reverses this pattern, showing no repetition before the stanza break but introducing it in the second half: ABCD/EFEF. This scheme is quite rare.

Almost half of the Occitan melodies are of the *oda continua* sort. The French compositions, on the contrary, are arranged above all in *pedes cum* either *versibus* or *cauda.* Still, the four basic schemes—whose variants, moreover, are numerous—do not account for the entire surviving repertory. Rather than frozen, fixed forms demanding strict conformity, these melodic patterns emerge as principles of construction from which the troubadours and trouvères were able to create varied formal combinations.

A word about text and music in the courtly song

The songs that the troubadours and trouvères crafted to celebrate their notion of love brought music and poetry together in a relation whose closeness and nature need to be examined. After an initial word here, the issue will be treated more fully in the following section.

As we have seen, the *canso* is defined as a sequence of stanzas, and it is the stanza (the *cobla*) that represents the arena of poetic, melodic, and vocal invention. According, again, to Dante's *De vulgari eloquentia,* the stanza is built out of three components: combinations of rhymes (*relatio rithimorum*), melodic division or compositional scheme (*divisio cantus*), and the interlacing of verses (*contextum carminum*). The principal organizing idea is the proportional arithmetic relation between the two parts of the stanza, which Dante calls the *habitudo partium*. This bipartition of the stanza is manifest not only in the ordering of the rhymes but also in the melodic scheme.

Two musical examples, one drawn from the Occitan tradition and the other from the French, will illustrate these numeric and technical constraints.

In his *canso* "En chantan m'aven a membrar," the troubadour Folquet de Marseilla uses a stanza of 10 heterometric lines (8 8 10 4 8 10 4 8 10 10) with a partially reinforcing rhyme scheme (aabb/ccccdd); it shows repetition of the first rhymes in the *pedes* (8a8a10b4b). All the stanzas of the poem contain the same rhymes, a pattern of recurrence known as *coblas unissonans*. The melody, varying between *d* and *g,* is through-composed (*oda continua*): ABCDEFGHIJ; its compositional scheme may therefore be called classic. The link with the rhyme scheme is limited to the ornamented cadence on *a* in lines 4 and 10.

The Châtelain de Coucy's *chanson d'amour* "A vous, amant, plus qu'a nulle autre gent" is built on an isometric stanza of 8 decasyllabic lines (10 10′ 10 10′ 10′ 10 10 10). The rhyme scheme (ababbaac) reflects the mid-stanza break (*diesis*) after the repetition of ab, but it is does so somewhat ambiguously, for 10′b serves not only to close the first section of the poem but also to open the *cauda*. Note that the stanza ends with a rhyme, c, that finds its echo only in the other stanzas. These are the metrical elements that underlie the melody. In the version of ms. U, the very regular melodic scheme, in *pedes cum cauda*, parallels the first half of the rhyme scheme, but not the second: ABAB/CDEF and abab/baac.

The construction of a song, as we shall see, does not, of course, depend exclusively on the two components, rhyme and melody, whose link to each other is clearly metrical in nature; it depends as well on the third factor, *contextum carminum,* whose relation to the others is more difficult to characterize. Numerous microcomponents, to various degrees, may be brought into use by the poet-musician: the resources of syntax and vocabulary, rhetorical figures, alliterations, likewise melodic ornamentation, broad intervals (a sixth or higher), line-end cadences, particular melodic structures. In a general sense, the principle of *habitudo partium* turns out to be less a strict rule than an organizing idea, a virtuality that gives some latitude to the poet-singer. This latitude involves relations between key words, meanings, and melody that belong to the unpredictable experience of vocal performance rather than the realm of formal necessity.

The voice in sung poetry

The stylization of vocal techniques has been characteristic of Western music ever since the Renaissance. This stylization cannot be attributed to the secular vocal art of the troubadours and trouvères. Depending on the anatomical possibilities and physiology of the individual singer, the medieval voice was no doubt of a quality that our modern taste would consider poor and untutored, with heavy breathing, "unmusical" pronunciations, unrefined timbres, and so forth.

To judge by Peire d'Alvernhe's humorous *sirventés* "Cantarai d'aqest trobadors," the voices of his fellow-troubadours were sometimes rather strange. Guiraut de Bornelh's way of singing, Peire says, is that of "an old woman water-carrier," and the voice of Guilhem de Ribas he considers so rough that "a dog could do as well." It is true, however, that the gallery of portraits in this song may be more reflective of Peire d'Alvernhe's caustic verve than of reality.

From the point of view of making song, the voice leads us back in part to the *mouvance* of the medieval lyric text and to the paradoxical situation that we are in as we study songs through written sources. "The voice is nomadic, whereas writing is fixed," said Paul Zumthor. At bottom, the physical act of singing is not only a way of expressing the uniqueness of a timbre or a subjective being, but is also, as Dante suggests in his discussion of the *cantio*, an act that constructs the song. Voicing is performance, the full forming of the song—the realization of what up to the moment of singing is an idea, however detailed. The medieval singer possessed the ability to give the lyric poem its true voice. It is up to us to see what variations of the courtly song the modern voice makes possible.

(Translated by Samuel N. Rosenberg)

Notes

1. Zumthor 1993, 112.
2. *Musica ficta* properly describes notes lying outside the diatonic gamut of medieval plainchant, but with reference to other early music the term is used more loosely. In certain melodic contexts, it was understood that a given tonal step indicated in writing as a whole tone might well be performed as a semitone or that a particular written semitone might well be executed as a whole tone. The notes affected, written without accidentals but made flat or sharp in performance, constitute *musica ficta,* also known as *musica falsa.*
3. See Page 1986, 111-138 and 160ff; Huot 1989; Arlt 1989, 59 and 72-73.
4. See Rohloff 1967, 124; also, Corbin 1972, 72-77; Seay 1974; Page 1993b.
5. Corbin 1972, 77.
6. Van der Werf 1972.
7. For a defense of homogeneous provenance, see Arlt 1989, 61.
8. See van der Werf 1977, 576.

9. Van der Werf 1972.

10. Zumthor 1972/1992 and 1987, resp.

11. Zumthor 1972, 72.

12. Van der Werf 1983, 147.

13. See, for example, Sachs 1961.

14. Pesce 1987, 59-68, discusses how the medieval theoreticians understood the concept of transposition. The word that often recurs in the 12th- and 13th-century treatises has to do with affinity: *affinales*.

15. Some medieval theoreticians—such as Aribo in his *De musica,* who is troubled by certain irregularities in pitch that he has observed—show reluctance to limit themselves to the concept of affinity, in which case they put forth either the notion of transformation or translation, or else the notion of transfer. See Pesce 1987, 36 and 39.

16. Parker 1977.

17. Gennrich 1932.

18. Dante, 2: 10. See, too, Perrin 1956.

MUSIC AND WORDS:
METHODOLOGIES AND SAMPLE ANALYSES

Margaret Switten

Song in the medium of the voice (and as received by the ear) does not separate music and words; it holds them together in a single artistic expression.[1] But song located only in the voice is ephemeral. Preservation and analysis of the song require that it be fixed by writing. Consequently, this discussion of words and music, focused on the troubadour and trouvère monophonic repertories, will chiefly engage texts and melodies as written. Yet the primary goal, paradoxical as it may seem, will be to encourage a better understanding of the songs as they might have been performed and heard.

Because it is usually assumed, though not proved or even provable, that troubadour and trouvère text attributions also apply to the tunes, I will normally speak as though melodies were composed by the author of the words. This practice is not without its pitfalls. If we cannot be sure that a given text and tune were placed together by a poet/composer, we must direct our attention away from concepts such as "author's original work" or "author's intention." As we have seen in the Introduction to the Anthology, the idea of a "correct," "original," or "fixed" version of a song is at odds with the variousness of the manuscript traditions. What this means for the study of words and music together is that when we speak of a "composer" or "author" of tunes and texts, it should be with full awareness that the medieval notions of "composer" or "author" might have been very different from ours. Further, we cannot presume that our analyses, although they may propose important connections between tunes and texts, will reveal the "only possible" or the "only intended" text-melody relationships for any given song. The types of relationships we can find between two different systems of expression will be diverse, not always necessarily predicated on a concept of total synthesis. We must be prepared both to seek imaginative interpretations and to rest our conclusions on uncertainty. Still, the effort to focus on words and music together, however perilous, is essential: it represents an attempt to seize the song in its very essence as a creation of the voice.

In this Anthology we have normally chosen to join a single melody version to an edited text. By so doing, we narrow the kinds of variability found in the medieval sources. However, it is hoped that the following discussion, by suggesting techniques that can be flexibly applied to various situations, will inspire curiosity to seek out the medieval sources themselves for further refinements.

For an initial contact with the songs

The medieval experience of troubadour and trouvère song cannot be reproduced. But some sense of words and music working together can be acquired, and listening skills developed, with the help of modern performances. For those whose interests are chiefly literary, the listening experience brings a new awareness of the sonorous dimension of the texts. To what should one attempt to attune one's ears? Many of the features that will be described in this essay can become a part of even the most untutored listening adventure. How does the melody move? Are there repetitions? Can one catch the text rhymes? Do text rhymes and melody seem to create some pattern? Often a melody reaches swiftly upward to a peak during the last portion of the stanza. Learning to appreciate the significance of this moment is a rewarding experience.[2] Nuances of tone and technique characteristic of different genres emerge upon attentive listening. And fundamental issues surrounding the songs are raised by solutions adopted by modern performers. Should one use instruments or not—what is the effect of their presence or absence? What conclusions about a song can be drawn from different performing styles? The performances available on the Compact Disc accompanying the present Anthology are intended to encourage exploration of the aural experience of songs. Further performances are listed in the Discography (but note that melodies or texts may be taken from different manuscripts and are therefore not necessarily identical to the songs in our Anthology). And new recordings appear regularly offering fresh realizations of sound and sense to the inquisitive neophyte as well as to the seasoned expert.

Basic approaches to analysis

The discussion that follows, offering a brief conspectus of concepts and methodologies pertinent to the work of the Anthology, is intended to serve the needs of those who would wish to emphasize poetry or music, even though its main purpose is to encourage examination of texts and tunes together. To this end, after reviewing basic approaches to the analysis of text-music relationships, I will consider text and music separately, and, following that, offer sample analyses of two songs that can serve to illustrate the application of techniques that will have been set forth.[3]

Before taking up approaches to analysis, I would like to single out some general features governing word/music relationships. The quite rigorous correlation between text syllables and notes or note groups that is characteristically found in the manuscripts, and the correlation between poetic line and musical phrase that has become normal in modern transcription, determine the framework within which music and poetry are usually discussed.[4] I will throughout equate line of verse and musical phrase and pay careful attention to the groupings of syllables and notes as a feature of musico/poetic style. Further, a central organizing principle operates in both melody and text but in different ways: repetition. Melodic repetition frequently engages entire phrases; texts cannot support such repetition except in special cases such as refrains. Analysis of repetition in melodies will feature the recurrence of entire phrases, but attention will also be given to the crucial function of smaller repeated motives.[5] The chief regular textual repetitions are the rhymes occurring at the ends of poetic lines. Coordinations of the different types of textual and melodic repetitions determine important structural relationships within most songs. In addition, other types of repetition—a varied array of rhetorical devices, for example—provide subtle compositional techniques on different levels.

Now to our subject: one may identify two basic approaches to the study of text-music relationships in troubadour and trouvère song: structural and rhetorical. The former emphasizes parallel patterns or shapes (metrical rather than semantic); the latter emphasizes the production and communication of meaning. The two are tendencies rather than mutually exclusive procedures, as we shall see.

The structural approach reposes on the analysis and comparison of metrical and melodic formal characteristics, chiefly repeated elements. The results of the analysis can be summarized by diagrams where specific pieces of information are represented by letters—capital letters for musical phrases, lowercase for rhyme sounds—and figures for the number of syllables in a line of verse (with a superior stroke for feminine lines). This analysis, carried out on the level of the stanza, yields important information about how stanzas are put together and how a variety of formal structures is created.

Structural analysis often draws upon the unfinished treatise by Dante Alighieri, *De vulgari eloquentia*, composed in Latin between 1303 and 1305. Since Dante uses troubadour and trouvère songs as models, his treatise has exerted a particularly strong influence on the way modern critics perceive text-music relationships in medieval song. Centering on the stanza (*stantia*) as the "receptacle," the "room" (*mansio*) where the art of song is forged, Dante's concern is with the proportioned arrangement and distribution of parts. He emphasizes particularly: (1) formal stanza structure (determined by divisions of the "melody" and by certain types of repetition); (2) the harmony (interweaving) of lines and syllables; and (3) the relationships between

rhymes (not, it must be pointed out, the rhymes themselves but their schemes).[6] The previous essay proposed some ways Dante's perceptions can operate for the *canso*.

Although Dante himself never uses such diagrams, his basic stanza divisions, as they have been interpreted by modern scholars, can be represented in abstract fashion by the customary letters and figures, for example:

1. *oda continua* melody, no rhyme repetition and the same number of syllables throughout;

A	B	C	D	E	F
a	b	c	d	e	f
8	8	8	8′	8	8′

2. *pedes* with *cauda* melody, initial rhyme repetition and a different number of syllables;

AB	AB	CD	E	F
a b	a b	c d	e	f
8 8	8 8	8 8	10	10

3. *pedes* with *versibus* melody, rhyme repetition in both parts and the same number of syllables.

AB	AB	CD	CD
a b	a b	c d	c d
7 7	7 7	7 7	7 7

As Dante's views have usually been understood, they would posit "agreement" between melodic and rhyme schemes as an ideal compositional model. The ideal is problematic, as we shall see. But let us recognize that Dante captured the medieval fascination—thinking of the troubadours, one could say the exuberant preoccupation—with form.

Useful though it may be, Dante's terminology raises numerous issues of interpretation because his terms, and the structural concepts that have been drawn from them, only partially correspond to the reality of medieval song.[7] Reduced to diagrams and strictly adhered to, these concepts tend to limit full awareness of formal flexibility and creativity. The notion, for example, that text-melody agreement is best expressed by the coincidence of letters designating rhymes with letters designating melodic lines (e.g. abab with ABAB), and that if such coincidence does not exist, then text and music do not "go together" is more appropriate to later trouvère repertories, where genres (such as *rondeau*) are defined by the correlation of musical and poetic form, than it is to the earlier experimental *canso*. There are many troubadour and trouvère songs that simply do not fit into the rigid schemes derived from Dante, and for which his terminology is inadequate. Such observations suggest that although Dante's schemes can continue to provide a point of departure, analysis should not be bound by them. Study of structure can profitably include the unusual as well as the usual coordinations of textual and musical elements, and it is precisely here that analysis of short repeated musical motives becomes crucial. Thus enlarged in scope, the structural approach becomes a primary avenue to understanding text-music relations, especially for songs where formal beauty and sophistication are predominant characteristics.

But if structural analysis provides insight into ways different song elements work together, it gives us little sense of how a song plays out in time. Abstract diagrams omit important information, often imposing on musical phrases a deceptive normalization. Furthermore, the emphasis on the stanza alone coming from Dante's basic approach, fails to take into account the important fact that because most of the songs in the troubadour/trouvère repertory are strophic, the stanzas are repeated, thus creating an ongoing temporal pattern, a movement that is irreversible: time-process is an integral part of the song. The repetition of stanzas, as the repetition of elements within the stanza, is not *mere* repetition: a restatement is different from an initial statement by virtue of the very fact that it *is* a re-statement. And although in strophic song basic melodic and metrical patterns are set by the first stanza, many intricate rhyme schemes and refrain patterns can only be fully deployed over the entire time of the song (a particular concern for non-strophic forms). Thus the unfolding *in time* of textual and musical elements is an issue that needs to be addressed.

The second type of basic approach, the rhetorical approach, allows us to confront this issue. We should first disengage the concepts of rhetorical purpose and the production of meaning from the idea of "text painting" or "madrigalism." Rarely can the melodies of our songs be said to "imitate" the meaning of the words directly. Rarely does medieval song exploit the mimetic possibilities of music. But that does not mean that melodies cannot reflect or enhance expressive values of texts. There are matchings of music and poetry that function on phonetic or syntactic levels and, through them, on the level of meaning.[8] The aim of rhetorical analysis is to discover combinations and coordinations of *all* the resources of language and music brought into play as the song unfolds. This opens up to analysis a wide range of musical responses to poetic texts. Musical patterns can be coordinated to patterns of language sounds, which reflect changes on the semantic or expressive levels. Ornamentation of the melodic line or the structure of intervals may relate to vocabulary or rhetorical figures. The possibilities are not easy to codify; we will provide some specific examples below. In the rhetorical approach to analysis of music and words, emphasis is placed on how all the diverse elements present in any given song create its meaning and expressiveness; the presence or absence of different elements and the weight accorded to each of them will vary in each individual song. The guiding analytical procedure is always the assessment of rhetorical purpose rather than the determination of any formal structure *per se*.

Those who seek primarily rhetorical interpretations, and sometimes consider the composer or performer as a "reader" or "interpreter" of the poem, frequently base their analysis on the first stanza of the song. Because that is usually the only stanza with music in the manuscripts (the assumption being that the same melody is then repeated for succeeding stanzas), one has the impression that the inventor of the melody might have had it in mind. This raises the issue of how the music can relate to succeeding stanzas. Indeed, the initial stanza has a special status. In the different manuscript traditions of any given song, the same stanza usually comes first: other stanzas may be interchangeable among themselves; the first stanza is almost never interchangeable with them. The first stanza sets the subject and the tone, preparing what is to follow.[9] But even if the first stanza conditions the rest, it cannot bear the entire weight of analysis. As the melody is repeated, it is cast in a new light by association with different texts in succeeding stanzas: here the concept of irreversibility, bringing with it the impossibility of exact repetition, can figure importantly. For all songs it is important, and for some crucial, to carry an examination of the song through to its conclusion to discover how its music and words function together. A fully effective rhetorical approach seeks to determine *how* the first stanza conditions the rest, how meaning is created through the entire time of the song.

Still, difficulties face the practitioner of rhetorical analysis. Among these is the widespread use of *contrafacta* or borrowing and exchange of tunes and texts. Sometimes a tune from, say, a *canso* (love song) has been borrowed for a *sirventes* (political song). If text and melody are related only on the level of form or shape, if, to adopt the words of John Stevens, "the musician did not set the words of the poem to music; he set its pattern,"[10] then texts and melodies can easily be exchanged, so long as formal structures correspond. If, however, specific melodies are *only* seen as responses to specific texts, then the practice of *contrafacta* problematizes this analytic approach. Further, the fluidity of the melodies in their manuscript preservation can raise difficult issues of interpretation in the detailed working out of rhetorical analyses, especially when there are multiple versions of a song, and the melody versions are so different as to constitute essentially different tunes. With rhetorical analyses, special care must be taken not to base interpretations on the concept of a fixed association between words and melodies, or on the notion of author's intention, narrowly defined. We need to assess for each song—and indeed for its several variations where there are variations—the full range of possible musico-poetic juxtapositions that can contribute to an understanding of the rhetorical effectiveness of the song.

Let us now take up specific elements of texts and tunes that are brought together in the song, beginning with the texts.

Textual elements

Versification. Study of troubadour and trouvère song requires some acquaintance with versification. Practices of troubadours and trouvères are sufficiently similar to permit discussion of both simultaneously. The chief feature—in contrast to English verse—is that for Old Occitan and Old French (as for the modern Romance languages), the line of verse is defined by number of syllables, with the result that the verse is syllabic before it is accentual. Accents play a role; but they have not at all the same function as in English verse, where accentual pattern defines the line.

Our first concern, then, will be identifying the types of line. This means counting syllables in order to define poetic meters (the term "meter" will throughout refer exclusively to number of syllables). Normally, according to a system that has been in place since at least the fourteenth century,[11] the basis for identifying types of meter is considered to be the oxytonic line. The oxytonic line ends with an accent on the final syllable; the oxytonic end-word is called "masculine." In contrast, an end-word with an accent on the next to last syllable, that is with paroxytonic accent, is called "feminine." In such a line, the final unaccented syllable *is not counted*. Thus for an 8-syllable line, the oxytonic model would be:

        1   2 3 4 5 6 7 8
        Anc/ non/ a/gui/ de/ me/ po/der
        ("Never have I had power over myself")

and the paroxytonic, or "feminine" equivalent would be:

        1 2 3 4   5 6 7 8 ′
        Qui/ en/ ce/lui/ n'a/ sa/ cre/an/ce
        ("Whoever has no belief in Him")

All lines are named according to number of syllables: thus, 8-syllable, or octosyllabic, 10-syllable, or decasyllabic, to give as examples the most frequently used meters. When the same meter is used throughout the stanza, one speaks of "isometric" stanzas; changes in meter within the stanza determine "heterometric" structures. Whether a stanza is isometric or heterometric and how it distributes masculine and feminine rhymes can have important consequences for its rhythm.

There are no entirely simple rules for counting syllables. Syllable count will be provided for many of the songs in the Anthology; complete information may be found in Frank 1953 for the troubadours and in Mölk-Wolfzettel 1972 for the trouvères. The important point here is to recognize the syllable as the central unit of measurement, not only for the poetry but also, it is to be remembered, for coordinations with music.

After number of syllables, the next prominent defining element is the rhyme, or identity of final sounds, which marks the end of the line, acting as a kind of punctuation. The rhyme further serves not only to show the end of one line but also to link lines together. And it becomes, in itself, when not just rhyme schemes but also rhyme sounds are considered, an essential musical resource.

The rhyme is also an accent, the one accent that is always required. Certain types of lines have internal accents, the most important of which is at the caesura. The caesura itself may be considered a pause; but the syllable preceding this pause is normally accentuated. (Exceptions to this accentuation pattern occur in two special types of paroxytonic caesurae, called "lyric" and "epic," when the syllable immediately preceding the pause is unable to bear stress, yet is not elided before a following vowel, and the stress then falls on the previous syllable : in the lyric caesura the unstressed syllable is counted to determine the meter; in the epic caesura, the unstressed syllable is not counted but is treated as a supernumerary element.) Caesurae are typically found in decasyllabic lines (after the fourth syllable, less often after the fifth or sixth) and in twelve-syllable lines called alexandrines (after the sixth). At the rhyme and at the caesura, accents are regular. But there are other, more fleeting accents determined by stress patterns. It is important here to distinguish Romance usage from English: in English, words are stressed as such; the word bears the same stress wherever it occurs. In Romance, there are stress (or breath) *groups* determined by grammar and meaning. The individual word disappears into the group; the accent comes only at the end of the *group*. Although the stress placed on individual words may have been heavier in medieval than in modern Romance languages, individual words still carried meaning chiefly as part of a stress group. And because rhythmic units corresponded to sense groups, rhythm and syntax went hand in hand. Further, there was a strong tendency for a line of verse to consist of elements that make a grammatical whole, so that syntactic unit and line of verse coincide. In violation of this tendency, poets sometimes used run-on lines (*enjambement* [enjambment]). This is a stylistic device, creating the effects of tension/resolution, surprise/satisfaction, and it is a source of rhythmic variety.

Lines of verse are generally grouped together in stanzas (*coblas*, in Occitan). If one takes into consideration only the formal elements—meters, rhyme schemes, rhyme sounds—the possibilities for variation are astounding, and the troubadours alone created over a thousand stanza forms. The stanza is defined by the number of its component lines of the same (isometric) or of varied (heterometric) meters and by the arrangement of its rhyme sounds into one of many repetitive patterns called schemes: ababddc, for example, or abbacdcd and so on. The sounds of the rhymes may be very common or extremely rare. Normally, the initial stanza configuration of a song is repeated exactly throughout, although some genres, such as the *descort*, require dissimilar stanzas (each stanza having a unique configuration). To describe the stanza, one should also consider syntax, although, as I have argued elsewhere,[12] it is a less easily definable component of the stanza than versification. Syntactical elements are not fixed; yet as they follow each other, they set up parallel or contrastive sequences, and they participate in determining the stanza's inner coherence.

The terminology we use for troubadour and trouvère stanzas comes from a fourteenth-century Occitan treatise called the *Leys d'amors*. The *Leys* furnish an exuberant collection of terms, only a few of which are in general use. These may be briefly defined. Two of these terms refer to stanzas considered without reference to interstanzaic grouping or ordering: *coblas singulars*, indicating that a new set of rhyme sounds is used for each stanza (but we should note that the rhyme scheme remains the same throughout: only the sounds change); and *coblas unissonans*, indicating that all rhyme sounds in all stanzas are the same and follow the same scheme. Other terms pertain to various ways of grouping or ordering stanzas: *coblas doblas* (where stanzas rhyme two by two), *coblas alternadas* (alternating rhymes from one stanza to the next), *coblas capcaudadas* (in which the last rhyme sound of one stanza becomes the first rhyme sound of the next), *coblas capfinidas* (where there is repetition of a final rhyme word, or a variation of the word, in the first line of the next stanza not necessarily at the rhyme), *coblas retrogradadas* (the same rhyme sounds appear in all the stanzas but with the order of rhymes reversed from one stanza to the next). Some terms refer to the rhymes themselves, such as *rim estramp* (a rhyme that is not repeated in the stanza itself but corresponds to the same rhyme sound, also isolated, in other stanzas), or *rims derivatius* (which are grammatical or derivative rhymes). Although such elements of versification may seem complex or conventional to us, the possibilities of combination and re-combination of these elements served as a powerful stimulus to creativity for the poet/composers in this Anthology.

Composition. Some of the terms from the *Leys d'amors* that engage grouping and ordering of stanzas point beyond the single stanza as a main locus of composition to the complete song, consisting of several stanzas in sequence. This conjoining of stanzas was an important aspect of the art of *trobar*. But stanzas are linked by more than rhyme schemes or rhyme sounds. Refrains, where they exist, are powerful elements of song structures. They are more prevalent in trouvère than in troubadour songs, and, indeed, in the thirteenth century circulate in such a way as to become almost a genre in themselves.[13] An important technique in the troubadour repertory is the word-refrain, the repetition at the rhyme of the same word in every stanza of the song. Refrains usually consist of an entire verse or verses, normally (but not always) found at the end of the stanza. Infrequently, refrains following each stanza are different; songs with such variable refrains are called *chansons avec des refrains*. More normally, stanzas end with the same refrain; and where we have the tune, the return of the same words with the same music, after contrasting differences in words and music, brings a powerful impulse to unity which always needs careful attention.

Beyond formal elements, examination of the composition of a complete song involves consideration of thematic development and division into parts. Thematic material is infinitely varied and engages notions of style and genre as well as motif and vocabulary. The *canso*, for example, treats the concept of *fin'amor*, "courtly" or "refined" love, in all its manifold aspects, from strongly sexualized eroticism to metaphysical longing. An important concept used in modern textual criticism is the "register."[14] A "register" is a collection of motives, words, rhetorical gestures that coalesce around and thus express attitudes or themes. For Pierre Bec, registers are socially as well as artistically determined; thus he distinguishes an aristocratic vs. a popular register, for example.[15] The very considerable thematic variety characteristic of troubadours and trouvères will emerge from the study of individual songs in our Anthology. Their organization into parts can be illustrated by the *canso*, against which other genres can be measured. We may divide the *canso* into three unequal parts. The first part is the first stanza: the *exordium*. In this stanza, as we saw above, the poet/composer justifies and explains his enterprise. The second part can be called the "body" of the song. It consists of the remaining stanzas which grow out of the first, relating to it and to each other in diverse ways. The order and number of these stanzas, unless they are held to a fixed order by genre or versification, can vary; a large array of rhetorical and compositional techniques are brought into play. In the troubadour tradition, there are frequently more stanzas in the development than in the trouvère tradition. The third part of the *canso*, where it exists, is the *tornada*, or *envoi*. This part brings closure, but it is a closure that sometimes invites the song to begin again. The *tornada* also frequently contains the names of identifiable people: it anchors the song, so to speak, in the real world. There may, on occasion, be several *tornadas*; in these circumstances, one can imagine that the song may have been used on more than one occasion and sent to more than one person. Since the *tornada* is a repetition of the final portion of the stanza, a kind of shortened stanza, it is assumed that it would have been performed to the last portion of the melody.

Musical elements

Drawing on the characterization of the music in the previous essay, we may now underscore those aspects that are of particular importance in the analysis of melody and text together. What questions can one ask of a tune that will help us understand how it works?

If we place the song in what we can know of contemporaneous musical contexts, we may perceive numerous relationships between secular song and liturgical (or Gregorian) chant, including Latin traditions such as the sequence or, particularly useful for the troubadours, the Aquitanian *versus*.[16] Important questions of analysis may be approached by reference to these repertories—as long as we bear in mind that the specific terms deriving from theoretical elaborations pertinent to chant usage are only partially applicable to secular tunes evolving outside such theoretical considerations—since the sonorous universe of chant constitutes a musical mentality in which secular poet/composers participated.

Useful questions one might ask of a tune seek to determine where it is going and how it achieves coherence. It is instructive to examine cadences, that is, the last note or notes of individual phrases and of the entire piece. Do these last notes or note groups seem to establish some pattern? Do they mark articulations of the stanza? Further, we may inquire how the individual phrases are linked together, how one line proceeds to another. Or again, phrasing things a bit differently, we could inquire how melodic syntax marks contrast, movement, tension, and resolution.

Scales and modes. These questions lead us to the much-vexed problem of tonality or modality. The previous essay emphasized the notorious ambiguity of tonal behavior in troubadour and trouvère music. Some melodies display from the start a strong tonal focus; others oscillate from one center to another without (to us) apparent reason. Still, recognizing the problems involved, we can set out some basic general concepts. We may attempt to relate both melodic movement and cadential patterns to a mode or a scale. The term "scale" in this context can refer to the general patterns embodied in the white keys of the piano (which produce the diatonic scale). Specific scale patterns are produced by different arrangements of the five whole tones (T) and two semi-tones (S) comprising the diatonic scale. Any of the pitches of the diatonic scale can be taken as a starting point for a specific scale. Thus a "scale on *d*" would be a scale starting on *d* and concluding on *d* an octave above. This starting point determines the order in which whole tones and half tones occur, that is, the interval structure of the specific scale. If one starts on *d* and moves through the white keys, one obtains the pattern TSTTTST. Similarly, if one starts on *g*, for a "scale on *g*," and moves again through the white keys, one obtains the pattern TTSTTST, and so on. Since by convention every scale is understood as bounded by an octave, there can, in theory, be seven versions of the diatonic scale, sometimes termed "octave species."[17] In practice, secular music does not use all possible versions. This concept of scale should be divorced from the modern notion of "key," applicable only to later tonal music.

Several of these octave species were organized with particular reference to the chant into the system of modes. It is neither possible nor pertinent to our work here to describe the modal system in any detail.[18] I shall single out only a few features and terms relevant to our analyses. The modal system established a hierarchy of tones: some tones became more important than others, acquiring special functions. The modal system also included certain melodic formulae or patterns specific to the various modes. Two tones are of particular importance because of their functions. First, the starting and ending scale degree, specifically the low boundary tone, called the *finalis* (final), a name that describes its function in establishing closure. The final, although often problematic in secular music, can still be useful as an indicator of mode. Second, a *tenor* or *reciting tone* which is used in psalm singing; this tone is usually a fifth above the final in what are called authentic modes, and a third or a fourth above the final in what are called plagal modes. In some cases, the reciting tone helps determine the tonal center of a composition because it can be considered a fundamental feature of the mode. It is necessary to distinguish this "reciting tone" from "psalm tone." The latter does not refer to a single tone but to the complete melodic formula to which a psalm is sung, consisting of an intonation formula, then a reciting tone, followed by a cadence. Since there are different formulae for the different modes, the intonation formula as well as the reciting tone can help define a mode. The tenor is sometimes also referred to as a "dominant" (not to be confused with the "dominant" of modern tonality). One last term: some melodies bring into play, especially in cadential formulae, the tone below the final, the *subfinalis* (subfinal). The properties briefly described in this paragraph constitute useful tools for musical analysis of secular songs and will serve not only the sample analyses of this essay but also the commentaries to individual songs of the Anthology.

Now to take up the notion of authentic and plagal mode which engages a concept of scale organization that has importance beyond the concept of mode itself. It also engages the important idea of range. If we return to our octave species, we can point out that the species themselves were subjected to a certain hierarchy in medieval modal theory. They were divided into four principal species, those beginning on *d*, *e*, *f* and *g*, called "authentic modes." Paired with these were four "subsidiary" or "plagal" modes beginning a fourth below the authentic modes, thus on *a* (fourth below *d*), *b* (fourth below *e*), *c* (fourth below *f*), and *d* (fourth below *g*). These different modes are characterized by range: plagal modes' range is from a fourth below to a fifth above the finals of the corresponding authentic modes. Each authentic mode has as important tones: (1) the final (or low boundary tone as defined above); and (2) a median tone, normally a fifth above (sometimes termed, except for the *g* mode, the co-final, because it could "stand in" for the final; it was usually the same as the tenor or reciting tone). Each plagal mode is divided into two segments by the final of its corresponding authentic mode, and has a reciting tone as described above. The important feature to be brought out by looking at the system in this way is that the octave appears as constituted by the joining of a fourth (tetrachord) and a fifth (pentachord): authentic modes have a fifth on the bottom and a fourth on the top; plagal modes have a fourth on the bottom and a fifth on the top. The interplay of conjoined fourths and fifths provides techniques for dynamic contrast and a way of organizing complete melodies into coherent structures.[19]

A final observation will help understand secular usage of modes. Classical medieval theory did not admit any modes other than those with finals on *d*, *e*, *f*, or *g*. However, gradually, scales on *c* and scales on *a* were brought into the theoretical system, and four other modes were added. Scales on *c* or *a* often undergird secular song, although they never acquired official importance for the chant.

The features just described are summarized in the diagram in figure 1.

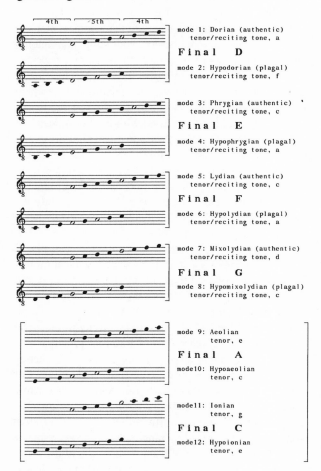

Figure 1

Third-chain principle. There is also another principle that can be used to good advantage in the analysis of monophonic melodies: the third-chain principle. This principle, simply stated, may be described as the division of the modal octave into two overlapping chains of thirds, one anchored in the final, the other in the tone above or below the final, identified as principal and secondary chains,

respectively. This differentiation provides a basis for creating dynamic contrast by juxtaposing third chains: the principal chain, containing both final and co-final (or tenor), projects resolution, stability, and closure, in contrast to the secondary chain, which projects tension, imbalance, and openness, implying a return to the principal chain.[20] The third-chain principle is schematized in figure 2.

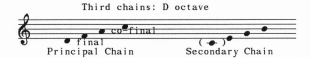

Figure 2

Although none of these analytic systems is perfectly adapted to the object we wish to analyze—troubadour and trouvère melodies—all can provide insight into melodic syntax and how that syntax can relate to poetic syntax. We can draw upon these systems to analyze the notions of statement and response, or question and answer, as these are expressed musically to articulate phrases and groups of phrases and bind them into a cohesive statement.

Contours of musical phrases. Whether or not we relate melodic movement to modes or scales, we can obtain important information about the nature of a melody by analyzing its contours. The general shape of a melodic phrase, its movement up or down, can serve as a principle of differentiation and contrast. Is the initial direction maintained throughout a phrase? Are there sharp reversals of direction? Looking at range in a slightly less technical way, one may ask if the range of a melodic phrase (defined as its highest and lowest note) is wide or limited. Playing that out across the entire song, one may seek to determine where the complete melody reaches the top of its range: at the outset? in the middle? Questions such as these lead to a better understanding of directional musical materials that determine a melody's structure and effectiveness as well as its expressiveness on the level of both the phrase and the stanza.

Style and interval structure. Melodic style, in the narrow sense, is usually described using three main terms: syllabic, neumatic, melismatic. Syllabic style means one note to a syllable on a regular basis. Neumatic refers to a slightly more ornate style, where, although basically there is one note to a syllable, a number of syllables carry several notes. A melisma is a group of several notes, sometimes as many as 6 or 7, set to a single syllable. Melismas used by themselves serve as ornaments, highlighting melodic and/or textual features (one frequently finds melismas at the ends of phrases, for example, or in the last line of the song). If these ornaments are prevalent throughout the song, that determines melismatic style. Stylistic concepts are fluid: the arrangement and positioning of melismas and single notes can be quite variable in the manuscript traditions. The ability to adorn and to vary a melody must have been an important technique in performance, because ornamentation could reflect an individual performer's skill as a singer and interpreter of texts.

Interval structure of a song can be a key to the expressive value of melodic gestures. Does the melody proceed in step-wise fashion? Or are there large skips? If there are skips, what intervals are used: thirds? fourths? fifths? etc. Is the skipping motion up or down? Where do the skips occur? Answers to these kinds of questions, as we shall see in the sample analyses and in the commentaries to individual songs, can reveal important aspects of melodic movement that serve both to determine the structure of a melody and to provide contrast and emotional tension.

A last feature must be mentioned. Our analyses progress without reference to musical rhythm. The question of musical rhythm in the monophonic repertories of this Anthology is controversial; we may take for our purposes the notion that melodic lines espouse text rhythms. Sufficient weight of critical opinion leans now in that direction.[21] The project for analysis is then carefully to relate musical features to text features: meters, poetic accents at rhyme and caesura, and more subtly elsewhere in the line, enjambment, the rhythmic effect of masculine and feminine rhymes, and the like, in order to determine a given song's *coordinated* rhythmic movements.

Genre

The analysis of words and music invites the consideration of genre as a very flexible principle. Medievals did not think in terms of the kinds of generic groupings prevalent in modern criticism. They used a bewildering variety of overlapping and highly specific designations, often unstable in meaning and application, and changing over time. Genres are thus best understood as historical products rather than as fixed categories; and their theoretical elaboration in medieval as well as modern treatises is more a sorting out that follows upon a development and maturing of traditions than a set of rules determining that development. But medieval poet/composers did have a sense of working within certain traditions, and many of the terms adopted by modern critics were drawn from the medieval songs. The major poetic genres have been briefly described in the Introduction to the Anthology; specific information about genres, as well as a sense of their early development, may be found in the commentaries to individual ascribed songs and in the introductions to the generic groupings of anonymous trouvère songs.

As a musical concept, genre is much more problematic. The semantic content that figures importantly in defining poetic genres does not exist in the music. Melodic genre is even more intimately connected to style. Perhaps the closest one can come to a generic designation that fits

both music and words is the *canso*; but in last analysis, there is no specific melodic style that can distinguish a *canso* from a *sirventes*, and the danger of using poetic designations to refer to melodic styles for our repertories has often been remarked. Still, some genres are music-specific; one thinks of the *motet*, or of dance songs such as the *rondeau* or *carole*, or even of certain types of *lai*. The preceding essay has proposed a musical typology; to it, one could add the remark that in broad stylistic terms, the simple designations "high" and "low," corresponding roughly to Pierre Bec's "aristocratic" and "popular" registers, when applied to tunes as well as texts, can provide rough analytic categories enabling us to make useful distinctions, particularly with respect to rhythm and general melodic movement.[22]

The motet. The motet became the main polyphonic genre of the 13th century, and into the 14th century, it continued to serve as the locus of new experiments. Because of the importance of the genre, three motets have been included in our Anthology. The motet belongs to a sonorous universe entirely different from that of the troubadours and trouvères. Its development depended on the discovery of a way to notate musical durations (or rhythms) so that music could clearly expand its rhythmic horizons independently of texts. The relationship between music and text was thereby profoundly modified. This is not the place to enter into the details of these modifications. The introduction to the motet section of the Anthology explains some of them. Here, I wish only to emphasize the excitement of a new listening experience. We do not, in fact, know how the audience for motets received these songs. The presence of polytextuality poses immense barriers to understanding the words. And yet the parodic intent, which many now see in the motet, depends on the intelligible manipulation of texts. Motets are related to Old French lyric in ways that have not been fully elucidated; motet versification, long looked upon with scorn, is now receiving renewed critical attention. Recent studies on the motet have opened fresh critical perspectives.[23] But perhaps the most rewarding initial contacts with these enigmatic but fascinating little songs come from listening: two compact discs in particular, *The Marriage of Heaven and Hell* and *Les escholiers de Paris*, listed in the Discography, provide both informed access to the motet and comparisons between motets and troubadour and trouvère songs.

Analysis of sample troubadour and trouvère songs

Marcabru *"Pax in nomine Domini!"*
This song is recorded on the Compact Disc that accompanies the Anthology.

Sources. This song illustrates the kinds of problems encountered in the effort to reconstruct troubadour songs. The text has been preserved in eight manuscripts; textual attribution is clear and the textual tradition relatively stable. The melody is only in the northern French Manuscrit du Roi (W), with only the first two stanzas, and it is anonymous—despite the fact that the name "Marcabru" appears there, too, in the first stanza. Because Marcabru states in the second line of the poem that he made the words and melody, we may with some confidence think of him as the composer of the tune as well as of the text. The problem is how to put the two together. Since only the W scribe provided a tune, we must use his tune. But his text is truncated. If we are to have a complete text, we must turn to a southern manuscript. Without entering into details of transmission, it may be observed that the melodies of some other early troubadours preserved in W match rather well the tunes in southern manuscripts. So the solution to the problem of reconstructing the song, imperfect perhaps but not unjustified, is to place the melody from W with the complete text from elsewhere as a basis for performance and analysis.

Listening to this song brings a powerful initial impression. The dramatic opening melodic gesture near the top of the range immediately captures one's attention. The return of this first gesture after a contrasting section that is lower in tessitura (portion of the range exploited), is followed by a further upward movement that heightens the drama. The harsh resonance of the words makes us understand that this will not be a song about a plaintive lover, even if we do not immediately grasp all the meanings. This sets a tone and a framework for closer analysis. The first stanza with melody and text is given here for convenience in following the analysis; the complete song will be found in the Anthology section.

Figure 3

Like many troubadour songs, Marcabru's *Pax* does not fall into any of Dante's categories. The poetic stanza form is unique (Frank N° 456.1); the melody is highly repetitive but not according to any usual scheme. One can make a diagram—which only confirms the stanza's unconventionality.

Melody:	A	B	C	D	D	A′	E(B′)	F	G
Rhymes:	a	b	a	c	d	c	d	e	f
Meters:	8	8	4	8	8	8	8	8	8

Most of the musical phrases contain at least some reminiscence of another. Phrases 4 and 5 are an expansion of 3. Particularly important is the return of an entire phrase, line 1 coming back in line 6, and the relationship of that phrase to line 8 in the use of a reciting tone. One might propose a musical division into four parts: AB CDD A′E FG.[24] But the irregular pattern of rhymes seems, at first, to lie athwart these divisions. Structures of syntax are very supple. Each stanza has an opening assertion; the short line is either a prolongation of that assertion or announces what is to come; then the stanza builds, but never in a rigid manner, toward a climax, particularly in the last four lines.

Let us now flesh out these initial findings through a detailed consideration of the song.

The melody first: how can we characterize the tonality of the song? If we examine the last notes of each phrase, we find cadences on *c* and *a* for lines 1-2 and 8-9, with *c* returning in line 6. Lines 3, 4, 5, in contrast, end on *e*. Pushing further the search for important tones leads us to observe that *c* functions as a reciting tone in lines 1 and 6, and it is prominent in lines 2, 7, 9; that *a* serves as reciting tone in lines 4 and 5; and that *e* is not only a very prominent repeated note in line 8 but also the initial (as well as concluding) note of lines 3, 4, 5. The diagram of modes (figure 1, above), shows one mode, if we take authentic and plagal dispositions together, that contains all the important tones we have observed: the Phrygian mode with a final on *e*. At this point, we may further note that the range extends from (*d*)*e* to *e*(*f*), and that a short repeated motive, *g*, *a*, *c*, in lines 1 and 6 (positions 6, 7, 8) and in line 2 (positions 3, 4, 5) is a mode 3 intonation formula. All of these observations suggest a tonal focus on *e*. But the song closes on *a*, which is not the final of the Phrygian mode. It is, however, an important structural tone, the tenor of mode 4; and one of the features of the modal system as loosely used by secular singers is that pieces do not necessarily end on the final. The last three lines, with a close on *g* in line 7 and the leap of a fifth in line 9 starting from *g* (positions 5-6), join the second-line movement from *g* to *a* to emphasize further the importance of *a* as a structural note. So we come to the conclusion that while the melody is best understood as built on *e*, it is colored by strong cadences on *a*. The *e* scale was infrequently used by troubadours; the tonality of the song is also unconventional.

Moving on, we may inquire: how does one melodic line proceed to another? Three moments are worth noting:

between lines 2 and 3, the downward leap of a fourth; between lines 5 and 6, a striking upward leap of a sixth; and from line 7 to line 8, the upward leap of a fourth. Otherwise, one line moves to another by repeating the same pitch, or by the interval of a second. The leaps define two tonal registers: lines 1-2 and lines 6-9 exploit the upper fifth of the octave; lines 3-5 remain in the lower fourth. This finding coincides with our initial impressions of the overall shape and with cadential patterns as described above. Stylistically, the melody is syllabic; but the last two cadences have important ornamentation, and the final line is more melismatic than syllabic.

We have here a melody that, despite its unusual structure, exhibits a high degree of internal coherence.

Let us now examine the text. The most striking feature is the short line, 3, which stands out among the otherwise regular sequence of octosyllables. The pattern of rhymes, all masculine, is particularly intricate. Alternating "a" rhymes group the stanzas two by two as in *coblas doblas*: rhyme a is "i" in stanzas 1-2 and 5-6, "es" in stanzas 3-4 and 7-8. The middle rhymes b= "o," c= "or," and d= "aus" do not change; b constitutes a *rim estramp* because it does not rhyme with other sounds in the stanza. The final rhymes e and f again alternate but this time for each stanza, and technically they, too, are *rims estramps*: in stanzas 1, 3, 5, 7, e= "as" and f= "ort," while for stanzas 2, 4, 6, 8, it is exactly the opposite: e= "ort" and f= "as." A further refinement is brought by rhyme sounds: "i" is high and tight, contrasting with the other more open sounds. Contrast of closed and open "o" creates subtle differentiations: rhyme "o" is closed; "or" is also closed but with an added consonant; "ort" is open.[25] These sound gradations create their own music, but also reinforce meaning, as we shall see. It should also be remembered that the character of the melodic line is affected by the sonic values of the text: changes in vowel sounds produce changing tone colors; and when, as here, the rhyme gradations are not organized around regular returns, the complete sonic image attains considerable complexity.

The foregoing observations reveal the kind of craftsmanship that is typical of the major troubadours. We may now ask: how do these subtle artistic procedures relate to the song's message, as it is expressed in the first stanza and carried through the others? The first line of text is in Latin, the only Old Occitan song with such a beginning. The words "Pax in nomine Domini" immediately set the cultural and political context of crusade and Peace movement, boldly drawn by the initial recitation on c, the sparse syllabic style, and the firm conclusion on c. The second phrase, naming the "author," is taut, confined to the third a-c with the supporting g. In the middle of this second phrase, the movement from c down to g and back to c, already heard in phrase 1 to the words "nomine Domini," recurs, shortened and slightly ornamented with the words "Marcabrus (los)." This repetition suggests that if the Lord

presides over peace in Latin, the poet takes over that function in the vernacular. He does this by creating a song: he, too, is a maker.

The first two strongly chiseled lines in the upper part of the range set the subject and the tone and place the poet in a position of authority. In the third line, the change in tonal register and the short line combine to set off the call to the audience. The Old Occitan "Aujatz que di" recalls the Old French "Oiez seignor" ("Harken, lords") familiar as an epic opening; the audience is likely to be knights. The speaking voice is the poet's; it is usual for poets to use the third person to refer to themselves: in an oral culture this is a way to sign one's name. We remain in the new tonal register as the description of the Lord's action begins and then leap up to the initial reciting tone, c, at a crucial moment (line 6): what is being offered to "nos"—the poet now includes himself among those to be affected—is close at hand; it is an extraordinary gift, a "lavador." The *lavador*, a cleansing place, is a polyvalent symbol capturing the essence of the journey toward salvation. As with all great symbols, the word suggests more than it states: cleansing, purification, baptism, paradise, remission of sins. The entire spectrum of religious motives is concentrated in this one prestigious word.

The musical phrase for the line in which the "lavador" appears is a repetition of the first. This repetition links the "lavador" to the bold initial invocation of the Peace of God. And it does even more: the g, a, c motive, our third-mode intonation formula and the kernel of the melodic gesture which has been heard to "nomine Domini" and "Marcabrus," now carries the "lavador." God, poet, and the subject of the poem are fused. The "lavador" is a gift of the sweetness of God: "doussor," line 4 rhymes with "lavador." Having spectacularly regained its initial tonal register, the melody proceeds to increase excitement by ascending motion. The call to sinners becomes more and more insistent, intensified by recitation on e in line 8, a third above the first recitation and the highest point of the stanza. The final line as it falls back to a is different from the others in the greater weight given to it by its melismas. It is a final exhortation and as such must be impressed on the minds of the listeners. At the end of the first stanza, the poet's authority and the subject of his song have been vigorously set forth by the conjoined effects of text and tune.

We do not realize until the second stanza that the word "lavador" is a refrain word, and not until the end of the song can we be certain it will recur in every stanza exactly as in the first. Only in the second stanza do we begin to sort out the stable and alternating rhyme sounds and recognize the sound "or" as the anchor sound, prepared by "o" and echoed with a slightly different quality by "ort." The notions of salvation and purification carried by the "lavador," linked always to the same textual and musical sounds (and through the music to the poet and to God), attain the permanence of eternity compared to the changing world of rhymes around them. Each stanza begins with a strong statement on the reciting tone *c* maintaining tension and energy. And the last two lines of each stanza bring a strong close, set off from the rest of the stanza by the alternating *rims estramps* and by the melodic climax moving into the emphatic melismas of the final phrase. Further examination of the ways text and tune combine to create meaning in each stanza (and, through the recording, of the effects of the singer's inflections) will bring fresh discoveries. Suffice it to point out that, by the last stanza, it has become clear that the exhortation to seek the washing place is both morally and politically motivated. A suitable response to the "lavador" in the religious sphere is comparable to observing courtly behavior in the secular sphere: mesure and virtue are as necessary to crusaders as to lovers. In this final stanza, we learn that the behavior of the degenerate French, the "desnaturat" boldly highlighted by the opening reciting tone, causes weeping for *Pretz* and *Valor*, the great moral courtly qualities. By such gestures, Marcabru presents himself, the singer, as a guide for society through the creative force and moral efficacy of his song.

The Châtelain de Coucy, "Li nouviauz tanz et mais et violete"

This song has been recorded by Gothic Voices (*Music for the Lion-hearted King*) with four stanzas (I, II, IV, III) and variations (as a singer might bring to performance) in the first part of the melody.

Sources. The song is found in 13 manuscripts, twelve with music. For both text and music M offers good readings so the text and music can easily be studied in the same manuscript; we have a different situation from that which pertained for Marcabru's song, a difference characteristic of the two repertoires involved. Problems regarding both text and melody nonetheless arise from the multiplicity of manuscript versions. The chief text problem is the variation in stanza order described in the Anthology commentary. For the music, problems are posed by sharply divergent melody versions. Viewing the multiple versions as a whole, we may observe that a large group of manuscripts, KLOPXMUTAa, is defined by similarity of readings for the first part of the song, and for the last line. In the second part of the song, melodic readings of this group are diverse; this is typical for the repertory. Contrasting to the relative homogeneity of this large group, R and V are both idiosyncratic, a frequent situation in trouvère manuscripts. Because they are peripheral and possibly later, we may exclude the V and R versions from detailed analysis, retaining them, however, in the synoptic chart (figure 4) for general comparison. This chart gives an idea of melodic variation within the main tradition, represented by K and M, and between this tradition and V and R.

An initial contact with this song through listening establishes an overall shape that is more regular and more readily grasped by the ear than was the case with Marcabru: repeated melodic phrases in the first part of the stanza; a second portion without repeats; a reach upward to a melodic climax in the second portion, followed by a return to the original tonal register to close. The sonorous features of the text are relatively homogeneous, the tone controlled

and mellow, but not without emotion. The sheer beauty of the melody is to be savored.

From this initial contact, we realize that the song fits one of Dante's most widely used categories: *pedes* with *cauda*:

Melody:	A B A B	C D E F
Rhymes:	a b a b	b b a b
Meters:	10′ 10 10′ 10	10 10 10′ 6

The second part of the stanza is not marked by a change in rhyme sound to "go with" the change in melody (as is usually the case with the troubadours for similar *pedes* constructions), but by a change in pattern using the same sounds: this is a technique typical of the trouvères. The repetition of the same rhyme sound with new music becomes a structural marker. The short final line is a prominent feature of the heterometric stanza. Syntax tends to reinforce a division of lines into two equal parts: 4 (2+2) + 4.

Now let us examine the tune more closely. The pattern of individual cadences affirms structural outlines: throughout the versions of the main group, the second, fourth, and last lines cadence on the final, with the first and third lines cadencing on the tenor or reciting tone. This establishes a clear tonal focus. Moreover, we find here a technique referred to as *ouvert* ("open") and *clos* ("closed") endings, where the first and second endings of a section to be repeated (here the AB section) establish a hierarchy of closure: the first inconclusive ending (here lines 1 and 3) leads to the second "closed" ending, usually on the final (here lines 2 and 4).

But if tonal focus is clear in separate versions, when we consider multiple versions, the issue of specific mode arises. The version of manuscript M (like the beginning of U) has been notated one fifth lower as compared to the other manuscripts. It thus closes on *c*; the others close on *g*. In troubadour and trouvère manuscripts, melodies are frequently notated at different pitch levels, often at a distance of a fourth or a fifth. We cannot entirely explain this phenomenon which can affect modal structure. It is true that in manuscripts, we are dealing with *writing*, and since writing did not then have the prescriptive force it now enjoys,[26] the kinds of precise interval relations prevalent in music controlled by writing seem not to have been a concern for medieval singers (or scribes) of our repertories. Multiple melody versions are not always preserved with exactly the same interval relations, and hence with the same modal structure, in all manuscripts: a scribe may have been more concerned with getting all the notes on the staff in a convenient manner than with notating precise intervals. However, in some manuscripts, accidentals rectify, as it were, apparent inconsistencies of interval structure. For the case at hand, we may observe that in MS U, the *b* is flatted throughout the notated portion (the final part of the melody is missing); in M, there is one b-flat in line one (this is the basis for the bracketed b-flat "key signature" in the transcription). If the *b* were consistently flatted in the M and U

Figure 4. The Châtelain de Coucy, "Li nouviauz tanz et mais et violete." Synoptic chart of multiple versions

versions, the exact pattern of whole steps and half steps that characterizes the *g* scale would occur in all melody versions. So this melody in all of its versions should probably be thought of as a Mixolydian melody. But since the version in M is notated on *c* with a single ambiguous accidental, and the M melody has a number of individual variants, it is better for our purposes to speak of the melody in M as built on *c* and the melody in K as built on *g*.

Now taking up the M version of this Anthology, we may observe that the setting out in phrases 1 and 2 and again in phrases 3 and 4 of an antecedent/consequent, or statement/response, relationship with *ouvert* and *clos* end-

ings is artfully balanced. Phrases 1 and 3, the antecedents, sweep in mostly stepwise fashion—except for the important leap of a third to the top *c*—through the full octave and part way back, describing an arch. This arch opens on *c*, suggests in passing a *d-f-a-c* secondary chain, and closes, after touching *f*, on the tenor, *g*. The responses, 2 and 4, remain within the sixth, *c - a*, emphasizing *c-e-g* as structural tones, and then close on the final *c*. The anticipated second-part contrast in line 5 is discreet at first: instead of moving from *e* to *g* as in lines 2 and 4, the opening gesture in line 5 moves a single step from *e* to *f*, then folds in on itself in a centrist, undulating motion, to approach a cadence on *g* from below, the first cadence with rising motion and the only one on *g* with a masculine rhyme. Then line 6 expands smoothly from *g*, outlining the only skip of a fourth, *g -c* (partially filled in by *a*) in the piece, until it touches on the *e* a tenth above the final. From there, it falls back in two waves to the final *c*. In line 7, a dip below *c* to the subfinal *b* ushers in the only cadence in the M melody on a note other than *c* or *g* and the only cadence not approached in stepwise motion. The third *b-d* frames and prepares the resolution of the short last line which functions as an elaborate final cadence.

To bring out the distinctive movement of this melody one may briefly compare it to the K melody. In K, the step-wise motion and narrower range of the *pedes*, the general absence of skips (none larger than a third) throughout, and the exact repetition of lines 5 and 6 produce a more placid tune. Some sense of climax is provided by the slightly higher tessitura of line 7, built on the secondary third chain (*a*)-*c-e*, and featuring the fourth *c-f* in ascending and descending stepwise motion as the apex of a center arch. As in M, the 7th line provides a new cadence, here on *c*, the only cadence not on *g* (the final of the K melody) or on *d*. And the last short line functions here, too, as an expanded cadence. But within a similar overall structure, the K melody in its details is clearly more compact than the M melody; comparison enables us fully to appreciate the captivating motion of M.

As is evident from the graphic representation of the song above, the clear outlines of melodic repetition are reinforced by a rhyme scheme constructed from only 2 sounds. In the first stanza, the feminine rhyme "ete" of lines 1 and 3, gracefully ornamented on the accented (pen-ultimate) syllable, is followed in lines 2 and 4 by the more focused masculine rhyme "er," set to a brief descending figure that returns, except for a slight variation in line 6, with every close on *c*. For stanzas 1, 2, and 4, the contrast between masculine and feminine rhyme, apart from the extra, unaccented syllable, is based on the open and closed "e," on the differing qualities of the same vowel rather than on contrast between dissimilar vowels. Stanzas 3, 5 and 6 preserve the closed "e" but in a feminine rhyme, thus immediately followed by an unaccented "e," and set it against the more somber nasal "on." As explained in the commentary to the song in this Anthology, the sequence of stanzas in our text follows neither the arrangement of *coblas doblas* (stanzas grouped two by two) nor that of *coblas ternas* (stanzas grouped three by three). Both of these techniques produce contrasting blocks of sound, with orderly passage from one block to the other. If the stanzas follow each other in the sequence of our Anthology text AABABB, the song begins and ends with blocks of two stanzas, while in the center (unlike the usual *coblas doblas* or *ternas* patterns) alternation prevails, and there is irregu-lar passage from one kind of stanza to another. On the other hand, the variant stanza order explained in the song com-

mentary offers a sequence AAAB(B). In this case, there is no alternation in the middle and a single progression from one sonorous block to the next which projects, although it does not completely realize it, a regular *coblas ternas* pat-tern. These two ways of performing the song produce dif-ferent experiences in sound, with the song as it appears in this Anthology offering an original variation of the *coblas doblas/ternas* technique. This song is less rich in its sonor-ities than *Pax*. But the kinds of subtle shadings we have observed bear witness to refined craftsmanship.

Now let us ask: does this craftsmanship carry mean-ing? Because of the word "outremer" in the last line of the first stanza, this song has been considered a crusade song. While that brief allusion is not enough to determine a generic identity, the reference to crusade in the first stanza conditions the song's thematic development. In its specific crusade coloring, this piece is very different from Marcabru's *Pax*. That song, from the time of the second crusade, represents a vigorous reaction to the idea of cru-sading, at the moment when crusading ideals were being elaborated. By the time of the third and fourth crusades, roughly 1189-92 and 1202-04 respectively, the period of the Châtelain's song, a certain disillusionment had begun to determine new poetic concerns. The anguish of departure and separation came to figure as prominently in crusading songs as the call to crusade itself, and poets took as their focus the emotional dilemma caused by the necessity of going overseas. "Li nouviauz tanz" represents this shift: departure is painful; if the crusader goes away to Jerusa-lem, he may never see the lady again. Precisely here we discover the importance of the first stanza's last short poetic line. The one mention of "outremer" is crucial because it establishes anxiety. One may note that the word is carefully prepared, and even prolonged into the second stanza, by textual phonetic patterns: repetition of the sound "ou" (lines 1, 2, 3, 4, 6 of stanza 1, and 1, 2, 3 of stanza 2) and of the consonant "m" (in almost every line of the first stanza). The word comes at the **end** of the stanza, in a line metrically opposed to all the other lines in the stanza, thus calling attention to itself. This enables it to color the entire song.[27] The simple initial suggestion—that going abroad could end forever the possibility of enjoying the lady's love—transforms that forced voyage into a kind of fate, sets up a conflict between lady and Jerusalem, and increases the anguish created by thwarted erotic desire.

In the light of these observations, let us ask what matchings of music and text might have been exploited in performance to generate meaning, beginning with the first stanza. To the antecedent/consequent movement of the melody correspond two poetic propositions, each stating a different source of the song's inspiration: first nature, then love. There is a perfect rhetorical fit between the melody and the syntax. Precisely at the climax of the melody, in the 6th line, comes the expression of desire, "cele u j'ai mon cuer." Then the word "nüete" at the end of line 7 falls on the one cadential formula that differs from the others. The presence of this new cadence creates the feeling that something else must follow: it arouses curiosity and prepares the conclusion—the final short text line, the one which, in this first stanza, links the song to crusade. The melodic gesture (and this would be true of all the main versions of the tune) throws the concept of "outremer" into sharp relief. And each time the line comes back in subsequent stanzas to a new text, the repeated melodic gesture subtly recalls initial associations to "outremer," infusing the entire song with a crusading context that would have been entirely familiar to a knightly audience, constantly recalling the danger of the trip, transformed here into the danger of losing the sweet present of love, an outcome foreshadowed only by this last line of the first stanza.

Once the main musical and textual ideas have been delineated, the experience of listening to the song becomes a matter of following their development. One can be attentive both to shifts in syntax and to the way melodic gestures underscore unfolding poetic ideas. In the second stanza, for example, the carrying over through the stanza break (lines 4 and 5) of the sentence that began in line 2 catches the importance of "M'orent . . . pris," the moment of capture, the sealing of the poet's fate. Or again, in the third stanza, the closing ornamentation of the third line offers the opportunity to give more weight both to the rhetorical question and to the word "plouree." Variations in stanza order bring different interpretations.[28] In the version with a full six stanzas, the last line of the last stanza echoes a crusading idea of pardon: crusaders were supposed to pardon all their enemies prior to departure. The syntactic detachment of this line (contrasting, for example, with the last two lines of the first stanza, where line 7 moves right into the dependent clause of line 8), places greater weight on the "incomplete" musical cadence (the only one not on the final or the reciting tone); the last spiteful wish acquires thereby great strength and bitterness. If the song ends with stanza three, the extra crusade resonance is absent, and if stanza five is not included, the theme of the wicked traitors is also absent. A conclusion with stanza three lays stress on the lady's refusal: she alone causes the poet's pain; and in that context the climax on "or sui suenz" acquires particular poignance.

A final brief observation may suggest shadings of interpretation brought by different melody versions. The melody versions in TAa preserve most of the dramatic features of the M version, but the drama is heightened in Aa where the sixth-line climax is more marked because the ascending motion reaches a step higher. K, as we have seen, is tamer, with a climax in the seventh line of the stanza and not the sixth. For the first stanza, this leads to projection of emphasis on "entre mes braz" more than on "cel'u j'ai." Nuances such as these offer a glimpse of how, in performance, a song might take on different colorings due to variations in both text and music.

Notes

1. Cf. Treitler 1992, 3: unity of poetry and music is a function of "the vocal production and aural reception of song."
2. Page 1995, ii.
3. For useful initial background to analysis of troubadour and trouvère lyric, beyond the main reference materials given at the beginning of the bibliography, one may consult: for **terminology**, Randel, *New Harvard Dictionary* 1986; for **general contexts** musical and/or poetic, Dronke 1968/1996, Zumthor 1972/1992, van der Werf 1972, Hoppin 1978, *New Grove*, "Troubadours and Trouvères" 1980, Stevens 1986, Switten 1988, Yudkin 1989, *New Oxford History*, "Medieval Song" 1990, Wilson 1990, Treitler, 1992; for **versification**, Lote 1949-55, Frank 1953-7, Mölk-Wolfzettel 1972, Chambers 1985; for **troubadours**, Marrou 1971, Topsfield 1975, Martín de Riquer 1975/1983, Switten 1985, *Handbook* 1995, Aubrey 1996; for **trouvères** Dragonetti 1960, Bec 1977-8.
4. But see *New Grove* "Trouvères," 203.
5. Switten 1985, 22-40; Aubrey 1996, 184-94. Not only repetition of phrases and motivic units but also reiteration of specific pitches in the same or different positions can provide structural unity; see van der Werf, *Handbook* 1995, 134, 147.
6. DVE, II, ix-x. Dante's treatise, since it is not clear, has given rise to considerable discussion among critics. For an examination of problematic terms, see Stevens, 1986, 19-25, Shapiro 1990. Although Dante's terminology has been widely applied to music, he does not base his concept of the stanza on music alone; indeed whether or not Dante was thinking of actual music is a subject of debate.
7. Cf Gonfroy 1982; Switten 1995, 111-113.
8. Treitler 1992, 3. See also Treitler 1983.
9. Treitler 1992, 8.
10. Stevens 1986, 499.
11. Chambers 1985, 13 ; Switten 1995, 87-8, 165n.175
12. Switten 1985, 53-63.
13. Doss-Quinby 1984; Butterfield 1991.
14. The term was initially proposed by Zumthor 1963, 141, taken up by Bec 1977-78. Note that the term "tonal register" in music makes a different use of the word; register here refers to a segment of the total range of pitches, thus "high" or "low" register.
15. Bec 1977-78, I, 30, 33-4.
16. The *versus* was a type of sacred monastic song characterized by syllable-counting, rhymed, strophic Latin poetry set to music, and cultivated at the Abbey of Saint Martial of Limoges. For a definition and for important relations between the *versus* and troubadour songs, see the article "versus" in the *New Grove* and also in Randel, *New Harvard Dictionary*; Switten 1988, Anthology I, 1-34; Treitler 1992. Troubadour song was certainly in contact with other repertories as well, notably Hispano-Arabic song and a putative "popular song" that is now entirely lost to us.
17. The "octave species" are laid out within the entire range of pitches available to medieval composers called the gamut. The gamut extends from G to e″ (including b flat), and it contains all the pitches theoretically recognized and accounted for. It should be noted that the Middle Ages did not think simply in terms of octave scales but rather conceived of the octave as a conjoined pentachord and tetrachord, as spelled out below. One might mention in addition the concept of the hexachord. Hexachords (collections of six pitches) figure prominently in the history of sight singing. The hexachord

always had one semi-tone in the middle; hexachords began on one of three notes: *c*, *f*, or *g*. Those beginning on *c* had as a semi-tone *e-f*; beginning on *f*, *a-b flat*; beginning on *g*, *b natural-c*. The hexachord system eventually permitted greater flexibility in the use of accidentals and for that reason is connected to *musica ficta*, or the singing of pitches, usually those altered by accidentals left unwritten but still performed, that were not in the gamut. For the concept of *musica ficta* applied to troubadours, see Aubrey 1996, 262-7.

18. A good description of church modes is provided in the article "Mode" in Randel, *New Harvard Dictionary*; for a fuller description, one may consult the article "Mode" in the *New Grove*. Discussion here draws on Treitler, *The Medieval Lyric* (Switten 1988), Commentary Volume, 12-20; Treitler 1991 & 1992. For a succinct discussion of composition of troubadour melodies, see van der Werf *Handbook* 1995, 131-139.

19. Treitler 1992, 5.

20. Treitler 1992, 5. Treitler further points out that the third-chain principle "never received explicit theoretical description in the Middle Ages as did the principle of the octave species."

21. For a recent discussion, see Aubrey 1996, 240-54.

22. See Page 1986; Stevens 1986, 460-91; Switten 1995, 119-33; Aubrey 1996, 80-131.

23. Butterfield 1993; Page 1993a; Everist 1994; Huot 1994, 1997.

24. Arlt 1988.

25. For a graph of these complexities, see Schulze-Busacker 1988, 987.

26. Treitler in Switten 1988, Commentary Volume, pp. 25-6.

27. Dijkstra 1995, 55-6.

28. For a fuller discussion of this question, see Switten 1985, 127-38.

PRONUNCIATION GUIDE

This guide to the pronunciation of Old Occitan (OO) and Old French (OF) takes Modern French (MF) as its point of departure. In other words, knowledge of MF pronunciation is assumed and the guide focuses on features that show a significant difference. The difference will naturally be much greater in the case of Occitan, which is, after all, a distinct, albeit closely related, language.

Both troubadour and trouvère texts show notable variation in spelling, some of it reflective of dialectal divergences in pronunciation. The guide will attempt to take such distinctions into consideration, but there will inevitably be a concentration on the usual. In the case of French, this means the "central" dialect; notes on the dialectal peculiarities of individual texts will be found among the comments on those pieces. The treatment of Occitan will be more inclusive.

Pronunciation, like other aspects of a language, changes in the course of time, and there is no doubt that shifts took place in both languages through the long period of troubadour and trouvère activity. For our present purpose, however, a temporally homogeneous approach seems appropriate. The pronunciation indicated here is therefore essentially that of a somewhat generalized 13th century (to the extent, of course, that scholars in historical linguistics, working from a variety of textual materials, have been able to reconstruct the pronunciation of that remote era).

Let it be noted that the following pages are intended to provide not a detailed description of OO or OF phonology but a practical guide to a reasonable approximation of authenticity in pronunciation.

Phonetic transcription follows the IPA model, with, however, certain simplifications. Closed *e* and *o* are indicated by an acute accent: [é], [ó]; open *e* and *o,* by a grave: [è], [ò]. The neutralization of the distinction between the front rounded vowels [œ] and [ø] is indicated by capital [Ö]. The symbol Ø means zero, not pronounced.

OLD OCCITAN

Stress may fall on the final syllable of a word or on the preceding syllable (the penult).

As a general rule, words ending with a consonant are stressed on the final: *auzelh, perdut, trobar.* There are numerous exceptions, however, especially in the case of flexional *-s*: *cantas, domnas, jutges,* and flexional *-n*: *aman, aguessen,* which are all stressed on the penult.

As a second general rule, words ending with a vowel are stressed on the penult: *canta, partía, domna, azori.* There are numerous exceptions, however, especially in the case of 1st- and 3rd-person preterite forms: *cantéi, partí,* and words whose vowel-endings are variants of vowel + *n*: *canso(n), certa(n).*

The acute accent will often be used to mark stress which is unusual.

Note that knowledge of French, Italian, and/or Spanish usually helps one locate the stressed syllable in Occitan. Cognates are countless and readily detected, and in almost every instance show the same accentual pattern.

Vowels

There are two classes: simple (monophthongs) and complex (diphthongs and triphthongs).

Monophthongs

There are eight such sounds, represented by five letters of the alphabet.

Letter	Pronunciation
a	[a]
e	[é] in unstressed syllables: *semblansa, menutz, trobaire*
	[é] or [è] in stressed position, depending principally on Latin etymon. Although not marked in spelling, the distinction is a significant one. Thus, *ser* 'evening' looks like *ser* 'servant', but the *e* of the first is closed [é] whereas the *e* of the second is open [è]. In addition to the guidance provided by dictionaries (e.g., Levy 1909) and grammars (e.g., Smith 1984) and by etymology, readers with French will find some limited help by considering French cognates. If modern French shows the vowel *oi,* the equivalent OO *e* is probably [é], as in *soir/ser* [é] 'evening' and *mois/mes* [é] 'month'.
i	[i]
o	[u] in unstressed syllables: *governa, mostrar*
	[u] or [ò] in stressed position, depending principally on Latin etymon. Although not marked in spelling, the distinction is a significant one. Thus, *cor* 'I run' looks like *cor* 'heart', but the *o* of the first is [u] whereas the *o* of the second is [ò]. In addition to the guidance provided by dictionaries (e.g., Levy 1909) and grammars (e.g., Smith 1984) and by etymology, readers with French will find some limited help by considering French cognates. If modern French shows the vowel *eu,* the equivalent OO *o* is probably [u], as in *fleur/flor* [u] 'flower' and *amoureuse/amorosa* [u] 'amorous'.
u	[y], as in French: *luna, perdut*

Diphthongs and triphthongs

Diphthongs and triphthongs are numerous in OO. Diphthongs are all of the falling type, i.e., opening with a stressed element and closing with an unstressed; triphthongs all show the pattern unstressed-stressed-unstressed. Note that a complex vowel must be distinguished from a string of vowels that have no intervening consonant (vowels "in hiatus"); the former is contained within a single syllable, whereas vowels in hiatus belong to two separate syllables.

ai	[aⁱ]	ei	[éⁱ] *or* [èⁱ]	oi	[óⁱ] *or* [òⁱ]		
au	[aᵘ]	eu	[éᵘ] *or* [òᵘ]	iu	[iᵘ]	ou	[óᵘ]
iei	[ⁱèⁱ]	ioi	[ⁱóⁱ]				
iau	[ⁱaᵘ]	ieu	[ⁱèᵘ]	iou	[ⁱóᵘ]		
uei	[ᵘèⁱ]	uoi	[ᵘóⁱ]				
ueu	[ᵘèᵘ]	uou	[ᵘóᵘ]				

NB. When the letter *u* occurs as part of a diphthong or triphthong, its value is never [y] but always [u].

Consonants

Letter-sound correspondences tend to be the same as in MF. Special cases are presented in the following table.

Letter(s)   Pronunciation

c	Before *e* and *i*, pronounced either [s] or [ts].
ch	Pronounced as in English *church*.
d	Between vowels, tends to be the equivalent of *z* [z]: *espada = espaza*
g	Before *e* and *i*, pronounced as in English *judge*.
gu	Before a vowel, pronounced [g], never [gw].
g (final)	= *ch* and pronounced as in English *touch*: *enueg = enuech*
h	Never pronounced and never "aspirate" as in MF, except in final position after a vowel, where = final *g* or *ch*: *enueh = enueg = enuech*
j, i	Pronounced as in English *judge*. Note that this consonant is sometimes indicated by the letter *i* in initial or intervocalic position: *ioi = joi* or *maior = major*.
lh, ll, gl	These spelling clusters may be preceded by an *i* which does not count as a vowel. They all represent palatal [l'], as in Italian *egli* or Spanish *llamar*.
nh, gn	May be preceded by an *i* which does not count as a vowel. Pronounced [n'], as in Italian *ogni* or Spanish *señor*.
qu	Pronounced [k], never [kw] except in dative *qui* (= *cui*).
r	Dental trill, as in Italian
z	= *tz* or *ts* at the end of a word and pronounced [ts]; elsewhere, [z].

OLD FRENCH

Stress is the same in OF as in MF: it falls on the final syllable unless the final contains a "mute" *e*. Note that,

whereas final unstressed *e* is truly mute in most cases in MF, it is normally pronounced in the medieval language.

Vowels

There are four classes, produced by the features oral and nasal, as in MF, and by the features simple (monophthongs) and complex (diphthongs and triphthongs): oral monophthongs, oral complex vowels, nasal monophthongs, and nasal complex vowels. In the following descriptive paragraphs, all nasal vowels will be treated together.

Oral monophthongs

Oral monophthongs—a few of which may be denoted by a sequence of two letters—should be pronounced as in MF. The following table will present only exceptional cases.

Note that the use of diacritical marks is quite restricted in OF. The acute accent is used only to indicate that a final *e* is stressed: *(il a) chanté* vs. *(il) chante*. It does not appear in non-final syllables: *desir*, or, more notably, in the two-syllable feminine ending *-ee: chantee*. The grave accent and the circumflex are not used. For the dieresis, see under Oral diphthongs.

Letter(s)   *Pronunciation*

e	Unstressed final *e* [ə] is elided before a word beginning with a vowel but is otherwise pronounced; thus, *une dame est* gives four syllables: *u-ne da-m(e) est*.
eu, ue, ueu	[Ö]: *peu, eu-re, fleur, estuet, vueut*
o	May be [ó] or [u] before final *r*: *amor, jor*
ou	[u]: *douce, amour, jour*
u	Normally [y]: *pur* 'pure', but sometimes [u]: *pur* 'for', *amur*
NOTE:	
ol, oul, ul	before a consonant = *ou* [u]: *dolce* or *doulce, mult*
al	before a consonant = *au* [aᵘ]; see Oral diphthongs.

Oral diphthongs and triphthongs

Oral diphthongs and triphthongs, more numerous in OF than in MF, either begin or end (or both) with an unstressed vocalic element. Note that a complex vowel must be distinguished from a string of vowels that have no intervening consonant (vowels "in hiatus"); the former is contained within a single syllable, whereas vowels in hiatus belong to two separate syllables. The dieresis is used to indicate that two contiguous vowels which might otherwise form a diphthong are syllabically distinct: *lié* 'glad' vs. dissyllabic *li-é* 'tied', *vueut* 'wants' vs. dissyllabic *crü-eus* 'cruel'. It is not normally used, however, to mark the separation of a final unstressed *e* (central [ə]) from a preceding monophthong or diphthong: *mi-e, jou-e, lë-u-e, es-toi-e*.

Letters	Pronunciation
au, al	[aᵘ]: *autre, altre*
eau	[əaᵘ]: *beaus*
iau	[ⁱaᵘ]: *biauté*
ie, ié	[ⁱé]: *pié, piez*

The acute accent is used in cases where it is useful to distinguish the diphthong from *ie* representing the monophthong [i] followed by the central, unstressed, but syllabic [ə]: *pié (s)* 'foot (feet)' vs. *pi-e(s)* 'magpie(s)'.

oi	[ᵘè]: *foi, estoit*
ieu, iel	[ⁱÖ]: *mieuz* or *mielz, sieu-e*
ui	[ʸi]: *nuit*

Nasal vowels

Nasal vowels, either monophthongs or diphthongs, are those preceding a nasal consonant. There are several differences from modern usage, the two most basic being the following. First, every nasal consonant nasalizes the preceding vowel, even when the consonant belongs to the following syllable: *a-ne-e* [ã], *da-me* [ã], *so-ner* [õ]. Second, the nasal consonant is pronounced, even when it belongs to the same syllable as the vowel: *don* [õn], *len-teur* [ãn]. Another matter to note in particular—see the table below—is that OF nasalizes *i* and perhaps even *u,* and does so without lowering them.

Letter(s)	Pronunciation
a	[ã]: *amer, grant, chambre*
e	[ã]: *tendre, lent, sembler*
i	[ĩ]: *fin, prince*
o	[õ]: *doner, home* (or *honme* or *homme*)
u	[ỹ]: *un, une*
ai	[ẽⁱ]: *aime, plaindre*
ei	[ẽⁱ]: *serein, sereine*
ie	[ⁱẽ]: *bien, criembre*
oi	[ᵘẽ]: *point, doigne, poign* (or *poingn* or *poing*)
ue	[ᵘẽ]: *buen, cuens*

Consonants

Letter-sound correspondences are largely the same as today. The most widely ranging distinction between 13th-century central French and the modern language concerns final consonants: in OF, they are pronounced. Differences of narrower range are presented in the following table.

Letter(s)	Pronunciation
h	Pronounced in words that in MF contain a so-called "aspirate" *h*: *haut* (but not *honme*).
l	Between a vowel and a consonant, usually has the same phonetic value as *u*: *altre* = *autre*. See Vowels above.
il (final), ill	Usually, palatal [l'] (like Italian *gl*): *vail, dueil, fille*
ing (final), ngn	Palatal [n']: *loing, seingnor*
r	Dental trill as in Italian
s	Within a word, pronounced before *p, t, c* (=k) and *qu*; before other consonants, *s* is silent: *espoir* [s] vs. *blasme* [Ø]. Remember to pronounce at the end of words, particularly at the end of a phrase.
x	[z] between vowels, [s] at the end of a word: *prixon, fix*
z	[s] or [ts] at the end of a word: *avez*

TROUBADOUR SONGS

Marcabru, "Pax in nomine domini" without music, f. 5a top (p. 51); "Lautrier iustuna sebissa" with music, f. 5a-b (p. 49). The letter P of *Pax* contains a head, the figure of Christ. The rubric states: "aisi comensa so de marc e bru que fo lo premier trobador que fos" ("here begin songs [melodies] of marc e bru who was the first troubadour who ever was"). Ms. R. Cliché Bibliothèque Nationale de France - Paris.

GUILHEM (William) IX DUKE OF AQUITAINE, VII COUNT OF POITIERS

Guilhem IX (1071-1126), usually identified in the *chansonniers* as Lo Coms de Peiteus, is the first known troubadour, the first important poet in any medieval vernacular. His compositions, in one way or another, inspired most later poets. He was also one of the most powerful feudal overlords of his day. This combination of political and poetic prominence has attracted a host of modern critics to the man and to his works (a rich harvest of studies is to be found in Hasenohr-Zink 1992). Eleven songs (one of doubtful authenticity) have been attributed to him. The songs encompass a range of themes and tones: Guilhem IX is a master of the extremes of bawdiness as of the fragile images of love. Singlehandedly, as far as we know, he forged a new, lay poetic voice to express the concerns of the southern urbanized aristocracy. No music survives with the poems. But in a 14th-century play, the *Jeu de Sainte Agnès*, there is a text that is to be sung, according to the stage directions, "in sonu del comte de Peytieu," "to the melody by the Count of Poitiers." The melody given there is incomplete; but enough of it survives to allow us to see that it would fit the poem "Pos de chantar m'es pres talentz."

EDITIONS: Jeanroy 1927; Pasero 1973; Bond 1982.

● "Ab la dolchor del temps novel": PC 183.1. Sources: mss. N 225 & 232, a^1 463 & 499. Text: Bond, 36. Although designated *canso* by modern scholars on thematic grounds, this song does not conform in all of its features, and especially not in its weight, to what will become the *grand chant courtois*. Note that in this song, the term *vers* does not seem to indicate a genre but rather corresponds to our modern idea of "verse," or "poem." The precise genre of the song cannot be specified. As regards versification, Guilhem IX tends to favor octosyllabic verses with masculine rhymes, as here; his rhyme schemes, however, are varied (Chambers 1985, 16-36). The song demonstrates a degree of complexity in its combination of what will come to be called *coblas doblas* and *coblas unissonans*: the first four stanzas are grouped two by two, as in *coblas doblas*; but instead of introducing new rhyme sounds in stanza 3, as would be required for *coblas doblas*, the same sounds are simply rearranged (a=c; b=a; c=b), thus maintaining *coblas unissonans*. Stanza 5 retains the formulation of 3 and 4. The thematics of the "new song"; the images of bird and flower and especially the exquisite comparison of love to hawthorn branch; the suggestion of the *lauzengier* theme at the end, all produce a *canso*-like song, the germ of much that is to come.

● "Companho, farai un vers tot covinen": PC 183.3. Sources: mss. C 231, E 115. Text: Bond, 2. Guilhem IX composed three *Companho* songs, so called because they begin with the same term and have the same metric pattern. They are generally grouped together; Pierre Bec has called them a "genre manqué" (Bec 1982, 37). They are all bawdy songs and stand somewhat apart from what will become common lyric structures. Guilhem IX calls this song a *vers*; but the term *vers,* despite considerable scholarly discussion, remains ambiguous. It has been related to the Latin *versus* (a type of monophonic monastic song, prominent in the repertory from the Abbey of Saint Martial, an important musical and literary center situated in the domains of William IX). *Vers* seems at first to have included what would become the *canso*, taking on later the more specialized meaning of poetry with a moralizing tone. Pierre Bec has argued that there is no real sense of genre in Guilhem's works: "Tout se passe . . . comme si la notion même de 'genre' est absolument absente chez le premier troubadour et que le terme de *vers* . . . est un terme globalisant désignant vraisemblablment toute sorte de poème chanté" (Bec 1982, 37). The structure of this and other *Companho* songs has sometimes been termed archaic: it is found nowhere else among the troubadours. The three-line stanzas have unusually long lines: 2 of 11 syllables and 1 with 14 syllables. The same masculine rhyme is carried all the way through, reminiscent of epic assonance. If the model for this poem comes from Saint Martial, from a Latin Christmas song whose structure this song strongly resembles (Chambers 1985; Chailley 1955), William's song can be considered a clever and particularly irreverent parody.

6.1: Confolens: a town in the Charente, northwest of Limoges, about 70 kilometers south of Poitiers.

8.3: N'Agnes, N'Arsen: unidentified ladies. N' is a contraction of the title *Na*, from the Latin *domina*.

9.1: Gimel is in the Corrèze, near Tulle.

9.2: The exact identity of Niol is not clear; it is probably southwest of Confolens and the place to which reference is made in stanza 6. It is likely that William here is asserting political as well as amorous hegemony.

● "Farai un vers de dreit nïen": PC 183.7. Sources: mss. C 230, E 114. Text: Bond, 14. This song has received abundant critical attention because its meaning constantly eludes the one who would pin it down. Again we find generic indeterminacy: is the song a *vers* (if we knew what that was)? Is it a conundrum? a riddle? a *fatrasie*? One can speak of parodic mode, but of what is it a parody? Of Guilhem's *Pos vezem*? (Chambers 1985, 25). Are we dealing with a serious investigation of psychological disarray? Or an ironic refusal to consider anything seriously? (Topsfield 1975, 30-4). The abrupt juxtapositions of tone leave interpretation open until one can find the *contraclau*, the key. This song, and *Pos vezem*, are possibly the first heterometric compositions we have in the vernacular. The number of syllables follows the pattern 888484. The rhyme scheme underscores this pattern. Change of rhyme and change of meter are coordinated: aaabab, and the fact that the b rhyme has the same sound (*au*) throughout, while the a rhyme (*en*) changes for each stanza, further underscores metric differences.

3.5-6: *Fromitz* means "ant"; in the version of C, we find *soritz* meaning "mouse." Both expressions are intended to convey insignificance; the translation uses an equivalent modern idiom. Saint Martial was a well-known saint in the Limousin, honored by the Abbey of Saint Martial at Limoges.

- "Pos de chantar m'es pres talentz": PC 183.10. Sources: mss. C 230, D^a 190, I 142, K 128, N 230 & 234, R 8, a^1 463. Text: Bond, 40. For the music, and a reconstruction of the song, see Bond, Appendix B, and Switten 1988, Anthology I, 42-3.

It is possible that this song was well known because it is attached to contemporary events. It was probably composed in 1117-9; it is often considered a farewell lament, reflecting Guilhem's awareness of the inevitability of death; it is sometimes connected with William's departure on a crusade to northern Spain in 1120. The four-line octosyllabic (isometric) stanzas have a rhyme scheme aaab whose only subtlety is the changing "a" rhyme and the constant "b" rhyme, a technique William often used.

1.3: *obedïenz*. For the translation "vassal," see Brunel 1973, glossary. In this passage it is a question of leaving "worldy service": the word can carry amatory as well as political meanings.

2: The order of lines in this stanza follows Pasero in maintaining DIK.

2:3: The son will become William X. He, in turn, will be succeeded, after a relatively short period, by his famous daughter Eleanor.

3.3: Foulques V the Younger, Count of Anjou. *Cozi* here means "relative": Foulques was not a cousin but a more distant relative of William IX.

4.1: The King of France, Louis VI (1108-37).

4.3: For this line, I follow Pasero.

6: A number of editors, including Jeanroy, have preferred the reading of CR for this stanza, given here. Pasero has proposed that the *compaignon* of 6.1 might be William's second wife, Philippa-Mathilde, who became a nun at Fontevrault (Pasero, 289; Bond, 80). Adopting Pasero's reading of the stanza: "Per merce prec mon conpaignon: / s'anc li fi tort, qu'il m'o perdon; / et il prec En Jezu del tron / en romans et en son lati," one can argue that the "il prec" refers to Philippa-Mathilde, who would then be invited to intercede for her former husband.

9:2: Although *cavalaria* is translated "chivalry," one should beware of reading into this word meanings appropriate to a later period (Switten, *Study of Chivalry* 1988, 414).

T.2 (4): These are symbols of earthly power.

- "Pus vezem de novelh florir": PC 183.11. Sources: mss. C 231, E 115, a^1 459, α 32435. Text: Bond, 28. This song develops in a somewhat paradoxical manner themes of "courtly conduct" (we see here what will become a familiar opposition of *cortes* and *vilan*), which are then juxtaposed to boasting about the artistic excellence of both words and music (stanza 7). In another song, not included in this Anthology, "Ben vueill que sapchon li pluzor," William proclaims his mastery of the art of *trobar* (which is also the art of love): "ieu port d'aicel mestier la flor" ("I take the prize in this profession"). From the very outset, troubadour song is a consciously cultivated craft.

T1.1 (6): *Narbona* is probably the city and not a *senhal* (Pasero, 209). William IX had political interests in Languedoc and pretentions to the Toulousain through his wife Philippa-Mathilde, who was related to the family of the Counts of Toulouse.

T2.1 (6): *Esteve*: unidentified *senhal* (or code-name).

Ab la dolchor del temps novel (PC 183.1)
Canso

Ab la dolchor del temps novel	With the sweetness of the new season
Foillo li bosc, e li aucel	The woods burgeon, and the birds
Chanton, chascus en lor lati,	Sing, each in their language
Segon lo vers del novel chan; 1.4	According to the verse of a new song;
Adonc esta ben c'om s'aisi	Then it is fitting that a man draw near
D'acho don hom a plus talan.	To that which he most desires.

De lai don plus m'es bon e bel	From the source of my greatest good and beauty
Non vei mesager ni sagel,	I see neither messenger nor letter,
Per que mos cors non dorm ni ri,	So that I neither sleep nor laugh,
Ni no m'aus traire adenan, 2.4	Nor do I dare go forward
Tro que eu sacha ben de la fi	Until I am sure, concerning the outcome,
S'el'es aissi com eu deman.	Whether it is such as I ask for.

La nostr'amor vai enaissi	Our love is like
Com la branca de l'albespi,	The hawthorn branch
Qu'esta sobre l'arbre tremblan	Which clings trembling on the tree
La nuoit, a la ploia ez al gel, 3.4	At night, in the rain and ice,
Tro l'endeman, que.l sols s'espan	Until the next day, when the sun spreads out
Per la fueilla vert el ramel.	Through the green leaves and the branches.

Enquer me menbra d'un mati	I yet remember one morning
Que nos fezem de guerra fi,	When we put an end to warring.
E que.m donet un don tan gran:	And she gave me so great a gift:
Sa drudari'e son anel; 4.4	Her love and her ring.
Enquer me lais Dieus viure tan	May God allow me still to live long enough
C'aia mas mans soz so mantel!	To place my hands beneath her cloak!

Qu'eu non ai soing d'estraing lati	And I care naught about the strange gibberish
Que.m parta de mon Bon Vezi;	Which could separate me from my *Bon Vezi,*
Qu'eu sai de paraulas, com van	For I know how words circulate
Ab un breu sermon, que s'espel, 5.4	From a short speech which spreads out.
Que tal se van d'amor gaban;	Some people go vainly boasting of love;
Nos n'avem la pessa e.l coutel!	We have the morsel and the knife.

Companho, farai un vers tot covinen (PC 183.3)
Vers

Companho, farai un vers tot covinen,	Companions, I'll make a suitable *vers*
Ez aura.i mais de foudatz no.i a de sen,	Containing more folly than sense,
Ez er totz mesclatz d'amor e de joi e de joven. 1.3	And it will be all mixed with love, joy, and youth.

E tenhatz lo per vilan qui no l'enten	And take him for a peasant who doesn't understand it,
O qu'ins en son cor voluntiers non l'apren;	Or doesn't learn it willingly in his heart;
Greu partir si fai d'amor qui la trob'a son talen. 2.3	It's difficult to part from love if you find it to your liking.

Dos cavals ai a ma seilla, ben e gen;	I have two horses for my saddle, well and good;
Bon son ez ardit per armas e valen,	They are fine, and skilled for feats of arms, and valiant,
Mas no.ls puesc tener amdos que l'uns l'autre	But I can't keep both because one won't accept
non consen. 3.3	the other.

Si.ls pogues adomesgar a mon talen,	If I could tame them to my desire,
Ja no volgr'aillors mudar mon garnimen,	Never would I wish to transfer my gear elsewhere,
Que meils for'encavalguatz de negun home viven. 4.3	For I would be better mounted than any man living.

Laüns fo dels montanhiers lo plus corren;	One was the swiftest of the mountain stock,
Mas aitan fera estranheza ha longuamen,	But for a long while it has been very skittish,
Ez es tan fers e salvatges que de bailar si defen. 5.3	And it is so wild and savage that it refuses currying.

L'autre fo noiritz sa jos, pres Cofolen,
Ez anc no vis belazor, mon essïen;
Aquest non er ja camjatz ni per aur ni
     per argen.   6.3

The other was raised down there by Confolens,
And never, in my opinion, did you see one so lovely;
This one will never be exchanged, neither for gold nor
     for silver.

Qu'ie.l donei a son senhor poilli paisen;
Pero si.m retinc ieu tant de covenen
Que s'il lo teni'un an, qu'ieu lo tengues
     mais de sen.   7.3

And I gave it to its lord, a colt in pasture;
However, I retained for myself this much by right,
That if he kept it a year, I could keep it more than
     a hundred.

Cavalier, datz mi cosseill d'un pensamen;
Anc mais no fui eisarratz de cauzimen:
E no sai ab cal mi tenha, de N'Agnes ho
     de N'Arsen.   8.3

Knights, give me advice about a dilemma,
Never was I more harassed in a choice:
I simply don't know with which one to stay, with Lady
     Agnes or with Lady Arsen.

De Gimel ai lo castel e.l mandamen,
E per Niol fauc ergueill a tota gen;
C'ambedui me son jurat e plevit per sagramen.   9.3

I have the castle and the command of Gimel,
And because of Niol, I act proud toward everyone,
For both are sworn and pledged to me by oath.

Farai un vers de dreit nïen (PC 183.7)
Vers (devinaill)

Farai un vers de dreit nïen:
Non er de mi ni d'autra gen,
Non er d'amor ni de joven,
     Ni de ren au,   1.4
Qu'enans fo trobatz en durmen
     Sus un chivau.

I'll make a *vers* of pure nothingness:
It will not be of me nor of others,
It will not be of love nor of youth,
Nor of anything else,
Rather was it composed while sleeping
On a horse.

No sai en qual hora.m fui natz,
No soi alegres ni iratz,
No soi estranhs ni soi privatz,
     Ni no.n puesc au,   2.4
Qu'enaisi fui de nueitz fadatz
     Sobr'un pueg au.

I know not at what hour I was born;
I am neither happy nor sad;
I am neither stranger nor intimate,
Nor can I be otherwise,
For to be thus was I fated, by night,
On a high hill.

No sai cora.m sui endormitz,
Ni cora.m veill, s'om no m'o ditz;
Per pauc no m'es lo cor partitz
     D'un dol corau;   3.4
E no m'o pretz una fromitz,
     Per Saint Marsau!

I know not when I fell asleep,
Nor when I wake, if I'm not told.
My heart is nearly broken
From heartfelt pain;
And I don't give a hoot for that,
By Saint Martial!

Malautz soi e cremi morir,
E re no sai mas quan n'aug dir;
Metge querrai al mieu albir,
     E no sai tau;   4.4
Bos metges er si.m pot guerir,
     Mas non si amau.

I am sick and fear to die,
And know nothing of it save what I hear;
I'll seek a doctor to my liking,
And I don't know who;
He'll be a good doctor if he can cure me,
But not if I grow sicker.

Amigu'ai ieu, no sai qui s'es,		I have a friend, I don't know who she is,
C'anc no la vi, si m'aiut fes;		For I never saw her, by my faith;
Ni.m fes que.m plassa ni que.m pes,		She has neither pleased me nor grieved me,
Ni no m'en cau,	5.4	Nor does it matter to me,
C'anc non ac Norman ni Franses		For I never had a Norman or a Frenchman
Dins mon ostau.		In my house.
Anc non la vi ez am la fort;		I never saw her and I love her greatly;
Anc non aic dreit ni no.m fes tort;		She has never done me right or wrong;
Quan no la vei, be m'en deport,		When I don't see her, I amuse myself just fine.
No.m prez un jau:	6.4	I don't care a cock,
Qu'ie.n sai gensor e belazor,		For I know a lady more noble and prettier
E que mais vau.		And who's worth more.
No sai lo luec ves on s'esta,		I don't know the place she inhabits,
Si es en pueg ho es en pla;		Whether it is on a hill or in a plain;
Non aus dire lo tort que m'a,		I dare not tell of the harm she's done me,
Abans m'en cau;	7.4	Rather do I remain silent;
E peza.m be quar sai rema,		And it saddens me to remain here,
Ab aitan vau.		For that reason I go.
Fait ai lo vers, no sai de cui;		I've made this *vers,* I don't know about whom;
E trametrai lo a celui		And I'll send it to the one
Que lo.m trametra per autrui		Who will send it for me through another
Enves Anjau,	8.4	There towards Anjou
Que.m tramezes del sieu estui		So that she might send me for her coffer
La contraclau.		The key.

Pos de chantar m'es pres talentz (PC 183.10)
Vers (planh)

Pos de chantar m'es pres talentz		Since I feel a need to sing
Farai un vers don sui dolenz:		I will make a song about my sorrow;
Mais no serai obedïenz		No longer will I be a vassal
En Peitau ni en Lemozi.	1.4	In Poitou and in Limousin.
Qu'era m'en irai en eisil:		For now I shall go into exile:
En gran paor, en grand peril,		In great fear, in great peril,
En guerra laisserai mon fil,		At war I will leave my son,
E faran li mal siei vezi.	2.4	And his neighbors will harm him.
Lo departirs m'es aitan grieus		The departure from the domain
Del senhoratge de Peitieus:		Of Poitiers is so difficult for me!
En garda lais Folco d'Angieus		I leave Foulques of Angers in charge
Tota la terr'e son cozi.	3.4	Of all the land and of his cousin.
Si Folcos d'Angieus no.l socor		If Foulques of Angers does not help him
E.l reis de cui ieu tenc m'onor,		And the king from whom I hold my domain,
Faran li mal tuit li pluzor,		Many people will bring him harm,
Felon Gascon et Angevi.	4.4	Treacherous Gascons and Angevins.

Si ben non es savis ni pros,	If he is neither wise nor valiant
Cant ieu serai partitz de vos,	When I will have left you,
Viatz l'auran tornat en jos,	Quickly they will have overturned him
Car lo veiran jov'e mesqui. 5.4	For they will see him young and feeble.
Merce quier a mon compaignon	I ask pity for my companion
S'anc li fi tort, qu'il m'o perdon,	If ever I wronged him, may he pardon me,
Et ieu prec en Jesu del tron,	And I pray to Lord Jesus on the throne
Et en romans et en lati. 6.4	In Romance and in Latin.
De proeza e de joi fui,	I have belonged to prowess and joy,
Mas ara partem ambedui,	But now we part company,
Et eu irai m'en a sellui	And I go away to the One
On tuit peccador troban fi. 7.4	With whom all sinners find rest.
Mout ai estat cuendes e gais,	I have been most charming and gay,
Mas Nostre Seigner no.l vol mais;	But our Lord wants that no more;
Ar non puesc plus soffrir lo fais,	Now I can no longer carry the burden,
Tan soi aprochatz de la fi. 8.4	So close have I come to the end.
Tot ai guerpit quant amar sueill,	I have left behind everything I used to love,
Cavalaria et orgueill,	Chivalry and pride,
E pos Dieu platz tot o acueill,	And since it pleases God, I accept all that
E prec li que.m reteing'am si. 9.4	And pray Him to retain me in His presence.
Toz mos amics prec a la mort	I pray all my friends, at the moment of death
Que vengan tuit e m'onren fort,	To come and render me high honor,
Qu'eu ai avut joi e deport	For I have known joy and pleasure
Loing e pres et e mon aizi. 10.4	Far and near and in my domain.
Aissi guerpisc joi e deport	Thus I leave joy and pleasure
E vair e gris e sembeli. T.2 (4)	And rich fur and sable.

Pus vezem de novelh florir (PC 183.11)
Vers

Pus vezem de novel florir	Since we see blossoming anew
Pratz, e vergiers reverdezir,	The meadows, and the orchards growing green again,
Rius e fontainas esclarzir,	Streams and fountains running clear,
Auras e vens, 1.4	Breezes and winds,
Ben deu cascus lo joi jauzir	Each rightly should enjoy the joy
Don es jauzens.	From which he is joyous.
D'amor non dei dire mas be.	I should say naught but good of love.
Quar no.n ai ni petit ni re?	Why have I not the smallest amount of it?
Quar ben leu plus no m'en cove.	Perhaps because more is not fitting for me.
Pero leumens 2.4	Yet easily
Dona gran joi qui be mante	It gives great joy to the one who maintains
Los aizimens.	The rules.

A totz jorns m'es pres enaisi
C'anc d'aquo c'amei no.m jauzi,
Ni o farai, ni anc no fi.
    C'az escïens   3.4
Fauc maintas rens que.l cor me di:
    "Tot es nïens."

Per tal n'ai meins de bon saber
Quar vueill so que no puesc aver,
E si.l reprovers me ditz ver:
    "Sertanamens   4.4
A bon coratge bon poder,
    Qui's ben suffrens."

Ja no sera nuils hom ben fis
Contr'amor, si non l'es aclis,
Ez als estranhs ez als vezis
    Non es consens,   5.4
Ez a totz sels d'aicel aizis
    Obedïens.

Obedïensa deu portar
A maintas gens, qui vol amar;
E cove li que sapcha far
    Faitz avinens,   6.4
E que.s gart en cort de parlar
    Vilanamens.

Del vers vos dic que mais ne vau,
Qui be l'enten, e n'a plus lau;
Que.ls motz son faitz tug per egau
    Comunalmens,   7.4
E.l sonetz, qu'ieu meteus m'en lau,
    Bos e valens.

A Narbona, mas ieu no.i vau,
    Sia.l prezens
Mos vers, e vueill que d'aquest lau
    Me sia guirens.   T1.4 (6)

Mon Esteve, mas ieu no.i vau,
    Sia.l prezens
Mos vers, e vueill que d'aquest lau
    Me sia guirens.   T2.4 (6)

Always it has befallen me thus
That never from the beloved did I have joy,
Nor will I, nor ever did I.
Quite knowingly
I do many things while my heart tells me
"All is nothingness."

And so I have less real pleasure
Because I want what I cannot have,
And the proverb tells me the truth:
"Certainly
Where there's a will, there's a way,
For the one who is patient."

Never will a man be entirely true
To love if he does not submit to it,
And if to both strangers and intimates
He is not obliging,
And to all in that domain
Obedient.

Obedience must he guarantee
To many people, he who wishes to love,
And it behooves him to know how to accomplish
Gracious deeds
And to refrain, at court, from speaking
Like a peasant.

Of this song I tell you that it is worth more,
If one understands it well, and it is praised more;
For the words are perfectly adjusted
Together
And the melody, for which I praise myself,
Fine and noble.

In Narbonne, although I'm not going there,
May my song
Be present; and I want it, of this praise,
To be my guarantor.

Before *Mon Esteve,* although I'm not going there,
May my song
Be present; and I want it, of this praise,
To be my guarantor.

MARCABRU

Among the troubadours, Marcabru (c. 1127-1150) was one of the most prolific and remains one of the most difficult. According to his *vida*, he was of humble birth. At the outset of his career, he probably benefitted from the patronage of William X, Duke of Aquitaine, son of the first known troubadour; subsequently, he seems to have travelled to other courts without attaching himself permanently to any. In all likelihood, he had the education of a cleric. Forty-two poems are attributed to him; four have been preserved with their music. Marcabru cultivated a "closed" style (known as *trobar clus*—although his "hermeticism" may be due more to gaps in our knowledge of the language than to any stylistic choice on his part), using a rich vocabulary, with a number of words he probably invented, and calling upon vivid resources of poetic image and symbol. Marcabru handles with consummate skill the weapons of the satirist: irony, invective, scathing criticism. He attacked what he considered to be false love and false lovers, those who did not live up to his ideals of true love (*fin'amor*) and civilized behavior. Marcabru's melodies show a diversity of construction that bears witness to a powerful formal imagination. He was an original versifier, continually experimenting with formal structures (Chambers 1985, 37-70). Like those of his predecessor Guilhem IX, his works have been much studied (see for example: Arlt 1988, Pollina 1991 and 1993, Harvey 1989; and for useful listings, Harvey and Gaunt 1988, as well as Hasenohr-Zink 1992).

EDITIONS: Dejeanne 1909; van der Werf 1984.

● "A la fontana del vergier": PC 293.1. Source: ms. C 173; no music. Text: Dejeanne, 3. (A more recent edition with numerous notes is Pirot 1973.) This song was probably composed between 1146-47 and has been linked to the second crusade, given the reference to King Louis (v. 26), doubtless Louis VII who led the crusade. It is a brief narration, not unrelated to what will become the *pastourelle*. Although it is called a *romance* by modern scholars, such a genre did not yet exist in Old Occitan. The narrator encounters a fair maiden whose favors he would surely enjoy if she would but let him. The poem has six stanzas, each with seven 8-syllable lines, all masculine. The rhymes follow the schema aaabaac, thus technically two *rims estramps*, b and c. The b-sound (ors) and the c-sound (atz) remain the same throughout the song, setting up a repetition that underscores key words. The a-sound changes with each stanza (determining *coblas singulars*), carrying the narrative forward. Thus is set up a delicate balance between stability and instability.

● "Bel m'es quan son li fruich madur": PC 293.13. Sources: mss. A 34, I 121, K 106, N 267, W 203, a¹ 297, d 308; music in W, with "frenchified" words, one stanza. Text: Dejeanne, 53. Several themes typical of Marcabru are bound up in this song: *fin'amor* (pure, refined love), nature, and song. The song is a firm defense of *fin'amor* against the *fals'amor* that disrupts both the natural and the moral order. The six *coblas unissonans* have a rhyme scheme ababcdcd; they are heterometric, mixing masculine and feminine endings: 888887'87'. The melody initially establishes a *d* mode in its authentic disposition, sweeping through the range of an octave in the first phrase, producing an eloquent opening gesture. The mode is further reinforced by the cadences, which could be considered musical rhymes, forming, as it were, a "scheme" abba (ending notes *dffd*) which is repeated, dividing the stanza into two parts, with the exception of the fifth phrase in which the concluding formula dips to *c*, a second below the *finalis* (Arlt 1988). This close and the prominence of the notes *c*, *e*, *g* in phrases 5 and 6 suggest a momentary change of tonal focus from *d* to *c*. The melody is characterized by a number of skips, by its relatively wide range and elegant ornamentation, and by a series of repetitions of small segments other than the cadences. Although there are no exact repetitions of entire lines, repetition of these small segments and the musical rhyme create a tight construction. One may note the subtly shifting sound coordinations between textual and musical "rhyme schemes," and the rhythmic shift that arises when the cadences of lines 6 and 8 accompany feminine rhymes when they had previously been heard to masculine rhymes.

3.2: The translation of "revolim" comes from Levy *Petit dictionnaire*. It could also be translated "change." For a discussion of the word, see Pollina 1991, 70.

4.5: The word "meillor" usually refers to the lady because by very definition, she is "the best."

● "Dirai vos senes duptansa": PC 293.18. Sources: mss. A 29, C 174, Dᵃ 189, I 177, K 103, M 142, R 5, a¹ 309, α 28231 & 28246; music in R. Text: Dejeanne, 77. This song has a troubled manuscript history, numerous variants, and divergent stanza orders. See Dejeanne, 77-86. The stanza order here is from AIK, closely seconded by D and R.

If the previous song is an ardent defense of good Love, this one, just as ardently, attacks bad Love—in Marcabru's best satirical manner, demonstrating his penchant for provocative imagery, double entendre, and unusual choice of words. Marcabru may have invented the *sirventes* although he did not use the term, designating instead such songs as *vers*. This song differs from the previous song in almost all of its features. Melody and text here converge angrily around a small number of sounds within a tightly circumscribed musical space. The melody is tersely syllabic, moving initially within the range of a third (*f-a*), expanding to a fifth (*d-a*), then to the sixth *c-a*. Stepwise motion predominates. The tonality of *f* is first suggested; but the piece closes on *d*, which is the final of the primary third chain *d, f, a, c*. The versification combines feminine and masculine 7-syllable lines with a brisk, 3-syllable masculine refrain, and two different rhyme sounds, thus: aaabab / 7'7'7'37'7. The shift from the feminine rhyme "ansa" to the masculine "atz," preserving the vowel sound but changing the consonants, strongly punctuates refrain and stanza close. The twelve stanzas present a series of assertions castigating false love, usually two per stanza. The assertions are paired with each other, offering, first, example or image (first three lines), followed by proverbial or moralistic declaration (last two lines) (Nichols 1976). They are separated by the refrain "Escoutatz!" which is set apart musically by a sparse descent to *c*, sketching a shift to the contrasting third *c-e*. Because only the refrain cadences on a note not from the primary third chain, it catches our attention to reinforce the moral lesson.

2: The rapaciousness of love seems to be the theme of this stanza. Some have suggested that Love here is compared to a bad lord. See Harvey 1989, 103.

3: The image of fire depicts both the attraction and the destructiveness of love. Harvey 1989, 51.

6.3-4: Ruth Harvey connects the meaning of these lines to the selfishness of love and offers an interesting parallel quotation from Hugh of Saint Victor. Harvey 1989, 102 and 229 n. 17.

8.1: Here is suggested again the notion of adulteration which Marcabru so often associates with false love.

9.1: The horse as a symbol of licentiousness is well known.

10.5-6: I follow Paterson 1975, 38 and Harvey 1989, 116 in the translation of "mosca" as "fly"; Dejeanne gives "abeille".

11.1-3: Both antifeminism and the importance of the Scriptures in Marcabru's works are evident in these lines. For comparison to Solomonic passages of the Scriptures and to the Book of Proverbs, see Harvey 1989, 113.

• "L'autrier jost'una sebissa": PC 293.30. Sources: mss. A 33, C 176, I 120, K 106, N 266, R 5, T 206, a^1 310, d 307; music in R. Text: Dejeanne, 137. This is one of the best known songs by Marcabru, in the Middle Ages as now, if one is to judge by the number of manuscripts in which it has been preserved and the number of modern editions and commentaries. It is the first known vernacular *pastorela* (not so named, however, by Marcabru). Marcabru was not working within established generic conventions; his song helped establish them. "L'autrier" demonstrates most of the features of future *pastourelles*: the marauding knight's attempt to seduce the shepherdess and her refusal (as in this case), acceptance, or rape (Pasero 1980, 1983).

The melody is preserved in manuscript R with a kind of ambiguous "semi-mensural" notation, demonstrating in all probability numerous hesitations on the part of the scribe; this notation has produced considerable discussion (van der Werf 1984, 18-9; Aubrey 1982 and 1996; Switten 1993). The song has been transcribed here with neutral black notes, without indication of rhythm; original note forms are represented above the staff. The state of the manuscript does not permit sure indication of the note forms, especially of the stems: some are practically illegible. Notes to the transcription indicate where most doubts arise.

Few subsequent *pastorelas* can match this one for sauciness, wit and handling of dramatic dialogue. It rewards close study of tone, imagery and dialectic. The *coblas doblas* (such stanzas are typical for dialogue songs) are constructed from a succession of 7-syllable lines with all feminine rhymes: aaabaab / 7'7'7'7'7'7'7'. The a rhyme changes every two stanzas; the b rhyme remains constant. It includes the refrain word "vilana" (in the even-numbered stanzas from 2-10, the refrain is a phrase: "so.m dis la vilana"). One could diagram the melody ABABCCD, but C starts out like A, and there are other similar features, such that the only entirely different line is D. At first, melody and verse seem of simple, unrelated construction; but the simplicity is deceptive. One cannot assume by the time of Marcabru the notion that a melodic scheme ABAB should be paired to a rhyme scheme abab. One must ask: what meaning does the joining of rhyme scheme and melodic scheme in this song generate? The key feature is the presence of a new rhyme sound (b) to a repeated melody (B) at line 4—just the moment of the appearance of the refrain word. This feature brings into contact a musical cadence already heard and a verbal sound that is new, and the effect—carried throughout the song—is to emphasize the defining refrain word: "vilana" (Switten 1988; 1995, 116). Tonally, the piece is ambiguous. The first segment, ABAB, explores the upper portion of the octave *a-a'* and cadences on *d* (A) or *c* (B), establishing an antecedent/consequent relationship. The second portion remains essentially within the fifth *a-e*, cadencing on *g* twice, then on a final *a*. *C* is not only the cadence of the 2nd and 4th phrases but also the initial reciting tone of phrases 1, 3, 5, and 6. It thus assumes special importance and establishes *c* as a tonal center. But since the song ends on *a*, it is reasonable to think not in terms of a single mode, but in terms of bi-tonality (Parker 1977, 24).

1.1: Melody position 1: The note could once have had a stem which was erased.

1.4: Melody position 3: The note is almost entirely covered by a smudge. Showing the note as here is merely a best guess. Melody position 4: There could be a very faint stem for this note. Van der Werf has no stem; Aubrey (1982, 139) puts one.

1.7: Melody position 1: The stem here is almost entirely absorbed by the letter "t," yet a faint line seems to descend below the letter. Van der Werf has a note without stem and a question mark; Aubrey places a stem. Melody position 2: There is a very faint suggestion of a stem. Van der Werf has no stem; Aubrey has one. Melody position 8: The stem is almost entirely covered by the flourish that marks the beginning of the second stanza.

T2.1: This line is unclear: the idea seems to be that the knight has false hopes, with the obvious further assumption that the *vilana* holds the truth. It is evident that these words are intended to close the debate and send the knight packing.

- *"Pax in nomine Domini"*: PC 293.35. Sources: mss. A 29, C 177, I 117, K 103, R 5, W 194, a¹ 293, d 303; music in W, with two stanzas and "frenchified" words. Text: Dejeanne, 169 (taking into consideration also Ricketts 1966 and Hamlin 1985). Performed on Anthology CD. This is the best known early vernacular crusade song; it enjoyed considerable success even among Marcabru's contemporaries (Schulze-Busacker 1988). If 1149 is accepted as a date (an earlier date had long been proposed), the song bathes in the climate of the Second Crusade preached at Vézelay by Saint Bernard. It reflects the continuing impor-

tance of the Peace movement and especially the new visibility of the crusade in Spain. From about 1115 the Spanish Theater became more and more important until, finally, around 1148, all aspects of crusade were associated with it: vows, taking the cross, penitential remissions. For a guide to analysis, see the introductory essay on music and words.

1.6: The *lavador* suggests any purifying rite, such as baptism, pilgrimage or crusade. Note that in Spain, crusading and pilgrimage motifs intertwine because of the famous pilgrimage route to Compostela, but the Orient is clearly suggested also (Antioch).

1.9: Melody position 8: The ms. has a natural sign on line 2 preceding the notes *b, c, a*. Since the natural sign served as both natural and sharp sign, it could here indicate a c-sharp, the only such use of a natural sign in troubadour sources (Van der Werf 1984, 38, 42, 277*). Arlt 1988, 185, gives b-natural.

2.9: That is, we will be in hell rather than in heaven.

3.9: Doubtless the devil.

4.4: Alfonso VII of Spain (1126-57).

7.1: Raimon-Berenguer IV, Count of Barcelona and Marquis of Provence.

7.2: The Knights Templars.

8:4-5: Here I follow Ricketts 1966.

8.7: William X of Aquitaine (VIII of Poitiers) who died in 1137 at Compostela.

A la fontana del vergier (PC 293.1)
Romance

A la fontana del vergier,		By the orchard fountain
On l'erb'es vertz josta.l gravier,		Where the grass is green along the sandy bank,
A l'ombra d'un fust domesgier,		In the shade of a domestic tree,
En aiziment de blancas flors	1.4	Adorned with white flowers,
E de novelh chant costumier,		And the new seasonal song,
Trobey sola, ses companhier,		I found alone, without companion,
Selha que no vol mon solatz.		The girl who does not want my solace.

So fon donzelh'ab son cors belh		She was a maiden of fair body
Filha d'un senhor de castelh;		Daughter of a castle lord,
E quant ieu cugey que l'auzelh		And when I thought the birds
Li fesson joy e la verdors,	2.4	Might bring her joy as well as the verdure
E pel dous termini novelh,		And the sweet springtime,
E quez entendes mon favelh,		And that she might hear my tale,
Tost li fon sos afars camjatz.		Suddenly her whole attitude changed.

Dels huelhs ploret josta la fon		Tears flowed from her eyes there by the fountain
E del cor sospiret preon.		And from her heart came deep sighs.
"Ihesus, dis elha, reys del mon,		"Jesus," said she, "King of the world,
Per vos mi creys ma grans dolors,	3.4	Because of You my great sorrow increases,
Quar vostra anta mi cofon,		Your shame confounds me,
Quar li mellor de tot est mon		For the best men in this world
Vos van servir, mas a vos platz.		Go to serve You, according to Your wish.

Ab vos s'en vai lo meus amicx,   With You goes my friend,
Lo belhs e.l gens e.l pros e.l ricx;   So handsome, fine, valiant and noble;
Sai m'en reman lo grans destricx,   Here remains with me great distress,
Lo deziriers soven e.l plors.   4.4   Endless desire and tears.
Ay! mala fos reys Lozoicx   Ah! May King Louis be damned
Que fay los mans e los prezicx   Who gave the commands and the pleas
Per que.l dols m'es en cor intratz."   That caused grief to enter my heart."

Quant ieu l'auzi desconortar,   When I heard her grieving
Ves lieys vengui josta.l riu clar: I went near her, down by the clear stream:
"Belha, fi.m ieu, per trop plorar   "Fair lady," I said, "too much weeping
Afolha cara e colors;   5.4   Will ruin your face and complexion;
E no vos cal dezesperar,   And you must not despair
Que selh qui fai lo bosc fulhar,   For He who makes the woods come into leaf
Vos pot donar de joy assatz."   Can give you great joy."

"Senher, dis elha, ben o crey   "My Lord," said she, "I do believe
Que Deus aya de mi mercey   That God may take pity on me
En l'autre segle per jassey,   In the world to come, forever,
Quon assatz d'autres peccadors;   6.4   As with many other sinners;
Mas say mi tolh aquelha rey   But here below he takes from me the one
Don joys mi crec; mas pauc mi tey   Who can increase my joy; but nothing matters
Que trop s'es de mi alonhatz."   Since he has gone away from me."

Bel m'es quan son li fruich madur (PC 293.13)

Sirventes-Canso

Bel m'es quan son li fruich madur   It pleases me when the fruit are ripe
E reverdejon li gaïm,   And the second crop grows green
E l'auzeill, per lo temps escur,   And the birds, as the days become darker,
Baisson de lor votz lo refrim   1.4   Lower the sound of their voices
Tant redopton la tenebror;   So fearful are they of the gloom;
  E mos coratges s'enansa,   And my heart is lifted up
Qu'ieu chant per joi de fin'Amor   For I sing for joy of noble Love
  E vei ma bon'esperansa.   1.8   And I see my good hope.

Fals amic, amador tafur,
Baisson Amor e levo.l crim;
E no.us cuidetz c'Amors pejur,
C'atrestant val cum fetz al prim;   2.4
Totz temps fon de fina color,
    Et ancse d'una semblansa;
Nuills hom non sap de sa valor
    La fin ni la comensansa.   2.8

Qui.s vol si creza fol agur,
Sol Dieus mi gart de revolim!
Qu'en aital Amor m'aventur
On non a engan ni refrim;   3.4
Qu'estiu et invern e pascor
    Estau en grand alegransa,
Et estaria en major
    Ab un pauc de seguransa.   3.8

Ja non creirai, qui que m'o jur,
Que vins non iesca de razim,
Et hom per Amor no meillur;
C'anc un pejurar non auzim,   4.4
Qu'ieu vaill lo mais per la meillor,
    Empero si.m n'ai doptansa,
Qu'ieu no.m n'aus vanar, de paor
    De so don ai m'esperansa.   4.8

Greu er ja que fols desnatur,
Et a follejar non recim
E folla que no.is desmesur;
E mals albres de mal noirim,   5.4
De mala brancha mala flor
    E fruitz de mala pesansa
Revert al mal outra.l pejor,
    Lai on Jois non a sobransa.   5.8

Que l'Amistat[s] d'estraing atur
Falsa del lignatge Caïm
Que met los sieus a mal ahur,
Car non tem anta ni blastim,   6.4
Los trai d'amar ab sa doussor,
    Met lo fol en tal erransa
Qu'el non remanria ab lor
    Qui.l donava[n] tota Fransa.   6.8

False friends, perfidious lovers,
Lower Love and elevate crime;
Don't think that love is getting worse,
For it is now worth as much as at the start;
It was always of noble color,
And always of the same appearance;
No one knows, concerning its worth,
The beginning or the end.

Whoever wants to may believe foolish omens,
Provided God protect me from the whirlwind!
For I venture into such Love
Where there is neither betrayal or gossip;
For summer and winter and spring
I remain in great happiness,
And I would be in greater happiness
With a bit of reassurance.

Never will I believe, whoever may swear it to me,
That wine does not issue forth from the grape,
And a man does not improve because of love;
We never heard of one growing worse (because of it),
For I am worth the most because of the best one,
But I am concerned about it,
And I dare not boast, for fear
Of that on which I set my hope.

It will be difficult for the fool to change his nature,
And never relapse into folly,
And for the foolish woman not to act immoderately;
A bad tree (comes) from a bad shoot,
From a bad branch a bad flower
And the fruit of a bad thought
Reverts to the worst kind of evil,
There where Joy holds no power.

Friendship of strange attachments
False, of the lineage of Cain
Which places its practitioners in an unhappy state
Because it fears neither shame or blame,
With its sweetness lures them away from true love,
And places the fool in such perplexity
That he would not remain with those
Who would give him the whole of France.

Dirai vos senes duptansa (PC 293.18)
Vers (Sirventes)

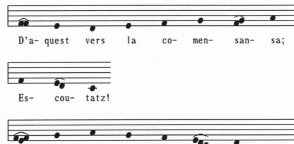

Di- rai vos se- nes dup- tan- sa / D'a- quest vers la co- men- san- sa; / Li mot fan de ver sem- blan- sa; / Es- cou- tatz! / Qui ves pro- e- za ba- lan- sa / Sem- blan- sa fai de mal- vatz.

Dirai vos senes duptansa	I'll tell you without fear
D'aquest vers la comensansa;	The beginning of this poem;
Li mot fan de ver semblansa;	The words seem true;
- Escoutatz! - 1.4	Listen!
Qui ves proeza balansa	He who hesitates in front of prowess
Semblansa fai de malvatz.	Gives the appearance of (being) evil.
Jovens faill e fraing e brisa,	Youth fails, falls, and is broken,
Et Amors es d'aital guisa	And love is of such nature
De totz cessals a ces prisa,	That it taxes all its subjects,
- Escoutatz! - 2.4	Listen!
Chascus en pren sa devisa,	Each pays his share
Ja pois no.n sera cuitatz.	With no dispensations.
Amors vai com la belluja	Love is like the spark
Que coa.l fuec en la suja	That keeps the fire smoldering beneath the soot
Art lo fust e la festuja,	Then burns wood and straw,
- Escoutatz! - 3.4	Listen!
E non sap vas qual part fuja	He knows not where to flee
Cel qui del fuec es gastatz.	The one who is devoured by the fire.
Dirai vos d'Amor com signa;	I'll tell you about Love's tricks;
De sai guarda, de la guigna,	He looks here, winks there,
Sai baiza, de lai rechigna,	Here he kisses, there makes a face,
- Escoutatz! - 4.4	Listen!
Plus sera dreicha que ligna	He will be straighter than a line
Quand ieu serai sos privatz.	When I will be his friend.
Amors soli'esser drecha,	Love used to be true
Mas er'es torta e brecha	But now it is twisted and chipped
Et a coillida tal decha	And has cultivated this defect:
- Escoutatz! - 5.4	Listen!
Lai ou non pot mordre, lecha	There where it can't bite, it licks
Plus aspramens no fai chatz.	With a rougher tongue than a cat's.

Greu sera mais Amors vera		Hardly will love be true again
Pos del mel triet la cera		Since he separated honey from wax;
Anz sap si pelar la pera;		For himself he peels the pear;
- Escoutatz! -	6.4	Listen!
Doussa'us er com chans de lera		Sweeter he will be than lyre's song,
Si sol la coa.l troncatz.		If only you cut off his tail.
Ab diables pren barata		He makes a pact with the devil
Qui fals'amor acoata,		Who accepts a false love,
No.il cal c'autra verga.l bata		No other stick is needed to beat him;
- Escoutatz! -	7.4	Listen!
Plus non sent que cel qui.s grata		He'll feel no more than the one who scratches
Tro que s'es vius escorjatz.		Until he flays himself alive.
Amors es mout de mal avi;		Love is of bad lineage;
Mil homes a mortz ses glavi,		He has killed a thousand men without a sword,
Dieus non fetz tant fort gramavi,		God made no greater sophist (grammarian),
- Escoutatz! -	8.4	Listen!
Que tot nesci del plus savi		For he makes a fool of the wisest
No fassa, si.l ten al latz.		If he catches him in his net.
Amors a usatge d'ega		Love resembles a mare
Que tot jorn vol c'om la sega		Who wants to be followed all day
E ditz que no.l dara trega		And says she will give no truce
- Escoutatz! -	9.4	Listen!
Mas que puej de leg'en lega,		Making you mount league after league,
Sia dejus o disnatz.		Whether hungry or full.
Cujatz vos qu'ieu non conosca		Do you think I don't know
D'Amor s'es orba ou losca?		If love is blind or cross-eyed?
Sos digz aplan'et entosca		His words are smooth and polished
- Escoutatz! -	10.4	Listen!
Plus suau poing qu'una mosca		Sweeter he pricks than a fly
Mas plus greu n'es hom sanatz.		But one is cured with greater difficulty.
Qui per sen de femna reigna		If you follow women's wisdom
Dreitz es que mals li.n aveigna		It is just that you come to ill,
Si cum la letra.ns enseigna;		As the Scripture teaches us
- Escoutatz! -	11.4	Listen!
Malaventura.us en veigna		Misfortune will come to you
Si tuich no vos en gardatz!		If you are not careful!
Marcabrus, fills Marcabruna,		Marcabru, son of Marcabruna
Fo engenratz en tal luna		Was sired beneath such a moon
Qu'el sap d'amor cum degruna.		That he knows how love behaves.
- Escoutatz! -	12.4	Listen!
Quez anc non amet neguna,		Therefore he's never loved a woman
Ni d'autra non fo amatz.		Nor been loved by any.

L'autrier jost'una sebissa (PC 293.30)
Pastorela

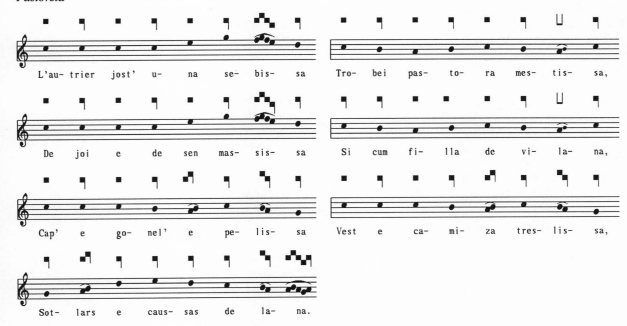

L'au-trier jost' u- na se-bis- sa | Tro- bei pas- to- ra mes- tis- sa,

De joi e de sen mas- sis- sa | Si cum fi- lla de vi- la- na,

Cap' e go- nel' e pe- lis- sa | Vest e ca- mi- za tres-lis- sa,

Sot- lars e caus- sas de la- na.

L'autrier jost'una sebissa		The other day beside a hedge
Trobei pastora mestissa,		I found a humble shepherdess
De joi e de sen massissa,		Full of joy and good sense
Si cum filla de vilana,	1.4	Like the daughter of a peasant girl;
Cap'e gonel'e pelissa		A cape, a coat and fur
Vest e camiza treslissa,		She wore, and a shirt of rough cloth,
Sotlars e caussas de lana.		Shoes and woolen stockings.

Ves lieis vinc per la planissa:		I came to her across the plain:
"Toza, fi.m ieu, res faitissa,		"Young girl," I said, "charming creature,
Dol ai car lo freitz vos fissa."		I am pained because the cold pierces you."
"Seigner, so.m dis la vilana,	2.4	"Sir," said to me the peasant girl,
Merce Dieu e ma noirissa,		"Thanks to God and my nurse,
Pauc m'o pretz si.l vens m'erissa,		If the wind ruffles my hair, I don't mind,
Qu'alegreta sui e sana."		For I am cheerful and healthy."

"Toza, fi.m ieu, cauza pia,		"Young girl," I said, "sweet thing,
Destors me sui de la via		I have turned out of my way
Per far a vos compaignia;		To keep you company,
Quar aitals toza vilana	3.4	For such a young peasant girl
No deu ses pareill paria		Should not, without a comrade,
Pastorgar tanta bestia		Pasture so many beasts
En aital terra, soldana."		In such a place, alone."

"Don, fetz ela, qui que.m sia,		"Sir," said she, "be what I may,
Ben conosc sen e folia;		I know common sense from folly;
La vostra pareillaria,		Your company,
Seigner, so.m dis la vilana,	4.4	Sir," so said to me the peasant girl,
Lai on se tang si s'estia,		"Should be offered where it is fitting,
Que tals la cuid'en bailia		For one who thinks she can hold it
Tener, no.n a mas l'ufana."		In her power, has nothing but the illusion."

"Toza de gentil afaire,
Cavaliers fon vostre paire
Que.us engenret en la maire,
Car fon corteza vilana.   5.4
Con plus vos gart, m'etz belaire,
E per vostre joi m'esclaire,
Si.m fossetz un pauc humana!"

"Don, tot mon ling e mon aire
Vei revertir e retraire
Al vezoig et a l'araire,
Seigner, so.m dis la vilana;   6.4
Mas tals se fai cavalgaire
C'atrestal deuria faire
Los seis jorns de la setmana."

"Toza, fi.m ieu, gentils fada,
Vos adastret, quan fos nada,
D'una beutat esmerada
Sobre tot'autra vilana;   7.4
E seria.us ben doblada,
Si.m vezi'una vegada,
Sobira e vos sotrana."

"Seigner, tan m'avetz lauzada,
Que tota.n sui enojada;
Pois en pretz m'avetz levada,
Seigner, so.m dis la vilana,   8.4
Per so n'auretz per soudada
Al partir: bada, fols, bada
E la muz a meliana."

"Toz'estraing cor e salvatge
Adomesg'om per uzatge.
Ben conosc al trespassatge
Qu'ab aital toza vilana   9.4
Pot hom far ric compaignatge
Ab amistat de coratge,
Si l'us l'autre non engana."

"Don, hom coitatz de follatge
Jur'e pliu e promet gatge:
Si.m fariatz homenatge,
Seigner, so.m dis la vilana;   10.4
Mas ieu, per un pauc d'intratge,
Non vuoil ges mon piucellatge
Camjar per nom de putana."

"Toza, tota creatura
Revertis a sa natura:
Pareillar pareilladura
Devem, ieu e vos, vilana,   11.4
A l'abric lonc la pastura,
Car plus n'estaretz segura
Per far la cauza doussana."

"Young girl of noble condition,
Your father was a knight
Who got your mother with child
For she was a courtly peasant girl.
The more I look at you, the prettier you seem,
And by your joy I am gladdened,
If only toward me you were more human!"

"Sir, all my lineage and my family
I see returning and going back
To sickle and plow,
Sir," so said to me the peasant girl;
"But some pass themselves off as knights
Who should be doing likewise
Six days of the week."

"Young girl," said I, "a noble fairy
Blessed you, when you were born,
With perfect beauty
Above any other peasant girl;
And it would be doubled
If I saw myself just once
Above and you below."

"Sir, you have praised me so much
That I am quite annoyed;
Since you have raised me in worth,
Sir," so said to me the peasant girl,
"You will have for recompense
On departure: gape, fool, gape
Vainly waiting at noonday."

"Young girl, a wild and skittish heart
One can tame by using it.
I certainly realize on passing by here
That with such a young peasant girl
A man can find noble company
With heartfelt friendship,
If neither deceives the other."

"Sir, a man pressed by madness
Swears and pledges and guarantees:
Thus you would do me homage,
Sir," so said to me the peasant girl;
"But I, for a cheap entrance fee,
Do not want to exchange my virginity
For the name of whore."

"Young girl, every creature
Reverts to its nature;
We should prepare to form a couple,
You and I, peasant girl,
Under cover beside the pasture,
For you will be in greater safety there
To do the sweet thing."

"Don, oc; mas segon dreitura		"Sir, yes; but according to what is right,
Cerca fols sa follatura,		The fool seeks his foolishness,
Cortes cortez'aventura,		The courtly, courtly adventures,
E.il vilans ab la vilana;	12.4	And the peasant boy, the peasant girl;
En tal loc fai sens fraitura		Wisdom is lacking in any place (circumstance)
On hom non garda mezura,		Where moderation is not observed,
So ditz la gens anciana."		So say the ancients."

"Toza, de vostra figura   "Young girl, about your face,
Non vi autra plus tafura   I never saw one more dishonest,
Ni de son cor plus trefana."   T1.3 (7)   Nor a heart more deceitful."

"Don, lo cavecs vos ahura,   "Sir, the owl promises you
Que tals bad'en la peintura   That one man gapes before the painting
Qu'autre n'espera la mana."   T2.3 (7)   While the other expects reward."

Pax in nomine Domini! (PC 293.35)
Crusade song

Pax in no- mi- ne Do- mi- ni!

Fetz Mar- ca- brus los motz e.l so.

Au- jatz que di:

Cum nos a fait, per sa dous- sor,

Lo Sein- gno- rius ce- les- ti- aus

Pro- bet de nos un la- va- dor,

C'anc, fors ou- tra- mar, no.n fon taus,

En de lai de- ves Jo- sa- phas:

E d'a- quest de sai vos co- nort.

Pax in nomine Domini!
Fetz Marcabrus los motz e.l so.
        Aujatz que di:
Cum nos a fait, per sa doussor,
Lo Seingnorius celestiaus   1.5
Probet de nos un lavador,
C'anc, fors outramar, no.n fon taus,
En de lai deves Josaphas:
E d'aquest de sai vos conort.   1.9

Lavar de ser e de mati
Nos deuriam, segon razo,
        Ie.us o afi.
Chascus a del lavar legor;
Domentre qu'el es sas e saus,   2.5
Deuri'anar al lavador,
Que.n es verais medicinaus;
Que s'abans anam a la mort,
D'aut en sus aurem alberc bas.   2.9

Mas Escarsedatz e No-fes,
Part Joven de son compaigno.
        Ai! cals dols es,
Que tuich volon lai li plusor,
Don lo gazaings es enfernaus!   3.5
S'anz non correm al lavador
C'ajam la boca ni.ls huoills claus,
Non i a un d'orguoill tant gras
C'al morir non trob contrafort.   3.9

Que.l Seigner que sap tot quant es
E sap tot quant er e c'anc fo,
        Nos i promes
Honor e nom d'emperador.
E.il beutatz sera,—sabetz caus—   4.5
De cels qu'iran al lavador?
Plus que l'estela gauzignaus;
Ab sol que vengem Dieu del tort
Que.ill fan sai, e lai vas Domas.   4.9

Probet del lignatge Caï,
Del primeiran home felho,
        A tans aissi
C'us a Dieu non porta honor;
Veirem qui.ll er amics coraus;   5.5
C'ab la vertut del lavador
Nos sera Jhesus comunaus;
E tornem los garssos atras
Qu'en agur crezon et en sort!   5.9

Pax in nomine Domini!
Marcabru made the words and the music.
Listen to what he tells:
How through His kindness
The Lord in Heaven has made,
Near us, a washing place,
Such that never was there one like it except overseas
Way yonder toward Jehoshaphat:
And to the nearby one, I exhort you.

Every morning and every evening
We should wash, according to reason,
I assure you.
Each one has the opportunity to do so;
While he is hale and hearty,
Each should go to the washing place,
Whence comes true medicine;
For if, before that, we go to death,
Rather than on high, we will have a low lodging.

But Niggardliness and Lack-of-Faith
Separate Youth from his companion.
Ah! what grief it is,
That most all fly there
Where the recompense is Hell!
If we do not run to the washing place
Before we have our mouth and eyes closed,
There is not one with pride so great
That in death he will not find the great enemy.

But the Lord who knows all that is
And knows all that will be and that ever was
Promised us there
Honor and the name of emperor.
And the beauty will be—do you know of what kind—
Of those who go to the washing place?
Greater than the morning star:
Provided that we avenge God of the wrong
They do him here, and there toward Damascus.

In the lineage of Cain,
Of that first treacherous man,
There are many,
Not one of whom honors God;
We shall see who will be a loyal friend to Him,
For by the virtue of the washing place
Jesus will be one with us;
And let us turn back those scoundrels
Who believe in omens and in sorcery!

E.il luxurios corna-vi,
Coita-disnar, bufa-tizo,
   Crup-en-cami
Remanran inz el felpidor;
Dieus vol los arditz e.ls suaus   6.5
Assajar a son lavador;
E cil gaitaran los ostaus;
E trobaran fort contrafort,
So per qu'ieu a lor anta.ls chas.   6.9

En Espaigna, sai, lo Marques
E cill del temple Salamo
   Sofron lo pes
E.l fais de l'orguoill paganor,
Per que Jovens cuoill avol laus.   7.5
E.l critz per aquest lavador
Versa sobre.ls plus rics captaus
Fraitz, faillitz, de proeza las,
Que non amon Joi ni Deport.   7.9

Desnaturat son li Frances,
Si de l'afar Dieu dizon no,
   Qu'ieu sai cum es:
Antiocha! Pretz e Valor
Sai plora Guiana e Peitaus.   8.5
Dieus, Seigner, al tieu lavador
L'arma del comte met en paus:
E sai gart Peitieus e Niort
Lo Seigner qui ressors del vas!   8.9

And the lechers, drunkards,
Eager-eaters, fireside-squatters,
Rumps-on-the-road
Will remain in their squalor;
God wants the brave and the kind
To test at his washing place,
And the rest will wait in their dwellings,
And they will find the great and mighty enemy;
That's why I chase them to their shame.

In Spain, nearby, the Marquis
And those of Solomon's temple
Bear the brunt
And the burden of pagan pride,
On account of which Youth reaps disgrace;
And the outcry for this washing place
Pours over the greatest leaders,
Broken, failed, weary of prowess,
Who love not Joy or Delight.

The French are degenerate
If they say no to the task of God;
I know how it is:
Antioch! Guyenne and Poitiers
Here weep for Merit and Valor.
Lord God, at your washing place
Grant peace to the soul of the count;
And here may he protect Poitiers and Niort,
The Lord Who rose from the grave!

JAUFRE RUDEL

Like Guilhem IX, Jaufre Rudel (c. 1130-1148) was of noble birth. There seems no reason to doubt the information given by his *vida* that he was lord of Blaye in southwestern France. The dukes of Aquitaine, William IX and William X, and William's daughter Eleanor, were his overlords. It is generally agreed that Jaufre Rudel took part in the crusade of 1147-8 and reached the Holy Land. There is no record that he ever returned to his native land. Jaufre Rudel is the earliest figure from whom we have a significant number of melodies with the poems: 6 (or 7) poems and 4 melodies.

The real Jaufre Rudel fades before the legend. The legend began with the 13th-century *vida* relating the trip to the Holy Land. The *vidas* or short biographies that accompany troubadour song in some (mostly Italian) manuscripts offer a mixture of reliable fact and wild fancy. This famous *vida* may serve to illustrate the genre (Meneghetti 1984, 235-77; Poe 1984a; Monson 1985; Poe, *Handbook* 1995, 185-97).

Jaufres Rudels de Blaia si fo mout gentils hom, princes de Blaia. Et enamoret se de la comtessa de Tripol, ses vezer, per lo ben qu'el n'auzi dire als pelerins que venguen d'Antiocha. E fez de leis mains vers ab bons sons, ab paubres motz. E per voluntat de leis vezer, el se croset e se mes en mar, e pres lo malautia en la nau, e fo condug a Tripol, en un alberc, per mort. E fo fait saber a la comtessa et ella venc ad el, al son leit e pres lo antre sos bratz. E saup qu'ella era la comtessa, e mantenent recobret l'auzir e.l flairar, e lauzet Dieu, que l'avia la vida sostenguda tro qu'el l'agues vista; et enaissi el mori entre sos bratz. Et ella lo fez a gran honor sepellir en la maison del Temple; e pois, en aquel dia, ella se rendet morga, per la dolor qu'ella n'ac de la mort de lui. (Boutière-Schutz 1964, 16-7)

Jaufré Rudel de Blaye was a noble man, Prince of Blaye. He fell in love with the Countess of Tripoli, without seeing her, on account of the fine things he heard about her from the pilgrims who came from Antioch, and he composed many *vers* about her with good melodies but poor words. And desiring to see her, he took the cross and set out over the sea. He fell ill in the ship and was taken to Tripoli, to an inn, as though dead. The Countess was informed of this; she came to him, right up to his bed, and took him in her arms. He recognized that it was the Countess and immediately he recovered his hearing and sense of smell; and he praised God who had kept him alive until he saw her. And in this manner he died in her arms. She buried him in the House of the Temple, with great honor, and then that very day, she took vows on account of the sorrow his death brought to her.

The *vida* takes most of its substance from the song "Lanquand li jorn." This song and the *vida* often appear together in the manuscripts. Ms. I has a superb illustration of the countess in the arms of the poet. Song and *vida* thus create a powerful poetic persona and an image that seems to encapsulate the notion of *fin'amor*.

EDITIONS: Jeanroy 1924; Pickens 1978; Wolf and Rosenstein 1983; van der Werf 1984; Chiarini 1985.

• "Lanquand li jorn son lonc en mai": PC 262.2. Sources: mss. A 127, B 77, C 214-15, D 88, E 149, I 121-22, K 107, M 165, R 63, S 182-83, Sg 108, W 189-90; X 81, a^1 498-99, e 186-90; Music in R, W, X. Melody from X. Text: Lejeune 1959, 416. This song well repays careful examination of poetic vocabulary and melodic idiom. Not yet so called by its composer, the song yet constitutes "une préfiguration typologique de la *canso*" (Bec 1982, 41). The key to thematic development is the refrain word *loing*, occurring in lines 2 and 4 of each stanza, and in most stanzas joined to the word *amor*, thus creating the mysterious linking of love and distance that dominates the poem. The elegant metric structure includes seven 8-syllable lines with a rhyme scheme ababccd. The rhyme sounds remain the same throughout the song, a technique called *coblas unissonans* (same-sounding stanzas). The d rhyme is a *rim estramp*, a rhyme sound that rhymes only with its counterparts in other stanzas. The melodic structure, ABAB CDB, constitutes in all likelihood the first appearance in medieval music of the ordering that Dante will later designate *pedes* with *cauda*. These features can be summarized:

Melody	A	B	A	B	C	D	B
Cadential notes	d	c	d	c	g	d	c
Rhyme scheme	a_8	b_8	a_8	b_8	c_8	c_8	d_8
Rhyme sounds	ai	*loing*	ai	*loing*	is	is	atz

The poetic text generates mystery by its studied ambiguities, by its constant crossing between sacred and profane, and by its exploitation of the notion of distance as at once physical, psychological, temporal. The key melodic device is the consistent structural linking of the same melodic gesture to the text's refrain words: *loing* or *amor de loing*. The melody reveals a degree of modal (or tonal) instability which can be best described if we take *d* as the final. The first phrase of the melody points clearly in the direction of *d*, with its emphasis on the notes *d* and *f* (as a reciting tone) with a cadence on *d*. The second phrase starts out like the first with movement from *d* to *f*, but rapidly veers toward a different configuration, emphasizing *g, e, c,* and closing on *c*. Compared to *d* as a final note and thus stability, *c* is unstable. The movement thus sketched from stability to instability is repeated for phrases 3 and 4. Phrases 5 and 6 constitute the climax of the melody, containing its highest note and its most dramatic melodic gestures. Phrase 6 cadences on the stable note *d*. Then phrase 7, by taking up again phrases 2 and 4, effects a firm conclusion, but at the same time, because it closes on *c*, it reconfirms the shift from stability to instability, so that the entire melody ends in an unresolved manner. Particularly striking is the final linking of *amor de loing* and *non fos amatz* in stanza 7. Musical syntax and poetic diction conspire to project the dominant theme of the song: the irreducibility of distance and love (Lejeune 1959; Zumthor 1963, 205-17; van der Werf 1972, 85-9; Topsfield 1975, 42-69; Le Vot, Lusson, Roubaud 1979; Switten 1988, 1992b; Treitler 1991, 1992).

• "Quan lo rius de la fontana": PC 262.5. Sources: mss. A 127, B 77, C 214, D 88, E 149, I 122, K 107-08, M 165, R 63, S 183-84, Sg 108, U 126, X 149, a^1 278-79; bI 6; e 180-82; Music in R. Text: Pickens, 100. For the complex transmission of this song, see Pickens 1978 and Wolf and Rosenstein, 1983. Thematically linked to "Lanquand li jorn," without possessing quite the same magic, this song differently develops the key notion of "distant love," *amors de terra lonhdana* (2.1), with its contrasting human and spiritual values (Rosenstein 1990). The chief differences here are the reference to the artistic quality of the poet's verses (1.6-7) and a more precise evocation of the lady (stanzas 3 and 4). The complex metric structure is based on the use of *coblas doblas* (in this case stanzas with 7 lines of 7 syllables each), in which the rhyme sounds change every two stanzas. But instead of *changing* rhymes, Jaufre reshuffles the same sounds: thus if abcdace stands for stanzas 1 and 2, 3 and 4 may be represented by cdabcae. Only the "e" rhyme keeps the same position throughout, effecting closure for each stanza. Rhymes a and c are repeated within the stanza; rhymes b, d and e constitute

rims estramps. A further refinement comes with the use of alternating masculine and feminine rhymes for the first part of the stanza. Since we have only 5 stanzas for his poem, the full flavor of *coblas doblas* is not present. Stanza 5, due to certain irregularities of versification, can best be understood as a *coblas singulars*. The initial melodic gestures of lines 1 and 3 and the overall range suggest the mode of *d* in its plagal disposition. As in "Lanquand li jorn," a number of lines, including the final line, cadence on *c*. But the musical rhetoric is quite unlike that of "Lanquand li jorn." Since all the the cadences are either on *c* (1, 3, 5, 7) or *e* (2, 4, 6), and the alternance is regular, the kind of tension set up between stable and unstable configurations in the former song do not function here. The melody is more compact, and although the contrast of an opening gesture going up from *d* to *g* in line 4 marks the climax of the song, the melody immediately settles back into earlier patterns moving toward a cadence on *c*. The melodic structure, which could be diagrammed ABAB CB'D, sets up in the first part a parallel between exchangeable rhymes of the text: *ana/ina* go with the A music, *ol/am* with the B music. In the second part, the rhyme sounds *ana*, *ina*, and the *rim estramp aigna* are heard to slightly different music. Thus we have a subtle play on shifting sounds which persuades us that the artistry of song, a central theme announced in the first stanza, is to be found in the joining of text and music.

3.5 Sarrazina was also the name of Hugh of Lusignan's wife (see 5.4 below). Jaufre Rudel may be saying to Hugh of Lusignan that not even his "Sarrazina" is the equal of the love the poet is describing (Rosenstein 1990, 231).

5.1-2 These lines have caused much comment on the manner of transmission of troubadour song, especially to support transmission through singing.

5.4 Hugh the Swarthy, Count of Lusignan. See Rosenstein 1990, 228-9. "Filhol" meaning "godson" is the name of the messenger, perhaps a jongleur.

Lanquand li jorn son lonc en mai (PC 262.2)
Canso

Lanquand li jorn son lonc en mai
M'es bels douz chans d'auzels de loing,
E qand me sui partitz de lai
Remembra.m d'un'amor de loing;   1.4
Vauc de talan enbroncs e clis,
Si que chans ni flors d'albespis
No.m platz plus que l'inverns gelatz.

Ja mais d'amor no.m gauzirai
Si no.m gau d'est'amor de loing,
Qe gensor ni meillor non sai
Vas nuilla part ni pres ni loing.   2.4
Tant es sos pretz verais e fis
Qe lai el renc dels Sarrazis
Fos eu per lieis chaitius clamatz.

Iratz e gauzens m'en partrai
Qan veirai cest'amor de loing,
Mas non sai coras la.m veirai,
Car trop son nostras terras loing: 3.4
Assatz i a portz e camis.
E per aisso no.n sui devis,
Mas tot sia cum a Dieu platz!

Be.m parra jois qan li qerrai
Per amor Dieu l'amor de loing.
E s'a lieis plai, albergarai
Pres de lieis, si be.m sui de loing.   4.4
Adoncs parra.l parlamens fis
Qand drutz loindas er tant vezis
C'ab bels digz jauzirai solatz.

When the days are long in May,
I like the sweet song of birds from afar,
And when I have departed from there,
I remember a love from afar;
I go sad and bowed with desire
So that neither song nor hawthorn flower
Pleases me more than icy winter.

Never in love shall I rejoice
Unless I enjoy this love from afar,
For nobler or better I do not know
In any direction, near or far,
Her worth is so true and perfect
That there in the kingdom of the Saracens
I would, for her, be proclaimed captive.

Sad and rejoicing I shall depart
When I shall see this love from afar,
But I do not know when I shall see her
For our lands are too far.
Many are the ports and roads,
And so I cannot prophesy,
But may all be as it pleases God!

Joy will surely appear to me when I seek from her,
For the love of God, this love from afar.
And if it pleases her, I shall lodge
Near her, although I am from afar.
Then will appear fine discourse,
When, distant lover, I shall be so close
That with charming words I shall take delight
                    in conversation.

Ben tenc lo seignor per verai
Per q'ieu veirai l'amor de loing,
Mas per un ben qe m'en eschai
N'ai dos mals, car tant m'es de loing.   5.4
Ai! car me fos lai peleris
Si que mos fustz e mos tapis
Fos pelz sieus bels huoills remiratz!

I consider that Lord as the true one
Through whom I shall see this love from afar;
But for one good that befalls me from it,
I have two ills, because she is so far.
Ah! Would that I might be a pilgrim there
So that my staff and my cloak
Might be seen by her beautiful eyes.

Dieus qe fetz tot qant ve ni vai
E fermet cest'amor de loing
Me don poder, qe.l cor eu n'ai,
Q'en breu veia l'amor de loing   6.4
Veraiamen en locs aizis,
Si qe la cambra e.l jardis
Me resembles totz temps palatz.

God who made all that comes and goes
And established this love from afar,
Give me the power, for the desire I have,
Quickly to see this love from afar,
Truly, in agreeable places,
So that chamber and garden
Might always seem to me a palace!

Ver ditz qui m'apella lechai
Ni desiran d'amor de loing,
Car nuills autre jois tant no.m plai
Cum jauzimens d'amor de loing;   7.4
Mas so q'eu vuoill m'es tant ahis
Q'enaissi.m fadet mos pairis
Q'ieu ames e non fos amatz.

He speaks the truth who calls me greedy
And desirous of love from afar,
For no other joy pleases me as much
As enjoyment of love from afar;
But what I want is so difficult,
For thus did my godfather decree my fate,
That I should love and not be loved.

Mas so q'ieu vuoill m'es tant ahis . . .
Toz sia mauditz lo pairis
Qe.m fadet q'ieu non fos amatz!   T.3 (7)

But what I want is so difficult
May the godfather be cursed
Who decreed my fate that I should not be loved.

Quan lo rius de la fontana (PC 262.5)

Vers (Canso)

Quan lo rius de la fontana
S'esclarzis si cum far sol,
E par la flors aiglentina,
E.l rossinholetz el ram   1.4
Volf e refraing et aplana
Son doutz chantar et afina
Dreitz es qu'ieu lo mieu refraigna.

When the stream from the fountain
Runs clear as it is wont to do,
And the wild rose blooms,
And the nightingale on the bough
Turns and smooths and polishes
His sweet song and refines it,
It is right that I polish my own.

Amors de terra loingdana,
Per vos totz lo cors mi dol;
E non puosc trobar meizina
Si non vau al sieu reclam   2.4
Ab atraich d'amor doussana,
Dinz vergier o sotz cortina,
Ab desirada compaigna.

Pois del tot me.n faill aizina,
No.m meravill s'ieu m'aflam,
Car anc genser Crestïana
Non fo, que Dieus non la vol,   3.4
Juzena ni Sarrazina;
Et es ben pagutz de manna
Qui ren de s'amor gazaigna.

De desir mos cors non fina
Vas cella ren q'ieu plus am,
E cre que volers m'engana
Si cobezesa la.m tol,   4.4
Que plus es poignens qu'espina
La dolors que ab joi sana,
Don ja non voill c'om me.n plaigna.

Senes breu de pargamina,
Tramet lo vers en chantan
Plan et en lenga romana
A.N Hugon Brun per Fillol.   5.4
Bon m'es, car gens Peitavina,
De Beiriu et de Bretaigna
S'esgau per lui, e Guianna.

Love from a far away land
For you my whole heart aches:
And I cannot find medicine
If not at her call,
With the temptation of sweet love
In an orchard or curtained chamber,
Beside the desired companion.

Since this is not possible,
I marvel not that I am aflame.
For fairer Christian
Never was, nor does God want one,
Nor Jewess nor Saracen;
And he is well fed with manna
Who wins anything of her love.

My heart never stops desiring
Her whom I most love
And I believe that desire tricks me
If lust takes her from me,
For it is sharper than a thorn
The pain that is healed by joy,
For which I don't want to be pitied.

Without parchment brief
I transmit the song in singing
Plainly and in romance tongue
To Lord Hugo Brun, by Fillol.
I am pleased because the people of Poitou
Of Berry and of Brittany
Are delighted by it, and of Guyenne.

Jaufre Rudel, *vida* and "Lanquand li jorn
son lonc en mai" (pp. 54 and 56): decorated
letter L showing, presumably, the poet and
the Countess of Tripoli. Ms. I, f. 121v. Cliché
Bibliothèque Nationale de France - Paris.

BERNART DE VENTADORN

Little is known about Bernart de Ventadorn (c.1145-1180). His *vida* would make of him the lover of Eleanor of Aquitaine, but this is legend and not life. The troubadour Peire d'Alvernhe speaks scornfully of him, saying that he was of poor birth (see below, "Cantarai d'aqestz trobadors"). This may have been the case. Bernart was possibly born in the castle of Eble II of Ventadorn (sometimes mentioned as one of the earliest Occitan poets, though no poems are extant) and more than likely began his career in Limousin and Poitou. He seems to have been a professional poet/composer. He may have travelled to England to the court of Eleanor and Henry II; he may have had the Count of Toulouse as a patron; possibly he visited Narbonne. He is said to have died in a Cistercian abbey.

If Bernart's life was humble, his songs were among the best known and most widely circulated of all troubadour *cansos* in the medieval period, and they remain so even today. With him, we can speak confidently of the *canso*: he used the term a number of times, twice with the term *vers* (for example, "A! tantas bonas chansos / et tan bo vers aurai faih"). Many would count him among the greatest poet/composers of any age. Some 45 songs have come down to us; around 20 have music, an astonishing number when one considers that Bernart de Ventadorn flourished in the mid-twelfth century, a hundred years before our first written records. The songs proceed from a rich lyric imagination, purely lyric: there are few political, philosophical, or satirical overtones. Bernart cultivates the "easy" or "clear" style, the *trobar leu*. Music and words communicate intense feeling through elegant patterns of poetic imagery and melodic gesture. He captures the essence of *fin'amor*, the losing of one's self in the contemplation of the beloved, and yet his vision is not without drama, irony, and humor born of the tension between love's ideal and the poet's experience, between deep poetic emotion and the "reality" of the professional singer whose business it is to create songs. (Topsfield 1975 provides a brief introduction to the poetry; Gossen 1988 to text-music relations; Hasenohr-Zink 1992 a full listing of important studies.)

EDITIONS: Appel 1915 and 1934; Nichols et al. 1965; Lazar 1966; van der Werf 1984.

• "Amics Bernartz de Ventadorn": PC 70.2. Sources: mss. A 177, D 143, E 212, G 100, I 155, K 141, L 51, W 190; music in W. Text: Appel, 11. A *tenso* is a debate in which each interlocutor defends a specific position usually on a question of moral or amatory interest. How lovers should behave is a favorite subject. This song has often been interpreted as a parodic reversal of the conventions of *fin'amor*: Bernart prefers sleeping to singing, and Peire tries to set him back on the correct poetic course. The notion that women should do the courting is perhaps to be placed in a larger debate represented also by the discussion between Maria de Ventadorn and Gui d'Ussel half a century later (see below, "Gui d'Ussel be.m pesa de vos"). The metric structure comprises 6 lines of 8 syllables each, divided into two sections of 4 (abba) and 2 (dd) lines separated by a shorter feminine line of seven syllables ending in a *rim estramp*, thus: a8b8b8a8 c7′d8d8. The melody has no repetition of complete phrases (in the troubadour repertory, the rhyme scheme abba is often joined to a melody without repetition, to which it can lend definition by creating a dialogue between recurrence and continued forward movement). The short line beginning the second section of the stanza is clearly set off, however, by the relatively rare leap of a minor seventh. The melodic style is for the most part syllabic, with ornamentation tending to occur toward the ends of phrases, so that the music underscores and does not obscure the argumentation. There is marked tonal ambiguity. *C* could be considered the final; it is the concluding note of the *frons*. *F* and *g* are the other cadence notes, however, and the several flats incline one toward *f*. The final cadence heads toward *f* and then by turning up to *g* to close seems to toss the question to the new speaker. The final melodic gesture destabilizes the tonality even as the text leaves the question under debate unresolved (Switten 1988).

2.1: Peire is generally considered to be Peire d'Alvernhe, to whom the song has been attributed in some manuscripts (and by Pillet-Carstens).

• "Lo tems vai e ven e vire": PC 70.30. Sources: mss. A 86, C 51, D 17, G 16, I 33, K 21, Q 28, R 12, a 103. Text: Appel, 181. This song treats the eminently lyric theme of the passage of time and the permanence of desire. One thinks of Guillaume Apollinaire's "Le Pont Mirabeau": "Vienne la nuit, sonne l'heure / Les jours s'en vont, je demeure." The metric structure reflects change and permanence. Four sets of *coblas doblas*, each *cobla* having 7 lines of 7 syllables, are anchored by the unchanging *rim estramp* that closes the stanza (Chambers 1985, 126). Alternating masculine and feminine rhymes and contrasts in rhyme sounds—*ire/ans*, or *ia/en* for example—sustain the ebb and flow of emotion. The opening and closing references to *tems*: "Lo tems vai e ven e vire" (1.1) and "Totz tems vos ai dezirada" (8.5) reflect both the circular movement of time through the seasons and the years and the transformation of time into the eternal force of desire.

4.2: Eble II, viscount of Ventadorn, vassal of Guilhem IX.

• "Non es meravelha s'eu chan": PC 70.31. Sources: mss. A 89, C 57, D 19, F 21, G 9, I 27, K 16, L¹ 22, L² 124, M 42, N 139, O 7, P 18, Q 28, R 57, S 46, U 88n, V 52, W 191, a 92; music in G and W. Unusually, music is given for the second stanza in G, but incorrectly. See van der Werf 1984, 54*. Melody from G. Text: Appel, 188. Performed on Anthology CD. This could be a signature song not only for Bernart de Ventadorn but for the courtly lyric: love is the source of song; love is the source of suffering; not to love is not to live; not to love is no longer to sing. For "Non es meravelha," as for many other songs, the stanza order varies in the different manuscript traditions (Appel, 187). Compared to the edition we have here, the stanza orders of the manuscripts which have music are as follows: G: 1 4 3 6 5 7 8; W 1 2 5 6 3 7. Two features may be emphasized: (l) the first stanza is always first, as is the case for almost all *cansos*—that alone gives the stanza a special status; and (2) no stanza order, unless it is guaranteed by versification, is immutable. Since the songs usually turn about a center, a different stanza order creates a different series of visions of that center and may determine a different tone. This kind of flexibility in ordering is typical of the troubadour repertory as we know it from manuscripts. Probably it reflects a performing reality (Switten 1985; van Vleck 1991). The metric structure comprises 8 lines of 8 syllables each, with two sets of *rimes embrassées*: abba cddc. The similarity in sound of the rhymes a (*an*) and c (*en*) create clear sonorous coherence. The *coblas* are both *unissonans* and *capcaudadas*: the rhyme sounds remain the same throughout, but a and c are regularly interchanged so that the last rhyme sound of one stanza becomes the first of the next; b and d remain constant. The melody is structured around the nearly exact repetition of phrase 1 for phrase 5, which divides the stanza melodically, and the return of phrase 4 in phrase 8, which brings closure. The cadences to which are heard the anchor sounds (*an* and *en*) are on *f* and *d* in both halves of the stanza, thus the text sounds are associated with the same musical sounds, even as the former alternate. *D* serves as a tonal focus, somewhat destabilized by the opening gesture moving up from *d* to *g* (a recitation on *f* or *a* might have been expected); the repeated use of *g* in phrase 5; the insistence on *e* in line 7; and the clear outline of the secondary third chain *c-e-g* in line 8. Thus the melody captures the bittersweet contrasts of the poetic text.

1.6: Melody position 6: One syllable is missing in the text of G, hence a missing note. In performance, the note *a* has been used for "ai."

T.1: *Senhal* for a patroness.

• "Pois preyatz me, senhor": PC 70.36. Sources: mss. A 90, C 52, D 16, E 103, F 22, G 20, I 29, K 18, M 40, N 140, Q 31, R 57, S 42, a 75; music in G and R. Melody from R. Text: Appel, 205. This song is addressed to knights, "senhor," whose language it uses: stanza 6 is one of the clearest examples of "feudal" metaphors applied to lyric situations. The poet uses this language and treats the usual

themes with a certain whimsy, however, which is underscored by the choice of short 6-syllable verses. There are three sets of *coblas doblas*, with a rhyme scheme abababb; each set is linked by the fact that the b rhyme of one set becomes the a rhyme of the next set, with a new b sound. The metric structure plays itself out over time; only when one has reached the transition from stanza 4 to stanza 5 is it clear. It has been argued that the melody matches the poem's whimsy (Sesini 1940, 53). The melody exhibits a highly repetitive structure that can be diagrammed ABAB CDCDC′, emphasizing the repetitive patterns of the rhyme sounds. This is unusual for the early troubadours, but Bernart de Ventadorn shows more variety than one might at first imagine in his exploration of different poetico-musical configurations. In the R version, the tonal focus settles on *f*, but only in the last line. The entire melody moves within a narrow range, for the most part syllabically. No flights of melodic—or emotional—imagination characterize the song. The first half of the song concentrates on the third *a - c*, cadencing on *a* for each phrase. The second half moves to a slightly lower tessitura, concentrating on movement from *f* to *a* (5 and 7) or from *a* to *f* (6 and 8), but cadencing on the contrasting tones *g* or *e*. The last line then swings back at the end to *f* (and a sense of closure can be reinforced by flatting the *b*).

3.9 People see only the shadow of the poet, not his "substance," his heart, which has been drawn to the beloved. For that reason, they do not really see him.

T1.1: A *senhal* for a friend, possibly a poet.

T2.3: A *senhal* for a person as yet unidentified.

• "Can vei la lauzeta mover": PC 70.43. Sources: mss. A 90, C 47, D 16, E 102, F 22, G 10, I 28, K 16, L 19, M 39, N 139, O 60, P 16, Q 25, R 56, S 53, U 89, V 55, W 190, X 148, a 91; music in G, R, W. Melody from G. Text: Appel, 250. There are numerous textual variations and shifts in stanza order (Appel, 249); the melody versions, however, are remarkably stable. We may attribute this musical stability to "a strong melodic structure" (van der Werf 1972, 90). This song vies with Jaufre Rudel's "Lanquand li jorn" for listing on the charts of the troubadours' greatest hits. Trouvères used the melody (RS 265, 349, 1460, 1934) as did Latin poets: comparative studies reveal wide circulation (van der Werf 1984). The song was cited in numerous works, including Jean Renart's *Roman de la Rose*. As Frank Chambers has remarked about the song, "its simple rhyme scheme (ababcdcd), its unassuming rhymes (*er, ai, e, on*), and its clarity constitute a perfect example of *trobar leu* in general, and, in particular, of the genius of Bernart de Ventadorn" (Chambers 1985, 130). From the initial powerful image of the lark to the somber despair of the closing lines, the poem's rhetorical energy never falters. Bernart de Ventadorn was the first to appropriate in a western vernacular the twin themes of Narcissus and the mirror to express the fatal attraction of passion, the desire of the inaccessible Other reflected back on the self. Although it does not utilize regular repetition of entire phrases, the melody possesses a balance and logic that make of it a classic (Treitler 1991, 27). The first phrase establishes *d-f-a* as main structural tones but by touching on *b* (which is not flatted in G, but usually is in performance) and closing on *g*, it sketches also the contrasting third chain (*g-b-[d]*). The second phrase picks up on *g* and moves to *c*, then back to *f*, ending on *a*, reinforcing the main structural tones. The third phrase closes on *f*, while the fourth phrase (in all manuscripts except R, which does not effect closure until the end of the stanza) concludes the first part with a cadence on *d*, firmly establishing tonal focus on *d*. The second part of the song marks contrast and climax. The 5th phrase ends with a strong gesture: the downward leap of a fifth, *d-g*, which prepares for the brooding tone of the conclusion. Phrase 7 repeats the initial rising gesture of phrase 2, and indeed this gesture somewhat varied opens phrases 1, 2, 4, 7 and 8, serving to unify the song. Then the final phrase, with the lowest tessitura of the song, lets all sink into despair. The oscillation between hope and pain, between desire and death that characterizes the poetic text seems admirably carried by the graceful yet firm outlines of the melody.

T.1: Tristan is here possibly the name of the hero of *Tristan et Iseut*, or it may be an unidentified *senhal*.

Amics Bernartz de Ventadorn (PC 70.2)
Tenso

Amics Bernartz de Ventadorn,		Friend Bernart de Ventadorn
Com vos podetz de chant sofrir		How can you stop singing
Can aissi auzetz esbaudir		When you hear rejoicing
Lo rossinholet noih e jorn?	1.4	The nightingale, night and day?
Auyatz lo joi que demena!		Listen to his joy!
Tota noih chanta sotz la flor;		All night he sings beneath the flower;
Melhs s'enten que vos en amor.		He understands love better than you do.

Peire, lo dormir e.l sojorn		Peire, sleep and repose
Am mais que.l rossinhol auvir,		I much prefer to hearing nightingales,
Ni ja tan no.m sabriatz dir		Nor for anything that you could say to me
Que mais en la folia torn.	2.4	Would I return to madness.
Deu lau fors sui de chadena,		Praise God I have no chain,
E vos e tuih l'autr'amador		And you and all the other lovers
Etz remazut en la folor.		Remain in madness.

Bernartz, greu er pros ni cortes
Qui ab amor no.s sap tener,
Ni ja tan no.us fara doler
Que mais no valha c'autre bes,   3.4
    Car, si fai mal, pois abena.
Greu a om gran be ses dolor,
Mas ades vens lo jois lo plor.

Bernart, scarcely will he be worthy or courtly
Who cannot stay firm in love,
Nor ever will it (love) cause you so much pain
That it will not be worth more than any other good,
For if it causes pain, it then compensates.
Seldom does one have real good without pain,
And joy soon conquers tears.

Peire, si fos dos ans o tres
Lo segles faihz al meu plazer,
De domnas vos dic eu lo ver;
Non foran mais preyadas ges,   4.4
    Ans sostengran tan greu pena
Qu'elas nos feiran tan d'onor
C'ans nos prejaran que nos lor.

Peire, if for two or three years
The world were run according to my desires,
I'll tell you how it would be with women;
They would never be courted at all,
Instead they would suffer such pain
That they would honor us
And court us rather than we, them.

Bernartz, so non es d'avinen
Que domnas preyon. Ans cove
C'om las prec e lor clam merce.
Et es plus fols, mon escien,   5.4
    Que cel qui semn'en l'arena
Qui las blasma ni lor valor,
E mou de mal ensenhador.

Bernart, it is not proper
For women to court. Rather it is fitting
For men to court them and cry for mercy.
And he is more foolish, I think,
Than one who sows in the sand
Who blames them or their merit,
And it comes from a bad teacher.

Peire, mout ai lo cor dolen
Can d'una faussa me sove
Que m'a mort, e no sai per que,
Mas car l'amava finamen.   6.4
    Faih ai longa carantena
E sai, si la fezes lonhor,
Ades la trobara pejor.

Peire, my heart aches
When I remember one false woman
Who killed me, I know not why,
Except that I loved her faithfully.
I have fasted long,
And I know that if I were to do it even longer,
I'd find her worse than ever.

    Bernartz, foudatz vos amena
Car aissi vos partetz d'amor
Per cui a om pretz e valor.   T1.3 (7)

Bernart, madness rules you
Since you thus abandon love
By which men gain merit and valor.

    Peire, qui ama, desena,
Car las trichairitz entre lor
An tout joi e pretz e valor.   T2.3 (7)

Peire, whoever loves loses his mind,
For the traitresses among them
Have stolen joy and merit and valor.

Lo tems vai e ven e vire (PC 70.30)
Canso

Lo tems vai e ven e vire
Per jorns, per mes e per ans,
Et eu, las, no.n sai que dire,
C'ades es us mos talans.   1.4
Ades es us e no.s muda,
C'una.n volh e.n ai volguda
Don anc non aic jauzimen.

Time comes and goes and turns
Through days, months and years,
And I, alas, do not know what to say of it,
For always my desire is one.
Always it is one, and does not change,
For one lady I want and I have wanted
From whom I have never had joy.

Pois ela no.n pert lo rire,
A me.n ven e dols e dans,
C'a tal joc m'a faih assire
Don ai lo peyor dos tans,   2.4
C'aitals amors es perduda
Qu'es d'una part mantenguda,
Tro que fai acordamen.

Be deuri'esser blasmaire
De me mezeis a razo,
C'anc no nasquet cel de maire
Que tan servis en perdo;   3.4
E s'ela no m'en chastia,
Ades doblara.lh folia,
Que fols no tem tro que pren.

Ja mais no serai chantaire
Ni de l'escola n'Eblo,
Que mos chantars no val gaire
Ni mas voutas ni mei so;   4.4
Ni res qu'eu fassa ni dia,
No conosc que pros me sia,
Ni no.i vei melhuramen.

Si tot fatz de joi parvensa,
Mout ai dins lo cor irat.
Qui vid anc mais penedensa
Faire denan lo pechat?   5.4
On plus la prec, plus m'es dura,
Mas si'n breu tems no.s melhura,
Vengut er al partimen.

Pero ben es qu'ela.m vensa
A tota sa volontat,
Que s'el'a tort o bistensa,
Ades n'aura pietat;   6.4
Que so mostra l'escriptura:
Causa de bon'aventura
Val us sols jorns mais de cen.

Ja no.m partrai a ma vida,
Tan com sia sals ni sas,
Que pois l'arma n'es issida,
Balaya lonc tems lo gras;   7.4
E si tot no s'es cochada,
Ja per me no.n er blasmada,
Sol d'eus adenan s'emen.

Ai, bon'amors encobida,
Cors be faihz, delgatz e plas,
Frescha chara colorida,
Cui Deus formet ab sas mas,   8.4
Totz tems vos ai dezirada
Que res autra no m'agrada,
Autr'amor no volh nien.

Since she doesn't stop laughing about it,
To me come both pain and suffering,
And she has made me sit down to such a game
That I have the worst twice over—
For such love is lost
That is on only one side upheld—
Until she makes peace.

I should indeed be the accuser
Of myself, and rightly so,
For never was one born of mother
Who served so much in vain.
And if she does not chastise me for it,
Then I will forever double my folly,
For a fool does not fear until he is caught.

Never will I be a singer,
Nor (belong to) the School of Lord Eble,
For my singing is of no avail,
Nor my vocalises nor my melodies;
And whatever I do or say,
I do not know that it will help me,
And I do not see improvement.

Although I make a show of joy,
In my heart I have great vexation.
Whoever saw such penance
Done before the sin?
The more I beg her, the harder she is to me,
But if in a short time she does not improve,
There will be a separation.

However, it is good that she bends me
To her will,
For if she is wrong or delays,
Soon she will have pity;
For the scriptures show:
In the matter of good fortune,
A single day is worth more than a hundred.

Never in my life will I quit,
As long as I am safe and sound,
For after the soul has gone,
The flesh swings (aimlessly) for a long time.
And although she has not hastened,
She will never be blamed by me for that,
Provided that from now on she make amends.

Ah, good and desirable love,
Well made body, slender and smooth,
Fresh skin and high color,
Which God formed with his hands,
Always I have desired you
For no other pleases me;
No other love do I want at all.

Dousa res ben ensenhada,
Cel que.us a tan gen formada
Me.n do cel joi qu'eu n'aten.   T.3 (7)

Sweet and learned creature,
May the one who formed you so graciously
Give me the joy I anticipate.

Non es meravelha s'eu chan (PC 70.31)
Canso

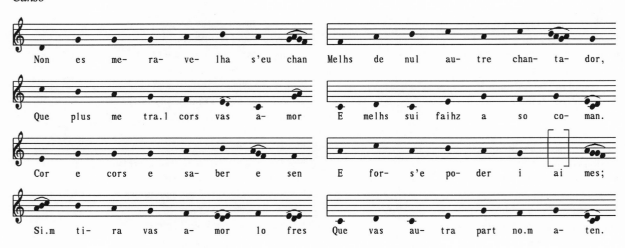

Non es me- ra- ve- lha s'eu chan

Melhs de nul au- tre chan- ta- dor,

Que plus me tra.l cors vas a- mor

E melhs sui faihz a so co- man.

Cor e cors e sa- ber e sen

E for- s'e po- der i ai mes;

Si.m ti- ra vas a- mor lo fres

Que vas au- tra part no.m a- ten.

Non es meravelha s'eu chan
Melhs de nul autre chantador,
Que plus me tra.l cors vas amor
E melhs sui faihz a so coman.   1.4
Cor e cors e saber e sen
E fors'e poder i ai mes;
Si.m tira vas amor lo fres
Que vas autra part no.m aten.   1.8

Ben es mortz qui d'amor no sen
Al cor cal que dousa sabor;
E que val viure ses valor
Mas per enoi far a la gen?   2.4
Ja Domnedeus no.m azir tan
Qu'eu ja pois viva jorn ni mes,
Pois que d'enoi serai mespres
Ni d'amor non aurai talan.   2.8

Per bona fe e ses enjan
Am la plus bel'e la melhor.
Del cor sospir e dels olhs plor,
Car tan l'am eu, per que i ai dan.   3.4
Eu que.n posc mais s'Amors me pren,
E las charcers en que m'a mes
No pot claus obrir mas merces,
E de merce no.i trop nien?   3.8

It is no marvel that I sing
Better than any other singer,
For my heart draws me more towards love
And I am better made for its command.
Heart and body, knowledge and sense,
Force and power have I placed in it.
The rein so leads me towards love
That elsewhere I do not turn my attention.

He is certainly dead who feels not of love
Within his heart the sweet taste.
And what is the use of living without merit
Except to annoy people?
May God not so hate me
That I may live a day or a month
After I am guilty of being a nuisance
Or have no desire of love.

In good faith and without deceit
I love the fairest and the best;
From the heart I sigh and from the eyes weep
Because I love her so much it brings me pain.
What more can I do if Love seizes me,
And the prison in which it has put me
No key can open except mercy,
And I find no mercy there?

Aquest'amors me fer tan gen
Al cor d'una dousa sabor;
Cen vetz mor lo jorn de dolor
E reviu de joi autras cen.   4.4
Ben es mos mals de bel semblan,
Que mais val mos mals qu'autre bes;
E pois mos mals aitan bos m'es,
Bos er lo bes apres l'afan.   4.8

Ai Deus, car se fosson trian
D'entrels faus li fin amador,
E.lh lauzenger e.lh trichador
Portesson corns el fron denan.   5.4
Tot l'aur del mon e tot l'argen
I volgr'aver dat, s'eu l'agues,
Sol que ma domna conogues
Aissi com eu l'am finamen.   5.8

Cant eu la vei, be m'es parven
Als olhs, al vis, a la color,
Car aissi tremble de paor
Com fa la folha contra.l ven.   6.4
Non ai de sen per un efan,
Aissi sui d'amor entrepres;
E d'ome qu'es aissi conques
Pot domn'aver almorna gran.   6.8

Bona domna, re no.us deman
Mas que.m prendatz per servidor,
Qu'e.us servirai com bo senhor,
Cossi que del gazardo m'an.   7.4
Ve.us m'al vostre comandamen,
Francs cors umils, gais e cortes.
Ors ni leos non etz vos ges
Que.m aucizatz s'a vos me ren.   7.8

A Mo Cortes, lai on ilh es,
Tramet lo vers, e ja no.lh pes
Car n'ai estat tan lonjamen.   T.3 (8)

This love wounds me so gently
In the heart with sweet savor;
A hundred times a day I die of grief,
And revive with joy another hundred.
Truly my anguish is of fine appearance,
And my anguish is worth more than any good;
And since my anguish seems so good to me,
Good will be the reward after suffering.

Ah God, if only one could distinguish
True lovers from among the false,
And if only slanderers and deceivers
Wore horns on their foreheads.
All the gold and silver in the world
I would have given, if I had it,
Provided my lady might know
How truly I love her.

When I see her, it certainly shows
In my eyes, my face, my color,
For I tremble with fear
Like the leaf in the wind.
I haven't the judgment of a child,
So overwhelmed am I by love,
And toward a man who is thus vanquished,
A lady could show great pity.

Fair lady, I ask you nothing
Except that you take me as your servant,
For I will serve you as a good lord,
Whatever the reward.
See me now at your command,
Noble figure, humble, gay and courtly.
You are not a bear or a lion
That you would kill me if I give myself to you.

To my *Cortes,* wherever she is,
I send the song, and never may it grieve her
That I have been away so long.

Pois preyatz me, senhor (PC 70.36)
Canso

Pois preyatz me, se- nhor,   Qu'eu chan, eu chan- ta- rai;

E can cuit chan- tar, plor   A l'o- ra c'o es- sai.

Greu vei- retz chan- ta- dor   Be chan si mal li vai.

Vai me doncs mal d'a- mor?   Ans melhs que no fetz mai!

E doncs, per que m'es- mai?

Pois preyatz me, senhor,		Since you ask me, my lords,
Qu'eu chan, eu chantarai;		To sing, I shall sing;
E can cuit chantar, plor		And when I think of singing, I weep
A l'ora c'o essai.	1.4	The moment I try.
Greu veiretz chantador		You will scarcely see a singer
Be chan si mal li vai.		Sing well if things go badly for him.
Vai me doncs mal d'amor?		Are things going badly for me in love?
Ans melhs que no fetz mai!		Rather better than ever!
E doncs, per que m'esmai?	1.9	Well then, why am I dismayed?
Gran ben e gran onor		Great good and great honor
Conosc que Deus me fai,		I know that God does me,
Qu'eu am la belazor		For I love the fairest
Et ilh me (qu'eu o sai).	2.4	And she me (as I know).
Mas eu sui sai, alhor,		But I am here, away,
E no sai com l'estai.		And I don't know how she is.
So m'auci de dolor,		Thus I die of sorrow
Car ochaizo non ai		Because I don't have a chance
De soven venir lai.	2.9	To go there often.
Empero tan me plai		However it so pleases me
Can de leis me sove,		When I remember her
Que qui.m crida ni.m brai,		That if someone cries or shouts to me,
Eu no.n au nula re.	3.4	I don't hear a thing.
Tan dousamen me trai		So sweetly the fair one draws
La bela.l cor de se,		My heart out from itself
Que tals ditz qu'eu sui sai,		That some say I am here,
Et o cuid et o cre,		And think it and believe it,
Que de sos olhs no.m ve.	3.9	Who do not see me with their eyes.

Amors, e que.m farai?		Love, what shall I do?	
Si guerrai ja ab te?		Shall I ever be cured with you?	
Ara cuit que.n morrai		Now I think that I shall die	
Del dezirer que.m ve	4.4	Of the desire which comes to me	
Si.lh bela lai on jai		If the fair one, there where she lies,	
No m'aizis pres de se,		Does not welcome me near her,	
Qu'eu la manei e bai		So that I may caress and kiss her	
Et estrenha vas me		And press against me	
So cors blanc, gras e le.	4.9	Her white body, plump and smooth.	

Ges d'amar no.m recre
Per mal ni per afan;
E can Deus m'i fai be,
No.l refut ni.l soan.　　　5.4
E can bes no m'ave,
Sai be sofrir lo dan,
C'a las oras cove
C'om s'an entrelonhan
Per melhs salhir enan.　　　5.9

Never do I renounce loving
On account of pain or trouble;
And when God is good to me,
I do not refuse or despise it.
And when good does not come to me
I know how to endure the harm,
For at times it is fitting
That one take one's distance
In order better to jump forward.

Bona domna, merce
Del vostre fin aman!
Qu'e.us pliu per bona fe
C'anc re non amei tan.　　　6.4
Mas jonchas, ab col cle,
Vos m'autrei e.m coman.
E si locs s'esdeve,
Vos me fatz bel semblan,
Que molt n'ai gran talan!　　　6.9

Good Lady, mercy
For your true lover!
For I pledge you in good faith
That never did I so love anyone.
Hands joined, head bowed,
I give and commend myself to you.
And if the occasion arises,
Show me the fair countenance
For which I have such great desire!

Mon Escuder e me
Don Deus cor e talan
C'amdui n'anem truan.　　　T1.3 (9)

To my Squire and to me.
May God give the courage and desire
To go on, disconsolate.

Et el en men ab se
So don a plus talan,
Et eu Mon Aziman.　　　T2.3 (9)

And he takes with him
What he most desires,
And I *Mon Aziman.*

Can vei la lauzeta mover (PC 70.43)
Canso

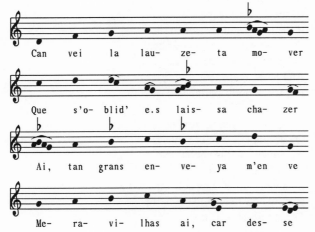

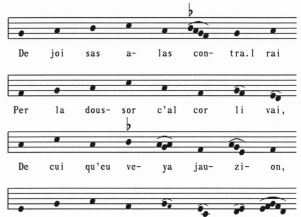

Can vei la lauzeta mover	When I see the lark beating
De joi sas alas contra.l rai	His wings, for joy, against the sun's ray
Que s'oblid'e.s laissa chazer	Until he forgets to fly and lets himself fall
Per la doussor c'al cor li vai, 1.4	For the sweetness which goes to his heart,
Ai, tan grans enveya m'en ve	Alas! such great envy comes over me
De cui qu'eu veya jauzion,	Of those whom I see rejoicing,
Meravilhas ai, car desse	I marvel that at once
Lo cor de dezirer no.m fon. 1.8	My heart does not melt from desire.
Ai las! tan cuidava saber	Alas! I thought I knew so much
D'amor, e tan petit en sai!	About love, and I know so little!
Car eu d'amar no.m posc tener	For I cannot keep myself from loving
Celeis don ja pro non aurai. 2.4	Her from whom I shall have no good.
Tout m'a mo cor e tout m'a me	She has stolen my heart, and stolen my self,
E se mezeis e tot lo mon;	And herself and all the world;
E can se.m tolc, no.m laisset re	And when she took herself away, she left me nothing
Mas dezirer e cor volon. 2.8	Except desire and a longing heart.
Anc non agui de me poder	Never have I had power over myself
Ni no fui meus de l'or'en sai	Or belonged to myself from the very hour
Que.m laisset en sos olhs vezer	That she let me see into her eyes,
En un miralh que mout me plai. 3.4	Into a mirror that pleases me greatly.
Miralhs, pus me mirei en te,	Mirror, since I mirrored myself in you,
M'an mort li sospir de preon,	Deep sighs have slain me;
C'aissi.m perdei com perdet se	I have destroyed myself just as the beautiful
Lo bels Narcisus en la fon. 3.8	Narcissus destroyed himself in the fountain.
De las domnas me dezesper;	I despair of ladies;
Ja mais en lor no.m fiarai;	No more will I trust them;
C'aissi com las solh chaptener,	And just as I used to defend them
Enaissi las deschaptenrai. 4.4	Now I shall abandon them.
Pois vei c'una pro no m'en te	Since I see that none aids me
Vas leis que.m destrui e.m cofon,	Against her who destroys and confounds me,
Totas las dopt'e las mescre,	I fear and distrust them all,
Car be sai c'atretals se son. 4.8	For well I know that they are all alike.

D'aisso.s fa be femna parer
Ma domna, per qu'e.lh o retrai,
Car no vol so c'om deu voler
E so c'om li deveda, fai.   5.4
Chazutz sui en mala merce
Et ai be faih co.l fols en pon,
E no sai per que m'esdeve
Mas car trop puyei contra mon.   5.8

Merces es perduda, per ver,
Et eu non o saubi anc mai,
Car cilh qui plus en degr'aver,
No.n a ges, et on la querrai?   6.4
A! can mal sembla, qui la ve,
Qued aquest chaitiu deziron,
Que ja ses leis non aura be,
Laisse morir, que no l'aon.   6.8

Pus ab midons no.m pot valer
Precs ni merces ni.l dreihz qu'eu ai,
Ni a leis no ven a plazer
Qu'eu l'am, ja mais no.lh o dirai.   7.4
Aissi.m part de leis e.m recre;
Mort m'a, e per mort li respon,
E vau m'en, pus ilh no.m rete,
Chaitius, en issilh, no sai on.   7.8

Tristans, ges no.n auretz de me,
Qu'eu m'en vau, chaitius, no sai on.
De chantar me gic e.m recre,
E de joi e d'amor m'escon.   T.4 (8)

In this, she surely shows herself to be a woman,
My lady; that is why I reproach her.
For she does not want what one ought to want,
And what one forbids her, she does.
I have fallen into ill favor,
And I have indeed acted like the fool on the bridge;
And I do not know why this happens to me,
Unless I tried to climb too high.

Mercy is lost, truly,
And I never knew it,
For she, who ought to have most of it,
Has none, and where shall I seek it?
Ah! how terrible it appears, to one looking at her,
That this poor, love-sick wretch,
Who will never have good without her,
She allows to perish, without helping him.

Since with my lady nothing avails me,
Neither prayers nor pity nor the rights I have,
And since to her it is no pleasure
That I love her, never shall I tell her again.
Thus I leave her and give up.
She has slain me, and by death I shall answer,
And I go away, since she does not retain me,
Wretched, into exile, I know not where.

Tristan, you will have nothing more from me,
For I depart, wretched, I know not where.
I forsake and give up singing,
And I hide myself from joy and love.

RAIMBAUT D'AURENGA

Probably the first troubadour from Provence proper, Lord (at least nominally) of Orange and of Courthézon, brought up under the watchful eye of the great feudal lords Bertran des Baux and Guilhem de Montpellier, Raimbaut d'Aurenga (c.1144-1173) was an original and unconventional poet, more concerned with play of words than with feats of battle. Although his economic situation was never brilliant, he maintained a court, likely at Courthézon where he seems to have spent most of his time, to which many other poets came. The circle of Raimbaut's acquaintances included Peire Rogier, Peire d'Alvernhe, Guiraut de Bornelh, and probably Bernart de Ventadorn. That Raimbaut was well educated in humane letters is attested by his mastery of rhetoric; the range of his knowledge of vernacular literature—including *chansons de geste* and romances (especially *Tristan*) as well as lyric poetry—was exceptional. He seems to have known well the early troubadours, particularly Guilhem IX and Marcabru. At the time of Raimbaut, stylistic questions were a focus of poetic debate. He joined in the controversy over *trobar clus* and *trobar leu* in the celebrated exchange with Guiraut de Bornelh, defending the closed, hermetic style of which he was one of the great masters. Yet, when he so desired, he could compose in the simpler style as well—calling attention to his own versatility at the beginning of one song: "Pos trobars plans / Es volguz tans / Fort m'er greu s'i non son sobrans" ("Since the simple style is so much in demand, I will be most displeased if I am not outstanding in it" PC 389.37, Pattison, 118). His poetry is full of humor and capriciousness with a virtuosic control of rhythms and sounds. We have from him around 40 songs, only one with a melody.

EDITION: Pattison 1952.

● "Ara.m platz, Giraut de Borneill": PC 389.10a. Sources: mss. D^a 183, E 221, N^2 18, R 24. Text: Pattison, 173. This debate song bears witness to troubadour concern with stylistic matters. It was probably composed at a time (Pattison proposes the date of 1170) when the *clus* style was about to pass out of fashion, giving way to the less hermetic poetry of the later troubadours. Unlike many debate songs, this one does not use *coblas doblas* but *coblas unissonans*, a heterometric 7-line stanza, and one *rim estramp*: a8 b8 b8 c4 c4 d8 d8. The song does not describe in any detail specific features of the different styles. It chiefly raises the general issue, as valid now as it was then: should the song be understood or not? should poetry be composed only for the discriminating few or attempt to reach a wider audience (termed "los faz," [3.4] by Raimbaut)? The poem does not

provide a definitive answer. (For discussions, see Topsfield 1975, 151-2; Paterson 1975, 145; Kay 1987, 125-28.)

2.1: "Lignaura" is a *senhal* used to designate Raimbaut d'Aurenga.

6.2-3: For Pattison, the sense of "amans contrarian" would be: "you are just arguing for the sake of argument." Then the following line would mean: "For that reason I am more dismayed than ever as to whether or not I should follow your advice" (174, 176). The last lines of this stanza seem to indicate on the part of Giraut a deferential stance towards Raimbaut, his patron and confrere: a singer may garble Giraut's words because they are not fit for a noble audience—in contrast to the words of Raimbaut which are (Pattison, 176). Some of the developments in this *tenso* are tinged with irony (Gaunt 1989, 122).

9.1: Saint Martial is a patron saint of the Limousin.

10.1: Probably one of the courts in Spain is intended here (Pattison, 176).

● "Ar resplan la flors enversa": PC 389.16. Sources: mss. C 198, D 90, E 176, I 145, K, 131, M 135, N^2 15, O 31, R 7, U 24, a 195, c 42. Text: Pattison, 199. Justly celebrated for its rich but harsh sounds, recherché vocabulary, and intricate construction, this song is a striking example of the *trobar ric*. I have endeavored in the translation to preserve something of the dynamism of the song carried by word repetition at the rhyme, but the grammatical aspect of these repetitions could not be reproduced. The rhyme words of the first stanza recur in all odd-numbered stanzas; those of the second stanza—which are the same as the first but in derivative form—recur in all even-numbered stanzas. Each rhyme word is a key word in the poem's thematic development: upside-down world ("enversa"); relations of nature and song ("tertres" "conglapis" "siscles" "giscles" "joy"); pain ("trenca"); and the exclusion of the undiscriminating ("croys"). In its use of recurring rhyme words, this song is related to the slightly later *sestina* of Arnaut Daniel. (Topsfield 1975, 154-7.)

● "Escotatz, mas no say que s'es": PC 389.28. Sources: mss. C 201, M 135, R 8, a 204. Text: Pattison, 152. With humor and a fine sense of the constraints of genre as well as the uselessness of "naming," of seeking strict categorizations, Raimbaut plays not only with generic designations (as in line 2) but even with separation into verse and prose. Nothing is sacrosanct. One of the intriguing mysteries of this song is that it appears in ms. R with empty staves. One wonders what kind of melody could have been invented for such a song, but a scribe of R evidently thought there was one. It has sometimes been argued that the more poetically difficult songs were not primarily intended to be sung. Yet Raimbaut himself in the first stanza of the poem quoted above, "Pos trobars plans," clearly suggests that original, and by extension difficult, verses were sung, when he compares verses never before heard to others one hears shouted out every day: "Car ben pareis / Qi tals motz fai / C'anc mais non foron dig cantan, / Qe cels c'om tot jorn ditz e brai / Sapcha, si.s vol, autra vez dir." ("It seems right that one who makes such verses as never before were sung should be able to compose, if he wishes, verses which people recite and shout about every day"). Thus it is not implausible that even a song such as this had a melody. Pattison proposes to call this song a *gap* (humorous or joking song), and relates it to "Farai un vers de dreit nïen" by William IX (in this Anthology). Particularly convincing is the argument that Raimbaut could here be making a direct reference (possibly ironic) to the opening line of the last stanza of William's poem: "Fait ai lo vers, no sai de cui" with a transposition of "about whom" into "of what kind" (Pattison, 154; Gaunt 1989, 134).

1.7: "ad home ni a femna" recalls the terminology of Southern French oaths of fidelity, for example, "e si hom era ni femena quel ti tolgues . . ." ("and if a man or a woman took it from you . . ." [Brunel 1973, N° 44]). Raimbaut juggles different discourses, and different languages: there is a phrase in Latin in stanza 4.

5.6: The *senhal "joglar"* was applied to Raimbaut d'Aurenga and to women he celebrated (see Azalais de Porcairagues). Lady Ayma, mentioned in the following prose, has not been identified but is possibly the person referred to in the scabrous story involving Truc Malec (Toja 1960, 181; Riquer 1975, 438; Bec 1984, 147).

Ara.m platz, Giraut de Borneill (PC 389.10a)
Tenso

Ara.m platz, Giraut de Borneill,
Que sapcha per c'anatz blasman
Trobar clus, ni per cal semblan.
    Aiso.m digaz,   1.4
    Si tan prezatz
So que es a toz comunal,
Car adonc tut seran egual.

Seign'en Lignaura, no.m coreill
Si qecs s'i trob'a son talan.
Mas eu son jujaire d'aitan
    Qu'es mais amatz   2.4
    E plus prezatz
Qui.l fa levet e venarsal;
E vos no m'o tornetz a mal.

Giraut, non voill qu'en tal trepeil
Torn mos trobars; que ja ogan
Lo lauzo.l bon e.l pauc e.l gran.
    Ja per los faz   3.4
    Non er lauzatz,
Car non conoisson (ni lor cal)
So que plus car es ni mais val.

Lingnaura, si per aiso veil
Ni mon sojorn torn en affan
Sembla que.m dopte del mazan.
    A que trobatz   4.4
    Si non vos platz
C'ades o sapchon tal e cal?
Que chanz non port'altre cabtal.

Now it would please me, Giraut de Borneill,
To know why you go blaming
The "closed" style, and for what reason.
Do tell me
Whether you prize so greatly
That which is common to all,
For then all will be equal.

My Lord Sir *Lignaura,* I don't complain
If each composes according to his desire.
But this much I judge,
That he is better liked
And prized more highly
Who makes it (his composition) easy and simple;
And do not take me wrong in this.

Giraut, I don't want my compositions
Turned into such confusion. Henceforth may
The good, the small and the great never praise them.
Never by fools
Will they be praised,
For they do not know (nor does it matter to them)
That which is most precious and worthy.

Lignaura, if for that I lie awake
And turn my pleasure into suffering
It seems that I fear applause.
Why do you compose
If it doesn't please you
That every one immediately understand?
A song has no other value.

Giraut, sol que.l miels appareil		Giraut, if only I prepare the best
E.l dig'ades e.l trag'enan,		And say it immediately and bring it forth
Mi non cal sitot non s'espan.		I don't care if it's not spread abroad.
C'anc granz viutaz	5.4	For nothing base
Non fon denhtatz:		Was ever worthy:
Per so prez'om mais aur que sal,		That is why one prizes gold more than salt,
E de tot chant es atretal.		And so it is with any song.

Lingnaura, fort de bon conseill,		*Lignaura,* excellent adviser,
Etz fis amans contrarian,		You are an argumentative lover,
E per o si n'ai mais d'affan.		And for that reason I have greater perplexity.
Mos sos levatz,	6.4	As for my lofty melody,
C'us enraumatz		Let a hoarse singer
Lo.m deissazec e.l diga mal,		Garble it for me and say it badly,
Que no.l deing ad home sesal.		For I do not find it suitable for a noble man.

Giraut, per cel ni per soleil		Giraut, by the sky and by the sun
Ni per la clardat que resplan,		And by the light which spreads,
Non sai de que.ns anam parlan,		I don't know what we're talking about,
Ni don fui natz,	7.4	Nor of whom I was born,
Si soi torbatz		I am so troubled
Tan pes d'un fin joi natural.		I think constantly about fine, natural joy.
Can d'als cossir, no m.es coral.		When I think of aught else, it is not wholeheartedly.

Lingnaura, si.m gira.l vermeil		*Lignaura,* she so turns towards me the scarlet
De l'escut cella cui reblan,		Side of the shield, the one whom I court,
Qu'eu voill dir "a Deu mi coman."		That I want to say "to God I commend myself."
Cals fols pensatz	8.4	What a foolish thought,
Outracuidatz!		Presumptuous!
M'a mes doptanza deslial!		It has placed in me disloyal doubt!
No.m soven com me fes comtal?		Do I not remember how she gave me a noble rank?

Giraut, greu m'es, per San Marsal,		Giraut, it is painful to me, by Saint Martial,
Car vos n'anatz de sai nadal.	T1.2 (7)	That you are leaving here by Christmas.

Lingnaura, que ves cort rial		*Lignaura,* towards a royal court,
M'en vauc ades ric e cabal.	T2.2 (7)	Rich and powerful, I now go.

Ar resplan la flors enversa (PC 389.16)
Vers

Ar resplan la flors enversa		Now shines the flower reversed
Pels trencans rancx e pels tertres,		Amidst the sharp cliffs and the hills,
Cals flors? Neus, gels e conglapis		What flower? Snow, ice and frost
Que cotz e destrenh e trenca,	1.4	Which burns and distresses and cuts,
Don vey morz quils, critz, brays, siscles		So that I see dead chirpings, cries, calls, warblings
En fuelhs, en rams e en giscles;		In the leaves, in the branches and in the twigs;
Mas mi ten vert e jauzen Joys		But Joy keeps me green and joyful
Er quan vey secx los dolens croys.	1.8	Now when I see dried up the sorrowing churl.

Quar enaissi m'o enverse
Que bel plan mi semblon tertre,
E tenc per flor lo conglapi,
E.l cautz m'es vis que.l freit trenque,   2.4
E.l tro mi son chant e siscle,
E paro.m fulhat li giscle.
Aissi.m suy ferm lassatz en joy
Que re non vey que.m sia croy—   2.8

Mas una gen fad'enversa
(Cum s'eron noirit en tertres)
Que.m fan pro pieigz que conglapis;
Q'us quecx ab sa lengua trenca   3.4
E.n parla bas et ab siscles;
E no y val bastos ni giscles
Ni menassas; —ans lur es joys
Quan fan so don hom los clam croys.   3.8

Qu'ar en baizan no.us enverse
No m'o tolon pla ni tertre,
Dona, ni gel ni conglapi,
Mas non-poder trop en trenque.   4.4
Dona, per cuy chant e siscle,
Vostre belh huelh mi son giscle
Que.m castion si.l cor ab joy
Qu'ieu no.us aus aver talan croy.   4.8

Anat ai cum cauz'enversa
Sercan rancx e vals e tertres,
Marritz cum selh que conglapis
Cocha e mazelh'e trenca: 5.4
Que no.m conquis chans ni siscles
Plus que folhs clercx conquer giscles.
Mas ar, Dieu lau, m'alberga Joys
Malgrat dels fals lauzengiers croys.   5.8

Mos vers an, qu'aissi l'enverse,
Que no.l tenhon bosc ni tertre,
Lai on hom non sen conglapi,
Ni a freitz poder que y trenque.   6.4
A midons lo chant e.l siscle
Clar, qu'el cor l'en intro.l giscle,
Selh que sap gen chantar ab joy
Que no tanh a chantador croy.   6.8

Doussa dona, Amors e Joys
Nos ajosten malgrat dels croys.   T1.2 (8)

Jocglar, granren ai meynhs de joy!
Quar no.us vey, en fas semblan croy.   T2.2 (8)

For so do I reverse things
That fair plains seem to me hills,
And I take for a flower the frost,
And it seems that cold by heat is cut
And thunderclaps are songs and warblings,
And in leaf appear to me the twigs.
I am so firmly bound up in joy
That I see nothing which is to me churl—

Except a stupid people reversed
(As if they had been reared in the hills)
Who do me service worse than frost
For each one with his tongue cuts
And speaks low and with warblings;
And of no avail is stick or twig
Or threats; —rather to them it is joy
When they behave so as to be called churls.

For now that in kissing I reverse
You is not denied me by plains or hills,
Lady, nor by ice or frost;
But by powerlessness from it I am cut.
Lady, for whom I sing and warble,
Your beautiful eyes are to me twigs
Which so chasten my heart with joy
That I daren't offer you desire of a churl.

I have gone like a thing reversed
Seeking crags and valleys and hills
Distressed like one whom frost
Torments and molests and cuts:
I am no more conquered by songs or warblings
Than foolish clergy by twigs.
But now, I praise God, I am sheltered by Joy
Despite the false, slanderous churls.

Let my verse go, thus reversed
So it is not detained by woods or hills,
There where one does not feel frost
Nor does cold have the power to cut.
To my lady may he sing it and warble
Clearly, so into her heart go its twigs,
Whoever knows how to sing nobly with joy,
For it does not suit a singing churl.

Sweet lady, may love and joy
Help us despite the churls.

Joglar, I have much less joy!
Since I don't see you, I seem a churl.

Escotatz, mas no say que s'es (PC 389.28)
No-sai-que-s'es

Escotatz, mas no say que s'es
Senhor, so que vuelh comensar.
Vers, estribot, ni sirventes
Non es, ni nom no.l sai trobar;
Ni ges no say co.l mi fezes   1.5
S'aytal no.l podi'acabar,
Que ia hom mays non vis fag aytal ad home ni a femna
en est segle ni en l'autre qu'es passatz.

Listen, but I don't know what it is,
Lords, that I want to begin.
Vers, estribot or *sirventes*
It is not, nor can I find a name for it;
Nor do I know how I should make it,
If I could not finish it in such a way
That never one saw its equal made by man or by woman
in this century or in the other which has passed.

Sitot m'o tenetz a foles
Per tan no.m poiria layssar
Que ieu mon talan non disses:
No m'en cujes hom castiar;
Tot cant es non pres un pojes   2.5
Vas so c'ades vey et esgar,
E dir vos ay per que. Car si ieu vos o avia mogut, e no.us
o trazia a cap, tenriatz m'en per fol. Car mais amaria seis
deniers en mon punh que mil sols el cel.

Although you think me mad,
On that account I could not stop
Telling you about my desire:
No one should blame me for this;
I do not care two bits for all that exists
Beside that which I now see and behold,
And I have to tell you why. For if I had begun it for you
and did not bring it to a conclusion, you would take me
for a fool. For I would prefer six deniers in my hand to a
thousands sous in heaven.

Ja no.m tema ren far que.m pes
Mos amicx, aisso.l vuelh prejar;
S'als obs no.m vol valer manes
Pus m'o profer'ab lonc tarzar;
Pus leu que selh que m'a conques   3.5
No.m pot nulh autre galiar.
Tot ayso dic per una domna que.m fay languir ab belas
paraulas et ab lonc respieg, no say per que. Pot me
bon'esser, senhors?

May he never fear to do anything which grieves me
My friend, this I want to beg him;
If he doesn't want to help me at once in my need,
Then may he offer me help after a long delay;
More easily than she who conquered me
Can no other deceive me.
All this I say for a lady who makes me languish with fine
words and long expectations, I don't know why. Can
good come of this, lords?

Que ben a passatz quatre mes,
(Oc! e mays de mil ans so.m par)
Que m'a autrejat e promes
Que.m dara so que m'es pus car.
Dona! Pus mon cor tenetz pres   4.5
Adossatz me ab dous l'amar.
Dieus, aiuda! *In nomine patris et filii et spiritus sancti!*
Aiso, que sera, domna?

A good four months have passed
(Yes! and it seems more than a thousand years)
Since she agreed and promised
To give me what I most desire.
Lady! Since you hold my heart prisoner
Relieve with sweetness my bitterness.
God, help! "In the name of the Father and the Son and of
the Holy Ghost!" What will become of all this, lady?

Qu'ieu soy per vos gays, d'ira ples;
Iratz-jauzens me faytz trobar;
E so m'en partitz de tals tres
Qu'el mon non a, mas vos, lur par;
E soy fols cantayre cortes   5.5
Tan c'om m'en apela ioglar.
Dona, far ne podetz a vostra guiza, co fes n'Ayma de
l'espatla que la estujet lay on li plac.

I am joyous because of you, and full of sorrow;
Sorrowful rejoicing you make me compose;
And for you I have left three women such
That except you, their equal does not exist.
And I am a foolish courtly singer
To such a degree that they call me "joglar."
Lady you can do as you want about it, as did Lady Ayma
with the shoulder [-bone] who stuck it there where it
pleased her.

Er fenisc mo no-say-que-s'es,
C'aisi l'ay volgut batejar;
Pus mays d'aital non auzi jes
Be.l dey enaysi apelar;
E diga.l, can l'aura apres,   6.5
Qui que s'en vuelha azautar.
E si hom li demanda qui l'a fag, pot dir que sel que sap
be far totas fazendas can se vol.

Now I finish my "I don't know what it is,"
For thus I have wished to baptize it,
Since I have never heard of such a thing
I certainly should so name it.
And may he recite it, when he has learned it,
Whoever wishes to amuse himself with it.
And if anyone asks him who made it, he can say one who
well knows how to do all sorts of deeds when he wants to.

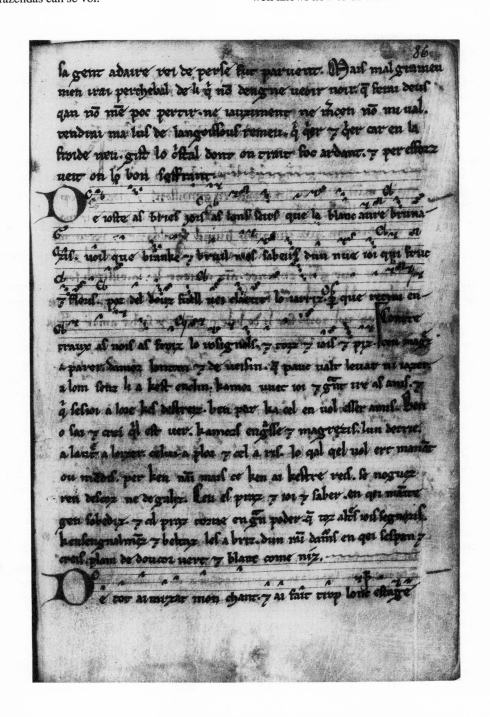

Peire d'Alvernhe, "De ioste as bries jors as lons seirs" (p. 78). Ms. X, f. 86r.
Cliché Bibliothèque Nationale de France - Paris.

PEIRE D'ALVERNHE

Peire d'Alvernhe flourished between 1150 and 1180, visiting the courts of Raimon V of Toulouse and Ermengard of Narbonne as well as the court of Castile. According to his *vida* (for the relationship of this *vida* to that of Guiraut de Bornelh, see Gruber 1983, 24-8), he was from Clermont, the son of a bourgeois, well educated and charming. Allusion is made to the fact that he was the first troubadour to be known "outra mon," ("beyond the mountains": the biographer was probably writing in Italy), and he was indeed the earliest troubadour mentioned by Dante in the *De vulgari eloquentia,* where he is placed with the "antiquiores doctores" (I, x, 2). The *vida* further asserts that Peire composed the best melodies for the *vers* ("sons de vers") that had ever been composed, quoting as an example the song "Dejosta.ls breus iorns e.ls loncs sers." It is then specified that Peire composed no *cansos* because "non era adoncs negus cantars appellatz cansos, mas vers" ("songs were not then called *cansos* but *vers*"). This remark is doubtless inspired by the use Peire makes of the term *vers* or *vers entiers* to characterize his songs (Paterson 1975, 58-74). Though not accurate in all respects, the *vida* situates Peire's art in contexts that modern criticism would not entirely reject. Peire knew well, and was well known by other troubadours, as his "Cantarai d'aqestz trobadors," or the *tenso* with Bernart de Ventadorn, "Amics Bernartz de Ventadorn," easily demonstrate (Gaunt 1989, 99-120). His verses are refined, often difficult in the manner of the *trobar clus*, often formally intricate. Some 20 songs have come down to us with one melody.

EDITIONS: Zenker 1900; Del Monte 1955; van der Werf 1984.

• "Cantarai d'aqestz trobadors": PC 323.11. Sources: mss. A214, C 183, D^{a}198, I 195, K 181, N^2 28, R 6. Text: Del Monte, 118. Although it has been classified as a *sirventes*, a more correct designation for this song, used by many scholars, would be a "literary gallery." Twelve troubadours are reviewed, one to a stanza, their foibles neatly sketched, with humor and, one wants to believe, accuracy. The caricatures selected for inclusion here, describing troubadours in the Anthology, give an idea of the method. The six-line *coblas singulars* have a rhyme scheme aabaab. The rhyme sounds chosen for each stanza are based on the name of (or on some specific reference to) the poet who is the subject of the stanza. This poem is thought to have been composed at a gathering of poets at Puivert: those satirized would have been present, so it is in the nature of a "roasting." The date of the song is not certain, probably between 1162 and 1170.

1.2: A reference to the colors of rhetoric.

1.6: This could be a reference to the melodic line which "rises" or "falls."

10.1: Raimbaut d'Aurenga

T.2: The identification of the place, Puivert, is not certain. It could be in Southern France (near Carcassonne) or in Catalonia.

• "Deiosta.ls breus iorns e.ls loncs sers": PC 323.15. Sources: mss. A 10, B 35, C 178, D 2, E 45, I 11, K 1, N^2 19, R 6, T 153, V 78, X 86; music in R and X. Melody from X. Text: Del Monte, 65. This song takes its place in the continuing discussion of "distant" love that animated many troubadour texts, notably Jaufre Rudel's "Lanquand li jorn," to which this song doubtless refers (1.1, 2.2), or (see the 5th stanza) Bernart de Ventadorn's "Can vei la lauzeta mover" (Topsfield 1975, 164-6). The stanzas are heterometric with lines of 8 and 10 syllables; the same rhyme sounds, all masculine, are maintained throughout, on the model of *coblas unissonans*, succeeding each other according to the scheme ababcdc. In both manuscript versions the melody is quite ornate; because X offers a more regular use of accidentals and a more coherent structure, it has been transcribed here. Repetition of complete melodic phrases in the first part of the melody followed by new material in the second part establishes the scheme ABAB CDE. Each phrase cadences on *c* except the last which falls on *g*. This means that, although a general correspondance pertains between melodic and metrical schemes, the different rhyme sounds in the first part of the stanza will be heard to the same final note *c* in each line—varied by the slight ornament for the rhyme "ers" (lines 1 and 3) and the stark simplicity of the single note for "is" (lines 2 and 4). Such sonorous subtleties are often found in troubadour songs. The movement of the first part of the melody corresponds to a kind of contraction and expansion: phrases A are narrower in range, while phrases B expand to an octave. Familiar techniques mark the beginning of the second part of the melody: the leap of a fourth from *c* to *g* between phrases 4 and 5, and the immediate return to *c* by a leap of a sixth at the beginning of 5, the more dramatic because these leaps are difficult to negotiate for a singer. In line 5, the poetic line expands to 10 syllables. That part of the stanza will thus be stressed, and one needs to listen carefully to the way meanings are colored by considering tune and text together. Only at the beginning of the second part does one sense an attraction for *c* as a tonal center, although it has been an important cadence all along. The final phrase is striking in its change of melodic color brought about by the use of the tritone (*f, g, a, b natural*) specifically indicated by the scribe.

Cantarai d'aqestz trobadors (PC 323.11)
Sirventes

Cantarai d'aqestz trobadors	I'll sing of those troubadours
Que canton de maintas colors	Who sing in many styles
E.l pieier cuida dir mout gen;	And the worst one thinks he speaks well.
Mas a cantar lor er aillors 1.4	But they will have to sing elsewhere,
Q'entrametre.n vei cen pastors	For among them I see a hundred yokels
C'us non sap qe.s mont'o.s dissen.	Not one knows if his song rises or falls.
. . .	. . .
E.l segonz, Girautz de Borneill,	And the second [is] Guiraut de Borneill,
Qe sembl'oire sec al soleill	Who resembles a goatskin dried in the sun
Ab son chantar magre dolen,	With his weak, pitiful singing,
Q'es chans de vieilla porta-seill; 3.4	Like the song of an old woman watercarrier;
Que si.s mirava en espeill,	And if he looked at himself in a mirror,
No.s prezari'un aiguilen.	He would not think much of himself.
E.l tertz, Bernartz de Ventedorn,	And the third [is] Bernart de Ventadorn,
Q'es menre de Borneill un dorn;	Who is a hand's width shorter than Borneill;
En son paire ac bon sirven	His father was a good servant
Per trair'ab arc nanal d'alborn, 4.4	Able to handle a laburnum bow well,
E sa mair'escaldava.l forn	And his mother heated the oven
Et amassava l'issermen.	And collected brushwood.
. . .	. . .
E.l novens es en Raembautz,	And the ninth is Lord Raimbaut
Qe.s fai de son trobar trop bautz;	Who is too proud of his own compositions;
Mas eu lo torni en nien,	But I have a low opinion of him
Q'el non es alegres ni chautz; 10.4	Because he is neither joyful nor warm;
Per so pretz aitan los pipautz	That's why I esteem as highly the pipers
Que van las almosnas queren.	Who go seeking alms.
. . .	. . .
Peire d'Alvernge a tal votz	Peire d'Alvernhe has such a voice
Que canta de sus e de sotz,	That he sings both high and low
E lauza.s mout a tota gen;	And praises himself to everyone;
Pero maïstres es de totz, 14.4	However, he is the master of all,
Ab c'un pauc esclarzis sos motz,	If he would make his words a bit clearer,
C'a penas nuils hom los enten.	Because hardly anyone understands them.
Lo vers fo faitz als enflabotz	The song was made for bagpipes
A Puoich-vert, tot iogan rizen. T.2 (6)	At Puivert, while playing and laughing.

Deiosta.ls breus iorns e.ls loncs sers (PC 323.15)
Vers (Canso)

De- ios- ta.ls breus iorns e.ls loncs sers,

Qan la blanc' au- ra bru- ne- zis,

Vuoill que branc e bruoill mos sa- bers

D'un nou ioi que.m frui- ch'e.m flo- ris;

Car del doutz fuoill vei clar- zir los gar- rics,

Per- qe re- trai en- tre.ls e- nois e.ls freis

Lo ros- si- gnols e.l tortz e.l gais e.l pics.

Deiosta.ls breus iorns e.ls loncs sers,	During the brief days and long evenings,
Qan la blanc'aura brunezis,	When the clear air darkens,
Vuoill que branc e bruoill mos sabers	I want to spread and branch out my knowledge
D'un nou ioi qe.m fruich'e.m floris; 1.4	Of a new joy that will bring me fruit and flowers;
Car del doutz fuoill vei clarzir los garrics,	For I see the oaks cleared of their sweet leaves;
Per qe retrai entre.ls enois e.ls freis	That's why from the discomfort and the cold
Lo rossignols e.l tortz e.l gais e.l pics.	Nightingale, thrush, jay and woodpecker withdraw.
Contr'aisso m'agrada.l parers	In contrast to this, the vision pleases me
D'amor loindan'e devezis	Of a love far-off and separated,
Car pauc val levars ni iazers	For of little value is standing or lying
A lui ses lieis cui es aclis; 2.4	To a man, without the one he venerates;
C'amors vol gaug e guerpis los enics,	Love wants joy and banishes the wicked,
E qui s'esgau a l'ora q'es destreis,	And whoever rejoices at the moment he is oppressed,
Be.m par q'a dreit li vol esser amics.	Rightfully, it seems to me, wants to be a friend.
Q'ieu vei e crei e sai q'es vers	For I see and believe and know it is true
C'amors engraiss'e magrezis	That love fattens and makes thin
L'un ab trichar, l'autr'ab plazers	The one through deceit, the other through pleasure
E l'un ab plor e l'autr'ab ris; 3.4	And the one with tears and the other with laughter;
Lo cals qe.s vol n'es manens o mendics,	Whoever it wishes is rich or poor,
Per qu'ieu n'am mais so qu'en ai q'esser reis	That's why I prefer what I have to being king
Assatz non—re d'Escotz ni de Galics.	—King of Scotland or Wales.

Ges ieu non sai los capteners
Mas soffre, c'una m'a conquis
Don reviu iois e nais valers,
    Tals que denan li.m trassaillis;   4.4
Car no m'enqier de dir, m'en ven destrics,
Tan tem qe.l mieils lais e prenda.l sordeis;
On plus n'ai cor, mi pens: car non t'en gics?

I certainly do not know [correct] behavior
But I am patient, for a lady has won me
Through whom joy revives and merit is born,
Such that before her I tremble;
Because I do not try to speak, harm comes to me,
I so fear that I'll leave the good and take worse;
When I have greatest desire, I think: why not give up?

A! car si fos dels mieus volers
Lo sieus rics coratges devis,
Desque ma dompna.m tol poders
    De so de q'ieu plus l'ai requis!   5.4
Mas no.ll sai dir lausengas ni prezics,
Mas meillor cor l'ai trop que non pareis;
S'ella no.l sap, morrai m'en totz antics.

Ah! if only my desires had been
Divined by her noble heart,
Since my lady took from me the possession
Of that which I have most requested of her!
But I don't know how to praise or flatter
So I have greater desire than it appears;
If she doesn't know, I'll die of it, quite aged.

Tant m'es doutz e fis sos vezers
Pel ioi qe.m n'es al cor assis,
E sobre tot lo bons espers
    Q'ieu n'ai, per que m'en enriquis;   6.4
C'anc tant non fui mais coartz ni mendics,
Ab q'ieu la vis alques, aqui mezeis
No.m saubes far de gran paubretat rics.

So sweet and pure is the sight of her
Because of the joy placed in my heart,
And above all because of the good hope
I have, through which I may become richer;
For never was I so cowardly or poor
That, provided I saw her a bit, at once
This did not bring me from great poverty to wealth.

So es gaugz e iois e plazers
Que a moutas gens abellis,
E sos pretz mont'a grans poders
    E sos iois sobreseignoris,   7.4
Q'enseignamens e beutatz l'es abrics:
Dompneis d'amor, q'en lieis s'espan e creis,
Plens de dousor, vertz e blancs, cum es nics;

This is a happiness, a joy and a pleasure
That to many people is attractive,
And its worth raises to great power
And its joy reigns supreme,
For distinction and beauty are its shelter:
Lady service, which in her spreads and grows,
[Is] full of sweetness, green and white like snow;

Per q'ieu mi pens: ia non t'en desrazics,
Quan mi conquis en loc on ilh me seis
Plus que se.m des Franssa lo reis Loics.   T1.3 (7)

That's why I think: never uproot yourself;
Since, where she won me, she invested me
With more than if King Louis had given me France.

En aqest vers sapcha vilans, Audrics,
Que d'Alvernge manda c'om ses dompneis
No val ren plus que bels malvatz espics.   T2.3 (7)

By this song may he know, the churl Audrics,
From Auvergne is bidden: a man not courting
Is worth no more than a fine wretched ear of corn.

GUIRAUT DE BORNELH

Guiraut de Bornelh (fl. c. 1165-1200) was called in his *vida* the master of troubadours ("maestre dels trobadors"). He was of humble birth but well educated, a professional poet/composer who sought patronage in many great courts of southern France and northern Spain. His immediate overlord was Adémar V, Viscount of Limoges. The large number of extant works bears witness to the favor he enjoyed in the Middle Ages and to his mastery of the art of *trobar*: seventy-seven poems are attributed to him, far more that for most troubadours. Only four melodies survive; but two of those melodies were taken over elsewhere: the celebrated dawn song, *Reis glorios*, and *Si.us quier conseil*, so that one can imagine he enjoyed musical as well as poetic prestige among his medieval confreres. Guiraut cultivated a variety of genres and joined in the debate over the merits of various styles (see Raimbaut d'Aurenga in this Anthology). He was adept in the *trobar leu* and may even have been the first to give it theoretical formulation (Paterson 1975, 88-144); but he was also a skilled practitioner of the allusive *trobar clus*, and his tastes inclined more toward difficult poetry, tinged with moral reflection. The austerity of his verses may account for the relative disfavor many of them have found with modern critics; and even Dante took a different view from the composer of the *vida*, reserving the designation of master for Guiraut's near contemporary, Arnaut Daniel (*Purgatorio*, XXVI, 119-20).

EDITIONS: Kolsen 1910 and 1935; van der Werf, 1984; Sharman 1989.

● "Can lo glatz e.l frechs e la neus": PC 242.60. Sources: mss. A 22, B 14, C 14, D 155, E 55, G 69, I 22, K 11, M 3, N 175, Q 82 and 106, R 82, Sg 87, T 239, a 25. Text: Kolsen, I 58. This song could be considered "typical" of Guiraut's treatment of the *canso* (van Vleck, *Handbook* 1995, 42-53, where one may find a detailed analysis of the text). It is neither radically original nor entirely conventional. The metrical structure is unique and demonstrates Guiraut's penchant for lengthy stanzas (one poem has 24 lines) cleverly held together by interweavings of rhyme and meter: thus here we have five *coblas unissonans*, abbaaccddeeff / 8888488884888. The rhymes in *eus* (with vocalization of the *l* of *els)* are rare; the others quite common. The mixture of what must by Guiraut's time have been perceived as the old (in this case the description of nature, beginning with "Qan . . .") and the new (into these familiar surroundings springs a leopard) is representative of Guiraut's style.

2.9 The most likely meaning of *de Bezers* is "a fool" (Sharman, 96).

● "Reis glorios, verais lums e clartatz": PC 242.64. Sources: mss. C 30, E 56, P 19, R 8, Sg 92, T 86; music in R. Text: Switten 1988, Anthology I, 77. This is the most famous of Guiraut's songs among modern specialists, although perhaps not among medieval scribes and compilers, judging by the manuscript record. It is a contender for the honor of being the most prestigious medieval *alba*. The genre is not easy to define (Saville 1972; Bec I 1977; Poe 1984b, 1984c, 1985; Dronke 1996). It is probably of Occitan origin: some 18 pieces in Old Occitan can be so categorized. The salient features are repetition of the word *alba*, usually as a refrain, and the playing out of the characteristic roles of "the sleeper," "the object of desire," and "the vigilant figure" (Poe 1984b, 148). The key theme is separation of lovers at dawn. But considerable thematic variety is characteristic. In *Reis glorios*, there is, in fact, no parting scene, and the song is sung by an outsider, the watchman, until the last stanza (not included in all manuscript versions or modern editions of the song) where the lover replies. Until this last stanza, there is no lady mentioned, although the lady as object of desire is evoked by generic expectations and the reference to the *gilos* (3.4). The final stanza is a rejection of the watchman's moral order and of the watchman himself, expressed by the transformation of the refrain, where the lover casts aside "lo fol gilos e l'alba" in favor of sensual pleasure. The metrical structure is unique to Guiraut: 10-syllable masculine and feminine lines followed by a 6-syllable refrain line, with the rhyme scheme aab'b'c', and *coblas doblas*. The melody belongs to a family of tunes, which could include the hymn *Ave maris stella* as well as the only other Occitan *alba* with music, Cadenet's "S'anc fui belha ni prezada," which in turn was used for a *cantiga* by Alfonso the Wise, and a lament from the 15th-century *Mystère de Sainte Agnes* whose stage directions indicate borrowing: "mater facit planctum in sonu albe Rei glorios, verai lums e clardat" (*Le Jeu de Sainte Agnès*, 16; Switten 1992). The opening repeated phrases of the melody propose tonal focus on *d* by the rising fifth *d-a* (a first mode intonation formula) and the ornamented recitation on *a*. The second portion of the stanza contains two phrases that make use of the contrasting notes *c-e-g* and close first on *c* and then on *e*, while at the same time repeating the fifth *d-a* first in descending motion (line 3) and then again in ascending motion (line 4). This leads to the refrain (a shortened version of line 4) which emphasizes again *d-f-a* and by its close on *d* reaffirms the tonal focus initially proposed, creating a pleasing clarity of melodic design.

• "S'ie.us quer conselh, bel'ami'Alamanda": PC 242.69. Sources: mss. A 18, B 18, C 8, D 11, G 70, H 37, I 23, K 12, N 181, Q 87, R 8, Sg 66, V 74, a 41; music in R. Text: Kolsen I, 366, except that lines 3.6,7,8; 4.3,5,6; 5.3,5,7; 6.4,7; 7.7 are taken from ms. A, rather than C which Kolsen uses as a base, following Schultz [-Gora]. (See also other editions of the trobairitz corpus, Rieger 1991; Bruckner 1995; Bec 1995). The song raises numerous problems. First the text is not clear; the major difficulties are addressed in the editions. Second, we don't know who Alamanda is. The song was long considered a fictitious *tenso* and Alamanda accordingly a fiction. However, recent criticism has tended to see in her a real woman, but who? A *razo* accompanies the song in two manuscripts. This *razo* tells how Guiraut long courted a certain Alamanda d'Estang, but when she sent him away, he turned to one of her servants, a *donzela* **also** named Alamanda to ask how he could get the first Alamanda back. The song is the advice given. In the *razo*, the first Alamanda is portrayed as clever and learned and a composer of words. Of the second Alamanda, it is said, "La donzela si era savia e cortesa, e sabia trobar ben et entendre" ("The maiden was wise and courtly and knew how to invent [songs] and appreciate [them]"), apparently indicating that she was a trobairitz. It is clearly the *donzela* who is "inventing" the advice in the song. Furthermore, the name "Alamanda" is found in other troubadour/trobairitz poems, which leads Pierre Bec to conclude that a lady named Alamanda must have enjoyed a certain celebrity in the world of the troubadours (1995, 138). So despite the fact that all the manuscripts attribute the *tenso* only to Guiraut de Bornelh, recent criticism has tended to think of Alamanda as an equal partner in the creation of the song. Angelica Rieger has proposed to identify this trobairitz as Alamanda of Castelnau, wife of William

of Castelnau, a member herself of the Alaman family whose possessions centered on the Albi/Toulouse region (Rieger 1991, 201-3). Alamanda might have grown up at the court of Raimon V of Toulouse, patron of poets such as Bernart de Ventadorn, where she could have encountered Guiraut de Bornelh. This hypothesis, though not provable, is nonetheless plausible. But the connections offered by this poem do not stop there. One of the mentions of "Alamanda" is in a *sirventes* by Bertran de Born (PC 80.19): Bertran claims to have composed his song "al son de N'Alamanda" thus recognizing a borrowing technique often encountered with the *sirventes*. This particular borrowing may be the first example of the technique (Chambers 1952-3), and the borrowing goes far beyond just the melody to the rhymes and some of the turns of phrase (Gruber 1983). Guiraut's song consists of 8 heterometric *coblas doblas* and 2 *tornadas*, thus four exchanges and a final summing up. The "a" rhyme establishes the *coblas doblas* by changing every two stanzas; the "b" rhyme "atz," closing the two short lines, remains the same. The melody is almost ungracious in its somewhat angular movement and stark syllabism, relieved by scattered melismas, more concentrated in the short lines. Phrases 3 and 4 repeat 1 and 2 almost exactly with alternating cadences on *e* and *d*. The scales suggested are *e* and *d* in their plagal dispositions; but the initial recitation on *f* in 1 and 3, the sketched third chain *b-d-f* and the lingering on low *a* in 2 and 4 incline the melody to a focus on *d*. Then the second part of the melody develops contrasting third chains *d-f-a* (ascending) and *g-e-c* (descending), especially in line 7 which oscillates around *e* with which it opens and closes. Tonal ambiguity is thus maintained until the end of the song with the close on *g* of line 8.

5.7 Na Berengera has not been identified.

Can lo glatz e.l frechs e la neus (PC 242.60)
Canso

Can lo glatz e.l frechs e la neus		When the ice and the cold and the snow
S'en vai e torna la chalors		Depart and the warm weather returns
E reverdezis lo pascors		And the Eastertide becomes green again
Et auch las voltas dels auzeus,	1.4	And I hear the trills of the birds,
M'es aitan beus		So pleases me
Lo dolz tems a l'issen de martz		The sweet time at the end of March
Que plus sui salhens que leupartz		That I am sprightlier than a leopard,
E vils non es chabrols ni cers.	1.8	And roe or deer is not quicker.
Si la bela cui sui profers		If the fair one to whom I am devoted
Me vol onrar		Wishes to honor me,
D'aitan que.m denhe sofertar		To the extent that she deigns to permit me
Qu'eu sia sos fis entendens,		To be her true suitor,
Sobre totz sui rics e manens.	1.13	Above all others am I noble and rich.

Tan es sos cors gais et isneus		Her body is so gay and nimble
E complitz de belas colors		And perfect with beautiful colors
C'anc de rozeus no nasquet flors		That never from a rose was born
Plus frescha ni d'altres brondeus,	2.4	A fresher flower, nor from any other bush,
Ni anc Bordeus		Nor did Bordeaux
Non ac senhor fos plus galhartz		Have a lord more gallant
De me, si n'era coltz ni partz		Than I, if I were received by her and tolerated
Tan que fos sos dominis sers,	2.8	So that I would be her own servant;
E fos apelatz de Bezers,		And let me be called a fool from Beziers
Can ja parlar		If I ever one hears
M'auziri'om de nulh celar		Me speak of any secret
Qu'ela.m disses, celadamens,		That she might tell me, privately,
Don s'aïres lo seus cors gens!	2.13	By which her noble self might be vexed.

Bona domna, lo vostr'aneus		Good lady, the ring
Que.m donetz, me fai gran socors;		Which you gave me is of great help to me
Qu'en lui refranhi mas dolors,		For with it I alleviate my sorrow
E can lo remir, sui plus leus	3.4	And when I look at it, I am livelier
C'us estorneus;		Than a starling;
E sui per vos aissi auzartz		And I am so bold on account of you
Que no tem que lansa ni dartz		That I fear not that lance or dart
Me tenha dan n'acers ni fers.	3.8	May harm me, nor steel nor iron.
E d'altra part sui plus despers		And yet on the other hand I am more confused
Per sobramar		Through overloving
Que naus, can vai torban per mar		Than a ship when it goes buffeted over the sea
Destrecha d'ondas e de vens;		Tormented by waves and winds;
Aissi.m destrenh lo pensamens.	3.13	So do my thoughts distress me.

Domna, aissi com us chasteus		Lady, like a castle
Qu'es assetjatz per fortz senhors,		Which is besieged by powerful lords,
Can la peirer'abat las tors		When the stone throwing machine beats down the towers,
E.ls chalabres e.ls manganeus	4.4	And the catapults and the mangonels,
Et es tan greus		And it is so fierce,
La guerra devas totas partz		The war, from all sides,
Que no lor te pro genhs ni artz		That neither trick nor artifice avails them,
E.l dols e.l critz es aitan fers	4.8	And the pain and the cries are so cruel
De cels dedins quez an grans gers,		Of those within who have great anguish,
Sembla.us ni.us par		It seems and appears to you
Que lor ai'obs merce clamar,		That they have need to beg for mercy,
Aissi.us clam merce umilmens,		So do I beg you for mercy humbly,
Bona domna pros e valens.	4.13	Good lady, noble and worthy.

Domna, aissi com us anheus		Lady, just as a lamb
Non a forsa contr'ad un ors,		Has no power against a bear
Sui eu, si la vostra valors		So am I, if your merit
No.m val, plus frevols c'us rauzeus,	5.4	Avails me not, more feeble than a reed,
Et er plus breus		And it will be shorter,
Ma vida; que de cartel chartz,		My life, than a quarter second,
S'oimais me pren negus destartz,		If now any harm befalls me
Que no.m fassatz drech de l'envers.	5.8	Without your righting the wrong.
E tu, fin'Amors, que.m sofers,		And you, noble love, who sustain me,
Que deus garar		Who should protect
Los fis amans de foleiar,		True lovers from foolish actions,
Sias me chabdeus e guirens		Be for me leader and defender
A ma domna, pos aissi.m vens.	5.13	With my lady, since she thus overpowers me.

Reis glorios, verais lums e clartatz (PC 242.64)

Alba

Reis glo-ri-os, ver-rais lums e clar-tatz,

Deus po-de-ros, Se-nher, si a vos platz,

Al meu com-panh sï-atz fi-zels a-iu-da,

Qu'eu non lo vi pos la nochs fo ven-gu-da,

Et a-des se-ra l'al-ba.

Reis glorios, verais lums e clartatz,	Glorious king, true light and clarity,
Deus poderos, Senher, si a vos platz,	Powerful God, Lord, if it please You,
Al meu companh sïatz fizels aiuda,	To my companion be a faithful aid,
Qu'eu non lo vi pos la nochs fo venguda,	For I have not seen him since the night came,
Et ades sera l'alba. 1.5	And soon it will be dawn.
Bel companho, si dormetz o velhatz,	Fine companion, whether you sleep or wake,
Non dormatz plus, suau vos ressidatz,	Sleep no longer, but softly rouse yourself,
Qu'en orïent vei l'estela creguda	For in the East I see the star arisen
Qu'amena.l jorn, qu'eu l'ai ben conoguda,	Which brings the day, I have indeed recognized it,
Et ades sera l'alba. 2.5	And soon it will be dawn.
Bel companho, en chantan vos apel:	Fine companion, in singing I call you:
Non dormatz plus, qu'eu aug chantar l'auzel	Sleep no longer, for I hear the bird sing
Que vai queren lo jorn per lo boscatge,	Which goes seeking the day through the woods,
Et ai paor que.l gilos vos assatge,	And I fear the jealous one may attack you,
Et ades sera l'alba. 3.5	And soon it will be dawn.
Bel companho, eissetz al fenestrel,	Fine companion, go to the window
E regardatz las estelas del cel;	And look at the stars in the sky;
Conoisseretz si.us sui fizels messatge:	You will know if I am your faithful messenger
Si non o faitz, vostres n'er lo damnatge,	If you don't do this, yours will be the harm,
Et ades sera l'alba. 4.5	And soon it will be dawn.
Bel companho, pos mi parti de vos,	Fine companion, since I left you
Eu non dormi ni.m moc de ginolhos,	I have not slept nor moved from my knees,
Ans preguei Deu, lo filh Santa Maria,	Rather I prayed God, the Son of Saint Mary,
Que.us mi rendes per leial companhia,	That He might give you back to me in loyal friendship,
Et ades sera l'alba. 5.5	And soon it will be dawn.

Bel companho, la foras als peiros
Me preiavatz qu'eu no fos dormilhos,
Enans velhes tota noch tro al dia;
Era no.us platz mos chans ni ma paria,
  Et ades sera l'alba. 6.5

Bel dous companh, tan sui en ric sojorn
Qu'eu no volgra mais fos alba ni jorn,
Car la gensor que anc nasques de maire
Tenc et abras, per qu'eu non prezi gaire
  Lo fol gilos ni l'alba. 7.5

Fine companion, out there on the steps
You begged me that I not be sleepy
But rather keep watch all night until the day;
Now neither my song nor my company please you,
And soon it will be dawn.

Fair sweet companion, I am in so rich a dwelling
That I would it were never dawn nor day,
For the noblest (lady) ever born of mother
I hold and embrace; therefore I heed not at all
The jealous fool or the dawn.

S'ie.us quer conselh, bel'ami'Alamanda (PC 242.69)
Tenso

S'ie.us quer conselh, bel'ami'Alamanda,
No.l me vedetz, qu'om cochatz lo.us demanda;
Que so m'a dich vostra dompna truanda
Que lonh sui fors issitz de sa comanda, 1.4
Que so que.m det m'estrai er'e.m desmanda.
  Que.m cosselhatz?
Qu'a pauc lo cors totz d'ira no.m abranda,
  Tan fort en sui iratz. 1.8

If I seek your advice, pretty friend Alamanda,
Don't deny it to me, for I'm a troubled man.
For your deceitful lady told me
That I've gone far away from her command,
And what she gave me she retracts now and reclaims.
What do you advise me?
For my body is almost aflame with anger
I'm so irritated about it.

Per Deu, Giraut, ges aissi tot a randa
Volers d'amic no.s fai ni no.s garanda,
Que, si l'us falh, l'autre conve que blanda,
Que lor destrics no cresca ni s'espanda   2.4
E s'ela.us ditz d'aut poi que sia landa,
      Vos la.n crezatz,
E plassa vos lo bes e.l mals que.us manda,
        Qu'aissi seretz amatz.   2.8

Non posc mudar que contr'orgolh no gronda,
Ja siatz vos donzela bel'e blonda.
Pauc d'ira.us notz e paucs jois vos aonda,
Mas ges non etz primera ni segonda.   3.4
Et eu que tem d'est'ira que.m confonda—
      Vos me lauzatz,
Si.m sent perir, que.m traia plus vas l'onda?
        Mal cre que.m chabdelatz.   3.8

Si m'enqueretz d'aital razon preonda,
Per Deu, Giraut, non sai com vos responda;
Vos m'apellatz de leu cor jauzionda—
Mais vuolh pelar mon prat qu'autre.l mi tonda;   4.4
Que s'ie.us era del plaich far dezironda,
      Vos escercatz
Com son bel cors vos esdui'e.us resconda.
        Ben par com n'etz cochatz.   4.8

Donzel'oimais non siatz trop parlera,
Qu'il m'a mentit mais de cinc vetz primera
Cudatz vos doncs qu'ieu totz temps lo sofera?
Semblaria qu'o fezes per nescera.   5.4
D'autr'amistat ai talan qu'ie.us enquera,
      Si no.us calatz;
Melhor cosselh dava na Berengera
        Que vos no me donatz.   5.8

L'ora vei ieu, Giraut, qu'ela.us o mera,
Car l'apeletz camjairitz ni leugera;
Per so cudatz que del plach vos enquera?
Ieu non cuig jes qu'il sia tant manera: 6.4
Ans er oimais sa promessa derrera,
      Que que.us digatz,
Si.s destrenh tant que contra vos sofera
        Trega ni fi ni patz.   6.8

Bela, per Deu, non perda vostr'aiuda—
Ja sabetz vos com me fo covenguda.
S'eu ai falhit per l'ira qu'ai aguda,
No.m tenga dan; s'anc sentitz com leu muda   7.4
Cor d'amador, bela, e s'anc fotz druda,
      Del plach pensatz!
Qu'eu sui be mortz, s'enaissi l'ai perduda
        Mas no.lh o descobratz!   7.8

In God's name, Guiraut, thus a lover's wishes
Are neither kept nor carried out,
For if one fails, the other should keep up appearances,
So that that their trouble doesn't spread or grow.
If she tells you that a high peak is a plain,
Believe her,
And accept the good and the bad she sends,
Thus you will be loved.

I can't keep from speaking out against pride,
Even if you are a beautiful and blond damsel.
The slightest pain hurts, the smallest joy overwhelms you,
And still you [the lover] are not in first or second place.
And I who am worried that this anger will destroy me—
You advise me,
If I feel I'm dying, that I should go nearer the water?
I think you lead me badly.

If you ask me about such profound questions,
By God, Guiraut, I don't know how to reply to you;
You call me with a joyful, easy heart,
But I want to mow my field before another clips it;
If I were willing to arrange a reconciliation,
You must try to understand
Why she keeps her lovely body hidden from you.
Rightly it appears you are troubled by that.

Now don't talk so much, young girl,
For she lied to me first, more than five times.
Do you think I can put up with this forever?
I'd be taken for an ignoramus.
I have a mind to seek another friendship
If you don't shut up;
Na Berengera gave me better counsel
Than you give me.

Now I see, Guiraut, how she rewards you,
Since you call her fickle and unfaithful;
Do you still think she seeks reconciliation?
I doubt she's that tame yet:
From now on she'll delay her promise,
Whatever you say.
If indeed she can bring herself to accept
Treaty, end to the dispute, or peace.

Beauty, for God's sake, don't let me lose your aid—
You already know how it was granted me.
If I've done wrong in being so irate,
Don't hold it against me; and if you've ever felt how fast
A lover's heart can change, or if you've ever loved,
Think of a reconciliation!
For I'm as good as dead if I have lost her—
But don't tell her that!

Senher Giraut, ja n'agr'eu fi volguda,
Mas ela ditz qu'a drech s'es irascuda,
Qu'autra.n prejetz com fols tot a saubuda
Que no la val ni vestida ni nuda.   8.4
Noi fara doncs, si no.us gic, que vencuda,
    S'autra.n prejatz?
Be.us en valrai, ja l'ai'eu mantenguda,
    Si mais no.us i mesclatz.   8.8

Bela, per Deu, si d'ela n'etz crezuda,
    Per me l'o affiatz!   T1.2 (8)

Ben o farai, mas, quan vos er renduda
    S'amors, non la.us tolhatz.   T2.2 (8)

Lord Guiraut, I would already have wanted an end,
But she says she has a right to be enraged,
Because you're openly courting someone else
Who next to her is worth nothing, clothed or nude.
If she didn't jilt you wouldn't she be acting weak,
Since you're courting someone else?
But I'll speak well of you to her—I always have—
If you do not do that again.

Beauty, for God's sake, if she has your trust,
Reassure her for me.

I'll gladly do so, but when she's given you her love again,
Don't take yours back.

ARNAUT DANIEL

Arnaut Daniel (fl. 1180-1210) came from the castle of Ribérac in the Périgord; he was probably of noble birth. He likely knew Bertran de Born and Guiraut de Bornelh who came from the same region. Arnaut's brief *vida* tells us that he first acquired "letters" and delighted in *trobar*, but then abandoned letters to become a *joglar*. His activities cannot be dated with certainty, but he appears to have been present at the coronation of Philip Augustus in 1180. The *razo* accompanying one of his poems ("Anc eu no l'aic") shows him taking part in a song competition:

> E fon aventura qu'el fon en la cort del rey Richart d'Englaterra, et estant en la cort, us autres joglars escomes lo com el trobava en pus caras rimas que el. Arnautz tenc so ad esquern e feron messios, cascus de son palafre, que no fera, en poder del rey. E.l reys enclaus cascu en una cambra. E.N Arnautz, de fasti que n'ac, non ac poder que lasses un mot ab autre. Lo joglars fes son cantar leu e tost; et els non avian mas X. jorns d'espazi, e devia.s jutgar per lo rey a cap de V. jorns. Lo joglars demandet a.N Arnaut si avai fag, e.N Arnautz respos que oc, passat a III. jorns; e no.n avia pessat. E.l joglars cantava tota nueg sa canso, per so que be la saubes. E.N Arnautz pesset co.l traysses isquern; tan que venc una nueg, e.l joglars la cantava, e.N Arnautz la va tota arretener, e.l so. E can foro denan lo rey, N'Arnautz dis que volia retraire sa chanso, e comenset mot be la chanso que.l joglars avia facha. E.l joglars, can l'auzic, gardet lo en la cara, e dis qu'el l'avia facha. E.l reys dis co.s podia far; e.l joglars preguet al rey qu'el ne saubes lo ver; e.l reys demandec a.N Arnaut com era estat. E.N Arnautz comtet li tot com era estat, e.l reys ac ne gran gaug e tenc so tot a gran esquern; e foro aquitiat li gatge, et a cascu fes donar bels dos. E fo donatz lo cantar a.N Arnaut Daniel, que di:

> Anc yeu non l'ac, mas ela m'a . . .
> Et aysi trobaretz de sa obra.
> (Boutière-Schutz 1964, 62-3)

And he was by chance at the court of the king Richard of England, and while he was at the court, another jongleur defied him claiming to compose with richer rhymes than he. Arnaut considered that mockery, and they made a bet, each one of his horse, that the other couldn't do it, under the supervison of the king. And the king closed each one up in a room. And Arnaut, out of annoyance, couldn't bind one word to the other. The jongleur made his song easily and quickly. And they had only ten days' time, and it [their work] was to be judged by the king at the end of five days. The jongleur asked

Arnaut if he had finished and Arnaut answered yes, three days ago; and he had not even thought of it. And the jongleur sang his song all night, to learn it well. And Arnaut thought how he could play a good joke on him; finally came one night when the jongleur was singing and Arnaut put himself to remembering it all with the melody. When they were in front of the king, Arnaut said that he wanted to recite his song, and he began very well the song the jongleur had made. And the jongleur, when he heard it, looked him in the eye and said he had made it. And the king asked how this could be; and the jongleur begged the king to find out the truth for him; and the king asked Arnaut how this had come to be. Arnaut told how it had come to be, and the king had a good laugh and thought the whole thing a good joke, and the bets were off and he had fine gifts given to each. And the song was given to Arnaut Daniel which says

> I never had her, but she has me . . .
> And here you will find the result of his work.

The story related in this *razo* may well be apocryphal. But the fact that it is given as "true" speaks to its usefulness as a witness to the role memory likely played in the invention and performance of songs. Moreover, the story links song competition, and Arnaut Daniel himself, to the prestigious court of Poitiers and Richard Lion-Heart (himself a trouvère), suggesting the kind of artistic patronage and rivalry that must have characterized troubadour song culture (Gruber 1983). Arnaut's artistic personality is sharply etched for us in a series of poems that demonstrate consummate control of poetic form and image and a mastery of the resources of language that inspired Dante to refer to him in the *Purgatorio* (XXVI, 127) as a foremost "craftsman of the mother tongue" (Old Occitan being considered the "mother tongue" of poetry). Eighteen (Toja 1960) or nineteen (Wilhelm 1981) songs have been attributed to him, with two melodies. He cultivated the *trobar clus* and especially the *trobar ric* with *caras rimas* (rich rhymes). He sang of idealized love but also of explicit sexual desire; he composed "courtly" *cansos* but also scabrous satire (Bec 1984). His valorization of carnal desire as part of the human experience of love may explain why Dante placed him in Purgatory rather than in Paradise.

EDITIONS: Toja 1960; Perugi 1978; Wilhelm 1981; Eusebi 1984; van der Werf 1984.

● "Chansson do.ill mot son plan e prim": PC 29.6. Sources: mss. A 40, B 28, C 206, D 51, E 61, G 73, H 9, I 67, K 52, L 105, N 194, N² 3, P 30, Q 39, R 94, S 187, Sg 84, c 40, α

32289; music in G. Text: Toja, 193. This song not only exemplifies Arnaut Daniel's mastery of poetic technique but also formulates a brief *ars poetica*. The metrical structure combines *coblas doblas* and *capfinidas* (imperfectly realized in some manuscripts) with a series of rich and rare rhymes whose disposition follows no set pattern, aaabbcddc, and a series of different meters, 884446'446', to create a subtly irregular stanza (Chambers 1985, 119). Each stanza closes on a feminine rhyme; the rhyme word is then taken up in the first line of the next stanza (not at the rhyme), as a masculine noun or verb form without the feminine ending. The "c" rhyme that generates the *capfinidas*, remains everywhere the same. The other rhymes change every two stanzas, thus generating *coblas doblas*, but no new sounds are introduced; the old ones are simply shifted around. This produces uncommon vocabulary difficulties. Arnaut sees his craft as that of the artisan who works to shape resistant materials into perfectly beautiful forms. The melody, like the other melody of Arnaut Daniel, is without exact phrase repetition. The most important structural tone is *a*, around which the melody seems to turn, as though about a center, and on which it cadences four times. Other important structural tones are *g* and *f*. The melody moves essentially within the space *f* to *c*, with important excursions up to *d*, and one dip to lower *d* (line 1). These features suggest a hypolydian modal coloring, with close on *a*, although Sesini proposes a kind of oscillation between focus on *f* and focus on *g* (1941, 85). The leap of a fourth from line 4 to line 5 seems to mark a structural division. However, line 5 is ambiguous; it again cadences on *a* and the rhyme sound is prolonged from the first part; thus it is as much transition as new departure. One could develop at length the correlations between poetic and musical artistry, but let us here mention just one: since the melody both opens and closes on *a*, the repetition of this note at the beginning of each stanza discreetly underscores picking up of text sounds from the last line of one stanza to the first line of the next: both text and tune define, in their own ways, *coblas capfinidas*.

1.1 The term *prim* may be a designation of style, like *trobar ric* or *car* (Paterson 1975, 201).

1.2 Melody, position 8. Pitches at the end of this phrase are unclear in the manuscript. Over the word *no.ill* appear the single notes *b* and *a*; over the word *vim* appears the note *c*. We agree with Sesini in considering this *c* an extra note because it follows the vertical line indicating the end of a phrase and so have not transcribed it. Van der Werf (1984, 13*) considers the notes *b* and *a* "two neumes over a contraction." Thus he preserves the *c* and concludes the second phrase: . This interpretation would slightly change the pattern of cadences.

• "L'aur'amara": PC 29.13. Sources: mss. A 42, C 206, D 51, H 9, I 65, K 50, N 193, N² 2, R 27, U 22, V 90, a 110.

Text: Toja, 254. It would be hard to imagine a more brilliant display of technical virtuosity than this piece, probably Arnaut's most difficult. The *coblas unissonans* have 17 short lines of different meters and irregular rhyme pattern: abcdefgbhhicjklcm / 3'4262154134424646'. Needless to say, this stanza structure is unique. But perhaps the most extraordinary feature is that the stanza also works as a set of 7 lines—4 octosyllables and 3 decasyllables—with inner rhyme, as the first stanza may illustrate and as some editors have preferred (Toja 1960, 259):

> L'aur'amara fa.ls bruoills brancutz
> Clarzir que.l dous'espeis'ab fuoills,
> E.ls letz becs dels auzels ramencs
> Ten balps e mutz pars e non pars;
> Per qu'eu m'esfortz de far e dir plazers
> A mains per liei que m'a virat bas d'aut
> Don tem morir si.ls afans no m'asoma.

Viewed this way, the stanza is made up of *rims estramps*, a rhyme scheme used as an example of *oda continua* in Dante's treatise. One can admire the rare words and the clusters of consonants, harsh perhaps, but rich and full, crisply setting off the short lines. It is surprising that the song has any meaning at all; the fact that it does is another tribute to Arnaut Daniel's skill at achieving the goal announced in the previous poem: "Obre e lim / Motz de valor / Ab art d'amor" ("I shape and refine / excellent words / by the art of love"). The sequence of stanzas is remarkably stable throughout the manuscript tradition: only IKNa deviate, placing the 5th stanza before the third.

5.17 For *Doma*, see Toja 1960, 264-5. Doma may have been a small town in the Périgord with a relatively insignificant monastery.

6.15 It is not clear that Arnaut Daniel ever went to Aragon. One can interpret this stanza as an evocation of the prestige of Aragon as a poetic center and of its king as patron.

• "Lo ferm voler q'el cor m'intra": PC 29.14. Sources: mss. A 39, B 28, C 202, D 53, E 61, G 73, H 12, I 66, K 51, M 143, Mc 3, N² 2, Q 39, R 27, S 184, Sg 82, U 29, V 25, Ve Ag 74, a 106, c 40, g¹ 90, g² 202; music in G. Text: Toja, 373. Arnaut Daniel likely invented the *sestina*, although the term itself may have come from Dante. This is one of the most famous poems in the troubadour repertory. The *sestina* stanza is constructed from six end-words, technically *rims estramps* because they rhyme only from stanza to stanza. Their relative order changes with the succeeding stanzas in such a way that by the end of the song all six words have been heard in all six end-line positions of the stanza. The rotation of rhyme words follows a regular formula: rhyme 6 of one stanza is rhyme 1 of the next; rhyme 1 becomes rhyme 2; 5 becomes 3; 2 becomes 4; 4 becomes 5; 3 becomes 6 as the diagram below will indicate. When the cycle is completed, the song is ready to begin again: a seventh stanza would be identical to the first. Since they recur in every stanza, the rhyme words carry the song's meaning. *Cambra* and *intra*, for example, tell us the song will be about entering closed space. *Verga* is first a symbol of agressivity, in stanza 4 of human frailty dominated by love, in stanza 5 an allusion to the tree of Jesse, and last an expression of the poet's desire. *Arma* means the soul, and by juggling *arma*, *cors* (which is both "body" and "heart"), and *verga*, the poet creates a complex tension between spiritual love and carnal desire. The word *Desirat* in the tornada seems to summarize the poem as it serves as a *senhal* for a lady (Toja, 382-3). The melody that carries these words is rigorously syllabic, without obvious divisions. The pattern of cadences suggests a tonal focus on *c*.

But the sequence of cadences is unlike any other troubadour melody: they follow each other 2 by 2, thus *g* for lines 1 and 2; *f* for lines 3 and 4; *c* for lines 5 and 6 (Switten 1991). Contrast of a sort is created by emphasis on the third chain *c-e-g* in lines 1-2 and 5-6, while lines 3-4 have a slightly higher tessitura and suggest (*d*)-*f-a-c*. Taken with the repeated end-words, the cadence repetition patterns create an elaborate interweaving of coordinated sounds, with each rhyme word being heard to different cadences in regular sequence. Thus is created a musico-poetic entity of impeccable craftsmanship and density of lyric expression. The entire structure may be summarized (with previous stanza order numbers in parentheses):

I		II		III		IV		V		VI,	
1 intra	*g*	1(6) cambra	*g*	1(6) arma	*g*	1(6) oncle	*g*	1(6) verga	*g*	1(6) enongla	*g*
2 ongla	*g*	2(1) intra	*g*	2(1) cambra	*g*	2(1) arma	*g*	2(1) oncle	*g*	2(1) verga	*g*
3 arma	*f*	3(5) oncle	*f*	3(5) verga	*f*	3(5) ongla	*f*	3(5) intra	*f*	3(5) cambra	*f*
4 verga	*f*	4(2) ongla	*f*	4(2) intra	*f*	4(2) cambra	*f*	4(2) arma	*f*	4(2) oncle	*f*
5 oncle	*c*	5(4) verga	*c*	5(4) ongla	*c*	5(4) intra	*c*	5(4) cambra	*c*	5(4) arma	*c*
6 cambra	*c*	6(3) arma	*c*	6(3) oncle	*c*	6(3) verga	*c*	6(3) ongla	*c*	6(3) intra	*c*

Chansson do.ill mot son plan e prim (PC 29.6)
Canso

Chans- son *do.ill* mot son plan e prim

Fa- rai puois que bo- to- no.ill vim

E l'aus- sor cim

Son de co- lor   De main- ta flor

E ver- de- ia la fuo- illa,

E.il chant e.il braill   Son a l'om- braill

Dels au- zels per la *bruo- illa*.

Chansson *do.ill* mot son plan e prim	A song whose words are smooth and fine
Farai puois que botono.ill vim	Shall I make, since the willows bud,
E l'aussor cim	And the highest peaks
Son de color	Take color
De mainta flor 1.5	From many flowers,
E verdeia la fuoilla,	And the leaves become green
E.il chan e.il braill	And the songs and cries
Son a l'ombraill	Of the birds are
Dels auzels per la *bruoilla.* 1.9	In the shadows of the *woodlands.*

Pel *bruoill* aug lo chan e.l refrim	Through the *woods* I hear the song and the refrain,
E per q'om no m'en fassa crim	And so that I be not accused of a crime
Obre e lim	I shape and refine
Motz de valor	Excellent words
Ab art d'amor 2.5	By the art of love
Don non ai cor qe.m tuoilla;	Of which I do not wish to be deprived;
Ans si be.m faill	Rather, although she (love) fails me
La sec a traill	I follow her closely
On plus vas mi s'*orguoilla.* 2.9	Where she is most *arrogant* to me.

Val *orguoill* petit d'amador	A lover's *arrogance* is worth little,
Que leu trabucha son seignor	For it readily overthrows its lord
Del luoc aussor	From the highest places
Ius al terraill	Down to the earth
Per tal trebaill 3.5	With such pain
Que de ioi lo despuoilla;	That it despoils him of joy;
Dreitz es lagrim	Rightly does he weep
Et ard'e rim	And burn and crack
Qi.'ncontr'amor *ianguoilla.* 3.9	Who *mocks* love.

Per *ianguoill* ges no.m vir aillor,	Never on account of *mockery* will I turn elsewhere
Bona dompna, ves cui ador;	Good Lady, whom I adore;
Mas per paor	But from fear
Del devinaill,	Of gossip,
Don iois trassaill, 4.5	Whence joy shudders,
Fatz semblan que no.us vuoilla;	I pretend not to want you;
C'anc no.ns gauzim	For never did we rejoice
De lor noirim:	Over their nourishment.
Mal m'es que lor *acuoilla.* 4.9	It is painful to *turn* to them in greeting.

Si ben m'*acuoill* tot a esdaill	Although I *turn* away
Mos pessamens lai vos assaill;	My thought assails you there;
Q'ieu chant e vaill	For I sing and am worthy
Pel ioi qe.ns fim	Through the joy we knew
Lai o.ns partim; 5.5	There where we parted;
Dont sovens l'uoills mi muoilla	For this reason often my eyes are wet
D'ir'e de plor	From sadness and tears
E de doussor	And sweetness,
Car per ioi ai qe.m *duoilla.* 5.9	For I *grieve* on account of the joy I have.

Ges no.m *duoill* d'amor don badaill		Never do I *grieve* for love, for which I sigh,
Ni non sec mesura ni taill;		Nor fail to follow moderation or proportion;
Sol m'o egaill		If only this were equalized for me,
Que anc no vim		For never did we see
Del temps Caym	6.5	From the time of Cain
Amador meins acuoilla		A lover who less welcomed
Cor trichador		A cheating heart
Ni bauzador,		Or treacherous,
Per que mos iois *capduoilla.*	6.9	So that my joy would *mount on high.*
Bella, qui qe.is destuoilla,		Fine Lady, whoever may turn away,
Arnautz dreich cor		Arnaut runs directly
Lai o.us honor		There where he may honor you,
Car vostre pretz *capduoilla.*	T.4 (9)	For your merit *mounts on high.*

L'aur'amara (PC 29.13)

Canso

L'aur'amara		The bitter breeze
Fa.ls bruoills brancutz		Makes the branching woodlands
Clarzir		Thin out
Qe.l dous'espeis'ab fuoills,	1.4	Which sweet air thickens with leaves,
El.s letz		And the joyful
Becs		Beaks
Dels auzels ramencs		Of birds in the branches
Ten balps e mutz,	1.8	It holds stammering and mute,
Pars		Paired
E non pars;		And unpaired;
Per q'eu m'esfortz		That is why I force myself
De far e dir	1.12	To do and say
Plazers		Pleasing things
A mains, per liei		To many, for her
Que m'a virat bas d'aut,		Who has brought me low from on high
Don tem morir		On whose account I fear to die
Si.ls afans no m'asoma.	1.17	If she does not end my suffering.
Tant fo clara		So clear
Ma prima lutz		Was my first luminous decision
D'eslir		To choose
Lieis don cre.l cors los huoills,	2.4	The one about whom my heart believes my eyes
Non pretz		I prize
Necs		Secret messages
Mans dos aguilencs:		Less than two brambles;
D'autra s'es dutz	2.8	On account of another is emitted
Rars		Rarely
Mos preiars;		My prayer;
Pero deportz		However it pleases
M'es ad auzir	2.12	Me to hear
Volers		The wishes
Bos motz ses grei		Fair words without complaint
De liei, don tant m'azaut		From her who so charms me
Q'al sieu servir		That in her service
Sui del pe tro c'al coma.	2.17	I place myself from toe to head.

Amors, gara,		Watch out, love,
Sui ben vencutz,		I am wholly vanquished,
C'auzir		Yet
Tem far, si.m desacuoills,	3.4	I fear that I would make known, if you abandon me,
Tals d'etz		Certain of those
Pecs		Sins
Que t'es mieills qe.t trencs;		That you would be better off curtailing;
Q'ieu soi fis drutz,	3.8	For I am a noble lover
Cars		Priceless
E non vars,		And not changeable,
Ma.l cors ferms fortz		But the firm strong heart
Mi fai cobrir	3.12	Makes me cover
Mains vers;		Many truths;
C'ab tot lo nei		For with all the "No"
M'agr'ops us bais al chaut		I would need a kiss to calm
Cor refrezir,		My feverish heart,
Que no.i val autra goma.	3.17	For any other balm is of no avail.
Si m'ampara		If she provides me,
Cill cui.m trahutz,		The one to whom I have offered myself,
D'aizir,		With shelter,
Si q'es de pretz capduoills,	4.4	She who is the summit of merit,
Dels qetz		For the silent
Precs		Prayers
C'ai dedinz a rencs,		That are disposed in ranks within me,
L'er fors rendutz	4.8	Then will be brought forth
Clars		Clearly
Mos pensars:		My thought:
Q'eu fora mortz,		That I would be dead,
Mas fa.m sofrir	4.12	Except that I am sustained by
L'espers		The hope
Qe.ill prec qe.m brei,		That I pray her to bring me shortly,
C'aisso.m ten let e baut;		And for which I keep myself happy and proud;
Que d'als iauzir		For joy coming from elsewhere
No.m val iois una poma.	4.17	Is not worth an apple.
Doussa car', a		Sweet woman with
Totz aips volgutz,		All desirable charms,
Sofrir		To bear
M'er per vos mainz orguoills,	5.4	Your many affronts will be my lot,
Car etz		For you are
Decs		The goal
De totz mos fadencs,		Of all my follies;
Don ai mains brutz	5.8	From which I have many hateful
Pars,		Equals;
E gabars;		And mockery
De vos no.m tortz		Does not turn me from you
Ni.m fai partir	5.12	Nor am I separated
Avers,		By money,
C'anc non amei		For never did I love
Ren tan ab meins d'ufaut,		Anyone so much with less vanity,
Anz vos desir		Rather I desire you
Plus que Dieu cill de Doma.	5.17	More than (the monks) of Doma desire God.

Era.t para,		Now get ready,
Chans e condutz,		Songs and conducti,
Formir		To run
Al rei qui t'er escuoills;	6.4	To the king who will greet you;
Car Pretz,		For *pretz,*
Secs		Dry
Sai, lai es doblencs,		Here, there is doubled,
E mantengutz	6.8	And maintained (are)
Dars		Giving
E maniars:		And banquets:
De ioi la.t portz,		Out of joy go there,
Son anel mir,	6.12	Admire his ring
Si.l ders,		If he raises it
C'anc non estei		For never have I been
Iorn d'Aragon q'el saut		A day from Aragon that in a jump
No.i volgues ir,		I did not want to go back there,
Mas sai m'an clamat: roma!	6.17	But here they persuade me to stay.
Faitz es l'acortz,		The pact is made,
Q'el cor remir	T.2 (12)	For in my heart I see
Totz sers		Every evening
Lieis cui dompnei		The one to whom I pay court
Ses parsonier, Arnaut,		Partnerless, Arnaut,
Q'en autr'albir		For any other thought
N'es fort m'entent'a soma.	T.7 (17)	Is too heavy a charge.

Lo ferm voler q'el cor m'intra (PC 29.14)
Canso (Sestina)

Lo ferm voler q'el cor m'intra
No.m pot ies becs escoissendre ni ongla
De lausengier, qui pert per mal dir s'arma;
E car non l'aus batr'ab ram ni ab verga,   1.4
Sivals a frau, lai on non aurai oncle,
Iauzirai ioi, en vergier o dinz cambra.

Qan mi soven de la cambra
On a mon dan sai que nuills hom non intra
Anz me son tuich plus que fraire ni oncle,
Non ai membre no.m fremisca, neis l'ongla,   2.4
Aissi cum fai l'enfas denant la verga:
Tal paor ai no.l sia trop de l'arma.

Del cors li fos, non de l'arma
E cossentis m'a celat dinz sa cambra!
Que plus mi nafra.l cor que colps de verga
Car lo sieus sers lai on ill es non intra;   3.4
Totz temps serai ab lieis cum carns et ongla,
E non creirai chastic d'amic ni d'oncle.

Anc la seror de mon oncle
Non amei plus ni tant, per aqest'arma!
C'aitant vezis cum es lo detz de l'ongla,
S'a liei plagues, volgr'esser de sa cambra;   4.4
De mi pot far l'amors q'inz el cor m'intra
Mieills a son vol c'om fortz de frevol verga.

Pois flori la seca verga
Ni d'En Adam mogron nebot ni oncle,
Tant fin'amors cum cella q'el cor m'intra
Non cuig fos anc en cors, ni eis en arma;   5.4
On q'ill estei, fors en plaz', o dins cambra,
Mos cors no.is part de lieis tant cum ten l'ongla.

C'aissi s'enpren e s'enongla
Mos cors en lei cum l'escorss'en la verga;
Q'ill m'es de ioi tors e palaitz e cambra,
E non am tant fraire, paren ni oncle: 6.4
Q'en paradis n'aura doble ioi m'arma,
Si ia nuills hom per ben amar lai intra.

Arnautz tramet sa chansson d'ongl'e d'oncle,
A grat de lieis que de sa verg'a l'arma,
Son Desirat, cui pretz en cambra intra.   T.3 (6)

The firm desire that enters
My heart cannot be torn from me by beak or nail
Of the slanderer who by evil talk loses his soul,
And since I dare not beat him with branch or rod,
I shall at least, in secret, where I will have no uncle,
Rejoice in joy, in an orchard or in a chamber.

But when I remember the chamber
Which, to my misfortune, I know no man enters
Instead all are worse than brother or uncle,
My entire body, even to my fingernail,
Trembles like a child before a rod,
Such fear I have of not being hers with all my soul.

Would that in body I were hers, but not in soul,
And that she'd hide me within her chamber;
For it wounds my heart more than blows of rod
That I, her serf, can never therein enter.
I shall be with her as flesh and nail
And heed no reproach of friend or uncle.

Even the sister of my uncle
I never loved like this, by my soul!
As close as is the finger to the nail,
If it pleased her, would I be to her chamber.
It can bend me to its will, that love which enters
My heart, better than a strong man with a frail rod.

Since flowered the dry rod,
Or from Adam issued nephew and uncle,
There never was a love so fine as that which enters
My heart, neither in body nor in soul;
And wherever she may be, outside or in her chamber,
My heart holds to her like flesh to the nail.

As if with tooth and nail
My heart grips her, or as the bark the rod;
To me she is of joy the tower, palace and chamber
Nor do I love as much brother, parent or uncle;
And in paradise will find double joy my soul,
If any man through loving well therein enters.

Arnaut sends his song of nail and uncle
By leave of her who has of her (his) rod the soul,
His *Desirat,* whose merit into the chamber enters.

The COMTESSA DE DIA

Although the argument has been made that the songs ascribed to the women poets called *trobairitz* might have been written by men, it is now generally acknowledged that there did exist in southern France, during the 12th and 13th centuries, a small group of some 20 women who engaged fully in the art of composing songs. If we include in their corpus a few anonymous works, we can arrive at a total of as many as 49 individual poems that have come down to us. Only two trobairitz, the Comtessa de Dia and Castelloza, are represented by more than one song, and for only one of these, "A chantar m'er" by the Comtessa de Dia, do we have music. Despite this scarcity of preserved melodies, there is ample evidence indicating that women sang as well as composed. The manuscript tradition suggests that the trobairitz were not well known in the north but that their songs travelled to Italy; indeed a few Italian and Catalan manuscripts group the women poets together as if to emphasize their cohesiveness (Bec 1979; Rieger 1985).

What we know of southern French society makes the activity of women poets entirely plausible. Placed against the background of the paradox often cited as undergirding troubadour song—a man sings to a woman portrayed as powerful and of higher status, while in reality women were of lower status than men and excluded from power—the poetry of the trobairitz must either be explained away or brought interpretatively into the orbit of male dominance. However, this paradox did not characterize Occitan society, for in Occitania, at least until the early 13th century, we do not find complete disjuncture between poetic discourse and the realities of power. To be sure, the number of powerful women was smaller than the number of powerful men; it was a patriarchical society. But numerous documents, such as oaths of fidelity or contracts of sale and gift, reveal that women participated fully in political life and held castles under the same obligations of fidelity and service as did men (Cheyette, unpublished paper). Oaths of fidelity were given to women, or even exchanged between women (Brunel 1973). It is instructive to note, for example, that in 1114 when a member of the prominent Trencavel family joined the Poitevans in their effort to hold Toulouse, claimed by William IX of Aquitaine because he had married Philippa, daughter of the count of Toulouse, it was to Philippa, the heiress, and not to her powerful husband that an oath of fidelity was taken. If the trobairitz used the language of oaths and charters in their poetry, it was not merely because they were adopting a poetic discourse elaborated by men, although they of course did that, but also because women, too, used such language in their society. And the trobairitz' ability to manipulate this discourse came not only from familiarity with a masculine poetic code but also from women's experiences as rulers and castellans. The phenomenon of the trobairitz (not repeated in any other European lyric repertory) is of a whole with the society in which it arose, and although poetry as an esthetic object is never a direct window opening onto "reality," awareness of the reality from which it springs can sometimes help us better situate its meaning.

Most of the trobairitz belonged to the aristocracy, as did the Comtessa de Dia (late 12th century). Confusion masks her precise identity. A brief *vida* tells us that she is the wife of a William of Poitiers and the lover of a Raimbaut d'Orange. None of this can be verified. Possibly the writer of the *vida* wished to surround her with prestigious names to make of her a kind of legend. Her poetic status is suggested by the rubric to the illuminator in ms. A: he is to portray "una dona que cante," "a lady singing." We have four songs attributed to her and the one melody.

EDITIONS: Schultz[-Gora], 1888; Kussler-Ratyé 1917; van der Werf 1984; Rieger 1991; Bruckner 1995; Bec 1995.

● "Ab joi et ab joven m'apais": PC.46.1. Sources: mss. A 167, B 104, D 85, H 49, I 141, K 126, T 197, a 232. Text: Kussler-Ratyé, 161 (with consideration of Schultz [-Gora] 1888; Rieger 1991; Bruckner 1995; Bec 1995). The metric scheme of thie song, a8 b7′ a8 b7′ b7′ a8 a8 b7′, is based on derivative rhymes, one set per paired stanzas following the model of *coblas doblas*: *ais, aia* (stanzas 1-2); *en, enssa* (stanzas 3-4). The change in pattern from abab to baab divides the stanza into two segments; division is marked by the repetition of the "b" sound (not unlike the effect created by the *huitain* used by François Villon). The poem develops the theme of the ennobling power of love which can only take place if the lover (male or female) choses a worthy love object. Stanza 3 insists on the lady's right to love openly. The thematic development of this poem, reinforced by the balanced and alternating succession of masculine and feminine rhymes, takes up the notion of equality in love that is developed by a number of trobairitz (Bruckner 1992, 878; but see Kay 1989, 1990, 109). In a song not in this Anthology, "Estat ai en greu cossirier," the Comtessa de Dia goes even further in stating her claim to equality: she speaks of holding her lover in her power (III, 17: "cora.us tenrai en mon poder"). She also insists that she would like to hold him in the place of her husband (III, 22), in a thematic development reminiscent of the *chanson de mal-mariée*. The trobairitz had a range of discourses from which to choose, and their *cansos* are sometimes colored by themes from other genres with feminine voices (Bec 1979, 252-59).

• "A chantar m'er de so qu'ieu non volria": PC.46.2. Sources: mss. A 168, B 104, C 371, D 85, G 114, I 141, K 127, L 120, M 204, N 229, R 22, W 204, a 231, bII 12, χ 134; music in W (G and R have staves but no music). Text: Kussler-Ratyé, 164 (with consideration of Schultz [-Gora], Rieger, Bruckner, Bec). This song has more manuscript witnesses than any other trobairitz song and is the only one to have made its way into a northern French chansonnier, where the melody is written also. This song (as do many troubadour songs) appears anonymously in W: one stanza of the text is provided in the Frenchified Old Occitan that is characteristic of northern manuscripts, under staves bearing notes. The northern scribe's handling of text and melody is somewhat erratic; we have here adjusted the melody to the Occitan text. The song as it appears in W is in van der Werf 1984.

This song has a stanza of 7 decasyllables that can be divided into *pedes* and *cauda*, producing the metrical scheme a10′ a10′ a10′ a10′ b10 a10′ b10 and the musical pattern ABAB CDB. The rhyme scheme juxtaposes two sounds only: a block, aaaa, then alternation, bab. The a rhyme changes for each stanza, the b rhyme remains. Technically, then, these constitute *coblas singulars*; but continuity between stanzas is assured by the reiterated b sound. The initial phrases of the melody (ABAB), using great economy of means and remaining within the lower pentachord except for a dip to *c* to reinforce the final *d*, stand in a complementary antecedent/consequent relationship (open ending on *e*, closed ending on *d*). This establishes the tonal focus on *d*. The *cauda* starts with recitation on *a*, reaches to the upper tetrachord in the sixth line, with the highest point attained as part of a rising triad *f-a-c*. After this contrast, the melody falls back into the pentachord for the conclusion. The final phrase rounds out the song since it exactly repeats phrases 2 and 4. Lines 5 and 6 contain the most dramatic portions of both melody and text: listening for this key moment in each stanza is an important part of learning to enjoy the song (Pollina 1988).

The text, in the direct style of the *trobar leu*, exploits the language of oaths and charters as well as the masculine discourse of troubadour song to develop a critique of male behavior and a poignant examination of the love relationship. It couches its developments in both emotional and political terms: fidelity and service are contrasted to deceit and discord. Terms key to both discourse systems (poetic and political) are crucial, particularly the term *covinens* (4.7), corresponding to the *convenientia* or *concordia* that was the name for agreements that ended conflicts in Occitania. The Comtessa de Dia situates herself as the *domna* of the male troubadour song: she has all the qualities needed to be loved: *beltatz, pretz, sens* (1.5), *paratges, fis coratges* (5.1-2). But she assumes also the role of the masculine "je" by insisting that she has made a wise choice of *amic*, assigning to him the great value usually attributed to the lady, reminding him that he, too, should choose wisely (stanza 4). In another discourse reversal, she removes from herself, in order to attach them to her *amic*, the defects attributed to the lady in male songs: pride and haughtiness (2.14; 3.1; 5.6-7). By this manipulation of troubadour conventions, the Comtessa suggests that she is above reproach and not guilty of betrayal (3.21-2); she is therefore within her right to demand fidelity of her *amic*, and to complain if she does not get it—just as a lord (man or woman) would demand fidelity of his vassal. The subtleties of this song allow us to become aware of the way in which this trobairitz, and other trobairitz as well, adopted but also adapted the poetic and political discourses available to them in order to "find" new female voices (Bruckner 1992).

2.11: Seguin is probably the hero of a lost romance, known for his love of Valensa. The Comtessa compares herself to a male lover.

3.4: Schultz[-Gora] read "qu'ie.us." Kussler-Ratyé and others have read as here. It is not clear whether *diga* and *acuoilla* are first person or third person. Rieger translates third person (as do Riquier 1975 and Dronke 1984b); Bruckner translates first person; Bec opts for a neutral translation, leaving the interpretation to the reader. I have followed Bec. The third person sets a context of rivalry (amorous with political overtones); the first person suggests the possibility of misinterpretation by the lover of the Countess's words or actions.

Ab joi et ab joven m'apais (PC 46.1)
Canso

Ab joi et ab joven m'apais		I am nourished by joy and youth
E jois e jovens m'apaia,		And joy and youth sustain me
Que mos amics es lo plus gais,		For my friend is the gayest,
Per qu'ieu sui coindet'e guaia;	1.4	And that is why I am charming and gay
E pois ieu li sui veraia,		And since I am true to him,
Bei.s taing qu'el me sia verais,		It is fitting that he be true to me
Qu'anc de lui amar non m'estrais		For never from loving him do I withdraw
Ni ai cor que m'en estraia.	1.8	Nor from it do I desire withdrawal.

Mout mi plai quar sai que val mais
    Cel qu'ieu plus desir que m'aia,
E cel que primiers lo m'atrais
    Dieu prec que gran joi l'atraia;   2.4
    E qui que mal l'en retraia,
No.l creza, fors so qu'ie.l retrais;
C'om cuoill maintas vetz los balais
    Ab qu'el mezeis se balaia.   2.8

Dompna que en bon pretz s'enten
    Deu ben pausar s'entendenssa
En un pro cavallier valen;
    Pois qu'ill conois sa valenssa,   3.4
    Que l'aus amar a presenssa;
Que dompna, pois am'a presen,
Ja pois li pro ni.ll avinen
    Non dirant mas avinenssa.   3.8

Qu'ieu n'ai chausit un pro e gen
    Per cui pretz meillur'e genssa
Larc et adreig e conoissen,
    On es sens e conoissenssa.   4.4
    Prec li que m'aia crezenssa.
Ni om no.l puosca far crezen
Qu'ieu fassa vas lui faillimen,
    Sol non trob en lui faillensa.   4.8

    Floris, la vostra valenssa
Sabon li pro e li valen,
Per qu'ieu vos quier de mantenen,
    Si.us plai, vostra mantenenssa.   T.4 (8)

I'm very pleased to know he's worth more
The one I most desire that he have me
And to the one who first gave him to me
I pray that God may give great joy;
And whoever tells him evil about it,
Let him not believe it, except what I told him;
For one picks many times the switch
With which one switches oneself.

A lady who understands true merit
Must place her understanding
In a fine and worthy knight;
Since she knows his worth,
Let her dare love him openly;
For of a lady, since she loves openly,
Never after will the worthy and the gracious
Say anything but gracious words.

For I have chosen one worthy and noble
Through whom merit improves and is ennobled,
Generous and skillful and knowledgeable,
Where resides good sense and knowledge.
I pray him that he believe in me.
And no one can make him believe
That I would commit toward him a fault
If I find in him no failing.

Floris, your worth
Is known by the valiant and the worthy,
That is why I seek from you now,
If it please you, your protection.

A chantar m'er de so qu'ieu non volria (PC 46.2)
Canso

A chan- tar m'er de so qu'ieu non vol- ri- a,

Tant me ran- cur de lui cui sui a- mi- a,

Car ieu l'am mais que nu- illa ren que si- a;

Vas lui no.m val mer- ces ni cor- te- si- a

Ni ma bel- tatz ni mos pretz ni mos sens,

C'a- tres- si.m sui en- ga- nad' e tra- hï- a

Com degr' es- ser, s'ieu fos de- sa- vi- nens.

A chantar m'er de so qu'ieu non volria,
Tant me rancur de lui cui sui amia,
Car ieu l'am mais que nuilla ren que sia;
Vas lui no.m val merces ni cortesia
Ni ma beltatz ni mos pretz ni mos sens,
C'atressi.m sui enganad'e trahïa
Com degr'esser, s'ieu fos desavinens.

D'aisso.m conort car anc non fi faillenssa,
Amics, vas vos per nuilla captenenssa,
Anz vos am mais non fetz Seguis Valenssa,
E platz mi mout quez eu d'amar vos venssa,
Lo mieus amics, car etz lo plus valens;
Mi faitz orguoill en ditz et en parvenssa,
E si etz francs vas totas autras gens.

Meravill me com vostre cors s'orguoilla
Amics, vas me, per qu'ai razon qu'ieu.m duoilla
Non es ges dreitz c'autr'amors vos mi tuoilla
Per nuilla ren qe.us diga ni acuoilla;
E membre vos cals fo.l comenssamens
De nostr'amor! ja Dompnedieus non vuoilla
Qu'en ma colpa sia.l departimens.

I am obliged to sing of that which I would not,
So bitter am I over the one whose love I am,
For I love him more than anything;
1.4   With him mercy and courtliness are of no avail
Not my beauty, nor my merit nor my good sense,
For I am deceived and betrayed
Exactly as I should be, if I were ungracious.

I comfort myself because never was I at fault,
Friend, towards you on account of any behavior,
Rather I love you more than Seguin [loved] Valensa,
2.4   And it pleases me greatly that I vanquish you in love,
My friend, because you are the most valiant;
You are haughty to me in words and appearance,
And yet you are so affable towards all others.

I am astonished at how you become haughty,
Friend, towards me, and I have reason to grieve;
It is not right that another love take you from me
3.4   On account of anything said or granted to you.
And remember how it was at the beginning
Of our love! May God never wish
That my guilt be the cause of separation.

Proesa grans qu'el vostre cors s'aizina
E lo rics pretz qu'avetz m'en ataïna,
C'una non sai, loindana ni vezina,
Si vol amar, vas vos non si'aclina;   4.4
Mas vos, amics, etz ben tant conoissens
Que ben devetz conoisser la plus fina,
E membre vos de nostres covinens.

The great valor which dwells in you
And your noble worth retain me,
For I know of no woman, far or near,
Who, if she wishes to love, would not incline toward you;
But you, friend, are so discerning
That you certainly must discern the finest,
And remember our agreement.

Valer mi deu mos pretz e mos paratges
E ma beltatz e plus mos fis coratges,
Per qu'ieu vos man lai on es vostr'estatges
Esta chansson que me sia messatges: 5.4
Ieu vuoill saber, lo mieus bels amics gens,
Per que vos m'etz tant fers ni tant salvatges,
Non sai, si s'es orguoills o maltalens.

My worth and my nobility,
My beauty and my faithful heart should help me;
That is why I send there to your dwelling
This song, that it may be my messenger.
I want to know, my fine and noble friend,
Why you are so cruel and harsh with me;
I don't know if it is haughtiness or ill will.

Mas aitan plus voill qe.us diga.l messatges
Qu'en trop d'orguoill ant gran dan maintas gens.   T.2 (7)

But I especially want the messenger to tell you
That many people are harmed by excess pride.

The Comtessa de Dia, "A chantar mes al cor que non deurie" (p. 98). The photograph shows both sides of folio 204, Ms. W. Clichés Bibliothèque Nationale de France - Paris.

AZALAIS DE PORCAIRAGUES

So far as we can judge from the information at our disposal—a *vida* and one remaining song, Azalais de Porcairagues composed at the end of the 12th century. The *vida* says she came from Montpellier; scholars have associated her with Portiragues near Béziers (Bec 1995, 65). It is probable that her *amic* was Raimbaut d'Aurenga and that the *senhal* of *Joglar* was used by Raimbaut to refer to her. Several parallels have been drawn between her work and that of the troubadour from Orange, and she was doubtless connected with his court. Despite the fact that only one poem has come down to us, iconographic evidence offered by miniatures in the manuscripts where she is represented suggests that Azalais was almost as important as the Comtessa de Dia or Castelloza, whose works are relatively more abundant. For this reason, considerable scholarly attention has been devoted to her song.

EDITIONS: Schultz[-Gora] 1888; Sakari 1949; Rieger 1991; Bruckner 1995; Bec 1995.

• "Ar em al freg temps vengut": PC 43.1. Sources: mss. C 385, D^a 190, H 57, I 140, K 125, N 233, d 314. Text: Schultz[-Gora], 16 (taking into consideration also Rieger 1991; Bruckner 1995; Bec 1995). This is a particularly difficult poem because its textual tradition is so troubled (Rieger published two versions of the song: one from N, the other from CDIKd). To explain the poem's apparent discontinuity, Rieger speculates that several fragments were combined into a single piece (494-5). The irregularities express themselves formally as well as thematically. The basic stanza structure consists of 8 7-syllable lines with a rhyme scheme ab'ab'ccd'd'. The stanzas follow each other according to the model of *coblas doblas*, except the last two, where there is a sudden switch to *coblas singulars*. Rhyme d remains the same throughout; rhyme c has the same vowel sounds, but the first two stanzas have a rhyme

in *ais*, while in the third stanza this changes to *ai*. The poem develops what is known as the *"ric ome* theme" (3.2): should a lady love a man who is above her in station? The notions of power and hierarchy associated with this theme are explored by a number of trobairitz. This poem may be compared to those of the Comtessa de Dia and especially to the debate between Maria de Ventadorn and Gui d'Ussel, or even, for the other side of the coin, to "Amics Bernartz" by Bernart de Ventadorn (all in this Anthology). The end of the song has been interpreted as a lament on the death of Raimbaut d'Aurenga (but see below). We probably do not have here anything like the preservation of an "author's original"; but through the song as it is, we may seek to understand one of the more important feminine voices coming to us from medieval Occitania.

6: This entire stanza refers to monuments from the region of Orange. Bel Esgar is probably Beauregard in the Vaucluse, close to Courthézon; Glorïette was a castle of the princes of Orange, as, in all likelihood was Caslar; 6.6 refers to the celebrated arch on whose frieze are sculpted various battles.

T.1: Joglar is probably a *senhal* possibly designating Raimbaut d'Aurenga; it is a *senhal* Raimbaut also used, possibly to designate Azalais (Sakari 1949, 196). However, Joglar here could simply refer to the messenger who is to carry the song.

T.2: The mention of Narbonne suggests that the one "cui jois e jovens guida" is Ermengard of Narbonne, one of the most powerful women (or men) of her time, mentioned by several troubadours. As Matilda Bruckner has pointed out, if *Joglar* is Raimbaut, and if he is urged to carry the song to Narbonne, the final stanza can hardly be a death lament (Bruckner 1995, 156); the loss must refer to the loss of love.

Ar em el freg temps vengut (PC 43.1)
Canso

Ar em al freg temps vengut,		Now we have come to the cold weather
Que.l gels e.l neus e la faingna,		With the ice, the snow and the mud,
E.l aucellet estan mut,		And the birds are silent:
C'us de chantar non s'afraingna;	1.4	Not one desires to sing;
E son sec li ram pels plais,		And the branches in the hedges are dry:
Que flors ni foilla no.i nais,		Neither flowers nor leaves bloom there,
Ni rossignols non i crida,		Nor does the nightingale warble,
Que l'am'en mai me reissida.	1.8	Who awakens my soul in May.

Tant ai lo cor deseubut,	My heart is so wronged
Per qu'ieu soi a totz estraingna,	That's why I am distant to all;
E sai que l'om a perdut	And I know that one loses
Molt plus tost que non gasaingna; 2.4	Much more rapidly than one wins;
E s'ieu faill ab motz verais,	And if I fail with true words,
D'Aurenga me moc l'esglais,	From Orange came my torment,
Per qu'ieu m'estauc esbaïda	That is why I am so dismayed
E.n pert solatz en partida. 2.8	And in part lose my joy.

Dompna met mot mal s'amor	A lady places very badly her love
Que ab ric ome plaideia,	Who gets on well with a rich man,
Ab plus aut de vavassor,	With one higher placed than a vavasour;
E s'il o fai, il folleia; 3.4	And if she does this she acts foolishly;
Car so diz om en Veillai	For they say in Velay
Que ges per ricor non vai,	That love does not go with riches,
E dompna que n'es chauzida	And a lady distinguished in this way
En tenc per envilanida. 3.8	I consider base.

Amic ai de gran valor	I have a friend of great merit
Que sobre toz seignoreia	Who reigns above all others
E non a cor trichador	And he has not a deceiving heart
Vas me, que s'amor m'autreia. 4.4	Towards me, the one who grants me his love.
Ieu dic que m'amors l'eschai,	I say that I accord my love to him
E cel que dis que non fai	And the one who says I don't
Dieus li don mal'escarida,	May God give him bad fortune
Qu'ieu m'en teing fort per guerida. 4.8	For I consider myself, in this respect, quite safe.

Bels amics, de bon talan	Handsome friend, of gracious manner,
Son ab vos toz jornz en gatge,	I am engaged in your service forever,
Cortez'e de bel semblan,	Courtly and of fine countenance,
Sol non demandes outratge; 5.4	Provided that you ask no outrage;
Tost en venrem a l'assai,	Soon we will come to the test,
Qu'en vostra merce.m metrai:	For I shall put myself in your mercy
Vos m'avetz la fe plevida,	You have sworn to me your fidelity,
Que no.m demandes faillida. 5.8	Do not ask failure of me.

A Dieu coman Bel Esgar	To God I commend Beauregard,
E plus la ciutat d'Aurenga	And the city of Orange,
E Glorïet'e.l Caslar	And Gloriette and the Caslar,
E lo seignor de Proenza 6.4	And the Lord of Provence,
E tot can vol mon ben lai	And all who are well disposed toward me there
E l'arc on son fag l'assai.	And the arch where are sculptured the exploits.
Celui perdiei c'a ma vida,	I have lost the one who has my life,
E.n serai toz jornz marrida. 6.8	And I will be forever troubled.

Joglar, que avetz cor gai,	Joglar, you who have a joyous heart,
Ves Narbona portatz lai	Carry down there towards Narbonne
Ma chanson ab la fenida	My song with the conclusion
Lei cui jois e jovens guida. T.4 (8)	To her who is a model of joy and youth.

BERTRAN DE BORN

Bertran de Born was born around 1140; he died sometime before 1215, having retired, like Bernart de Ventadorn, into the monastery of Dalon. He belonged to the lesser nobility; his family owned the castle of Hautefort in the Périgord, and after evincing his brother, Bertran became sole master of the property. It was situated within Plantagenet domains but near possessions of the King of France. To maintain his hold on the castle, Bertran engaged in constant political intrigue, shifting alliances as his interests dictated. He was associated in diverse ways (sometimes fomenting trouble among them) with the sons of Henry II and Eleanor of Aquitaine, particularly with their second son, also named Henry and called the "Young King" (because his father had him crowned already in 1170, but he died before he could rule), and with Richard Lion-Heart who became Duke of Aquitaine and, after 1189, king of England. Bertran was twice married and had five children.

Bertran de Born was an original poet and a colorful figure. He sang of love, but his real love seems to have been war. One finds in his poems a sense of the immediacy of war and of its necessity: war, for him, had moral value; it was part of the knightly ethic that Bertran elaborated more vigorously than any other troubadour. He was considered by Dante the outstanding poet of arms (*De vulgari eloquentia* 2.2.9), but at the same time placed in Hell among those who created discord (*Inferno*, 118-42; Barolini 1984, 153-73). In uniting poetry and politics, love and war, Bertran richly represented the contradictions of his time (Paden et al. 1986). Bertran was probably the first poet to use the term *sirventes* to indicate a moral or satirical poem; he designates several of his poems that way. We have from him a substantial number of poems, around 45, and a single melody. One of the characteristics of the *sirventes* which Bertran chiefly cultivated was the taking over of melodies from other songs according to the technique of *contrafactum*. Indeed, Bertran was an innovator in the use of formal imitation (Paden et al. 1986, 45-8; and see Guiraut de Bornelh, "S'ie.us quer" in this Anthology).

EDITIONS: Stimming 1913; Appel 1932; van der Werf 1984; Gouiran 1985 & 1987; Paden et al. 1986.

• "Bel m'es, quan vei chamjar lo senhoratge": PC 80.7. Sources; mss. C 139, M 228. Text, Stimming, 137. This song, called *sirventes* by Bertran (6.1), wittily develops themes of youth and old age using techniques of enumeration. The qualities are defined more as moral than as physical attributes: the poem serves as a definition of courtly virtues. The *tornada* suggests that the song may be offering advice to Richard Lion-Heart (T.2) on how he should behave. The jongleur, Arnaut, mentioned in the *tornada* has not been identified, but Paden et al. propose that it might be the poet Arnaut Daniel who was a jongleur according to his *vida* (1986, 299).

2.1: This line is unclear. Paden et al. propose a text: "Velha la tenc pus c'a pel laya" and a translation "Old is a lady, I think, when she has ugly skin" (296-7). Gouiran proposes a text "Vielha la tenc dona, pus capel atge" and a translation "Je tiens une dame pour vieille si elle a mauvaise réputation" (534-5).

• "Be.m platz lo gais temps de pascor": PC 80.8a. Sources: mss. A 213, B 123, C 130, D 142, G 130, I 176, K 161, M 242, N 85, P 1, Q 108, Sg 107, T 171, U 137, V 77, a^1 443, d 280, e 158, α 32135. Text: Stimming, 139 (with consideration of Gouiran and Paden et al.). Both the attribution and the number of stanzas in the song have caused considerable critical comment. Recent editors have reaffirmed the attribution of the song to Bertran, although only 5 manuscripts place his name with it. Gouiran suggests that it is likely that the song circulated in several versions and may have been sent to several different individuals (1985, 730; 1987, 37).

The song is Bertran de Born's most successful evocation of war and often quoted for that reason. But if one adopts the entire range of preserved stanzas, as we have here, themes of love and war are intertwined, so that the poem contains within itself the main themes characteristic of Bertran's poetry. Conservative in its versification, although the heterometric *coblas unissonans* (combining 8 and 6 syllables) do not lack grace, the song is chiefly distinguished by the vigor and power of its imagery.

6: This stanza, contained in 6 manuscripts (CNQVa^{1}α), is rejected from the main body of the poem by both Stimming and Gouiran, added as an appendix. Paden et al. include it.

7: This stanza is found in 9 of the 19 manuscripts (ABCMPUVa^{1}e). It is included in both Gouiran and Paden, but not in Stimming.

7.5: Beatriz cannot be identified.

T1: This stanza, contained only in 3 manuscripts (PMe), is included in the main body of the text only by Paden et al.

T3: The final tornada is also in 3 manuscripts (SgTV), but in all of them it has too many syllables in the last line. Both Gouiran (in his notes) and Paden et al. emend this line. I have followed Gouiran's emendation.

T3.1: Papiol is the name given to a jongleur by Bertran de Born. Among the troubadours, Bertran made perhaps the most overt use of jongleurs, if one is to judge by how the poets speak of sending their songs to the recipients.

T3.2: Oc-e-No is the name given by Bertran to Richard Lion-Heart. This last line might suggest that a state of war is not only pleasing to Bertran, but the best way he can maintain his independence: as long as the kings are busy fighting each other, they are less likely to give him trouble.

• "Si tuit li dol e.lh plor e.lh marrimen": PC 80.41. Sources: mss. T 169, a¹ 425, c 72. Text: Stimming, 76. This song also presents problems of attribution. The two recent editors are divided: Paden et al. exclude the song from Bertran's corpus (93-4); Gouiran includes it (1985, 181-2), with persuasive arguments, as did Stimming.

The song laments the death of the "jove rei engles," the "Young King," who died at age twenty-eight. It was a

devastating blow for Bertran de Born. Young Henry was not only a protector but also a charming and generous man and a brilliant fighter. The *planh*, or funeral lament, was modeled on the medieval Latin *planctus*, which in turn originated with the Greeks and Romans. At its inception, the lament was predominantly religious. The Occitan lament differed from the Latin in that it was composed for a lay public and meant to be sung outside the Church. One may consider the *planh* a kind of *sirventes*: it concerns a recent event and usually develops themes of praise and (more rarely) blame. This stately lament unfolds the poet's pain in verses of 10 syllables with 3 refrain words at the rhyme: "marrimen," "jove rei engles," and "ira," the latter two forming *rims estramps*. Thus the young king is entirely enclosed in the misery and sorrow his death provoked.

Bel m'es, quan vei chamjar lo senhoratge (PC 80.7)
Sirventes

Bel m'es, quan vei chamjar lo senhoratge		It pleases me to see power change hands
E.lh vielh laissan a.ls joves lor maisos,		And the old leave to the young their dwellings
E chascus pot giquir a son linhatge		And each can leave to his lineage
Aitans d'enfans que l'us puosch'esser pros:	1.4	Enough children so that one may be excellent:
Adoncs m'es vis que.l segles renovel		Then it seems to me that the world is renewed
Mielhs que per flor ni per chantar d'auzel;		Better than by flower or by song of bird;
E qui domna ni senhor pot chamjar,		And whoever can change lady or lord,
Vielh per jove, ben deu renovelar.	1.8	Old for young, should indeed effect renewal.
Per vielha tenh domna, puois qu'a pelatge,		Old I consider a lady after she's bald
Et es vielha, quan chavalier non a;		And she's old when she has no knight;
Vielha la tenh, si de dos drutz s'apatge		Old I consider her if she takes two lovers
Et es vielha, si avols hom lo.lh fa;	2.4	And she's old if a lout does it to her;
Vielha la tenh, si ama dintz son chastel,		Old I consider her if she loves within her castle
Et es vielha, quan l'a ops de fachel;		And she's old when she needs witchcraft
Vielha la tenh, puois l'enoian joglar,		Old I consider her when jongleurs bore her
Et es vielha, quan trop vuolha parlar.	2.8	And she's old when she wants to talk too much.
Joves es domna que sap honrar paratge		Young is a lady who knows how to honor nobility
Et es joves per bos fachs, quan los fa,		And she's young through good deeds when she does them
Joves si te, quan a adrech coratge		Young she keeps herself when she has a frank heart
E ves bo pretz avol mestier non a;	3.4	And to get fine merit has no evil scheme;
Joves si te, quan guarda son cors bel,		Young she keeps herself by maintaining a beautiful body
Et es joves domna, quan be.s chapdel;		And the lady is young when she conducts herself well
Joves si te, quan no.i chal divinar,		Young she keeps herself when gossip doesn't interest her,
Qu'ab bel joven si guart de mal estar.	3.8	And with fine youth refrains from doing wrong.

Joves es hom que lo sieu ben enguatge		Young is a man who pawns his possessions	
Et es joves, quan es be sofrachos;		And he's young when he is very needy;	
Joves si te, pro.lh costan ostatge,		Young he keeps himself when hosting costs him plenty	
Et es joves, quan fai estragatz dos;	4.4	And he's young when he makes extravagant gifts	
Joves si te, quan art l'arch'e.l vaissel		Young he keeps himself when he burns chests and vases	
E fai estorn e vouta e cembel;		And fights battles and jousts and tournaments;	
Joves si te, quan li platz domneiar,		Young he keeps himself when it pleases him to court,	
Et es joves, quan be l'aman juglar.	4.8	And he's young when he's liked by jongleurs.	

Vielhs es rics hom, quan re no met en guatge
E li sobra blatz e vis e bacos;
Per vielh lo tenh, quan liura uous e fromatge
A jorn charnal se e sos companhos;   5.4
Per vielh, quan vest chapa sobre mantel,
E vielh, si a chaval qu'om sieu apel;
Vielhs es, quan vol un jorn en patz estar,
E vielhs, si pot guandir ses baratar.   5.8

Old is a rich man when he risks nothing
And he has grain, wine, and bacon in excess;
Old I consider him when he offers eggs and cheese
On meat-eating days to himself and his friends;
Old when he wears a cape over his cloak,
And old if he has the horse of another;
He's old when he wants to spend a day in peace
And old if he can leave without foolish spending.

Mo sirventesc port'e vielh e novel,
Arnautz joglars, a Richart, que.l chapdel,
E ja tesaur vielh no vuolh'amassar,
Qu'ab tesaur jove pot pretz guazanhar.   T.4 (8)

Take my sirventes old-and-new,
Arnaut, jongleur, to Richard, that it may guide him,
May he never want to amass an old treasure
For with a young treasure he can win prestige.

Be.m platz lo gais temps de pascor (PC 80.8a)
Sirventes

Be.m platz lo gais temps de pascor,
Que fai fuolhas e flors venir,
E platz mi, quan auch la baudor
Dels auzels, que fan retentir
        Lor chan per lo boschatge,   1.5
E platz mi, quan vei sobre.ls pratz
Tendas e pavilhos fermatz,
        Et ai gran alegratge,
Quan vei per champanha rengatz
Chavaliers e chavals armatz.   1.10

I am pleased by the gay season of spring
Which brings forth leaves and flowers,
And I am pleased when I hear the merriment
Of the birds making their song
Resound through the woods;
And I am pleased when I see the meadows
Covered with tents and pavilions;
And great is my joy
When I see ranged over the countryside
Knights and horses in armor.

E platz mi, quan li corredor
Fan las gens e l'aver fugir,
E platz mi, quan vei apres lor
Gran re d'armatz ensems venir,
        E platz m'en mon coratge,   2.5
Quan vei fortz chastels assetjatz
E.ls barris rotz et esfondratz
        E vei l'ost el ribatge,
Qu'es tot entorn claus de fossatz
Ab lissas de fortz pals serratz.   2.10

And I am pleased when I see scouts
Making people flee with their belongings
And I am pleased when I see after them
Great hosts of armed men come together,
I am pleased in my heart
When I see strong castles besieged,
With the ramparts broken and crumbled,
And I see the troops on the bank
Surrounded by the moat,
With palisades of strong stakes crowded together.

Et autresi.m platz de senhor.
Quan es primiers a l'envazir
En chaval, armatz, ses temor,
Qu'aissi fai los sieus enardir
    Ab valen vassalatge;   3.5
E puois que l'estorns es mesclatz,
Chascus deu esser acesmatz
    E segre.l d'agradatge,
Que nuls hom non es re prezatz,
Tro qu'a maintz colps pres e donatz.   3.10

Massas e brans, elms de color,
Escutz trauchar e desguarnir
Veirem a l'entrar de l'estor
E maintz vassals ensems ferir,
    Don anaran arratge   4.5
Chaval dels mortz e dels nafratz;
E quan er en l'estorn entratz,
    Chascus hom de paratge
No pens mas d'asclar chaps e bratz,
Que mais val mortz que vius sobratz.   4.10

Ie.us dic que tan no m'a sabor
Manjar ni beure ni dormir
Com a, quan auch cridar: "A lor!"
D'ambas las partz et auch ennir
    Chavals vochs per l'ombratge,   5.5
Et auch cridar; "Aidatz! Aidatz!"
E vei chazer per los fossatz
    Paucs e grans per l'erbatge,
E vei los mortz que pels costatz
An los tronzos ab los cendatz.   5.10

Amors vol drut cavalgador,
Bon d'armas e larc de servir,
Gen parlan e grand donador
E tal qi sapcha far e dir
    Fors e dinz son estatge   6.5
Segon lo poder qi l'es datz.
E sia d'avinen solatz,
    Cortes e d'agradatge.
E domna c'ab aital drut jatz
Es monda de totz sos pechatz.   6.10

Pros comtessa, per la meillor
C'anc se mires ni mais se mir
Vos ten hom e per la genssor
Dompna del mon, segon q'auch dir.
    Biatriz d'aut lignage,   7.5
Bona dona en ditz et en fatz,
Fons lai on sortz tota beutatz,
    Bella ses maestratge,
Vostre rics pretz es tant poiatz
Que sobre totz es enansatz.   7.10

And I am pleased, too, when a baron
Is the first to attack,
On horseback, armed, without fear,
Thus by his valor and bravery
Giving courage to his men;
And when the battle's underway,
Each one should be ready
To follow him with pleasure,
For no man is worthy
Until he has received and given many blows.

Clubs, swords, many-colored helmets
And shields broken and shattered
We will see at the start of the battle,
Along with vassals striking each other,
So that the horses of the dead
And wounded wander aimlessly about.
And when he is in the thick of battle,
Each nobleman thinks only
Of breaking heads and arms, for it is better
To be dead than alive but vanquished.

I tell you that I find less pleasure
In eating, drinking or sleeping
Than when I hear the cry of "Charge!"
From both sides, and hear riderless
Horses whinnying in the shade,
And hear shouts of "Help! Help!"
And I see the great and small
Fall in grassy moats,
And see the dead with bits of lances
And banners through their sides.

Love wants a chivalric lover,
Good at arms and generous with service,
Noble of speech and a liberal giver
And one who knows what to do and say
Outside and inside his domain
According to the power given him.
And let him be of good conversation
Courtly and pleasing.
And the lady who lies with such a lover
Is purified of all her sins.

Noble countess, you are held to be the best
Who has ever been or will be seen,
And held to be the noblest
Lady in the world, according to what I hear.
Beatrice of high lineage,
Fine lady in words and actions,
Source of all beauty,
Beautiful without rival,
Your noble worth is so elevated
That it surpasses all others.

Donzella d'aut lignatge,		A lady of high lineage
Tal en cui es tota beutatz,		In whom is all beauty
Am fort, e sui per leis amatz;		I love deeply, and am loved by her;
E dona.m tal coratge		And she gives me such courage
Que ja no pens esser sobratz		That I think I will never be vanquished
Per un dels plus outracujatz.	T1.6 (10)	By the most presumptuous.
Baro, metetz en guatge		Barons, better to pawn
Chastels e vilas e ciutatz,		Your castles, towns and cities
Enanz qu'usquecs no.us guerreiatz.	T2.3 (10)	Rather than stop making war!
Papiol d'agradatge		Papiol, cheerfully,
Ad Oc-e-No t'en vai vaitz		To Sir Yes-and-No go promptly
Dire qe trop estai en patz	T3.3 (10)	To tell him he remains too much in peace.

Si tuit li dol e.lh plor e.lh marrimen (PC 80.41)
Planh

Si tuit li dol e.lh plor e.lh marrimen		If all the grief and the tears and the misery
E las dolors e.lh dan e.lh chaitivier		And the anguish and the pain and the misfortune
Qu'om anc auzis en est segle dolen		That one ever heard of in this sad world
Fossen ensems, sembleran tot leugier	1.4	Were put together, they would seem as nothing
Contra la mort del jove rei engles,		Beside the death of the young English King,
Don rema pretz e jovens doloros		Whereat merit and youth remain grieving,
E.l mons oscurs e teintz e tenebros,		And the world obscure, dark and gloomy,
Sems de tot joi, ples de tristor e d'ira.	1.8	Deprived of joy, full of sadness and sorrow.
Dolen e trist e ple de marrimen		Grieving and sad and full of misery
Son remasut li cortes soudadier		Stand the courtly retainers left behind,
E.lh trobador e.lh joglar avinen,		And the charming troubadours and jongleurs,
Trop an agut en mort mortal guerrier;	2.4	Death has been for them too deadly a foe;
Que tout lor a lo jove rei engles,		For it has taken from them the young English King
Ves cui eran li plus larc cobeitos;		Beside whom the most generous were miserly;
Ja non er mais ni no crezatz que fos		Ne'er will there be, nor do I think there was,
Ves aquest dan el segle plors ni ira.	2.8	Like pain in this world for tears and sorrow.
Estenta mortz, plena de marrimen,		Mighty death, full of misery,
Vanar ti potz que.l melhor chavalier		You can boast that the best knight
As tout a.l mon qu'anc fos de nula gen,		There ever was, among any people, you've taken;
Quar non es res qu'a pretz aia mestier,	3.4	For there is nothing pertaining to merit
Que tot no fos el jove rei engles,		Which was not wholly in the young English King,
E fora mielhs, s'a dieu plagues razos,		And it were better, if reason had pleased God,
Que visques el que maint autre enoios		That he had lived rather than many other bores
Qu'anc no feiron a.ls pros mas dol et ira.	3.8	Who never gave the worthy aught but pain and sorrow.
D'aquest segle flac, ple de marrimen,		From this stale world, full of misery
S'amors s'en vai, son joi tenh menzongier,		If love goes, I consider its joy false,
Que re no.i a que no torn en cozen,		For there is nothing which does not turn to pain;
Totz jorns veuzis e val mens huoi que hier;	4.4	Each day worsens; today is worth less than yesterday;
Chascus si mir el jove rei engles,		Let everyone contemplate the young English king
Qu'era del mon lo plus valens dels pros;		Who was, in this world, the worthiest of the worthy;
Ar'es anatz sos gens cors amoros,		Now has passed away his noble, loving person,
Don es dolors e desconortz et ira.	4.8	Whence comes sadness, dismay, and sorrow.

Celui que plac pe.l nostre marrimen
Venir el mon nos traire d'encombrier
E receup mort a nostre salvamen,
Com a senhor humil e drechurier   5.4
Clamem merce, qu'al jove rei engles
Perdo, si.lh platz, si com es vers perdos,
E.l fassa estar ab honratz companhos
Lai on anc dol non ac ni aura ira.   5.8

To the One whom it pleased, on account of our misery,
To come into the world and deliver us from evil,
And who received death for our salvation,
As to a charitable and just lord,
Let us beg mercy, that the young English king
Be pardoned, if it please Him, as He is true pardon,
And that he be placed with honored companions
There where never was pain nor will be sorrow.

PEIRE VIDAL

According to his *vida*, Peire Vidal (fl 1175-1205) was the son of a furrier from Toulouse, and he sang better than anyone in the world. He began his career at the court of Raimon V of Toulouse; he was later associated with the courts of Viscount Barral of Marseille, of King Alfonso II of Aragon, and, still later, after the demise of his southern French and Spanish patrons, with the court of Boniface of Montferrat in Italy. Peire more than likely visited the court of Bela III (1172-96), king of Hungary, at Esztergom (near what is now Budapest), or the court of Bela's son, Imre (1196-1204). Bela married his son to the daughter of Alfonso II of Aragon. Peire might have met Bela during the negotiations. Peire turned up finally in Malta, after which there is no more trace of him.

Medieval sources represent Peire Vidal as somewhat eccentric. He is said to have crafted verses with great skill and invented beautiful melodies. He is also described as a madcap who spread malicious gossip and said crazy things about arms and love. His 45 remaining songs are difficult to classify; they are marked by unexpected juxtapositions of tone and theme; serious developments can be tinged with irony; the poignant and the boastful are intermingled. Peire seems to speak through a series of masks that both conceal and reveal a highly original personality. The 12 remaining melodies bear witness to his musical gifts.

EDITIONS: Anglade 1923; Avalle 1960; van der Werf 1984.

• "Anc no mori per amor ni per al": PC 364.4. Sources: mss. A 95, B 60, C 31, D 22, D^c 248, F 17, G 41, I 42, K 29, L 16, M 58, N 88, P 21, Q 68, R 46, S 9, U 102, X 85, c 64, c^a 27, e 7, f 57, α 29795; music in GRX. Melody from G. Text: Avalle II, 327. Performed on Anthology CD. For the complicated manuscript tradition of this song, see Avalle II, 327-8. Anglade, 76, offers another stanza order. For stanza V, both editors furnish two versions; I have taken here the Avalle version based on CLMRc^a. This song has more manuscript witnesses than most other songs by Vidal, and the melody (in versions that are essentially the same) is found in three sources. This circumstance and the presence of several tornadas suggest that the song was well known; it might have had multiple performances, for each of which the tornadas could have been adjusted to the audience and to the performer's intentions. Avalle speculates that the second tornada, found in only one manuscript, might have been added later to bring the poet back into the good graces of the Count of Poitiers, Richard Lion-Heart, after the harsh tone of the first tornada. The song was probably composed after the fall of Jerusalem in 1187 (7.7) and before Richard became king. The main theme is the inaccessible

lady (but note the possibly ironic tone with which the song opens, 1.1). The imagery is on occasion unusual, for example, 4.5-8, or most of stanza 6. When there is nothing else for the poet to do, he heads off on crusade; the song shifts into another thematic register. The metric structure, seven *coblas unissonans*, a10 b10 b10 a10 c10 c10 d10 d10, is not unusual: many other songs share it. The first tornada is irregular in its formal structure; some manuscripts have only lines 57, 58, and 60, thus a normal structure. The opening melodic gesture exhibits the fondness for thirds typical of Peire Vidal. The intervals connecting the first six phrases tend to be skips of a fourth or a fifth (Vidal also had a fondness for ascending fifths), and skips within phrases are fairly numerous. The melody thus has a quixotic character that underscores the tone of the poem. Tonal focus on *c* is initially suggested, and the first four lines are sufficiently homogeneous to delineate a melodic division corresponding to the ryhme scheme. The melody rises to its highest point in phrase 6, then falls back to what one fully expects to be a final cadence on *c*, only to turn up to *d* at the end, closing with a whimsical suspension.

• "Baron, de mon dan covit": PC 364.7. Sources: mss. C 45, E 27, M 63, Q 73, R 65, e 95; music in R. Text: Avalle II, 189. This song reflects Peire Vidal's penchant for mixing thematic registers: in it are blended love, combat, and moral criticism; it partakes of the *canso*, of the *sirventes* and of the *gap* (a humorous boast). The fourth stanza (4.2) connects this song to the court of Barral, Viscount of Marseille. The metric structure combines 7- and 10-syllable lines with a rhyme scheme ababccdde. Melodic repetition is the chief musical structuring device. Phrase repetition is exact for 1-3 and 2-4; it is slightly more diversified for 5-6 and 7-8; line 9 follows a substantially different pattern, isolated like the rhyme sound. Melodic differentiation at cadence points reinforces repetition patterns in grouping the lines (except the last) two by two. The initial phrases constitute a recitation on *a*; this is recalled in 5 and 6 but on *d*. F tonality is suggested throughout; noteworthy is the *b* flat the scribe has included in the last line.

1.2: I follow Anglade for this line; the meaning of 1 and 2 is not clear.

1.6 Melody position 11: the last *f* in brackets, is a proposed addition, since the manuscript has one note fewer than the syllable count would require.

1.8 Melody position 8: The text version in R was hypometric; the melody has one note fewer than would be needed. To perfom the song, one could simply place the note *e* between *d* and *f*.

- "A per pauc de chantar no.m lais": PC 364.35. Sources: mss. C 38, Dᵃ163, H 25, I 44, K 31, N 99, Q 72, R 16, S 247. Text: Avalle I, 68. This song probably belongs to the period 1193-4 when Philip Augustus had left the third crusade (stanza 3) and Richard Lion-Heart was a prisoner in Austria (stanza 4). The church in Rome was not strong enough to contain heresy (stanza 2), and the Spanish kings fight among themselves (stanza 5). Only joy and love can save the world. The lady associated with Carcassonne is possibly Na Loba (Avalle, 67), who may have been well known among poets. For the *razos* to songs by Peire Vidal and Raimon de Miraval in which she appears, see Boutière-Schutz (1964).

- "Pus tornatz sui em Proensa": PC 364.37. Sources: mss. A 95, B 60, C 35, D 22, E 23, G 42, H 23, I 41, J 3, K 29, M 52, N 97, P 21, Q 70, R 63, S 7, T 255, U 100, b1 5, c 60, e 9, χ 54. Music in G. Text: Avalle II, 361. This, too, is a widely known song if one is to judge by the manuscript tradition. It develpes a theme often associated with Peire Vidal: the love of Provence (see also "Ab l'alen tir vas me l'aire"). The text speaks of love service in cleverly turned conventional topoi that are colored by Peire's special overtones. It is thought that the song was composed for Barral of Marseille, who is customarily designated by the *senhal* "Rainier" in Peire's works. A lively and extravagant *razo* provides an interpretation that links the story of the stolen kiss (stanza 2) to Barral's wife Azalais. (See Poe 1984a, 50-65.) The melody immediately captures the listener's attention by the initial recitation on *c* and the cascading gesture, emphasizing thirds (filled in or not), falling through the octave. Although there is no repetition of entire phrases, the melody exhibits strong coherence by the sequence of cadences defining a tonal focus on *c,* and by motivic repetition. The initial note of the song, *c*, situated at the top of the scale, is the same as the final (bottom note of the scale) that appears as the cadential tone of lines 4 and 9. The song consistently exploits the full octave, with two excursions up to *e*, making the total range a 10th. Phrases 1 and 3 are similar, sketching a structure ABA(B). Since the rhymes move a'bba', the overall sonorous patterning is more varied than straightforward metrical and musical coordinations such as ABAB / abab (Switten 1985, 102-4). But the entire first part of the melody is best understood as an ample 4-line rhetorical gesture with changes in motivic patterning in line 4 and the cadence on *c* effecting closure. Perhaps the most eloquent manipulation of motive links lines 3, 6 and 7. The stepwise ascending motion that opens line 3 is expanded at a different pitch level in 6, and taken up immediately in 7 at the original pitch level to create a climax on the highest note of the song. The melody then falls back through ornamented cascades to close. This kind of bravura passage is typical of many of Vidal's melodies; indeed in his "Be.m pac d'ivern et d'estiu" (PC 364.11), the second part of the melody sweeps through almost a double octave, an ample development that has no counterpart anywhere else in the troubadour repertory.

Anc no mori per amor ni per al (PC 364.4)
Canso

Anc no mori per amor ni per al,
Mais ma vida pot be valer murir
Quan vei la ren qu'eu plus am e dezir
E ren no.m fai mas quan dolor e mal.   1.4
Ben me val mort, mais enquer m'es plus grieu,
Qu'en breu serem ja vielh et ilh et ieu:
E s'aissi pert lo mieu e.l sieu joven,
Mal m'es del mieu, mais del sieu per un cen.   1.8

Anc mais no vi plag tan descomunal,
Que quant ieu puesc nulla ren far ni dir,
Qu'a lieis degues plazer ni abellir,
Ja mais no voill far nulh autre jornal.   2.4
E tot quan fas par a lieis vil e lieu,
Que per merce ni per amor de Dieu
No.i puesc trobar ab lei nulh chauzimen;
Tort a de me e peccat ses conten.   2.8

I never died for love or for aught else,
But my life is surely the equal of death
When I see the creature I most love and desire,
And it brings me only pain and suffering.
Death can be of value to me, but it is more grievous
That soon we will be old, she and I,
And if thus she loses my youth and hers,
It's bad for mine, but a hundred times worse for hers.

Never did I see such a disagreeable quarrel
As when I can do or say nothing
That might please or delight her;
Never do I want to attempt anything else.
And whatever I do appears to her vile and base,
Neither for mercy nor for love of God
Can I find with her any compassion;
Without question she wrongs and sins against me.

Bona domna, vostr'home natural
Podetz, si.us plai, leugeiramen aucir:
Mas a la gen vos faretz escarnir
E pois auretz en peccat criminal.   3.4
Vostr'om sui be, que ges no.m tenc per mieu,
Mas ben laiss'om a mal senhor son fieu;
E val ben pauc rics hom, quan pert sa gen,
Qu'a Daire.l rei de Persa fon parven.   3.8

Estiers mon grat am tot sol per cabal
Lieis que no.m denha vezer ni auzir.
Que farai doncs, pus no m'en puesc partir,
Ni chauzimens ni merces no mi val?   4.4
Tenrai.m a l'us de l'enuios romieu,
Que quier e quier, quar de la freja nieu
Nais lo cristals, don hom trai fuec arden;
E per esfortz venson li bon sufren.   4.8

Doncs que farai? sufrirai per aital,
Co.l pres destregz, cui aven a sufrir,
S'om li fai mal, mas ben saupra grazir
Qui.m fezes be en luec d'amic leial.   5.4
E s'ieu volgues, domna, penr'autrui fieu,
Honrat plazer agra conquist em brieu;
Mas res ses vos no.m pot esser plazen
Ni de ren als gaug entier non aten.   5.8

Per so m'en sui gitatz a no m'en cal,
Cum l'om volpilhs que s'oblid'a fugir
Que no s'auza tornar ni pot gandir,
Quan l'encausson siei enemic mortal.   6.4
No sai conort, mas aquel del Juzieu,
Que si.m fai mal, fai om adeis lo sieu;
Aissi cum sel qu'a orbas si defen,
Ai tot perdut la fors'e l'ardimen.   6.8

Lai vir mon chan, al rei celestial,
Cui devem tug onrar et obezir,
Et es mestier que l'anem lai servir,
On conquerrem la vid'esperital;   7.4
Que.lh Sarrazi, deslial Caninieu,
L'an tout son rengn'e destruita sa plieu,
Que sazit an la crotz e.l monimen:
Don devem tug aver gran espaven.   7.8

Coms de Peitieus, de vos mi clam a Dieu
E Dieus a mi per aquel eis coven,
Qu'amdos avetz trazitz mout malamen,
Lui de sa crotz e me de mon argen,
Per qu'en devetz aver gran marrimen.   T1.5 (8)

Coms de Peitieus, bels seigner, vos et ieu
Avem lo pretz de tota l'autra gen,
Vos de ben far et eu de dir lo gen.   T2.3 (8)

Fair lady, your true man
You can, if it pleases you, easily kill;
But you will be blamed by everyone
And then you will be in mortal sin.
I am your man; I belong not to myself;
But one rightly abandons his fief to an evil lord;
And a nobleman is worth little when he loses his men,
As became evident to Darius the King of Persia.

In spite of myself I love with all my heart
The lady who does not deign to see or hear me.
What will I do then since I cannot leave,
And compassion and pity do not help me?
I shall adopt the habits of the annoying pilgrim
Who begs and begs, for from the cold snow
Is born the crystal whence one draws burning fire.
And through their efforts the good lovers triumph.

What then shall I do? I will suffer anyway,
Like the distressed prisoner who must suffer
If one harms him; but I would surely receive gratefully
The one who would treat me well as a loyal friend.
And if I wished, lady, to take another fief,
Rapidly I would have conquered honorable pleasure;
But nothing without you can please me,
Nor do I expect total joy from anyone else.

That's why I have become indifferent
Like the coward who forgets to flee
And does not dare turn nor can he escape
When his mortal enemies chase him.
I know no comfort but that of the Jew:
He who hurts me hurts also himself;
Like the one who blindly defends himself,
I have lost all force and courage.

I turn my song there towards the King of Heaven
Whom we should all honor and obey,
And we must go there to serve him
Where we will conquer spiritual life;
For the Saracens, disloyal Canaanites,
Have taken his kingdom and destroyed his realm,
For they have seized the cross and the sepulchre
Whence we should all have great horror.

Count of Poitou, I complain about you to God
And God to me on account of this agreement,
For you have betrayed both very badly:
Him for his cross and me for my money;
That's why you should have great anguish.

Count of Poitou, fine Lord, you and I
Have everyone's merit:
You for acting well and I for speaking well.

Baron, de mon dan covit (PC 364.7)
Canso-gap

Baron, de mon dan covit
Fals lauzengiers deslials,
Qu'en tal domna ai chauzit,
Ont es fis pretz naturals.
Et ieu am la de cor e ses bauzia   1.5
E sui totz sieus, quora qu'ilh sia mia,
Qu'a sa beutat e sa valor pareis,
Qu'en lieis amar honraz fora us reis,
Per que.m tieng ric sol que.m deinh dire d'oc.   1.9

Anc res tan no m'abellit
Cum sos adreitz cors lials,
On son tug bon aip complit
E totz bes senes totz mals.
E pus tot a quan tainh a drudaria,   2.5
Ben sui astrucs, sol que mos cors lai sia;
E si merces, per que totz bos aips creis,
Mi val ab lieis, be.us puesc dir ses totz neis,
Qu'anc ab amor tant ajudar no.m poc.   2.9

Barons, I scorn harm caused
By the treacherous slanderers,
For I have chosen such a lady
In whom there is fine, true merit.
And I love her truly and without deceit
And I am entirely hers, whenever she may be mine,
For it appears from her beauty and her worth
That to love her would do honor to a king;
That's why I consider myself rich if she deigns to say yes.

Nothing ever so pleased me
As her adroit, loyal person
In whom are all fine accomplishments,
And all good without any evil.
And since she has all that is fitting to love,
I am very fortunate, if I were only there;
And if mercy, through which all good increases,
Avails me with her, I can certainly say to you
That it (mercy) never did help me so much with love.

Chant e solatz vei fallit,
Cortz e dous e bos hostals,
E domnei no vei grazit,
Si.lh domn'e.l drutz non es fals.
Aquel n'a mai que plus soven galia.   3.5
No.n dirai plus, mas cum si vuelha sia.
Mas peza me quar ades non esteis
Lo premiers fals que comenset anceis:
E fora dreitz, qu'avol eixample moc.   3.9

    Mon cor sent alegrezit,
    Quar me cobrara'N Barrals.
    Ben aja selh que.m noirit,
    E Dieus!, quar ieu sui aitals,
Que mil salut mi venon cascun dia   4.5
De Cataluenha e de Lombardia,
Quar a totz jorns pueja mos pretz e creis;
Que per un pauc no mor d'enveja.l reis,
Quar ab donas fas mon trep e mon joc.   4.9

    Ben es proat et auzit,
    Cum ieu sui pros e cabals,
    E pus Dieus m'a enriquit,
    Non tanh qu'ieu sia venals.
Cent domnas sai que cascuna.m volria   5.5
Tener ab se, si aver me podia.
Mas ieu sui selh qu'anc no.m gabei ni.m feis
Ni volgui trop parlar de mi meteis,
Mas domnas bais e cavaliers derroc.   5.9

    Mainht bon tornei ai partit
    Pels colps qu'ieu fier tan mortals,
    Qu'en luc non vau qu'om no crit:
    "So es En Peire Vidals,
Selh qui manten domnei e drudaria   6.5
E fa que pros per amor de s'amia;
Et ama mais batallas e torneis
Que monje patz, e sembla.l malaveis
Trop sojornar et estar en un loc."   6.9

Plus que non pot ses aigua viure.l peis,
Non pot esser ses lauzengiers domneis,
Per qu'amador compron trop car lur joc.   T.3 (9)

I see song and conversation neglected,
Court-assemblies, sweet and fine hospitality,
And I do not see lady-service favored,
Unless ladies and lovers are not false.
He has most who betrays most often.
I will say no more of it: be it as it will.
But it pains me that he was not destroyed
The first traitor who began at the start;
And it would be right, for he set a bad example.

My heart feels happiness
For Lord Barral will take me back.
Good fortune to the one who nourished me,
And God! for I am such
That a thousand greetings come to me each day
From Catalonia and Lombardy,
And every day my merit rises and increases;
And the king almost dies of envy,
For with ladies I dance and play.

It is well proven and understood
How I am worthy and distinguished,
And since God has richly endowed me,
It is not fitting that I be corrupt.
A hundred ladies I know who each would want
To keep me with her, if she could have me.
But I am one who never boasted or dissembled
Nor wanted to talk too much of myself,
But I kiss ladies and unhorse knights.

Many a fine tourney have I decided
By the mortal blows I strike,
So that I go no place without being hailed:
"That is Lord Peire Vidal
The one who maintains courting and loving
And acts nobly for the love of his lady,
And he likes better battles and tournaments
Than a monk peace, and it seems sickly to him
To stay too long in one place."

No more than the fish can live without water,
Courting cannot exist without slanderers;
That's why lovers buy too dearly their game.

A per pauc de chantar no.m lais (PC 364.35)
Sirventes-canso

A per pauc de chantar no.m lais,	I'm about ready to give up singing
Quar vei mort joven e valor	Since I see youth and valor dead,
E pretz, que non trob'on s'apais	And merit, for it finds no nourishment
C'usquecs l'enpeinh e.l gieta por; 1.4	Since everyone repulses it and throws it out;
E vei tant renhar malvestat	And I see evil reign so fully
Que.l segl'a vencut e sobrat,	That it has conquered and dominated the world,
Si qu'apenas truep nulh paes	So that one can scarcely find a country
Qu'el cap non aj'a son latz pres. 1.8	Whose head is not caught in its trap.
Qu'a Rom'an vout en tal pantais	In Rome, they have stirred up such trouble—
L'Apostolis e.lh fals doctor	The Pope and the false doctors—
Sancta Gleiza, don Dieus s'irais;	In the Holy Church that God is angered;
Que tan son fol e peccador, 2.4	For they are so foolish and sinful,
Per que l'eretge son levat.	That's why heretics have sprung up.
E quar ilh commenso.l peccat,	And because they initiate sin,
Greu es qui als far en pogues;	It's difficult for one to do anything else;
Mas ieu no.n vuelh esser plaies. 2.8	But I don't want to be their advocate.
E mou de Fransa totz l'esglais,	And from France comes all the trouble,
D'els qui solon esser melhor,	From those who used to be superior,
Que.l reis non es fis ni verais	For the king is neither loyal nor true
Vas pretz ni vas Nostre Senhor 3.4	Towards merit or towards Our Lord;
Que'l Sepulcr'a dezamparat	And he has left the Sepulchre
E compr'e vent e fai mercat	And buys and sells and haggles
Atressi cum sers o borzes:	Just like a serf or a bourgeois;
Per que son aunit siei Frances. 3.8	That's why the French are shamed.
Totz lo mons torn'en tal biais	The whole world has gone such a way
Qu'ier lo vim mal et huei peior;	That yesterday we saw it bad and today worse;
Et anc pus lo guit de Dieu frais,	And never since he broke the law of God,
Non auzim pueis l'Emperador 4.4	Have we heard of the Emperor
Creisser de pretz ni de bontat.	Increasing in merit or goodness.
Mas pero s'ueimais laiss'en fat	However, if henceforth he leaves to his fate
Richart, pus en sa preizon es,	Richard, since he is in his prison,
Lor esquern en faran Engles. 4.8	The English will scorn him.
Dels reis d'Espanha.m tenh a fais,	I find it vexing about the kings of Spain
Quar tant volon guerra mest lor,	That they want so much to fight among themselves,
E quar destriers ferrans ni bais	And that bay or grey horses
Trameton als Mors per paor: 5.4	They send to the Moors out of fear.
Que lor erguelh lor an doblat,	For they have doubled their (the Moors') pride
Don ilh son vencut e sobrat;	Whence they [themselves] are conquered and dominated;
E fora miels, s'a lor plagues,	And it would be better, if it pleased them,
Qu'entr'els fos patz e leis e fes. 5.8	That there were peace among them and law and faith.

Mas ja non cug hom qu'ieu m'abais
Pels rics, si.s tornon sordeyor;
Qu'us fis jois me capdell'e.m pais
Qui.m te jauzent en gran doussor   6.4
E.m sojorn'en fin'amistat
De lieis que plus mi ven a grat:
E si voletz saber quals es,
Demandatz la en Carcasses.   6.8

Et anc no galiet ni trais
Son amic ni.s pauzet color,
Ni.l cal, quar selha qu'en leis nais
Es fresca cum roz'en pascor.   7.4
Bell'es sobre tota beutat
Et a sen ab joven mesclat:
Per que.s n'agrado.l plus cortes
E.n dizon laus ab honratz bes.   7.8

But let no one think that I am abased
By the nobles, though they become worse;
For a true joy guides and nourishes me
And keeps me joyous in great sweetness
And allows me to reside in true friendship
With her who most pleases me;
And if you want to know who she is
Ask for her in the Carcassonne region.

Never did she deceive or betray
Her friend, nor put on color,
Nor need to, for the one natural to her
Is fresh as an Easter rose.
She is beautiful above all beauty
And she has wisdom mingled with youth:
That's why the most courtly welcome her
And speak her praises in most honorable terms.

Pus tornatz sui em Proensa (PC 364.37)

Canso

Pus tornatz sui em Proensa
Et a ma dona sap bo,
Ben dei far gaia chanso,
Sivals per reconoissensa:
Qu'ap servir et ab honrar   1.5
Conquier hom de bon senhor
Don e benfag et honor,
Qui bel.l sap tener en car;
Per qu'ieu m'en dei esforsar.   1.9

Since I have returned to Provence
And it is pleasing to my lady,
I certainly must compose a joyous song
At least out of gratitude;
For by serving and paying honor
One can win from a good lord
Gift, reward and honor,
If one knows how to cherish him;
That's why I wish to do my best.

E sel que long'atendensa
Blasma, fai gran falhizo;
Qu'er an Artus li Breto
On avion lur plevensa.
Et ieu per lonc esperar   2.5
Ai conquist ab gran doussor
Lo bais que forsa d'amor
Me fetz a ma domn'emblar,
Qu'eras lo.m denh'autreiar.   2.9

E quar anc non fis failhensa,
Sui en bona sospeisso
Que.l maltragz me torn en pro,
Pus lo bes tan gen comensa.
E poiran s'en conortar   3.5
E mi tug i'autr'amador,
Qu'ab sobresforciu labor
Trac de neu freida fuec clar
Et aigua doussa de mar.   3.9

Ses pechat pris penedensa
E ses tort fait quis perdo,
E trais de nien gen do
Et ai d'ira benvolensa
E gaug entier de plorar   4.5
E d'amar doussa sabor,
E sui arditz per paor
E sai perden gazanhar
E, quan sui vencutz, sobrar.   4.9

Estiers non agra guirensa,
Mas quar sap que vencutz so,
Sec ma domn'aital razo
Que vol que vencutz la vensa;
Qu'aissi deu apoderar   5.5
Franc'humilitatz ricor,
E quar no trop valedor,
Qu'ab lieis me puosc'aiudar,
Mas precs e merce clamar.   5.9

E pos en sa mantenensa
Aissi del tot m'abando,
Ja no.m deu dire de no;
Que ses tota retenensa
Sui sieus per vendr'e per dar.   6.5
E totz hom fai gran folor
Qui di qu'ieu me vir alhor;
Mais am ab lieis mescabar
Qu'ab autra joi conquistar.   6.9

The one who speaks of a long wait
Critically, is in great error;
For now the Bretons have Arthur
In whom was their faith.
And I, on account of long hoping,
Have conquered with great sweetness
The kiss that love's force
Made me steal from my lady,
Since she now deigns to grant it to me.

And since I never committed a sin
I am in good hope
That the anguish will turn to advantage for me
Since the good begins so sweetly.
And they will be able to take comfort
From my example, the other lovers,
For with superhuman effort
I have drawn a clear fire from the cold snow
And sweet water from the sea.

Without sin I did penance
And without wrong sought pardon
And drew from nothing a noble gift
And I have from anger benevolence
And perfect joy from weeping
And from bitterness sweet savor
And I am bold on account of fear
And know how to win losing
And when I am vanquished, I conquer.

Otherwise I would not have help;
But because she knows I am vanquished
My lady follows such a reasoning,
That she knows that vanquished I vanquish her;
For thus must be conquered,
By true humility, power;
And I do not find a helper
Who can aid me with her
Except prayers and crying for pity.

And since into her power
I completely abandon myself,
Never should she say no to me;
For without any reservation
I am hers to sell and to give.
And any man speaks great folly
Who says that I turn elsewhere;
I prefer to fail with her
Than to conquer joy with another.

Bel Rainier, per ma crezensa,		*Bel Rainier,* by my faith
No.us sai par ni companho,		I do not know your equal or companion,
Quar tug li valen baro		For all the valiant barons
Valon sotz vostra valensa.		Have less valor than your valor.
E pos Dieus vos fetz ses par	7.5	And since God made you without equal
E.us det mi per servidor,		And gave me to you for servant,
Servirai vos de lauzor		I will serve you with praise
E d'als, quant o poirai far,		And with all else that I can do,
Bel Rainier, car etz ses par.	7.9	*Bel Rainier,* for you are without equal.

Peire Vidal, "Pois tornaz sui en Proenza" (p. 115). Ms. G, ff. 42v-43r. Biblioteca Ambrosiana R 71 Sup., Milan.

RAIMON DE MIRAVAL

Raimon de Miraval (fl. 1185-1213) was a poor knight from the region of Carcassonne. He became a favorite poet of Raimon VI, Count of Toulouse, but he was also associated with the courts of Peter II of Aragon and Alfonso VIII of Castile. He seems to have owned only a quarter of the small castle of Miraval which was situated in the central area of the Cathar heresy; it was taken by Simon of Montfort in 1209 or 1211 during the Albigensian Crusade. After the disaster of Muret in 1213, Raimon fled to Spain where he seems to have died.

Raimon de Miraval was a poet of social behavior. He placed equal obligations on lady and lover to behave worthily; if they did not, he sharply criticized both. He cultivated the *trobar leu*, clearly affirming his desire to be understood and accepted by the elite society of which he was a part. We have from him some 45 pieces and 22 melodies, more melodies than for any other troubadour except Guiraut Riquier (for a study of all the melodies with their texts, see Switten 1985).

EDITIONS: Topsfield 1971; van der Werf 1984; Switten 1985.

● "Aissi cum es genser pascors": PC 406.2. Sources: mss. A 43, B 31, C 81, D 97, D^c 252, E 31, F 26, G 68, H 15, I 69, J 14, K 53, L 137, M 114, N 216, O 73, Q 55, R 85, U 93, V 45, a^1 319, β^1 575; music in G and R. Text and melody: Switten, 144. In this song, typical Miraval themes are allied with grace and skill. One could speak of composition by paired stanzas (Switten, 132-3): after an introduction, stanzas 2 and 3 explain how the poet's happiness has been destroyed; 4 and 5 shift from the particular to the general to criticize ladies who torment their lovers; 6 then concludes with the poet's reaffirmation of hope. A fragile narrative thread binds the stanzas together enough to insure a single stanza order in almost all 22 manuscripts. Both melody versions are presented here. Comparison of these versions raises interesting questions of sameness and difference in melodic movement. In both versions, the first four phrases constitute an integrated and balanced unit, defined by antecedent-consequent relationships (1-2; 3-4), closing on *d* in line 4. But whereas the MS G version exhibits perfectly regular phrase repetitions, ABAB, the R version is more varied, though still suggesting the pattern of repetitions characteristic of *pedes*, and by flirting with the secondary third chain *c-e-g-b* flat, offers a melodic vivacity that G does not have. In the *cauda*, differences in melodic contour and gesture are more marked; both versions close, however, on the final *d*, establishing clear tonal coherence. We may think of the two melodies as simply "different"; a medieval imagination might have thought of them as musi-

cal formulations of the same generic idea, even though they are not, in themselves, identical. Taking into consideration patterns of ornamentation, more noticeable in G, one could propose that varied ways of singing the song may have left their mark on the written versions. When the tunes are combined with the metric scheme, a8 b8 b8 a8 a8 c7 c7 d7 d7, subtly contrasting sonorous patterns emerge for each melody. The leap of a ninth between lines 8 and 9 in R is particularly striking because of the run-on text line, strong in the first stanza but reappearing in other stanzas as well. The descending leap of a sixth in the last line of G serves a similar expressive purpose. (Switten 1985, 23-5, 112-3; 1988 Anthology I, 100-2; Treitler 1991, 29-30.)

For a discussion of problems of syllable count in manuscript text versions as they affect the melody, see Switten, 147.

8.1: Peter II of Aragon.

9.2: *Audiart* is a *senhal* for Raimon VI of Toulouse.

● "Bel m'es q'ieu chant e coindei": PC 406.12. Sources: mss. A 43, C 75, D 95, E 34, F 25, H 15, I 69, K 54, L 106, M 111, N 217, P 31, Q 62, R 85, S 138, U 95, V 46, a^1 318, f 40, α 30574; music in R. Text and melody: Switten, 160. Performed on Anthology CD. Just before the disaster of Muret in 1213, Miraval wrote this eloquent plea to Peter of Aragon, calling upon him for help against Simon of Montfort. Raimon was sure Peter could destroy the enemy; but history decreed otherwise and Peter was killed, a terrible loss for all of Occitania. This song expresses a hope that is the more poignant because it will not be fulfilled. The first six stanzas develop traditional themes of the *canso*, but the 7th stanza brings a different twist because it makes clear what *political* effect the song should have. In the light of this 7th stanza, we realize that love and joy are political and cultural as well as emotional values. The melody opens with a motive, *d-a-c-d(c)*, that immediately proposes a *d* mode in its plagal disposition, and the second mode intonation formula *c-d-f* becomes a structural device of considerable importance, uniting lines 2, 4, and 8. The second part offers contrast with a rising fifth, *d-a*, that momentarily suggests the authentic *d* mode; but the song remains within the plagal range and particularly exploits the sixth *c-a*. The song is divisible into two parts with an ample first section stretching over 4 lines and cadencing on *d*, followed by contrast and a return to *d* to close. Although initial repetitions are not exact, and there is exact repetiton in the second part (lines 6-7), a structure of *pedes* with *cauda* seems to underlie the song's movement. The *coblas unissonans*, a7 b7 b7 a7 c7 d7' d7' c7 c7, offer a gradation of rhyme sounds which, when combined with the melody, create a sophisticated sound pattern and a pleasing unity of construction (Switten, 29, 49, 111-2, 136).

1.2: Melody position 4: the position of this note on the staff is ambiguous; it is high enough on the staff to be a *g*, yet *f* is also possible. I have opted for *g* given the similarity of initial melodic movement in lines 2, 4, and 8. Van der Werf has *f*.

7.1: Peter II of Aragon.

7.5: The castle of Montégut in the region of Albi.

7.6: Carcassonne had fallen to Montfort in 1209.

7.9: The armies of Montfort are the French; the Muslims in Spain are Peter's other enemies.

T1.4-5: Although he had only a quarter of a castle, Miraval constantly speaks of holding it from his lady (see the Monge de Montaudon satire below).

T2.3: *Audiart* is a *senhal* for Raimon VI of Toulouse.

• "D'amor es totz mos cossiriers": PC 406.24. Sources: mss. A 47, C 79, D 96, I 71, K 56, M 110, N 223, R 87, T 180, a¹ 322, b II 26, f 67, α 27908; music in R. Text and melody: Switten, 198. This song sets forth Miraval's overriding preoccupation with love and with how lovers should behave. The first two lines, in a compact musical and textual statement beginning and ending with "D'amor" and the notes *e-f*, encapsulate the thematic development. Indeed, the first two lines of most stanzas offer pithy precepts to lovers. The melody has regular repetition in the first part; the syllabic, stepwise motion initially ascending in lines 1 and 3, descending in lines 2 and 4 creates an almost perfect equilibrium of statement/response formulations. The climax comes only in the 7th line, where ascending thirds open briefly a new tonal space and the text lines expand to 10 syllables. The final line brings ingenious close by telescoping the 2-phrase statements of the first part into a single statement with added ornamentation.

4.1: For the use of the word *lausengier* here, see Switten, 82-6. It is entirely unusual that a poet should call himself a *lausengier*, although that is the reading of a majority of the manuscripts. Topsfield has "ieu sui tengutz per parliers" (212).

T1.1, T2.1: *Mais d'amic* and *Mantel* are *senhals* for ladies whose identities have not been fully established.

T3.1: *Pastoret* is a *senhal* for a patron.

Aissi cum es genser pascors (PC 406.2)

Canso

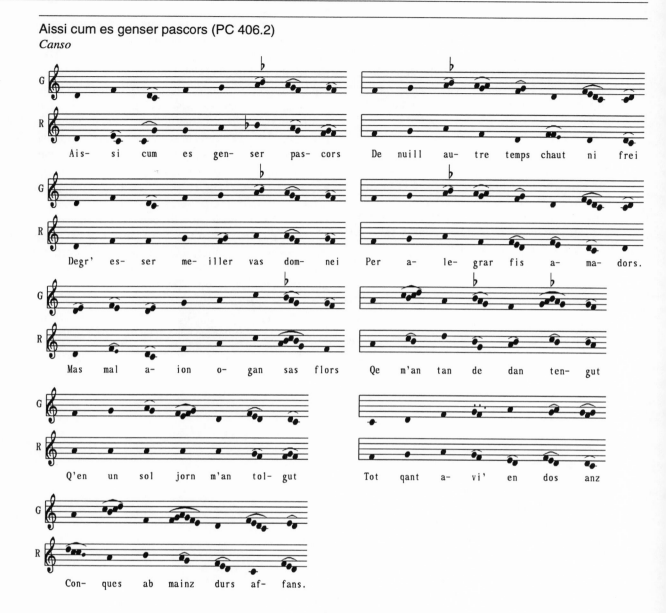

Aissi cum es genser pascors
De nuill autre temps chaut ni frei
Degr'esser meiller vas domnei
Per alegrar fis amadors.
Mas mal aion ogan sas flors   1.5
   Qe m'an tan de dan tengut
   Q'en un sol jorn m'an tolgut
   Tot qant avi'en dos anz
   Conques ab mainz durs affans.   1.9

Just as the spring is more beautiful
Than any other season hot or cold,
So it should be more favorable toward courting,
To delight true lovers.
But this year, woe unto its flowers
Which have done me so much harm
That in a single day they have taken from me
All that I had over two years
Conquered by many painful efforts.

Ma domna et eu et Amors
Eram pro d'un voler tuich trei,
Tro c'aras ab lo dols aurei
La ros'e.l chanz e la verdors
Ll'an remenbrat que sa valors   2.5
  Avia trop desendut
  Car volc so q'eu ai volgut.
  Pero no.i ac plasers tanz,
  Q'anc res fos mas sol demanz.   2.9

Aquel m'era gaugz et honors,
Mas no.ill plaz que plus lo m'autrei,
E puois midonz vol q'eu sordei,
Be.m pot baissar car il m'a sors.
Las, per que no.ill dol ma dolors   3.5
  Puois aissi.m troba vencut?
  Q'eu ai tant son prez cregut
  Q'enanzat ai sos enanz
  E destarzat toz sos danz.   3.9

Un plait fan domnas q'es follors:
Qant troben amic qe.s mercei,
Per assai li movon esfrei,
E.l destreingnon tro.s vir'aillors;
E qant an loingnat los meillors,   4.5
  Fals entendedor menut
  Son per cabal receubut,
  Don se chala.l cortes chanz
  E.n sorz crims e fols mazanz.   4.9

Eu non faz de totas clamors,
Ne m'es gen c'ab domnas gerrei,
Ne ges lo mal qu'ieu dir en dei
No lor es enois ni temors.
Mais s'ieu disia dels peiors,   5.5
  Tost seria conogut
  Cals deu tornar en refut,
  Qe torz e pechaz es granz
  Qan domn'a prez per enianz.   5.9

C'ab leis q'es de toz bes sabors
Ai cor c'a sa merce plaidei,
E ges per lo primer desrei,
Don faz mainz sospirs e mainz plors,
No.m desesper del ric socors   6.5
  C'ai lonjament atendut.
  E si.ll plaz q'ella m'aiut,
  Sobre toz leials amanz
  Serai de joi benananz.   6.9

Domna, per cui me venz amors,
  Cals que m'ai'enanz agut,
  A vostr'ops ai retengut
  Toz faiz de druz benestanz,
  E Miraval e mos chanz.   T1.5 (9)

My Lady and I and Love
Were all three of one mind
Until now, when with the mild air
The rose and the song and the verdure
Have reminded her that her merit
Had sunk too low
Because she wanted what I wanted.
However, there were not so many pleasures,
For never was there anything but wooing.

That was for me joy and honor,
But it no longer pleases her to grant it to me,
And if my lady wants me to diminish in worth,
She can certainly debase me for she has elevated me.
Alas, why is my suffering not painful to her
Since she thus finds me vanquished?
For I have increased her prestige so much
That I have improved her advantages
And deferred all harm.

Ladies adopt one procedure that is foolishness:
When they find a lover who implores mercy,
For a test, they inspire fear in him,
And oppress him until he turns elsewhere;
And when they have estranged the best,
False and insignificant suitors
Are surpassingly well received,
For which reason courtly song falls silent,
And gossip and foolish noise arise.

I do not complain of all ladies,
Nor does it please me to fight with ladies,
Nor ever is the evil I must say of them
A cause of annoyance or fear to them.
But if I spoke of the worst ones,
Soon it would be known
Which should be scorned,
For fault and sin are great
When a lady gains merit through trickery.

For from the one who is the essence of all virtues
I wish to seek mercy,
And not on account of the first difficulty,
That causes me many sighs and many tears,
Do I despair of the noble succor
That I have long awaited.
And if it pleases her to aid me,
Above all loyal lovers
I shall be blessed with joy.

Lady for whom love conquers me,
Whoever may have possessed me previously
For you I have reserved
All deeds befitting worthy lovers
And Miraval and my songs.

Al rei d'Aragon vai de cors,   To the King of Aragon go quickly,
    Cansos, dire qe.l salut,   Song, to say that I salute him,
    E sai tant sobr'altre drut   And that I know so much more than another lover
    Qe.ls paucs prez faz semblar granz   That I make insignificant merits seem important
    E.ls rics faz valer dos tanz.   T2.5 (9)   And important ones twice as valuable.

    E car lai no m'a vegut,   And he has not seen me there,
    Mos Audiartz m'a tengut,   Because my *Audiart* has held me back,
    Qe.m tira plus q'adimanz   For he (*Audiart*) attracts me more than a magnet
    Ab diz et ab faiz prezanz.   T3.4 (9)   With distinguished words and actions.

Bel m'es q'ieu chant e coindei (PC 406.12)
Canso

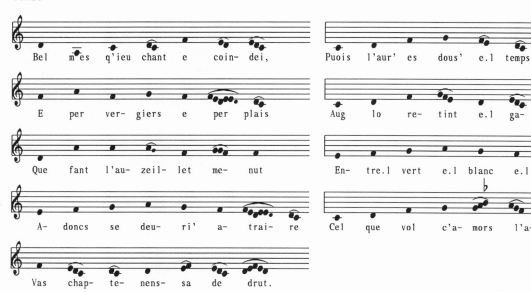

Bel m'es q'ieu chant e coindei,   It pleases me to sing and rejoice
Puois l'aur'es dous'e.l temps gais,   Since the air is warm and the weather fine,
E per vergiers e per plais   And in the orchards and hedges
Aug lo retint e.l gabei   I hear the chirping and warbling
Que fant l'auzeillet menut   1.5   Poured forth by the little birds
Entre.l vert e.l blanc e.l vaire;   Through the multicolored (foliage);
Adoncs se deuri'atraire   At that time he should strive—
Cel que vol c'amors l'aiut   The one who wants love to help him—
Vas chaptenenssa de drut.   1.9   To adopt the behavior of a lover.

Eu non sui drutz, mas dompnei,   I am not accepted as a lover, but I pay court,
Ni non tem pena ni fais,   And I do not fear suffering or burden,
Ni.m rancur leu ni m'irais,   Nor do I complain easily or become angered
Ni per orguoill no m'esfrei.   Nor lose courage on account of arrogance.
Pero temenssa.m fai mut,   2.5   However, fear makes me silent,
C'a la bella de bon aire   For to the fair high-born lady
Non aus mostrar ni retraire   I dare not show or expose
Mon cor q'ieu.l tenc rescondut,   My heart, which I keep secret from her
Pois aic son pretz conogut.   2.9   Since I have known her great merit.

Ses preiar e ses autrei	Without entreaty and without concession
Sui intratz en greu pantais	I have entered into grievous torment
Cum pogues semblar verais	(Trying to find) how I might seem truthful
Si sa gran valor desplei;	If I set forth her great merit.
Q'enquer non a pretz agut　3.5	For until now never has a lady
Dompna c'anc nasqes de maire	Born of woman had merit
Que contra.l sieu valgues gaire,	Which might be worth anything beside hers,
E si.n sai maint car tengut,	And I know many a one highly valued,
Qe.l sieus a.l meillor vencut.　3.9	Yet hers has vanquished the best.
Ben vol q'om gen la cortei,	She is willing to be nobly courted
E platz li solatz e jais,	And conversation and joy please her,
E no.ill agrad'om savais	And the boor does not please her
Que s'en desgui ni fadei.	Who turns from these and acts the fool;
Mas li pro son ben vengut,　4.5	But the worthy are welcome
Cui mostra tant bel veiaire,	To whom she is so charming
Si que chascus n'es lauzaire	That all praise her
Qan son d'enan lieis mogut,	Upon going out from her presence
Plus que s'eron siei vendut.　4.9	More than if they were her slaves.
Ja non cre c'ab lieis parei	I do not believe one can compare to her
Beutatz d'autra dompna mais,	The beauty of any other lady,
Que flors de rosier qan nais	For the newborn rose
Non es plus fresca de liei:	Is not fresher than she is:
Cors ben fait e gen cregut,　5.5	Well made and gracefully formed body,
Boch'et oills del mon esclaire,	Mouth and eyes the light of the world,
C'anc Beutatz plus no.i saup faire,	Such that Beauty could do no more,
Se.i mes tota sa vertut,	Having used therein all her power
Que res no.il n'es remasut.　5.9	So that nothing remained to her.
Ja ma dompna no.is malei	May my lady not get angry
Si a sa merce m'eslais,	If I throw myself on her mercy,
Q'ieu non ai cor qe.m biais	For it is not my intention to be unfaithful
Ni vas bass'amor desrei;	Or turn towards an inferior love,
C'ades ai del mieills volgut,　6.5	For I have always wanted the best
Defors e dins mon repaire,	Outside and inside my dwelling place;
E de lieis non sui gabaire,	And I am not boastful about her,
Que plus non ai entendut	For I have desired no more
Mas gen m'acuoill'e.m salut.　6.9	Than that she receive and greet me graciously.
Chanssos, vai me dir al rei	Song, go for me and tell the king
Cui jois guid'e vest e pais,	Whom joy guides and clothes and nourishes
Q'en lui non a ren biais,	That in him there is nothing improper,
C'aital cum ieu vuoill lo vei.	For I see him just as I want him to be.
Ab que cobre Montagut　7.5	Provided that he recover Montagut
E Carcasson'el repaire,	And return to Carcassonne,
Pois er de pretz emperaire,	Then he will be emperor of merit,
E doptaran son escut	And they will fear his shield—
Sai Frances e lai Masmut.　7.9	Here the French and there the Muslims.
Dompn'ades m'avetz valgut	Lady you have always helped me
Tant que per vos sui chantaire,	So much that for you I am a singer,
E non cuiei chanson faire	And I did not think I would make a song
Tro.l fieu vos agues rendut	Until I had given back to you the fief
De Miraval q'ai perdut.　T1.5 (9)	Of Miraval which I have lost.

Mas lo reis m'a covengut	But the king has promised me
Q'ieu.l cobrarai anz de gaire,	That I will recover it before long
E mos Audiartz Belcaire;	And my *Audiart*, Beaucaire.
Puois poiran dompnas e drut	Then will ladies and lovers be able
Tornar el joi q'ant perdut. T2.5 (9)	To return to the joy they have lost.

D'amor es totz mos cossiriers (PC 406.24)
Canso

D'amor es totz mos cossiriers	About love is all my concern
Per qu'ieu non cossir mas d'amor,	Because I am concerned only about love,
E diran li mal parlador	And evil tongues will say
Que d'als deu pessar cavaliers. 1.4	That a knight should think of other things.
Mas ieu dic que no fai mia,	But I say that is not so,
Que d'amor mou, qui qu'o dia,	For from love comes, whatever one may say,
So que val mais a foudat et a sen,	What is best for both folly and wisdom,
E tot quant hom fai per amor es gen. 1.8	And everything done on account of love is good.
Amors a tans de bos mestiers	Love has so many good qualities
Qu'a totz faitz benestans secor	That it helps all suitable actions
Qu'ieu no vey nulh bon servidor	Such that I see no good servant
Que no.n cug esser parsoniers, 2.4	Who does not believe he shares in it;
Qu'en luec bos pretz no s'abria	For nowhere does merit find shelter
Leu, si non ve per amia,	Easily, if it does not come from an *amia,*
Pueys dizon tug quant hom fai falhimen,	Since everyone says when a man sins
Bem par d'aquest qu'en donas non enten. 2.8	It certainly seems he does not court ladies.

Dona no pot aver estiers	A lady cannot otherwise have
Si non ama, pretz e valor;	If she does not love, merit and value;
Qu'atressi quom li amador	And just as lovers
An mais de totz bos aips sobriers, 3.4	Have more of all superior qualities,
Selha que trop no s'en tria	So she who does not choose too carefully
En val mais qui la.n castia,	Becomes better if one chastises her for this;
Adoncs fai mal si mielhs no s'i enpren,	Then she does badly not to improve her conduct,
Mas creire deu adreg castiamen. 3.8	Rather should she obey a just admonition.
Qu'ieu sui mainhtas vetz lauzengiers:	And I am many times a *lausengier:*
Quar a dona ni a senhor	Because to a lady or to a lord
Non deu cossentir dezonor	No faithful counselor
Neguns sos fizels cosselliers, 4.4	Should permit dishonor,
Non laissarai qu'ieu non dia,	I shall not cease to mention,
Qu'ieu tostemps non contradia,	Nor constantly to forbid,
So que faran domnas contra joven	What ladies do against youth
Ni.m semblara de mal captenemen. 4.8	And what seems to me bad manners.
E ja d'aquestz drutz messongiers	And let not one of the lying lovers
Que cuion aver gran lauzor,	Who think they receive great praise,
Ni dona que s'aten a lor,	Nor a lady who pays attention to them,
Uns per so no.m sia guerriers; 5.4	Attack me because of this;
Qu'enemics ni enemia	For no enemy, male or female,
No.m notz lo pretz d'una fia,	Harms my merit one iota,
Sol que m'aia ma dona ferm talen	Provided my lady has toward me firm desire,
E meinhs d'erguelh e mais de chauzimen. 5.8	Less pride and more pity.
De gaug li fora plazentiers	Joyfully would I be agreeable to her,
Mas trop mi ten en gran error;	But she torments me too much;
Pero per semblan del melhor	However in hope of the best,
N'ai ieu jogat cinc ans entiers; 6.4	I have dallied with her five whole years;
Mas una dona mendia	But a perfidious lady
Falsa, que Dieus la maldia,	And false, may God curse her,
Mes entre nos aquest destorbamen	Put between us this disturbance
Don mainhtas vetz n'ai pueys plorat greumen. 6.8	Over which I have often wept bitterly.
Mais d'amic, Dieus benezia	*Mais d'amic,* may God bless
Qui vol que.m siatz amia,	The one who wants you to be my friend,
E s'ie.us ai fag plazer ni onramen,	And if I have given you pleasure and honor,
Enquer si.us platz o farai per un cen. T1.4 (8)	I shall, if you wish, give you a hundred times more.
Mantelh, qui aital n'abria,	*Mantel,* about her who shelters such a one (as I)—
Ben er cregutz, quals qu'o dia,	It will be believed, whoever says it—
Qu'anc no.l conques per aur ni per argen,	That never she won him by gold or silver
Mas per valor e per pretz e per sen. T2.4 (8)	But by excellence, merit, and wisdom.
Pastoret, no.us laissetz mia,	*Pastoret,* do not fail,
Si Dieus vos don joy d'amia,	And may God give you joy in love,
Qu'a ma dona no mostretz cum l'es gen	To show my lady how fine it is for her
Si Miravalh sap tener franchamen. T3.4 (8)	If she knows how to hold Miraval freely.
Chansoneta, ves midons vai corren,	Little song, run toward my lady
Qu'ilh mante pretz e reman en joven. T4.2 (8)	For she upholds worth and retains her youth.

GAUCELM FAIDIT

According to his *vida*, Gaucelm Faidit (fl. 1170-1205) was from Uzerche in the Limousin. He seems to have belonged to the petty nobility. An unusually lengthy collection of *razos* traces an unflattering portrait: Gaucelm composed well but sang worse than any man alive; he became a jongleur because he lost all his money gambling; he and his wife ate too much and got too fat; his son had a disagreeable character; he traveled a great deal in the effort to establish himself (on *razos* as "contre-textes," see Poe, *Handbook* 1995, 191). Most of these statements are surely fiction; but it is clear from the patrons mentioned in Gaucelm's poems that he did travel widely in Occitania as well as to France, Brittany, Hungary and the Holy Land, taking part in the third and fourth crusades. He found patronage at the courts of Raimon d'Agout, Maria de Ventadorn, and Boniface of Montferrat. He knew the sons of Henry II and Eleanor of Aquitaine from his sojourn in Brittany. At the outset of his career, he was likely influenced by Bernart de Ventadorn, but knowledge of the work of other troubadours is demonstrated by exchanges in his *partimens* (with Aimeric de Peguilhan, Perdigon, Raimbaut d'Aurenga, for example) and poetic borrowings (Gruber 1983, 142-4, 245). One of his songs uses Old French: he is thus entitled to be called a trouvère as well as a troubadour. The number of documents we have about him and the number of preserved poems and melodies, at least 65 and 14 respectively, bear witness to a remarkable reputation.

EDITIONS: Mouzat 1965; van der Werf 1984.

● "Fortz chausa es que tot lo major dan": PC 167.22. Sources: mss. A 80, B 50, C 64, D 36, G 29, I 197, K 183, Kp 107, M 85, Q 52, R 44, S 111, U 59, W 191, X 87, a 155, μ 353, η 89; music in G W X η. Melody from G. Text: Mouzat, 415. Richard Lion-Heart, son of Henry II and Eleanor, died from an arrow wound in a battle against rebelling Limousins in March of 1199. This *planh* laments Richard's death in a poetic homage that is both elegant and moving. It is Gaucelm's most celebrated song and one of the few laments for which music is extant. The song has six *coblas unissonans,* each stanza consisting of nine 10-syllable lines with the rhyme scheme abac'c'ddee. The poetic line (with its epic associations) befits a subject of dignified gravity. Gaucelm was among the first troubadours to make extensive use of 10-syllable lines, contributing to their wider adoption in the south. Noteworthy here is the handling of the caesura, which would normally fall after the fourth syllable. It is delayed until the sixth for emphasis in 1.6, 1.9, 2.2, 2.3, 2.6, and 2.8, and 4.1 (with displaced accent: *séigner*). In 3.4 and 5, it is extended until after the 7th syllable to follow the syntax and underline the major themes

of death (*mortz*) and the futility of the efforts made by humanity. Noteworthy also is the unusual concentration of lyric caesuras. This caesura falls after an unstressed syllable, thus the accent is moved back, as, for example, in 4.2, 4.6, and 5.6: *ármas*, *éran*, *Sepúlcres*. Skilful use of enjambment is found in 1.6-7, or 4.1-2. The poem expresses Gaucelm's sorrow, justifying that sorrow by a description of Richard's prowess in battle, his generosity, and his courtliness. The melody is preserved in four manuscripts, unusual within the troubadour corpus; there is also an Old French contrafact (van der Werf 1984, 115*-123*). The manuscript tradition exhibits variants of detail among melody versions, and often these variants will influence specific ways text and music work together, but the overall outlines of the melody remain stable through the different versions (Pollina 1989). There are no exact repetitions of entire phrases in the G version of the melody here presented. The intonation formula of line 1 and the final cadence suggest a tonal focus on *d*. But the tonality remains ambiguous due to the varying final cadences of the other phrases (*e*, lines 2, 4, 5; *c*, line 3; *b*, line 7). The unusual suppleness of the melody, the varied gestures using disjunct and conjunct motion (the expressive downward leap of a third in 1.7 has often been noticed) with frequent ornamentation, allow the melody to join with metric and syntactic elements to create an eloquent tribute to the dead king (Switten 1988, Anthology I, 86-7; Pollina 1989).

● "Mon cor e mi e mas bonas chanssos": PC 167.37. Sources: mss. A 71, B 48, C 69, D 35, E 11, I 36, K 24, M 81, N 113, P 16, Q 51, R 44 (95: Guillem de Cabestaing), S 106, U 49, V 27, X 84, a 154, ι 35; music in RX. Melody from X. Text: Mouzat, 161 (Frenchified text of X, 165). This song was likely first composed in Provence at the court of Raimon d'Agout (Mouzat, 166). Its multiple *tornadas* may indicate that it circulated widely (an observation supported by the manuscript tradition). The different *tornadas* would correspond to different "editions" of the poem: one to Raimon d'Agout, another to Raimbaut d'Orange, another, later, to Maria de Ventadorn, and so forth (Mouzat, 168). This state of affairs shows at least one way multiple variations of a song, melodic and textual, may have come into existence: the poet/composer made them himself. The theme of love is here developed in sufficiently abstract terms, even though a little story is involved, that it could apply to any lady. The two melody versions we have (van der Werf, 123* offers a comparative chart) seem initially of quite different construction. X is notated a fourth higher than R. The R scribe (as is often his wont) has recorded a pattern of initial repeated phrases followed by diversity: ABABCDEF; the X scribe offers a melody without strict phrase repetition, thus ABCDEFGH. But upon closer inspection, one can discern also in the X version given here a basic model ABABCDEF, suggested by the cadences on *g*, lines 2, 4, 8; the contrasting cadences on *a* and *f* in lines 1 and 3 (sketching a more interesting statement/response relationship for the first four lines than obtains in R); the return to *f* for the beginning of line 3, recalling 1; and a shift in tonal coloring in line 5, indicated by the natural sign in the manuscript, to mark the second part of the melody. The song illustrates two different and equally successful melodic coordinations with the rhyme scheme a10 b10 a10 b10 c10′ d10 d10 c10′ (Pollina 1992). The main cadences in the X version are on *g*. But the frequent use of the *b* flat suggests an underlying *d*-mode interval structure; one might think here of transposed dorian, the mode of the R version.

1.2: Melody position 7: van der Werf has a ligature *b-c*.

1.2: Melody position 1, and 1.3 position 9: the flat sign here occurs after a change of clef.

1.4: Melody position 6, and 1.6 position 4: the flat sign occurs after a change of staff.

T1.1: *Linhaure* is Raimbaut d'Aurenga.

T1.3: Raimon d'Agout.

T2.1: *Doussa Res* has not been identified; possibly a lady to whom the song was sent.

T3.1: *Plus Avinens* refers to a protector who probably frequented the court of Maria de Ventadorn.

T4.1: Na Maria is Maria de Ventadorn.

T5.1: *Bels Maracdes* is possibly Uc IX of Lusignan who likely also frequented Maria's court.

● "Si anc nuills hom per aver fin coratge": PC 167.52. Sources: mss. A 74, C 70, E 13, G 27, H 49, I 37, K 25, M 82, N 118, P 14 (anonymous, 39), Q 58, R 45, S 95, T 145, V 32, X 86, a 158, f 59; music in GRX. Melody from X. Text: Mouzat, 336 (Frenchified text of X, 339). The first part of this song sets out the perfect courtliness of the lover; the fifth and sixth stanzas address carnal vs "courtly" love; the sixth is frankly critical of what seems to be a lady of loose virtue. For that reason, the song was designated *mala canso* by the author of a colorful, fabliau-like *razo* (Boutière-Schutz 1964, 180). The *tornada* assures us that Lady Maria would never behave like the subject of stanza 6. The melody follows the "through-composed" construction favored by Gaucelm. A *d*-mode tonality is proposed by the cadences of lines 2, 4, 6, 7, 9, and 10. The melody is adroitly adjusted to the metric structure, a10′ b10′ a10′ b10′ c5 c7 d7′ c7 d7′ c7, by a scaling down of the scope of phrases 5-10. (Lines 5-6 might be considered one musical phrase, especially where the syntax carries over also, as in stanza 1.) Noteworthy is the ascending melodic sweep of line 3, covering the octave *d-d′*, balanced by a more graduated descent in line 4 and echoed in lines 9 and 10 with the repeated close on the final.

1.5: Melody positions 4-5, and 1.7 positions 5-8: these notes were added in the margin of the manuscript, but the note for 1.7 position 5 disappeared, probably in a subsequent trimming of the manuscript page (van der Werf, 143*). Its loss is indicated by brackets.

T1.1: Maria de Ventadorn.

Fortz chausa es que tot lo major dan (PC 167.22)

Planh

Fortz chausa es que tot lo major dan		'Tis a terrible thing that the greatest pain
E.l major dol, las! q'ieu anc mais agues,		And the greatest sorrow, alas, that I have ever had,
E so don dei totztemps plaigner ploran,		And which I must henceforth lament tearfully,
M'aven a dir en chantan, e retraire —		I must relate in singing and recount—
Car cel q'era de valor caps e paire,	1.5	For he who was the chief and father of merit,
Lo rics valens Richartz, reis dels Engles,		The noble, valiant Richard, King of England,
Es mortz — Ai Dieus! cals perd'e cals dans es!		Is dead—Ah God! what a loss and how distressing it is!
Cant estrains motz, e cant greus ad auzir!		What a dreadful word and how grievous to hear!
Ben a dur cor totz hom q'o pot sofrir.	1.9	Any man who can bear it has a hard heart.

Mortz es lo reis, e son passat mil an	The king is dead, and not for a thousand years
C'anc tant pros hom non fo, ni no.l vi res,	Has there been so fine a man, nor did one see his like,
Ni mais non er nulls hom del sieu semblan,	Nor will there ever be a man like unto him,
Tant larcs, tant rics, tant arditz, tals donaire,	So generous, so noble, so brave and so munificent,
Q'Alixandres, lo reis qui venquet Daire,	And Alexander, the king who vanquished Darius,
Non cre que tant dones ni tant meses;	I do not believe that he gave or spent as much;
Ni anc Karles ni Artus plus valgues,	Nor were ever Charlemagne or Arthur more worthy,
C'a tot lo mon si fetz, qui.n vol ver dir,	For throughout the world he made himself, truth to tell,
Als us doptar et als autres grazir.	Feared by some and cherished by others.

2.5 ... 2.9

Meravill me del fals segle truan,	I am astonished concerning this false, cruel century
Co.i pot estar savis hom ni cortes,	That in it a wise or courtly man can exist,
Puois re no.i val beill dich ni faich prezan,	Since fine words and glorious deeds are of no avail,
E doncs per que s'esfors om, pauc ni gaire?	Why then should one make an effort, even the slightest?
Q'eras nos a mostrat Mortz que pot faire,	For now Death has shown us what it can do
Q'a un sol colp a.l meillor del mon pres,	For in one fell swoop it has taken the best in the world,
Tota l'onor, totz los gaugs, totz los bes;	All honor, all joy, all virtue;
E pos vezem que res no.i pot gandir,	And since we see that nothing can escape from it
Ben deuri'hom meins doptar a morir!	One must certainly fear less to die!

3.5 ... 3.9

Ai! valens reis seigner, e que faran	Ah! noble lord, what will now become
Oimais armas ni fort tornei espes,	Of arms, or hotly contested tournaments,
Ni richas cortz ni beill don aut e gran,	Rich courts or splendid, magnificent gifts,
Pois vos no.i etz, qui n'eratz capdelaire,	Since you are not there, who were their guiding spirit,
Ni que faran li liurat a maltraire,	And what will they do, those delivered unto suffering,
Cill que s'eran en vostre servir mes,	Who had placed themselves in your service,
C'atendion que.l guizerdos vengues;	And who were waiting for the reward to come;
Ni que faran cill, qe.is degran aucir,	And what will they do, who should kill themselves,
C'aviatz faitz en grand ricor venir?	Whom you had brought to great power?

4.5 ... 4.9

Longa ira et avol vid'auran,	Long suffering and a miserable life they will have
E totztemps dol, q'enaissi lor es pres;	And endless grief, for such is their fate;
E Sarrazin, Turc, Paian et Persan,	And Saracens, Turks, Pagans and Persians,
Qe.us doptavon mais c'ome nat de maire,	Who dreaded you more than any man born of woman,
Creisseran tant en orguoil lor afaire,	Will so greatly increase their arrogant attitude
Qe.l Sepulcres n'er trop plus tart conques —	That the Holy Sepulchre will be conquered much later—
Mas Dieus o vol; que, s'el non o volgues,	But God wills it; for, if he had not wanted this,
E vos, seigner, visquessetz, ses faillir,	And if you, Lord, had lived, without fail,
De Suria los avengr' a fugir.	They would have had to flee Syria.

5.5 ... 5.9

Oimais no.i a esperanssa qe.i an	Henceforth there is no hope that they will go there
Reis ni princeps que cobrar lo saubes!	Kings and Princes who might know how to recover it!
Pero, tuich cill qu'en luoc de vos seran	However, all those who will be in your place
Devon gardar cum fotz de pretz amaire,	Must contemplate how you loved merit,
Ni cal foron vostre dui valen fraire,	And who were your two valiant brothers,
Lo Joves Reis e.l cortes Coms Jaufres;	The Young King and the courtly Count Geoffrey;
Et qui en luoc remanra de vos tres	And he who will remain in place of you three there
Ben deu aver aut cor e ferm cossir	Must surely have high courage and the firm will
De far bos faitz e de socors chausir.	To do fine deeds and to choose (to offer) assistance.

6.5 ... 6.9

Ai! Seigner Dieus! vos q'etz vers perdonaire,	Ah! Lord God! you who are a true pardoner,
Vers Dieus, vers hom, vera vida, merces!	True God, true man, true life, have mercy!
Perdonatz li, que ops e cocha l'es,	Pardon him who is needy and desirous,
E no gardetz, Seigner, al sieu faillir,	And pay no heed, Lord, to his sins,
E membre vos cum vos anet servir!	And remember how he went about serving you.

T.5 (9)

Mon cor e mi e mas bonas chanssos (PC 167.37)
Canso

Mon cor e mi e mas bonas chanssos
E tot qant sai d'avinen dir e far,
Conosc q'ieu teing, bona dompna, de vos,
A cui non aus descobrir ni mostrar   1.4
L'amor q'ie.us ai, don languisc e sospire;
E pos l'amor no.us aus mostrar ni dir
Ni.l ben q'ie.us vuoill, greu m'auser'enardir,
Si.us volges mal, de mon coratge dire.   1.8

Al prim q'ie.us vi, m'agr'ops, dompna, que fos,
Per c'Amors tant no.us mi fezes amar,
Que non fossetz tant bella ni tant pros
Ni saubessetz tant avinen parlar,   2.4
C'aissi.m pasmei, qan vos vi dels huoills rire,
D'una doussor d'amor qe.m venc ferir
Al cor, qe.m fetz si tremblar e fremir,
C'a pauc denan no.n mori de desire.   2.8

My heart and myself and my good songs,
And all gracious things I can say and do,
I know that I hold from you, Fair Lady,
To whom I dare not reveal or show
The love I bear you, for which I languish and sigh;
And since I dare neither show nor tell you my love
Nor the good I wish you, how could I dare be so bold,
If it displeased you, as to reveal my heart.

When first I saw you, Lady, it would have been necessary,
In order that Love might not make me love you so,
For you not be so beautiful or so worthy,
Or know how to speak with such charm,
For thus I fainted, when with my eyes I saw you laugh,
For the sweetness of love which came to strike
My heart, and which made me so tremble and quiver
That in front of you I almost died from longing.

Adoncs parti destreitz et envejos	Then, distraught and yearning, I left
De vos, dompna, cui desir e teing car,	You, Lady, whom I desire and cherish,
Si quez anc pois seigner ni poderos	And never since have I been lord and master
No fui de mi, mas de mon cor celar; 3.4	Of myself, except to hide my heart;
Per so conosc c'Amors mi vol aucire,	That's why I know that Love wants to kill me,
E, pois li platz, mout m'es bons a sofrir,	And since it pleases him, good is the suffering to me,
Car autramen non porri'eu morir	For otherwise I could not die
Tant bonamen, ni ab tant doutz martire. 3.8	So well, nor with such sweet martyrdom.

Ai! cum m'a traich mos fis cors amoros	Ah! how my loyal and loving heart drew me on!
C'anc mais non fo leus ad enamorar;	Never did I fall in love easily;
E qand ieu vei, dompna, luocs ni sazos,	And when I see, Lady, a place and a time,
Per nuilla ren no.us aus dir mon penssar; 4.4	Not for anything do I dare tell my thought,
Ni vos non platz conoisser mon cossire;	Nor does it please you to know my concern;
Pero saber podetz leu lo desir	However, you can easily perceive the desire
Q'ieu ai de vos, ab maint cortes sospir	That I have for you, by the many courtly sighs
Qe.m vezetz far qand vos vei ni.us remire. 4.8	That you see me make when I look or glance at you.

Tot cant m'acort en un mes o en dos	All that I arrange over a month or two
De cal guisa.us pogues genseitz prejar,	Concerning how I might most nobly court you
M'oblit qan vei vostras bellas faissos,	Leaves me when I see your beautiful face,
Qe no m'en pot sovenir ni membrar; 5.4	So that I can neither recall nor remember it
Tant, cant vos vei, soi del vezer jauzire,	So joyous am I at the sight of you, when I see you;
E, qan m'en part, soi en aital cossir	And, when I leave, I am in such a state
Qe jes la nuoich non puosc el lieig dormir,	That in bed at night I can never sleep,
Ni sai als far, mas plaing e.m volv e.m vire! 5.8	Nor can I do aught else but moan and turn and toss.

Dompna l'afans e.l cossirs m'es tant bos	Lady the pain and the worry are to me so good
Qu'on plus i pens e mais i vuoill pensar;	That the more I think of them the more I want to think;
Et ai ab mi maintas vetz compaignos	And I have companions with me many times
Q'ieu volria mais totz soletz estar, 6.4	When I would prefer to be all alone,
Que tant m'es bos quan mi pens ni m'albire	For it so pleases me when I think of or reflect
Vostra valor, mas aqui eis m'azir	Upon your merit; but at the same time I hate myself
E muor quar sai que no.us aus descobrir	And die, because I know that I dare not reveal to you
So don lonctemps crei q'ieu serai sofrire. 6.8	That from which I believe I shall suffer for a long time.

Linhaure, mout ai estat en cossire,	*Linhaure,* I have been sorely troubled
Mas eras sent mon coratg'esclarzir,	But now I feel my heart lighten
Car ab N'Agout sui, don no.m puosc partir,	For I am with Agout, whom I cannot leave,
De cui nuills hom non pot trop de ben dire. T1.4 (8)	And about whom one cannot say too much good.

Ai, Doussa Res, per vos sui en cossire,	Ah, *Doussa Res,* for you I am sorely troubled
Quar ieu no.us puesc mon coratg'esclarzir,	For I cannot explain my heart to you
Mas vostres sui, e no m'en vuelh partir,	But I am yours, and I don't wish to leave you
Quar hom de vos no pot sobre-ben dire. T2.4 (8)	For no man can say too much good about you.

Plus Avinens, ben sai senes falir	*Plus Avinens,* I well know without fail
Que.l jorn non pot a nulh home venir	That no harm can come to any man
Mal, que de cor vos veya ni.us remire. T3.3 (8)	The day he sees and contemplates you wholeheartedly.

Na Maria, tantz bes faitz de vos dir,	Lady Maria, you have so much good said of you
Per qe no.n cal a mi de vos ben dire. T4.2 (8)	That it does not matter to me to speak well of you.

Bels Maracdes, tan son vostre desire
Onrat e car, qu'ab joi devez soffrir
Lo ben e.l mal e l'ausar e.l grasir,
Lo pensamen e.l trebaill e.l cossire.   T5.4 (8)

Bels Maracdes, your wishes are so
Honorable and refined that with joy you should bear
The good and the bad and the daring and the grateful
The worry and the pain and the trouble.

Si anc nuills hom per aver fin coratge (PC 167.52)
Canso

Si anc nuills hom, per a- ver fin co- ra- tge

Ni per a- mar lei- al- men ses fal- su- ra,

Ni per so- frir fran- cha- men son dam- pna- tge,

Ac de si- donz nuill' on- rad' a- ven- tu- ra,

Ben degr' eu a- ver

Al- cun co- vi- nen pla- zer,

Qe.l ben e.l mal, cal q'ieu n'a- ia,

Sai so- frir, et ai sa- ber

De far tot qant mi- dons pla- ia,

Si qe.l cor no.n puosc mo- ver.

Si anc nuills hom per aver fin coratge
Ni per amar leialmen ses falsura,
Ni per sofrir franchamen son dampnatge,
Ac de sidonz nuill'onrad'aventura,
    Ben degr'eu aver   1.5
    Alcun covinen plazer,
    Qe.l ben e.l mal, cal q'ieu n'aia,
    Sai sofrir, et ai saber
    De far tot qant midons plaia,
    Si qe.l cor no.n puosc mover.   1.10

De fin'amor sai segre.l dreich viatge,
Si que tant am mi donz outra mesura
Qe far en pot tot qant l'es d'agradatge;
Qu'eu no.ill deman, tan tem dir forfaitura,
    Baisar ni jazer;   2.5
    Pero si sai tant valer
    Ad ops d'amar, qui q'en braia,
    C'onrat jorn e plazen ser
    Et tot so c'a drut s'eschaia
    Aus desirar e voler.   2.10

Si tot lo vuoill, ieu non ai autre gatge,
Don ni autrei ni paraula segura;
Mas ill es tant franch'e de bel estatge
Que la valors e.l pretz, c'a lieis s'atura
    Fai a totz parer   3.5
    C'Amors i aia poder,
    Qe lai on es valors gaia
    Deuria merces caber —
    Vec vos tot so qe.m n'apaia
    E.m tol, qe no.m desesper.   3.10

Mas e que.m val? qu'ieu non ai vassalatge
Ni ardimen don l'aus dir ma rancura;
Qe tan dopte s'onor e son paratge,
Son gai joven e sa bella faitura,
    Qu'aisso.m fai temer   4.5
    Qu'a leis non deigna caler
    De mal ni d'afan qu'ieu traia;
    E si.m volgues retener
    No volgr'esser reis de Maia,
    Tan cum ab lieis remaner!   4.10

Auzit ai dir, de savi ses follatge,
Q'om ora mal celui don non a cura,
E ditz que.l don Dieus jove seignoratge;
Aqest oratz sia tortz o drechura,
    Ai d'amor per ver,   5.5
    E, si l'ai, no.m pot doler;
    Que, de pro dompna veraia,
    Val mais c'om ric dan esper
    Qu'aia don d'avol savaia
    Qu'om non deu en grat tener.   5.10

If ever a man, on account of noble heart,
Loyal love without deceit,
Or courageous endurance of torment,
Had from his lady honorable favors,
I should certainly have
Some suitable pleasure,
For whatever good or harm I may have
I know how to bear, and I have the ability
To do whatever may please my lady,
Such that I cannot move from her my heart.

I know how to follow the path of true love
So that I love my lady to such excess
That she can do with me as she pleases;
And I do not ask her, so do I fear to speak wrongly,
For kissing or lying;
However, I have so much merit
In love, whoever may decry it,
That an honorable day and a pleasurable night
And all that befits a lover
I dare desire and wish.

Although I wish it, I have no other pledge,
Gift or grant or certain promise;
But she is so noble and of high rank
That merit and worth which attach themselves to her
Make it clear to all
That Love may have power over her,
For there where is charming merit
Should reside mercy—
See then all that nourishes
And enraptures me, to keep me from despairing.

But what does it avail me? For I have not the bravery
Nor the daring to tell her of my torment;
I so dread her high and noble rank,
Her charming youth and her fine features
That this makes me fear
That she will not deign to concern herself
With the pain and the anguish I bear.
If she wished to retain me,
I would not want to be the King of May
As long as I stayed with her.

I have heard tell by a wise man without folly
That one wishes harm to those one cares not for
And tells God to give them a meager domain;
Whether this wish be wrong or right
I truly have love,
And if I have it, it cannot pain me;
For from a noble and true lady
It is preferable to hope for a rich suffering,
Than to have a gift from a boorish lady
To whom one need not be grateful

Q'ieu.n sai una q'es de tant franc usatge
C'anc non gardet honor sotz sa centura,
Sieus es lo tortz s'ieu en dic vilanatge!
Qe, senes geing e senes cobertura,
    Fai a totz vezer   6.5
   Cum poing en se deschazer;
   E dompna q'ab tans s'essaia
   Non cuich ja qe m'alezer,
   Que ja de lieis ben retraia,
   Ni.m vuoill qe.m deia eschazer.   6.10

   Na Maria, dompna gaia,
   Vos non etz de tal saber,
   Car non faitz ren que desplaia,
   Anz plai tot e deu plazer.   T.4 (10)

For I know such a one who is so free
That she takes no care of honor under her belt,
Hers be the wrong if I speak ill of her!
For without ceremony or secrecy
She makes all see
How she pushes towards decadence;
And a lady who tests herself like that
Cannot ever, I think, make me happy,
And never can I speak well of her
Or wish that she may fall to me.

Lady Maria, charming lady,
You are not of that sort
For you do nothing displeasing,
Rather does all in you please and must please.

PEIROL

If we are to believe his *vida*, Peirol was a poor knight ("uns paubres cavaliers"), from the castle of the same name located in the territory of the counts of Auvergne. He may have been born around 1160; he is generally considered to have composed most of his works between 1188 and 1222. The *vida* also tells us that Peirol was accomplished and courtly and that towards the end of his life, he became a jongleur. Reference is made to Peirol as a performer in a song by another troubadour, Albertet de Sestairon (PC 16.8): "Peirol violatz et chantatz cointamen / de ma chanson los motz e.l son leugier" ("Peirol played [on the vielle] and sang graciously / the words and the melody of my song"). This is one of the very few indications we have of a jongleur playing and singing at the same time (Cohen, 1990). Peirol cultivates the style of the *trobar leu* which he handles with ease and grace, and with a certain originality in the use of comparison and metaphor. We have from him some 34 songs (including 2 of doubtful authenticity) and a surprising number of melodies: 17. The melodies normally make ample use of repetition; few are "through-composed." Yet there is faithful attention to nuance and adroit handling of detail, and the sheer tunefulness of the songs can help explain why so many have been preserved.

EDITIONS: Aston 1953; van der Werf 1984.

● "Per dan que d'amor mi veigna": PC 366.26. Sources: mss A 150, C 105, D 59, F 30, G 46, H 15, I 59, K 44, M 179, N 75, O 35, Q 79, R 89, S 94, T 159, V 94, c 90; music in G. Text: Aston, 97. This song plays out through a particularly successful union of seven-, five-, and four-syllable lines in three sets of *coblas doblas* the typical lover's dilemma—to love and be not loved—which becomes the source of his song. The melody is essentially syllabic with principal tonal focus on *g* (cadences for verses 2, 4, and 8). Some contrast is afforded in the second part by the close on *d* for verses 5 and 7, leading first to *c* (verse 6) and then back to the final conclusion on *g*. In the first part of the stanza the 7-syllable feminine line followed by a 4-syllable masculine line creates a hesitant equilibrium, a forward momentum with the rising fifth, immediately cut off, that conveys the poet's emotion. The second half of the stanza is firmer: masculine and feminine rhymes change about, and the now masculine 7-syllable line has a more equal partner in the 5-syllable feminine line. The tune is almost entirely built on repetition and can be diagrammed ABA′B′ CDC′E(D′). Apparently well known in the Middle Ages (Sesini considers it one of Peirol's best melodies [1941-2, 39]), it was taken up again for a trouvère song (R 41) and as the lower voice of a 2-part conductus "Vite perdite" (Pluteus 29.1), both transcribed by van der Werf (1984, 269*).

● "Si be.m sui loing et entre gent estraigna": PC 366.31. Sources: mss A 148, B 92, C 101, D 59, F 18, G 50, I 59, K 45, M 175, N 78, O 31, O¹ 46, P 25, Q 80, R 88, S 74, V 93, a 167; music in G. Text: Aston, 121. The repeated melodic phrases and pattern of rhyme sounds create an architecture that is ingenious and original. Repetition of melodic phrases does not follow any set type: ABC A′C A″B′. The second repetition of A is made up of A and A′; the B phrase, heard first to a masculine rhyme, returns a second time to close with a feminine rhyme that provides space for a final melodic flourish. Tonal focus is again on *g*, with regularly recurring cadential notes: *b, g, f, b, f, b, g*. The 10-syllable lines are organized into the rhyme pattern a′bbccd′d′ which subtly underscores the melodic repetitions. Stanzas are *unissonans* and *capcaudadas,* and since the inner rhymes b and c turn about as well, the even numbered stanzas reproduce the odd numbered stanza rhymes in exactly reverse order (abbccdd:dccbbaa). All of this seems effortless as the poem weaves through the themes of distance and love and the poet's pride in his own artistry.

4-5: these stanzas take into account the corrections proposed by Lecoy 1956 concerning both the text and the translation.

Per dan que d'amor mi veigna (PC 366.26)
Canso

Per dan que d'amor mi veigna
    Non laissarai
Que joi e chan no manteigna
    Tan cant viurai;   1.4
E si.m sui en tal esmai
    Non sai que.m deveigna,
Car cil on mos cors m'atrai
    Vei q'amar no.m deigna.   1.8

Neguna bon'entresseigna
    De lieis non ai
Que ja merces pro m'en teigna
    Del mal qu'ieu trai.   2.4
Pero si la preiarai
    Que de mi.l soveigna;
Que, s'amors no la.m atrai,
    Merces la.m destreigna.   2.8

Bona domna, si.us plazia
    Fort m'amistatz,
Quals miravilha seria
    Si m'amavatz!   3.4
Mas aoras quar no.us platz,
    Si jois m'en venia
Conosc que mout majer gratz
    Vos en taigneria.   3.8

Lo nuoich mi trebaill e.l dia
    No.m laiss'en patz,
Si m'angoissa.l cortesia
    E la beutatz.   4.4
Las! que farai mais que fatz
    Tro.l desirs m'aucia
O l'en prenda pietatz
    Que plus franca.m sia?   4.8

Though harm comes to me from love
I will not cease
To uphold joy and song
As long as I live;
And I am in such trouble
I don't know what will become of me,
For she who has my heart,
I see that she does not deign to love me.

No good sign
Do I have from her
That mercy may ever help me
In the pain I bear.
However I will beg her
To remember me;
For if love does not draw her to me
Then may pity so constrain her.

Good lady, if it really pleased you,
My friendship,
What a marvel it would be
If you loved me!
But now since it does not please you,
If joy came to me
I know that even greater thanks
Would appropriately be yours for it.

At night she torments me and by day
She does not leave me in peace,
So much does her courtliness torture me
And her beauty.
Alas, what will I do more than I'm doing
Until desire kills me
Or pity for me seizes her
So that she is more gracious to me?

Tant ai en lieis ferm corage		So firmly is my heart set on her	
Qu'en als non pes.		That I think of no one else.	
Et anc, ses talan volatge,		And never, without fickle intent,	
Mieills n'amet res.	5.4	Did anyone love better.	
Per so.m degra venir bes,		That's why good should come to me,	
E ai eu dampnatge!		And I have harm!	
Gardatz s'en amor agues		Behold if in love there has been	
De pejor usatge!	5.8	Worse treatment.	

Chanssos, vai t'en dreich viatge		Song, go directly	
Lai on ill es,		Where she is,	
Qu'el mon non ai mais messatge		For I have no other messenger in the world	
Que.l trameses.	6.4	That I might send.	
E puois del tot me sui mes		And since I have placed myself completely	
El sieu seignoratge,		In her seigneury,	
Preia li non aia ges		Beg her not to show	
Vas mi cor salvatge.	6.8	A cruel heart towards me.	

A! dompna, calsque merces		Ah lady, may some mercy	
Vos n'intr'el coratge,		Enter your heart,	
C'aleviar pot petitz bes		For a little good can alleviate	
Lo mieu gran dampnatge.	T.4 (8)	My great sorrow.	

Si be.m sui loing et entre gent estraigna (PC 366.31)

Vers (Canso)

Si be.m sui loing et en- tre gent es- trai- gna

Eu ai pen- sier d'a- mor en que.m co- nort,

E pens d'un vers cos- si.l fas- s'e l'a- cort

Tal que si- a bos e va- lens e fis;

Et on hom plus mos chan- tars mi gra- zis

E mieils me dei gar- dar que no.i mes- pren- da

Ni di- ga ren don sa- vis me re- pren- da.

Si be.m sui loing et entre gent estraigna
Eu ai pensier d'amor en que.m conort,
E pens d'un vers cossi.l fass'e l'acort
Tal que sia bos e valens e fis;   1.4
Et on hom plus mos chantars mi grazis
E mieils me dei gardar que no.i mesprenda
Ni diga ren don savis me reprenda.

Non es nuills jorns qu'en mon cor non dissenda
Una dolsors qe.m ven de mon pais.
Lai joing mas mans e lai estau aclis,
E lai, sapchatz, que volri'esser fort,   2.4
Pres de midonz, sitot a vas mi tort;
C'ab bel semblan et ab doussa compaigna
Me dauret gen so qu'aora m'estaigna.

Ar ai assatz que plor e que complaigna,
C'a pauc lo cor no.m part quan mi recort
E mi soven del ris e del deport
E dels plazers qu'ela.m fetz e que.m dis.   3.4
A! cum fora garitz s'adoncs moris!
Que quand li prec que de mi merce.ill prenda
Sol vejaire non fai qu'ella m'entenda.

Ben ai razon que sofra et atenda.
Cum atendrai, pois lieis non abellis?
Miels me fora, so cre, que m'en partis.
Partir? Non ges! Trop n'ai pres lonc acort.   4.4
Bona dompna, vostr'om sui tot a fort;
Et no.us cuidetz l'amors en mi remaigna,
Qu'a vos amar tem que temps mi soffraigna.

Lieis non faill res c'a pro dompna s'ataigna,
C'om no la ve que de lieis laus non port.
Bell'e gai'es e pros, per que l'am fort.
E doncs amors, cui totz temps sui aclis,   5.4
Plairia.il ja c'una vetz m'en jauzis?
Aquesta.il quier per don e per esmenda
O ja d'autra mais guizerdon no.m renda.

D'autre trebaill prec Deu que la defenda,
Mas sol un jorn volgra qu'ela sentis
Lo mal qu'ieu trac per lei sers e matis;
Qu'en greu perill m'a laissat loing del port.   6.4
E non vuoill ges qu'autra m'en ai'estort,
Car s'a lieis platz que ja vas mi s'afraigna
Anc hom non fetz d'amor genssor gazaigna.

Non laissarai, dompna, lo vers no.us port;
Qu'enaissi.m ten lo desirs en greu laigna,
Non pot esser que ja plus sai remaigna.   T.3 (7)

Although I am far away among strangers
I have a thought of love which comforts me,
And I think of how to make and arrange a *vers*
So that it will be good and noble and fine;
For the more my songs are well received
The more I must strive not to err
Or say anything criticizable by a learned man.

There is no day that into my heart does not descend
A sweetness coming from my country.
In that direction, I join my hands and bow,
And be it known that I would fain be there
Near my lady, although she does me wrong;
For with her fine appearance and sweet companionship
She nobly gilded for me what now she now tarnishes.

Now I have reason to weep and lament
For my heart almost breaks when I remember
And recall the laughter, the amusement
And the pleasure she gave in word and deed.
Ah! how I would be saved if I had then died!
For when I entreat her to take pity on me
She doesn't even seem to hear me.

I have reason to suffer and wait.
Why will I wait, since it doesn't please her?
It would be better for me, I believe, if I left.
Leave? Not at all! I have waited too long.
Fair lady, I am yours entirely;
And do not think that love will cease in me;
I fear there will not be time enough to love you.

In her nothing fitting a noble lady is lacking
For no one sees her who does not praise her.
Fair and gay she is and worthy, so I love her.
And so to love, to whom I am ever submissive,
Could it be pleasing to let me once know joy?
I ask her this as a gift and as a recompense
Or never may she grant the reward of another lady.

From other anguish I pray God to preserve her,
But just one day I would like for her to feel
The pain I bear for her evening and morning;
For in dire peril she has left me far from the port.
And I do not want another to deliver me,
For if it please her ever to weaken toward me,
Never would one have from love nobler gain.

I will not fail, lady, to bring the *vers* to you;
For since desire holds me in grievous pain,
It cannot be that I should remain here any longer.

The MONGE DE MONTAUDON

The Monge de Montaudon, whose works one can date to around 1180-1215, was one of the more colorful figures among the troubadours. He was probably born at Vic (Vic-sur-Cère, near Aurillac in the Auvergne), and he seems to have belonged to a noble family. Montaudon itself has not been identified. He was probably a member of a Benedictine order. From his poems, one can learn that he traveled widely, notably in Spain, and that he entertained relations with well known persons of his day such as Maria de Ventadorn, Richard Lion-Heart, or the Emperor Otto IV (1175-1216). The fact that he knew the troubadours of his day is clearly demonstrated by the *sirventes* in the manner of Peire d'Alvernhe. Almost 20 songs remain, *cansos*, *sirventes*, *tensos*, and the lesser known genres of *enueg* and *plazer*. There are two melodies.

EDITIONS: Philippson 1873; Klein 1885; Lavaud 1910; Routledge 1977; van der Werf 1984.

- "Autra vetz fui a parlamen": PC 305.7. Sources: mss. A 187, C 187, R 54; f 75. Text: Lavaud II, 268. This *tenso* is a particularly original composition: the freewheeling exchanges are like nothing else in the Occitan repertory. The interlocutors are the monk and God. The painted statues of God's saints have complained that ordinary women (doubtless those who ply the oldest profession in the world) should not use "paint." The monk takes the side of the "dompnas que.s van peignen" (1.4) and defends their right to use "paint" against God's wish to deny them that right in order to satisfy his saints. The ensuing dialogue is both amusing and racy: one thinks of Rabelais.

T4.2-3: Elys of Montfort was one of the three daughters of the viscount of Turenne, sister of Maria de Ventadorn; she married Bernart de Montfort.

- " Pus Peire d'Alvernh'a cantat": PC 305.16. Sources: mss. A 214, C 183, Dᵃ166, I 135, K 121, L 33, M 146, R 40, a¹ 470, d 298, α 28167, χ 131. Text, Hamlin et al., 168 (with consideration of Routledge 1969 and 1977, Grassano 1975, Riquer 1983). Some thirty years later, the Monge de Montaudon here imitates Peire d'Alvernhe's satirical review of fellow troubadours, choosing 16 confrères at whom he pokes sometimes not so gentle fun. Eight troubadours are included here, those in this Anthology, with the *tornadas*.

T1.6: Caussade is probably the one in Tarn-et-Garonne, or perhaps in the Hautes-Pyrénées (Chambers 1971, 97).

T2.5-6: These names have not been identified.

Autra vetz fui a parlamen (PC 305.7)
Tenso

Autra vetz fui a parlamen		Another time I was at a meeting
El cel, per bon'aventura;		In Heaven, by chance;
E feiron li vout rancura		And the statues were complaining
De las dompnas que.s van peignen;	1.4	Of ladies who paint themselves;
Qu'eu los en vi a Dieu clamar		I saw them complain to God
D'ellas, qu'an faich lo teing carzir,		About the women who heighten their complexion
Que se fan la cara luzir		And make their flesh shine
Del teing qu'om degr'en els pauzar.	1.8	With paint that should be used on statues.
Pero dis Dieus mout franchamen:		Then God said quite sincerely
"Monges, ben auch qu'a tortura		"Monk, I hear that wrongly
Perdon li vout lor dreitura;		The statues lose their rights;
E vai lai per m'amor corren,	2.4	Go running there for love of me
E fai m'en las dompnas laissar,		And tell the ladies to stop,
Que ieu no.n vuoill ges clam auzir,		For I don't want to hear complaints.
E si no s'en volon giquir		And if they don't want to cease,
Eu las anarai esfassar."	2.8	I will go wash them."

"Seigner Dieus," fi m'ieu, "chausimen
  Devetz aver e mesura
  De las dompnas, cui natura
Es que lor caras teingan gen,   3.4
E a vos no deu enojar;
Ni.l vout no.us o degran ja dir:
Que jamais no volran ufrir
Las dompnas denan lor, so.m par."   3.8

"Monges," dis Dieus, "gran faillimen
  Razonatz e gran falsura,
  Que la mia creatura
Se genssa ses mon mandamen.   4.4
Doncs serion cellas mieu par,
Qu'ieu fatz totz jorns enveillezir,
Si per peigner ni per forbir
Podion plus joves tornar!"   4.8

"Seigner, trop parlatz ricamen,
  Car vos sentetz en l'autura,
  Ni ja per so la peingtura
No remanra ses un coven: 5.4
Que fassatz lor beutatz durar
A las dompnas tro al morir,
O que fassatz lo teing perir,
Qu'om no.n puosc'el mon ges trobar."   5.8

"Monges, ges non es covinen
  Que dompna.s genz'ab penchura,
  E tu fas gran desmesura,
Car lor fas tal razonamen.   6.4
Si tu o volguesses lausar,
Ellas non o degran sofrir:
Aital beutat que.l cuer lor tir,
Que perdon per un sol pissar."   6.8

"Seigner Dieus, qui be peing be ven,
  Per qu'ellas se donon cura
  E fan l'obra espessa e dura,
Que per pissar no.s mou leumen.   7.4
Pois vos no las voletz genssar,
S'ellas se genson, no vos tir;
Abanz lor o devetz grazir,
Si.s podon ses vos bellas far."   7.8

"Monges, penhers ab afachar
Lor fai manhs colps d'aval sofrir,
E no.us pessetz ges que lur tir
Quan hom las fai corbas estar?"   T1.4 (8)

"Senher, fuecs las puesca cremar,
Qu'ieu non lur puesc lur traucs omplir,
Ans quan cug a riba venir,
Adoncs me cove a nadar."   T2.4 (8)

"Lord God," said I, "pity
Should you have and a moderate attitude
Toward ladies, whose nature
Is that they should tint their skin,
And that should not bother you;
And the statues should not even tell you,
For never will the women give offerings
To them, it seems to me."

"Monk," said God, "great sin
You set forth and great falsehood
That my creature
Embellishes herself without my command.
Soon would they be like me,
Those whom I make grow older each day,
If by painting and by make-up
They could become younger!"

"Lord, you speak too proudly,
For you feel yourself on high;
Never will the painting
Cease without an agreement:
Make beauty last
In ladies 'til death,
Or have make-up perish
So that no one can find any on earth."

"Monk, never has it been agreed
That ladies should beautify themselves with paint,
And you act unreasonably
When you give such reasons.
Even if you wanted to praise it,
They should not accept
Beauty that wrinkles their skin,
And that they lose on pissing once."

"Lord God, who paints well, sells well,
That's why they take care
And make the stuff thick and hard,
Which does not yield to the first piss.
Since you don't want to beautify them,
If they beautify themselves, don't be angry;
Rather should you be grateful to them
If they can make themselves beautiful without you."

"Monk, this painting
Makes them endure many blows down below,
And do you think it pleases them
When men make them bend over?"

"Lord, may fire cremate them,
For I cannot fill their holes;
Rather when I think I've come to shore
I have to swim more than ever."

"Monges, tot las n'er a laissar,
Pos pissars pot lo tenh delir;
Qu'ieu lur farai tal mal venir
Qu'una non fara mais pissar."   T3.4 (8)

"Monk, they will have to stop,
Since pissing can destroy their paint,
For I will make them catch such a sickness
That they will do nothing but piss."

"Seigner, cuy que fassatz pissar,
A Na Elys devetz grazir
De Montfort, qu'anc no.s volc forbir,
Ni n'ac clam de vout ni d'autar."   T4.4 (8)

"Lord whoever you make piss
You must spare Lady Elise
Of Montfort for never did she paint herself,
Or inspire complaints from statues or altars."

Pus Peire d'Alvernh'a cantat *(extracts)* (PC 305.16)
Vers (Sirventes)

Pus Peire d'Alvernh'a cantat
Dels trobadors que son passat,
Cantarai ieu al mieu escien
D'aquels que pois se son levat;   1.4
E ja no.n aian cor irat,
S'ieu lor malvatz fagz lor repren.

. . . .

Since Peire d'Alvernhe has sung
Of troubadours now past,
I shall sing as best I can
Of those who have come since;
And let them not be angry
If I criticize their misdeeds.

E lo tertz es de Carcasses
Miravalhs qui.s fai mout cortes,
E dona son castelh soven;
E no.y esta l'an ges un mes,   4.4
Et anc mais kalendas no.y pres,
Per que no.lh ten dan qu'il se pren.

And the third is from the Carcassès
Miraval, who takes on courtly airs,
And often gives his castle;
He's not there more than one month per year,
And never did he spend Christmas there,
So it's no loss to him to give it away.

Lo quartz, Peirols, us Alvernhatz,
Qu'a trent'ans us vestirs portatz,
Et es plus secs que lenh'arden,
E totz sos cantars pejuratz;   5.4
Qu'anc pus si fon enbaguassatz
A Clarmon, no fetz chan valen.

The fourth, Peirol, an Auvergnat,
Who wore one set of clothes for thirty years
And is drier than burning wood,
And his singing debased,
For since he became a rake
In Clermont, he hasn't made a decent song.

E.l cinques es Gauselms Faiditz,
Qui de drut s'es tornatz maritz
De lieys que sol anar seguen;
No.n auzim pueys voutas ni critz,   6.4
Ni anc sos chans no fon auzitz
Mas d'Userca entro qu'Agen.

. . . .

And the fifth is Gaucelm Faidit
Who from lover changed to husband
Of the one he used to go following;
We haven't heard since trills or cries,
Nor were his songs ever heard
Except from Uzerche to Agen.

Ab Arnaut Daniel son set,
Qu'a sa vida ben non cantet,
Mas us folhs motz qu'om non enten;
Pus la lebre ab lo buou casset,   8.4
E contra suberna nadet,
No valc sos chans un aguilen.

. . . .

With Arnaut Daniel, that's seven
Who in his life never sang anything
Except crazy words no one understands;
And since he hunted the hare with the ox
And swam against the tide
His songs have been worthless.

E lo dotzes sera Folquetz
De Marcelha, us mercadairetz;
Et a fag un folh sagramen,
Quan juret que chansos no fetz;   13.4
Ans dizon ben que fo per vetz
Que.s perjuret son escien.

. . . .

And the twelfth will be Folquet
Of Marseille, a little merchant;
He made a foolish agreement
When he swore not to make songs;
Rather they say it's happened many times
That he knowingly perjured himself.

Peire Vidals es dels derriers,
Que non a sos membres entiers;
Et agra.l ops lengua d'argen
Al vilan qu'era pelleciers,   15.4
Que anc pus si fetz cavalliers,
Non ac pueys membransa ni sen.

. . . .

Peire Vidal is among the last
Who doesn't have all his members;
He would need a tongue of silver
This peasant who was a furrier,
For ever since he became a knight
He has had neither memory nor sense.

Ab lo sezesme i agra pro
Lo fals Monge de Montaudo,
Qu'ab totz tensona e conten,
Et a laissat Dieu per baco;   17.4
E quar anc fetz vers ni canso,
Degra.l hom tost levar al ven.

With the sixteenth, there will be enough,
The false Monk of Montaudon
Who argues and quarrels with all
And left God for bacon;
And because he ever made *vers* and *cansos,*
One should quickly blow him away in the wind.

Lo vers fe.l Monges, e dis lo
A Caussada primeiramen.   T1.2 (6)

The Monk wrote and spoke the *vers*
For the first time at Caussade.

E trames lo part Lobeo
A.N Bernat, son cors, per prezen.   T2.2 (6)

And transmitted it beyond Lobeo
To Sir Bernart, himself, as a present.

FOLQUET DE MARSEILLA

Folquet was probably born in 1160, the son of an Italian merchant who had settled in Marseille. He was first a merchant himself, and a poet, but then suddenly abandoned the way of life he had followed and entered the Cistercian monastery of Le Thoronet with his wife and children. In 1205, he became bishop of Toulouse, in which position he remained until he died in 1231. Folquet actively persecuted heretics during the Albigensian Crusade; he was a friend of Saint Dominic and helped found the Dominican Order; but if Dante placed him in Paradise, the Occitan poem on the Crusade describes him chiefly as a man responsible for killing thousands of people. Because he was a public figure, Folquet's life is reasonably well known; but in the end, he remains enigmatic: there is no easy explanation for his abrupt changes of heart.

He composed his songs during the period 1180-95, before his conversion. After his conversion, he rejected poetry entirely, even fiercely. Many of his contemporaries are mentioned in his songs: Alfonso II of Aragon, the powerful Guilhem family of Montpellier, Barral de Marseille, Richard Lion-Heart, Peire Vidal, Raimon de Miraval, Bertran de Born. His poetry is well preserved: some 19 songs can be securely attributed to him, for the most part *cansos*, with 13 melodies. Though a bourgeois, he was very learned. His poetry tends toward abstract analysis of sentiment and intricate syntax. It is distinguished by masterful control of rhythms and sounds and a rich—some would say over-rich—interlacing of conceits.

EDITIONS: Stronski 1910; van der Werf 1984.

● "En chantan m'aven a membrar": PC 155.8. Sources: mss. A 65, B 44, C 5, D 42, D^c 245, E 7, G 5, I 63, K 48, L 25, M 33, N 58, O 76, P 8, Q 19, R 43, T 230, U 37, V 34, W 189, c 13; music in G. Text: Stronski, 27. The metrical structure of this poem is unique: a8 a8 b10 b4 c8 c10 c4 c8 d10 d10. The formulation sets off the two short 4-syllable lines and brings the stanza to a stong conclusion with the final decasyllabic couplet. The rhymes are all masculine, but there are gradations: the first four lines change vowel but not consonant; the final two rhymes take up the closed "o" of rhyme b; only the c rhyme is distinctly different. The melody is without repetition of entire phrases, and thus may be diagramed ABCDEFGHIJ. It shows a capriciousness that has been related to the metric structure. The tonal focus oscillates between *d* and *g*, but without any rigor, as the sequence of cadential notes demonstrates: *d, d, g, a, a, g, d, d*(octave above), *e, a*. One may note, however, that the recurrence of the same cadence in lines 4 and 10, as well as a similar formula in line 7 suggest stanza divisions ABCD EFG HIJ (coinciding nicely with the position of the 4-syllable lines and the final close). The extraordinary ascent, almost entirely syllabic, of line 8,which reaches *f* in line 9 only to fall back in a series of brief melismas through a ninth to *e*, is a bravura passage for a singer. But there are significant leaps in the beginning as well: line 2, two ascending fourths; line 3, a descending fifth. The entire melody spans a wide range, from middle *c* to high *f*. Sesini has remarked of this melody "Per inventiva, per ampiezza, per aderenza al testo, è questa una delle più belle melodie di Folchetto et del repertorio trobadorico tutto" (1940, 23). The text develops the conceit of the lover's heart holding an image of the lady, superbly and amusingly illustrated in ms. N (Pierpont Morgan Library) by the portrait of a lover with a lady's head inside his chest (Huot 1992).

T1.8: Aziman is a reciprocal senhal used for eath other by Folquet de Marseilla and Bertran de Born (Chambers 1971, 62).

T2.8-9: William VIII of Montpellier is the intended recipient of the song.

● "Sitot me soi a tart aperceubutz": PC 155.21. Sources: ms. A 61, B 39, C 1, D 41, D^c 246, F 44, G 3, I 61, K 46, M 31, N 59, O 77, P 23, Q 19, R 51, S 26, U 32, V 86, W 188, c 15, f 41, α 28181; music in G and W. Melody from G. Text: Stronski, 52. In its series of comparisons and metaphors, this song furnishes a good illustration of Folquet's style. The two *tornadas* establish relations with prominent troubadours: Aziman is a *senhal* for Bertran de Born; Totztemps is possibly Raimon de Miraval, but the identification is not certain (Stronski, 41*); Plus-Leial is a *senhal* for the troubadour Pons de Capduelh. The melody of this song and of the one following are simpler than the first tune and more gracefully ornamented, particularly at the ends of lines. Folquet's songs seem to fall into two different categories: "En chantan" represents one category; "Si tot me soi" and "Tan m'abellis" the other. Although there are no exact repetitions of entire phrases, one may discern similarities of short motifs, particularly at cadence points: lines 1 and 4; lines 2, 3, 6, and 8, with lines 2 and 8 forming a "musical rhyme." Lines 2, 4 and 8 cadence on *d*, thus providing a sense of structure, reinforced by the almost exact repetition of lines 6 and 8. The sequence of cadences suggests a tonal focus on *d*. One may note subtle coordinations of meter and tune: the cadences in the first four lines underscore the rhyme sequence abba, while the cadences of the last three lines of the melody reflect the rhyme sequence cdc. This leaves line 5 separated from the others: it marks change to open the second part, and in it the melody reaches its highest point, a typical procedure in troubadour songs. For the most part, these melodic configurations are supported by syntax.

- "Tant m'abellis l'amoros pessamens": PC 155.22. Sources: mss. A 62, B 40, C 3, D 40, E 1, F 43, G 2, I 62, K 47, L 125, M 29, N 54, O 56, P 22, Q 18, R 42, S 25, U 36, V 83, W 188, bI 2, c10, f 49, χ 104; music in GRW. Melody from G. Text: Stronski, 15. Folquet de Marseilla is the only lyric poet in Dante's Paradise. He is initially evoked in the *Purgatorio* by a line echoing this song: "Tan m'abellis vostre cortes deman" (XXVI, 140)—which Dante had previously cited in the *De vulgari eloquentia* (II, vi, 6). In the *Purgatorio*, Folquet is placed alongside Arnaut Daniel, among the poets who seek carnal satisfaction. But because he has renounced his lustful ways, he returns in the *Paradiso* (IX; Barolini 1984, 115-23). "Tant m'abellis" was much admired by Dante for its rhetoric, at least; we do not know whether Dante knew the music. The metrical scheme is unique: a10 b10′ c10 a10 b10′ b10′ d10 d10. One should note, however, the similarity of the a and d rhymes: *ens* and *en*. This creates an effect not unlike *coblas capcaudadas* because *almost* the same *sound* at the rhyme links the last line of one stanza with the first line of the next. The melodies in the three manuscripts are similar. Following techniques typical of Folquet, the tune is structured not around ABAB-type melodic repetitions, but around coordinated cadences, such as for lines 3 and 7 (which share similarities in their approach to the cadence as well), and, in this case, one completely repeated line: 8 duplicates 4. These techniques clearly divide the stanza into two parts and determine a tonal focus on *d*. There is no real melodic peak in the second part of the stanza, but the fifth line does seem to sketch a tonal shift, especially if the *b*'s are not flatted, and thus it provides change after the initial portion. The juxtapositions of rhyme sounds and cadential motifs provide subtle sound patterns (Schlager 1984; Arlt 1988).

Folquet de Marseilla, "En chantan m'aven a membrar" (p. 145). The Pierpont Morgan Library, New York. M.819, f. 59r, upper right detail. Marginal illustration of the word "cor," stanza 1, line 9.

En chantan m'aven a membrar (PC 155.8)

Canso

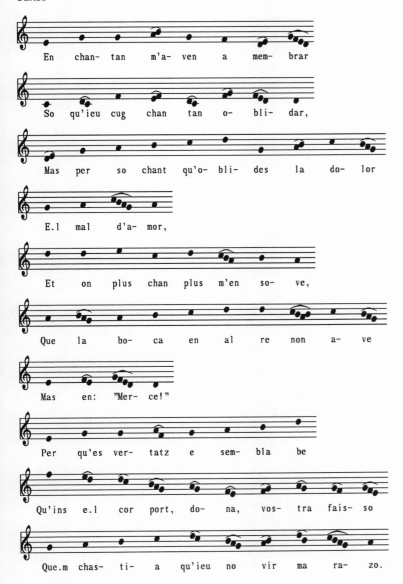

En chan- tan m'a- ven a mem- brar

So qu'ieu cug chan tan o- bli- dar,

Mas per so chant qu'o- bli- des la do- lor

E.l mal d'a- mor,

Et on plus chan plus m'en so- ve,

Que la bo- ca en al re non a- ve

Mas en: "Mer- ce!"

Per qu'es ver- tatz e sem- bla be

Qu'ins e.l cor port, do- na, vos- tra fais- so

Que.m chas- ti- a qu'ieu no vir ma ra- zo.

En chantan m'aven a membrar		In singing it befalls me to remember
So qu'ieu cug chantan oblidar,		What I expected in singing to forget,
Mas per so chant qu'oblides la dolor		But I sing in order to forget the pain
E.l mal d'amor,		And the anguish of love.
Et on plus chan plus m'en sove,	1.5	Yet the more I sing, the more I remember,
Que la boca en al re non ave		For my mouth can say naught else
Mas en: "Merce!"		But: "Mercy!"
Per qu'es vertatz e sembla be		That's why it is true and seems fitting
Qu'ins e.l cor port, dona, vostra faisso		That in my heart, lady, I carry your image
Que.m chastia qu'ieu no vir ma razo.	1.10	Which exhorts me not to change my attitude.

E pos Amors mi vol honrar
Tant qu'e.l cor vos mi fai portar,
Per merce.us prec que.l gardetz de l'ardor,
     Qu'ieu ai paor
De vos mout major que de me,   2.5
E pos mos cor, dona, vos a dinz se,
     Si mals li.n ve,
Pos dinz etz, sufrir lo.us cove;
Empero faitz del cors so que.us er bo
E.l cor gardatz si qom vostra maizo.   2.10

     Qu'el guarda vos e.us ten tan car
Que.l cors en fai nesci semblar,
Que.l sen hi met, l'engienh e la valor,
     Si qu'en error
Laissa.l cors pe.l sen qu'el rete;   3.5
Qu'om mi parla, manthas vetz s'esdeve,
     Qu'ieu no sai que,
E.m saluda qu'ieu no.n aug re;
E ja per so nuls hom no m'ochaizo
Si.m saluda et ieu mot non li so.   3.10

     Pero lo cors no.s deu blasmar
Del cor, per mal que.il sapcha far,
Que tornat l'a al plus honrat senhor
     E tolt d'alhor
On trobav'enjan e no fe;   4.5
Mas dregz torna vas so senhor ancse;
     Pero no cre
Que.m denh, si merces no.m mante,
Que.lh intr'e.l cor tan qu'en luec d'un ric do
Denh escoutar ma veraia chanso.   4.10

     E si la denhatz escoutar,
Dona, merce.i deurai trobar;
Pero ops m'es qu'oblides sa ricor
     E la lauzor
Qu'ieu n'ai dig e dirai jasse,   5.5
Mas autre pro mos lauzars noca.m te
     Com que.m malme;
Que l'ardors mi creis e.m reve,
E.l fuex, qui.l mou, sai que creis a bando,
E qui no.l mou, mor en pauc de sazo.   5.10

     Morir puesc be
     N'Azimanz, qu'ieu no.m planh de re,
Neis si.m doblava.l mals d'aital faisso
Com dobla.l pointz del taulier per razo.   T1.4 (10)

     Chansos, desse
     Vas Monpeslier, vai de part me
A don Guillem dir, si tot no.il sap bo,
Sos pretz, car creis, li.m fai querre perdo.   T2.4 (10)

And since Love wants to honor me
So much that in my heart it makes me carry you,
For mercy's sake I pray you to keep it from burning
For I fear
More for you than for me,
And since my heart, lady, has you in it
If harm comes to it,
Since you are inside, you will have to bear it;
Do with the body then what you will
And preserve the heart as your dwelling.

For it keeps you and holds you so dear
That it makes the body look like a fool,
For it uses wisdom, skill and merit,
So that in error
It places the body by retaining wisdom;
It often happens that someone speaks to me
And I know not about what,
Or greets me and I don't hear a thing;
And so may no man accuse me
If he greets me and I don't say a word.

But the body should not blame
The heart, whatever harm the latter has done,
For it has turned it toward the most honorable lord
And taken it from another
Where it found deceit and faithlessness.
Thus right turns always toward its lord;
However I do not believe
That she will receive me if mercy does not help;
May it enter her heart so that, instead of a rich gift
She will deign to listen to my true song.

And if you deign to listen
Lady, I should find mercy;
However I must forget her high rank
And the praise
That I have said of her and will always say,
For no other profit does my praise bring me
Except mistreatment;
For the ardor increases and returns to me
And the fire, if stirred, grows, I know, greatly,
And if not stirred, dies in a short time.

I can well die
Lord *Aziman,* for I complain of nothing
Not even if pain doubles for me just as
The point of the gaming table doubles by right.

Song, quickly
Towards Montpellier, go for me
To tell Sir William, although it displeases him,
His merit, by increasing, makes me beg his pardon.

Sitot me soi a tart aperceubutz (PC 155.21)

Canso

Sitot me soi a tart aperceubutz,		Although I realized only very late,
Aissi cum cel qu'a tot perdut e jura		Like the one who lost all and swears
Que mais non joc, a gran bonaventura		Never again to gamble, yet fortunate
M'o dei tener car me sui conogutz	1.4	Must I consider myself to have recognized
Del gran engan qu'Amors vas mi fazia;		The great mischief Love has done to me;
C'ab bel semblan m'a tengut en fadia		For with fine glance he kept me waiting
Mais de detz ans a lei de mal deutor		More than ten years, like a bad debtor
C'ades promet mas re no pagaria.	1.8	Who always promises but would pay nothing.

Ab bel semblan que fals'Amors adutz   By the fine appearance that false love brings
S'atrai vas lieis fols amans e s'atura,   The foolish lover is attracted and fixes himself
Co.l parpaillos qu'a tant folla natura   Like the butterfly who has such a foolish nature
Que.is fer e.l foc per la clardat qe lutz;   2.4 That he flies into the fire on account of the shining light;
Mas eu m'en part e segrai autra via,   But I depart and will follow another road,
Sos mal pagatz, q'estiers no m'en partria;   Badly paid, for otherwise I would not leave,
E segrai l'aip de tot bon sofridor   And I will follow the example of any good sufferer
Que s'irais fort si com fort s'umelia.   2.8 Who is greatly angered just as he is greatly humbled.

Pero no.is cuig, si be.m sui irascuz
Ni faz de leis en chantan ma rancura,
Ja.l diga ren que no semble mesura;
Mas be sapcha c'a sos ops sui perdutz,   3.4
C'anc sobre fre no.m volc menar un dia,
Anz mi fetz far mon poder tota via,
Et anc sempre cavals de gran valor,
Qui.l biorda trop soven, cuoill feunia.   3.8

Fels for'ieu ben, mas sui m'en retengutz,
Car qui ab plus fort de si.s desmesura
Fai gran foudat; e neis en aventura
N'es de son par, qu'esser en pot vencutz;   4.4
E de plus freul de si es vilania;
Per q'anc no.m plac ni.m platz sobranssaria,
Pero en sen deu hom gardar honor,
Car sen aunit no pretz plus que foillia.   4.8

Per so, Amors, mi soi ieu recrezutz
De vos servir, que mais no.n aurai cura;
Q'aissi cum prez'om plus laida peintura
De loing, no fai qand l'es de pres venguz,   5.4
Prezav'ieu vos mais qand no.us conoissia,
E s'anc vos volc, mais n'ai qu'er no volria:
C'aissi m'es pres cum al fol qeridor
Que dis c'aurs fos tot qant el tocaria.   5.8

Bels N'Azimans, s'Amors vos destreignia,
Vos ni.N Totztemps, eu.s en conseillaria:
Sol vos membres qant ieu n'ai de dolor
Ni qant de be, ja mais no.us en calria.   T1.4 (8)

En Plus-Leial, s'ab los huoills vos vezia,
Aissi cum fatz ab lo cor tota via,
So q'ieu ai dig porri'aver valor,
Q'ieu qier conseill e conseill vos daria.   T2.4 (8)

However, let him not think, although I am irate,
Or express my rancor in singing,
That ever I may say anything immoderate;
But may he recognize that by him I am lost,
For never has he wished to lead me by the bridle,
Rather he let me do as I wished always,
And a horse of great value inevitably
Garners remorse if one lets him play too often.

I would be irritated, but I restrained myself:
Who acts immoderately with stronger than himself
Behaves foolishly; and there is even danger
With his equal, for he can be vanquished;
And with weaker than oneself, it is villainy;
That's why arrogance never pleased nor pleases me,
But in wisdom must one preserve honor,
For dishonored wisdom I prize no more than folly.

Thus, Love, have I given up
Serving you, so that never more will I care for it;
For just as one esteems more an ugly painting
From afar than when one is close up,
So I esteemed you more when I did not know you,
And if ever I desired you, now I have more than I wanted;
So it happened to me as to the foolish questioner
Who said that all he would touch would become gold.

Fine Sir *Aziman,* if Love oppresses you,
You and Sir *Totztemps,* I would advise you:
If only you remember how much pain I have
And how much good, no more would it bother you.

Sir *Plus-Leial,* if with my eyes I saw you
As I always do with my heart,
What I said could be of value,
For I seek counsel and counsel I would give you.

Tant m'abellis l'amoros pessamens (PC 155.22)

Canso

Tant m'a-bel-lis l'a-mo-ros pes-sa-mens

Que s'es ven-gutz e mon fin cor as-si-re

Per que no.i pot nuills au-tre pes ca-ber

Ni mais ne-gus no m'es dous ni pla-zens;

Qu'a-donc viu sas quan m'au-ci-zo.l cos-si-re

E fin' a-mors a-leu-ja.m mo mar-ti-re

Qe.m pro-met joi, mas trop lo.m do-na len,

Qu'ap bel sem-blan m'a trai-nat lon-ga-men.

Tant m'abellis l'amoros pessamens	I am so pleased by the loving thought
Que s'es vengutz e mon fin cor assire	Which has come to place itself in my noble heart
Per que no.i pot nuills autre pes caber	That no other thought can be therein contained
Ni mais negus no m'es dous ni plazens; 1.4	Nor is any other sweeter or more agreeable to me;
Qu'adonc viu sas quan m'aucizo.l cossire	For now I live in good health when care slays me
E fin'amors aleuja.m mo martire	And true love lightens my martyrdom
Que.m promet joi, mas trop lo.m dona len,	By promising joy but gives it to me too slowly,
Qu'ap bel semblan m'a trainat longamen. 1.8	For with fine airs it has made me wait a long time.
Be sai que tot quan faz es dreiz niens!	I know well that everything I do is as nothing!
Eu qu'en puesc mais s'Amors mi vol aucire?	What can I do if Love wants to kill me?
Qu'az escien m'a donat tal voler	For knowingly it has given me a desire
Que ja non er vencutz ni el no vens; 2.4	That never will be conquered nor conqueror;
Vencutz si er, qu'aucir m'an li sospire,	But it will be conquered, for sighs will kill me,
Tot soavet, quar de liey cui dezire	Sweetly, since from her whom I desire
Non ai socors, ni d'allors no l'aten,	I have no help, nor expect any from elsewhere,
Ni d'autr'amor no puesc aver talen. 2.8	Nor can I wish for another love.

Bona dona, si.us platz, siatz sufrens
Del ben qu'ie.us vuel qu'ieu sui del mal sufrire,
E pueis lo mals no.m poira dan tener
Ans m'er semblan que.l partam egalmens;   3.4
Pero, si.us platz qu'az autra part me vire,
Ostatz de vos la beutat e.l dous rire
E.l bel semblan que m'afollis mon sen:
Pueis partir m'ai de vos, mon escien.   3.8

A totz jorns m'etz plus bel'e plus plazens;
Per qu'ie.n vuel mal als huels ab que.us remire,
Quar a mon pro no.us poirian vezer
Et a mon dan vezon trop sotilmens;   4.4
Mos dans non es, sivals pos no.m n'azire,
Ans es mos pros, dona, per qu'ieu m'albire,
Si m'aucisetz, que no.us estara gen,
Quar lo mieus dans vostres er eissamen.   4.8

Per so, dona, no.us am saviamens
Qu'a vos sui fis et a mos ops trayre:
E vos cug perdr'e mi no puesc aver,
E.us cug nozer et a mi sui nozens;   5.4
Pero, no.us aus mon mal mostrar ni dire,
Mas a l'esgart podetz mon cor devire,
Qu'ar lo.us cuich dir et aras m'en repen
Et port n'als huels vergonh'e ardimen.   5.8

Trop vos am mais, dona, qu'ieu no sai dire,
E quar anc jorn aic d'autr'amor desire
No m'en penet, ans vos am per un cen,
Car ai proat l'autrui captenemen.   T1.4 (8)

Vas Nems t'en vai, chanssos, qui qe.s n'azire,
Que gauch n'auran, per lo meu escien,
Las tres donnas a cui ieu te presen.   T2.3 (8)

Good lady, if it please you, suffer
The good I wish you since I suffer the pain,
And then the pain will not be able to harm me
Rather it will seem to me that we share equally;
However, if it pleases you that I turn elsewhere,
Take away your beauty and your sweet laugh
And charming look which drive me mad:
Then I will leave you, surely.

Every day you are more beautiful and more pleasing.
That's why I curse the eyes with which I look on you,
For never to my advantage could they see you,
And to my harm they see too subtly;
Yet it is not my harm, at least since I am not sad,
Rather it is my advantage, lady, so that I think
That if you kill me, that will not be good for you,
For my harm is also yours.

Thus, lady, I do not love you wisely
For I am true to you and traitor to myself;
And I think I'll lose you and cannot have myself,
And I think I'll harm you and I harm myself;
However, I dare not show or tell you my pain
But from my glance you can guess my heart,
Now wanting to tell you and then repenting
And carrying in the eyes both shame and daring.

I love you much more, lady, than I can say
And if any day I had desire of another love
I do not repent, rather love you more a hundred fold
Because I have tested the behavior of others.

Go song toward Nimes, whoever gets mad,
For they will be glad, I feel sure,
The three ladies to whom I present you.

MARIA DE VENTADORN and GUI D'USSEL

Maria de Ventadorn (late 12th century) was a knowledgeable and celebrated patroness of song and protectress of poets. She was the daughter of Raimon II of Torena, one of three sisters referred to by Bertran de Born as the most beautiful in the world: "De tota beltat terrena / ant pretz las tres de Torena" ("Of all earthly beauty / the three ladies of Turenne have the prize" [PC 80.9]). As the second wife of Eble V of Ventadorn, she married into an illustrious poetic family: Eble's ancestor, Eble II of Ventadorn (1096-1147) may have been the first troubadour, although no songs by him have survived. Many poets mention Maria: Bertran de Born, the Monk of Montaudon, Pons de Capduelh, Gaucelm Faidit, and Gui d'Ussel, her partner in this song, to recall only the best known. It would seem that Maria de Ventadorn held what might be called a veritable "salon littéraire." She had two sons. She died after 1221, the year in which she entered a monastery, likely with her husband. We know her own poetic talents only from this *tenso*, which may date from 1196-8 (Bec 1995, 167).

Gui d'Ussel (end of the 12th century) belonged to a family of troubadours from Ussel in the Limousin, called the "four brothers," although there were in fact three brothers and a cousin. Gui was the best known. We have a number of songs from him, including *pastorelas* and *tensos* as well as *cansos*.

EDITIONS: Schultz[-Gora] 1888; Audiau 1922; Rieger 1991; Bec 1995; Bruckner et al. 1995. For the *razo*, Boutière-Schutz 1964.

• "Gui d'Ussel, be.m pesa de vos": PC 194.9; 295.1. Sources: mss. A 185, C 389, D 149, E 220, H 53, R 78, T 83, a¹ 548, χ 134. Text: Audiau, 73; *razo* Boutière-Schutz, 212. This *tenso* seems to belong to a series of sometimes tangled exchanges reported in several songs and *razos*. "Si be.m partetz," mentioned in this *razo*, is "explained" in another *razo* connected with Gui d'Ussel (Boutière-Schutz, 205-6), where we learn that this *mala canso* was composed because Gui d'Ussel's lady wanted him to marry her, but after a debate on the relative merits of lover or husband (PC 194.2), Gui decided it was better to be a lover, thus refused marriage. His lady then went off and found a husband, with the parting shot that she didn't anyway want a lover who was not a knight (Gui d'Ussel was a cleric, and even for that reason, according to his *vida*, a papal legate had told him to stop singing ["lo legatz del papa li fetz jurar que mais non fezes cansos," Boutière-Schutz, 202]). Still another *razo* (Boutière-Schutz, 208-9), explaining Gui d'Ussel's side of the *tenso* exchanged with Maria, tells us that Gui's sad situation had become a *cause célèbre*. The *razo* here, then, is the third on the subject: it tells the story from Maria's point of view, raising yet another issue (involving Hugh IX, Count of La Marche) that engages power, politics and poetic discourse. Maria's *razo* appears in MS H, where a whole section is devoted to trobairitz, and it is accompanied by a portrait of the countess. The beginning of the *razo*, "Ben avetz auzit . . . ," presupposes a *vida* already in existence, or to be composed; but no *vida* has come down to us. One cannot of course claim that *razos* give realistic descriptions; they do furnish, however, a medieval "interpretation" that can help us understand song contexts as they were then perceived. It is likely that the *vidas* and *razos* pertaining to events prior to about 1250 were collected, and in some cases composed, by Uc de Saint Circ (fl 1217-53). Uc may have known the brother of Maria de Ventadorn; he likely gathered information on his travels in southern France (Poe, *Handbook* 1995, 188, 194-5). Thus the discussions and debates connected by the *razos* to the *tenso* between Maria and Gui reflect a reasonably contemporaneous view of poetic composition at her court, and of the purposes of singing, that can inform our thinking even if the view may not be factually accurate.

The *tenso* itself raises the issue of equality vs. hierarchy in love and in song. Maria maintains the hierarchical position that is the source of her power, as a poet and as a suzerain. Gui seeks equality. The play on feudal terminology in stanza V has often been considered ironic. But the song lacks the normal summarizing *tornadas*, and its final interpretation must remain ambiguous. It invites comparison to other trobairitz songs and to the exchange between Bernart de Ventadorn and Peire ("Amics Bernartz" above).

Gui d'Ussel, be.m pesa de vos (PC 194.9; 295.1)
Tenso

RAZO

Ben avetz auzit de ma dompna Maria de Ventedorn com ella fo la plus preziada dompna qe anc fos en Lemozin, et aqella qe plus fetz de be e plus se gardet de mal. E totas vetz l'ajudet sos senz, e follors no.ill fetz far follia. Et onret la Deus de bel plazen cors avinen, ses maestria.

En Guis d'Uisels si avia perduda sa dompna, si com vos avetz ausi[t] en la soa canson qe dis:

[PC 194.19]   Si be.m partetz, mala dompna, de vos;

don el vivia en gran dolor et en gran tristessa. Et avia lonc tems q'el no avia chantat ni trobat; don totas las bonas dompnas d'aqella encontrada n'eron fort dolentas, e ma dompna Maria plus qe totas, per so q'En Guis d'Uisels la lauzava en totas sas cansos. E.l coms de la Marcha, lo cals era apellatz N'Ucs lo Brus, si era sos cavalliers, et ella l'avia fait tant d'onor e d'amor com dompna pot far a cavalier.

Et, un dia, el dompnejava com ella, e si ag[r]on una tenson entre lor: qe.l coms de la Marcha dizia qe totz fis amaire, pois qe sa dompna li dona s'amor ni.l pren per cavalier ni per amic, tant com el es leials ni fis vas ella, deu aver aitan de seignoria en ella e de comandamen com ella de lui; e ma dompna Maria defendia qe l'amic[s] no devia aver en ella seignoria ni comandamen. En Guis d'Uisels si era en la cort de ma dompna Maria; et ella, per far lo tornar en cansos et en solatz, si fetz una cobla en la cal li mandet si se covenia qe l'amics ages aitant de seignoria en la soa dompna com la dompna en lui. E d'aqesta rason ma dompna Maria si l'escomes de tenson e dis enaissi:

Gui d'Uisel, be.m pesa de vos.

You have certainly heard about my lady Maria de Ventadorn how she was the most esteemed lady who ever lived in Limousin, and the one who did the most good and who most refrained from evil. And her good sense always helped her, and folly never made her act foolishly. And God honored her with a beautiful, attractive body, without artifice.

Lord Gui d'Uisel had lost his lady, as you have heard in his song which says:

If you separate me, evil lady, from you

so he lived in great grief and in great sadness. And he had not sung or composed for a long time, and all the good ladies from that region were very grieved about it, and Lady Maria more than all others, because Lord Gui d'Uisel praised her in all his songs. And the Count of La Marche, who was called Lord Uc lo Brun, was her knight, and she had given him as much honor and love as a lady can give a knight.

And one day he was courting her, and there arose a dispute between them: the Count of La Marche said that every true lover, since his lady gives him her love and takes him as her knight and friend, so long as he is loyal and true to her, must have as much suzerainty and authority over her as she has over him. And Lady Maria argued that the friend should not have suzerainty or authority over her. Lord Gui d'Uisel was in the court of Lady Maria and she, to make him return to songs and joy, composed a couplet in which she asked him if it was suitable for the friend to have as much suzerainty over the lady as she had over him. And on this subject my lady Maria challenged him to a *tenso,* and said thus:

Gui d'Ussel, I'm quite concerned

Gui d'Ussel, be.m pesa de vos,		Gui d'Ussel, I'm quite concerned
Car vos etz laissatz de chantar,		Because you've given up singing,
E car vos i volgra tornar,		And since I wish you'd take it up again,
Per que sabetz d'aitals razos,	1.4	Because you know about such things,
Vuoill que.m digatz si deu far egalmen		I want you to tell me if a lady
Dompna per drut, can lo qier francamen,		Should do equally for a lover, if she courts him,
Cum el per lieis tot cant taing ad amor		As he for her, all that befits love,
Segon los dreitz que tenon l'amador.	1.8	According to the rights of lovers.

Dompna Na Maria, tenssos
  E tot cant cuiava laissar,
  Mas aoras non puosc estar
  Qu'ieu non chant als vostres somos;   2.4
E respon vos de la dompna breumen
Que per son drut deu far comunalmen
Cum el per lieis, ses garda de ricor:
Qu'en dos amics non deu aver maior.   2.8

Gui, tot so don es cobeitos
  Deu drutz ab merce demandar,
  E dompna pot o comandar,
  E deu ben pregar a sazos;   3.4
E.l drutz deu far precs e comandamen
Cum per amig'e per dompn'eissamen,
E.il dompna deu a son drut far honor
Cum ad amic, mas non cum a seignor.   3.8

Dompna, sai dizon de mest nos
  Que, pois que dompna vol amar,
  Egalmen deu son drut onrar,
  Pois egalmen son amoros;   4.4
E s'esdeven que l'am plus finamen,
Els faichs, els dichs en deu far aparen,
E si ell'a fals cor ni trichador,
Ab bel semblan deu cobrir sa follor.   4.8

Gui d'Uissel, ges d'aitals razos
  Non son li drut al comenssar,
  Anz ditz chascus, can vol preiar,
  Mans jointas e de genolos: 5.4
"Dompna, voillatz que.us serva franchamen
Cum lo vostr' om," et ell'enaissi.l pren;
Ieu vo.l jutge per dreich a trahitor,
Si.s rend pariers e.s det per servidor.   5.8

Dompna, so es plaitz vergoignos,
  Ad ops de dompn'a razonar,
  Que cellui non teigna per par
  Ab cui a faich un cor de dos.   6.4
O vos diretz, e no.us estara gen,
Que.l drutz la deu amar plus finamen,
O vos diretz qu'il son par entre lor,
Que ren no.il deu lo drutz mas per amor.   6.8

Lady Maria, *tensos*
And all manner of song I thought I'd given up,
But now I cannot refuse
To sing when you summon;
My reply is that the lady
Ought to do exactly for her lover
As he does for her, without regard to rank;
Between two friends one should not be better.

Gui, the lover, by prayer, ought to ask
For everything he desires,
And the lady may grant his request
And she should woo on occasion;
And the lover ought to entreat and command
As toward a friend and a lady equally,
And a lady should honor her lover the way
She would a friend, but never as a lord.

Lady, here among us it is said
That when a lady wants to love
She should honor equally her lover,
Since they're equally in love.
And if it happens that she loves him better,
In words and deeds she should make it show;
But if she's fickle or untrue
She ought to hide it with a fine appearance.

Gui d'Ussel, never of such a mind
Are lovers at the beginning,
To the contrary, each says when he seeks to woo,
Hands joined and kneeling,
"Grant that I may freely serve you, lady,
As your man," and she thus receives him;
I rightly judge to be a traitor
A man who says he's her equal and her servant.

Lady, it's a shameful opinion
For a lady to defend
That she will not hold as equal
The one with whom she's made one heart of two.
Either you'll say (and this won't flatter you)
That the man should love the lady more faithfully,
Or else you'll say that they're the same,
Because the lover owes her nothing except by love.

RAIMBAUT DE VAQUEIRAS

Raimbaut de Vaqueiras flourished between 1180 and 1205. He was from Vaqueiras, near Orange, in the region of the Vaucluse, a member of the petty nobility. He spent a major part of his career at the court of Boniface of Montferrat whom he accompanied to the Orient and with whom he probably participated in the Fourth Crusade. The *senhal Bel Cavalier* which appears in many of Raimbaut's songs probably refers to a lady of high rank at the court of Montferrat, although her exact identity remains conjectural. He was both a soldier and a poet: perhaps he was knighted by Boniface; in his poetry, he claims his knighthood has been won through song. Raimbaut played an important role in the spread of troubadour song to Italy. It is not known when he died; it is probable that he was mortally wounded, along with his patron Boniface, in 1207 near Salonika (Linskill 1964, 36-7).

More than 30 songs have been attributed to Raimbaut. They exhibit great formal and linguistic variety. Raimbaut excelled in drawing surprising results from unpretentious materials; he demonstrates originality of theme and genre as well as complete mastery of the craft of poetry. His corpus includes, beside the multilingual *descort*, the *estampida*, and the *canso* presented here, a fictitious *tenso* with a Genoese lady, a poem on a mock battle between a lady and a number of other ladies envious of her beauty, an *alba*, a *partimen*, and other *cansos*. Raimbaut also composed an epic letter to his patron, a text of considerable historical as well as poetic interest. Seven melodies have been preserved, one of which, "Kalenda maia," has taken its place among the most celebrated troubadour inventions.

EDITION: Linskill 1964; van der Werf 1984.

● "Eras quan vey verdeyar": PC 392.4. Sources: mss. C 125, E 187, M 108,251, R 62, Sg 50, a^1 334, f 76. Text: Linskill, 192. On the problems of editing this multilingual text, see Linskill, 192. This may well be one of the first *descorts* we have. The stanzas are composed successively in Occitan, Italian, French, Gascon, Galician-Portuguese, and the *tornada* (really a series of five *tornadas*) is in all five languages. Raimbaut calls his text a *descort* (1.3) so named because he is going to make "discordant" the words, melodies and languages. No music remains; one wonders if there would have been a different melody for each stanza; this is the view of Raimbaut's editor. The *coblas singulars* are all alike in regard to versification (normally a *descort* would have different stanza shapes): 8 lines of 7 syllables, alternating masculine and feminine rhymes (except for stanza 5), and two rhyme sounds to a stanza. Thematically, the song displays no particular originality except perhaps in the very notion of making discord

between lovers not only a theme but a form. The song is a precious linguistic document, however: the stanzas in Italian, Gascon, and Galician-Portuguese are among the earliest, if not the earliest, literary examples of these languages.

6.8: Saint Quiteria was a well-known Gascon saint.

● "Kalenda maia": PC 392.9. Sources: mss. C 125, M 106,250, R 62, Sg 49; music in R. Text: Linskill, 184. This is one of the most famous of all troubadour songs; the *razo*, equally famous, is given here with the song. The *razo* contains one of the best known references to instrumental music in the troubadour corpus; indeed, it can be argued that the tune for "Kalenda maia" might be the only surviving pre-13th-century piece of instrumental music. The song designates itself as an *estampida* (in the last line of the text). However, it is rather more a variant of the *canso*: its melody would have been repeated for each stanza, following the conventions of the *canso*. Moreover, it does not correspond to the definition given of the *estampida* in treatises such as Grocheio's *De Musica*. The *estampida* and its French counterpart the *estampie* have been much discussed in both their musical and poetic dimensions, but definitive conclusions still elude scholars (Linskill 1964, 189; Bec 1977 I, 243; Cummins 1982; Chambers 1985, 152-3; Billy 1987; McGee 1989; Aubrey 1996; instrumental *estampies* have been frequently recorded; two are on the Compact Disc accompanying the Anthology). The learned sound-architecture of "Kalenda maia," moving artfully through six 14-line heterometric *coblas singulars*, defies both description and translation. There is one main rhyme per stanza; the lines of 8 and 6 syllables are further divided by internal rhymes. The whole song dances through a virtuosic whirlwind of rhyming sounds that seem to take on a life of their own. This sophisticated verse structure contrasts curiously with the idea of a popularizing May ceremony suggested by the first verse, and indeed by the melody which has the characteristics of a dance tune and remains joyously focused on *c*. The total effect is unconventional and somewhat humorous (Page 1986, 47-9). According to the *razo*, the piece was composed at the court of Boniface of Montferrat. Lady Beatrice is identified in Raimbaut's *vida* as well as in the *razo* as the sister of Boniface. She was more likely his daughter (Linskill 1964, 22-5). Possibly she is the person designated by *Bel cavalier*. *Engles* is the Marquis Boniface.

● "Eissamen ai gerreiat ab amor"; PC 392.13. Sources: mss. A 162, B 99, C 123, D 106, D^c 252, E 35,183, F 28, G 56, I 77, J 6, K 61, N^2 11, P 13, Q 49, R 61, S 128, Sg 49, a^1 328, β^1 784; music in R. Text: Linskill, 159. In the Middle Ages, this song had far wider circulation than "Kalenda maia," but it has found far less favor with modern critics. It illustrates Raimbaut's fondness for images comparing love and chivalry: the poet/lover/knight fights with love as a noble vassal fights with his ungrateful lord, and in the end, war itself turns back upon the lover. The conceit governing this poem is found elsewhere in troubadour poetry and is echoed in the song by the trobairitz Azalais de Porcairagues: the poor lover/knight is to be preferred to the rich nobleman. The versification is unusual without being contrived. The *coblas unissonans* have 8 10-syllable lines with the ryhme scheme aab'ccb' dd. There is no immediately apparent metrical stanza division. The rhyme sounds are not rich, but considerable use is made of alliteration. Like the rhyme scheme, the melody is unconventional; it does not have the kind of phrase repetition that would define a regular structure. It does, however, exhibit ample use of motivic recurrences: phrase 6 telescopes 1 and 3; 7 resembles 4; 8 recalls 5 except for the final cadence, creating a sense of internal coherence. One may note also frequent use of the interval of a fourth in stepwise motion: *g-c* ascending in lines 1 and 6, but also suggested by descending gestures in lines 3, 4, 5 (ornamented) and 7; *c-f* ascending in lines 5 and 8; *d-g* ascending in lines 4 and 7. One could speak, especially for the last lines, of chains of fourths. Tonal focus is on *g* in its plagal disposition; but the final cadence moves unexpectedly up to *b*. Can we see in this final destabilizing flourish a tinge of wit?

Eras quan vey verdeyar (PC 392.4)
Multilingual descort

Eras quan vey verdeyar		Now when I see greening
Pratz e vergiers e boscatges,		Meadows and orchards and woods
Vuelh un descort comensar		I want to begin a "discord"
D'amor, per qu'ieu vauc aratges;	1.4	About love, about which I am distressed;
Q'una dona.m sol amar,		One lady used to love me
Mas camjatz l'es sos coratges,		But her heart has changed,
Per qu'ieu fauc dezacordar		That's why I make discordant
Los motz e.ls sos e.ls lenguatges.	1.8	The words and the melodies and the languages.
Io son quel que ben non aio		I am one who has not good
Ni jamai non l'averò,		Nor ever will I have it,
Ni per april ni per maio,		Not in April nor in May,
Si per ma donna non l'ò;	2.4	If I don't have it from my lady;
Certo que en so lengaio		It is certain that in her language
Sa gran beutà dir non sò,		I cannot describe her great beauty,
Çhu fresca qe flor de glaio,		Fresher than gladiolus,
Per qe no m'en partirò.	2.8	That's why I shall not leave her.
Belle douce dame chiere,		Fair, sweet, dear lady
A vos mi doin e m'otroi;		To you I give and commit myself;
Je n'avrai mes joi'entiere		I will never have perfect joy
Si je n'ai vos e vos moi.	3.4	If I don't have you and you me.
Mot estes male guerriere		You are a very bad warrior
Si je muer per bone foi;		If I die through good faith;
Mes ja per nulle maniere		But never for any reason
No.m partrai de vostre loi.	3.8	Will I leave your sovereignty.
Dauna, io mi rent a bos,		Lady, I surrender to you
Coar sotz la mes bon'e bera		For you are the best and fairest
Q'anc fos, e gaillard'e pros,		Who ever was, joyous and worthy,
Ab que no.m hossetz tan hera.	4.4	If only you were not so cruel to me.
Mout abetz beras haisos		You have a most beautiful face
E color hresc'e noera.		And color fresh and young.
Boste son, e si.bs agos		I am yours, and if I had you
No.m destrengora hiera.	4.8	Nothing would be lacking to me.

Mas tan temo vostro preito,		But I so fear your anger
Todo.n son escarmentado.		That I am entirely in despair.
Por vos ei pen'e maltreito		On your account, I have pain and torture
E meo corpo lazerado:	5.4	And my body is racked:
La noit, can jatz en meu leito,		At night, when I lie in bed,
So mochas vetz resperado;		I am many times awakened;
E car nonca m'aprofeito		And because there is for me no advantage
Falid'ei en mon cuidado.	5.8	I have failed in my desire.
Belhs Cavaliers, tant es car		Fair Knight, so dear is
Lo vostr'onratz senhoratges		Your honorable sovereignty
Que cada jorno m'esglaio.		That every day I am distressed.
Oi me lasso! que farò		Ah! miserable! What will I do
Si sele que j'ai plus chiere	6.5	If the one I hold dearest
Me tue, ne sai por quoi?		Kills me, and I know not why?
Ma dauna, he que dey bos		My lady, by my faith,
Ni peu cap santa Quitera,		And by the head of Saint Quiteria
Mon corasso m'avetz treito		You have drawn my heart from me
E mot gen favlan furtado.	6.10	And stolen it with your sweet speech.

Kalenda maia (PC 392.9)
Estampida (Canso)

RAZO

Ben avetz auzit de Rambaut qi el fo ni don, et si com el fo fait cavalier del marqes de Monferrat, et com el s'entendia en ma dompna Biatrix et vivia jausen per lo so amor.

Et auiatz com el ac um pauc de temps gran tristessa. Et aiso fon per la falsa jen enueiosa a cui nom plasia amors ni dopneis, qe dizion paraolas a ma dompna Biatrix et encontra las autras dompnas, disen aisi: "Qi es aqest Rambaut de Vaqera, si tot lo marqes l'a fait cavalier? Et cuja entendre en tan auta dompna con vos o ez! Sapchatz qe no.n vos es onor, ni a vos ni al marqes." Et tan disseron mal, qe d'una part qe d'autra, si con fan las avols genz, qe ma dompna Biatrix s'en corecet contra Rambaut de Vaqera. Qe qant Rambaut la pregava d'amor e.l clamava merce, ella non entendea sos precs, anzi li dis q'el se degues entendre en autra dompna qe fos per ell, et als non entendria ni auziria d'ella. Et aqest'es la tristessa qe Rambautz ac un pauc de temps, si com eu dis al comenzamen d'aqesta rason.

Dont el se laisset de chantar et de rire et de toz autres faitz qe.l deguesson plager. Et aiso era gran danz. Et atot aqest ac per la lenga dals lausengiers, si com el dis en una cobla de la stampida qe vos ausiret.

En aqest temps vengron dos joglars de Franza en la cort del marqes, qe sabion ben violar. Et un jorn violaven una stampida qe plazia fort al marqes et als cavaliers et a las dompnas. Et en Rambaut no.n s'allegrava nien, si qe.l marqes s'en perceupet et dis: "Senher Rambaut, qe es aiso qe vos non chantatz ni.us allegraz, c'ausitz aisi bel son de viola et veitz aiqi tan bella dompna com es mia seror, qe vos a retengut per servidor et es la plus valen dompna del mon?" Et en Rambautz respondi qe no.n faria nien. E.l marqes saubia ben l'acaison, et dis a sa seror: "Ma dopna Biatrix, per amor de mi et de totas aqestas genz, vol qe vos deignat pregar Rambaut q'el, per lo vostro amor et per la vostra graçia, se deges alegrar et chantar et star alegre, si com el fazia denan." Et ma dompna Biatrix fu tan cortes' et de bona merce qu'ella lo preget e.l confortet q'el se deges, per lo so amor, rallegrar et q'el feses de nou una chanson.

Dont Rambaut, per aqesta raison qe vos avez ausit, fet la stampida, et dis aisi:

[First stanza of "Kalenda maia"]

Aqesta stampida fu facta a las notas de la stampida qe.l joglars fasion en las violas.

You have certainly heard who Raimbaut was and where he came from and how he was knighted by the Marquis of Montferrat and how he paid court to Lady Beatrice and on account of his love lived joyously.

And hear how he experienced during a short time great sadness. This was caused by the false jealous ones who found love and courting displeasing. They spoke to Lady Beatrice in the presence of the other ladies saying: "Who is this Raimbaut de Vaqueiras even though the Marquis made him a knight? And how dare he court so high born a lady as you are? Be it known that it is not an honor either for you or for the Marquis." They said so many evil things (as bad people do) that Lady Beatrice became angry at Raimbaut de Vaqueiras. So when Raimbaut tried to woo her and ask her pity, she did not listen to his prayers, but to the contrary told him that he should woo another lady who would be more appropriate for him and that she would no longer listen to him. And that is the sadness Raimbaut had during a short time just as I told you at the beginning of this *razo*.

So he stopped singing and laughing and withdrew from all activities that might please him. That was too bad. All this was caused by the tongues of gossips, just as he tells it in one stanza of the estampie you will hear.

At that time two jongleurs came from France to the court of the marquis who were skilled at playing the vielle. And one day they played an estampie that much pleased the marquis, the knights and the ladies. But Raimbaut did not enjoy it. The marquis noticed this and said to him: "Sir Raimbaut, why do you not sing and rejoice since you are listening to a fine sound of the vielle, you see here so beautiful a lady as my sister who has retained you as her servant, and she is the noblest lady in the world?" And Raimbaut replied that he would do nothing. Now the marquis knew why, and he said to his sister: "Lady Beatrice, for the love of me and of all these people, I want you to agree to beg Raimbaut, in the name of your love and your grace, that he be happy, that he sing, and that he enjoy himself, like he used to." And Lady Beatrice was so courtly and of such good grace that she begged Raimbaut, encouraging him, for her sake, to be happy again and to again make a song.

So Raimbaut, for the reason you've just heard, made the *estampida* that runs like this:

[First stanza of "Kalenda maia"]

This *estampida* was made to the notes of the *estampida* that the jongleurs played on their vielles.

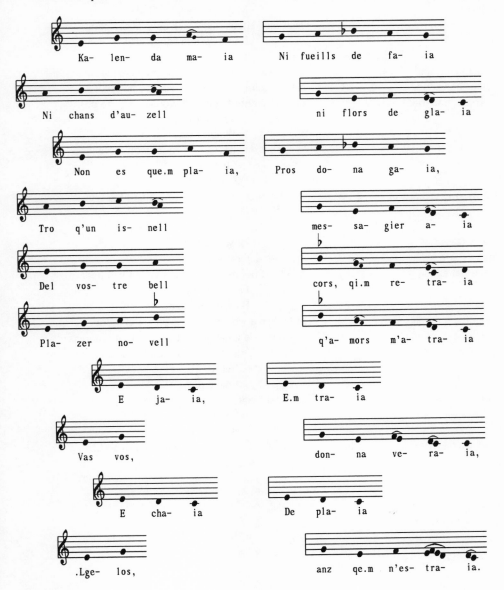

Kalenda maia
Ni fueills de faia
Ni chans d'auzell   ni flors de glaia
Non es qe.m plaia,
Pros dona gaia,   1.5
Tro q'un isnell   messagier aia
Del vostre bell   cors, qi.m retraia
Plazer novell   q'amors m'atraia
E jaia,
E.m traia   1.10
Vas vos,   donna veraia,
E chaia
De plaia
.L gelos,   anz qe.m n'estraia.   1.14

Neither Mayday
Nor beach-tree leaf
Nor bird's song   nor gladiolus
Can please me
Noble lady
Until a speedy   messenger comes to me
From your fair   person, who can tell me
Of new pleasure   that love brings me
With joy,
And I repair
To you   true lady,
And he falls
Wounded,
The jealous one,   ere I depart.

Ma bell' amia,
Per Dieu non sia
Qe ja.l gelos   de mon dan ria,
Qe car vendria
Sa gelozia,   2.5
Si aitals dos   amantz partia;
Q'ieu ja joios   mais non seria,
Ni jois ses vos   pro no.m tenria;
Tal via
Faria   2.10
Q'oms ja   mais no.m veiria;
Cell dia
Morria,
Donna   pros, q'ie.us perdria.   2.14

My fair friend
May it not be, by God
That the jealous one   laughs at my pain
For he would sell dearly
His jealousy
If two such   lovers were parted;
Never again   would I be joyous,
For joy without you   would bring no profit;
Such a road
Would I take
That one never   more would see me;
That day
I would die,
Lady   fine, that I lost you.

Con er perduda
Ni m'er renduda
Donna, s'enanz   non l'ai aguda?
Que drutz ni druda
Non es per cuda;   3.5
Mas qant amantz   en drut si muda,
L'onors es granz   qe.l n'es creguda,
E.l bels semblanz   fai far tal bruda;
Qe nuda
Tenguda   3.10
No.us ai,   ni d'als vencuda;
Volguda,
Cresuda
Vos ai,   ses autr' ajuda.   3.14

How shall I lose
Or regain
A lady, if before   I have not had her?
For one is not a lover
By mere thought;
But when a wooer   is changed to lover,
The honor is great   that is for him increased,
For a sweet glance   produces such fame;
Yet naked
I have not
Held you,   nor won aught else;
I have wanted
And trusted
You   without other aid.

Tart m'esjauzira,	Scarcely would I rejoice
Pos ja.m partira,	If I were to depart,
Bells Cavalhiers, de vos ab ira,	Fair Knight, from you with sorrow,
Q'ailhors no.s vira	My heart does not turn
Mos cors, ni.m tira 4.5	Elsewhere, nor does my desire
Mos deziriers, q'als non dezira;	Draw me, for naught else do I desire;
Q'a lauzengiers sai q'abellira,	To *lauzengiers* I know it would be pleasing,
Donna, q'estiers non lur garira:	Lady, otherwise they could not recover:
Tals vira,	One of them would see
Sentira 4.10	And feel
Mos danz, qi.lls vos grazira,	My troubles, and be grateful to you—
Qe.us mira,	One who admires you,
Cossira	And meditates
Cuidanz, don cors sospira. 4.14	Presumptuously, for which (my) heart sighs.

Tant gent comensa,	Your worth,
Part totas gensa,	Nobler than all,
Na Beatritz, e pren creissensa	Lady Beatrice, so sweetly begins
Vostra valensa;	And increases;
Per ma credensa, 5.5	By my belief,
De pretz garnitz vostra tenensa	You adorn with merit your might
E de bels ditz, senes failhensa;	And with fine words, without fault,
De faitz grazitz tenetz semensa;	And of pleasing deeds you are the source;
Siensa,	Knowledge,
Sufrensa 5.10	Compassion
Avetz e coneissensa;	You have, and discernment;
Valensa	Worth
Ses tensa	Without dispute,
Vistetz ab benvolensa. 5.14	You dress (yourself) in benevolence.

Donna grazida,	Gracious lady
Qecs lauz' e crida	Each praises and proclaims
Vostra valor q'es abellida,	Your merit which is pleasing,
E qi.us oblida,	And to the one who forgets you
Pauc li val vida, 6.5	Life is worth little;
Per q'ie.us azor, Donn' eissernida;	And so I adore you, distinguished lady;
Qar per gençor vos ai chauzida	For as the noblest I have chosen you
E per meilhor, de prez complida,	And as the best, of perfect merit,
Blandida,	I have wooed
Servida 6.10	And served (you)
Genses q'Erecs Enida.	Better than Erec did Enide.
Bastida,	I have composed
Finida,	And finished
N'Engles, ai l'estampida. 6.14	Lord *Engles*, the *estampida*.

Eissamen ai gerreiat ab amor (PC 392.13)

Canso

Eissamen ai gerreiat ab amor
Co.l francs vassals gerrei'ab mal seignor,
Qe.il tol sa terr'a tort, per que.l gerreia,
E qan conois qe.il gerra pro no.il te,   1.4
Pel sieu cobrar ven puois a sa merce;
Et eu ai tant de joi cobrar enveia
C'ad amor qier merce del sieu pechat
E mon orgoill torn en humilitat.   1.8

Gauch ai cobrat, merce de la meillor,
Qe.m restaura lo dan q'ai pres aillor,
E s'amistat per plaich d'amor m'autreia
Ma bella dompn'e per sieu mi rete   2.4
E.m promet tant per qe.l reprovier cre
Que ditz: "qui ben gerreia, ben plaideia";
Q'en chantan ai ab amor gerreiat
Tant c'ab midonz n'ai meillor plait trobat.   2.8

I have made war on love
As the noble vassal makes war on an evil suzerain,
Who wrongfully takes his land so he'll make war,
And then when he learns war is profitless,
To regain his rights, he asks for pardon;
And I have such longing to regain joy
That I beg love's pardon for its own sin
And change my pride to humility.

I have recovered joy and the pity of the best (lady),
Who compensates for the hurt received elsewhere,
And she grants me her friendship in loving agreement,
My fine lady, and retains me in her service,
And promises me so much that I believe the proverb
That says: "Who fights well, agrees well,"
For in singing I have fought with love
So long that I reached a better agreement with my lady.

El mon non a rei ni emperador
Q'en lieis amar non agues plaich d'onor,
Car sa valors e sos pretz seignoreia
Sobre totas las pros dompnas c'om ve,   3.4
Car mieills s'enanss'e plus gen si capte
E mieills acuoill e mieills parl'e dompneia,
E mostr'als pros son pretz e sa beutat,
Salva s'onor, e reten de totz grat.   3.8

Dompna, ben sai, si merces no.m socor,
Qu'eu non vaill tant qe.us taign'ad amador,
Car tant valetz, per que mos cors feuneia
Car non puosc far tant rics faitz co.us cove   4.4
A mi qe.us am; empero no.m recre
De vos amar, que vassals, puois derreia,
Deu poigner tant tro fassa colp honrat,
Per q'ie.us enquis pois m'aguetz conseill dat.   4.8

S'ieu non sui rics segon vostra ricor
Ni pro valens a vostra gran valor,
Mon poder fatz, e sui cel qe.us merceia
E.us serv e.us blan e vos am mais que re   5.4
E.m gart de mal e m'esfortz de tot be
Per vostr'amor, e mieills mi par que deia
Pros dompn'amar bon cavallier prezat
Endreich d'amor c'un ric outracujat.   5.8

Vostre beill huoill plazen, galiador,
Rizon d'aisso don eu sospir e plor,
E l'adreitz cors q'ades genss'e coindeia
M'auci aman, tals enveia m'en ve;   6.4
E si ab vos non trob amor e fe,
Mais no.m creirai en ren c'auia ni veia,
Ni.m fiarai en dompna d'aut barat,
Ni ja non vuoill c'autra.m don s'amistat.   6.8

Bels Cavalliers, vostr' amors mi guerreia,
E prec merce e franc'humilitat
C'aissi.us venssa cum vos m'avetz sobrat.   T1.3 (8)

Na Beatritz, las melhors an enveya
De vostre pretz e de vostra beutat,
Que gensa vos e.l don de Monferrat.   T2.3 (8)

There is no king or emperor in the world
Who in loving her would not reach honorable agreement
For her worth and merit hold dominion
Over all the excellent ladies one sees,
For she advances herself, behaves more graciously,
And receives and speaks better and courts better,
And shows worthy (men) her merit and beauty
Without harming her honor, and is approved by all.

Lady, well I know that if pity does not help me,
I have not such worth as befits your lover,
For you are so worthy that my heart is sad
Since I can't accomplish all the high deeds
That, as your lover, I should; however, I don't stop
Loving you, for a vassal, once he's got behind,
Must spur on until he strikes an honorable blow;
That's why I wooed you after you had counseled me.

If I am not noble to match your noble birth
Nor worthy to equal your great worth,
I do all in my power, and I ask your pity,
And serve and praise you and love you above all else,
And refrain from evil and apply myself to all good
On account of your love, and it seems to me
That a worthy lady must love a worthy knight
More than a presumptuous nobleman.

Your beautiful eyes, pleasing, deceiving,
Laugh at what makes me sigh and weep,
And your shapely body ever sweeter and prettier
Kills me, even as I love you, such desire overcomes me;
And if with you I do not find love and true faith,
I shall no longer believe anything I hear or see,
Nor trust a lady of high degree,
Nor do I want another to give me her friendship.

Fair Knight, my love for you wars with me
And I pray that pity and true humility
May vanquish you as you have conquered me.

Lady Beatrice, the best (ladies) are envious
Of your merit and of your beauty
Which adorn you and the Lord of Montferrat.

CASTELLOZA

The poetic activity of Castelloza can probably be dated to the first third of the 13th century. As with other trobairitz, we know very little about the woman herself. According to her *vida*, she was from the Auvergne, married to a man named Truc or Turc Mairona, mentioned in a sirventes by the Dauphin d'Auvergne (PC 119.9). She may well have been associated with the court of the Dauphin (1155-1235), who was both poet and patron, and she may have met there the troubadour Peirol, whose works she seems to have known. The first line of a song that can be attributed to Castelloza, although it is anonymous in the one manuscript that has preserved it, "Per ioi que d'amor m'avegna," recalls Peirol's "Per dan que d'amor mi veigna" (in this Anthology).

It is difficult, given the few songs we have, to characterize Castelloza's talent. Three songs are attributed to her, and the one anonymous song mentioned above is usually included in her corpus. The songs are all *cansos*; she cultivated established troubadour discourse as did the Comtessa de Dia, to whom she can be compared. But her songs are less varied than those of the Comtessa. They constitute intensely personal meditations on the main theme of love's betrayal seen from the woman's point of view (Paden et al. 1981-82, Dronke 1984a, Bruckner 1992).

EDITIONS: Schultz[-Gora] 1888; Paden et al. 1981-82; Rieger 1991; Bec 1995; Bruckner et al. 1995.

• "Mout avetz faich long estatge": PC 109.3. Sources, mss. A 169, I 125, K 111, N 228, d 311. Text: Schultz[-Gora],

24. The five *coblas unissonans* with 10-line stanzas and alternating masculine and feminine rhymes (a7′ b7 a7′ b7 c7′ d7 d7 c7′ e7′ e7′) carry an argument intended to bring the trobairitz' lover back to her. Their relationship is initially set out in terms of "feudal" fidelity: though he has pledged and sworn his faith to her (1.4), he has deceived her by doing "castle guard" ("estatge") for another. Hers is a female speaking voice that takes on certain attributes of the male speaking voice (she loves him even if he gives harm for good, 2.6; she is enriched and ennobled by love 3.8; without love she will die 4.10) but remains situated in feminine space, requiring that the man send her messages (3.3).

5.1-4: These lines are not clear. Paden proposed a reading for line 1: "Tot lo maltrag e.l dampnatge" giving the translation "I endure all the suffering and the loss that is destined to me through you—my family makes you welcome, and especially my husband!" (179). This reading has not been accepted by other editors, however. Dronke (1984a, 150) offers the translation "All the affliction and harm that have been my lot because of you, my birth makes me thank you for these—and my husband above all." As Pierre Bec points out, the only thing we can be sure of is that Castelloza presents herself as having a husband. From there, we may either think that her love has ennobled her family and even her husband, or in a severely ironic mode we can think that the husband is quite happy about his wife's suffering, which turns her into a *malmariée* (Bec, 87).

Mout avetz faich long estatge (PC 109.3)
Canso

Mout avetz faich long estatge,	You have made a long sojourn
Amics, pois de mi.us partitz,	Friend, since you left me,
Et es me greu e salvatge,	And it is painful and cruel to me,
Quar me juretz e.m plevitz	For you swore and pledged
Que als jorns de vostra vida 1.5	That all the days of your life
Non acsetz dompna mas me;	You would receive no lady but me;
E si d'autra vos perte,	And if another has your attention,
M'avetz morta e trahida,	You have killed and betrayed me,
Qu'avi'en vos m'esperanssa	For I had my hope in you
Que m'amassetz ses doptanssa. 1.10	That you might love me without deceit.

Bels amics, de fin coratge
Vos amei, pois m'abellitz,
E sai que faich ai follatge,
Que plus m'en etz escaritz;
Qu'anc non fis vas vos ganchida,   2.5
E si.m fasetz mal per be:
Be.us am e non m'en recre;
Mas tan m'a amors sazida
Qu'ieu non cre que benananssa
Puosc'aver ses vostr'amanssa.   2.10

Mout aurai mes mal usatge
A las autras amairitz:
Qu'om sol trametre messatge
E motz triatz e chausitz.
Et ieu tenc me per garida,   3.5
Amics, a la mia fe,
Quan vos prec, qu'aissi.m cove;
Que.l plus pros n'es enriquida
S'a de vos qualqu'aondanssa
De baisar o d'acoindanssa.   3.10

Mal aj'ieu, s'anc cor volatge
Vos aic ni.us fui camjairitz,
Ni drutz de negun paratge
Per me non fo encobitz;
Anz sui pensiv'e marrida   4.5
Car de m'amor no.us sove,
E si de vos jois no.m ve,
Tost me trobaretz fenida:
Car per pauc de malananssa
Mor dompna, s'om tot no.il lanssa.   4.10

Tot lo maltraich e.l dampnatge
Que per vos m'es escaritz
Vos fai grazir mos linhatge
E sobre totz mos maritz;
E s'anc fetz vas me fallida,   5.5
Perdon la.us per bona fe;
E prec que venhatz a me,
Despois quez auretz auzida
Ma chanson, que.us fatz fiansa
Sai trobetz bella semblansa.   5.10

Fine friend, with noble heart
I loved you, since you pleased me,
And I know I have acted foolishly,
For you are more aloof from me as a result;
Never have I refused you
And if you give me harm for good
Still I love you and do not recant;
But love has so captured me
That I do not believe that happiness
Can be mine without your love.

I will have shown a very bad example
To the other women in love,
For the man usually sends a message
And distinctive and choice words.
And I deem myself satisfied
Friend, by my faith,
When I entreat you, for so it suits me;
The most worthy woman is enriched
If she has from you a good amount
Of kissing or greeting.

May harm strike me if ever a fickle heart
I showed you or was unfaithful to you,
Or if a lover of any rank
Was coveted by me;
Rather am I pensive and troubled
Because you do not remember my love,
And if from you joy does not come to me,
Soon you will find me dead;
For from her malady
A lady all but dies if no one helps her.

All the mistreatment and the harm
That have come to me from you
Make my family thank you
And above all my husband;
And if ever you sinned towards me,
I pardon you in good faith;
And I pray that you may come to me,
When you will have heard
My song, for I assure you
Here you will find a handsome greeting.

The COMTESSA DE PROENSA (Garsenda de Forcalquier) and GUI DE CAVAILLON

The Comtessa de Provence, who has been securely identified as Garsenda de Forcalquier, held from 1213-1220 the most important county in Provence. She followed in a long line of strong women who exercised political power in that region. She presided over a court at Aix-en-Provence mentioned by a number of troubadours. In his *Abrils issi'e mays intrava* (l. 626, Field 1971), the Catalan troubadour Raimon Vidal refers to a visit to the Count and Countess of Provence, doubtless Garsenda and her husband, and not Beatrice of Savoy as was earlier thought (Field, 179; Page 1989, 52, but see Rieger 1991, 208; Bec 1995, 146). The only piece we have from Garsenda is this *cobla* exchanged with Gui de Cavaillon, a troubadour who flourished between 1205 and 1229, who defended the cause of the Counts of Toulouse during the Albigensian Crusade, and from whom we have a number of songs (PC 192).

EDITIONS: Schultz[-Gora] 1888; Rieger 1991; Bec 1995; Bruckner et al. 1995.

● "Vos que.m semblatz dels corals amadors": PC 187.1; 192.6. Sources: mss. F 47, T 86. Text: Schultz[-Gora], 21. The *cobla* is a mixed genre. It may have from one to three stanzas, sometimes with a *tornada*. *Coblas* may be invented by one poet or, as here, become an exchange between poets. *Coblas* were intended for singing, if we may believe the 13th-century troubadour Bertran Carbonel: "Cobla ses so es enaissi / col molis que aigua non a; / per que fai mal qui cobla fa / si son non li don'atressi." ("A *cobla* without a melody / is like a mill without water; / he does badly who makes a *cobla* / if he does not give it a tune." PC 82.83 [the statement has been erroneously attributed to Folquet de Marseilla]). As a genre, the *cobla* is difficult to circumscribe since the term refers also, and more usually, to a stanza that is part of a longer poem. The generic designation *cobla* first appears in the late 12th century; in the 13th century, *coblas* were widely cultivated.

The *cobla* exchange between the Comtessa and her *amador* is in the nature of a *tenso*. The problem debated is the appropriate conduct of lovers and ladies: who should woo whom, in what way and with what result. It is instructive to compare this exchange to other songs in which similar questions are raised. These *coblas* take the metrical structure of Gaucelm Faidit's "Ja mais nuill temps no.m pot ren far amors"; Garsenda may have been deliberately referring to Gaucelm's poem (Rieger, 211-2).

Vos que.m semblatz dels corals amadors (PC 187.1; 192.6)
Coblas

Vos que.m semblatz dels corals amadors,		You seem to me so sincere a lover,
Ja non volgra que fossetz tan doptanz;		I do wish you wouldn't be so hesitant;
E platz mi molt quar vos destreing m'amors,		But I'm glad my love torments you,
Qu'atressi sui eu per vos malananz.		Otherwise I'm the one to suffer.
Ez avetz dan en vostre vulpillatge	1.5	Still, you are harmed by your cowardice
Quar no.us ausatz de preiar enardir,		If you're not brave enough to woo,
E faitz a vos ez a mi gran dampnatge;		And you do both of us great harm;
Que ges dompna non ausa descobrir		For a lady doesn't dare uncover
Tot so qu'il vol per paor de faillir.	1.9	Her true will, for fear of being at fault.
Bona dompna, vostr'onrada valors		Good lady, your esteemed merit
Mi fai temeros estar, tan es granz,		Makes me fearful, so great it is,
E no.m o tol negun'autra paors		And no other fear prevents me
Qu'eu non vos prec; que.us volria enanz		From wooing you; for I should prefer
Tan gen servir que non fezes oltratge —	2.5	To serve you so well that you would not be outraged
Qu'aissi.m sai eu de preiar enardir —		(You see, I do know how to find the courage to woo),
E volria que.l faich fosson messatge,		And I should wish that deeds were messengers to you,
E presessetz en loc de precs servir:		And you accepted them in wooing's place:
Qu'us honratz faitz deu be valer un dir.	2.9	For a noble deed should be as good as words.

PEIRE CARDENAL

Peire Cardenal's life covered almost the entire span of the 13th century; he wrote most of his poems between 1200 and 1272, during the period of the Albigensian crusade. He was probably born in Puy-en-Velay, a member of a noble family. After having first studied at the cathedral school to prepare for a career in the church, he became a court poet and stayed for some time at the courts of Raimon VI and Raimon VII of Toulouse, briefly visited the court of Uc de Baux, and travelled to Spain, to the court of James I of Aragon, possibly even to the celebrated court of Alfonso the Wise. Evidence indicates that he was married and had several children.

Peire Cardenal was a master of the political and the moral *sirventes*. He cultivated much less the *canso*; the ones we have tend to be heavily ironic with regard to the courtly universe. Other pieces, most of them *coblas*, speak of women, not always in flattering terms. Several new designations were adopted by Cardenal, such as the *estribot* (a satire of religious orders: Vatteroni 1990) or the *faula* (a short moral narrative). He selected for his particular targets the hypocrisy of the church, the cruelty of Simon de Montfort, and the corruption of the French. His work constitutes a sharp reaction against the historical events and forces—the Albigensian Crusade, the Inquisition—that would help undermine Occitan society and the brilliant culture it had supported. But he also unleashed his vigorous rhetoric on the foibles of private individuals and the weaknesses of social groups. He can be compared to Marcabru among the Occitan poets or to his northern French contemporary Rutebeuf. His corpus includes over 90 poems; three melodies have been preserved.

EDITIONS: Lavaud 1957; van der Werf 1984.

• ''Ar me puesc ieu lauzar d'Amor'': PC 335.7. Sources: mss. C 273, D^b 233, I 170, K 156, R 72, T 98, d 331, f 34, α 34277; music in R. Text: Lavaud, 2. According to Lavaud this would be an early song, demonstrating both mastery of courtly themes and a witty disavowal of those themes along with the vocabulary used to express them. The last two stanzas following the poet's ''escape'' (3.10) turn toward a moralizing critique of unbridled sexual desire (''lo faitz desmezuratz,'' 4.7) and the ever more frenetically repeated words and sounds seem to become a linguistic reflection of the poet's anger. The formal structure of the poem (a8 b8 a8 b8 c6' d8 d8 c6' d8 d8, with rhymes *or, ir, atge, atz*) is used by 10 other poets (Frank, 424:1-11). Ms. R attributes the same melody to both Guiraut de Bornelh (''Non puesc sofrir'') and Peire Cardenal. Peire Cardenal's song can be thought of as a parodic imitation of Guiraut de Bornelh, which deepens its ironic intent. With Peire Cardenal as with Bertran de Born, imitation of form (and music) was an important device (Marshall 1978-79 and 1980). The melody is syllabic throughout with few melismas. *D* is established as a tonal focus, chiefly by the cadences. Repetitions of melodic phrases are not regular. One can note similarities of concluding motion in phrases 1 and 5, and again in 2 and 6; one may also note that 3 and 4 are exactly or almost exactly repeated for phrases 5 and 6. This isolates 7 and 8 which resemble each other, conclude both on *d*, and with the repeated rhyme ''atz'' bring a strong close. Line 5 plays a pivotal role; it is both a return and a new departure. Since each stanza of this song is made up of a series of statements reaching at the end a conclusion, the somewhat ambiguous relationship of the melody to the metrical pattern allows each statement to stand alone, while the strong repetition at the end affirms the conclusion. One cannot say that Peire Cardenal intended specific coordinations of words and melody since this is in all likelihood a borrowed melody. One can propose, however, that the combined melodic and metrical structures function as well for the Cardenal poem as they do for the Bornelh poem, and this may be a part of Peire's imitative and parodic technique.

• ''Tartarassa ni voutour'': PC 335.55. Sources: mss. C 286, I 169, K 154, R 68, d 329. Text: Lavaud, 490. This is one of Peire Cardenal's best known songs, and it is a good illustration of his manner. The criticism of particular groups is elevated to a moral discourse on the human condition and man's relation to God. The ''clerc e prezicador'' (1.3) probably refer to the newly founded Dominicans, established in Toulouse in 1216. The idea that Peire Cardenal could at the end of the poem ask God's forgiveness for those very persons he had attacked so bitterly at the outset of the poem has seemed abrupt to some critics. But the ability to attain a wider vision than the specific focus of the beginning makes of the song more than a simple poem of circumstance. This poem shares metrical structure and rhyme sounds with a song by Bernart de Ventadorn, ''Ara.m cosselhatz, seignor''; imitation may here, too, be involved.

Ar me puesc ieu lauzar d'Amor (PC 335.7)
Canso

Ar me puesc ieu lauzar d'Amor,	Now I can boast about love
Que no.m tol manjar ni dormir;	That it doesn't stop me from eating or sleeping;
Ni.n sent freidura ni calor	Nor am I, on account of it, cold or hot
Ni non badail ni no.n sospir	Nor do I yawn or sigh
Ni.n vauc de nueg arratge. 1.5	Or wander about at night.
Ni.n soi conquistz ni.n soi cochatz,	Nor am I conquered by it nor desirous,
Ni.n soi dolenz ni.n soi iratz	Neither am I sad or irritated,
Ni no.n logui messatge;	Nor do I hire a messenger;
Ni.n soi trazitz ni enganatz	Neither am I tricked or betrayed,
Que partitz m'en soi ab mos datz. 1.10	For I came away with all my dice.
Autre plazer n'ai ieu maior,	I have from it another pleasure greater:
Que no.n traïsc ni fauc traïr,	I do not betray or cause (others) to betray,
Ni.n tem tracheiris ni trachor,	Nor do I fear traitress or traitor,
Ni brau gilos que m'en azir;	Nor disagreeable jealous one who hates me for it;
Ni.n fauc fol vassalatge, 2.5	Nor do I perform foolish exploits,
Ni.n soi feritz ni derocatz,	Nor am I wounded or destroyed,
Ni no.n soi pres ni deraubatz,	Nor am I captured or robbed,
Ni no.n fauc lonc badatge,	Nor do I engage in vain waiting
Ni dic qu'ieu soi d'amor forsatz,	Nor say that I am dominated by love,
Ni dic que mos cors m'es emblatz. 2.10	Nor say that my heart is taken from me.
Ni dic qu'ieu mor per la gensor,	Nor do I say that I die for the noblest lady,
Ni dic que.l bella.m fai languir,	Nor say that the fair one makes me languish,
Ni non la prec ni non l'azor,	Nor do I entreat her or adore her,
Ni la deman ni la dezir;	Nor ask her nor desire her;
Ni no.l fas homenatge, 3.5	Nor do I pay homage to her,
Ni no.l m'autrei ni.l me soi datz,	Nor do I octroy or give myself to her,
Ni non soi sieus endomenjatz,	Nor am I her vassal,
Ni a mon cor en gatge,	Nor have I pledged my heart,
Ni soi sos pres ni sos liatz,	Nor am I her prisoner or bound to her,
Anz dic qu'ieu li soi escapatz. 3.10	Rather I say that I have escaped from her.

Mais deu hom lauzar vensedor	But one should praise the victor
No fai vencut, qui.l ver vol dir,	Not the vanquished, truth to tell;
Car lo vencens porta la flor	For the victor bears the flower
E.l vencut vai hom sebelir;	And the vanquished they are going to bury;
E qui venc son coratge 4.5	And he who vanquishes his heart
De las desleials voluntatz	(By surmounting) disloyal desires,
Don ieis lo faitz desmezuratz	Whence comes the unreasonable act
E li autre outratge,	And the other offenses,
D'aquel venser es plus onratz	For this victory is more honored
Que si vensia cent ciutatz. 4.10	Than if he had vanquished a hundred cities.

Pauc pres prim prec de pregador,	I prize little the prayer of an aspirant,
Can cre qu'il, cuy quer convertir,	When I believe that the one he seeks to convert
Vir vas vil voler sa valor,	Turns towards vile wishes her value,
Don dreitz deu dar dan al partir;	Whence right must give harm at the beginning;
Si sec son sen salvatge, 5.5	If he follows his untamed wisdom
Leu l'er lo larcx laus lag loinhatz;	Soon will the fervent praise be hatefully banished;
Plus pres lauzables que lauzatz.	I prize more the praiseworthy than the praised.
Trop ten estreg ostatge	He is in too narrow a dwelling
Dreitz drutz del dart d'amor nafratz.	The true lover pierced by love's dart.
Pus pauc pres, pus pres es compratz. 5.10	I prize less when the prize is purchased.

Non voilh voler volatge	I do not want a fickle will
Que.m volv e.m vir mas voluntatz	Which turns and twists my desire
Mas lai on mos vols es volatz. T.3 (10)	Except there where my will has flown.

Tartarassa ni voutor (PC 335.55)
Sirventes

Tartarassa ni voutor	Neither buzzard nor vulture
No sent tan leu carn puden	Smells stinking flesh
Quom clerc e prezicador	As rapidly as clergy and preachers
Senton ont es lo manen. 1.4	Smell out where the rich man is.
Mantenen son sei privat,	Immediately they are his intimates
E quant malautia.l bat,	And when sickness strikes
Fan li far donassïo	They have him make a donation
Tal que.l paren no.i an pro. 1.8	Such that his relatives have no advantage.

Franses e clerc an lauzor	Frenchmen and clergy are praised
De mal, quar ben lur en pren;	For evil, since good comes to them from it.
E renovier e trachor	And usurers and traitors
An tot lo segl'eissamen, 2.4	Likewise own the world.
C'ab mentir et ab barat	With lying and cheating
An si tot lo mon torbat	They have so confused the world,
Que no.i a religïo	That there is no religious order
Que no.n sapcha sa leisso. 2.8	Which does not know their lesson.

Saps qu'endeven la ricor
De sels que l'an malamen?
Venra un fort raubador
Que non lur laissara ren: 3.4
So es la mortz, que.ls abat,
C'ab catr'aunas de filat
Los tramet en tal maizo
Ont atrobon de mal pro.   3.8

Hom, per que fas tal follor
Que passes lo mandamen
De Dieu, quez es ton senhor
E t'a format de nïen?   4.4
La trueia ten al mercat
Sel que ab Dieu si combat,
Qu'el n'aura tal guizardo
Com ac Judas lo fello.   4.8

Dieus verais, plens de doussor,
Senher, sias nos guiren!
Gardas d'enfernal dolor
Peccadors e de turmen,   5.4
E solves los del peccat
En que son pres e liat,
E faitz lur veray perdo,
Ab vera confessïo!   5.8

Do you know what becomes of the wealth
Of those who gain it through evil?
There will come a great robber
Who will leave them nothing:
That is Death who strikes them down
And with four yards of cloth
Transports them to such a house
Where they find plenty of anguish.

Man, why do you engage in such folly
As to transgress the commandment
Of God who is your Lord
And created you out of nothing?
He takes his sow to market,
The one who fights God,
And he will have the same reward
As Judas the traitor.

True God full of sweetness,
Lord be our protector!
Keep from infernal pain
And torment all sinners,
And absolve them from the sin
In which they are caught and bound,
And give them true pardon
With true confession!

GUIRAUT RIQUIER

Guiraut Riquier, whose works date from 1254-1292, is often called the "last of the troubadours." He creates in his works the impression of a poet/composer struggling to maintain the true art of *trobar* in difficult times. The impression is not entirely false: although composing verses continued in southern France well beyond the time of Guiraut, the brilliant tradition of Occitan *song* increasingly faded in the next century with the rise of a writerly poetics. The works of Guiraut strikingly demonstrate the beginning of this poetics. Exceptionally in the troubadour repertory, these songs have been preserved as a collection in the two manuscripts which contain them (C and R), grouped and dated as though by Guiraut's own hand (Bossy 1991). Riquier began his career in Narbonne, moving then to Spain around 1270, to the prestigious court of Alfonso X of Castile, where he spent ten years before returning to southern France, to Rodez and possibly again to Narbonne. His more than 100 surviving songs include 48 melodies, more than for any other troubadour. The melodies largely exploit the by now settled paradigm ABABX (Dante's *pedes cum cauda*) but they are often richly ornamented and careful attention to written detail tends to reduce the role of "improvisation" (Phan 1987). Religious themes are significantly more in evidence in Guiraut's works than was the case with earlier troubadours and tend to displace secular love motifs in his later pieces. By the time of Guiraut, genres had been elaborated theoretically; he gives to each of his songs a specific generic designation. There is great variety of genre: *tenso*, *alba*, *retroencha*, epistles composed in rhymed couplets, as well as *vers* (designated *sirventes* by most modern editors) and *canso*. A series of *pastorelas* is linked by a story in which the poet dialogues on several occasions with the same shepherdess.

Guiraut was a formidable technician. He left the only song we have where an attempt is made to create both poetic *and* melodic *coblas capcaudadas*: *Pus sabers no.m val* (PC 248.66). The directions and the first stanza will demonstrate the method:

> Canson redonda ez encadenada de motz e de son d'en Guiraut Riquier, facha l'an M CC LXXXII en abril, e·l sos de la segonda cobla pren se el mieg de la primeira e sec se tro la fin, pueys torna al comensamen de la primeira e fenis en la mieja de la pri[mi]meira aissi, quon es senhat; pueys tota la cansos canta se aissi: la primeira et la tersa e la quinta d'una maneira, et la segonda et la quarta et la sexta d'autra maneira; ez aquesta cansos es la XXa IIIa.

Canson redonda ez encadenada, both words and melody, by Guiraut Riquier, made in the year 1282 in April, and the melody of the second stanza takes up in the middle of the first and follows along to the end, then returns to the beginning of the first and ends in the middle of the first as is indicated by the sign; then the whole song is sung thusly: the first and the third and the fifth in one way, and the second and the fourth and the sixth in another manner; and this song is the 23rd.

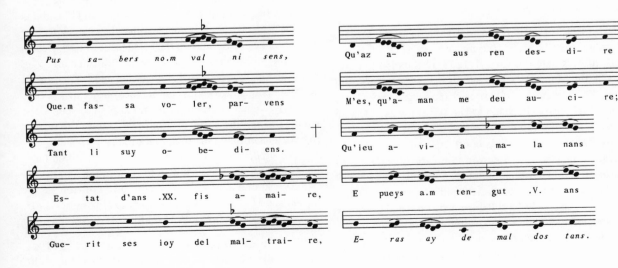

For the entire poem, this produces the following schema:

ens	ire			ans	aire		
ans	aire			ens	ire		
a	b	a b	a	c	d	c d	c
7	7′	7 7′	7	7	7′	7 7′	7
A	B	A B	C	D	E	D E	F

Stanzas 1, 3, 5, begin here

Stanzas 2, 4, 6, begin . . . . here

Combined intricacy of metrical and musical structures can scarcely be carried beyond this point. It is to be noted that the instructions concerning how the song is to be performed appear in ms. C (given here) although there is no music. This has been taken to indicate that the scribe of C used an exemplar with music but did not himself have the means to notate the melodies (Bertolucci 1978, 239).

EDITIONS: Pfaff, 1853; Anglés 1926; Mölk 1962; Longobardi 1982-3; van der Werf 1984.

• "Be.m degra de chantar tener": PC 248.17. Source: ms. C 307. Text: Pfaff, 78. Since this piece bears the latest date of all Guiraut's works, it has often been looked upon as his farewell to song. Thematically it serves that purpose. The five octosyllabic stanzas constructed on one of the most widely used rhyme schemes, abbaccdd, are chiefly distinguished by the use of *coblas capcaudadas* and *retrogradadas*: the last rhyme sound of one stanza becomes the first rhyme sound of the next and then the following rhymes are repeated in inverse order. Because the rhyme scheme is different in both halves of the stanza, the exact pattern of the first stanza can only come back again in the fifth, where it effects closure. From a rejection of what he perceives to be a degenerate courtly world—he has come too late to participate in an art he could admire (2.8)—Guiraut moves to a prayer to the Virgin, a trajectory that retraces, as it were, his career.

• "Humils, forfaitz, repres e penedens": PC 248.44. Sources: mss. C 295, R 106; music in R. Text: Pfaff, 31. Both rubrics date the song to 1273. C calls it "lo quint vers" ("the fifth *vers*"); R identifies it as a "*vers* de Nostra Dona." The second *tornada* situates the song at the brilliant court of Alfonso X El Sabio ("The Wise") where Occitan works were admired and to which Guiraut had betaken himself about 1270. At this court, Alfonso compiled the extraordinary song collection, the *Cantigas de Santa María,* in which troubadour inspiration figures prominently. Yet even this court, when Guiraut arrived, was past its prime. The stately 10-syllable poetic lines and the richly ornamented melody are responsible for the reputation the song has attained among modern critics as an example of the transformation in Guiraut's works of secular themes into songs of praise of the Virgin Mary. The melody sets a tonal focus on *d*, defined initially by the opening on *a*, the coming to rest on *d* at the caesura, and the regularly alternating cadences *f / d* in the first part of the song, confirmed by the final cadence of line 7. Syntactical groupings are flexible; noteworthy, for example, are the run-on line from 2 to 3 in the first stanza, a *rejet* of the verb by means of which it is highlighted, and the weaker carry-over of sense from lines 4 to 5, emphasizing the words *Maires de Crist.* Such syntactical subtleties soften the cadences on *d* of lines 2 and 4. True closure comes only at the end with the extensive ornamentation of the feminine rhyme.

• "Pus astres no m'es donatz": PC 248.65. Sources: mss. C 306, R 110; music in R. Text: Pfaff, 80. Performed on Anthology CD. Both manuscripts date this "first *retroencha*" to 1262 (the dating in Pfaff and in Martín de Riquer's anthology [1975] is incorrect). Although this song can no longer be considered a farewell to Narbonne, it was doubtless composed there and suggests that already in the early 1260s Riquier was thinking of turning elsewhere to seek the inspiration he no longer found at home. That he would turn to Catalonia is not surprising, given its close linguistic and political ties to southern France; if Guiraut did visit Catalonia, however, he did not stay, but pushed on to Castile. The *retroencha* is unusual in the troubadour repertory (there are only two others besides the three composed by Riquier); it is considered to be of French inspiration (Chambers 1985, 233); this song is the first known Occitan example. The distinguishing feature of the genre is the refrain, here of 2 lines. The refrain does not rhyme with any other verses in the stanza; all the other rhyme sounds change following a sequence of *coblas singulars*. Thus both for sound and for sense, the refrain anchors the piece. The melody, both sprightly and restrained, plays out, within the range of the sixth *c - a*, a series of exact and nearly exact repetitions: phrases 3 and 4 repeat 1 and 2; 7 and 8 closely follow 5 and 6; the two lines of the refrain are similar. The first four phrases open on *d*, that note occurs most frequently in lines 2 and 4, and *d* is the final cadence; but it is not clear that the piece will close on *d* until the end because of the persistence of cadences on *e* and the prominence of the secondary third chain *c-e-g*. Thus the tonality is somewhat uncertain and the ending all the more poignant. The line before the refrain always contains a reference to *Cataluenha*, and in the last stanza, the rhyme of that line is the feminine version of the refrain rhyme, thus bringing the song to a strong conclusion.

3.3: *Belh Deport* is a senhal for an unidentified lady; but Guiraut himself uses it also to refer to the Virgin (PC 248.88), so one may see in it a conflation of troubadour *domna* and Mother of God. (Chambers 1971; Anglade 1905, 297; see especially Bossy 1991 for the role of *Belh Deport*)

• "Tant m'es plazens le mals d'amor": PC 248.82. Sources: mss. C 288, R 103; music in R. Text: Mölk, 20. This is the first song in Guiraut's book, dated 1254 and marked, in R, by a decorated letter. The decoration portrays a woman, wearing a crown, whose features are similar to those of the Christ figure with which the manuscript inaugurated the first song of Marcabru. The woman is thus simultaneously queen and Virgin. The themes developed in the song are typical of the *canso*. If, however, *Belh Deport* can be this early identified as the Virgin, *Tant m'es plazens* announces the kinds of thematic transformations of the secular love song that will become typical of Riquier. The melody remains quite resolutely focused on *d* with a structure of phrase repetitions that follows a basic pattern ABAB CDEF. There are brief repeated motives for incipits, notably for the transition between lines 4 and 5 , and for the opening notes of line 6, which return at the same pitch level in line 7 (both times realizing the third chain *f-a-c*), and are echoed though not exactly repeated a third lower in line 8.

This structures both the climax and the close of the second part of the melody. The syntax generally supports a division of the stanza into two equal parts; the run-on line in 5.4-5 becomes all the more striking an evocation of love-death, and at this point the repeated melodic incipit takes on fresh expressive value.

1.2: Melody position 4: The text in R has one syllable too many, thus one note too many. The notes in brackets accompany two syllables in the manuscript.

7.1: Bernat d'Orlargue is probably the father-in-law of Guilhem d'Andusa who became the brother-in-law of Amalric of Narbonne (Chambers 1971).

7.4: Oupia is in the Hérault; Bertran was doubtless a knight from that region (Chambers 1971).

Guiraut Riquier, "Tant mes plazens lo mal damor" (p. 176). Ms. R, f. 103v. The decorated letter shows the lady's head with a white crown, stylistic details matching f. 5r. The rubric states: "aiso es la primieira canso den Gr. Riquier lan M.CC.LIII." Cliché Bibliothèque Nationale de France - Paris.

Be.m degra de chantar tener (PC 248.17)
Vers

Lo XXVII vers d'En Guiraut
Riquier, fag en l'an MCCLXXXXII.

The 27th *vers* by Guiraut
Riquier made in the year 1292.

Be.m degra de chantar tener,
Quar a chan coven alegriers,
E mi destrenh tant cossiriers
Que.m fa de totas partz doler;   1.4
Remembran mon greu temps passat,
Esgardan lo prezent forsat
E cossiran l'avenidor,
Que per totz ai razon que plor.   1.8

I should certainly refrain from singing;
For to song, happiness is fitting,
And worry constrains me so much
That it causes pain from all sides;
Remembering my cruel past
Looking at the oppressive present
And considering the future,
For all that I have reason to weep.

Per que no.m deu aver sabor
Mos chans, qu'es ses alegretat;
Mas Dieus m'a tal saber donat
Qu'en chantan retrac ma folhor,   2.4
Mo sen, mon gauch, mon desplazer,
E mon dan et mon pro per ver,
Qu'a penas dic ren ben estiers;
Mas trop suy vengutz als derriers.   2.8

That's why I have no taste
For my song, for it is without happiness;
But God has given me such skill
That in singing I retrace my folly
My sense, my joy, my displeasure
My pain and my profit truly,
For I scarcely say anything else good;
But I have come too late, at the last.

Qu'er non es grazitz lunhs mestiers
Menhs en cort que de belh saber
De trobar; qu'auzir e vezer
Hi vol hom mais captenhs leugiers   3.4
E critz mesclatz ab dezonor;
Quar tot, quan sol donar lauzor,
Es al pus del tot oblidat,
Que.l mons es quays totz en barat.   3.8

For now no ability is received
Less well at court than the fine art
Of composition; for hearing and seeing
Are preferably devoted to frivolous conduct
And cries mixed with dishonor;
All that used to elicit praise
Is completely forgotten,
For the world is given over to deceit.

Per erguelh e per malvestat
Dels Christias ditz, luenh d'amor
E dels mans de Nostre Senhor,
Em del sieu Sant Loc discipat   4.4
Ab massa d'autres encombriers;
Don par qu'elh nos es aversiers
Per desadordenat voler
E per outracujat poder.   4.8

On account of the pride and the wickedness
Of so-called Christians, far from love
And from the commands of Our Lord,
We are now put out of the Holy Sepulchre
With a great number of other setbacks;
From which it seems that He is against us
On account of disordered desire
And overweening power.

Lo greu perilh devem temer
De dobla mort, qu'es prezentiers,
Que.ns sentam Sarrazis sobriers,
E Dieus que.ns giet a non chaler;   5.4
Et entre nos, qu'em azirat,
Tost serem del tot aterrat;
E no.s cossiran la part lor,
Segon que.m par, nostre rector.   5.8

We should fear the grievous peril
Of double death which is present;
Let us feel the Saracens dominating
And God forgetting us;
And we who are hateful among ourselves,
Quickly we will be completely struck down;
And they do not think of their duty,
As I see it, our leaders.

Selh que crezem en unitat,
Poder, savïeza, bontat,
Done a sas obras lugor,
Don sian mundat peccador.   T1.4 (8)

May He in whom our belief finds oneness,
Power, wisdom, goodness,
Cast light on His works
By which sinners may be purified.

Dona, Maires de caritat,
Acapta nos per pïetat
De ton filh, nostre redemptor,
Gracia, perdon et amor.   T2.4 (8)

Lady, Mother of charity
Secure for us, out of pity,
From your son, Our Redeemer,
Grace, pardon and love.

Humils, forfaitz, repres e penedens (PC 248.44)
Vers

Lo quint vers d'En Guiraut
Riquier, l'an MCCLXXIII.

The fifth *vers* by Guiraut
Riquier, in the year 1273.

Hu- mils, for- faitz, re- pres e pe- ne- dens,

En- tris- te- zitz, mar- ritz de re- ve- nir

So, qu'ay per- dut de mon temps per fa- lhir.

Vos clam mer- ce, Do- na, Ver- ges pla- zens,

Mai- res de Crist, filh del Tot po- de- ros,

Que no gar- detz cum suy for- faitz vas vos;

Si.us plai, gar- datz l'ops de m'ar- ma mar- ri- da.

Humils, forfaitz, repres e penedens,
Entristezitz, marritz de revenir
So, qu'ay perdut de mon temps per falhir.
Vos clam merce, Dona, Verges plazens,   1.4
Maires de Crist, filh del Tot poderos,
Que no gardetz cum suy forfaitz vas vos;
Si.us plai, gardatz l'ops de m'arma marrida.

Qu'a penas truep nulh peccat de mi mens,
Sal desesper e raubar et aucir;
Que dels autres mos cors no.s pot complir,
Don suy avutz mantas vetz malsabens;   2.4
Quar si espers ab bona fe no fos,
Per trop peccatz greus, vils e vergonhos,
Fora m'arma del tot de Dieu partida.

Humble, guilty, accused and repentant,
Saddened, unhappy to return
I am, for I have lost my time on account of sin.
I beg mercy, Lady, gracious Virgin,
Mother of Christ, son of the all-powerful,
That you take no account of my sin towards you;
If it please you, consider the need of my miserable soul.

I find scarcely no sin lacking to me
Save desperation, robbery and murder;
For of the others my body cannot get its fill
Whence has come to me many times displeasure.
For if there were not hope with good faith,
On account of grievous sins, vile and shameful,
My soul would have completely left God.

Mas esper ai que.m siatz vos guirens
Del greu perilh mortal que.m fa marrir,
De que no puesc per ren ses vos issir:
Tans e tan greus trobi mos fallimens!   3.4
E donc pregatz vostre filh glorïos
Que.m fassa far sos plazers e mos pros,
Qu'aissi.m podetz tornar de mort a vida.

Quar Jhezus Cristz vos es obedïens
Quan lo pregatz de peccadors guerir,
Sol que.l vuellan be fazen obezir;
Per que per mi e per mos benvolens   4.4
E per totz selhs de be far deziros
Vos prec, Dona, que.l preguetz qu'elh a nos
Don per anar a lhuy veraya guida.

Que.l camis es de comensar cozens,
Tant es estreitz et aspres per fromir;
E quar del mon se fa tan greu partir,
Es del camin greus sos comensamens,   5.4
E l'acabars es pus greus per un dos:
Tans hi trob'om de passes perilhos
Que nuls ses guit no va tro la guandida.

Per nos, Dona, Verges regina, fos
Maires del filh de Dieu tot poderos:
Doncx acaptatz d'elh a nos esta guida.   T1.3 (7)

Dieu prec del rey de Castella N'Anfos,
Que a son cors don honramens e pros
Lonc temps ab grat et espirital vida.   T2.3 (7)

But I have hope that you may protect me
From the grievous mortal peril that afflicts me,
From which I cannot at all come out without you;
So numerous and so grievous I find my sins!
And so pray your glorious Son
That he lead me to his pleasure and my profit,
So that you may turn me from death to life.

For Jesus Christ obeys you
When you pray him to cure sinners,
Provided they wish to obey by doing good;
That's why for me and for my friends
And for all those desirous of doing good
I pray you, Lady, that you pray that He
Give us a true guide to go to Him.

For the road is painful to begin
And is so narrow and harsh to complete;
And because it is so difficult to leave the world,
The beginning of the road is grievous,
And the completion is two times more difficult:
One finds along it so many perilous passes
That no one without a guide reaches salvation.

For us, Lady, Virgin Queen, you were
Mother of the Son of God all-powerful:
Therefore obtain from Him that He guide us.

I pray God that to the King Alphonse of Castile
He give honors and merit
For a long time, with pleasure and spiritual life.

Pus astres no m'es donatz (PC 248.65)
Retroencha

La primeira retroencha d'En Guiraut
Riquier, facha en l'an MCCLXII.

The first *rotrouenge* by Guiraut
Riquier made in the year 1262.

Pus as- tres no m'es do- natz

Ni nulhs mos pla- zers no.l platz,

Ops m'es qu'ieu si- a fon- datz

E puesc n'a- pen- re as- satz

En- tre.ls Ca- ta- lans va- lens

Que de mi- dons bes m'es- cha- ia,

Ni ai po- der que.m n'es- tra- ia,

En vi- a d'a- mor ve- ra- ia;

En Ca- ta- luen- ha la ga- ia,

E las do- nas a- vi- nens.

Pus astres no m'es donatz
Que de midons bes m'eschaia,
Ni nulhs mos plazers no.l platz,
Ni ai poder que.m n'estraia,
Ops m'es qu'ieu sia fondatz   1.5
En via d'amor veraia;
E puesc n'apenre assatz
En Cataluenha la gaia,
Entre.ls Catalans valens
E las donas avinens.   1.10

Quar dompneis, pretz e valors,
Jois e gratz e cortesia,
Sens e sabers et onors,
Belhs parlars, bela paria,
E larguesa et amors,   2.5
Conoissensa e cundia
Troban mantenh e secors
En Cataluenha a tria,
Entre.ls Catalans valens
E las donas avinens.   2.10

Per qu'ieu ai tot mon acort
Que d'elhs lurs costums aprenda,
Per tal qu'a mon Belh Deport
Done razon, que m'entenda,
Que non ai autre conort   3.5
Que de murir me defenda,
Et ai cor, per penre port,
Qu'en Cataluenha atenda,
Entre.ls Catalans valens
E las donas avinens.   3.10

E s'ieu entr'elhs non aprenc
Ço per qu'amors gazardona
Servir als sieus, don dan prenc,
No.i a mas qu'om me rebona;
Quar tant d'afan ne sostenc   4.5
Que m'a gitat de Narbona,
E per gandir via tenc
En Cataluenha la bona,
Entre.ls Catalans valens
E las donas avinens.   4.10

Tan sui d'apenre raissos
Ço que d'amar ai falhensa,
Que nulhs pessars no m'es bos
Mas celh qu'als verais agensa;
E quar no.l sai, ad estros   5.5
Vau per bona entendensa
Querre e trobar cochos
En Cataluenha valensa,
Entre.ls Catalans valens
E las donas avinens.   5.10

Since fate has not willed
That good come to me from my lady,
And none of my pleasures pleases her,
Nor can I give her up,
It is necessary that I be instructed
In the way of true love;
And I can learn a great deal
In Catalonia, the joyous,
Among the noble Catalans
And gracious ladies.

For lady service, merit and worth,
Joy and agreeableness and courtliness
Sense and knowledge and honor
Fine speech, beautiful company
And generosity and love
Manners and charm
Find support and sustenance
Fully in Catalonia
Among the noble Catalans
And gracious ladies.

That's why I have put all my effort
To learning from them their customs,
So that to my *Belh Deport*
I may give a reason to listen to me,
For I have no other comfort
Which may keep me from dying,
And to arrive safely in port, I intend
To look toward Catalonia
Among the noble Catalans
And the gracious ladies.

And if among them I do not learn
Why love rewards
Her servants, since I suffer from it,
There will remain only to bury me;
For I endure torment
Because it cast me out from Narbonne,
And to escape I take the road
To Catalonia the good,
Among the noble Catalans
And the gracious ladies.

I am so eager to learn
That which in loving I lack
That no thought is sweet to me
Except the one which pleases true (lovers);
And because I do not know it, quickly
I go for the sake of good understanding,
To seek and find as soon as possible
Help in Catalonia
Among the noble Catalans
And the gracious ladies.

Tant m'es plazens le mals d'amor (PC 248.82)
Canso

La primeira canso de Guiraut Riquier
de Narbona, facha en l'an de la
encarnation de Ihesu Christ que hom
comtava MCCLIIII.

The first *canso* by Guiraut Riquier
of Narbonne, made in the year
from the incarnation of Jesus Christ
that one counts 1254.

Tant m'es plazens le mals d'amor,
Que si tot say que.m vol aucir
No.m vuelh ni m'aus ni.m puesc partir
De midons ni virar alhor;　　　　　　　1.4
Quar tals es qu'ieu penray honor
Si fis lieys aman puesc murir,
O, si.m rete, cen tans maior;
Doncx no.m dey tarzar al servir.　　　　1.8

Quar plazent m'es so que.n dezir,
E.l servirs e.l mals m'an sabor,
E.m play quan ren puesc far ni dir
Que.s tanha endreg sa valor,　　　　　　2.4
E.m play mais quar lunhs hom folhor
No.n pot dir ni mal ses mentir,
E.m play per so l'afans sufrir,
Tan que mortz no m'en fay paor.　　　　2.8

Pero no suy ges ses dolor,
Mas, qui.s vuella, sal Dieus, m'azir,
Sol que midons me denh grazir
E.m tenha per so servidor;　　　　　　　3.4
Qu'adoncx sobre.ls ricx de ricor
Serai manens a mon albir,
Qu'er no say, qui m'ai per senhor,
Tant me fa.l cujars esjauzir.　　　　　　3.8

The pain of love is so agreeable to me
That, although I know she wants to kill me,
I do not want to nor dare I nor can I leave
Her, or turn elsewhere;
For she is such that I would hold it to be an honor
If loving her truly I can die,
Or, if she retains me, a hundred times greater;
Therefore I must not delay serving.

For what I desire is pleasing to me,
And the service and the harm delight me,
And it pleases me when I can say or do something
Which is fitting as regards her merit,
And it pleases me more that no man can
Speak folly or evil of her without lying,
And it pleases me therefore to suffer torment
So great that death holds no fear for me.

However, I am not without pain,
But let whoever may wish to, except God, hate me,
Provided that my lady deign to receive me
And retain me as her servant;
For then above the rich in richness
Shall I be wealthy in my opinion,
For I now do not know whom I have as lord,
So happy does the thought make me.

Que, folhs, ai dig? yeu mi reiruelh,
Quar ben sai, que dos senhors ay,
Midons ez amor, de cuy vuelh
Tener mon cors, qu'aissi s'eschay;   4.4
Quar s'ieu ren far d'avinen sai
Ni dir, de lor ai lo capduelh;
Per que lunh vil fag no m'acuelh
Mon cor, que tenon, de que.m play.   4.8

Aitant de ben amors m'atray,
Que de malestar m'en destuelh,
E tant de mal, que no m'en duelh,
Don crey que deziran murray   5.4
Leys aman tant que m'en dechai;
Ez ab tot suy aitals, cum suelh;
Quar esper que so que quist l'ay
Me torn tot mon cen en vert fuelh.   5.8

Doncx ia no guar lo mieu escuelh
Merces si.m deu pro tener may:
Qu'ab amor abaisse l'erguelh
Qu'a midons, quar no.m reten sai;   6.4
Qu'als no.l deman ni ges no sai,
Que per tant de pretz s'en despuelh,
Ni non l'er honors, si.m recuelh
Mortz per lieys, mas ieu la.i penray   6.8

A.n Bernat d'Olargue t'en vai,
Qu'a de saber razitz e bruelh,
Chanson, mas d'en Bertran no.m tuelh
D'Opian lauzar, quan poiray.   T1.4 (8)

Mos Belhs Deportz tot quant qu'ieu vuelh
En est mon tant cum vos no.m play.   T2.2 (8)

What, fool, have I said? I despise myself,
For I well know that I have two lords,
My lady and love, from whom I want
To hold my self, for thus it is fitting;
And if I know how to do anything gracious
Or speak [well], it is under their control;
That's why no vile deed is received
By my heart, which they hold, which pleases me.

So much good love draws to me
That I turn away from impropriety,
And so much harm, which does not grieve me,
Whence I believe that I shall die desiring
Loving her so much that it destroys me;
And withal I am as I used to be;
For I hope that that which I have asked her
May turn all my thoughts to green leaves.

May therefore no account be taken of my behavior
By Mercy if she is ever to favor me:
For with love she lowers the pride
My lady has, because she does not retain me near her;
Naught else do I ask her nor do I think
That on account of so great merit she would undress,
Nor will it be honorable if she receives me
Dead for her; but I will take it [merit] from her.

Go to Bernat d'Olargue—
Who has of knowledge the root and the branch—
My song, but I do not stop
Praising Sir Bertran of Oupia, when I can.

My *Belh Deport*, nothing do I want
In this world as long as it does not please you.

TROUVÈRE SONGS

Thibaut de Champagne, "Ausi cum lunicorne sui" (p. 307). The historiated letter A shows the unicorn being traitoriously slain as he lies before the lady with his head in her lap. Ms. O, f. 1r.
Cliché Bibliothèque Nationale de France - Paris.

BALLETTES

The *ballette* is a structurally simple form derived, as its name implies, from dance; it is in origin a song intended to accompany dancing in a round. It opens with a brief refrain, which then circles back after every stanza. The stanzas usually number no more than three; each contains three relatively short, monorhymed (or assonanced) verses followed by a shorter verse linked by rhyme to the refrain. This characteristic structure—with its brevity, lightness, swift movement—is well illustrated in the first of our two examples, "Por coi me bait mes maris": 7A 2B   7a 7a 7a 2b   7A 2B   7c 7c 7c 2b   7A 2B   7d 7d 7d 2b   7A 2B.

The second example, "Amis, amis," is clearly of the same basic structure, though it shows a greater number of stanzas, longer lines, and no formal link between stanza and refrain: 4A 10A   10b 10b 10b 10b   4A 10A   10c 10c 10c 10c   4A 10A, etc. The atypical length of the verses, as of the entire composition, produces a slowness of movement that accords well with the seriousness of the poem's subject-matter. Other examples of the genre reveal further modifications, such as prolonged stanzas and varied line-lengths.

Ballettes tend to be women's songs and in any case concerned with matters of love. They are basically first-person lyrics sung by unhappy wives or young girls awakening to passion, but the type makes room for the occasional male lover just as it does for a narrative framework (see "Quant ce vient en mai ke rose est panie," under CHANSONS DE RENCONTRE). The tone of the *ballettes* is popular and their authorship typically unknown. As our second piece reveals, the type may also be borrowed for the rather sensual expression of a woman's spiritual longing.

STUDY: Bec 1977, chapters 1, 2, 17.

• "Por coi me bait mes maris": L 265-1346, RS 1564, MW 417, B 1515. Single source: ms. I; no music. RT 2-3/80-81; Bartsch 1870, 20-21. A truncated version of this text occurs as the tenor in Guillaume de Machaut's 14th-century motet, "Lasse, comment oublieray," where it is accompanied by music.

Dialectal features: Lorraine, including *bait* = Central Fr. *bat, laisette = lassette; acolleir = acol(l)er, dureir = durer; amin = ami; lou = le.* Note, too, that *r* is silent in *certes.*

This is a *chanson de mal mariée,* typically threading together the motifs of brutal husband, threatened revenge, and adulterous lover with whom to "mener bonne vie."

• "Amis, amis": L 265-978, RS 747, MW 78, B 123. Single source: ms. i; music. RT 9-11/90-93; Järnström-Långfors 1927, 195-197.

This is one of a number of *chansons pieuses* composed in imitation of secular songs. In this case, the secular model is evident not only in the choice of *ballette* form, but also in the sensuality that pervades the entire text and in the estrangement decried in the refrain.

Mutilation of the manuscript is responsible for the fact that parts of the melody and st.1 text, presented here in parentheses, are reconstructed—in the case of the melody, by analogy between lines 1 and 2.

Melodically, the refrain and the first two lines of the stanza are built on *g,* while the third and, particularly, fourth lines are on *d.* The scheme, like that of the early *ballade* is: refrain/AABC/refrain.

Por coi me bait mes maris?   (L 265-1346)
Ballette, chanson de femme

Por coi me bait mes maris?	*Why does my husband beat me?*
Laisette!	*Poor girl!*
Je ne li de rienz meffis,	I haven't done him any harm
Ne rien ne li ai mesdit	or said anything wrong —
Fors c'acolleir mon amin	just embraced my boyfriend
Soulette.	all alone.
Por coi me bait mes maris?	*Why does my husband beat me?*
Laisette!	*Poor girl!*

1.4

Et s'il ne mi lait dureir
Ne bone vie meneir,
Je lou ferai cous clameir
        A certes.   2.4
Por coi me bait mes maris?
        Laisette!

Or sai bien que je ferai
Et coment m'an vangerai:
Avec mon amin geirai
        Nüete.   3.4
Por coi me bait mes maris?
        Laisette!

If he doesn't let me be
and let me enjoy life,
I'll make sure he's called
a cuckold.
Why does my husband beat me?
Poor girl!

Now I know what to do
and how to get back at him:
I'll go to bed with my boyfriend
naked.
Why does my husband beat me?
Poor girl!

Amis, amis   (L 265-978)
Ballette, chanson de femme, chanson pieuse

A- mis, a- mis, Trop me lais- sie(z en) es- tran- ge pa- ïs.

L'a- me qui quiert Dieu de (ve- raie en-) ten- te

Sou- vent se plaint (et) for- ment se de- men- te

Et (s)on a- mi, cui ve- nue est trop len- (te),

Va re- gre- tant que ne li a- ta- len- te.

        Amis, amis,
Trop me laissiez en estrange païs.

L'ame qui quiert Dieu de veraie entente
Souvent se plaint et forment se demente
Et son ami, cui venue est trop lente,
Va regretant que ne li atalente.   1.4
        Amis, amis,
Trop me laissiez en estrange païs.

Trop me laissiez ci vous longuement querre.
En ciel regnés et en mer et en terre;
Enclose sui en cest cors qui me serre,
De ceste char qui souvent me fait guerre.   2.4
        Amis, amis,
Trop me laissiez en estrange païs.

My love, my love,
you leave me too long in an alien land.

The soul that seeks God in earnest
often complains and bitterly laments
and, as her belovèd is long in arriving,
she grieves that she doesn't attract him.
My love, my love,
you leave me too long in an alien land.

Too long you leave me here seeking you.
You reign in heaven and on land and sea;
I am locked in this confining body,
in this flesh that remains at war with me.
My love, my love,
you leave me too long in an alien land.

Dieus, donnez moy ce que mes cuers desirre,
Pour cui languis, pour cui sui a martire.
Jhesucrist est mes amis et mon sire,
Li biaus, li bons, plus que nul ne scet dire.   3.4
      Amis, amis,
Trop me laissiez en estrange païs.

Mon createur, quar je sui sa faiture,
Qui me nourrit et de tout me procure,
Mes amis est, quar en moy mist tel cure
Que par amour se joint a ma nature.   4.4
      Amis, amis,
Trop me laissiez en estrange païs.

Il m'apela ains que je l'apelasse,
Si me requist ainz qu'aprez lui alasse.
Or est bien drois qu'en lui querre me lasse
Si que cest mont pour lui trouver trespasse.   5.4
      Amis, amis,
Trop me laissiez en estrange païs.

Et quant j'avray passé ceste bruïne
Ou li jour faut et le vespre decline,
Cilz qui les cuers alume et enlumine
Se moustrera; lors avray joie fine.   6.4
      Amis, amis,
Trop me laissiez en estrange païs.

God, give me what my heart desires,
what I long for and leaves me martyred.
Jesus Christ is my belovèd and my lord,
more beautiful and good than anyone can say.
My love, my love,
you leave me too long in an alien land.

My creator (for I am his creature),
who attends to me and provides all my wants,
is my lover, for he has shown me such care
that through his love he is now fused to my nature.
My love, my love,
you leave me too long in an alien land.

He called me before I could call him,
and summoned me before I could go to him.
Now it is right that I should toil toward him
and pass beyond this world to find him.
My love, my love,
you leave me too long in an alien land.

And once I have passed this mist
where day declines and evening darkens,
he who brings brightness and light to our hearts
will appear; then I shall have pure joy.
My love, my love,
you leave me too long in an alien land.

CHANSONS DE TOILE

The *chansons de toile*, or *chansons d'histoire*, consti-
tute a genre indigenous to northern France rather than one
inspired by an Occitan model. They combine narrative and
dialogue with their lyric interest, as their brief, simple stan-
zas relate tales of frank and insistent, "pre-courtly," desire
experienced by young noble women. The songs vary in
length but are all characterized by three- to five-line mono-
rhymed (or assonanced) stanzas, each followed by a pro-
sodically different, normally invariable, refrain; the stanza
verses are decasyllabic.

The genre is represented by a score of compositions,
mostly anonymous, preserved in thirteenth-century
songbooks or as interpolations in romances (notably Jean
Renart's *Guillaume de Dole*). Only some of them—four
anonymous pieces as well as the more elaborate ones com-
posed by Audefroi le Bâtard—survive with music. It is not
certain how or why the *chansons de toile* originated, but
they appear to have arisen at the time of the early epics as
an accompaniment to women's needlework or the like;
indeed, a few of the poems, such as our "Bele Yolanz,"
mention such activity in their narration.

STUDIES: Bec 1977, chapter 4; Zink 1978.

EDITION: Zink 1978.

● "Quant vient en mai que l'on dit as lons jors": L 265-
1485, RS 2037, MW 43, B 869. Single source: ms. U; no
music. RT 12-14/92-95; Bartsch 1870, 3-4; Zink 1978,
93-95.

The only notable dialectal features are the Lorraine
forms *meis* = Central Fr. *mes* and *lo* = *le*.

1.2: The term *Franc de France*, borrowed from epic
poetry, designates the Franks of the limited territory of Car-
olingian France in contrast to those from the rest of the
empire; it is no doubt to be understood as connoting special
distinction.

The final stanza contains only four verses instead of
the usual five and thus poses the problem of a lacuna. It is
not certain, however, that all the stanzas of a *chanson de
toile* must adhere absolutely to a fixed number of verses,
and, from the point of view of meaning, this stanza is, in
any case, clear and complete as it stands.

● "Lou samedi a soir fat la semainne": L 265-1048, RS
143, MW 302, B 1830. Single source: ms. U; no music. RT
14-16/94-97; Bartsch 1870, 8; Zink 1978, 85-88.

Dialectal features: Lorraine, including *fat* = Central Fr.
faut; Gerairs = *Gerars, laise* = *lasse; crollet* = *crol(l)e,
chosit* = *choisi, vat* = *va, laxiét* = *laissié; soweif* = *souef,
torneit* = *torné, citeit* = *cité; lou* = *le*. Note particularly the
verb forms *ait* = *a, remainra* = *remainrai, j'a* = *j'ai*.

The treatment of the decasyllabic line is unusual, in
that the caesura occurs at the sixth syllable rather than the
fourth.

The modern poet Apollinaire no doubt had this text in
mind when he composed his well-known poem, "Le pont
Mirabeau," whose refrain in particular is evocative of the
medieval source: *Vienne la nuit sonne l'heure,/ Les jours
s'en vont je demeure*. (See Roques 1949, 144-146.)

● "Bele Doette as fenestres se siet": L 265-215, RS 1352,
MW 61, B 716. Single source: ms. U; music. RT 18-
20/102-105; Bartsch 1870, 5-6; Zink 1978, 89-92; Switten
1988, 162-166.

Dialectal features: Lorraine, including *nomeie* = Cen-
tral Fr. *nomee, fauseie* = *faussee, entreie* = *entree; drecie* =
dreciee, adrecie = *adreciee, correcie* = *correciee*. In 1.7,
s'est is to be understood as a rewriting of *s'ait*, Lorraine for
si a 'and he has'.

Note the unusual activity of Doette at the beginning of
the poem: not needlework, but reading. Also unusual in this
chanson de toile is the expansion of the refrain in stanzas 6
and 7, with further expansion in the final stanza.

The melody, notated in Messine neumes, is rather
sophisticated in its extensive range (a ninth) and its consid-
erable ornamentation. Melismas occur not only at the
opening and in the cadences of lines 1 and 3, but also at the
caesura in lines 2 and 4. The scale of *a* is a transposed Dor-
ian, or *d*, scale, and the melodic scheme is regular:
ABAB/refrain C. The performance of this song no doubt
required vocal virtuosity, which brings into question the
supposed functionality of the genre.

● "Bele Yolanz en ses chambres seoit": L 265-223, RS
1847, MW 74, B 571. Single source: ms. U; music. RT 20-
21/106-109; Bartsch 1870, 10; Zink 1978, 76-79.

Dialectal features: Lorraine, including *boen* = Central
Fr. *bon; se* = *si; lo* = *le; a (tor)* = *au*.

6.4: *Au tour françois* is a well-attested term for some
riding maneuver the exact nature of which is unclear; its
precise metaphoric value here is consequently unclear as
well, though the general sense is obvious. The grammati-
cally unspecified subject and the epicene direct object (*l'*)
of *estent* lend further obscurity to the verse.

The melody, notated in Messine neumes, is of archaic
style. Starting with two lines in the Phrygian, or *e*, scale, it
develops through the stanza according to the scheme
AABC/refrain B'B". In the refrain, earlier editors have
often emended the cadence on *d* to *e;* the change is unjusti-
fied, and the modal ambiguity stemming from the cadence
on *d* is hardly without beauty.

Quant vient en mai que l'on dit as lons jors   (L 265-1485)
Chanson de toile

Quant vient en mai que l'on dit as lons jors,
Que Franc de France repairent de roi cort,
Reynauz repaire devant el premier front;
Si s'en passa lez lo meis Arembor,   1.4
Ainz n'en dengna le chief drecier amont.
    E Raynaut, amis!

With the coming of May — long-dayed, as they say —
the French of France come home from the king's court,
and Raynaud rides back at the head of the line.
He rode past the house of Erenborg
but did not deign to raise his eyes.
Ah, Raynaud, my love!

Bele Erembors a la fenestre au jor
Sor ses genolz tient paile de color,
Voit Frans de France qui repairent de cort
Et voit Raynaut devant el premier front.   2.4
En haut parole, si a dit sa raison:
    E Raynauz, amis!

Lovely Erenborg, at the window in the light,
has on her knees a cloth of bright color;
she sees the French of France riding home from court
and sees Raynaud at the head of the line.
She raises her voice and speaks her mind:
Ah, Raynaud, my love!

"Amis Raynauz, j'ai ja veü cel jor
Se passissoiz selon mon pere tor,
Dolanz fussiez se ne parlasse a vos."
"Ja.l mesfaïstes, fille d'empereor;   3.4
Autrui amastes, si obliastes nos."
    E Raynauz, amis!

"Raynaud, my love, I once saw the day
when, if you came past my father's tower,
you would have been hurt if I had not spoken to you."
"You have done wrong, emperor's daughter;
you have loved someone else and forgotten us."
Ah, Raynaud, my love!

"Sire Raynauz, je m'en escondirai;
A cent puceles sor sainz vos jurerai,
A trente dames que avuec moi menrai,
C'onques nul home fors vostre cors n'amai.   4.4
Prennez l'emmende et je vos baiserai."
    E Raynauz, amis!

"Raynaud, sir, I will deny that charge;
before a hundred maidens, I will swear on relics,
before thirty ladies that I will bring along,
that I have never loved any man but you.
Accept that justification, and I'll kiss you."
Ah, Raynaud, my love!

Li cuens Raynauz en monta lo degré,
Gros par espaules, greles par lo baudré;
Blonde ot lo poil, menu recercelé.
En nule terre n'ot si biau bacheler.   5.4
Voit l' Erembors, si comence a plorer.
    E Raynauz, amis!

Count Raynaud went up the stairs;
broad at the shoulders, narrow at the waist,
he had blond hair in tiny curls;
in no other land was there a young man so handsome.
Erenborg sees him and begins to weep.
Ah, Raynaud, my love!

Li cuens Raynauz est montez en la tor,
Si s'est assis en un lit point a flors;
Dejoste lui se siet bele Erembors.
Lors recomencent lor premieres amors.   6.4
    E Raynauz, amis!

Count Raynaud is up in the tower
and sitting on a bed trimmed with flowers;
Erenborg sits down beside him.
Then they fall in love all over again.
Ah, Raynaud, my love!

Lou samedi a soir fat la semainne   (L 265-1048)
Chanson de toile

Lou samedi a soir fat la semainne;
Gaiete et Oriour, serors germainnes,
Main et main vont bagnier a la fontainne.
    Vante l'ore et la rainme crollet;
      Ki s'antrainment soweif dorment.   1.5

Saturday evening, and the week is over;
Gayette and Orior, sisters by father and mother,
hand in hand go to bathe at the spring.
Let the wind blow and the branches bend;
couples in love sleep in peace.

L'anfes Gerairs revient de la cuitainne,
S'ait chosit Gaiete sor la fontainne;
Antre ses bras l'ait pris, soueif l'a strainte.
    Vante l'ore et la rainme crollet;
        Ki s'antrainment soueif dorment.   2.5

Young Gerard is back from quintain training
and has noticed Gayette at the spring;
he takes her in his arms, gently holds her close.
    Let the wind blow and the branches bend;
    couples in love sleep in peace.

"Qant avras, Orriour, de l'ague prise,
Reva toi an arriere, bien seis la ville;
Je remainra Gerairt, ke bien me priset."
    Vante l'ore et la rainme crollet;
        Ki s'antrainment soweif dorment.   3.5

"When you have taken enough water, Orior,
go back to the village; you know the way.
I'll stay with Gerard, who holds me dear."
    Let the wind blow and the branches bend;
    couples in love sleep in peace.

Or s'an va Oriour, stinte et marrie;
Des euls s'an vat plorant, de cuer sospire,
Cant Gaie sa seror n'anmoinnet mie.
    Vante l'ore et la rainme crollet;
        Ki s'antrainment soweif dorment.   4.5

Orior now turns back, pale and sad,
with tears in her eyes and sighs in her heart,
because she is leaving behind her sister Gayette.
    Let the wind blow and the branches bend;
    couples in love sleep in peace.

"Laise," fait Oriour, "com mar fui nee!
J'a laxiét ma serour an la vallee,
L'anfes Gerairs l'anmoine an sa contree."
    Vante l'ore et la rainme crollet;
        Ki s'antrainment soweif dorment.   5.5

"Alas," says Orior, "that I was ever born!
I have left my sister in the valley,
and young Gerard is taking her home with him."
    Let the wind blow and the branches bend;
    couples in love sleep in peace.

L'anfes Gerairs et Gaie s'an sont torneit,
Lor droit chemin ont pris vers sa citeit;
Tantost com il i vint, l'ait espouseit.
    Vante l'ore et la rainme crollet;
        Ki s'antrainment soweif dorment.   6.5

Young Gerard and Gayette went on their way;
they took the road that goes straight to his city;
as soon as he arrived, he married her.
    Let the wind blow and the branches bend;
    couples in love sleep in peace.

Bele Doette as fenestres se siet   (L 265-215)
Chanson de toile

Be - le Do - ette   as   fe - nes - tres se siet,

Lit   en   un   li - vre mais au   cuer   ne   l'en   tient;

De   son   a - mi   Do - on   li   re - so - vient

Q' en   au - tres   ter - res   est   a - lez   tor - noi - er.

E   or   en   ai   dol!

Bele Doette as fenestres se siet,
Lit en un livre mais au cuer ne l'en tient;
De son ami Doon li resovient
Q'en autres terres est alez tornoier.   1.4
    E or en ai dol!

Uns escuiers as degrez de la sale
Est dessendu, s'est destrossé sa male.
Bele Doette les degrez en avale,
Ne cuide pas oïr novele male.   2.4
    E or en ai dol!

Bele Doette tantost li demanda:
"Ou est mes sires, que ne vi tel pieç'a?"
Cil ot tel duel que de pitié plora;
Bele Doette maintenant se pasma.   3.4
    E or en ai dol!

Bele Doette s'est en estant drecie;
Voit l'escuier, vers lui s'est adrecie;
En son cuer est dolante et correcie
Por son seignor dont ele ne voit mie.   4.4
    E or en ai dol!

Bele Doette li prist a demander:
"Ou est mes sires cui je doi tant amer?"
"En non Deu, dame, ne.1 vos quier mais celer:
Morz est mes sires, ocis fu au joster."   5.4
    E or en ai dol!

Bele Doette a pris son duel a faire:
"Tant mar i fustes, cuens Do, frans debonaire,
Por vostre amor vestirai je la haire,
Ne sor mon cors n'avra pelice vaire.   6.4
    E or en ai dol!
Por vos devenrai nonne en l'eglyse saint Pol.

"Por vos ferai une abbaïe tele,
Qant iert li jors que la feste iert nomeie,
Se nus i vient qui ait s'amor fauseie,
Ja del mostier ne savera l'entreie."   7.4
    E or en ai dol!
Por vos devenrai nonne a l'eglise saint Pol.

Bele Doette prist s'abaiie a faire,
Qui mout est grande et adés sera maire;
Toz cels et celes vodra dedanz atraire
Qui por amor sevent peine et mal traire.   8.4
    E or en ai dol!
Por vostre amor devenrai nonne a l'eglise saint Pol.

Lovely Doette is sitting by the window
reading a book, but her thoughts are elsewhere;
she is thinking of her belovèd Do,
who has gone to tourney in foreign lands.
Oh, what grief I feel!

At the stairs to the great hall, a squire
has dismounted and untrussed his bags.
Lovely Doette runs down the stairs;
she does not expect to hear bad news.
Oh, what grief I feel!

Lovely Doette asked him right away:
"Where is my lord, whom I've not seen for so long?"
The man was so grieved that he was moved to weep;
lovely Doette suddenly fainted away.
Oh, what grief I feel!

Lovely Doette has stood back up;
she sees the squire and walks up to him;
in her heart she is upset and disappointed
not to see any sign of her lord.
Oh, what grief I feel!

Lovely Doette began to question the man:
"Where is my lord, whom I rightfully love?"
"By God, my lady, I'll not keep it from you anymore:
my lord is dead; he was killed in the joust."
Oh, what grief I feel!

Lovely Doette began her mourning:
"Alas you ever went there, noble gracious Count Do!
For love of you I will now wear a hairshirt,
and no fur-lined cloak will cover my body."
Oh, what grief I feel!
For you I'll become a nun at St. Paul's.

"For you I will found an abbey such
that, when its day of dedication comes,
if anyone appears who has betrayed his love,
he will not find his way into the church."
Oh, what grief I feel!
For you I'll become a nun at St. Paul's.

Lovely Doette proceeded to build her abbey,
which is very large and will grow larger;
she wants to draw all men and women there
who know the pain and woe of love.
Oh, what grief I feel!
For love of you I'll become a nun at St. Paul's.

Bele Yolanz en ses chambres seoit   (L 265-223)
Chanson de toile

Be- le Y- o- lanz en ses cham- bres se- oit ;

D' un boen sa- miz u- ne ro- be co- soit ;

A son a- mi tra- met- tre la vo- loit .

En sos- pi- rant , ces- te chan- çon chan- toit :

Deus , tant est douz li nons d' a- mors ,

Ja n' en cui- dai sen- tir do- lors .

Bele Yolanz en ses chambres seoit;
D'un boen samiz une robe cosoit;
A son ami tramettre la voloit.
En sospirant, ceste chançon chantoit: 1.4
    Deus, tant est douz li nons d'amors,
    Ja n'en cuidai sentir dolors.

"Bels douz amis, or vos voil envoier
Une robe par mout grant amistié.
Por Deu vos pri, de moi aiez pitié."
Ne pot ester, a la terre s'assiet.   2.4
    Deus, tant est douz li nons d'amors,
    Ja n'en cuidai sentir dolors.

A ces paroles et a ceste raison
Li siens amis entra en la maison.
Cele lo vit, si bassa lo menton;
Ne pot parler, ne li dist o ne non.   3.4
    Deus, tant est douz li nons d'amors,
    Ja n'en cuidai sentir dolors.

"Ma douce dame, mis m'avez en obli."
Cele l'entent, se li geta un ris;
En sospirant, ses bels braz li tendi;
Tant doucement a acoler l'a pris.   4.4
    Deus, tant est douz li nons d'amors,
    Ja n'en cuidai sentir dolors.

Lovely Yolande was sitting in her room;
she was sewing a robe of fine silk;
she meant to send it to her lover.
Sighing all the while, she was singing this song:
God, how sweet is the name of love!
I never thought it would bring me sorrow.

"My dear love, I want to send you
a robe out of deepest love.
By God, I beg you to take pity on me."
She could not stand but sat on the floor.
God, how sweet is the name of love!
I never thought it would bring me sorrow.

At these words, at this statement,
her lover came into the house.
She saw him and lowered her head;
she could not speak, not say Yes or No.
God, how sweet is the name of love!
I never thought it would bring me sorrow.

"My dear lady, you have forgotten me."
She heard this and gave him a smile;
with a sigh, she held out her lovely arms;
she took and embraced him so sweetly!
God, how sweet is the name of love!
I never thought it would bring me sorrow.

"Bels douz amis, ne vos sai losengier,
Mais de fin cuer vos aim et senz trechier.
Qant vos plaira, si me porrez baisier;
Entre voz braz me voil aler couchier." 5.4
    Deus, tant est douz li nons d'amors,
    Ja n'en cuidai sentir dolors.

"My dear love, I cannot flatter you,
but I love you with a pure and true heart.
You may kiss me whenever you like;
I want to go lie in your arms."
God, how sweet is the name of love!
I never thought it would bring me sorrow.

Li siens amis entre ses braz la prent;
En un biau lit s'asïent seulement.
Bele Yolanz lo baise estroitement;
A tor françois en mi lo lit l'estent. 6.4
    Deus, tant est douz li nons d'amors,
    Ja n'en cuidai sentir dolors.

Her lover takes her in his arms;
they sit down, alone together, on a fine bed.
Lovely Yolande presses close and kisses him;
she (he?) lays him (her?) down *à la française.*
God, how sweet is the name of love!
I never thought it would bring me sorrow.

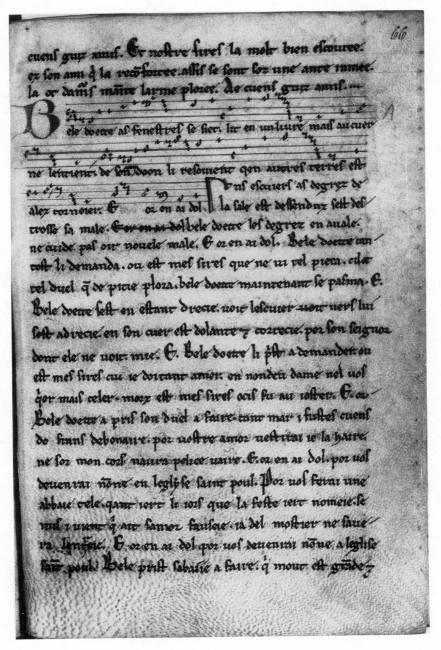

"Bele Doette as fenestres se siet" (p. 186). Ms. U, f. 66r. Cliché Bibliothèque Nationale de France - Paris.

AUBES

Dawn-songs did not have the success among the trouvères that, in the form of *albas,* they had among the troubadours. There are only five of them; two are somewhat fragmentary motet texts; authorship is unknown except for one piece, whose attribution is improbable; and they show considerable diversity in form and in their handling of the basic theme of lovers' separation at dawn. Though the genre did not prosper in French, it produced as many as three pieces that are widely regarded as notable poetic achievements; we present all three. Note that two of them present the experience of separation from the woman's point of view.

STUDIES: Hatto (Woledge) 1965; Dronke 1968, chapter 5; Saville 1972; Bec 1977, chapter 3.

● "Gaite de la tor": L 265-722, RS 2015, MW 475, B 884. Single source: ms. U; music. RT 24-28/114-119.

This song has provoked more interpretative commentary than perhaps any other in Old French, the principal questions being, first, whether it is essentially a dramatic work, even meant to be choreographed, or a purely lyric composition, and, second, whose voices are heard in the various stanzas. Since the ms. offers nothing beyond text and music, speculation has ranged rather broadly from Jeanroy 1889, p. 79, through Woledge 1965, pp. 388-389, and Bec 1973, as well as others. It is Bec's distribution of the stanzas, together with his view that the refrains form a lyric entity independent of the speakers, that we consider the most persuasive, viz., stanza 1: the lover, stanzas 2-5: the watchman, stanzas 6-7: the lover.

1.8: The pronoun *l'*, without antecedent, no doubt designates the "jaloux," the lady's husband, referred to as *traïtor* in 2.5 and explicitly left nameless in 4.5.

2.2: *Blancheflor* is the name of the heroine in a number of medieval romances, most notably *Floire et Blancheflor.* It is likely that the name is mentioned here for its generally evocative value rather than some reason specifically relevant to the context.

With its broad range of an eleventh, the melody appears light and lively. Cadences in *c* (lines 2, 4, and 11)

alternate with cadences in *d,* which are more traditional for the period. The tonal focus on *c* works with the rising contours of lines 3 and 7 to produce an effect of simplicity.

Structurally, there is no strong opposition between the stanza and the refrain, both of which are heterometric: ABCAB'C'/refrain DEFD'G. The melody of the refrain, unlike that of the stanza, seems to call for a certain swaying movement in performance. Although the piece is notated in neumes with no indication of rhythmic mode, we have therefore chosen, in order to underline the contrast with the stanza, to make such movement explicit in a mensural transcription of the refrain. This is, of course, an interpretation.

● "Entre moi et mon amin": L 265-665, RS 1029, MW 2240, B 892. Single source: ms. I; no music. RT 29-29/118-121; Bartsch 1870, 27-28.

Dialectal features: Lorraine, including *mairdi* = Central Fr. *mardi, lai = la; leis = les; amin = ami; neut = nuit; juwant = jouant; vocexiens = vousissiens* (modern *voulussions*), *dixant = disant, sant = cent.* Note in particular the verb forms *ajornait = ajorna, chantait = chanta; durest = durast.*

2.8: *Mais* 'moreover'.

● "Cant voi l'aube dou jor venir": L 65-12, RS 1481, MW 369, B 1453. Single source: ms. C; no music. RT 240-241/120-123; Dyggve 1951, 441-442; Rosenberg 1985, 266-269. The ms. attributes this song to the well-known and prolific Gace Brulé, but the attributions of ms. C are often so unreliable and the composition is so unlike the others ascribed to Gace that it is better to consider its authorship unknown.

Dialectal features: Lorraine, including *depairt* = Central Fr. *depart; poent = point; amin = ami;* adverbial *se = si; lou = le.*

2.4: We translate *enuious* as 'envious' (modern Fr. *envieux*) taking the first *u* to represent *v,* as it usually does in medieval mss. The word may well be understood, however, as the old form of modern *ennuyeux* —in its medieval sense of 'wrong-doers, those who harm'.

Gaite de la tor   (L 265-722)
Aube

Gai- te de la tor,   Gar- dez en- tor

Les murs, se Deus vos voi- e!

C'or sont a se- jor   Dame et sei- gnor,

Et lar- ron vont en proi- e.

Hu et hu et hu et hu!   Je l'ai ve- ü

La jus soz la cou droi- e.

Hu et hu et hu et hu!

A bien pres l'o- cir- roi- e.

Gaite de la tor,	Watchman in the tower,
Gardez entor	be on the lookout around
Les murs, se Deus vos voie!	the walls (may God protect you!),
C'or sont a sejor	for lady and lord
Dame et seignor, 1.5	have now retired
Et larron vont en proie.	and thieves are on the prowl.
Hu et hu et hu et hu!	*Hoot and toot, hoot and toot!*
Je l'ai veü	*I've seen him*
La jus soz la coudroie.	*over there under the hazels.*
Hu et hu et hu et hu! 1.10	*Hoot and toot, hoot and toot!*
A bien pres l'ocirroie.	*I would gladly kill him.*

D'un douz lai d'amor
De Blancheflor,
Compains, vos chanteroie,
Ne fust la poor
Del traïtor   2.5
Cui je redotteroie.
Hu et hu et hu et hu!
Je l'ai veü
La jus soz la coudroie.
Hu et hu et hu et hu!   2.10
A bien pres l'ocirroie.

Compainz, en error
Sui, k'a cest tor
Volentiers dormiroie.
N'aiez pas paor!
Voist a loisor   3.5
Qui aler vuet par voie.
Hu et hu et hu et hu!
Or soit teü,
Compainz, a ceste voie.
Hu et hu! Bien ai seü   3.10
Que nos en avrons joie.

Ne sont pas plusor
Li robeor;
N'i a c'un que je voie,
Qui gist en la flor
Soz covertor,   4.5
Cui nomer n'oseroie.
Hu et hu et hu et hu!
Or soit teü,
Compainz, a ceste voie.
Hu et hu! Bien ai seü   4.10
Que nos en avrons joie.

Cortois ameor
Qui a sejor
Gisez en chambre coie,
N'aiez pas freor,
Que tresqu'a jor   5.5
Pöez demener joie.
Hu et hu et hu et hu!
Or soit teü,
Compainz, a ceste voie.
Hu et hu! Bien ai seü   5.10
Que nos en avrons joie.

A tender tale
of Blanchefleur's love
I'd sing you, friend,
if not for fear
of the traitor
whom I would dread.
Hoot and toot, hoot and toot!
I've seen him
over there under the hazels.
Hoot and toot, hoot and toot!
I would gladly kill him.

Friend, I am
worried; at this point
I'd gladly go to sleep.
Don't be afraid!
Let whoever wants to
go on his way in peace.
Hoot and toot, hoot and toot!
No more noise now,
friend, at this time.
Hoot and toot! I knew
it would turn out well.

There are not many
robbers:
only one, as far as I can see,
lying among the flowers
under a cover,
whom I wouldn't dare name.
Hoot and toot, hoot and toot!
No more noise now,
friend, at this time.
Hoot and toot! I knew
it would turn out well.

Courtly lovers
who are now lying
restfully in a quiet room,
have no fear!
You can enjoy your pleasure
until daybreak.
Hoot and toot, hoot and toot!
No more noise now,
friend, at this time.
Hoot and toot! I knew
it would turn out well.

Gaite de la tor,	Watchman in the tower,
Vez mon retor	here I am back
De la ou vos ooie;	from the place where I heard you;
D'amie et d'amor	when it comes to belovèd and love,
A cestui tor 6.5	I have now had
Ai ceu que plus amoie.	what I love most.
Hu et hu et hu et hu!	*Hoot and toot, hoot and toot!*
Pou ai geü	*I have spent a short while*
En la chambre de joie.	*in the chamber of joy.*
Hu et hu! Trop m'a neü 6.10	*Hoot and toot! I have been badly hurt*
L'aube qui me guerroie.	*by dawn, which is at war with me.*
Se salve l'onor	With no disrespect
Au Criator	to the Creator,
Estoit, tot tens voudroie	I keep wishing
Nuit feïst del jor:	He would turn day into night:
Jamais dolor 7.5	I would have no more
Ne pesance n'avroie.	sorrow or trouble.
Hu et hu et hu et hu!	*Hoot and toot, hoot and toot!*
Bien ai veü	*I have really seen*
De biauté la monjoie.	*the paragon of beauty.*
Hu et hu! C'est bien seü. 7.10	*Hoot and toot! It's clear.*
Gaite, a Deu tote voie.	*Watchman, God be with you always.*

Entre moi et mon amin   (L 265-665)

Aube, chanson de femme

Entre moi et mon amin,	My love and I,
En un boix k'est leis Betune,	in a wood outside Bethune,
Alainmes juwant mairdi	spent all night Tuesday
Toute lai nuit a la lune, 1.4	playing in the moonlight,
Tant k'il ajornait	until day broke
Et ke l'alowe chantait	and the lark sang,
Ke dit: "Amins, alons an."	saying: "Lover, let's go."
Et il respont doucement: 1.8	My love answered softly:
Il n'est mie jours,	*It is not day,*
Saverouze au cors gent;	*my sweet and fair;*
Si m'aït Amours,	*so help me Love,*
L'alowette nos mant. 1.12	*the lark is lying.*
Adont se trait pres de mi,	Then he drew close to me,
Et je ne fu pas anfrune;	and I was not unwilling;
Bien trois fois me baixait il,	he gave me a good three kisses,
Ausi fix je lui plus d'une, 2.4	and I gave him more than one,
K'ainz ne m'anoiait.	for it was certainly no trouble.
Adonc vocexiens nous lai	Then we would have wished
Ke celle neut durest sant,	the night to last a hundred nights,
Mais ke plus n'alest dixant: 2.8	with no more need to say:
Il n'est mie jours,	*It is not day,*
Saverouze au cors gent;	*my sweet and fair;*
Si m'aït Amours,	*so help me Love,*
L'alowette nos mant. 2.12	*the lark is lying.*

Cant voi l'aube dou jor venir   (L 65-12)
Aube, chanson de femme, rotrouenge

Cant voi l'aube dou jor venir,
Nulle rien ne doi tant haïr,
K'elle fait de moi departir
Mon amin, cui j'ain per amors.   1.4
Or ne hais riens tant com le jor,
Amins, ke me depairt de vos.

When I see the dawn of day appear,
there is nothing I am bound to hate so much,
for it takes away my belovèd,
whom I love truly.
I hate nothing now so much as day,
for it parts me from you, belovèd.

Je ne vos puis de jor veoir,
Car trop redout l'apercevoir,
Et se vos di trestout por voir
K'en agait sont li enuios.   2.4
Or ne hais riens tant com le jor,
Amins, ke me depairt de vos.

I cannot see you in the daytime,
for I fear we'll be noticed;
and this I tell you in truth:
the envious are watching.
I hate nothing now so much as day,
for it parts me from you, belovèd.

Quant je me gix dedens mon lit
Et je resgairde encoste mi,
Je n'i truis poent de mon amin,
Se m'en plaing a fins ameros.   3.4
Or ne hais riens tant com le jor,
Amins, ke me depairt de vos.

When I lie in my bed
and look to my side,
I find no trace of my belovèd,
and I lament to all true lovers.
I hate nothing now so much as day,
for it parts me from you, belovèd.

Biaus dous amis, vos en ireis;
A Deu soit vos cors comandeis.
Por Deu vos pri, ne m'oblieis!
Je n'ain nulle rien tant com vos.   4.4
Or ne hais riens tant com le jor,
Amins, ke me depairt de vos.

Dear sweet love, you will go away;
may God watch over you.
I beg you, by God, don't forget me!
I love nothing so much as you.
I hate nothing now so much as day,
for it parts me from you, belovèd.

Or pri a tous les vrais amans
Ceste chanson voixent chantant
Ens en despit des mesdixans
Et des mavais maris jalos.   5.4
Or ne hais riens tant com lou jor,
Amins, ke me depairt de vos.

Now I beg all true lovers
to go singing this song
in spite of the slanderers
and mean, jealous husbands.
I hate nothing now so much as day,
for it parts me from you, belovèd.

REVERDIES

The *reverdies* constitute a lyric type native to the land of the trouvères rather than inspired by Occitan poetry. They are not numerous, only about a dozen surviving, and they are quite varied in structure, including a motet and a *lai* along with regular strophic forms. Almost all are anonymous. Diverse as they are, they all fundamentally express a celebration of spring, whose colorful return is of course linked to the rebirth of amorous joy. This celebration tends to veer into fantasy and dreaming, as well as allegorical expression.

In addition to the anonymous *reverdie* that follows, we later present one by Colin Muset.

STUDY: Bec 1977, chapter 6.

● "Volez vous que je vous chant": L 265-1737, RS 318, MW 562. Sources: ms. K, also NX; music in all. RT 30-32/122-127; Bartsch 1870, 23-24; Spanke 1925, 241-242; Switten 1988, 158-161.

This *reverdie*, strange and charming, has always been considered the gem of the genre and is, indeed, one of the most alluring of all trouvère compositions. Note that the female vision so amply described in stanzas 2-4 is not identified even by a subject pronoun: only later is she named, quite simply, *Bele*. This lends particular mystery to the relation of the characters in stanza 1 to those that follow. The versification is no less striking than the content, for it mixes rhyme and assonance (including one case of only approximate homophony, *soie*: *chauçade*), varies the rhyme scheme, makes a metrical change in the last three stanzas, and introduces Occitanized participles in *-ade* into an otherwise purely French text.

Simple and light-hearted, built on a heterometric stanza, this syllabic melody, transposed from the *d* (Dorian) scale to *g,* is through-composed: ABCDEF. Like the versions in mss. NX, it readily lends itself to interpretation in the ternary meter (in our transcription, the first rhythmic mode) that some modern musicologists have tended to ascribe to it. No doubt intended for dancing, this *son d'amors* (1.2) may well be accompanied in performance by such instruments as the fiddle, flageolet, or tambourine.

Volez vous que je vous chant   (L 265-1737)
Reverdie

Vo- lez vous que je vous chant

Un son d'a- mors a- ve- nant ?

Vi- lain ne.l fist mi- e,

Ainz le fist un che- va- lier

Souz l'on- bre d'un o- li- vier

En- tre les braz s'a- mi- e.

Volez vous que je vous chant
Un son d'amors avenant?
          Vilain ne.l fist mie,
Ainz le fist un chevalier   1.4
Souz l'onbre d'un olivier
          Entre les braz s'amie.

Chemisete avoit de lin
Et blanc peliçon hermin
          Et blïaut de soie,
Chauces ot de jaglolai   2.4
Et sollers de flors de mai,
          Estroitement chauçade.

Çainturete avoit de fueille
Qui verdist quant li tens mueille;
          D'or ert boutonade.
L'aumosniere estoit d'amor;   3.4
Li pendant furent de flor,
          Par amors fu donade.

Si chevauchoit une mule;
D'argent ert la ferreüre,
          La sele ert dorade;
Seur la crope par derrier   4.4
Avoit planté trois rosiers
          Por fere li honbrage.

Si s'en vet aval la pree;
Chevaliers l'ont encontree,
          Biau l'ont saluade:
"Bele, dont estes vous nee?"   5.4
"De France sui, la löee,
          Du plus haut parage.

"Li rosignous est mon pere
Qui chante seur la ramee
          El plus haut boscage;
La seraine, ele est ma mere   6.4
Qui chante en la mer salee
          El plus haut rivage."

"Bele, bon fussiez vous nee,
Bien estes enparentee
          Et de haut parage;
Pleüst a Dieu nostre pere   7.4
Que vous me fussiez donee
          A fame espousade."

Do you wish me to sing you
a sweet song of love?
No rustic composed it,
but rather a knight
in the shade of an olive tree
in the arms of his sweetheart.

She wore a linen shift,
a white ermine wrap,
and a tunic of silk;
she had stockings of iris
and shoes of mayflowers,
fitting just right.

She wore a sash of leaves
whose green deepened in the rain;
it had buttons of gold.
Her purse was of love,
with pendants of flowers:
it was a love-gift.

She was riding a mule;
its shoes were of silver
and its saddle of gold;
on the crupper behind her
three rosebushes grew
to provide her with shade.

So she went down through the field;
some knights came upon her
and greeted her nicely:
"Lovely lady, where were you born?"
"From France I am, the renowned,
of the highest birth.

"The nightingale is my father,
who sings on the branches
high in the forest;
the siren is my mother,
who sings high on the shore
of the salt sea."

"Lovely lady, may such birth bode well!
You are of fine family
and high birth;
would to God our father
that you were given me
as my wedded wife!"

PASTOURELLES

Of twelfth-century troubadour origin, the *pastourelle* was widely cultivated only by thirteenth-century trouvères, who left over one hundred fifty such compositions, a third of them anonymous. The genre presents a sort of antithesis to the *grand chant courtois*, in that it directs the knightly persona's libido not toward a noble lady, with the attendant stimulation of social constraints and a consequent refinement of desire into love, but toward a shepherdess, apparently representative of an unfettered, natural sensuality that has the effect of turning the man's desire into undisguised sexual aggressiveness. The poet-knight moves out of his courtly milieu, and the expression of his desire changes radically. While the *grand chant*, moreover, is a purely lyric genre, the *pastourelle* combines lyric with narrative and dialogue; indeed, the verbal exchange between the male persona and the country woman that he chances to encounter forms a significant part of the poetic experience, very different from the often tremulous one-way communication characteristic of the courtly songs. The tone is meant to be light and the pace lively, which is manifested as much in versification as in content and vocabulary, for the *pastourelles* show a high frequency of heterometric stanzas and of quite varied rhyme schemes.

The poet-knight's chance meeting with a shepherdess is followed by his attempt to seduce her, the attempt sometimes taking on the humorously transgressive appearance of courtly wooing and sometimes eliciting from the woman a defensive wit that clearly gives her the intellectual as well as moral advantage. The knight may succeed, whether by suasion or by force, and in either case the woman may ultimately be depicted as satisfied by her experience. Or he may fail, whether because the woman's arguments are convincing or because one or more of her companions come, or threaten to come, to her rescue. The little drama is intended to be entertaining whatever the outcome may be and whether the last laugh is on the shepherdess or on the knight. There are, of course, numerous variations on the basic scenario, as our four anonymous compositions reveal.

In a small subgroup of *pastourelles*, the so-called *bergeries*, the poet-knight comes upon a group of peasants singing and dancing; he simply observes their activity and ostensible lack of constraint, which he tends to envy. If he lets his presence be known, it is made immediately evident that the peasants regard him as an unwelcome interloper. As shown in the fourth song in our series, "L'autrier a

doulz mois de mai," the *bergerie* may be combined with the more usual type of *pastourelle*.

In a final, very minor, subgroup, the knight out riding encounters a shepherd, with whom he enters into a conversation on the trials of love; see Thibaut de Blaison's "Hui main par un ajournant" (in this Anthology).

STUDIES: Zink 1972; Bec 1977, chapter 5.

EDITIONS: Bartsch 1870; Rivière 1974-76; Paden 1987.

- "L'autrier quant je chevauchoie, desouz l'onbre d'un prael": L 265-1037, RS 1698a, MW 2. Single source: ms. K; music. RT 41-42/140-143; Bartsch 1870, 194-195; Spanke 1925, 174-175; Rivière 1975 (2), 121-122.

The unusually long lines are composed of two hemistichs of seven syllables each, the first sometimes augmented by a final unstressed *-e* not counted in the verse meter but certainly counting in the music.

5.4: This concluding statement, in the third person, represents (perhaps together with the preceding line) a shift from the first-person narrative of the beginning of the song. Some earlier editors, perceiving a scribal mistake, emended to *mes braz l'ai*. However, since the same shift occurs in several other *pastourelles*, we prefer to respect the ms. reading.

The melody, syllabic, built on *g*, shows great simplicity and regularity in its scheme: ABAB CDD′.

- "Enmi la rousee que nest la flor": L 265-632, RS 1984, MW 518. Sources: ms. K, also NPX; music in all. RT 43-45/142-147; Bartsch 1870, 184-185; Spanke 1925, 32-33; Rivière 1975 (2), 111-113; Paden 1987 (1), 284-287.

The metric structure of the decasyllabic lines is a bit free, as is sometimes the case in *pastourelles* and similar compositions. Thus, 1.1 shows $5 + e + 4$; 1.2 and 2.1, $5 + e + 4$; 2.2 and 3.1, $5 + 5$; 3.2, $5 + e + 5$, and so forth. Note that the poem also shows irregularities in rhyming, e.g., *arbroie : s'envoysent, baudor : amors, destre : damoisele*.

2.7: There is irony in addressing the rustic as *damoisele*; the same device recurs in 3.4 and 3.5, where Robin's mother is called *dame* and the peasant boyfriend himself, *cortois*.

The melody, syllabic, with no ornamentation, shows the prevalence of the Lydian, or *f*, scale in both the opening and the final cadence, even though the internal cadences are on *a, g,* and *e*. The scheme is regular: AA BCD B′CE. The other manuscript versions are of the same family.

● "La douçors del tens novel": L 265-971, RS 580, MW 461, B 1854. Single source: ms. U; music. RT 57-60/164-169; Bartsch 1870, 135-137; Rivière 1975 (2), 77-80.

The meaning of the refrain word *pickenpot*, which we have translated as 'popinjay', is actually not at all certain.

Built on *g* and *c*, the melody shows consistently moderate ornamentation, in the neumatic style. The scheme of the stanza is regular: ABCABC DDEAB/refrain FG.

● "L'autrier a doulz mois de mai": L 265-1009, RS 89, MW 1878, B 478 and 1679. Single source: ms. C; no music. RT 62-64/174-179; Bartsch 1870, 112-113; Rivière 1975 (2), 33-35.

Dialectal features: Lorraine, including *ameit* = Central Fr. *amé, chanteir = chanter; poent = point; oxelet = oiselet, fix = fis; lou = le*. Note particularly the verb forms *ait = a, laissait = laissa, rescriait = rescria*.

L'autrier quant je chevauchoie, desouz l'onbre d'un prael   (L 265-1037)
Pastourelle

L'autrier quant je chevauchoie,
    desouz l'onbre d'un prael
Trouvai gentil pastorele,
    les euz verz, le chief blondel,
        Vestue d'un blïaudel,
La color fresche et vermeille;
    de roses fet un chapel.   1.4

Je la saluai, la bele;
    ele me respont briément.
"Bele, avez vous point d'ami
    qui vous face biau senblant?"
        Tantost respont en riant:
"Nenil voir, chevalier sire,
    mes g'en aloie un querant."   2.4

The other day, as I was out riding,
    in a shady meadow
I found a fine shepherdess,
    sparkling-eyed and blonde,
dressed in a tiny tunic,
fresh and pink of complexion,
    making a garland of roses.

I greeted the lovely girl;
    she didn't take long to answer.
"My dear, don't you have a boyfriend
    who looks good to you?"
With a laugh, she answered right away:
"No indeed, sir knight,
    but I've been looking for one."

"Bele, puis qu'ami n'avez,
　　dites se vos m'amerez."
Ele respont conme sage:
　　"Oïl, se vous m'espousez.
　　　　Lors ferez voz volentez,
Et, se querez autre chose,
　　ce seroit desloiauté."　　　　　　　3.4

"Bele, ce lessiez ester;
　　n'avons cure d'espouser!
Ainz demerrons nostre joie
　　tant com la porrons mener,
　　　　De besier et d'acoler,
Et je vous ferai fiance
　　que je n'avrai autre a per."　　　　4.4

"Sire, vostre biau senblant
　　va mon cuer si destraignant
Vostres sui, que que nus die,
　　des cestui jour en avant."
　　　　N'ala pas trois pas avant;
Entre ses braz l'a sesie
　　deseur l'erbe verdoiant.　　　　　　5.4

"My dear, since you have no boyfriend,
　　what about loving me?"
She answered sensibly:
　　"Yes, if you marry me;
then you can have your way with me;
but if you want anything else,
　　it wouldn't be fair."

"My dear, forget that;
　　we don't care about marriage!
Let's instead go enjoy life
　　as long as we can,
embracing and kissing,
and I'll promise you
　　not to have another mate."

"My lord, you look so good
　　to my throbbing heart
that I am yours as of this very day,
　　whatever others may say."
She didn't take three steps forward
before he seized her in his arms
　　on the green grass.

Enmi la rousee que nest la flor   (L 265-632)
Pastourelle

En- mi la rou- se- e que nest la flor,

Que la rose est be- lë au point du jor !

Par mi cele ar- broi- e

Cil oi- sel- lon s'en- voi- sent

Et mai- nent grant bau- dor .

Quant j'oi la leur joi- e,

Pour riens ne m'i ten- droi- e

D'a- mer bien par a- mors .

Enmi la rousee que nest la flor,
Que la rose est belë au point du jor!
Par mi cele arbroie
Cil oisellon s'envoisent   1.4
Et mainent grant baudor.
Quant j'oi la leur joie,
Pour riens ne m'i tendroie
D'amer bien par amors.   1.8

La pastore ert belë et avenant;
Ele a les euz verz, la bouche riant.
Benoet soit li mestre
Qui tele la fist nestre,   2.4
Bien est a mon talent.
Je m'assis a destre,
Si li dis: "Damoisele,
Vostre amor vous demant."   2.8

In the dew where the flowers grow,
how lovely is the rose at daybreak!
In the grove
young birds frolic
and fly about gaily.
When I hear their cheerful song,
nothing could stop me
from falling in love.

The shepherdess was lovely and charming;
she had bright eyes and a smiling mouth.
Blessèd be the master
who created her that way,
for she is just as I like!
I sat down on her right
and said: "Young lady,
I ask for your love."

Ele me respont: "Sire champenois,
Par vostre folie ne m'avrois des mois,
    Car je sui amie
      Au filz dame Marie,   3.4
      Robinet le cortois,
    Qui me chauce et lie
    Et si ne me let mie
Sanz biau chapiau d'orfrois."   3.8

Quant vi que proiere ne m'i vaut noient,
Couchai la a terre tout maintenant,
    Levai li le chainse,
      Si vi la char si blanche,   4.4
      Tant fui je plus ardant,
    Fis li la folie.
    El ne.l contredist mie,
Ainz le vout bonement.   4.8

Quant de la pastore oi fet mon talent,
Sus mon palefroi montai maintenant,
    Et ele s'escrie:
      "Au filz sainte Marie,   5.4
      Chevalier, vos conmant;
    Ne m'oublïez mie,
    Car je sui vostre amie,
Mes revenez souvent."   5.8

She answered: "Knight of Champagne,
you won't ever have me for your lust.
I am the sweetheart
of lady Mary's son,
courteous young Robin,
who gives me shoes and belts
and never leaves me
without a fine gold-trimmed garland."

When I saw that I'd be urging in vain,
I pulled her right down on the ground,
lifted her shift,
saw her white flesh,
burned all the hotter,
and did the lusty thing.
She made no protest
but went along with delight.

When I'd done what I liked with the girl,
I jumped back up in the saddle
and she cried out:
"I commend you, knight,
to holy Mary's Son!
I am your sweetheart;
don't forget me,
but come back often!"

La douçors del tens novel   (L 265-971)
Pastourelle

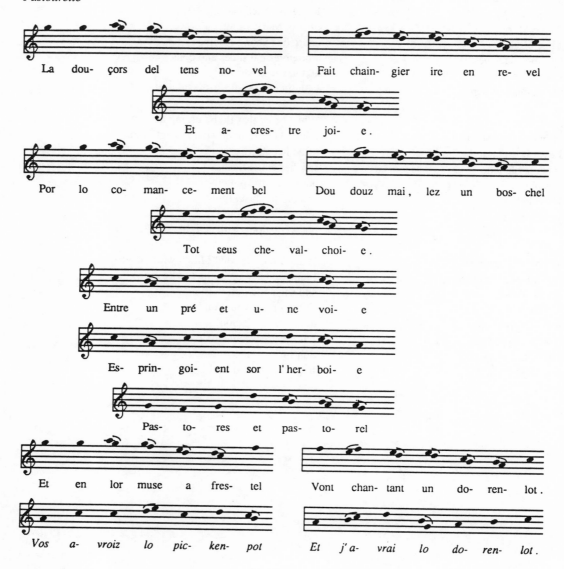

La dou- çors del tens no- vel   Fait chain- gier ire en re- vel

Et a- cres- tre joi- e.

Por lo co- man- ce- ment bel   Dou douz mai, lez un bos- chel

Tot seus che- val- choi- e.

Entre un pré et u- ne voi- e

Es- prin- goi- ent sor l'her- boi- e

Pas- to- res et pas- to- rel

Et en lor muse a fres- tel   Vont chan- tant un do- ren- lot.

Vos a- vroiz lo pic- ken- pot   Et j'a- vrai lo do- ren- lot.

La douçors del tens novel	The fairness of the new season
Fait chaingier ire en revel	changes gloom to cheer
Et acrestre joie.	and heightens joy.
Por lo comancement bel 1.4	To taste the fine beginning
Dou douz mai, lez un boschel	of fair May, I went out riding
Tot seus chevalchoie.	all alone near a wood.
Entre un pré et une voie	Between a field and a lane
Espringoient sor l'herboie 1.8	shepherdesses and shepherds
Pastores et pastorel	were dancing on the grass
Et en lor muse a frestel	and with their fluted bagpipe
Vont chantant un dorenlot.	went singing a ditty.
Vos avroiz lo pickenpot 1.12	*You shall have the popinjay*
Et j'avrai lo dorenlot.	*and I will have the ditty.*

Por faire le cointerel
Ot chascuns un vert chapel
  Et blanche corroie
Et ganz couez et coutel   2.4
Et cotte d'un gros burel
  A diverse roie.
S'ot chescuns lez lui la soie
Et chescune se cointoie   2.8
Por son cointe vilenel.
Biatris, estroit graislel,
Va chantant un dorenlot.
Vos avroiz lo pickenpot   2.12
Et j'avrai lo dorenlot.

Entre Guibor et Ansel
Marchent del pié lo prael,
  Guioz lez Maroie
Refasoit lo lecherel,   3.4
Et font croller le cercel
  Si qu'il en peçoie.
Cil et cele se desroie,
Fierent del pié sor l'arboie,   3.8
Chescuns i fait son merel
Et Guis en son chalemel
Cointoie lo dorenlot.
Vos avrez lo pickempot   3.12
Et j'avrai lo dorenlot.

Senz semonse et senz apel,
De mon palefroit morel
  Dessent lez l'arbroie;
En la dance molt isnel   4.4
Me mis lez un sotterel
  Cui forment ennoie,
Car de celi l'esloignoie
Qui l'amoit, si s'en gramoie, 4.8
Si a dit: "Seignor tousel,
Cil qui fait lo damoisel
Nos tout nostre dorenlot."
Vos avrez lo pickenpot   4.12
Et j'avrai lo dorenlot.

Dist Perrins: "Sire donzel,
Querez aillors vostre avel,
  Lassiez autrui proie!"
Kant cil oï son aidel,   5.4
En sa main prist un caillel,
  Vers moi lo paumoie;
Kant vi la force n'iert moie,
Sor mon cheval remontoie, 5.8
Mais l'un d'aus oing lo musel,
D'un baston li fis borsel,
Puis guerpi lo dorenlot.
Vos avroiz lo pikenpot   5.12
Et j'avrai lo dorenlot.

To play the dandy,
 each fellow wore a green garland
 and white belt,
fringed gloves and a knife
 and a thick homespun coat
 with varied stripes.
Each one had his girl beside him,
 and each girl primped
 for her country dandy.
Beatrice, in a high voice,
 went singing a ditty.
You shall have the popinjay
and I will have the ditty.

Guibor and Ansel
 were both stomping on the ground
 while, alongside Marie, Guiot
was playing the gallant,
 and they were shaking the tambourine
 so hard that it broke;
one couple stepped out of the line
 to dance jigs on the grass.
Everyone did his leaps and skips,
 and Guiot with his shawm
 dressed up the ditty.
You shall have the popinjay
and I will have the ditty.

Uninvited and unaddressed,
 I dismounted from my jet-black horse
 at the edge of the grove;
I slipped swiftly into the dance
 alongside one of the dunces,
 whom it bothered badly,
for I was parting him from the girl
 who loved him; he flared up
 and said: "Boys, sirs,
this fellow dressed like a lordlet
 is stealing our ditty!"
You shall have the popinjay
and I will have the ditty.

Perrin said: "Sir, young lord,
 go somewhere else for what you want;
 leave others' game alone!"
When the first one heard this support,
 he picked up a little stone
 and flung it straight at me;
when I saw that strength was theirs,
 I mounted on my horse again
 but I bloodied the nose of one of them;
with a stick I gave him a good bump —
 and then gave up the ditty.
You shall have the popinjay
and I will have the ditty.

Lors me sui mis a la voie		Then I set out on my way
Et chascuns d'els me convoie		and they all escorted me
De baston ou de chaillel;		with sticks and stones;
Lors chiens Tancre et Mansael	E.4 (10)	their dogs Tancre and Mansael
M'ont hüé senz dorenlot.		chased me with barks but no ditty.
Vos avrez lo pikenpot		*You shall have the popinjay*
Et j'avrai lo dorenlot.		*and I will have the ditty.*

L'autrier a doulz mois de mai   (L 265-1009)
Pastourelle

L'autrier a doulz mois de mai		The other day in the fair month of May,
Ke nest la verdure,		when everything comes up green,
Ke cil oxelet sont gai,		when the little birds are lively
Plain d'envoixeüre,	1.4	and full of good cheer,
Sor mon cheval l'ambleüre		I was out riding, ambling
M'alai chevalchant;		along on my horse;
S'oï pastoure chantant		I heard a shepherdess singing
De jolit cuer amerous:	1.8	*with a glad and loving heart:*
Se j'avoie ameit un jor,		*If I had loved one day,*
Je diroie a tous		*I would tell everyone*
Bones sont amors.		*that love is good.*

Ausi tost com j'entendi		As soon as I heard
Ceste chansonnete,		this little song,
Tout maintenant descendi		I jumped right down
Per desor l'erbete,	2.4	onto the ground
Si resgardai la tousete		and watched the girl
Ke se desduisoit		as she amused herself
Et ceste chanson chantoit		singing the song
De jolif cuer amerous:	2.8	*with a glad and loving heart:*
Se j'avoie ameit un jor,		*If I had loved one day,*
Je diroie a tous		*I would tell everyone*
Bones sont amors.		*that love is good.*

Tantost comme j'entendi		No sooner had I heard
Celle bergerete,		the shepherdess
Maintenant me trais vers li		than I drew up close to her
Soz une espinete;	3.4	under an evergreen tree;
Et Robins de sa musete		while Robin was playing
Davant li musoit,		his musette for her,
Et elle se rescrioit		she was singing out
De jolit cuer amerous:	3.8	*with a glad and loving heart:*
Se j'avoie ameit un jor,		*If I had loved one day,*
Je diroie a tous		*I would tell everyone*
Bones sont amors.		*that love is good.*

Lors m'escriai a haut ton,
　　Sens poent d'arestence:
"Li lous enporte un mouton!"
　　Et Robins s'avance, 4.4
S'ait deguerpie la dance;
　　La blonde laissait,
Et elle se rescriait
De jolit cuer amerous: 4.8
Se j'avoie ameit un jor,
　　Je diroie a tous
　　Bones sont amors.

La pastourelle enbraissai,
　　Ki est blanche et tendre;
Desor l'erbe la getai,
　　Ne s'en pout desfendre. 5.4
Lou jeu d'amors sens atendre
　　Li fix per delit,
Et elle a chanteir se prist
De jolit cuer amerous: 5.8
Se j'avoie ameit trois jors,
　　Je diroie a tous
　　Bones sont amors.

Then, without a pause,
　　I cried out loud:
"The wolf is stealing a sheep!"
　　Robin ran off,
abandoning the dance;
　　he left the blonde girl behind
and she sang out
with a glad and loving heart:
If I had loved one day,
　　I would tell everyone
　　that love is good.

I embraced the shepherdess,
　　who was white and tender;
I pushed her down to the ground,
　　and she could not protest.
With no delay I played her
　　the pleasant game of love,
and she began to sing
with a glad and loving heart:
If I had loved three days,
　　I would tell everyone
　　that love is good.

CHANSONS DE RENCONTRE

The small group we call encounter songs is a hybrid that has no formal definition and only a loose thematic unity. Like the *pastourelles*, these compositions begin with a poet-knight unexpectedly coming upon a woman, but this one is a lady or maiden, a bourgeoise or a nun—in any case, not a shepherdess. She may be accompanied by a female friend or by a male lover, and there is talk of love in the form of an overheard debate, as in our first piece, "Au renouvel du tens que la florete," or a monologue, as in the second, "Quant ce vient en mai ke rose est panie," or an exchange between the poetic persona and the female figure. There is no attempted seduction. The point of the *pastourelle*-like opening seems to be little more than the staging of a dialogue or monologue that does not involve the poet-knight, who is here an observer rather than an actor. Structurally, the *chansons de rencontre* vary considerably, ranging from the simplicity of *ballettes* to long, heterometric stanzas.

- "Au renouvel du tens que la florete": L 265-185, RS 980, MW 102. Sources: ms. K, also NPX; music in all. RT 68-70/184-189; Spanke 1925, 107-109.

In four metrically complex stanzas, this poem combines a (presumably male) narrator's springtime introduction and staging of an overheard dilemmatic exchange, the women's exchange reported in direct discourse, and a woman's amatory monologue incorporating the substance of an envoy.

The melody is syllabic, with almost no ornamentation; it is built on *d,* with internal cadences on *e* and *a.* The scheme is close to that of a *lai-sequence* melody: AA BB CCD CCD BB'.

- "Quant ce vient en mai ke rose est panie": L 265-1482, RS 1156, MW 353, B 1126. Sources: ms. C, also U; no music. RT 78-79/200-201. The form of this composition is that of a *ballette* without initial refrain or a *rotrouenge.*

Dialectal features: Lorraine, including *leis* = Central Fr. *lez, moneir* = *mener; senturete* = *ceinturete; lou* = *le, jeu* = *je; seux* = *sui; amaixe* = *amasse.* Note in particular the verb forms *ait* = *a; escriait* = *escria, getait* = *geta.*

Au renouvel du tens que la florete   (L 265-185)

Chanson de rencontre

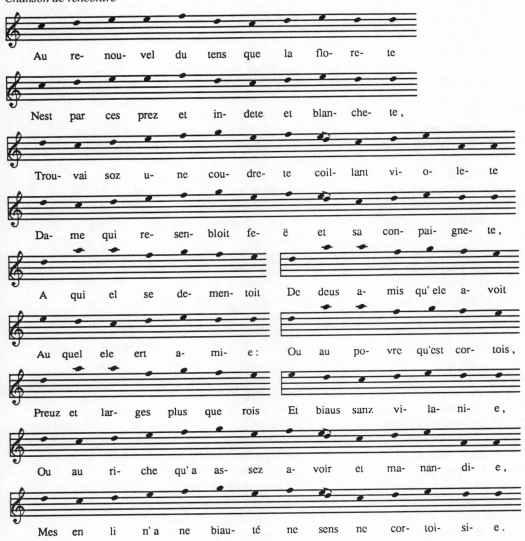

Au re- nou- vel du tens que la flo- re- te	
Nest par ces prez et in- dete et blan- che- te,	
Trou- vai soz u- ne cou- dre- te coil- lant vi- o- le- te	
Da- me qui re- sen- bloit fe- ë et sa con- pai- gne- te,	
A qui el se de- men- toit	De deus a- mis qu'ele a- voit
Au quel ele ert a- mi- e:	Ou au po- vre qu'est cor- tois,
Preuz et lar- ges plus que rois	Et biaus sanz vi- la- ni- e,
Ou au ri- che qu'a as- sez a- voir et ma- nan- di- e,	
Mes en li n'a ne biau- té ne sens ne cor- toi- si- e.	

Au renouvel du tens que la florete	At the return of the season when new flowers
Nest par ces prez et indete et blanchete,	india-blue and white blossom in the fields,
Trouvai soz une coudrete coillant violete	I found, as they were gathering violets in a hazel grove,
Dame qui resenbloit feë et sa conpaignete,	a lady who looked like a fay and her companion,
A qui el se dementoit 1.5	with whom she was pondering
De deus amis qu'ele avoit	which one of two suitors
Au quel ele ert amie:	of hers to love:
Ou au povre qu'est cortois,	the poor man who was refined,
Preuz et larges plus que rois	upright, and generous even more than a king,
Et biaus sanz vilanie, 1.10	and flawlessly handsome,
Ou au riche qu'a assez avoir et manandie,	or else the rich man with money and land
Mes en li n'a ne biauté ne sens ne cortoisie.	but with no beauty or brains or refinement.

"Ma douce suer, mon conseil en creez:
   Amez le riche, grant preu i avrez;
Car se vous volez deniers, vous en avrez assez;
Ja, de chose que il ait, mes soufrete n'avrez.
     Il fet bon le riche amer,   2.5
      Q'il a assez a donner;
       Je seroie s'amie.
      Se je lessoie mantel
      D'escarlate por burel,
       Je feroie folie;   2.10
Car li riches veut amer et mener bone vie,
Et li povres veut jöer sanz riens donner s'amie."

   "Or ai oï ton conseil, bele suer,
    Du riche amer; ne.l feroie a nul fuer!
Certes, ja n'iert mon ami par deseure mon cuer.
Dame qui a cuer joli ne.l feroit a nul fuer.
     Dames qui vuelent amer   3.5
      De bone amor sanz fausser,
       Conment que nus me die,
      Ne doivent riens demander,
      Pour nus qu'en sache parler,
       Fors bons amor jolie.   3.10
Toutes fames je les hé, et Jhesus les maudie,
Qu'aiment honme pour doner; c'est grant ribauderie.

   "E! fine Amor, tant m'avez oublïee
    Que nuit ne jor ne puis avoir duree,
Tant m'a sa tres grant biauté tainte et descoloree;
Tant pens a li nuit et jor que toute en sui müee.
     Rosignol, va, si li di   4.5
      Les maus que je sent pour li,
       Et si ne m'en plaing mie;
      Di li q'il avra m'amor,
      Car plus bele ne meillor
       De moi n'avra il mie;   4.10
Di li q'il avra assez puis que je sui s'amie,
Q'il ne lest pas pour deniers a mener boune vie."

"Sister, my dear, trust my advice:
love the rich one; the benefit will be great,
for if money's what you want, you'll have a lot;
you'll never lack for anything he has.
It's good to love the rich man,
since he has much to give;
I would be his mistress.
If I gave up a cloak
of silk for homespun,
I'd be making a foolish mistake;
the rich man wants to enjoy life and love,
and the poor one wants to play but not pay."

"I've now heard your advice, dear sister,
to love the rich man. I'd never do it!
He'll never be my lover; my heart would refuse.
A lady with a lively heart would never do it.
Ladies who want to love
truly and sincerely,
whatever anyone may tell me,
mustn't ask for anything,
whatever anyone may say,
save true and lively love.
I hate all women — and Jesus curse them! —
who trade love for money; that's plain wantonness.

"Ah, true Love, you have so forgotten me
that I can't last through day or night,
so drained and wan has his beauty left me;
day and night I think of him so much that I'm all changed.
Nightingale, go tell him
the pains that I feel because of him,
(and yet I have no complaint);
tell him that he shall have my love,
that he will never have a woman
better and more beautiful than I;
tell him that he will be rich with my love,
that money must not keep him from enjoyment."

Quant ce vient en mai ke rose est panie   (L 265-1482)
Chanson de rencontre, ballette? rotrouenge?

Quant ce vient en mai ke rose est panie,
Je l'alai coillir per grant drüerie;
En pouc d'oure oï une voix serie
Lonc un vert bouset pres d'une abïete: 1.4
Je sant les douls mals leis ma senturete.
Malois soit de Deu ke me fist nonnete!

When May arrives and roses bloom,
I go a-picking with love on my mind;
in little time I hear a lovely voice
in a green grove near a convent.
I feel the pleasant pains below my waist.
God curse whoever made a nun of me!

"Ki nonne me fist, Jesus lou maldie!
Je di trop envis vespres ne complies;
J'amaixe trop muels bone compaingnie
Ke fust deduissans et amerousete."   2.4
Je sant les douls mals leis ma senturete.
Malois soit de Deu ke me fist nonnete!

Elle s'escriait: "Com seux esbaihie!
E Deus! ki m'ait mis en ceste abaïe?
Maiz jeu en istrai, per sainte Marie!
N'i vestirai mais souplis ne gonnete."   3.4
Je sant les douls mals leis ma senturete.
Malois soit de Deu ke me fist nonnete!

"Celui manderai a cui seux amie
K'il me vaigne querre en ceste abaïe;
S'irons a Parix moneir bone vie,
Car il est jolis et je seux jonete."   4.4
Je sant les douls mals leis ma senturete.
Malois soit de Deu ke me fist nonnete!

Quant ses amis ot la parolle oïe,
De joie tressaut, li cuers li fremie;
A la porte en vient de celle abaïe,
Si en getait fors sa douce amïete.   5.4
Je sant les douls mals leis ma senturete.
Malois soit de Deu ke me fist nonnete!

"Whoever made a nun of me be cursed by Jesus!
Compline and vespers I sing against my will;
I'd much rather have good company,
fun-loving and ready to love."
I feel the pleasant pains below my waist.
God curse whoever made a nun of me!

She cries out: "I am mortified here!
God, who placed me in this convent?
But, by holy Mary, I'll get out!
Nor will I wear habit or surplice anymore."
I feel the pleasant pains below my waist.
God curse whoever made a nun of me!

"I'll send word to the man I love
that he should come get me in this convent;
we'll go to Paris to enjoy our life,
for he is high-spirited and I am young."
I feel the pleasant pains below my waist.
God curse whoever made a nun of me!

When her friend hears the message,
he jumps with joy and his heart flutters;
he comes to the gate of the convent
and frees his young sweetheart.
I feel the pleasant pains below my waist.
God curse whoever made a nun of me!

CHANSONS DE FEMME

The traditional term "women's songs" covers a broad spectrum of formal and thematic possibilities, for their only common characteristics are female voice and a preoccupation with love. Indeed, the category may even be stretched to include compositions not in the voice of a woman—that is, with a female poetic "I"—but songs that nevertheless present a woman's point of view or are associated with performance by women. *Chansons de femme* comprise, then, the laments or invective of unhappy wives, the regrets of bourgeois or aristocratic ladies who have said no once too often, the yearnings of girls discovering desire, the frustrations of young nuns too sensual for their habit or the spiritualized longings of those who prefer the love of God, the poignancy of parting from one's lover whether because the night is over or because a crusade is beginning; the category also makes room for narrative lyrics sung by women at their work and whose central figures are women in love. The great majority of these numerous compositions are anonymous, and those that are not are almost all attributed by the ms. sources to male trouvères, the land of *langue d'oïl* never having developed an identifiable counterpart of the southern trobairitz. Many of the pieces are readily seen as belonging to other, more strictly defined lyric types or genres and are normally so classified; thus, in the present collection, women's songs will be found under BALLETTES, AUBES, CHANSONS DE TOILE; elsewhere they will appear as crusade songs, *chansons de mal mariée*, even an occasional *grand chant courtois*, or *chanson d'amour* of the high style. The category covers both works created in the tradition of the troubadours and works of purely French origin.

In this section we present a small set of anonymous women's songs that do not readily fit under our other rubrics. The first, "L'on dit qu'amors est dolce chose," is in the form of a courtly *chanson* and, except for the reversal of genders, could readily be the plaint of a typical male poet-lover. The second, "Lasse, pour quoi refusai," expresses a specifically feminine experience in a somewhat lighter, more varied structure. The last, "Jherusalem, grant damage me fais," is a song of separation, a *chanson de croisade* not of exhortation but of pain.

STUDIES: Dronke 1968, chapter 3; Bec 1977, chapters 1, 2 et passim.

● "L'on dit qu'amors est dolce chose": L 265-1235, RS 1937, MW 827, B 1716. Sources: ms. U, also C; music in U. RT 82-84/208-211.

3.6-8: The reference here is to the fate of Pyramus and Thisbe, recounted in Ovid's *Metamorphoses* IV:142-146

and very likely known to the poet through the anonymous twelfth-century French adaptation:

"Piramus, ves ci vostre amie.
Car l'esgardez, si ert garie."
Li jovenciaus, la ou moroit,
Entr'oevre les iex et si voit
Que ce iere Tisbé s'amie
Qui l'apeloit toute esmarie.

("Pyramus, this is your belovèd.
Look at her, and she will be healed."
The youth, as he was dying,
half-opened his eyes and saw
that it was Thisbe his belovèd
who in distress was addressing him.)

—*Piramus et Tisbé*, ed. C. de Boer
(Paris, 1921), ll. 892-897

Note that it is to the male figure that the female speaker in this song compares herself; note, moreover, that the song makes no mention of the death which in the story immediately follows Pyramus's glance at Thisbe.

The melody, relatively unornamented, shows a *pedes cum cauda* scheme with added refrain: ABAB CDEF/GH. The opening of the piece is on *c* (lines 1 and 3), and the principal cadences of both stanza and refrain are on *g* (lines 1, 3, 8, and 10).

● "Lasse, pour quoi refusai": L 265-990, RS 100, MW 2024, B 1040. Sources: ms. K, also NPX; music in all. RT 102-104/244-249; Spanke 1925, 114-116.

This seems to be a Central French transcription of a text composed in Lorraine dialect. Graphic variety and dialectal adaptation mask the unusual fact that, with the exception of the last two lines of the refrain, there is essentially only one rhyme in this poem: *a* is -[e], and *b* is simply its feminine equivalent. The *a* rhyme is represented by *-ai, -é, -er, -ez*, and even *-ier*. To this list must be added *-a* (2.5-6), for the rhyme words *pria* and *a* in stanza 2 are no doubt Central rewritings of the Lorraine verb forms *priait* and *ait*.

The melody, built on the Lydian, or *f*, scale (with cadences on *f* and *a*), shows a *pedes cum cauda* scheme with added refrain: ABAB CDEFG/D'E'H.

● "Jherusalem, grant damage me fais": L 265-939, RS 191, MW 596. Single source: ms. M; no music. RT 107-108/250-253; Bédier-Aubry 1909, 275-279. The rubric attributes this piece to Gautier d'Epinal and the ms. table of contents ascribes it to Jean de Neuville; these attributions have been rejected by the modern editors of the two trouvères, and we have no reason not to accept their judgment. As for the particular crusade that inspired the song, there is no way to identify it. For a detailed textual analysis, see Dijkstra 1995, 174-177.

The poem is no doubt a fragment. The occurrence of identical rhymes in stanzas 2 and 3 indicates that the song, composed in *coblas doblas*, should contain at least four stanzas, of which the surviving st. 1 would be either the first or the second. Normally, however, poems in *coblas doblas* contain five or six stanzas; and the fact is that, after st. 3 (originally st. 4), the ms. shows a blank space large enough to accommodate two more stanzas.

This moving lament has much in common with Guiot de Dijon's "Chanterai por mon corage," which is also a crusade song of separation in a woman's voice, and should be compared as well with the male-voiced compositions "Ahi, Amours! com dure departie" by Conon de Béthune and "A vous, amant, plus qu'a nulle autre gent" by the Châtelain de Coucy. All these songs appear in the present volume.

3.4: *n'a pas c'une*, which we have rendered as 'has more than one' (lit. 'has not only one') is ambiguous in Old French, where it may also mean 'has only one'. Our interpretation follows that of Bédier-Aubry 1909.

L'on dit qu'amors est dolce chose   (L 265-1235)
Chanson de femme

L'on dit qu'amors est dolce chose,
Mais je n'en conois la dolçor;
Tote joie m'en est enclose,
N'ainz ne senti nul bien d'amor.
Lasse! mes mals ne se repose,   1.5
Si m'en deplaing et faz clamor.
Mar est batuz qui plorer n'ose,
N'en plorant dire sa dolor.
Ses duels li part qui s'ose plaindre;
Plus tost en puet son mal estaindre.   1.10

De ce me plaing qu'il m'a traïe;
S'en ai trop grant duel acoilli,
Quant je qui sui leals amie
Ne truis amor en mon ami.
Je fui ainçois de lui baisie,   2.5
Si lo fis de m'amor saisi;
Mais tels baise qui n'aime mie:
Baisier ont maint amant traï.
Ses duels li part qui s'ose plaindre;
Plus tost en puet son mal estaindre.   2.10

Estre cuidai de lui amee
Quant entre ses braz me tenoit;
Cum plus iere d'amors grevee,
A son parler me refaisoit;
A sa voiz iere si sanee   3.5
Cum Piramus quant il moroit:
Navrez en son flanc de s'espee,
Au nom Tisbé les iauz ovroit.
Ses duels li part qui s'ose plaindre;
Plus tost en puet son mal estaindre.   3.10

They say that love is a sweet thing,
but I am a stranger to its sweetness;
all its joy is barred to me,
and I have never felt its pleasure.
Alas! my pain knows no pause
and so I lament and raise my cry.
You are woefully beaten if you dare not weep
or express your sorrow in tears.
One who dares lament drives his sorrow away;
he can sooner put an end to his pain.

My complaint is that he betrayed me;
and I have endured great sorrow,
since I who love loyally
find no love in my belovèd.
I was once kissed by him,
and I made him master of my love;
but there are those who kiss without loving:
kisses have betrayed many a lover.
One who dares lament drives his sorrow away;
he can sooner put an end to his pain.

I believed myself loved by him
when he held me in his arms;
when I was most oppressed by love,
his words gave me back my strength.
I was revived by his voice
like Pyramus dying:
wounded in the side by his sword,
at the name of Thisbe he opened his eyes.
One who dares lament drives his sorrow away;
he can sooner put an end to his pain.

Lasse, pour quoi refusai   (L 265-990)
Chanson de femme

Las- se, pour quoi re- fu- sai   Ce- lui qui tant m'a a- me- e?

Lonc tens a a moi mu- sé   Et n'i a mer- ci trou- ve- e.

Las- se, si tres dur cuer ai !   Qu' en di- rai ?

Fors- se- ne- e   Fui, plus que des- ve- e,

Quant le re- fu- sai .   G' en fe- rai

Droit a son ple- sir   S' il m' en daigne o- ïr .

Lasse, pour quoi refusai		Alas, why did I reject
Celui qui tant m'a amee?		the man who loved me so?
Lonc tens a a moi musé		He whiled away much time with me
Et n'i a merci trouvee.	1.4	and never found mercy.
Lasse, si tres dur cuer ai!		Alas, what a hard heart I have!
Qu'en dirai?		What shall I say?
Forssenee		I was out of my mind,
Fui, plus que desvee,	1.8	more than mad,
Quant le refusai.		to reject him.
G'en ferai		*I will do*
Droit a son plesir,		*justice to his wishes,*
S'il m'en daigne oïr.	1.12	*if he deigns to hear me.*
Certes, bien me doi clamer		I must indeed call myself
Et lasse et maleüree		wretched and unfortunate
Quant cil ou n'a point d'amer,		that the man who knows no spite
Fors grant douçor et rousee,	2.4	but only gentleness and warmth
Tant doucement me pria		courted me so gently
Et n'i a		yet found in me
Recouvree		no mercy;
Merci; forssenee	2.8	I was out of my mind
Fui quant ne l'amai.		not to love him.
G'en ferai		*I will do*
Droit a son plesir,		*justice to his wishes,*
S'il m'en daigne oïr.	2.12	*if he deigns to hear me.*

Bien deüst avoir trouvé		He should have found	
Merci quant l'a demandee;		mercy when he sought it;	
Certes, mal en ai ouvré		I certainly did wrong	
Quant je la li ai vëee;	3.4	to deny it him;	
Mult m'a mis en grant esmai.		this has greatly distressed me.	
G'en morrai,		I shall die	
S'acordee		if I am not soon	
Sanz grant demoree	3.8	reconciled	
A lui ne serai.		with him.	
G'en ferai		*I will do*	
Droit a son plesir,		*justice to his wishes,*	
S'il m'en daigne oïr.	3.12	*if he deigns to hear me.*	

A touz ceus qui l'ont grevé		To all those who have troubled him	
Dont Deus si fort destinee		may God give the harsh fate	
Q'il aient les euz crevez		of having their eyes plucked out	
Et les orilles coupees!	4.4	and their ears cut off!	
Ensi ma dolor perdrai.		In that way I'll lose my sorrow.	
Lors dirai:		Then I will say:	
Genz desvee,		Madmen,	
Ma joie est doublee,	4.8	my joy is doubled	
Et se mesfet ai,		and, if I did wrong,	
G'en ferai		*I will do*	
Droit a son plesir,		*justice to his wishes,*	
S'il m'en daigne oïr.	4.12	*if he deigns to hear me.*	

Chançon, va sanz delaier		Song, go with no hesitation	
A celui qui tant m'agree.		to the man who is so dear to me.	
Pour Dieu li pri et reqier		Ask him, by God, and entreat him	
Viengne a moi sanz demoree.	5.4	to come to me without delay.	
En sa merci me metrai,		I will throw myself at his mercy;	
Tost avrai		I will recover	
Pes trouvee,		my peace of mind	
Se il li agree,	5.8	if he accepts,	
Car je trop mal trai.		for I am deeply troubled.	
G'en ferai		*I will do*	
Droit a son plesir,		*justice to his wishes,*	
S'il m'en daigne oïr.	5.12	*if he deigns to hear me.*	

Jherusalem, grant damage me fais   (L 265-939)
Chanson de femme, chanson de croisade

Jherusalem, grant damage me fais,		Jerusalem, you do me great harm,	
Qui m'as tolu ce que je pluz amoie.		taking away what I have loved the most.	
Sachiez de voir ne vos amerai maiz,		You may be sure I will love you no more,	
Quar c'est la rienz dont j'ai pluz male joie;		because that is what gives me the most doleful joy;	
Et bien sovent en souspir et pantais	1.5	often it leaves me sighing and so short of breath	
Si qu'a bien pou que vers Deu ne m'irais,		that I almost turn on God in anger,	
Qui m'a osté de grant joie ou j'estoie.		for He has stripped me of the great joy I had.	

Biauz dous amis, com porroiz endurer
La grant painne por moi en mer salee,
Quant rienz qui soit ne porroit deviser
La grant dolor qui m'est el cuer entree?
Quant me remembre del douz viaire cler   2.5
Que je soloie baisier et acoler,
Grant merveille est que je ne sui dervee.

Si m'aïst Deus, ne puis pas eschaper:
Morir m'estuet, teus est ma destinee;
Si sai de voir que qui muert por amer
Trusques a Deu n'a pas c'une jornee.
Lasse! mieuz vueil en tel jornee entrer   3.5
Que je puisse mon douz ami trover
Que je ne vueill ci remaindre esguaree.

My dear belovèd, how can you endure
your great pain as you sail away from me,
if nothing on earth could express
the great woe that has entered my heart?
When I remember the sweet, smiling face
that I used to kiss and caress,
it is a wonder that I don't lose my mind.

So help me God, I have no way out:
I must die, for that is my fate;
yet I well know that whoever dies for love
has more than one day's journey to God.
Alas! I would rather set out on such a journey
in order to recover my dear belovèd
than remain here adrift.

SOTTES CHANSONS

Like other kinds of nonsense or burlesque poetry—*resveries* and *fatrasies,* for example—the *sottes chansons,* or silly songs, are probably less well represented in the surviving written sources than more serious compositions and surely less than strict respect for the medieval reality would have demanded. There is only one manuscript that transmits any significant number of these thirteenth-century compositions, and it contains only twenty legible pieces, none accompanied by music.

The genre, unknown to the troubadours and cultivated—anonymously—only in French, offers a racy parody of the courtly love song, within whose formal framework the highminded topoi of *fin'amors* are grotesquely mocked. Our single, characteristic example is thus a sequence of five *coblas unissonans* in *pedes cum cauda* form, with a first-person poet-lover who begins by identifying the motive of his song and goes on to describe his lady and the effects of love; the result, however, can hardly be thought a *grand chant courtois.*

STUDY: Bec 1977, chapter 9.

EDITION: Långfors 1945.

• "Chans de singe ne poire mal pellee": L 265-320, RS 537, MW 1835. Single source: ms. I; no music. RT 109-110/254-257; Långfors 1945, 40-42.

Dialectal features: Lorraine, including *varroit* = Central Fr. *vauroit, chafee = chaufee, xadee = (es)chaudee; chainge = change, faice = face; chanteir = chanter, teil = tel; biauteit = beauté; plaixans = plaisanz, fuxiés = fussiez; lou = le, ceu = ce, ju = je.* Note particularly the verb form *ait = a.*

The model of this *sotte chanson* is a song by Adam de la Halle, "Au repairier en la douce contree" (L 2-4).

1.4: *Adangier* is no doubt the same as Audigier, the coarse hero of an epic parody or fabliau whose name came to be used as a term of scorn.

Chans de singe ne poire mal pellee   (L 265-320)
Sotte chanson

Chans de singe ne poire mal pellee		Neither monkey song nor unpeeled pear
Ne me font pas a chanteir revenir,		makes me return to singing,
Mais ma dame qui est trop mal büee		but my lady, poorly laundered,
Me fait chanter d'Adangier lou martir.		makes me sing of Audigier the martyr.
Sor piez ne me puis tenir	1.5	I can't remain standing
Cant elle vers moi coloie,		when she cranes her neck toward me;
Dont ait mes cuers si grant joie		my heart enjoys it so much
C'a poc tient je ne m'oci		that I come close to suicide
Por l'amour de li.	1.9	for love of her.
Moult est plaixans, bien samble forcenee,		She is very appealing, seems out of her mind,
Sovant me fait presant d'un teil sopir		often presents me with such a deep sigh
Ke bien varroit une reupe et demee		that it would fetch a belch and a half
Ki au chainge la vandroit par loixir.		if one were free to make the exchange.
Et Deus li voille merir	2.5	May it please God to reward her
Toz les biens k'elle m'anvoie,		for all the good things she sends me,
Car se je mualz estoie,		for even if I were mute
Ce diroie ju ensi:		I would say this:
"Dame, grant merci."	2.9	"Many thanks, my lady."

Dame d'onor, blanche con poix chafee,
A vos loeir ne doi je pas mantir.
La faice aveis brune, noire et ridee;
C'a main vos voit lou soir devroit morir.
    Ceu me fait resovenir,   3.5
    De vos forment mesferoie
    Se a vos servir failloie,
    Car vos m'aveis enrichi
        D'estre bien chaiti.   3.9

Vint ans cinc mois avant ke fuxiés nee,
Vostre biauteit se vint an moi flaitir
Si aprement, j'an ai la pance anflee.
Nes an sonjant ne me puet sovenir
    De vous, si fort vos desir   4.5
    Ke, se les fievres avoie,
    Dame, je les vos donroie
    Volantiers de cuer joli.
        N'est ce dons d'ami?   4.9

Encor vos don, dame hallegoutee,
De mes jualz, ne.s voil plus retenir,
Boutons mal keus et prunelle xadee,
Tot ceu en boins a vostre eus por tucir.
    Cant vos voi vers moi venir,   5.5
    A poc ke Deu ne renoie,
    Car plus volantiers vairoie
    Venir un louf dever mi.
        Amors en graci.   5.9

Honorable lady, white as hot pitch,
I mustn't lie in praising you.
Your face is brown and black and wrinkled:
See you in the morning — die that night!
This makes me realize
I'd be doing you a great wrong
if I failed in your service,
for you have enriched me
by making me a wretch.

Twenty years five months before your birth,
your beauty came and flung itself at me
so harshly that my belly's still full of gas.
Even in my dreams I can't think of you
without thinking I yearn for you so much
that, if I had a fever,
my lady, I would gladly and eagerly
pass it on to you.
Isn't that a lover's gift?

I'll also give you, tattered lady,
from treasures I no longer care to keep,
half-cooked hips and a scalded plum —
and do it good-naturedly, to help you cough.
When I see you come near,
I almost give up God,
for I would much rather see
a wolf appear.
My thanks to Love!

CHANSONS PIEUSES

Non-liturgical religious songs borrow their forms from various secular genres and have only their piety in common. They are in fact deeply imitative, not only copying general forms but also taking particular lay compositions as structural and even lexical models and adopting their melodies as well: so-called *contrafacta* abound in this category. The favorite focus of the approximately one hundred fifty *chansons pieuses*—all from the thirteenth century—is devotion to the Virgin Mary, which further defines their imitative, reactive character, since the love they express for the heavenly Lady is often a deliberate substitution, sometimes involving playful ambiguity, for the love elsewhere directed toward ladies of the court. Others are inspired by Latin hymns of praise for the Virgin. A small set of devotional songs take on the voice of a woman desiring union with the heavenly Bridegroom, and we have in fact presented one such composition, "Amis, amis," among the BALLETTES; still fewer coincide with *chansons de croisade*. The following pieces both take Mary as their subject.

STUDY: Bec 1977, chapter 7.

EDITION: Järnström 1910 (vol. 1) and Järnström-Långfors 1927 (vol. 2).

- "L'autrier m'iere rendormiz": L 265-1029, RS 1609, MW 1155. Sources: ms. V, also C; no music (see below). RT 133-135/292-297; Järnström 1910, 26-28.

While many *chansons pieuses* are clearly contrafacta of secular songs, it is extraordinary to find one that incorporates an acknowledgment of its model. The song identi-fied in st. 2 is known (L 38-15) and in fact includes among its ms. sources both of the codices that contain the present work. It was composed by either the Châtelain de Coucy or Raoul de Ferrières. It is this song, as transmitted in ms. O, that furnishes our melody.

4.3: The *Lys* is a tributary of the Escaut, in northern France and Belgium. Since it is hardly so well known outside its own region as the Rhone, its presence in this text suggests the locus of the poet's activity.

The melody is built on *d* and *g,* and its seventh line is notated in the second rhythmic mode. It has a *pedes cum cauda* scheme: ABAB' CDEFGH. The ornamentation is quite uniformly distributed over lines 1, 3, and 8; in the other lines, it occurs at or near the rhyme.

- "Douce dame virge Marie": L 265-555, RS 1179, MW 1360. Single source: ms. X; music. RT 136-138/300-303; Järnström-Långfors 1927, 149-150.

This *chanson pieuse* is striking not only for its apparently personal nature, but also because it leaves unexplained why an ardent would-be convert to Christianity should have been refused baptism.

Recalling, in its openings, certain *cantigas de Santa Maria* (Nos. 21, 34, 136, etc.), this song moves between two melodic poles: on one hand, the scale of *f* (opening of lines 1, 3, 6, 8, and cadence of line 5); on the other hand, a kind of suspended cadence on *d* transposed to *g* (lines 2, 4, and especially, at the end of the stanza, line 8). The melody shows a regular scheme: ABAB CDEF.

L'autrier m'iere rendormiz   (L 265-1029)
Chanson pieuse

L'autrier m'iere rendormiz
Par un matin en esté;
Adonques me fu avis
Que la douce mere Dé
M'avoit dit et commandé   1.5
Que seur un chant qui jadis
Soloit estre mout joïs
Chantasse de sa bonté,
Et je tantost l'ai empris.
Dieus doint qu'il li viegne en gré.   1.10

"Quant li rossinoil jolis
Chante seur la flour d'esté"
C'est li chans seur quoi j'ai mis
Le dit que je ai trouvé
De celi qui recouvré   2.5
Nos a le saint paradis,
De quoi nos fusmes jadis
Par Evain desherité.
Ceste dame nos a mis
De tenebres en clarté.   2.10

A la chaste flour de lis,
Reprise en humilité,
Fu li sains anges tramis
De Dieu, qui humanité
Prist en sa virginité   3.5
Pour rachater ses amis.
En li fu noz rachaz pris
Dou saint sanc de son costé;
Mout doit estre de haut pris
Li hons qui tant a costé.   3.10

Not long ago, I'd gone back to sleep
on a summer morning;
it seemed to me then
that the sweet mother of God
had said and commanded
that to a certain tune which once
used to be in favor
I should sing about her goodness,
and I undertook to do so right away.
God grant that it please her!

"When the bright-voiced nightingale
sings among the summer's flowers"
is the tune to which I have set
the poem that I've composed
about the one who has gained
us back the holy paradise
from which we were once
dispossessed by Eve.
This lady has brought us
from darkness into light.

To the chaste lily flower,
renewed in humility,
the holy angel was sent
by God, who took on
human form in her virginity
in order to redeem those dear to Him.
In Him was our redemption effected,
with the holy blood of his flank;
mankind must be valuable
to have cost so much.

Se roches et quaillous bis	If rocks and dark stones
Erent frait et destrempé	were crushed and mixed
Dou ru dou Rosne et dou Lis,	with the rivers Rhone and Lys
Et d'arrement attempré,	and then worked into ink,
Em parchemin conreé 4.5	and heaven and earth
Fussent ciel et terre mis,	were turned into parchment,
Et chascun fust ententis	and everyone were careful
D'escrire la verité,	to write down the truth,
Ja si bien par ces escriz	her virtues would still never
Ne seroient recordé. 4.10	be adequately recorded.
Glorïeuse empereriz,	Glorious empress,
Chambre de la deïté,	chamber of the deity,
Ja ne sera desconfiz	the one who serves you sincerely
Qui vos sert sanz fauseté.	will never be vanquished.
Aiez dou monde pité, 5.5	Take pity on this world,
Qui s'en va de mal en pis;	which goes from bad to worse;
Et moi, qui vos aim et pris	and lead me, who love and esteem you
D'enterine volenté,	with all my will,
En vostre riche païs	lead me to salvation
Conduisiez a sauveté! 5.10	in your splendid land!

Douce dame virge Marie   (L 265-555)
Chanson pieuse

Dou- ce da- me vir- ge Ma- ri- e,

La ro- ï- ne de pa- ra- dis,

Vos- tre con- seil et vos- tre a- ï- e

Re- quier et re- quer- rai touz dis

Que vos prï- ez vos- tre chier filz

Bap- tes- me ne me fail- le mi- e;

Trop en ai es- té es- con- dix,

Si le re- quier sanz vi- la- ni- e.

Douce dame virge Marie,
La roïne de paradis,
Vostre conseil et vostre aïe
Requier et requerrai touz dis   1.4
Que vos prïez vostre chier filz
Baptesme ne me faille mie;
Trop en ai esté escondix,
Si le requier sanz vilainie.   1.8

Douce dame, j'ai grant fiance
En cil qui en crois fu penés.
Qui en celui n'a sa creance,
Certes, por droit noient est nez;   2.4
Son esperit si ert dampnez
Ens el puis d'enfer sanz faillance.
Cil qui ert crestïens clamez,
Il n'a d'enfer nule doutance.   2.8

Hé las, je l'ai tant desiree,
Et si ne la puis avoir.
Toute est m'entente et ma pensee
En crestïenté recevoir;   3.4
Feme, or et argent ne avoir
Ne nule riens tant ne m'agree
Con fait crestïenté, por voir,
Si ne me veut estre donee.   3.8

A vos, douce virge honoree,
Proi et requier mout bonement
Que vostre fiz sanz demoree
Proiés por moi prochainement   4.4
Que de ceus m'achat vengement
Qui crestïenté m'ont vëee,
Si con je croi veraiement
Celui qui fist ciel et rosee.   4.8

Dear Lady, virgin Mary,
queen of heaven,
I seek and will always seek
your counsel and your aid;
please pray to your dear Son
to grant me baptism;
I have been too long denied it,
though I seek it honorably.

Dear Lady, I have great trust
in the One who suffered on the cross.
Whoever has no belief in Him
was surely born for nothing;
his spirit will without a doubt
be damned in the depths of hell;
but anyone called a Christian
has no fear of hell.

Alas, I have so yearned for it
and yet cannot have it.
I put all my care and all my thought
into receiving Christianity;
woman, gold and silver, wealth —
nothing appeals to me, indeed,
as much as Christianity,
yet it is refused me.

To you, dear honored Virgin,
I pray and ask quite simply
that very soon, without delay,
you pray to your Son for me;
may He avenge me on those
who have denied me Christianity,
as I truly believe in the One
who created heaven and compassion.

CHANSONS D'AMOUR

The *chanson d'amour*, or *chanson courtoise*, or *grand chant courtois*, is the trouvères' version of the troubadours' *canso*, the courtly love song, the voice of *fin' amors*, and the highest expression of their lyric art. We have discussed its features at some length in the general introduction and will present numerous examples of the corpus in the sections devoted to individual trouvères. What follows here is simply a pair of anonymous pieces, each exceptional in its own way and both contributing to an appreciation of the considerable variety of expression obtaining within the genre.

STUDIES: Dragonetti 1960; Zumthor 1972, chapter 5.

● "Au nouviau tens, toute riens s'esjoïst": L 265-178, RS 1645, MW 662. Single source: ms. K; music. RT 92-94/226-229; Spanke 1925, 224-225.

This is one of a mere handful of Old French songs that speak, and with apparently personal reference, of marriage.

Two elements of the poet's craft merit particular attention. Note, first, the words rhyming in *-ire*, only one of which occurs in each stanza; the distant echo of these *rims estramps* is reinforced by their semantic association. Second, there is a tendency to break the normal rhythmic flow of the 4 + 6 decasyllabic verse: see the treatment of the caesura in 1.5, 2.1, 2.7, 4.5 and the instances of enjambment, or relative enjambment, at the end of 1.7, 1.8, 2.6, 2.7, 4.6.

4.3ff: It is unusual to find an Old French poet-lover blaming his lady's family for the failure of their love. A second such instance occurs in the following song, and a third in the single poem attributed to one Jacques d'Autun (L 126-1).

The melody has a regular *pedes cum cauda* scheme: ABA′B CDEFG. It has the modal peculiarity of fluctuating between the Gregorian *f* scale (lines 1, 3, 8) and a signature on *g* (lines 2, 4, 6, 9).

● "Li chastelains de Couci ama tant": L 265-1054, RS 358, MW 1227. Sources: ms. K, also NPX; music in all. RT 157-159/332-335; Spanke 1925, 20-21.

As the trouvère indicates in the first three verses, this is a contrafactum, modeled on the Châtelain de Coucy's song "A vous, amant, plus qu'a nulle autre gent" (which appears in the present volume). Whereas the Châtelain laments a separation caused by his departure on a crusade, the anonymous emulator faces the loss of his belovèd through death.

The song is one of the very few lyric death-laments in Old French, where the thematic type never developed into a distinct genre, as was the case in Occitan. We present two others elsewhere in this volume, one by Jean Erart and one by the Duchess of Lorraine.

Note the use of *rims estramps*, as in the preceding composition.

1.7-8: For this charge brought against the lady's family, see our note to the preceding song.

The melody is, as indicated above, a variant of the Châtelain de Coucy's original. It has a regular *pedes cum cauda* scheme: ABAB CDEF. The recitation tone of the first four lines is *a,* and the principal cadences are on *g*.

Au nouviau tens, toute riens s'esjoïst   (L 265-178)

Chanson d'amour

Au nou- viau tens, tou- te riens s'es- jo- ïst :

Cil oi- sel- lon con- men- cent nou- viaus sons,

En ces ver- giers vi- o- le- te flo- rist,

Et par a- mours chan- tent a- manz chan- çons.

Si ne m'est pas. Tou- te joi- e me nuist ;

Quant plus en voi et il mains m'en- be- list,

Quant pas n'a- tent a a- voir gue- ri- son

De la be- le, mes so- vent a lar- ron

De cuer plore et sous- pi- re.

Au nouviau tens, toute riens s'esjoïst:	In the new season, every creature rejoices:
Cil oisellon conmencent nouviaus sons,	the young birds begin new songs,
En ces vergiers violete florist,	violets bloom in the gardens,
Et par amours chantent amanz chançons. 1.4	and lovers sing songs out of love.
Si ne m'est pas. Toute joie me nuist;	But I do not. Every joy hurts me;
Quant plus en voi et il mains m'enbelist,	the more joy I see, the less pleased I am,
Quant pas n'atent a avoir guerison	because I do not expect any healing
De la bele, mes sovent a larron	from my lady; instead, in secret,
De cuer plore et souspire. 1.9	I often weep and sigh in my heart.

Je cuidai bien avoir, s'estre poïst,
En aucun tens de ma dame pardon,
Ne qu'a nul jor autre mari ne prist
Fors moi tot seul, qui sui ses liges hon;   2.4
Car si senblant, oncor ne.l me desist,
Me disoient qu'avant touz me vousist
Amer. Por ce ai mis en sa prison
Moi et mon cuer, et ore a pris baron!
            S'en muir de duel et d'ire.   2.9

Riens ne me plest en cest siecle vivant,
Puis que je ai a la bele failli,
Qu'ele donoit a moi par son senblant
Sens et honor, hardement, cuer joli.   3.4
Ore est torné ce derrieres devant,
Car a touz jorz avrai cuer gemissant,
Plain de dolor, plorant, tristre et marri,
Ne ja nul jor ne.l metrai en oubli;
            S'en sui en grant martire.   3.9

Biau sire Deus, par son faintis senblant
M'a ma dame confondu et traï;
Mes ce ont fet li sien, apertement:
Pour son avoir l'ont donee a celui   4.4
Qui ne deüst pas aler regardant.
Dolenz en sui; mes s'el m'amast autant
De loial cuer com je fesoie li,
Maugré aus touz i eüst il failli:
            Ja, pour ce, n'en fust pire.   4.9

I thought I would one day have,
if possible, my lady's pardon
and that she would never marry
anyone but me, who am her liegeman;
for appearances told me, though not her words,
that above all other men she wanted to love
me. That is why I surrendered to her prison
both self and heart — and now she has a husband!
I am dying of sorrow and rage.

Nothing alive appeals to me in this world
now that I have lost my lady,
for she gave me every appearance
of intelligence and honor, boldness and high spirits.
Now everything is turned upside down,
and I shall always have a groaning heart
sorrowful and weeping, sad and afflicted,
but I will never forget her;
this is agony for me.

Dear lord God, with her false appearances
my lady confounded and betrayed me.
But surely it was her family that did it!
For his riches, they gave her to a man
whom she should never have considered.
I am crushed. But if she had loved me
as wholeheartedly as I did her,
despite all of them he would not have won her:
that is why the situation could not be worse.

Li chastelains de Couci ama tant   (L 265-1054)
Chanson d'amour, plainte funèbre

Li chas- te- lains de Cou- ci a- ma tant

Qu'ainz por a- mor nus n'en ot do- lor grain- dre;

Por ce fe- rai ma con- plainte en son chant

Que ne cuit pas que la moi- e soit main- dre.

La mort m'i fet re- gre- ter et con- plain- dre

Vos- tre cler vis, bele, et vos- tre cors gent;

Mor- te vos ont frere et mere et pa- rent

Par un tres fol de- se- vre- ment mau- vés.

Li chastelains de Couci ama tant
Qu'ainz por amor nus n'en ot dolor graindre;
Por ce ferai ma conplainte en son chant
Que ne cuit pas que la moie soit maindre.   1.4
La mort m'i fet regreter et conplaindre
Vostre cler vis, bele, et vostre cors gent;
Morte vos ont frere et mere et parent
Par un tres fol desevrement mauvés.   1.8

Por qui ferai mes ne chançon ne chant,
Quant je ne bé a nule amor ataindre?
Ne jamés jor ne qier en mon vivant
M'ire et mon duel ne ma dolor refraindre.   2.4
Car venist or la mort por moi destraindre
Si que morir m'esteüst maintenant!
C'onques mes hom n'ot un mal si tres grant
Ne de dolor au cuer si pesant fais.   2.8

The Châtelain de Coucy loved so well
that no man, for love, ever suffered more deeply;
I will therefore set my lament to his tune,
for I do not believe I suffer any less.
Death makes me regret and lament,
my love, your fair face and gracious being;
mother and brother and kin caused your death
with a rash and wicked separation.

For whom shall I now compose poem or tune,
since I no longer aspire to love?
Never more in my life do I wish
to soften my rage, my grief, and my sorrow.
Come, let death now lay its hand on me
and make me die forthwith!
For no man has ever felt woe so great
or such a heavy weight of sorrow in his heart.

Mult ai veü et mult ai esprouvé,
Mainte merveille eüe et enduree,
Mes ceste m'a le cors si aterré
Que je ne puis avoir longue duree.   3.4
Or maudirai ma male destinee
Quant j'ai perdu le gent cors acesmé
Ou tant avoit de sens et de bonté,
Qui valoit melz que li roiaumes d'Ais.   3.8

Je departi de li outre mon gré;
C'estoit la riens dont je plus me doloie.
Ore a la mort le depart confermé
A touz jorz mes, c'est ce qui me tout joie.   4.4
Nule dolor ne se prent a la moie,
Car je sai bien jamés ne la verré.
Hé las, chetis, ou iré, que feré?
S'or ne me muir, je vivrai touz jorz mais.   4.8

Par Dieu, Amors, je ne vos pris noient,
Car morte est cele pour qui je vous prisoie.
Je ne pris riens, ne biauté ne jouvent,
Or ne argent ne chose que je voie.   5.4
Pour quoi? Pour ce que la mort tout maistroie.
Je quit amors et a Dieu les conmant.
Jamés ne cuit vivre fors en torment;
Joie et deduit tout outreement lais.   5.8

I have seen so much, lived through so much,
witnessed many a wonder and survived them all,
but this one has so overwhelmed my being
that I cannot endure any longer.
Now I will curse my evil fate,
for I have lost the gracious, lovely being
who so abounded in intelligence and goodness,
who was more precious than the kingdom of Aix.

I left her against my will;
that was the source of my greatest sorrow.
Now death has confirmed our parting
forever, and I am stripped of joy.
No suffering is so deep as mine,
for well I know I shall never see her again.
Alas, wretch, where can I go, what shall I do?
If now I don't die, I shall live on forever.

By God, Love, you have lost my esteem,
for she is dead who was its source.
I esteem nothing, neither beauty nor youth,
gold nor silver nor anything else I see.
Why? Because death is master of all.
I renounce love and commend it to God.
Henceforth I shall live only in torment,
leaving behind all pleasure and joy.

DEBATE SONGS

The occasional *joc-partit,* or *partimen,* of the troubadours blossomed into a thirteenth-century trouvère corpus of almost two hundred *jeux-partis,* about half preserved with music. The earliest is due to Thibaut de Champagne, whose renown no doubt contributed to the genre's success among the poet-musicians of Arras, especially Jean Bretel and Adam de la Halle. In six alternating stanzas of identical form and of the courtly chanson type, two poets debate a dilemmatic question posed by one of them at the outset. The question normally concerns amorous behavior and is often playful as well as reflective of bourgeois circumstances. The song concludes with two envoys, in which the poets separately ask two judges for their verdict—which is never recorded.

Several *jeux-partis* will be presented among the compositions attributed to known trouvères. In the two anonymous pieces that follow, we present examples of other kinds of debate poetry.

The first song, "Trop sui d'amors enganez," is a *tenson,* derived from the more widely cultivated Occitan *tenso.* This is basically a *jeu-parti* without the initial posing of a dilemma and without the concluding appeal to judges. The second, "Consilliés moi, signor," is a freer type, in which the speaker debates with himself but turns to an audience for counsel.

STUDY: Jeanroy 1889, chapter 2.

• "Trop sui d'amors enganez": L 265-1712, RS 925, MW 996. Sources: ms. P, also X; music in both. RT 161-163/338-341; Spanke 1925, 79-80.

This melody is of the two-step kind, based on two tones, chiefly *d* (all finals) and *g.* Its scheme is of the litany type: AA'AA' BCDA.

• "Consilliés moi, signor": L 265-381, RS 2014, MW 451. Sources: ms. C, also U; no music. An Occitan version of the first two stanzas appears in Raimon Vidal de Bezaudan's work, *So fol el tems c'om era jays.* RT 163-164/340-345.

Dialectal features: Lorraine, including *aiour* = Central Fr. *aour, jai* = *ja; perti* = *parti; keil* = *quel, ameir* = *amer; doingier* = *dongier; poene* = *peine; fuxe* = *fusse, pouxans* = *puissanz; otriat* = *otria; seux* = *sui.* Note particularly the verb form *avrait* = *avra.*

A ms. rubric identifies this composition as a *jeu-parti,* which is echoed in the second verse. The debate being univocal, however, it does not belong to that quite rigidly defined genre.

Trop sui d'amors enganez (L 265-1712)
Tenson

Trop sui d'amors enganez
Quant cele ne m'aime mie
A qui je me sui donez;
Si fet trop grant musardie   1.4
Cuer qui en fame se fie
S'il n'en a grant seürtez,
    Quar tost est müez
Cuer de fame et tost tornés.   1.8

— Conpaign, ne vos esmaiez!
Lessiez ester la folie,
Car s'el ne vos veut amer,
Tost avrés plus bele amie;   2.4
Et s'el s'est de vos partie,
D'autretel gieu li jouez;
    Si vos en partez,
Car bien voi ja n'en jorés.   2.8

— Mauvés conseil me donés
De lessier si bele amie;
Mon cuer a enprisoné,
Ravoir ne.l pouroie mie.   3.4
Ainz vaintra sa felonie
Ma grant debonereté
    Et ma loiauté,
Si serai amant clamé.   3.8

— Conpains, se tant atendez,
Dont vos est joie faillie.
Que de li soiez amez!
Il est bien honis qui prie,   4.4
Et si muert a grant haschie
Qui pent; autretel ferez,
    Se tant atendez
Que de li soiez amez.   4.8

— Conpains, vos me ranponez,
Si fetes grant vilanie,
Quant departir me voulez
De ma douce conpaignie;   5.4
C'est la riens ou plus me fie.
Je cuit que vos i baez,
    Si me sui pensez
Que departir m'en voulés.   5.8

I am too deceived by love
if the one to whom I am devoted
does not love me;
and a heart that trusts a woman
makes a stupid mistake
if it receives no solid assurance,
for a woman's heart
is quickly changed and quickly turned.

— Friend, don't be dismayed!
Do not be rashly upset:
if she does not care to love you,
you will soon have a fairer one;
and if she has left you,
play the same game with her;
leave her, then, for I see
that you'll never have joy of her.

— You give me bad advice,
to give up so fair a sweetheart;
she has put my heart in prison
and I could never have it back.
Instead, her treachery will be undone
by my great generosity
and my fidelity,
and I will be recognized as lover.

— Friend, if you wait so long,
you will never succeed.
The idea that she would love you!
A man who begs loses his honor,
and the hanged man dies
in great distress; you will do likewise,
if you wait
for her to love you.

— Friend, you are laughing at me,
and it is indecent of you
to try to part me
from my dear companion;
I place my greatest trust in her.
I think you fancy her yourself,
and it occurs to me
you want to part me from her.

Consilliés moi, signor   (L 265-381)
Débat

Consilliés moi, signor,
D'un jeu perti d'amors
A keil je me tanrai.
Sovant sospir et plour
Por celle cui j'aiour   1.5

Give me your advice, my lords,
about a love dilemma;
I will take the side you say.
I often sigh and weep
for the woman I adore,

Et grief martyre en ai;
Maiz une autre en proiai
(Ne sai se fix folour)
Ke m'otriat s'amor
Sens poene et sens delai.   1.10

Se jai celle m'atour,
Je ferai traïtour
De mon fin cuer verai.
Losengier jangleour
Voldroient ke des lour   2.5
Fuxe, maiz ne.l serai.
A celi me tanrai
Por cui seux en errour:
Se tenrai a gringnor
Ma joie, se je l'ai.   2.10

Or ai je trop mal dit,
Quant celi ke m'ocist
Veul ameir et proier,
Et celi ki ait dit
Ke m'aime sens respit   3.5
Veul guerpir et laissier.
La poene et li doingier
M'avrait mort et traï;
Nonporcant, Deus aïst
Celi cui j'ai plux chier!   3.10

K'est ceu, Deus! c'ai je dit?
Por ceu se m'escondist,
Je ne la doi laissier:
Siens seux sens contredit,
De si fin cuer eslit   4.5
Ke pertir ne m'en quier.
Nuls ne doit avancier
Ke son signor renist,
Maix celle ke m'ocist
Ain plux ke riens sous ciel.   4.10

Andous sont avenans,
Maix l'une est plux pouxans
De ma joie doneir;
Trop serai mescheans
S'a celi seux faillans   5.5
Ne l'autre lais aleir;
Celle veul aquiteir
As felons medixans,
Car l'autre est plux vaillans.
Se me doignoit ameir!   5.10

and I am in great torment;
but I sought out another
(was it a foolish thing to do?)
who granted me her love
easily and quickly.

If I ever turn toward the second,
I'll be making a traitor
of my sincere and true heart.
Hypocrites and slanderers
would like me to join
their ranks, but I never will.
I will stand by the woman
who leaves me bewildered:
if I ever have joy, I will
value it all the more.

Now I have said the wrong thing,
if I want to love and court
the one who kills me
and want to leave and abandon
the one who has said
she does not cease to love me.
Effort and resistance
will have betrayed and slain me;
still, may God grant his help
to the woman I love best!

What is this, God? what have I said?
Even if she rejects me,
I mustn't abandon her:
I am unreservedly hers,
with so pure and true a heart
that I have no wish to leave her.
No one should advance
through the denial of his lord,
but the woman who kills me
I love more than anything on earth.

Both are charming,
but one succeeds better
in bringing me joy;
I will be unhappy
if I fail one
or let the other go;
I am willing to yield one
to the treacherous slanderers,
for the other is more worthy.
If only she deigned to love me!

ARTHURIAN LAIS

The term *lai* is somewhat confusing in the context of French poetry of the twelfth and thirteenth centuries, for it is applied to three quite different types. There is, first of all, the lai of the sort composed by Marie de France, which is a narrative of some hundreds of lines, not, to our knowledge, accompanied by music, and having no place in a collection of songs. The other two are lyric, though only one—the heterostrophic *lai,* or *lai-descort*—is traditionally considered to belong to the trouvère repertory. That is, only this type is found in the various manuscript sources that have preserved songs of divers genres; an example is Colin Muset's composition, ''Sospris sui d'une amorette'' (included in the present volume).

The so-called Arthurian *lais* stand outside the normal lyric corpus in that they are transmitted only as lyric interpolations within Arthurian prose narratives, most notably the anonymous Prose *Tristan,* where they are explicitly intended as comment on some aspect of the story by particular characters. These pieces are isostrophic, consisting of monorhymed, isometric stanzas, generally quatrains, which makes them remarkably different in form from the *lais-descorts,* highly varied in both stanzaic structure and verse meter. The Arthurian *lais* differ considerably from one another in length; they are said to be accompanied on the harp.

STUDY: Bec 1977, chapters 13, 14.

EDITION: Fotitch 1974.

● ''Aprés chou que vi victoire'': Sources: ms. Vienna 2542 et al. Other edition: Fotitch 1974, 112-116/172-173.

According to the *Tristan* narrative, the hero is entertained one evening by a young maiden who sings him the victory song that he, Tristan, composed to mark his triumph in the tournament at Louveserp.

The melody, like most melodies of Arthurian lais, has a four-line scheme of three phrases (AABC), derived from the liturgical hymn pattern. It is very simple, in the scale of *g,* and, rather unusually, notated in its entirety, thus revealing a number of divergences through the nine stanzas of the piece. These variants stem from three causes. First, the cadential variants in lines 1, 2, and 4 are an inevitable outcome of the fact that the feminine-verse, i.e., nine-position, melody in the opening stanza is adapted for use with the masculine, i.e., eight-position, lines in stanzas 2 through 8. Then, in lines 3 and 4 of st. 7, scribal carelessness is no doubt responsible for substituting phrases AB for BC. Finally, the rest of the divergences, all affecting line 3, may be viewed as variants in ornamention/transposition and in metric adaptation; such variants no doubt originate in vocal, rather than written, transmission.

● ''D'Amours vient mon chant et mon plour'': Sources: ms. Vienna 2542 et al. Other edition: Fotitch 1974, 120-122/177-178.

This piece is sung by Tristan, who is said to have composed it while riding through a forest and thinking about his love.

The melody is built on the Lydian, or *f,* scale, with most cadences on *f* or *c.* Its structure is rather elaborate, not like that of a *lai-descort* (with its *discord* in place of *accord*) but somewhat reminiscent of the organization of a sequence: ABAB CC′DEFGC″HIJ.

Aprés chou que je vi victoire
Arthurian lai

Aprés chou que je vi victoire,
Fist si grant valour en estoire
Amours, si me met en tel gloire
Mon lay fas et met en memoire.   1.4

D'Amours muet mes lays et mes vers:
Se Amours m'a esté divers
Et en esté et en yvers,
Or ne m'a pas esté divers.   2.4

Se jou ai longement jeü
En doleur et traveil eü,
Pour chou voel jou qu'il soit seü
Et en mains lieus ramenteü.   3.4

Se ne disoie la bonté
D'Amours, jou seroie ahonté;
Pour chou voel jou qu'il soit conté
En quel pris Amours m'a monté.   4.4

After I had seen victory,
love fashioned that great valor
into a tale and brought me such glory
that I composed and memorized my lay.

My lay and my poem come from love:
though love has been inconstant
in summer and winter,
it has not been cruel to me now.

If I have long suffered
pain and travail,
I want the fact known
and recalled in many places.

If I did not speak of the goodness
of love, I would be disgraced;
and so I want it recounted
how love made me rise to fame.

Amours m'a tenu longement
En doel, en ire et en tourment,
Mais or ai je asouagement;
Amendé m'a mout longement,   5.4

Quant entre la flour des morteus
Me mist Amours, que jou fui teus
Mieudres ne fu ne autres teus,
Et pour çou di c'Amours est deus.   6.4

Quant a Louveserph oi le pris
Que tous li mons avoit empris,
Que jou i fui au mieudre pris
Et il i furent tout mespris,   7.4

Bien doi d'Amours estre avoués,
Pour tant sui par Amours löés.
Ha, vous qui chi mon dit öés,
Amours du tout en tout amés!   8.4

Quant Amours se veut entremetre
Qui m'a fait en si grant pris metre
Que encor sera mis en letre,
Du tout me doi a lui sousmetre.   9.4

Love held me for long
in distress, in sorrow, in torment,
but now I have relief;
it has greatly restored me,

for love set me among the flower
of mortals so that I became such
as to have no superior or peer,
and so I say that love is a god.

Since at Louveserp I won the prize
for which everyone had striven,
and I was judged the best
while they were all rejected,

I must needs be love's defender,
and for this reason I am valued by love.
Ah, you who hear this song of mine,
be sure to love love!

Since love wants engagement
— love that brought such fame to me
that it will yet be written down —
I must submit myself to him wholly.

D'Amours vient mon chant et mon plour

Arthurian lai

D'Amours vient mon chant et mon plour,
D'illuecques prennent naissement.
Chele fait que orendroit plour
Et m'i atort, se Dieus m'ament.   1.4

Et quant je voi apertement
Qu'el me mainne si a son tour
Que je sui sers, ele signour,
Je l'aour con mon sauvement.   2.4

Li serf tout enterinement,
Car je n'ai autre sauveour.
A lui aclin, a lui aour,
D'autre signeur nen ai paour.   3.4
A lui serf si veraiement
Qu'il n'i a point de faussement.

From love come my song and my tears;
that is where they were born.
She now makes me weep
and welcome it, so help me God.

And when I clearly see
that she so leads me in her way
that I am her servant and she my lord,
I worship her as my salvation.

I serve her entirely,
for I have no other savior.
I bow to her; I worship her;
I have no fear of another lord.
I serve her so truly
that there is no dishonesty.

MOTETS

Motets form a class apart from the general body of Old French lyric. Their origin was Latin and liturgical, and though the genre was profoundly secularized and vernacularized in the course of its development in the thirteenth century, it apparently remained within the fairly restricted confines of literate society. This tendency toward segregation can be seen in the fact that the various manuscript songbooks that transmit the trouvère repertory do not normally include motets, which survive in a quite separate set of sources (in the Bamberg, Montpellier, and Wolfenbüttel codices, for example). Unlike the other works, in which music, for all its importance, has the subordinate function of communicating a verbal text, the motets are primarily musical compositions, in which words provide a means for the expression of melody. Melody, moreover, is in this case multiple, for the most distinguishing characteristic of motets is that they are polyphonic, including at least two concurrent voices (the low *tenor* and the higher *motetus*), very often complemented by a third (the *triplum*), and sometimes by a fourth (the *quadruplum*). Along with polyphony, motets are marked by polytextuality; that is, each voice sings different words. In most instances, the *tenor* text is both extremely brief—but prolonged musically—and in Latin, while the higher voices sing poems in French; these texts are usually single, notably heterometric stanzas, more often than not drawn from normally unacknowledged, existing compositions. These may belong to almost any lyric type, but motet composers tended to favor pieces of a somewhat popular stamp, such as *pastourelles;* their reasons for collocating particular texts in a given motet are frequently not clear.

Our first motet is of the simplest kind: to a single-word Latin *tenor* is joined a French *motetus* which is the first stanza of a known *pastourelle.* The second has a *motetus* comprising two stanzas of an otherwise unknown courtly *chanson,* and is missing its *tenor* text. Our final example has a Latin *tenor,* along with a *motetus* and a *triplum* that are of unknown origin and metrically different but clearly related in theme and spirit.

STUDIES: Bec 1977, chapter 15; Huot 1994; Everist 1994.

EDITIONS: Raynaud 1881-83; Tischler 1978.

- ''Pensis, chief enclin'': L 265-1319; MW 1228,1; Gennrich 1957, no. 677. Single source: Montpellier; music. No attribution. Other editions: Raynaud 1881, 200; Tischler 1978 (3), 50. Performed on Anthology CD.

The text comes from a *pastourelle* (L 59-2) by the thirteenth-century trouvère Ernoul le Vieux de Gastinois.

The *motetus,* which carries the poem, is in the first rhythmic mode (long-short). It opens with the intonation of the first Gregorian tone. The principal cadence is *d* (lines 2, 4, 6, 7, 9, 10, 13). The *tenor,* also in the first rhythmic mode, is built on a religious melody in *d* plagal, "Flos filius eius."

- "Bien m'ont Amours entrepris": L 265-261; RS 1532; MW 1116; Gennrich 1957, no. 942a. Single source: ms. O; music. No attribution. Performed on Anthology CD.

Cf. Hans Tischler, *The Earliest Motets* (New Haven: Yale UP, 1982), II, no. 362, pp. 1559-1560. This motet remains very close to the courtly *chanson* in its syllabism and in its melodic scheme of the *pedes cum cauda* type: ABAB CEDF. The upper melody is in the scale of *d* and in the fifth rhythmic mode; the tenor, with no title specified, is in the second mode.

- ''Il n'a en toi sens ne valour''/''Robins, li malvais ouvriers'': L 265-789; MW 689,30/793,1; Gennrich 1957, no. 21/22; B 1236/1373. Sources: Bamberg, also Montpellier; music in both. No attribution. Other editions: Raynaud 1881, 147; Tischler 1978 (2), 184. Tenor: "Omnes."

Cf. Gordon A. Anderson, *Compositions of the Bamberg Manuscript,* in Corpus Mensurabilis Musicae 75 (American Institute of Musicology, 1977), p. 82. The religious *tenor,* "Omnes," at the base of this composition is in the scale of *f* and in the fifth rhythmic mode (3 longs). The *triplum,* like the *motetus,* has a relatively limited ambitus. The main tones of these two parts are *c* and *f.*

Our transcription preserves the arrangement in the manuscript, an arrangement which has a certain relevance to the synchronization of the voices. In the 13th century, such synchronization was in the main accomplished aurally and gesturally (by tactus) rather than visually (by reading), which of course entailed a degree of rhythmic imprecision; this was naturally increased by the musicians' ignorance of what we today call measure. With our transcription, we are suggesting to musicians that they give up part of their reliance on their eyes to achieve synchronization and give more attention to their ears.

Pensis, chief enclin   (L 265-1319)

Motet

Pen- sis , chief en- clin , Ier ma- tin er- roi- e ;

Les un au- bes- pin , De- jouste un ar- broi- e , Pas- tou- re trou- vai .

O- ïe l'ai , sa- lu- ai : *Do- ren- lot !*

Mes on- ques ne me dit mot , Car Ro- bin en- tro- ï ot ,

Qui per- du- e l'a , Si chan- toit pour li ra- voir :

Dieus , li cuers me fau- dra ja , Tant la de- sir ve- oir !

Pensis, chief enclin,		Pensive, head bowed,	
Ier matin erroie;		I was out riding yesterday morning;	
Les un aubespin,		next to a hawthorn,	
Dejouste un arbroie,	4	alongside a grove,	
Pastoure trouvai.		I found a shepherdess.	
Oïe l'ai, saluai:		I heard her and greeted her:	
Dorenlot!		*Dorenlot!*	
Mes onques ne me dit mot,	8	But she said never a word to me,	
Car Robin entroï ot,		because Robin, who had lost her,	
Qui perdue l'a,		had just come along	
Si chantoit pour li ravoir:		and he was singing to get her back:	
Dieus, li cuers me faudra ja,	12	*God, my heart will soon fail me,*	
Tant la desir veoir!		*so much do I yearn to see her!*	

Bien m'ont Amours entrepris   (L 265-261)
Motet

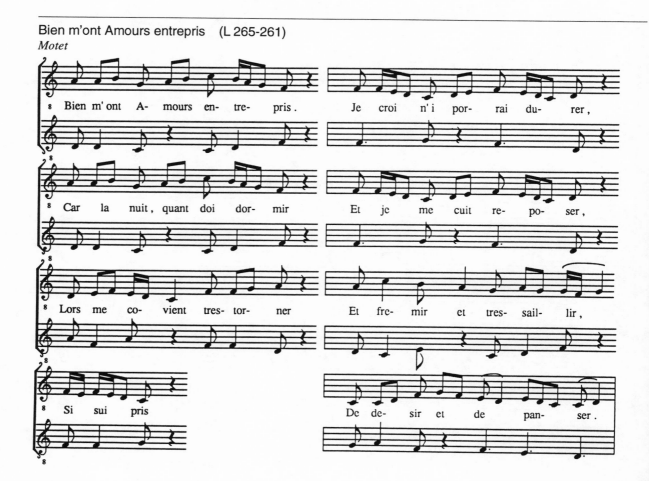

Bien m'ont Amours entrepris.		Love has taken hold of me.
Je croi n'i porrai durer,		I think I cannot last,
Car la nuit, quant doi dormir		for at night, when I should sleep
Et je me cuit reposer,	1.4	and I expect to rest,
Lors me covient trestorner		I find myself tossing and turning,
Et fremir et tressaillir,		shivering and trembling,
Si sui pris		so gripped am I
De desir et de panser.	1.8	by desire and brooding.

Dame, je vos cri merci.	My lady, I beg your mercy.
Bien voi n'en puis eschaper.	I clearly see I cannot escape.
A mains jointes je vos pri	With hands clasped, I pray
Que faciez vos volentez 2.4	you do what you will
De moi, et il ert mes grez	with me, and it will be my wish
Et me vendra a plesir.	and bring me pleasure.
Sanz partir	Unendingly
Vos servirai mon aé. 2.8	I will serve you all my life long.

Il n'a en toi sens ne valour   (L 265-789)
Motet

TRIPLUM

Il n'a en toi sens ne va- lour,

Ro- bins, ne cour-toi- si- e,

Qui d'un bai- sier par ta fo- lour

As es- con-dit t'a- mi- e.

Il n'a pas a- tente en a- mour,

Fo- le chievre es- ba- hi- e:

Li plus has- tis est li meil- lour,

A- mours het cou- ar- di- e.

MOTETUS

Ro- bins, li mal- vais ou- vriers,

A es- con- dit s'a- mi- e,

Qui de-man-doit un bai- sier

Pour es- tre plus jo- li- e;

Si res-pon- di li ber- giers

Ni- ce- té a fo- li- e:

Ne vous has- tés mi- e,

Be- le, ne vous has- tés mi- e.

TENOR :
OMNES

TRIPLUM

Il n'a en toi sens ne valour,
    Robins, ne courtoisie,
Qui d'un baisier par ta folour
    As escondit t'amie.   4
Il n'a pas atente en amour,
    Fole chievre esbahie:
Li plus hastis est li meillour,
    Amours het couardie.   8

In you, Robin, there is no sense
or virtue or courtliness,
you who, for a kiss, foolishly
turned your sweetheart away.
There is no waiting in love,
you foolish, frightened goat:
He is best who gets there first;
love hates faint-heartedness.

MOTETUS

    Robins, li malvais ouvriers,
        A escondit s'amie,
    Qui demandoit un baisier
        Pour estre plus jolie;   4
    Si respondi li bergiers
        Niceté a folie:
        Ne vous hastés mie,
    Bele, ne vous hastés mie.   8

Robin, the poor worker,
turned away his sweetheart,
who was asking for a kiss
to cheer her up;
the shepherd gave a silly answer
with a bad result:
Not so quick, my dear,
not so quick.

BLONDEL DE NESLE

Blondel de Nesle was one of the earliest trouvères, credited with the composition of at least twenty-four songs. Long thought, but without firm evidence, to be Jean II, lord of Nesle in Picardy, he was more likely the latter's father, Jean I, who was born ca. 1150 and died sometime between 1197 and 1200, not long after his return from the Third Crusade. However, the trouvère's identity is far from certain. What is clear is that he was part of the lyric coterie that included Conon de Béthune, Gace Brulé, and the Châtelain de Coucy. Blondel's songs, all preserved with music, belong to the tradition of the *grand chant courtois* derived from the Occitan troubadours.

EDITIONS: Wiese 1904; van der Werf 1977; Lepage 1994; Bahat-Le Vot 1996.

● "Cuer desirrous apaie": L 24-8, RS 110, MW 2050. Sources: ms. M, also CTUZa; music in MTZa. Attribution to Blondel in MTa; to Guiot de Dijon in C. RT 174-177/356-361; Wiese 1904, 150-152; van der Werf 1977, 6-9; Lepage 1993, 138-156; Bahat-Le Vot 1996, 92-97.

The only notable dialectal features are the Picard *jou = je* and imperfect subjunctive *-aisse = -asse*.

The melodies in MTZ are comparable; the music in ms. a is less ornate but preserves an analogous melodic movement. In all versions, the scheme is of the *pedes cum cauda* type and tends to reflect the metrical and rhyme schemes:

A	B	A′	B′	C	D	E	F
6	5	6	5	8	8	6	6
a′	b′	a′	b′	c	c	c	a′

Like the reading of M, which we present, the others too are rather composite in modality but show a preponderant cadence on *d* (lines 2, 4, 8). Note that the seventh position in line 2 occurs without music in ms. M; the *a* is supplied by analogy with line 1.

Cuer desirrous apaie   (L 24-8)
Chanson d'amour

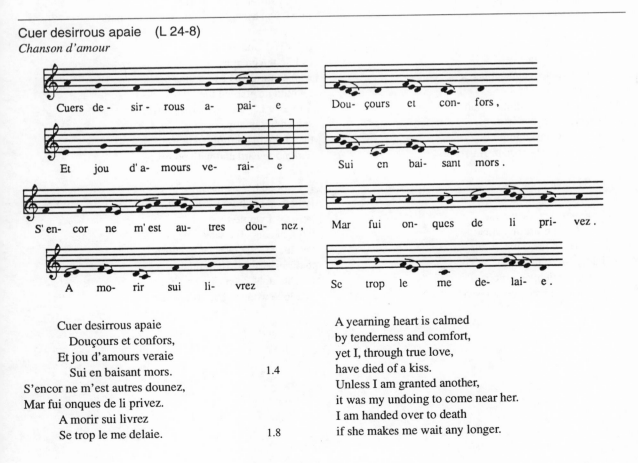

Cuer desirrous apaie	A yearning heart is calmed
Douçours et confors,	by tenderness and comfort,
Et jou d'amours veraie	yet I, through true love,
Sui en baisant mors. 1.4	have died of a kiss.
S'encor ne m'est autres dounez,	Unless I am granted another,
Mar fui onques de li privez.	it was my undoing to come near her.
A morir sui livrez	I am handed over to death
Se trop le me delaie. 1.8	if she makes me wait any longer.

Privez baisiers est plaie
   D'amours dedenz cors;
Mout m'angoisse et esmaie,
   Si ne pert dehors.   2.4
Ha las! pour quoi m'en sui vantez,
Quant ne m'en puet venir santez
   Se ce dont sui navrez
   Ma bouche ne rassaie?   2.8

Amours, vous me feïstes
   Mon fin cuer trichier,
Qui tel savour meïstes
   En son douz baisier.   3.4
A morir li avez apris
Se pluz n'i prent qu'il i a pris,
   Dont m'est il bien avis
   Qu'en baisant me trahistes.   3.8

Certes, mout m'atraisistes
   Juene a cel mestier,
N'ainc nului n'i vousistes
   Fors moi engignier.   4.4
Je sui li plus loiauz amis
Cui onques fust nus biens pramis.
   Hé las! tant ai je pis!
   Amours, mar me nourristes.   4.8

Se je Dieu tant amasse
   Com je fais celi
Qui si me painne et lasse,
   J'eüsse merci;   5.4
Qu'ainc amis de meilleur voloir
Ne la servi pour joie avoir
   Com je fais tout pour voir
   Sanz merite et sanz grasse.   5.8

Se de faus cuer proiasse
   (Dont je ne la pri),
Espoir je recouvrasse,
   Maiz n'est mie einsi;   6.4
Ne ja Dieus ne me doint voloir
De li deçoivre sanz doloir.
   Ce me tient en espoir:
   Qu'amours blece et respasse.   6.8

A kiss in private is a wound
love makes inside the body;
it fills me with anguish and dismay,
though nothing shows on the surface.
Alas, why did I ever boast of it,
when I cannot recover my health
unless the thing that wounded me
touches my lips again?

Love, you let my faithful heart
be tricked
when you put such sweetness
into her tender kiss.
You prepared my heart to die
unless it has more of what it had,
and so it is clear to me
that you betrayed me with a kiss.

I was indeed very young
when you drew me into this life,
and I am the only one
you have ever tried to delude.
I am the most faithful lover
ever promised happiness.
Alas, I suffer all the more!
Love, you brought me up only to undo me.

If I loved God as much
as I do the creature
who so torments and drains me,
I would be granted mercy;
for never has a more earnest lover
served her in hope of joy
than I do, in all truth,
with no reward and with no grace.

If I wooed her with a false heart
(which is not how I woo her),
perhaps I would recover,
but that is not the way it is;
and may God never let me wish
to deceive her with impunity.
One thought keeps me hopeful:
that love wounds but also heals.

CONON DE BÉTHUNE

Conon de Béthune (fl. from ca. 1180 to 1219-20) is now remembered as one of the classic generation of trouvères that included Gace Brulé and the Châtelain de Coucy, with whom he had friendly ties. Born into a noble family of Artois, he was better known during his lifetime, however, as a warrior, diplomat, and statesman. A participant in the Third Crusade, he was a major figure in the Fourth, esteemed by the French for his wisdom and eloquence in dealing with recalcitrant allies. After the capture of Constantinople, he served the Latin (Flemish) emperors devotedly and was even named regent of the empire in 1219.

Ten songs, all preserved with music, are attributed to Conon with reasonable certainty. These include two crusade songs and a satirical love-dialogue along with courtly love songs of an unusually personal stamp. One poem is noteworthy for evoking the difference between Conon's dialect and that of the royal court.

EDITIONS: Wallensköld 1921; van der Werf 1977.

● "Ahi, Amours! com dure departie": L 50-1, RS 1125, MW 1347. Sources: ms. M, also CHKNOPRTVXa and za, as well as two other, minor sources; one melody in MTO, a second in KNPX, a third in R, a fourth in V, a fifth in a; no music in CHza. Attribution to Conon in CMRTa; to the Châtelain de Coucy in KNPX. RT 182-187/368-371; Bédier-Aubry 1909, 27-37; Wallensköld 1921, 6-7; van der Werf 1977, 285-292.

To judge by the scope and complexity of the ms. tradition, this work was one of the most popular of the *chansons de croisade*. Earlier editors have convincingly ascribed it to Conon rather than the Châtelain de Coucy and dated it to 1188.

The various versions of this song pose problems that make it reasonable to intervene more than is strictly necessary in the establishment of a critical text. Though the redaction of ms. M, then, is our base, we have modified it significantly in accordance with variant readings in other sources. Most notably, we have re-ordered the stanzas, which occur in M as follows: 1 2 5 6 3 4, and have added the envoy, which appears only in C. Our sequence stems from several considerations: First, the mss. all agree on the placement of stanzas 1 and 2. Second, the pattern of stanzaic linking is that of *coblas doblas*, which means that stanzas 3 and 4 are inseparable, that stanzas 5 and 6 are equally inseparable, and that stanzas 5 and 6, whose rhymes are repeated in the envoy, must immediately precede the latter. Third, stanzas 2, 3, and 4 form a meaningful progression, in that st. 3 develops the idea of reward first expressed at the end of st. 2, and st. 4 takes the final line of st. 3 as its point

of departure for a shift of focus to the crusading enterprise. Fourth, stanza 5 follows from st. 4, in that it further develops the ideas, expressed in st. 4, of besieged Jerusalem and of the shame of those who will not join the crusade; the stanzas are linked, moreover, by the openings of their first two verses: *D(i)eus* and *Or i parra*. Fifth, stanza 6 continues the enumeration of types of men who will or will not participate; it then shifts to the women left behind, which both relates it to the envoy and represents a return to the theme that opened the poem. (Further details and references to other interpretations may be found in RT 186-187/968-969 and Dijkstra 1995, 83-92.)

5.4: The Saracens captured Jerusalem in 1187.

As indicated above, five different melodies are found with this song. Unlike the text, which, variants aside, can be attributed to the single trouvère Conon de Béthune, no particular melody—or melodies—among the five can be so ascribed. The one we present, that of M, shows a *pedes cum versibus* scheme: ABAB CDCD; this scheme is quite rare in so regular a configuration. The principal scale is Mixolydian, or *g*. Note that the melodic contours of lines 1, 3, 7, and 8 follow the 4 + 6 pattern of the decasyllabic verse.

● "Chançon legiere a entendre": L 50-5, RS 629, MW 1666. Sources: ms. T, also Re; one melody in T, another in R; no music in e. Attribution to Conon in TR. RT 187-189/372-375; Wallensköld 1921, 1-3; van der Werf 1977, 283-284.

Dialectal features: Picard, including *le* = Central Fr. *la*; *millor* = *meilleur*; *çou* = *ce*; *ochirre* = *ocirre*, *cançons* = *chançons*; *retaut* = *retout*.

According to Dyggve 1951, 45-53, this song was probably written around 1185 and, in any case, before 1201, when Conon left France for the Fourth Crusade. *Noblet*, named in the envoy, appears to have been Guillaume de Garlande V, friend to Conon de Béthune as well as Gace Brulé and Pierre de Molins, and a recipient of songs composed by each of them.

For this song we present both melodies preserved, which are fundamentally different in both tune and compositional scheme. T is in the scale of *g*, while R is tonally quite erratic (with cadences on *c, g, d, a, g*). T, moreover, shows a regular *pedes* pattern: ABAB CDA, whereas R is rather atypical for the trouvère tradition: ABCA′B′CD. On the one hand, R presents the melodic repeat A′B′ one line later than the corresponding prosodic feature; on the other hand, it shows an interval of a sixth between lines 5 and 6, marking a kind of melodic transfer to a higher pitch for the last two lines of the song.

● "Ce fut l'autrier en un autre païs": L 50-6, RS 1574, MW 626. Sources: ms. K, also CHIMNOPTU; one melody in KNP, a second in M, a third in O, a fourth in T; no music in CHIU. Attribution to Conon in CMT, to Richard de Fournival in KN. RT 189-194/376-379; Wallensköld 1921, 17-18 and 31-33; van der Werf 1977, 306-309; Lepage 1981, 131-136.

The only notable dialectal feature is Picard *aront* = Central Fr. *avront*.

This remarkable little dialogue, with its delight in the revenge of the spurned courtly lover, is wholly exceptional in the works of the early trouvères.

4.7: The "heresy" in question is homosexuality; see the lady's accusation in 3.7-8.

5.7-8: The allusion is to two historical figures: the Marquis Boniface II of Montferrat (d. 1207), one of the heroes of the Fourth Crusade, and Guillaume des Barres, a knight renowned for his physical strength and his victory over Richard Lion-Heart in single combat in 1188.

6.4: Carthage exemplifies the highest nobility.

We normally print only one melody with each song even in the case of compositions transmitted with more than one. For the sake of demonstration, we offer in the present instance three of the four melodies preserved in the manuscript sources. Schematically, the three are regular and relatively close: (mss. K and M) ABAB AB'BB'' and (ms. O) ABAB CA'DD'. Otherwise, they are quite different, diverging chiefly through transposition. This is a kind of transposition of pitches that should in fact be regarded as a "translation" of notes (in the sense meant by some of the music theorists of the Middle Ages) varying in range from one verse to another. For example, K, with its main cadences on *a,* and M, with its main cadences on *g,* are separated from each other in the A segment by a second but in the B segment by a fifth. As for ms. O, it transmits its melody in mensural notation (in the third dactylic mode), as opposed to the non-mensural readings in the other manuscripts. Ms. T, not transcribed here, presents other variants in transposition and ornamentation.

Ahi, Amours! com dure departie   (L 50-1)
Chanson d'amour, chanson de croisade

A- hi, A- mours ! com du- re de- par- ti- e

Me con- ven- dra fai- re de la meil- lour

Qui on- ques fust a- me- e ne ser- vi- e !

Deus me ra- maint a li par sa dou- çour

Si voi- re- ment que m'en part a do- lour .

Las ! qu'ai- je dit ? Ja ne m'en part je mi- e !

Se li cors vait ser- vir nos- tre Sei- gnour ,

Li cuers re- maint du tout en sa bail- li- e .

Ahi, Amours! com dure departie
Me convendra faire de la meillour
Qui onques fust amee ne servie!
Deus me ramaint a li par sa douçour   1.4
Si voirement que m'en part a dolour.
Las! qu'ai je dit? Ja ne m'en part je mie!
Se li cors vait servir nostre Seignour,
Li cuers remaint du tout en sa baillie.   1.8

Pour li m'en vois souspirant en Surie,
Quar je ne doi faillir mon Creatour.
Qui li faudra a cest besoing d'aïe,
Sachiez que il li faudra a greignour;   2.4
Et sachent bien li grant et li menour
Que la doit on faire chevalerie
U on conquiert paradis et honour
Et pris et los et l'amour de s'amie.   2.8

Qui ci ne veut avoir vie anuieuse
Si voist pour Dieu morir liez et joieus,
Que cele mors est douce et savereuse
Dont on conquiert le regne precïeus;   3.4
Ne ja de mort nen i morra uns seus,
Ainz naistront tuit en vie glorïeuse;
Et sachiez bien: qui ne fust amereus,
Mout fust la voie et bone et deliteuse.   3.8

Deus! tant avom esté preu et huiseuse!
Or i parra qui a certes iert preus;
S'irom vengier la honte dolereuse
Dont chascuns doit estre iriez et honteus,   4.4
Quar a no tanz est perduz li sains lieus
U Dieus soufri pour nous mort angoisseuse;
S'or i laissom nos anemis morteus,
A tous jours maiz iert no vie honteuse.   4.8

Dieus est assis en son saint hiretage;
Or i parra com cil le secourront
Cui il jeta de la prison ombrage
Quant il fu mors en la crois que Turc ont.   5.4
Sachiez, cil sunt trop honi qui n'iront,
S'il n'ont poverte u vieillece u malage;
Et cil qui sain et joene et riche sont
Ne pueënt pas demorer sanz hontage.   5.8

Touz li clergiez et li home d'aage
Qui en aumosne et en bienfais manront
Partiront tuit a cest pelerinage —
Et les dames qui chastement vivront   6.4
Et loiauté portent ceus qui iront;
Et s'eles font par mal conseill folage,
A lasches gens mauvaises le feront,
Quar tuit li bon iront en cest voiage.   6.8

Ah, love! how hard it will be to part,
as I must, from the finest woman
who was ever loved and served!
May God in his goodness bring me back to her
as surely as I part in sorrow.
But what have I said? This is no parting!
Though my body goes off to serve our Lord,
my heart remains here, ruled by her.

I sigh for her as I leave for Syria,
bound not to fail my Creator.
Whoever fails Him in this need for help
will surely see Him fail *him* in greater need;
and let all know, both great and humble,
that knightly deeds should be performed
where heaven and honor can be won,
and praise and renown and the love of your lady.

Whoever wants to avoid a troubled life
should go with joy and gladness to die for God,
for death is delicious and sweet
when it wins you the precious Kingdom;
and not one man will die of that death,
but all will be born into glorious life.
Know this: if you were not in love,
the journey abroad would be delightful and good.

God! how pointless our prowess has been!
Now we shall see what real prowess is;
we will go avenge the painful offense
that must leave everyone angry and ashamed,
for we have lived to see the holy place lost
where for our sake God suffered torment and death;
if we now leave our deadly enemies there,
our lives will be shamed forever.

God is under siege in his holy dwelling;
now we shall see how He is rescued
by those that He freed from the dark prison
when He died on the cross now held by the Turks.
Know that those who do not go will lose all honor
unless they are too poor or old or infirm;
and those who are well and young and rich
cannot stay back and escape disgrace.

The whole clergy and all men of great age
who give themselves up to alms and good deeds
will be taking part in this pilgrimage,
together with the ladies who live chaste lives
and remain faithful to those who go;
and if they let bad counsel lead them astray,
they will be straying with the cowardly and wicked,
for all good men will have undertaken this journey.

Las! je m'en vois plorant des euz du front	Alas, I go off with weeping eyes to the place
La ou Deus veut amender mon corage,	where God wants to set right my heart.
Et sachiez bien qu'a la meillour du mont	Know, though, that I shall be thinking less
Penserai plus que ne faz au voiage. E.4 (8)	of the journey than of the finest woman in the world.

Chançon legiere a entendre   (L 50-5)
Chanson d'amour

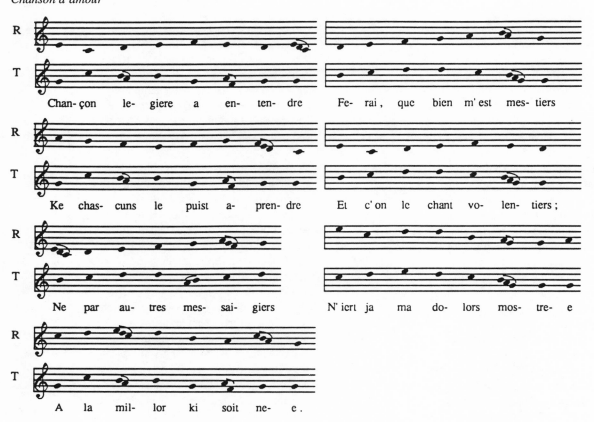

Chan-çon le- giere a en- ten- dre   Fe- rai, que bien m'est mes- tiers

Ke chas- cuns le puist a- pren- dre   Et c'on le chant vo- len- tiers;

Ne par au- tres mes- sai- giers   N'iert ja ma do- lors mos- tre- e

A la mil- lor ki soit ne- e .

Chançon legiere a entendre		I'll compose a song easy to grasp,
Ferai, que bien m'est mestiers		for it is important to me
Ke chascuns le puist aprendre		that everyone be able to learn it
Et c'on le chant volentiers;	1.4	and be glad to sing it;
Ne par autres messaigiers		and by no other messenger
N'iert ja ma dolors mostree		will my suffering be relayed
A la millor ki soit nee.	1.7	to the finest woman ever born.
Tant est sa valors doblee		Her worth is so great
C'orgeus et hardemens fiers		that it would be arrogant and too
Seroit se ja ma pensee		bold if I were the first
Li descovroie premiers;	2.4	to speak my mind;
Mais besoins et desiriers		but need and desire
Et çou c'on ne puet atendre		and the inability to wait
Fait maint hardement emprendre.	2.7	make for many a bold move.

Tant ai celé mon martire
Tos jors a tote la gent
Ke bien le devroie dire
A ma dame solement,   3.4
K'Amors ne li dist noient;
Neporquant s'ele m'oblie,
Ne l'oublïerai je mie.   3.7

Por quant, se je n'ai aïe
De li et retenement,
Bien fera et cortoisie
S'aucune pitiés l'em prent.   4.4
Au descovrir mon talent
Se gart bien de l'escondire,
S'ele ne me velt ochirre.   4.7

Fols sui, ki ne li ai dite
Ma dolors ki est si grans.
Bien deüst estre petite
Par droit, tant sui fins amans;   5.4
Mais je sui si meschaans
Ke quanques drois m'i avance,
Me retaut ma mescheance.   5.7

Tous i morrai en soffrance,
Mais sa beautés m'est garans,
De ma dame, et la samblance
Ki tos mes maus fait plaisans,   6.4
Si ke je muir tous joians,
Ke tant desir sa merite
Ke ceste mors me delite.   6.7

Noblet, je sui fins amans,
Si ai la millor eslite
Dont onques cançons fu dite.   E.3 (7)

I have always so carefully hidden
my agony from everyone
that I should reveal it
at least to my lady,
since love has told her nothing.
She may yet forget me,
but I will never forget her.

That is why, even if she does not
aid or retain me,
she will be kind and courteous
if pity so moves her.
If I reveal my desire,
let her take care not to deny it
unless she wants to kill me.

I am mad not to have told her
how great my suffering is.
I am so true a lover
that it should by rights be trifling;
but I am so luckless
that whatever I rightfully gain
Is stripped away by my ill luck.

I will die in distress,
but I find an assurance in my lady's
beauty and in her demeanor
that turns all my pain into pleasure,
so that I can die in joy;
so much do I yearn for her reward
that such a death delights me.

Noblet, I am a true lover
and I have chosen the finest woman
ever praised in song.

Ce fut l'autrier en un autre païs (L 50-6)

Débat

K Me- né vous ai par pa- ro- le mains dis;

Ore est l'a- mor co- ne- üe et do- ne- e:

Des or mes sui tout a vos- tre de- vis."

Ce fut l'autrier en un autre païs
Q'uns chevaliers ot une dame amee.
Tant com la dame fu en son bon pris,
Li a s'amor escondite et vëee,   1.4
Jusqu'a un jor qu'ele li dist: "Amis,
Mené vous ai par parole mains dis;
Ore est l'amor coneüe et donee:
Des or mes sui tout a vostre devis."   1.8

Li chevaliers la regarda el vis,
Si la vit mult pale et descoloree.
"Par Dieu, dame, mort sui et entrepris
Quant des l'autrier ne soi ceste pensee.   2.4
Li vostre vis, qui senbloit flor de lis,
M'est si torné du tout de mal en pis
Ce m'est avis que me soiez enblee.
A tart avez, dame, cest conseil pris."   2.8

Quant la dame s'oï ramponer,
Grant duel en ot, si dist par felonnie:
"Danz chevaliers, on vous doit bien gaber.
Cuidiez vous donc qu'a certes le vous die?   3.4
Nenil, certes, onc ne l'oi en penser!
Voulez vous donc dame de pris amer?
Nenil, certes, ainz avrïez envie
D'un biau vallet besier et acoler."   3.8

It happened not long ago in another land
that a knight was in love with a lady;
as long as the lady watched her reputation,
she held him off and denied him her love.
At last, though, one day she said, "My friend,
I have long led you on with words.
Now I accept your love and offer my own;
from now on I am yours."

The knight looked at her face
and saw she was pale and her color had gone.
"By God, my lady, it breaks my heart
that I never heard such words before.
Your face, which was like a lily,
has now so gone from bad to worse
it seems to me you're not the person I knew;
your change of heart, my lady, comes too late."

When the lady heard his rebuke,
she was stung and answered wickedly,
"Sir knight, I have to laugh at you.
do you really think I meant what I said?
Really, now, what a thought!
Do you really care to love a woman of repute?
Really, now, you would rather be kissing
and hugging some handsome young fellow."

"Dame," fet il, "j'ai bien oï parler
De vostre pris, mes ce n'est ore mie;
Et de Troie ai je oï conter
Qu'ele fu ja de mult grant seignorie: 4.4
Or n'i puet on fors les places trouver.
Par tel reson vous lo a escuser
Que cil soient reté de l'yresie
Qui des or mes ne vous voudront amer."   4.8

"Danz chevaliers, mar i avez gardé
Quant vous avez reprouvé mon aage.
Se j'avoie tout mon jouvent usé,
Si sui je tant riche et de haut parage   5.4
Qu'on m'ameroit a mult pou de biauté,
Qu'oncor n'a pas, ce cuit, un mois passé
Que li Marchis m'envoia son message
Et li Barrois a pour m'amor ploré."   5.8

"Dame," fait il, "ce vous a molt grevé
Que vous fïez en vostre seignorage;
Mais tel set ont ja pour vouz sospiré,
Se vous estiés fille au roi de Cartage,   6.4
Qui ja mes jour n'en aront volenté.
On n'aimme paz dame pour parenté,
Maiz quant ele est bele et cortoise et sage.
Vous en savroiz par tanz la verité."   6.8

"My lady," he said, "I know your good
reputation well, but you don't deserve it now.
Of Troy, too, I have heard it said
that it was once a city of great power,
yet now there is only a trace of it left.
I therefore advise you to refrain
from throwing a charge of heresy
at men who do not wish to love you."

"Sir knight, it was wrong of you
to speak so disparagingly of my age;
even if I had no youth left,
I am still so rich and high-born
that men would love me with far less beauty.
It was hardly a month ago, I think,
that the Marquis sent me his messenger,
and Barres has wept for my love."

"My lady," he said, "it hasn't helped you
to put so much stock in your high station;
many a man has sighed for you
who, were you the princess of Carthage,
won't ever feel the same longing again.
A lady is not loved for her birth
but for being beautiful, courteous, and bright;
you will soon see the truth of this."

The CHÂTELAIN DE COUCY

One of the major early trouvères, Guy de Thourotte was governor of Coucy castle in Picardy from 1186 until his death as a crusader in 1203. Of more than thirty compositions ascribed to him in medieval songbooks, only fifteen or so seem authentic. All texts survive with music, and all the pieces are courtly lyrics in the tradition of the troubadours. Like his friend and fellow-trouvère Gace Brulé, the Châtelain sings invariably of love, but his songs are more poignant than despairing and suggest an erotic reality. By the end of the thirteenth century, the Châtelain had been mythified into a great tragic lover, whom Jakemes, an otherwise unknown writer, made the hero of his *Roman du Castelain de Couci et de la dame de Fayel*.

EDITIONS: Lerond 1964; van der Werf 1977.

• "A vous, amant, plus qu'a nulle autre gent": L 38-1, RS 679, MW 1228. Sources: ms. M, also ACKOPRTUVX, also quoted whole or in part in several 13th-c. romances. Music in all mss. except C. Attribution to the Châtelain in CKPTX. RT 199-204/384-389; Bédier-Aubry 1909, 99-106; Lerond 1964, 57-62; van der Werf 1977, 224-231.

Like the three other *chansons de croisade* presented in this volume, the Châtelain's expresses the pain of separation from the speaker's belovèd. The crusade to which it refers is either the Third (1189) or the Fourth (1202). For a detailed textual analysis, see Dijkstra 1995, 147-152.

4.5-6: The charge that God has cruelly separated two faithful lovers occurs in several other crusade songs; cf. the anonymous "Jherusalem, grant damage me fais" under CHANSONS DE FEMME and Guiot de Dijon's "Chanterai por mon corage" in this Anthology.

5.3-4: This statement alludes to the vow taken by departing crusaders ("pilgrims") to forgive all the offenses of their enemies.

The numerous readings of the music all present essentially the same melody, with variants concerning mainly the ornamentation in the second half of the stanza. This is clearly a song as closely identified with a particular melody as with a particular text, and we might well hypothesize that the music was no less the Châtelain's own than was the poem. This idea is supported by the re-use of the same melody in the anonymous lament, "Li chastelains de Couci ama tant" (see CHANSONS D'AMOUR above), which pays homage to the Châtelain.

Mutilation of a section of ms. M, our source for the text, renders it necessary to have recourse to another manuscript for the music. This is U, whose melody, in *g*, presents ornamentation somewhat at variance with the rest of the tradition; insofar as *musica ficta* is concerned, U is, as

always, very precise. The scheme is that of *pedes cum cauda*: ABAB CDEF.

• "Li nouviauz tanz et mais et violete": L 38-9, RS 985, MW 1507. Sources: ms. M, also ACKLOPRTUVXa, also quoted in part in two 13th-c. romances. Music in all mss. except C. Attribution to the Châtelain in MAKPTXa, to "Muse en Borse" in C. RT 204-208/388-393; Bédier-Aubry 1909, 89-96; Lerond 1964, 76-81; van der Werf 1977, 243-250.

Normally, a six-stanza poem three of whose stanzas repeat one set of rhymes (set A) while three repeat another (set B) has the stanzas arranged in the order AAABBB; this is the sequence of *coblas ternas*. The present text is innovative in showing the order AABABB. It should be noted, however, that not all readings of the poem agree on this order. Mss. ORTa have it, and ms. A has it as well, except that A is missing the final stanza. On the other hand, KLPVX (which, like A, contain only five stanzas) arrange the stanzas in the order 1 2 4 5 3, which means strophic linkage in the pattern AAABB; and CU, with only four stanzas, have the arrangement 1 2 4 3, which gives the pattern AAAB. It is interesting to compare the different poetic statements arising from such variation in the number and sequencing of the stanzas.

1.8: It is apparently because of this verse that "Li nouviauz tanz" has been considered a crusade song and included in the Bédier-Aubry edition of such compositions. The allusion is no doubt to a crusade, either the Third or the Fourth, but strikes us as insufficient to warrant that generic designation.

The numerous musical readings reveal significant differences. M and U are a fifth lower than the rest; KLXPO diverge from M halfway through the stanza; R and V have melodies of their own, with schemes tending toward the through-composed. The melodies may thus be shown grouped as follows: KLOPX-Aa-MTU/R/V. The melody of M, presented here, is built on *c*, with which lines 2, 4, 6, and 8 end, and it has a *pedes cum cauda* scheme: ABAB CDEF; its ornamentation tends to appear in the second half of the individual lines.

• "La douce voiz du rosignol sauvage": L 38-7, RS 40, MW 1051. Sources: ms. K, also ACFMOPTVXa, also quoted in a 13th-c. romance. Music in all mss. except C. Attribution to the Châtelain in all mss. except OV. RT 209-212/392-395; Lerond 1964, 68-71; van der Werf 1977, 186-193. Performed on Anthology CD.

For a detailed textual analysis of this song, see Zumthor 1972, 194-204 and 240-241.

The numerous musical readings show M with a melody of its own; the others differ through transposition in the second half of the stanza. The general scheme is that of *pedes cum cauda:* ABAB CDA'E. The melody of K, presented here, is constructed on two tones: *c* for line-openings and *d* for the principal cadences, particularly halfway through the stanza (*diesis*) and at the end. Note that the final notes of the eight lines show an exact reflection of the rhyme scheme: *cdcd dccd = a'ba'b ba'a'b.*

A vous, amant, plus qu'a nulle autre gent   (L 38-1)
Chanson d'amour, chanson de croisade

A vous, amant, plus qu'a nulle autre gent,
Est bien raisons que ma doleur conplaigne,
Quar il m'estuet partir outreement
Et dessevrer de ma loial conpaigne;   1.4
Et quant li pert, n'est rienz qui me remaigne.
Et sachiez bien, Amours, seürement,
S'ainc nuls morut pour avoir cuer dolent,
Donc n'iert par moi maiz meüs vers ne laiz.   1.8

To you, lovers, more than anyone else,
it is only right that I should voice my lament,
for I must leave and go abroad
and part from my faithful companion;
and once I've lost her, I have nothing left.
You may be certain, love, without a doubt,
that, if ever a man has died of a broken heart,
no more poems or songs will come from me.

Biauz sire Dieus, qu'iert il dont, et conment?
Convenra m' il qu'en la fin congié praigne?
Oïl, par Dieu, ne puet estre autrement:
Sanz li m'estuet aler en terre estraigne.   2.4
Or ne cuit maiz que granz mauz me soufraigne,
Quant de li n'ai confort n'alegement
Ne de nule autre amour joie n'atent
Fors que de li; ne sai se c'iert jamaiz.   2.8

Biauz sire Dieus, qu'iert il du consirrer
Du grant soulaz et de la conpaignie
Et de l'amour que me soloit moustrer
Cele qui m'ert dame, conpaigne, amie?   3.4
Et quant recort sa simple courtoisie
Et les douz moz que seut a moi parler,
Conment me puet li cuers u cors durer?
Quant ne s'en part, certes il est mauvaiz.   3.8

Ne me vout pas Dieus pour neiant doner
Touz les soulaz qu'ai eüs en ma vie,
Ainz les me fet chierement conparer;
S'ai grant poour cist loiers ne m'ocie.   4.4
Merci, Amours! S'ainc Dieus fist vilenie,
Con vilainz fait bone amour dessevrer;
Ne je ne puiz l'amour de moi oster,
Et si m'estuet que je ma dame lais.   4.8

Or seront lié li faus losengeour,
Qui tant pesoit des biens qu'avoir soloie;
Maiz ja de ce n'iere pelerins jour
Que ja vers iauz bone volenté aie.   5.4
Pour tant porrai perdre toute ma voie,
Quar tant m'ont fait de mal li trahitour,
Se Dieus voloit qu'il eüssent m'amour,
Ne me porroit chargier pluz pesant faiz.   5.8

Je m'en voiz, dame. A Dieu le creatour
Conmant vo cors, en quel lieu que je soie.
Ne sai se ja verroiz maiz mon retour;
Aventure est que jamaiz vous revoie.   6.4
Pour Dieu vos pri, quel part que li cors traie,
Que nos convens tenez, vieigne u demour,
Et je pri Dieu qu'ensi me doint honour
Con je vous ai esté amis verais.   6.8

Dear Lord God, what will happen, and how?
Must I, in the end, take my leave?
Yes, by God, there is no other way:
I must leave for a foreign land without her.
Now I don't think I can ever escape great pain:
I will not have her comfort and solace,
and from no one else can I expect the joy of love,
only from her — and I don't know if it will ever be.

Dear Lord God, what will happen without
the great closeness and companionship
and love that I used to know with the one
who was my lady, my companion, my friend?
When I recall her unaffected courtesy
and the tender words she would speak,
how can my heart stand still within me?
If it does not tear itself away, it is worthless.

Not for nothing was it God's will to give me
all the pleasures that I have had in life;
no, He is making me pay dearly now,
and I am afraid the price will kill me.
Mercy, love! If ever God has done something foul,
it is foul of Him to separate good lovers;
I cannot drive my love out of my heart,
yet I am forced to leave my lady.

Now the liars and tale-bearers will be delighted,
who were so nettled by my happiness;
I can never be a pilgrim holy enough
to bear them any good will,
even if I thus lose the fruit of my journey.
The traitors have done me so much harm
that, if God wanted me to love them,
He could not burden me with a heavier load.

I am leaving now, my lady. To the Creator
I commend you, wherever I may be.
I am not sure you will ever see me return;
it may be that I shall never see you again.
Wherever we may be, I ask, for God's sake,
that you honor our vows whether I return or not,
and I ask God that He recognize
how true a lover I have been to you.

Li nouviauz tanz et mais et violete   (L 38-9)
Chanson d'amour

Li nou- viauz tanz et mais et vi- o- le- te

Et lous- sei- gnolz me se- mont de chan- ter,

Et mes fins cuers me fait d'une a- mou- re- te

Si douz pre- sent que ne l'os re- fu- ser .

Or me lait Dieus en tele ho- neur mon- ter

Que cele u j'ai mon cuer et mon pen- ser

Tieigne u- ne foiz en- tre mes braz nü- e- te

Ainz que j'aille ou- tre- mer .

Li nouviauz tanz et mais et violete
Et lousseignolz me semont de chanter,
Et mes fins cuers me fait d'une amourete
Si douz present que ne l'os refuser.   1.4
Or me lait Dieus en tele honeur monter
Que cele u j'ai mon cuer et mon penser
Tieigne une foiz entre mes braz nüete
       Ainz que j'aille outremer.   1.8

Au conmencier la trouvai si doucete,
Ja ne quidai pour li mal endurer;
Mes ses douz vis et sa bele bouchete
Et si vair oeill bel et riant et cler   2.4
M'orent ainz pris que m'osaisse doner;
Se ne me veut retenir ou cuiter,
Mieuz aim a li faillir, si me pramete,
       Qu'a une autre achiever.   2.8

The new season, may and violets,
  the nightingale, all bid me sing,
  and my pure heart has presented me
  with a sweet new love that I dare not refuse.
May God now let me rise to such honor
  that my heart's desire and object of my every thought
  will at last lie naked in my arms
  before I sail abroad.

At first, I found her so sweet and kind
  I never thought I would ache for her;
  but her sweet face and her lovely mouth
  and her smiling eyes sparkling and bright
  captured me before I could surrender;
  unless she wants to keep me or to let me go,
  I would rather fail with her (but with a promise)
  than succeed with someone else.

Las! pour coi l'ai de mes ieuz reguardee,
La douce rienz qui Fausse Amie a non,
Quant de moi rit et je l'ai tant plouree?
Si doucement ne fu trahis nus hom.   3.4
Tant com fui mienz, ne me fist se bien non;
Mes or sui suenz, si m'ocit sans raison,
Et c'est pour ce que de cuer l'ai amee!
              N'i set autre ochoison.   3.8

De mil souspirs que je li doi par dete,
Ne m'en veut pas un seul cuite clamer;
Ne Fausse Amours ne lait que s'entremete,
Ne ne me lait dormir ne reposer.   4.4
S'ele m'ocit, mainz avra a guarder;
Je ne m'en sai vengier fors au plourer;
Quar qui Amours destruit et desirete
              Ne s'en set ou clamer.   4.8

Sour toute joie est cele courounee
Que j'ai d'Amours. Dieus! i faudrai je dont?
Oïl, par Dieu, teus est ma destinee,
Et tel destin m'ont doné li felon.   5.4
Si sevent bien qu'il font grant mesprison,
Quar qui ce tolt dont ne puet faire don,
Il en conquiert anemis et mellee:
              N'i fait se perdre non.   5.8

Si coiement ai ma doleur celee
Qu'a mon samblant ne la coneüst on;
Se ne fussent la gent maleüree,
N'eüsse pas souspiré en pardon: 6.4
Amours m'eüst doné son guerredon.
Maiz en cel point que dui avoir mon don,
Lor fu l'amour descouverte et moustree.
              Ja n'aient il pardon!   6.8

Alas! why did I ever catch sight of her,
that sweet creature named False Belovèd,
who laughs at all the tears I have shed for her?
So easily has no man ever been betrayed.
As long as I was free, she made me happy;
but now I am hers, she kills me for no reason,
only because I have loved her with all my heart!
She has no other grounds.

Of the thousand sighs that are my debt to her
she will not free me of even one;
and false love, with its endless meddling,
lets me neither sleep nor rest.
If she kills me, she'll have fewer prisoners to watch.
Weeping is the only revenge I know,
for no one crushed and disinherited by love
knows where to seek redress.

Greater than any other joy is the supreme one
that comes to me from love. God! will I fail at it?
Yes, by God, such is my fate,
the fate that the wicked have sought for me
aware though they are of their great mistake,
for he who steals what he cannot give to another
gains enemies and battles thereby:
he can only lose.

So subtly have I concealed my pain
that you would not detect it in my looks;
if not for that accursed race,
I would never have sighed for love in vain:
love would have granted me its prize.
But just when I was to have my reward,
our love was uncovered and exposed.
May they never be forgiven!

La douce voiz du rosignol sauvage   (L 38-7)

Chanson d'amour

La dou- ce voiz du ro- si- gnol sau- va- ge

Qu' oi nuit et jor coin- toi- er et ten- tir

Me ra- dou- cist mon cuer et ras- sou- a- ge ;

Lors ai ta- lent que chant pour es- bau- dir .

Bien doi chan- ter puis qu' il vient a ple- sir

Ce- le qui j' ai de cuer fet lige hon- ma- ge ;

Si doi a- voir grant joie en mon co- ra- ge ,

S' e- le me veut a son oés re- te- nir .

La douce voiz du rosignol sauvage
Qu'oi nuit et jor cointoier et tentir
Me radoucist mon cuer et rassouage;
Lors ai talent que chant pour esbaudir.   1.4
Bien doi chanter puis qu'il vient a plesir
Cele qui j'ai de cuer fet lige honmage;
Si doi avoir grant joie en mon corage,
S'ele me veut a son oés retenir.   1.8

Onques vers li n'oi faus cuer ne volage,
Si me deüst por ce melz avenir;
Ainz l'aim et serf et aor par usage,
Si ne li os mon penser descouvrir.   2.4
Car sa biauté me fet si esbahir
Que je ne sai devant li nul langage;
Ne regarder n'os son simple visage,
Tant en redout mes euz a departir.   2.8

The sweet voice of the forest nightingale
that night and day I hear warble and trill
brings sweetness and balm to my heart;
then I cannot keep from rejoicing in song.
I am bound to sing because it brings pleasure
to the lady whose vassal of the heart I've become;
and I am bound to have a heart full of joy
if she cares to keep me and call me her knight.

Never, for her, has my heart been false or unsteady,
which should make my chances much better;
indeed, I love and I serve her, always adore her,
yet I dare not confess the love on my mind.
I am so abashed by her beauty
that in her sight I am tongue-tied and mute;
I dare not glance at her innocent face,
so much do I fear then looking away.

Tant ai en li ferm assis mon corage
Qu'ailleurs ne pens, et Deus m'en dont joïr,
C'onques Tristans, cil qui but le buvrage,
Si coriaument n'ama sanz repentir.   3.4
Car g'i met tot: cuer et cors et desir,
Sens et savoir — ne sai se faz folage,
Ançois me dout qu'en trestout mon aage
Ne puisse li ne s'amor deservir.   3.8

Je ne di pas que je face folage,
Nes se pour li me devoie morir,
Qu'el mont ne truis si bele ne si sage
Ne nule riens n'est tant a mon plesir.   4.4
Mult aim mes euz qui me firent choisir:
Lués que la vi, li lessai en ostage
Mon cuer qui puis i a fet lonc estage,
Ne jamés jor ne l'en quier departir.   4.8

Chançon, va t'en pour fere mon message
La ou je n'os trestorner ne guenchir,
Que tant redout la male gent honbrage
Qui devinent, ainz que puist avenir,   5.4
Le bien d'amors. Deus les puist maleïr,
Qu'a maint amant ont fet ire et outrage!
Mes j'ai de ce touz jorz mal avantage
Q'il les m'estuet seur mon cuer obeïr.   5.8

So firmly have I set my heart on her
that I can think of no one else. God grant me success!
Never did Tristan, for all the draught he had drunk,
love so deeply and with no hesitation.
For I give my all, body and heart, my desire,
my mind and my learning; perhaps it is folly,
but I fear that I may never in life
come to merit her love.

I don't say what I am doing is folly,
even were I to die for her sake,
for nowhere else do I find such beauty and judgment
and no other creature can bring me such pleasure.
I love my eyes for first letting me see her:
no sooner glimpsed than she held my heart hostage,
and hers it has been all this while;
nor would I ever tear it away.

Song, go now, carry my message
to the place where I don't dare take my way
for fear of the sinister knaves
who ferret out love and its joy even before
it has happened. May God curse them!
They have angered and wronged many a lover;
but I always face this disadvantage,
that I have to deny my heart and do their bidding.

GACE BRULÉ

The most illustrious of the early trouvères, Gace Brulé (fl. ca. 1185-1210), born into the lower nobility of Champagne, has been credited with one of the most extensive bodies of monophonic compositions in Old French. The texts—over eighty of them, with the great majority surviving accompanied by their melodies—are almost all courtly *chansons* in a style derived from the Occitan tradition. Their usual theme, persistent but unrequited and despairing love for a socially superior lady, is often interwoven with the theme of poetic and musical creation: loving and singing express each other. Though almost nothing is known of Gace's life, it is clear that his circle included other major lyric poets and that his patrons—Marie de Champagne, first of all—were among the most powerful feudal figures of his time. Textual and melodic evidence shows that he was widely admired and emulated by both contemporary and later trouvères, in Germany as well as France.

EDITIONS: Dyggve 1951; van der Werf 1977, 315-554; Rosenberg 1985.

● "Les oxelés de mon païx": L 65-45, RS 1579, MW 586. Sources: ms. C, also KLMNPRTUVX; music in all mss. except CU. Attribution to Gace in KMNPTX; to Guiot de Provins in C. RT 213-217/396-401; Dyggve 1951, 189-193; Rosenberg 1985, 4-9.

Dialectal features: Lorraine, including *lais* = Central Fr. *las, jai* = *ja, pailli* = *pali, compaireir* = *comparer, penseir* = *penser, leivres* = *levres, jueir* = *jouer; pués* = *puis; poent* = *point; oxelés* = *oiselez, païx, païs, baixant* = *baisant; ceu* = *ce; lou* = *le; seux* = *sui*. Note in particular the verb forms *ait* = *a, avrait* = *avra*.

Of all the songs of Gace Brulé, this is no doubt the best known today. In discussing the structure of the first stanza, one scholar calls it "un exemple très caractéristique des raffinements formels dont les trouvères se montrent capables" (Dragonetti 1960, 403). It is interesting to note that this song appears not to have had in the Middle Ages the same renown that it enjoys today. While it survives in many manuscripts, the redactions tend to be poor and incomplete (which is why we have had to combine text from one ms. with music from another in the present edition); it is not quoted in the thirteenth-century romances that quote various other poems by Gace; and there is no later composition—be it French, German, or Latin—for which anyone has been able to claim it as a model.

1.2: The reference is to a period, sometime between 1181 and 1186, spent at the court of Geoffrey Plantagenet, count of Brittany, half-brother of Marie de Champagne.

5.8-10: The meaning seems to be that the lady is so pure and innocent that the treacherous suitors can influence her unduly.

Among the various musical readings, only R and V diverge somewhat (through partial transpositions and occasional ornamentations) from the tradition. The highly ornamented line-ends are in general the places where the various readings prove divergent. In line 5, K, presented here, is missing a note for the second syllable. The music of ms. K, in the scale of *d*, close to the other versions, displays great homogeneity in its use of melodic mode. The *pedes cum cauda* scheme, ABAB CDEFGH, shows a cauda with extended development. Note in this regard the vocal sweep of a ninth in line 8, from *c* all the way up to *d*.

● "De bone amour et de lëaul amie": L 65-25, RS 1102, MW 2052. There are two quite different redactions of this song, one complete and the other abridged; we present only the complete version, the sources of which are: ms. O, also CHLU and za; music in LOU. Attribution to Gace in C (and five of the mss. containing the abridged version). RT 217-223/400-407; Dyggve 1951, 272-279; van der Werf 1977, 447-454; Rosenberg 1985, 236-243.

In its complete version, this poem is a masterly achievement of complex versification, bringing into play the various patterns of stanzaic linking known as *coblas capcaudadas, capfinidas, retrogradadas,* and *retronchadas*. Note, for example, that, while the rhymes are the same in all stanzas (*coblas unissonans*), the *a* and *b* rhymes are transposed in the even-numbered stanzas; note as well that the rhyme-words of each odd-numbered stanza are repeated in the following even stanza, though in a different order. See Dragonetti 1960, 454-457 for further examination of the poem's structural complexity.

The incipit, like that of another of Gace's poems (L 25-77), is quoted in a song (L 88-3) by Gilles de Viés-Maisons. That the present work was well known and admired in Gace's time is indicated by the fact that it served as model or inspiration for several compositions by other trouvères: a *chanson pieuse* perhaps by Thibaut de Champagne (L 265-443), another such by Jacques de Cambrai (L 121-6), two anonymous pieces (L 265-1637 and L 265-334), and a German song by Rudolf von Fenis.

The persons named in the second envoy, *Huet* and *Bertree*, are unknown.

If we consider both the complete and the abridged redactions of this song, we find a relatively complex musical tradition, with eleven variant melodies. The nature of the variation is chiefly transpositional, with melodic passages of differing lengths being affected. Ms. O has a semi-mensural version in the third rhythmic mode. The melody in U, which we present, is similar to that of O. Both are in the Mixolydian, or *g*, scale, with a higher-pitched development after the mid-stanza *diesis*. They show a *pedes cum cauda* scheme: ABAB′ CDEF, which is compatible with the rhyme scheme: a′b′a′b′ cccb′.

• "A la douçor de la bele seson": L 65-2, RS 1893, MW 1277. Sources: ms. N, also CKLOPVX; one melody in KLNX, another in O, a third in V; no music in CP. Attribution to Gace in KNPX. RT 236-238/422-425; Dyggve 1951, 366-368; van der Werf 1977, 538-540; Rosenberg 1985, 130-133.

Mss. LOPX conclude this poem with an envoy:

Li quens Jofroiz, qui me doit consoillier,
Dist qu'il n'est amis entierement
Qui nule foiz pense a amour laissier.

(Count Geoffrey, who must advise me,
says that no man is fully a lover
who at any time thinks of abandoning love.)

The reference is to Geoffrey Plantagenet, son of Henry II of England and Eleanor of Aquitaine, count of Brittany, who was the half-brother of Gace's patroness Marie de Champagne and whom Gace names or alludes to in several songs.

We present all three melodies, which share a *pedes cum cauda* scheme: (ms. K) ABA′B′ CDB″, (ms. O) ABAB CDE, (ms. V, with hypermetric lines 3 and 7) ABA′B′ CDE. In the *pedes*, the melodies are all analogous, their reference tones being *g* (lines 1, 3) and *d* (lines 2, 4). In the *cauda*, however, there are clear differences, which the distribution of melodic formulas shows to be due to the transposition of fragments of melody. This is especially obvious in V, the second part of whose melody tends to rise in contrast to the other readings (a fourth in line 5, a seventh at the line 7 cadence).

Les oxelés de mon païx   (L 65-45)

Chanson d'amour

Les o- xe- lés de mon pa- ïx

Ai o- ïs en Bre- tai- gne .

A lors chans m'est il bien a- vis

K'en la dou- ce Cham- pai- gne

Les o- ï ja- dis,   Se n'i ai mes- pris .

Il m'ont en si douls pen- seir mis

K'a chan- son fai- re m'en seux pris

Tant que je pe- ra- tai- gne

Ceu k'A- mors m'ait lonc tens pro- mis .

Les oxelés de mon païx	The little birds of my land
Ai oïs en Bretaigne.	I have heard in Brittany.
A lors chans m'est il bien avis	When I hear their song, it seems to me
K'en la douce Champaigne	that in fair Champagne
Les oï jadis, 1.5	I heard them long ago,
Se n'i ai mespris.	if I am not mistaken.
Il m'ont en si douls penseir mis	They have put me into such a gentle mood
K'a chanson faire m'en seux pris	that I have begun to sing
Tant que je perataigne	till I at last secure
Ceu k'Amors m'ait lonc tens promis. 1.10	what love has long promised me.

En longue atente me languis
    Sens ceu ke trop m'en plaigne;
Ceu me tolt mon jeu et mon ris,
    Ke nuls c'Amors destraigne
      N'est d'el ententis.   2.5
      Mon cors et mon vis
Truis si per oures entrepris
Ke fol semblant en ai enpris.
      Ki k'en Amors mespraigne,
Je seux cil k'ains riens n'i forfix.   2.10

En baixant, mon cuer me ravi
    Ma douce dame gente;
Moult fut fols quant il me guerpi
    Por li ke me tormente.
      Lais! ains ne.l senti   3.5
      Quant de moy parti;
Tant doulcement lou me toli
K'en sospirant le traist a li;
      Mon fol cuer atalente,
Maix jai n'avrait de moy merci.   3.10

Del baixier me remenbre si,
    Ke je fix, en m'entente
Il n'est hore — ceu m'ait traï —
    K'a mes leivres ne.l sente.
      Quant elle sousfri   4.5
      Ceu ke je la vi,
De ma mort ke ne me gueri!
K'elle seit bien ke je m'oci
      En ceste longue atente,
Dont j'ai lou vis taint et pailli.   4.10

Pués ke me tolt rire et jueir
    Et fait morir d'envie,
Trop sovant me fait compaireir
    Amors sa compaignie.
      Lais! n'i ous aleir,   5.5
      Car por fol sembleir
Me font cil fauls proiant dameir.
Mors seux quant je.s i voi pairleir,
      Ke poent de tricherie
Ne puet nulz d'eaus en li troveir.   5.10

I languish in long expectation
without much complaining;
it takes away my cheer and smile,
for no one tormented by love
is mindful of anything else.
My body and my face
I quite often find in such a sorry state
that I have taken on the look of a madman.
Others, perhaps, may misbehave toward love,
but I am one who has never transgressed.

With a kiss, she stole my heart away,
my sweet gentle lady;
my heart was mad to abandon me
for her who torments me.
Alas, I hardly felt it
when it left me;
she took it from me so gently,
drawing it away with a sigh;
she has inspired my mad heart with love,
but she will never have mercy on me.

So well do I remember the kiss
I gave that in my mind
there is no moment — and this betrays me —
when I do not feel it on my lips.
When she permitted me
to see her,
why did she not save me from my death!
For she well knows that I am dying
of this long delay
which leaves me with a pale and ashen face.

Since it takes away my cheer and laughter
and makes me die of longing,
love too often makes me
pay dearly for her company.
Alas, I dare not go to her,
for, with my madman's look,
those false suitors bring discredit upon me.
I die when I see them talk to her,
for no guile
can any of them find in her.

De bone amour et de lëaul amie   (L 65-25)

Chanson d'amour

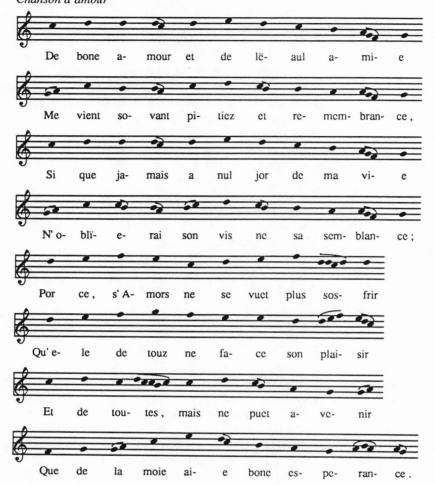

De bone a- mour et de lë- aul a- mi- e

Me vient so- vant pi- tiez et re- mem- bran- ce,

Si que ja- mais a nul jor de ma vi- e

N' o- blï- e- rai son vis ne sa sem- blan- ce ;

Por ce, s' A- mors ne se vuet plus sos- frir

Qu' e- le de touz ne fa- ce son plai- sir

Et de tou- tes, mais ne puet a- ve- nir

Que de la moie ai- e bone es- pe- ran- ce.

De bone amour et de lëaul amie	Good love and loyal belovèd
Me vient sovant pitiez et remembrance,	so often stir deep feeling and remembrance
Si que jamais a nul jor de ma vie	that at no moment in my life
N'oblïerai son vis ne sa semblance; 1.4	will I forget her face or her appearance;
Por ce, s'Amors ne se vuet plus sosfrir	and so, if love is no longer willing to refrain
Qu'ele de touz ne face son plaisir	from doing as it pleases to all men
Et de toutes, mais ne puet avenir	and all women, it cannot ever happen
Que de la moie aie bone esperance. 1.8	that I will have good hope for my love.
Coment porroie avoir bone esperance	How could I have good hope
A bone amor et a leal amie,	for good love and loyal belovèd,
Ne a biaus yeux n'a la douce semblance	or beautiful eyes and fair appearance
Que ne verrai jamés jor de ma vie? 2.4	that I will never see again in my life?
Amer m'estuet, ne m'en puis plus sosfrir,	I must love — I can no longer refrain from it —
Celi cui ja ne vanra a plaisir;	the one my love will never please;
Siens sui, coment qu'il m'en doie avenir,	I am hers, whatever may happen to me,
Et si n'i voi ne confort ne aïe. 2.8	though I foresee neither comfort nor aid.

Coment avrai je confort ne ahie
Encontre Amour, vers cui nus n'a puissance?
Amer me fait ce qui ne m'aimme mie,
Donc ja n'avrai fors ennui et pesance;   3.4
Ne ja nul jor ne l'oserai gehir
Celi qui tant de maus me fait sentir;
Mais de tel mort sui jugiez a morir
Dont ja ne quier veoir ma delivrance.   3.8

Je ne vois pas querant tel delivrance
Par quoi amors soit de moi departie,
Ne ja n'en quier nul jor avoir poissance;
Ainz vuil amer ce qui ne m'aimme mie.   4.4
N'il n'est pas droiz je li doie gehir
Por nul destroit que me face sentir;
N'avrai confort, n'i voi que dou morir,
Puis que je voi que ne m'ameroit mie.   4.8

Ne m'ameroit? Ice ne sai je mie,
Que fins amis doit par bone atendance
Et par soffrir conquerre haute amie;
Mes je n'i puis avoir nulle fiance,   5.4
Que cele est teus, por cui plaing et sopir,
Que ma dolor ne doigneroit oïr;
Si me vaut mieuz garder mon bon taisir
Que dire riens qui li tort a grevance.   5.8

Ne vos doit pas trop torner a grevance
Se je vos aing, dame, plus que ma vie,
Que c'est la riens ou j'ai greignor fiance,
Que par moi seul vos oi nommer amie.   6.4
Et por ce fais maint doloros sopir
Qu'assez vos puis et veoir et oïr,
Mais quant vos voi, n'i a que dou taisir,
Que si sui pris que ne sai que je die.   6.8

How will I have comfort and aid
to resist love, which no one has power to resist?
It makes me love one who does not love me;
I will therefore never have but pain and grief;
and I will never dare confess it
to her who makes me feel so many ills;
but I am condemned to die a death
such that I do not desire to see my deliverance.

I do not go seeking deliverance
such that love would thereby leave me,
nor do I ever wish to have that power;
instead, I want to love one who does not love me.
Nor is it right that I confess it to her,
whatever the torment she may make me feel;
I will have no comfort; all I foresee is death,
since I see that she would never love me.

Never love me? I do not know that,
for only through long patience and suffering
does a true lover win a noble belovèd;
but I can have no trust in that,
for she is such, the one for whom I lament and sigh,
that she would not deign to hear my sorrow;
thus it is better for me to keep a wise silence
than to say anything that might offend her.

It must not offend you too much
if I love you, my lady, more than my life,
for this is the thing in which I have the greatest trust:
that I hear you called belovèd by me alone.
And yet I utter many a sad sigh,
because I can often see and hear you,
but, when I see you, all I can do is be silent,
for I am so overcome that I do not know what to say.

A la douçor de la bele seson   (L 65-2)
Chanson d'amour

K   A la dou- çor de la be- le se- son,

K   Que tou- te riens se res- plent en ver- dor,

K   Que sont biau pré et ver- gier et buis- son

K   Et li oi- sel chan- tent de- seur la flor,

K   Lors sui joi- anz quant tuit les- sent a- mor,

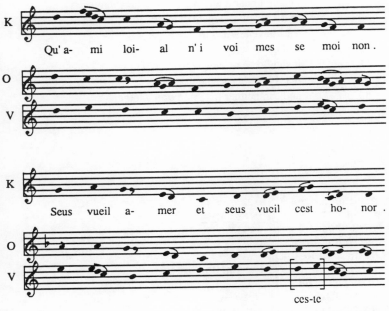

K Qu' a- mi loi- al n' i voi mes se moi non .

O

V

K Seus vueil a- mer et seus vueil cest ho- nor .

O

V

ces-te

A la douçor de la bele seson,
Que toute riens se resplent en verdor,
Que sont biau pré et vergier et buisson
Et li oisel chantent deseur la flor,   1.4
Lors sui joianz quant tuit lessent amor,
Qu'ami loial n'i voi mes se moi non.
Seus vueil amer et seus vueil cest honor.   1.7

Mult m'ont grevé li tricheor felon,
Mes il ont droit, c'onques ne.s amai jor.
Leur deviner et leur fausse acheson
Fist ja cuidier que je fusse des lor;   2.4
Joie en perdi, si en crut ma dolor,
Car ne m'i soi garder de traïson;
Oncore en dout felon et menteor.   2.7

Entor tel gent ne me sai maintenir
Qui tout honor lessent a leur pouoir;
Tant com je m'aim, les me couvient haïr
Ou je faudrai a ma grant joie avoir.   3.4
C'est granz ennuis que d'aus amentevoir,
Mes tant les hé que ne m'en puis tenir;
Ja leur mestier ne leront decheoir.   3.7

Or me dont Deus ma dame si servir
Q'il aient duel de ma joie veoir.
Bien me devroit vers li grant lieu tenir
Ma loiauté, qui ne puet remanoir;   4.4
Mes je ne puis oncore apercevoir
Qu'ele des biens me vuelle nus merir
Dont j'ai sousfert les maus en bon espoir.   4.7

In the sweetness of spring,
when everything turns resplendently green,
when meadows, orchards, and groves are beautiful
and the birds sing among the flowers,
then I rejoice, for everyone else has abandoned love,
so that I no longer see any loyal lover but myself.
I alone wish to love and I alone wish that honor.

Treacherous villains have hurt me much,
but they have the right, for I have never loved them.
Their gossip and their false accusation
once caused me to be thought one of them;
and so I lost my joy and pain grew,
for I did not know how to shield myself from betrayal;
even now I fear villains and liars.

I cannot remain among such people
who do their best to forsake all honor;
so long as I respect myself, I am bound to hate them
or else I shall fail to have my great joy.
It pains me to remember them,
but so much do I hate them that I cannot help it;
they will never give up their ways.

May God grant me now to serve my lady so well
that they will suffer to see my joy.
My loyalty, which cannot come to an end,
should make her look upon me with favor;
but I still cannot perceive
that she is willing to reward me with any of the favors
for which I have suffered such pains in good hope.

Je n'en puis mes se ma dame consent
En ceste amour son honme a engingnier,
Car j'ai apris a amer loiaument,
Ne ja nul jour repentir ne m'en qier;
Si me devroit a son pouoir aidier
Ce que je l'aim si amoureusement,
N'autre ne puis ne amer ne proier.

I cannot bear it any more if my lady agrees
to deceive her liegeman in this love,
for I have learned to live loyally,
and never wish to change my ways;
it should be of the greatest help to me
that I love her so passionately
and can neither love nor woo another.

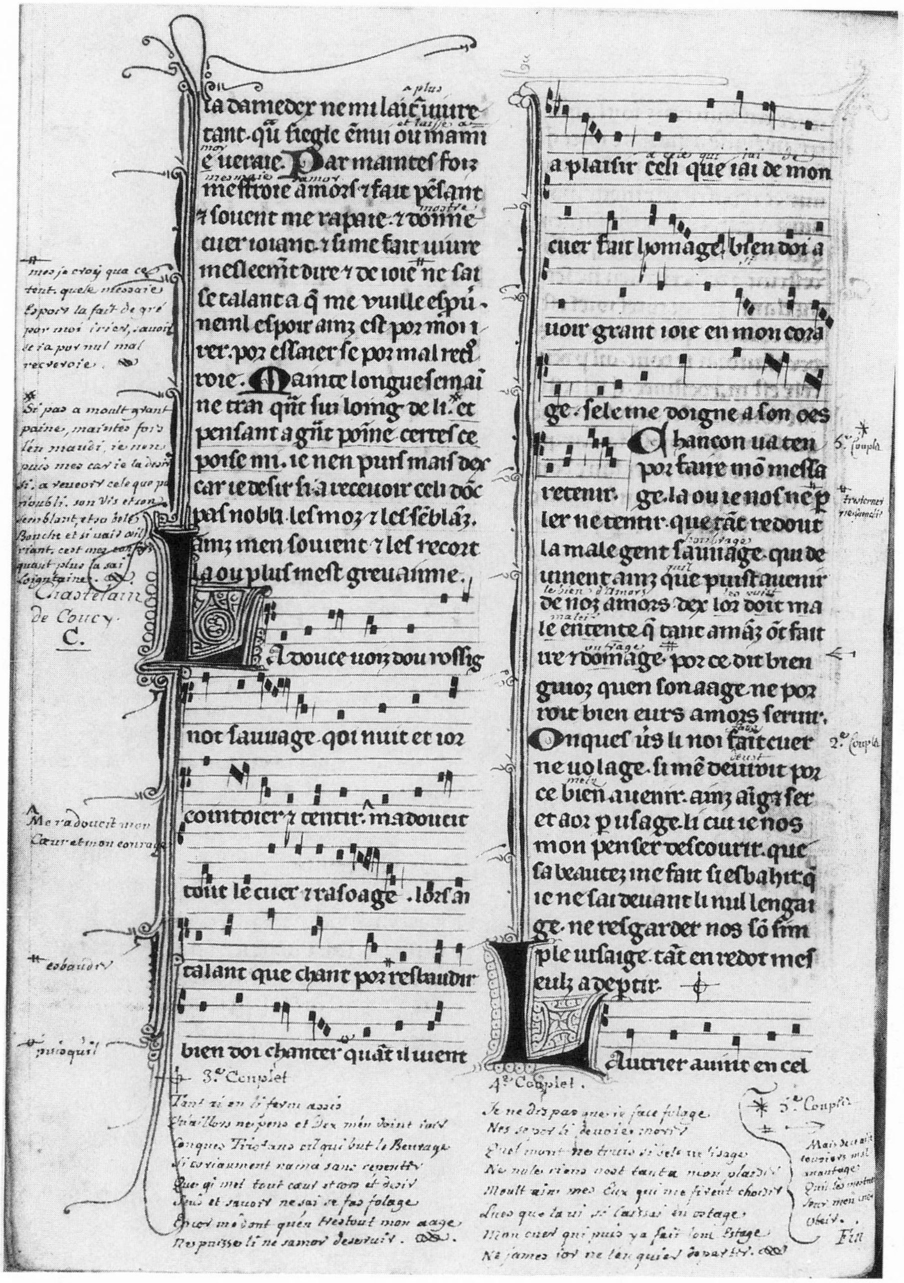

The Châtelain de Coucy, "La douce voiz dou rossignot sauuage" (p. 254). Ms. O, f. 74v.
Cliché Bibliothèque Nationale de France - Paris.

JEAN BODEL

Jean Bodel was a well-known professional writer of Arras, born ca. 1165; he died of leprosy in 1209-1210. He composed works in various genres, notably fabliaux, the epic *Chanson des Saisnes*, the *Jeu de saint Nicolas*, and his illness-provoked *Congés*. The five lyric pieces attributed to him are all *pastourelles*.

STUDY: Foulon 1958, 143-242.

● "Les un pin verdoiant": L 132-5, RS 367, MW 463, B 1408. Sources: ms. M, also T; music in both. Attribution to Jean Bodel in M. RT 242-244/430-435; Bartsch 1870, 288-290.

The first nine verses, along with their music, have been cut out of ms. M; our text therefore takes them, like the melody, from T.

The melody, homogeneous (built on *g*) and relatively syllabic, lends itself to dancing. The scheme, regular and well developed, approximates that of a ballade: ABCABC DEFD'E'F'/refrain GG'. The refrain has an ouvert-clos arrangement.

Les un pin verdoiant   (L 132-5)
Pastourelle

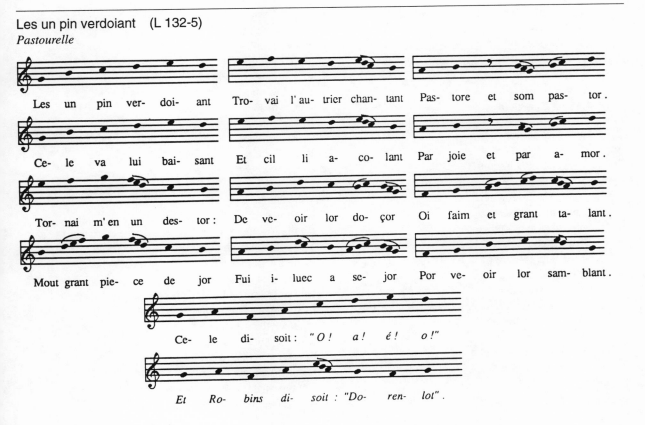

Les un pin ver- doi- ant   Tro- vai l'au- trier chan- tant   Pas- tore et som pas- tor.

Ce- le va lui bai- sant   Et cil li a- co- lant   Par joie et par a- mor.

Tor- nai m'en un des- tor: De ve- oir lor do- çor   Oi faim et grant ta- lant.

Mout grant pie- ce de jor   Fui i- luec a se- jor   Por ve- oir lor sam- blant.

Ce- le di- soit: "O! a! é! o!"

Et Ro- bins di- soit: "Do- ren- lot".

Les un pin verdoiant		Under a dark-green pine
Trovai l'autrier chantant		not long ago, I found a shepherdess
Pastore et som pastor.		and her shepherd singing.
Cele va lui baisant	1.4	She was kissing him
Et cil li acolant		and he was embracing her
Par joie et par amor.		in all the bliss of love.
Tornai m' en un destor:		I turned toward a secluded spot:
De veoir lor doçor	1.8	I was eager and hungry
Oi faim et grant talant.		to see their caresses.
Mout grant piece de jor		Much of the day
Fui iluec a sejor		I spent there quietly
Por veoir lor samblant.	1.12	watching their behavior.

Cele disoit: *"O! a! é! o!"* — She would say, *"Oh, ah, eh, oh!"*
Et Robins disoit: "Dorenlot!" — *And Robin would say, "Dorenlot!"*

Grant piece fui ensi,		I remained a long while like that,
Car forment m'abeli		for I found it a pleasure
Lor gieus a esguarder,		to watch them at play.
Tant que je departi	2.4	At last I saw the fellow
Vi de li son ami		take leave of the girl
Et ens el bois entrer.		and go into the woods.
Lors eu talent d'aler		Then I felt urged to go
A li por salüer;	2.8	forward and greet her;
Si m'assis delez li,		I sat down beside her,
Pris a li a parler,		started to speak
S'amor a demander,		and ask for her love,
Maiz mot ne respondi.	2.12	but she spoke not a word.

Ançois disoit: *"O! a! é! o!"* — Instead, she said, *"Oh, ah, eh, oh!"*
Et Robins el bois: "Dorenlot!" — *And Robin, in the woods, "Dorenlot!"*

"Touse, je vos requier,		"Shepherdess, give me a kiss,
Donez moi un baisier;		won't you, please?
Se ce non, je morrai.		I'll die if you don't.
Bien me pöez laissier	3.4	You will be leaving me here
Morir sanz recovrier		to die a certain death
Se je le baisier n'ai.		if I don't have your kiss.
Sor sains vos jurerai:		I swear to you by all that's holy:
Ja mal ne vos querrai	3.8	I won't try to harm you
Ne forceur destorbier."		or do anything worse."
"Vassal, et je.l ferai;		"All right then, young sir;
Trois fois vos baiserai		I'll give you three kisses
Por vos rassoagier."	3.12	to make you feel better."

Ele redit: *"O! a! é! o!"* — She repeated, *"Oh, ah, eh, oh!"*
Et Robins el bois: "Dorenlot!" — *And Robin, in the woods, "Dorenlot!"*

A cest mot, pluz ne dis;
Entre mes bras la pris,
Baisai l' estroitement;
Maiz au conter mespris,   4.4
Por les trois en pris sis.
Ele dit en riant:
"Vassal, a vo creant
Ai je fait largement   4.8
Pluz que ne vos pramis;
Or vos proi bonement
Que me tenez covent,
Si ne me querez pis."   4.12
Cele redit: *"O! a! é! o!"*
Et Robins el bois: "Dorenlot!"

Li baisier par amor
Me doublerent l'ardor
Et pluz en fui destrois.
Par desous moi la tor,   5.4
Et la touse ot paor
Si s'escria trois fois.
Robins oï la vois,
Gautelos et Guifrois   5.8
Et cist autre pastor;
Corant issent du bois
Et je, gabez, m'en vois,
Car la force en fu lor.   5.12
Puis n'i ot dit: *"O!" n' "a! é! o!"*
Robins ne dit puis: "Dorenlot!"

At that, I stopped speaking;
I took her in my arms
and kissed her with passion;
but my counting was wrong
and, rather than three, I took six.
She said with a laugh,
"Young sir, for your pleasure
I've given you many more kisses
than I had promised;
now I beg you, please,
keep your promise
and don't ask for anything more."
She repeated, *"Oh, ah, eh, oh!"*
And Robin, in the woods, "Dorenlot!"

Those loving kisses
had fanned my desire
and I was more aroused than before.
As I climbed atop her,
the girl took fright
and cried out three times.
Robin heard her voice,
as did Walt and Geoff
and the other shepherds;
They came running out of the woods,
and I, hearing their jeers, ran off.
Strength was on their side!
There was no more *"Oh, ah, eh, oh!"*
And Robin stopped saying, "Dorenlot!"

GONTIER DE SOIGNIES

Of Walloon origin, Gontier de Soignies was a professional trouvère, active between ca. 1180-1190 and ca. 1210-1220. About thirty lyric pieces are attributed to him, notably *rotrouenges* and other refrain songs.

EDITIONS: Scheler 1879; Formisano 1980.

● "Chanter m'estuet de recomens": L 92-3, RS 636, MW 178, B 1926. Single source: ms. T; music. Attribution to Gontier. RT 285-287/452-455; Scheler 1879, 11-12; Formisano 1980, 114-118.

Dialectal features: Picard, including *coraige* = Central Fr. *corage, faice = face; faus = fous; cose = chose, doche = douce, merchi = merci; aroit = avroit.*

The final stanza identifies this song as a *rotrouenge,* a term used in self-identification by half a dozen other trouvère compositions. Without much certainty or agreement, scholars have at one time or another called various other pieces, too, *rotrouenges,* including songs otherwise recognized as *ballettes* or *chansons de toile.* The term comes from the troubadours and may be of musical rather than prosodic relevance. The type, however ill-defined, is very simple and apparently of folkloric inspiration, its stanza being basically a series of monorhymed isometric lines followed by a refrain with a different rhyme; the last line of the stanza or the first line of the refrain may be linked to the other part by showing the same rhyme. For a detailed treatment of the *rotrouenge,* see Bec 1977, ch. 12.

This song is unusual in placing its refrain not at the end of the stanza but within it. Given the rest of its form as well, it thus appears to be an imitation of the song "Dirai vos senes duptansa" by the troubadour Marcabru (in this Anthology).

3.1-3: Instead of a period at the end of the first verse and a comma following the second, it would be perfectly reasonable to have no punctuation after line 1 and a full stop at the end of line 2. The translation would then be: "I cannot hide my feelings about what I most want and yearn for; I should surely give up."

The melody is in the scale of *g,* with the exception of line 5, in *a.* The scheme is of the litany type: AA′A″BCD.

● "Li tans nouveaus et la douçors": L 92-12, RS 2031, MW 79, B 312. Single source: ms. T; music. Attribution to Gontier. RT 290-292/460-463; Scheler 1879, 43-44; Formisano 1980, 84-87.

Dialectal features: Picard, including *millor* = Central Fr. *meilleur; pensieu = pensif; boin = bon; tenroit = tendroit; jou = je, çou = ce; le = la.*

Though it does not identify itself as such, this song, like our preceding selection, may be considered a *rotrouenge;* see note there. Its message is exceptional for a love song, since the poet complains of the disappointment produced by an easy conquest.

6.1: *Gontier* is surely meant as a playful reference to the trouvère himself. In fact, Gontier names himself in two other songs as well.

6.2-3: This proverb-like statement is echoed in the Old French refrain (B 1528), *Pou puet on le chastel prisier/Qui est prins du premier assault* ('A castle taken at the first attack cannot be greatly admired').

The melody is built on the scale of *d,* stated here with the classic homogeneity that also characterizes the scheme, ABAB CD.

Chanter m'estuet de recomens   (L 92-3)

Rotrouenge

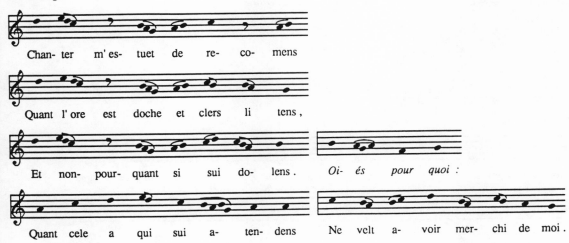

Chanter m'es- tuet de re- co- mens

Quant l'ore est doche et clers li tens ,

Et non- pour- quant si sui do- lens .   Oi- és pour quoi :

Quant cele a qui sui a- ten- dens   Ne velt a- voir mer- chi de moi .

Chanter m'estuet de recomens	I need to sing once again
Quant l'ore est doche et clers li tens,	since the time is mellow and the air is bright,
Et nonpourquant si sui dolens.	and yet I am sad.
Oiés pour quoi:	*I'll tell you why:*
Quant cele a qui sui atendens	because the lady I am courting
Ne velt avoir merchi de moi.	denies me mercy.
Molt aim ma dame et voil et pri,	I love my lady and want her and woo her,
Mais d'une cose m'a traï:	but one thing betrays me:
Quant li paroill, si m'entrobli.	when speaking to her, I forget myself.
Oiés pour quoi:	*I'll tell you why:*
Tant par desir l'amor de li	so much do I yearn for her love
Ke tous sui faus quant je la voi.	that I lose my mind when I see her.
Ne puis mon coraige covrir.	I cannot hide my feelings.
De ço ke plus voil et desir,	I should surely give up
Bien m'en devroie repentir.	what I most want and yearn for.
Oiés pour quoi:	*I'll tell you why:*
Car molt voi a noient venir	because I often see what's most exciting
Çou dont on fait plus grant desroi.	come to naught.
Se ma dame seüst le voir	If my lady knew in truth
Com je sui siens a mon pooir,	how completely I belong to her,
De moi aroit merci, espoir.	she would have mercy, perhaps.
Oiés pour quoi:	*I'll tell you why:*
Car ne me puis de li movoir;	because I can't take leave of her.
Som plaisir faice, je l'otroi.	Let her do as she likes; I don't mind.
Iceste amors me fait soulas	This love gives me pleasure
Sol del penser, quant plus n'en fas,	just thinking of it (for that's all I do),
Et si resui dolans et mas.	and yet I am sad and dejected.
Oiés pour quoi:	*I'll tell you why:*
Quant je me gis, si m'en porchas;	when I go to bed, I worry;
Por el ne.l di ne m'i anoi.	I say so only because it doesn't trouble me.

Line numbers in margin: 1.5, 2.5, 3.5, 4.5, 5.5

Ma rotruenge finera;
Bien puet savoir ki amé a
Se bien ou malement m'esta.
           Oiés pour quoi:
Car je sui chil ki l'amera,   6.5
Si n'en fera plus grant effroi.

My rotrouenge is ending;
anyone who has loved can understand
if I am doing well or not.
I'll tell you why:
because I am a man in love,
yet will make no more noise about it.

Li tans nouveaus et la douçors   (L 92-12)
Rotrouenge

Li tans nou- veaus et   la dou- çors   Ki nous re- trait her- bes et   flors

Me fait es- tre pen- sieu d'a- mors   Et re nou- vel- le mes do- lors.

Ce dont me plaing sor to- te rien   Ten- roit uns au- tres a grant bien.

Li tans nouveaus et la douçors
Ki nous retrait herbes et flors
Me fait estre pensieu d'amors
Et renouvelle mes dolors.   1.4
Ce dont me plaing sor tote rien
Tenroit uns autres a grant bien.

The new season, with its mildness,
brings back grass and flowers
but makes me brood over love
and revives my sorrows.
That which I complain of most
someone else would call a blessing.

Vers une dame de haut pris
Avoie mon coraige mis;
Trop legierement le conquis,
Autrui fust boin et moi est pis.   2.4
Ce dont me plaing sor tote rien
Tenroit uns autres a grant bien.

I had set my mind
on a lady of great standing;
it was very easy to win her;
good for someone else, but not for me!
That which I complain of most
someone else would call a blessing.

Savés por quoi je m'en deshait?
Ele estoit molt de riche fait;
Or croi ke mains de bien i ait,
Quant jou si tost i trovai plait.   3.4
Ce dont me plaing sor tote rien
Tenroit uns autres a grant bien.

Do you know what disturbs me?
She was a woman of great appeal;
now I find she has less of it,
since I so quickly gained satisfaction.
That which I complain of most
someone else would call a blessing.

Un grant termine li celai
C'onques jehir ne li osai;
Et tantost ke jou li proiai,
Tout quanques je quis i trovai.   4.4
Ce dont me plaing sor tote rien
Tenroit uns autres a grant bien.

For a long while I hid from her
what I never dared confess,
but as soon as I sought her love,
I was given whatever I asked for.
That which I complain of most
someone else would call a blessing.

Molt li seüsse millor gré	I would have been more grateful
S'un petit m'eüst refusé	if she had held me off for a moment
Ou tart ou a envis doné	and given me later, reluctantly,
Çou ke jou avoie rové. 5.4	the favors I had sought.
Ce dont me plaing sor tote rien	*That which I complain of most*
Tenroit uns autres a grant bien.	*someone else would call a blessing.*
Or proi Gontier ke chant en haut	Now I ask Gontier to sing forth
Et si li die ke poi vaut	and tell her that there is little worth
Chasteaus c'om prent par un assaut;	in a castle that falls at the first attack.
K'il se tiene, ou autrui n'en chaut! 6.4	Let it hold out — or else no one wants it!
Ce dont me plaing sor tote rien	*That which I complain of most*
Tenroit uns autres a grant bien.	*someone else would call a blessing.*

Gontier de Soignies, "Chanter mestuet de recomens" (p. 269). Ms. T, f. 115r.
Cliché Bibliothèque Nationale de France - Paris.

RICHARD DE SEMILLY

Probably a cleric, Richard de Semilly seems to have moved from Champagne to Paris. His literary activity has been traced to the very end of the twelfth century. Eleven lyric compositions of various types have been attributed to him, notably three *pastourelles*.

EDITIONS: Bartsch 1870; Steffens 1902; Johnson 1992.

● "L'autrier chevauchoie delez Paris": L 224-5, RS 1583, MW 27; B 537/620/1900/1282/462. Sources: ms. N, also KPVX; one melody in KNPX, another in V. Attribution to Richard in KN. RT 249-252/436-441; Bartsch 1870, 242-243, Steffens 1902, 354-356, Johnson 1992, 27-32.

Variable refrains put this composition into the category known as *chansons avec des refrains*, in contradistinction to *chansons à refrain*, which repeat the same refrain after each stanza.

The metric structure of the decasyllabic lines is variable, as is sometimes the case in *pastourelles* and similar compositions; cf. "Enmi la rousee que nest la flor," presented under the anonymous PASTOURELLES. Johnson 1992, 31, discusses the issue with reference to this particular text.

The melody in K, which we present, shows, like the readings in NPX, *pedes* in the scale of *d* and a refrain in *c*. The scheme, AA′AA′BCB′CD/refrain D′D, is based on the principle of melodic repetition with ouvert (cadences on *e* in lines 1, 3, 5, 7) and clos (cadences on *d* in lines 2, 4, 6, 8). These ouverts and clos, like the syllabic character of the music, make it clear that the song is meant for dancing.

● "Par amors ferai chançon": L 224-10, RS 1860, MW 1237, B 417. Sources: ms. K, also NPVX; one melody in KNPX, another in V. Attribution to Richard in KNPX. RT 254-256/444-449; Steffens 1902, 360-362; Johnson 1992, 37-41.

For an early courtly *chanson*, this piece is unusual—and less than courtly—in several ways. It has a refrain; the refrain material is of the invariable type but clearly admits, especially in the first half, some degree of variation (which means that it is not quite a *chanson à refrain* but is certainly not a *chanson avec des refrains* either); finally, it gives a voice (stanza 4) to the poet-lover's lady, normally a silent figure—and the regretful words it predicts she will utter reveal a poet-lover whose awe of his lady is moderated by a certain frankness. The theme of a woman's ultimate regret at not having yielded is expressed in several other Old French poems (in, for example, "Lasse, pour quoi refusai" under CHANSONS DE FEMME or, more mockingly, in Conon de Béthune's debate-song, "Ce fut l'autrier en un autre païs") but nowhere does it come so close as here to foreshadowing Ronsard's famous "Quand vous serez bien vieille, au soir, à la chandelle. . .".

The melody of K, presented here, is syllabic and in the Lydian, or *f*, scale. The principal cadences—at the *diesis* (end of line 4) and at the end of the stanza—are on *f*, and the secondary cadences are on *b*, *c*, and *a*. The melodic scheme is: ABAC DEFG/refrain FG.

L'autrier chevauchoie delez Paris (L 224-5)

Pastourelle

L'au- trier che- vau- choi- e de- lez Pa- ris.

Trou- vai pas- to- re- le gar- dant ber- biz;

Des- cen- di a ter- re, lez li m'as- sis

Et ses a- mo- re- tes je li re- quis.

El me dist: "Biau si- re, par saint De- nis,

J'aim plus biau de vos et mult meuz a- pris.

Ja, tant conme il soit ne sains ne vis,

Au- tre n'a- me- ré, je le vos ple- vis,

Car il est et biaus et cor- tois et se- nez.

Deus, je sui jo- nete et sa- dete et s'aim tes

Qui joen- nes est, sa- des et sa- ges as- sez!

L'autrier chevauchoie delez Paris,
Trouvai pastorele gardant berbiz;
Descendi a terre, lez li m'assis
Et ses amoretes je li requis.
El me dist: "Biau sire, par saint Denis,   1.5
J'aim plus biau de vos et mult meuz apris.
Ja, tant conme il soit ne sains ne vis,
Autre n'ameré, je le vos plevis,
Car il est et biaus et cortois et senez."
Deus, je sui jonete et sadete et s'aim tes   1.10
Qui joennes est, sades et sages assez!

Not long ago, as I was riding outside Paris,
I came upon a shepherdess guarding her flock;
I dismounted, sat down beside her,
and asked for her affection.
She said, "By Saint Dennis, dear sir,
I love a fellow handsomer than you and better bred.
Never, as long as he is alive and well,
will I love anyone else, I assure you,
for he is handsome and courteous and clever."
God, I am pretty and young, and I love a fellow
who is young and good-looking and bright.

Robin l'atendoit en un valet,
Par ennui s'assist lez un buissonet,
Qu'il estoit levez trop matinet
Por cueillir la rose et le muguet,
S'ot ja a s'amie fet chapelet   2.5
Et a soi un autre tout nouvelet,
Et dist: "Je me muir, bele" en son sonet,
"Se plus demorez un seul petitet,
    Jamés vif ne me trouverez."
Tres douce damoisele, vos m'ocirrez   2.10
            Se vos volez!

Robin was waiting for her down in a hollow;
out of weariness he sat down by a small bush,
for he had risen early that morning
to gather roses and lily-of-the-valley;
he had already made a garland for his sweetheart
and a new one for himself.
He sang a little tune, saying, "I'll die, my darling,
if you hold off even a little while longer;
you will never again see me alive."
My sweet young lady, you will kill me
if you wish!

Quant ele l'oï si desconforter,
Tantost vint a li sanz demorer.
Qui lors les veïst joie demener,
Robin debruisier et Marot baler!
Lez un buissonet s'alerent jöer,   3.5
Ne sai qu'il i firent, n'en quier parler,
Mes n'i voudrent pas granment demorer,
Ainz se releverent por meuz noter
            Ceste pastorele:
Va li durëaus li durëaus lairrele!   3.10

When she heard him so comfortless,
she ran to him right away.
You should have seen how joyful they were,
with Robin's antics and Marion's dancing!
They continued their play beside a little bush;
whatever they did there, I am not about to tell,
but they did not remain there for long;
instead they got up, the better to sing
this pastourelle:
Go durel, go durel, lerrelle!

Je m'arestai donc illec endroit
Et vi la grant joie que cil fesoit
Et le grant solaz que il demenoit
Qui onques Amors servies n'avoit,
Et dis: "Je maudi Amors orendroit,   4.5
Qui tant m'ont tenu lonc tens a destroit;
Je.s ai plus servies qu'onme qui soit
N'onques n'en oi bien, si n'est ce pas droit;
            Por ce les maudi."
Male honte ait il qui Amors parti   4.10
            Quant g'i ai failli!

I stopped then at that spot
and saw how joyful he was
and what a good time he was having,
that fellow who had never served love;
and I said, "I curse love now
for the long torment it has brought me;
I have served love better than any man,
but all in vain; it isn't right!
And so I curse it."
Shame and woe to anyone favored by love
when I have failed at it!

De si loing conme li bergiers me vit,
S'escria mult haut et si me dist:
"Alez vostre voie, por Jhesu Crist,
Ne vos tolez pas nostre deduit!
J'ai mult plus de joie et de delit   5.5
Que li rois de France n'en a, ce cuit;
S'il a sa richece, je la li cuit
Et j'ai m'amïete et jor et nuit,
            Ne ja ne departiron."
            Danciez, bele Marion!   5.10
            Ja n'aim je riens se vos non.

As soon as the shepherd spotted me,
he cried out and said,
"Move along, by Jesus!
Don't spoil our pleasure!
I have much more happiness and fun
than the king of France, I'm sure;
he may well be rich, but I don't care:
I've got my darling night and day,
and we will never part."
Dance, lovely Marion!
I love no one but you.

Par amors ferai chançon   (L 224-10)
Chanson d'amour

Par a- mors fe- rai chan- çon
Pour la tres be- le lö- er;
Tout me sui mis a ban- don
En li ser- vir et a- mer;
Mult m' a fet maus en- du- rer,
Si. n a- tent le guer- re- don,
N' on- ques n' en oi se mal non.
Hé las! si l' ai je tant a- me- e!
Dame, il fust mes bien se- son
Que vostre a- mor me fust do- ne- e.

Par amors ferai chançon
Pour la tres bele löer;
Tout me sui mis a bandon
En li servir et amer;
Mult m'a fet maus endurer,   1.5
Si.n atent le guerredon,
N'onques n'en oi se mal non.
Hé las! si l'ai je tant amee!
  Dame, il fust mes bien seson
Que vostre amor me fust donee.   1.10

Onques riens mes cuers n'ama
Fors la bele pour qui chant,
Ne jamés riens n'amera,
Ce sai je bien, autretant.
Ma douce dame vaillant,   2.5
Bien sai, quant il vos plera,
En pou d'eure me sera
Ma grant paine guerredonnee.
  Dame qui je aim pieç'a,
Et quant m'iert vostre amor donee?   2.10

Dame ou touz biens sont assis,
Une riens dire vos vueil:
Se vous estes de haut pris,
Pour Dieu, gardez vous d'orgueil
Et soiez de bel acueil   3.5
Et aus granz et aus petiz;
Vos ne serez pas touz dis
Ensi requise et demandee.
  Dame ou j'ai tout mon cuer mis,
Et quant m'iert vostre amor donee?   3.10

I will compose a song of praise
out of love for my darling;
I have thrown myself
into serving and loving her;
she has made me suffer greatly,
and I am awaiting my reward,
but I have had nothing but pain.
Alas, and I have loved her so much!
My lady, it is really time
I were given your love.

My heart has never loved anyone
but the beauty for whom I sing,
and it will never love anyone else
so much, I am sure.
Sweet and worthy lady,
I am sure that, once you are ready,
my great struggle will be
promptly rewarded.
Lady whom I have loved for long,
when will I be granted your love?

Lady in whom all virtues dwell,
I want to tell you something:
if you merit high esteem,
for God's sake, beware of arrogance
and be gracious
to both the great and the humble:
You will not always be
so courted and desired as now.
Lady I have set my heart on,
when will I be granted your love?

Se vous vivez longuement,
Dame, il ert oncore un tens
Ou viellece vous atent.
Lors diroiz a toutes genz:
"Lasse, je fui de mal sens,   4.5
Que n'amai en mon jouvent,
Ou requise iere souvent;
Or sui de chascun refusee."
Dame que j'aim loiaument,
Et quant m'iert vostre amor donee?   4.10

Chançon, va tost sanz delai
A la tres bele au vis cler
Et si li di de par moi
Que je muir por bien amer,
Car je ne puis plus durer   5.5
A la dolor que je trai;
Ne ja respas n'en avrai,
Puis que ma mort tant li agree.
Dame que j'aim de cuer vrai,
Et quant m'iert vostre amor donee?   5.10

If you live a long life,
my lady, a time will yet come
when old age is there for you.
Then you will say to everyone,
"Alas, I was badly mistaken
not to love in my youth,
when I was so often courted;
now everyone rejects me."
Lady whom I love loyally,
when will I be granted your love?

Song, go now, with no delay,
to my fair-faced beauty
and tell her from me
that I am dying of true love,
for I can no longer endure
the pain that I feel;
nor shall I ever be made well,
since she is so pleased by my dying.
Lady whom I love with a faithful heart,
when will I be granted your love?

GAUTIER DE DARGIES

Gautier de Dargies was a knight of the lower nobility, born between 1170 and 1175 in the Beauvaisis; he was still living in 1236. He had ties with several trouvères, notably the major figure, Gace Brulé, to whom two of his songs are addressed. Twenty-five lyric compositions are attributed to Gautier, including three *descorts,* which are probably the earliest French examples of the genre.

EDITIONS: Huet 1912; Raugei 1981.

● "La douce pensee": L 73-16, RS 539, MW 689,60. Sources: ms. M, also CT; music in MT. Attribution to Gautier in MT. RT 257-260/464-469; Jeanroy 1901, 5-6; Huet 1912, 61-63; Raugei 1981, 288-296.

Unlike all the other strophic genres that constitute the Old French lyric corpus (except the *estampie*), the *descort,* or *lai-descort,* comprises structurally different stanzas, and just as the versification changes from stanza to stanza, so does the melody. See ARTHURIAN LAIS and see Bec 1977, chapter 13, for an extensive discussion of the origin, definition, and development of the genre.

1.4: Despite its six syllables, this verse is only apparently hypermetric, for the final *e* of *entree* in the preceding line is elided before *A,* which thus does not appear in the syllable-count of line 4.

3.8: The allusion is to Hector, the tragic leader of the Trojans in the Trojan War, well known in medieval France not only through the twelfth-century romances of *Troie* and *Thèbes* but through several other works as well. In the later Middle Ages, Hector would be regarded, along with Alexander and Julius Caesar, as one of the three ancient heroes among the *Neuf Preux*, the Nine Worthies.

Of the two readings of the melody, we present T rather than the more ornamented M. Cf. the transcription in Stevens 1986, 478-480. The seven heterometric, "discordant" stanzas are melodically individuated, but are all in the scale of *g*. The scheme shows considerably less development than that of other French *lais-descorts,* relying chiefly on melodic repetitions of the sequence type:

1. (5' 5) ABAC ABAC
2. (10 10') DD' DD' DD' (D ouvert on *b*, D' clos on *g*)
3. (6' 6) EF EF' EF' EF'
4. (7 7') GH G'H' G"H"
5. (5') II'I'I"
6. (7' 7) JK JK JK JK
7. (7 7') LLMNM'N'O

On the subject of rhythm, Stevens 1986, p. 484, offers the following opinion: "what fits best, in my view, with the 'aesthetic' of the *lai* is a *metrical but not a measured rhythm,* [italics in original] in transcription and for performance."

● "Desque ci ai touz jorz chanté": L 73-9, RS 418, MW 2396. Sources: ms. K, also CMNPTUXa; music in all except C. Attribution to Gautier in all mss. except U. RT 260-263/470-473; Huet 1912, 8-10; Raugei 1981, 135-145.

For a study of the rhetorical development of this text, see Dragonetti 1960, 299-303.

Note that the envoy addresses the song to Gautier's fellow-trouvère, Gace Brulé.

The melody, in the scale of *f,* is identical in all manuscripts; we present that of ms. U. Ornamentation is abundant and, in line 7, occurs even at the beginning of the verse, which is quite rare for the trouvères. The scheme is through-composed: ABCDEFGH. In its cleanly sculpted lines, with contrasting syllabism, ornamentation, and agogic rises (cf. the two halves of lines 6 and 7), this melody recalls the music of the troubadours.

La douce pensee   (L 73-16)

Descort

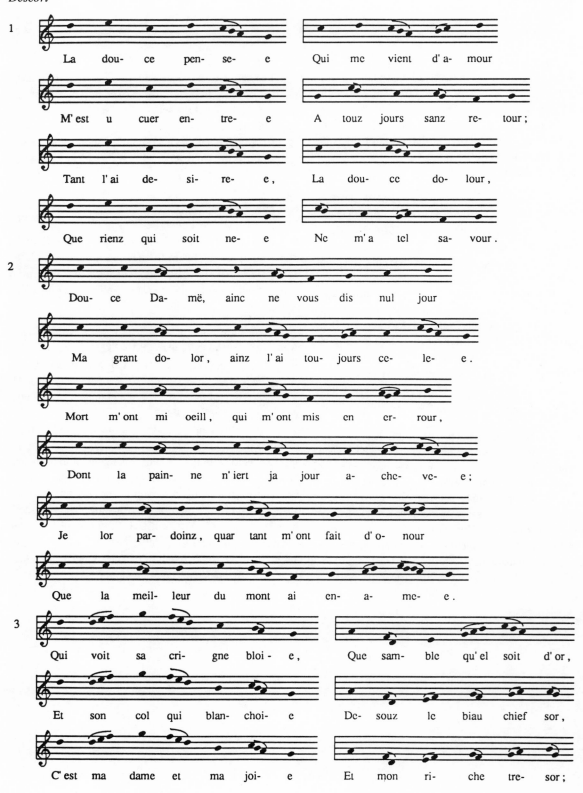

1

La dou- ce pen- se- e   Qui me vient d'a- mour

M'est u cuer en- tre- e   A touz jours sanz re- tour;

Tant l'ai de- si- re- e,   La dou- ce do- lour,

Que rienz qui soit ne- e   Ne m'a tel sa- vour.

2

Dou- ce Da- më, ainc ne vous dis nul jour

Ma grant do- lor, ainz l'ai tou- jours ce- le- e.

Mort m'ont mi oeill, qui m'ont mis en er- rour,

Dont la pain- ne n'iert ja jour a- che- ve- e;

Je lor par- doinz, quar tant m'ont fait d'o- nour

Que la meil- leur du mont ai en- a- me- e.

3

Qui voit sa cri- gne bloi- e,   Que sam- ble qu'el soit d'or,

Et son col qui blan- choi- e   De- souz le biau chief sor,

C'est ma dame et ma joi- e   Et mon ri- che tre- sor;

Cer- tes, je ne vou- droi- e   Sanz li va- loir Hec- tor.

4   De si bel- le da- me a- mer   Ne se por- roit nus des- fen- dre;

Puiz qu'a- mours m'i fait pen- ser,   El mi de- vroit bien a- pren- dre

Con- ment por- roie a- che- ver,   Puiz qu'ail- leurs ne puis en- ten- dre.

5   Se je li di- soi- e   Que s'a- mours fust moi- e,

Grant or- gueill fe- roi- e,   Ne- ïs se.l pen soi- e.

6   Ainz sou- fer- rai mon mar- ty- re!   Ja ne sa- vra mon pen- ser,

Se par pi- tié ne re- mi- re   Les maus que me fait por- ter,

Car tant re- dout l'es- con- di- re   De sa tres grant vo- len- té;

Tel cho- se por- roi- e di- re   Dont el me sa- vroit mal gré.

7   La ou Deus a as- sam- blé   Pris et va- leur et bon- té

T'en va, des- cors, sanz pluz di- re   Fors i- tant, pour l'a- mour Dé,

C'on puet bien par toi es- li- re   Que je ne chant fors pour lé,

Dont Deus me doint es- tre a- mé.

La douce pensee
Qui me vient d'amour
M'est u cuer entree
A touz jours sanz retour;   1.4
Tant l'ai desirree,
La douce dolour,
Que rienz qui soit nee
Ne m'a tel savour.   1.8

The sweet thought
that comes to me from love
has entered my heart
never to leave;
I have so yearned
for this sweet pain
that nothing else in existence
tastes so good to me.

Douce damë, ainc ne vous dis nul jour
Ma grant dolor, ainz l'ai toujours celee.
Mort m'ont mi oeill, qui m'ont mis en errour,   2.3
Dont la painne n'iert ja jour achevee;
Je lor pardoinz, quar tant m'ont fait d'onour
Que la meilleur du mont ai enamee.   2.6

Sweet lady, I have never told you
of my great pain, but have always concealed it.
My eyes killed me, bewildering me
with a pain that will never abate.
I forgive them, for they have done me the high honor
of making me love the finest woman in the world.

Qui voit sa crigne bloie,
Que samble qu'el soit d'or,
Et son col qui blanchoie
Desouz le biau chief sor,   3.4
C'est ma dame et ma joie
Et mon riche tresor;
Certes, je ne voudroie
Sanz li valoir Hector.   3.8

Whoever sees her blond hair,
which is like gold,
and her neck, glowing white
beneath that flaxen crown,
sees my lady and my joy
and my rich treasure;
I would refuse to be another Hector
if I had to live without her.

De si belle dame amer
Ne se porroit nus desfendre;
Puiz qu'amours m'i fait penser,   4.3
El mi devroit bien aprendre
Conment porroie achever,
Puiz qu'ailleurs ne puis entendre.   4.6

No one could stop himself
from loving a lady of such beauty;
since love makes me think of her,
love should surely teach me
how to win her,
for no other woman can fill my thoughts.

Se je li disoie
Que s'amours fust moie,
Grant orgueill feroie,
Neïs se.l pensoie.   5.4

If I told her
that her love should be mine,
I would be far too presumptuous,
even if I thought it.

Ainz souferrai mon martyre!
Ja ne savra mon penser,
Se par pitié ne remire
Les maus que me fait porter,   6.4
Car tant redout l'escondire
De sa tres grant volenté;
Tel chose porroie dire
Dont el me savroit mal gré.   6.8

I will suffer my martyrdom instead!
She will never know my thoughts
unless she takes pity and considers
the suffering she causes me,
for, strong-willed as she is,
I dread her rejection;
I might well say something
that she would not appreciate.

La ou Deus a assamblé
Pris et valeur et bonté
T'en va, descors, sanz pluz dire
Fors itant, pour l'amour Dé,   7.4
C'on puet bien par toi eslire
Que je ne chant fors pour lé,
Dont Deus me doint estre amé.

To the one in whom God has gathered
worth and virtue and goodness
go now, descort, and carry,
for the love of God, this one message:
that it is obvious, through you,
all my singing is for her alone.
God grant me, then, to have her love!

Desque ci ai touz jorz chanté   (L 73-9)

Chanson d'amour

Des- que ci ai touz jorz chan- té

De mult bon cuer fin et loi- al en- tier

N' ainc de chan- gier

N' oi de- denz mon cuer vo- len- té,

Ne ma pai- ne ne m'i ot onc mes- tier.

Bien m'a A- mors a son oés es- prou- vé;

De- te- nu m'a; ja ne la qier les- sier,

Et s'en voit on les plu- seurs mes tar- gier.

Desque ci ai touz jorz chanté	Till now I have always sung
De mult bon cuer fin et loial entier,	with a fully sincere and faithful heart;
N'ainc de changier	I have never had any desire in my heart
N'oi dedenz mon cuer volenté, 1.4	to do otherwise,
Ne ma paine ne m'i ot onc mestier.	yet my pains have been to no avail.
Bien m'a Amors a son oés esprouvé;	Love has done its best to try me;
Detenu m'a; ja ne la qier lessier,	it has me in thrall; I never want to give it up,
Et s'en voit on les pluseurs mes targier. 1.8	even if most people are now seen to avoid it.
Ne sont cil fol maleüré	Aren't those many people luckless fools,
Dont il est trop por Amors guerroier?	who go to war against love?
Par lor pledier	With their claims
Avront maint amant destorbé, 2.4	they will have disturbed many a lover,
Ne ja nul d'aus n'i verrez gaaignier.	yet you will never see any of them win thereby.
De ce deüssent estre porpensé:	They should bear this in mind:
Que tels puet nuire qui ne puet aidier;	that he who cannot help may do harm;
Mes envïeus ne se puet chastoier. 2.8	but an envious person cannot be corrected.

Tele gent ont petit amé
Qui se painent de nos contralïer.
　　　Ce n'a mestier,
　　　Car ja tant n'avront devisé   3.4
Que nus doie pour els Amors lessier.
Non fera il, s'en li n'a fausseté.
Deus! qui n'aime, de quoi se set aidier?
Voist soi rendre, qu'au siecle n'a mestier.   3.8

　　　Je me tieng mult a honoré
De ce qu'onc jor n'oi talent de trichier
　　　Ne de boissier;
　　　Ainz me truis tous tens alumé   4.4
Si freschement com fui au conmencier,
Oncore m'ait guerredons demoré.
Je me confort en ce qui puet aidier:
En loiauté vueil perdre ou gaaignier.   4.8

　　　L'en m'en a mainte foiz blasmé
De ce que trop me sui mis en dangier,
　　　Mes foloier
　　　Voi touz ceus qui le m'ont moustré;   5.4
Car nus ne puet melz sa poine enploier:
Tost a Amors le plus haut don doné.
Si ne s'en doit nus hons trop merveillier:
Pour sa joie se doit on travaillier.   5.8

A vous le di, compains Gasse Brullé:
Pensés d'Amors, de son non essaucier,
Que mesdisant le veulent abaissier.   E.3 (8)

Those people who take pains to oppose us
have not loved much.
It is useless,
for they will never have prattled so much
that anyone should give up love on their account.
No one will do so unless he is a hypocrite.
God! what profit is there for anyone not in love?
Let him become a monk, since he is useless in the world.

I consider myself greatly honored
never to have desired to lie
or deceive;
in fact, I still find myself as fresh
and glowing as I was at the start,
even though my reward has not come.
I take comfort in that which can help:
in fidelity, whereby I mean to win or lose.

I have often been rebuked
for being so submissive,
but I see all those who reproach me
behaving senselessly,
for one's efforts cannot be better deployed:
love soon enough grants the greatest gift.
And so no one should be too surprised:
to reach fulfillment, you must go through torment.

I'll tell you, Gace Brulé, my friend:
give thought to extolling the name of love,
for slanderers want to disparage it.

THIBAUT DE BLAISON

Born sometime before 1200 in the region of Anjou, Thibaut de Blaison was active in political and military life, becoming seneschal of Poitou for the king of France in 1227; he died in 1229. He had friendly ties with the great feudal lord and trouvère, Thibaut de Champagne. Almost a dozen love songs and *pastourelles* are attributed to him.

EDITIONS: Pinguet 1930; Newcombe 1978.

• "Hui main par un ajournant": L 255-8, RS 293, MW 1492. Sources: ms. M, also KNPTVXa; one melody in V, another in all others. Attribution to Thibaut in all mss. except Va. RT 273-275/486-491; Bartsch 1870, 227-228; Pinguet 1930, 42-46; Newcombe 1978, 86-90.

This subtype of pastourelle replaces the shepherdess with a shepherd and the poet-knight's quest for an amorous adventure with a discussion of love. Note, esp. in 6.4-6, the comic intrusion into the shepherd's speech of language belonging to the courtly register.

The melody in ms. K, which we present, is in *c,* as are all the other readings in this group except that of M, which is in *f.* Its extreme simplicity is of a popular stamp. Indeed, the range, only a fifth, is very narrow; its syllabism lends itself to dancing, as does the melodic scheme, ABAB CDABE, with its return of AB in lines 7-8. In the last line of the stanza, if one accepts a danced performance of the song, the ornamentation of the E phrase suggests a decelerating conclusion.

Hui main par un ajournant   (L 255-8)
Pastourelle

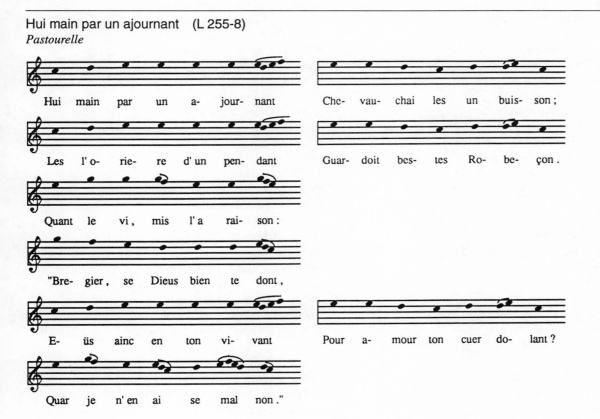

Hui main par un a- jour- nant

Che- vau- chai les un buis- son;

Les l'o- rie- re d'un pen- dant

Guar- doit bes- tes Ro- be- çon.

Quant le vi, mis l'a rai- son:

"Bre- gier, se Dieus bien te dont,

E- üs ainc en ton vi- vant

Pour a- mour ton cuer do- lant?

Quar je n'en ai se mal non."

Hui main par un ajournant
Chevauchai les un buisson;
Les l'oriere d'un pendant
Guardoit bestes Robeçon.   1.4
Quant le vi, mis l' a raison:
"Bregier, se Dieus bien te dont,
Eüs ainc en ton vivant
Pour amour ton cuer dolant?
Quar je n'en ai se mal non."   1.9

"Chevalier, en mon vivant
Ainc n'amai fors Marion,
La courtoise, la plaisant,
Qui m'a doné riche don,   2.4
Panetiere de cordon,
Et prist mon fermaill de plom.
Or s'en vait apercevant
Sa mere qui li deffant,
Si l'en a mise a raison."   2.9

A pou ne se vait pasmant
Li bregiers pour Marion.
Quant le vi, pitiez m'en prent,
Si li dis en ma raison: 3.4
"Ne t'esmaie, bregeron;
Ja si ne l'enserreront
Qu'ele lait pour nul tourment
Qu'ele ne t'aint loiaument,
Si fine amours l'en semont."   3.9

"Sire, je sui trop dolens
Quant je voi mes compaignons
Qui vont joie demenant;
Chascuns chante sa chançon   4.4
Et je sui seus environ;
Affuble mon chaperon,
Si remir la joie grant
Qu'il vont entour moi faisant.
Confors n'i vaut un bouton."   4.9

"Bregier, qui la joie atent
D'amours fait grant mesprison,
Se les maus en gré n'en prent
Touz sanz ire et sanz tençon: 5.4
En mout petit de saison
Rent amours grant guerredon,
S'en sunt li mal plus plaisant
Que on a soufert devant
Dont on atent guarison."   5.9

This morning at daybreak
I rode alongside a hedge;
near the edge of a slope
Robin was guarding his flock.
When I saw him, I spoke:
"Shepherd — God keep you! —
has love ever in your life
brought sorrow to your heart?
To me it has brought nothing but pain."

"Knight, in my whole life
I've never loved anyone but Marion,
who is courtly and appealing;
she gave me a fine present,
a string-bag for bread,
and accepted my lead clasp.
Now her mother has become
aware of it and spoken to her
and forbidden her to see me."

The shepherd had almost fallen
into a swoon, thinking of Marion.
Seeing this, I was deeply moved
and spoke these words to him:
"Don't be dismayed, shepherd;
she will never be so tightly confined
as to let suffering stop her
from loving you faithfully,
as long as true love urges her."

"Sir, I am full of sorrow
when I see my companions
having a merry time;
everyone is busy singing his song
while I stand around all alone;
I pull up my hood
and watch their merry-making
all around me.
There is not a bit of comfort in it."

"Shepherd, whoever expects joy
of love is making a great mistake
if he doesn't take love's pains in stride
without anger and without protest:
in a very short while
love brings a great reward,
and the pains become more pleasurable
that you suffered beforehand
in the hope of a remedy."

"Chevalier, pour rienz vivant
N'os parler a Marion
Et si n'ai par cui li mant
Que je muir en sa prison   6.4
Pour les mesdisans felons
Qui ne dïent se mal non,
Ainz vont trestout racontant
Que j'aim la niece Coustant,
La fillastre dant Buevon."   6.9

"Knight, for nothing in the world
do I dare speak to Marion,
nor have I anyone to carry the news
that I am dying in her prison
because of the slanderous scoundrels
who can only speak ill;
they go around with the tale
that I love Constant's niece,
sir Beuvon's stepdaughter."

AUDEFROI LE BÂTARD

One of the trouvères of Arras, Audefroi le Bâtard was active in the early thirteenth century. The compositions attributed to him, all preserved with their melodies, include ten *chansons d'amour,* a *jeu-parti,* a lyrico-narrative dialogue with a forlorn lover, and five *chansons de toile.* The last constitute Audefroi's only notable contribution, representing a unique attempt to renew that apparently old genre, partly through innovations in meter and homophony but chiefly through narrative amplification and an accumulation of detail.

STUDY: Zink 1978.

EDITIONS: Cullmann 1914; Zink 1978; van der Werf 1979, 446-482.

● "Bele Ysabiauz, pucele bien aprise": L 15-5, RS 1616, MW 397, B 712. Sources: ms. M, also CT; music in MT. Attribution to Audefroi in all mss. RT 245-248/498-505; Bartsch 1870, 57-59; Cullmann 1914, 99-101; Zink 1978, 107-112; van der Werf 1979, 476-477.

This song should be compared with the anonymous CHANSONS DE TOILE presented earlier in this volume.

The two musical readings are closely related, with T a fifth below M. The melody, in the scale of *g,* is relatively ornamented, and its scheme recalls that of the early ballade: AA'BCD/refrain E.

Bele Ysabiauz, pucele bien aprise   (L 15-5)
Chanson de toile

Bele Ysabiauz, pucele bien aprise,
Ama Gerart et il li en tel guise
C'ainc de folour par lui ne fu requise,
    Ainz l'ama de si bone amour   1.4
    Que mieuz de li guarda s'ounour.
      Et joie atent Gerars.

Lovely Isabel, a well-bred maiden,
loved Gerard, and he loved her in such a way
that he never asked her for anything improper;
indeed, his love was so true
that he guarded her honor even better than she.
And Gerard waited for his bliss.

Quant pluz se fu bone amours entr'eus mise,
Par loiauté afermee et reprise,
En cele amour la damoisele ont prise
    Si parent et douné seignour,   2.4
    Outre son gré, un vavassour.
        Et joie atent Gerars.

Quant sot Gerars, cui fine amour justise,
Que la bele fu a seigneur tramise,
Grains et mariz fist tant par sa maistrise
    Que a sa dame en un destour   3.4
    A fait sa plainte et sa clamour.
        Et joi atent Gerars.

"Amis Gerart, n'aiez ja couvoitise
De ce voloir dont ainc ne fui requise.
Puis que je ai seigneur qui m'aimme et prise,
    Bien doi estre de tel valour   4.4
    Que je ne doi penser folour."
        Et joie atent Gerars.

"Amis Gerart, faites ma conmandise:
Ralez vous ent, si feroiz grant franchise.
Morte m'avriez s'od vous estoie prise.
    Maiz metez vous tost u retour;   5.4
    Je vous conmant au Creatour."
        Et joie atent Gerars.

"Dame, l'amour qu'ailleurs avez assise
Deüsse avoir par loiauté conquise;
Maiz pluz vous truis dure que pierre bise,
    S'en ai au cuer si grant dolour   6.4
    Qu'a biau samblant souspir et plour."
        Et joie atent Gerars.

"Dame, pour Dieu," fait Gerars sanz faintise,
"Aiez de moi pitié par vo franchise.
La vostre amour me destraint et atise,
    Et pour vous sui en tel errour   7.4
    Que nus ne puet estre en greignour."
        Et joie atent Gerars.

Quant voit Gerars, qui fine amours justise,
Que sa dolour de noient n'apetise,
Lors se croisa de duel et d'ire esprise,
    Et pourquiert einsi son atour   8.4
    Que il puist movoir a brief jour.
        Et joie atent Gerars.

Tost muet Gerars, tost a sa voie quise;
Avant tramet son esquïer Denise
A sa dame parler par sa franchise.
    La dame ert ja pour la verdour   9.4
    En un vergier cueillir la flour.
        Et joie atent Gerars.

When each was sure of the other's true love,
faithfully declared and repeated,
just then the young lady's parents took her
and married her off, against her will,
to a country squire.
And Gerard waited for his bliss.

When Gerard, in the grip of pure love, learned
that his sweetheart now had a husband,
stunned and dejected he did whatever he could
to meet his lady in a secluded spot
and cry out his sorrow.
And Gerard waited for his bliss.

"Dear Gerard, put aside any desire
to seek from me that which you have never sought.
Now that I have a husband who loves and respects me,
I am duty-bound to guard my virtue
and put folly out of my mind."
And Gerard waited for his bliss.

"Dear Gerard, do as I ask:
go home now, and you will be doing a noble thing.
You would only kill me to take me away.
Now start on your way back;
I commend you to God."
And Gerard waited for his bliss.

"My lady, my loyalty should have won me
the love that you have given to another man;
I find you harder than stone,
and there is such pain in my heart
that, as you see, I can only sigh and weep."
And Gerard waited for his bliss.

"My lady, for God's sake," said Gerard earnestly,
"take pity on me, noble soul that you are.
Love for you torments me with its flames,
and because of you I am more bewildered
than any man has ever been."
And Gerard waited for his bliss.

When Gerard, tortured by true love, saw
that his pain was not in the least abating,
then, in sorrow and grief, he took the cross
and began making ready
to set out very soon.
And Gerard waited for his bliss.

Gerard started out, Gerard was on his way;
he sent his squire Dennis ahead
to announce him to his lady.
The lady, with everything in bloom,
was in her garden picking flowers.
And Gerard waited for his bliss.

Vestue fu la dame par cointise;
Mout ert bele, grasse, gente et alise;
Le vis avoit vermeill come cerise.
    "Dame," dit il, "que tres bon jour   10.4
    Vous doint cil qui j'aim et aour!"
        Et joie atent Gerars.

"Dame, pour Deu," fait Gerars sanz faintise,
"D'outre mer ai pour vous la voie emprise."
La dame l'ot, mieus vousist estre ocise.
    Si s'entrebaisent par douçour   11.4
    Qu'andui cheïrent en l'erbour.
        Et joie atent Gerars.

Ses maris voit la folour entreprise;
Pour voir cuide la dame morte gise
Les son ami. Tant se het et desprise
    Qu'il pert sa force et sa vigour   12.4
    Et muert de duel en tel errour.
        Et joie atent Gerars.

De pasmoisons lievent par tel devise
Qu'il firent faire au mort tout son servise.
Li deus remaint. Gerars par sainte eglise
    A fait de sa dame s'oissour.   13.4
    Ce tesmoignent li ancissour.
        Or a joie Gerars.

The lady was wearing elegant clothes; she was
full of body, lovely, smooth-skinned and graceful;
Her cheeks were cherry-red.
"My lady," he said, "may God, whom I love and
worship, grant you a good day!"
And Gerard waited for his bliss.

"My lady, for God's sake," said Gerard earnestly,
"I have decided, because of you, to go across the sea."
At those words, the lady would have rather been killed.
The two locked together in such an ardent embrace
that they both fell to the ground.
And Gerard waited for his bliss.

Her husband saw the folly under way
but truly believed the lady lay dead
beside her lover. He so blamed and berated himself
that he lost all his strength and vitality
and in his bewilderment died of grief.
And Gerard waited for his bliss.

The lovers rose from their swoon and saw to it
that the dead man was properly buried.
Their grieving came to an end. With holy blessing
Gerard took his lady to wife.
That is the story that has come down to us.
Now Gerard had his bliss.

GUIOT DE DIJON

A Burgundian trouvère active during the first third of the thirteenth century, Guiot de Dijon is known for about a dozen songs of several types; several are of only doubtful attribution. (In addition to the following composition, see "De moi dolereus vos chant," which we present as a song of Gillebert de Berneville.)

EDITION: Nissen 1928.

● "Chanterai por mon corage": L 106-4, RS 21, MW 861, B 552. Sources: ms. M, also CKOTX; music in all except C. Attribution to Guiot in M; to the Dame de Fayel (fictitious heroine of the *Roman du Chastelain de Couci*) in C. RT 293-296/504-509; Bédier-Aubry 1909, 107-117; Spanke 1925, 188-190; Nissen 1928, 1-3. Performed on Anthology CD.

This *chanson de croisade, chanson de femme, chanson à refrain,* and, according to some, *rotrouenge* cannot be attributed with certainty to Guiot de Dijon, who is not known to have composed any other songs touching on a crusade or voicing the sentiments of a woman.

As a crusade-inspired song of separation, this text calls for comparison with several others in the present volume: "Jherusalem, grant damage me fais" under CHANSONS DE FEMME, Conon de Béthune's "Ahi, Amours! com dure departie" and "A vous, amant, plus qu'a nulle autre gent" by the Châtelain de Coucy. For a detailed textual analysis, see Dijkstra 1995, 166-174.

The cry of *"Outree"* in the refrain occurs in several crusaders' songs.

Note that three of the sources of this song, mss. KOX, present the five stanzas in a divergent order: 1 3 2 5 4. From the point of view of strophic linking, this arrangement replaces the common sequence AABBC (*coblas doblas*) with the unusual and apparently disordered sequence ABACB. The arrangement also disturbs the neat linkage

effected by the five stanza openings: "Chanterai - Souffrerai / De ce - De ce - De ce." The development of the poetic message is, of course, quite different as well.

4.3-5: The motif of the breeze blowing from the land of the belovèd is found in various sources, most pertinently a song by the troubadour Bernart de Ventadorn, "Quan le douss' aura venta/ Deves vostre païs." Note that the rhymes of this stanza, *-ente* and *-is,* are the same as those opening Bernart's poem.

5.2-3: According to Bédier-Aubry 1909, 117, "La *chemise* est une tunique qui recouvrait les autres vêtements. Les croisés s'équipaient en pèlerins . . . et partaient, accompagnés jusqu'à une certaine étape par leurs parents et amis, d'ordinaire 'dechauz, a pié et en langes'. A l'étape, cette sorte de cérémonie prenait fin; le croisé se rechaussait et reprenait ses vêtements ordinaires. Ce que notre pèlerin a ici envoyé à sa dame, c'est sans doute la *chemise,* portée sur ses autres vêtements, qui avait symbolisé au départ son voeu de pèlerin." (The *chemise* is a tunic that covered the other garments. The crusaders fitted themselves out as pilgrims . . . and departed, accompanied up to a certain stopping place by their relatives and friends, usually "barefoot, walking, and dressed in rough woolens." At the stop, this ceremony of sorts came to an end; the crusader put his shoes back on and dressed again in his ordinary clothes. What our pilgrim has here sent to his lady is no doubt the *chemise,* worn over his other garments, that had symbolized his pilgrimage vow at the time of departure.)

The melody is built on the intonation of the eighth Gregorian tone (8 occurrences in 12 lines). The final cadence is on *g.* Despite the refrain, the scheme belongs to the litany type: ABABABCD/refrain ABC'E. Note that in line 4, ms. M shows no music for the sixth syllable; our note is supplied from the other manuscripts.

Chanterai por mon corage   (L 106-4)

Chanson de femme, chanson de croisade

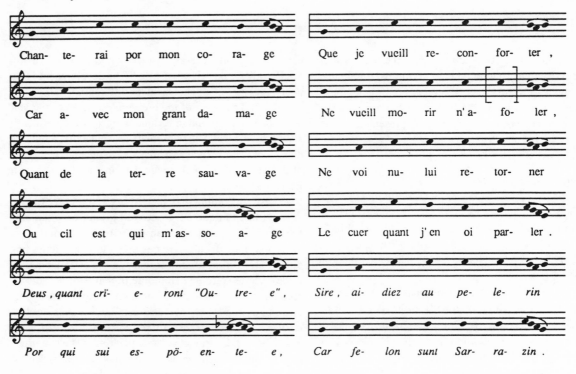

Chanterai por mon corage	I will sing for the sake of my heart,
Que je vueill reconforter,	which I want to console;
Car avec mon grant damage	with all my suffering
Ne vueill morir n'afoler, 1.4	I don't want to go mad or die,
Quant de la terre sauvage	as I see no one come back
Ne voi nului retorner	from that brutish land
Ou cil est qui m'assoage	where he is whose name calms
Le cuer quant j'en oi parler. 1.8	my heart when I hear it spoken.
Deus, quant crïeront "Outree",	*God, when they shout "Forward!",*
Sire, aidiez au pelerin	*help, Lord, the pilgrim*
Por qui sui espöentee,	*for whom I tremble,*
Car felon sunt Sarrazin. 1.12	*for the Saracens are ruthless.*

Souffrerai en tel estage	I will suffer just as I am
Tant que.l voie rapasser.	until I see him come home.
Il est en pelerinage,	He is on a pilgrimage,
Dont Deus le lait retorner! 2.4	and God grant he return!
Et maugré tot mon lignage	Despite my whole family,
Ne quier ochoison trover	I have no wish to find
D'autre face mariage;	another man to marry;
Folz est qui j'en oi parler. 2.8	anyone I hear suggest it is a fool.
Deus, quant crïeront "Outree",	*God, when they shout "Forward!",*
Sire, aidiez au pelerin	*help, Lord, the pilgrim*
Por qui sui espöentee,	*for whom I tremble,*
Car felon sunt Sarrazin. 2.12	*for the Saracens are ruthless.*

De ce sui au cuer dolente
Que cil n'est en cest païs
Qui si sovent me tormente;
Je n'en ai ne gieu ne ris.   3.4
Il est biaus et je sui gente.
Sire Deus, por que.l feïs?
Quant l'une a l'autre atalente,
Por coi nos as departis?   3.8
Deus, quant crïeront "Outree",
Sire, aidiez au pelerin
Por qui sui espöentee,
Car felon sunt Sarrazin.   3.12

De ce sui en bone atente
Que je son homage pris;
Et quant la douce ore vente
Qui vient de cel douz païs   4.4
Ou cil est qui m'atalente,
Volentiers i tor mon vis;
Adont m'est vis que je.l sente
Par desoz mon mantel gris.   4.8
Deus, quant crïeront "Outree",
Sire, aidiez au pelerin
Por qui sui espöentee,
Car felon sunt Sarrazin.   4.12

De ce fui mout deceüe
Que ne fui au convoier.
Sa chemise qu'ot vestue
M'envoia por embracier.   5.4
La nuit, quant s'amor m'argüe,
La met delez moi couchier,
Toute nuit a ma char nue,
Por mes malz assoagier.   5.8
Deus, quant crïeront "Outree",
Sire, aidiez au pelerin
Por qui sui espöentee,
Car felon sunt Sarrazin.   5.12

What pains my heart
is that he is not here at home
for whom I ache so much;
I have no delight or laughter.
He is handsome and I, lovely.
Lord God, why have you done this?
With so much desire for each other,
why have you parted us?
God, when they shout "Forward!",
help, Lord, the pilgrim
for whom I tremble,
for the Saracens are ruthless.

What gives me hope
is that I received his homage;
and when the sweet breeze blows
from that sweet land
where he is whom I desire,
I gladly turn to face it;
then I seem to feel his touch
under my grey cloak.
God, when they shout "Forward!",
help, Lord, the pilgrim
for whom I tremble,
for the Saracens are ruthless.

What leaves me disappointed
is that I was not there to escort him out.
The pilgrim's tunic that he wore
he then sent back for me to caress.
At night, harried with love for him,
I lay it out beside me
for the night, next to my naked flesh,
to soothe away my pain.
God, when they shout "Forward!",
help, Lord, the pilgrim
for whom I tremble,
for the Saracens are ruthless.

SIMON D'AUTHIE

Simon d'Authie was canon of Amiens as of 1224 and served as advocate of the abbey of Saint Vaast in Arras; he died in 1231. He knew several other trouvères of Picardy and the Artois, and three of his nine or ten surviving songs are *jeux-partis* composed with members of that literary world of the North.

EDITION: Gennrich 1951.

● "Quant li dous estez define": L 252-6, RS 1381, MW 2288, B 1882. Sources: ms. M, also TU; music in all. Attribution to Simon in MT. RT 330-332/564-569; Bartsch 1870, 137-138; Gennrich 1951, 84-87; Paden 1987 (1), 130-133.

The only notable dialectal forms are Picard *envoisie* = Central Fr. *envoisiee, assaïe = assaiee*.

According to Gennrich 1951, 62-64, this *pastourelle* of the early thirteenth century, the only one attributed to Simon d'Authie, is one of the first in French depicting honest and forthright—and successful—resistance to the knight's advances. Indeed, Gennrich considers it symbolic of the decline of aristocratic song and the ascent of Northern bourgeois lyric, noting that the very setting in which the knight's unsuccessful venture takes place (1.1-5) is, exceptionally, autumnal. It is true, however, that in troubadour poetry such an approach to the genre is found at the very beginning of the tradition, in the work of Marcabru.

Note the unusual inclusion of the refrain within the body of each stanza rather than at the end.

The melodies in MT are similar to the one presented, that of U. The music alternates between the scales of *f* and *d,* but this bipolarity is underplayed in U, which favors *d* (see the cadences of lines 4, 7, 8, 11). The scheme shows an extended *cauda,* with as many as seven phrases: ABAB CDEFGHI.

Quant li dous estez define   (L 252-6)
Pastourelle

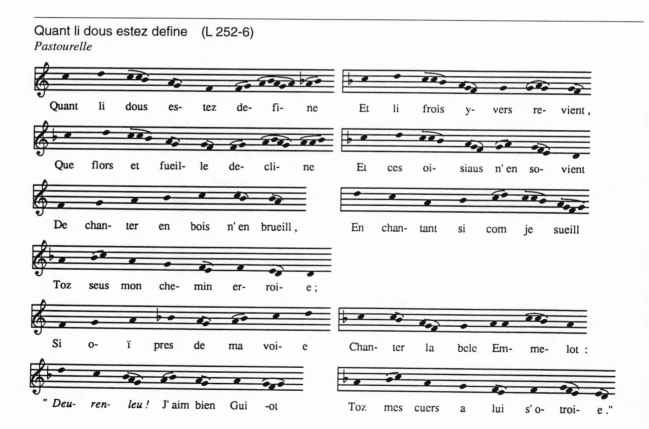

Quant li dous es- tez de- fi- ne

Et li frois y- vers re- vient,

Que flors et fueil- le de- cli- ne

Et ces oi- siaus n'en so- vient

De chan- ter en bois n'en brueill,

En chan- tant si com je sueill

Toz seus mon che- min er- roi- e;

Chan- ter la bele Em- me- lot:

Si o- ï pres de ma voi- e

Toz mes cuers a lui s'o- troi- e."

" Deu- ren- leu! J'aim bien Gui -ot

Quant li dous estez define
Et li frois yvers revient,
Que flors et fueille decline
Et ces oisiaus n'en sovient
De chanter en bois n'en brueill,   1.5
En chantant si com je sueill
Toz seus mon chemin erroie;
Si oï pres de ma voie
Chanter la bele Emmelot:
"*Deurenleu!* J'aim bien Guiot,   1.10
Toz mes cuers a lui s'otroie."

Grant joie fait la meschine
Quant de Guiot li sovient;
Je li dis: "Amie fine,
Cil vous saut qui tot maintient!
Vostre amor desir et vueill,   2.5
A vous servir toz m'acueill.
Se volez que vostres soie,
Robe vous donrai de soie,
Si laissiez cel vilain sot,
Deurenleu! c'ainc ne vous sot   2.10
Bien amer ne faire joie."

"Or parlez vous de folie,
Sire, foi que je doi vous,
Ja, se Dieu plaist, de s'amie
Ne sera mes amis cous.
Tournez vous! Fuiés de ci!   3.5
Ja ne lairai mon ami
Pour nul home que je voie;
Ne m'a pas dit que je.l doie
Pour autrui entrelaissier.
Deurenleu! Pour un baisier   3.10
M'a doné gans et corroie."

"Hé, douce rienz envoisie,
Cuers debonaires et douz,
Recevez par cortoisie
Mon cuer qui se rent a vous,
En qui je del tout m'afi;   4.5
Mains jointes merci vous cri,
Mes que vostre amour soit moie
Qui mon cuer destraint et loie
Si que ne l'en puis sachier.
Deurenleu! Pour embracier   4.10
Mes cuers au vostre se loie."

As sweet summer was ending
and cold winter coming back,
when leaves and flowers had faded
and the birds no longer thought
to sing in woods and groves,
I, singing as I often do,
was riding all alone along my way;
near the path I heard
the song of lovely Emmy:
"*Dorenlot!* I'm in love with Guy;
my whole heart is his."

The girl was full of joy
at the thought of Guy.
I said, "True belovèd,
God save you, the All-powerful!
I desire and want your love;
I am all ready to serve you.
If you want me to be yours,
I'll give you a silken robe —
and you leave that boorish dunce
— *Dorenlot!* — who's never known
how to love you or bring you joy."

"You're out of your mind, sir,
with all due respect:
never, please God, will my lover
be betrayed by his belovèd.
Turn around and ride away!
I won't leave my Guy
for any other man I see;
he hasn't told me I should
give him up for someone else.
Dorenlot! For a kiss
he gave me gloves and a belt."

"Ah, sweet smiling creature,
sweet and noble heart,
be courteous and accept
my heart, which surrenders to you;
to you I pledge my faith.
I beg you, hands joined, for mercy:
let your love be mine,
your love that so grips and binds my heart
that I cannot pull it back.
Dorenlot! My heart, to embrace you,
binds itself to yours."

"Bien m'avez ore assaïe,
Mes pou i avez conquis.
Mainte autre en avez proïe:
Ne l'avez pas ci apris,
N'encore ci ne.l lairoiz.   5.5
N'est pas li cuers si destrois
Com il pert a la parole;
Teus baise feme et acole
Qui ne l'aime tant ne quant.
Deurenleu! Alez avant!   5.10
Ja ne mi troveroiz fole."

"You have made a bold attempt
but have gained very little.
You have tried as much with many a woman:
this was not your first time
and it won't be your last;
your heart is not so tormented
as your words make it appear.
Many a man kisses and embraces a woman
who doesn't love her in the slightest.
Dorenlot! Away with you!
You'll never find me a wanton fool."

Moniot d'Arras, "Dame ains ke ie voise en ma contree" (p. 298). Ms. T, f. 120r.
Cliché Bibliothèque Nationale de France - Paris.

MONIOT D'ARRAS

Moniot d'Arras, from the region of the Artois, was apparently a monk before becoming a trouvère. His poetic activity can be situated in the years between 1213 and 1239 and was centered in the feudal courts of the North. He is credited with about fifteen lyric pieces of various genres, including a motet.

EDITIONS: Dyggve 1938; van der Werf 1979.

● "Amors mi fait renvoisier et chanter": L 185-3, RS 810, MW 1469, B 1555. Sources: ms. MTa. Music in M but mutilated; see below. Attribution to Moniot in all mss. RT 298-300/512-517; Dyggve 1938, 83-86; van der Werf 1979, 366.

The only notable dialectal form is Picard *enforcie* = Central Fr. *enforciee.*

This *chanson de femme* must have been composed before 1227-1229, for its first stanza is quoted in Gerbert de Montreuil's *Roman de la Violette,* written during those years.

Mutilation of ms. M makes a reliable reading of the first two lines and more impossible. After a probable opening on *g,* the principal cadences are on *c,* which is the preponderant tone of the piece. We may assume a *pedes cum cauda* scheme, which would give: ABAB CDEE'E.

● "Dame, ains ke je voise en ma contree": L 185-7, RS 503, MW 315, B 197/1102/321/405/392. Sources: ms. T, also M; music in both. Attribution to Moniot in both mss. RT 302-305/522-527; Dyggve 1938, 101-103; van der Werf 1979, 347-349.

Dialectal features: Picard, including *cançons* = Central Fr. *chançons, merchi = merci, ochist = ocist; çou = ce; ens = en; vo = vostre.*

Like many of the refrains that appear in *chansons avec des refrains,* two of the present ones occur not only in this song but in other contexts as well. Thus, the third refrain (B 321) also figures in a motet, and the fourth (B 405) is used in both a motet and in a *salut d'amours.*

The melodic tradition of this song is somewhat complicated when it comes to the refrains. T preserves the melodies of the first three and M that of the fourth. Neither ms. has music for the fifth refrain. The melodies of the two manuscripts, similar in shape, alternate between the preponderant tone of *c* and *d* as expressed in the cadences of lines 3, 5, and 6. The melodic scheme of the piece, according to T, is of the *frons cum cauda* type: AABCDEF/GH.

Amors mi fait renvoisier et chanter (L 185-3)
Chanson d'amour, chanson de femme

Amors mi fait renvoisier et chanter
Et me semont ke plus jolie soie,
Et mi doune talent de mieuz amer
C'onques ne fis. Pour c'est fous qui m'en proie,
Quar j'ai ami, n'en nul fuer ne voudroie   1.5
De bone amor mon voloir trestourner,
Ains amerai et serai bien amee.
Quant pluz me bat et destraint li jalous,
Tant ai je pluz en amours ma pensee.   1.9

Love makes me rejoice and sing
and urges me to be more lively
and makes me want to be a better lover
than ever before. So anyone's a fool to seek my favor,
since I have a lover and would at no price
let my desire turn away from true love.
No, I will love and I'll be loved.
The more my jealous husband beats and hounds me,
the more my mind is fixed on love.

Mon cuer voudrai metre en amor guarder,
Quar sanz amour ne puet nus avoir joie
Et d'amours doit bele dame amender;
Pour c' est fole qui son tanz n'i emploie.
Quant li jalouz me bat pluz et chastoie,   2.5
Lors me fait pluz esprendre et alumer,
Qu'amours n'iert ja pour jalous oublïee.
Quant pluz me bat et destraint li jalous,
Tant ai je pluz en amours ma pensee.   2.9

Quant je mi doi dormir et reposer,
Lors me semont amours qui me maistroie
Et si me fait et veillier et penser
A mon ami en cui braz je voudroie
Estre touz jours; et quant a moi dosnoie   3.5
Et il me veut baisier et acoler,
Lors est ma joie enforcie et doublee.
Quant pluz me bat et destraint li jalous,
Tant ai je pluz en amours ma pensee.   3.9

Biau m'est quant puiz ochoison controuver
Par quoi g'i puisse aler, c'on ne m'i voie,
A mon ami conseillier et parler.
Et quant j'i sui, partir ne m'en voudroie,
Et quant n'i puis aler, si i envoie   4.5
Mon cuer au mainz; ce ne puet trestourner
Qu'il ne voist la u j'ai m'amour dounee.
Quant pluz me bat et destraint li jalous,
Tant ai je pluz en amours ma pensee.   4.9

Nus ne me doit reprendre ne blasmer
Se j'ai ami, car plevir vous porroie
C'on ne porroit en mon mari trouver
Nule teche dont on amer le doie.
Il me gaite, maiz son tans pis emploie   5.5
Que cil qui veut sour gravele semer,
Quar il iert cous, ja n'iere si guardee.
Quant pluz me bat et destraint li jalous,
Tant ai je pluz en amours ma pensee.   5.9

Trestuit li bien c'on porroit deviser
Sont en celui a cui del tout m'otroie;
Bien set son cuer envers autrui celer
Et envers moi volentiers le desploie.
Non pluz c'on puet Tristan n'Yseut la bloie   6.5
De lor amour partir ne dessevrer,
N'iert ja l'amours de nous deus dessevree.
Quant pluz me bat et destraint li jalous,
Tant ai je pluz en amours ma pensee.   6.9

I want to store love in my heart,
for there is no joy without love
and with love a lovely lady is lovelier;
so anyone's a fool to give it no attention.
When my jealous husband berates and beats me most,
that's when I become most stirred up and aroused,
for jealousy can never make me forget my love.
The more my jealous husband beats and hounds me,
the more my mind is fixed on love.

When I am about to lie down and sleep,
then love summons me and takes over;
it makes me lie awake and think
of my lover, in whose arms I would like
to be forever. And when he makes love to me
and wants to embrace and kiss me,
then my joy deepens and redoubles.
The more my jealous husband beats and hounds me,
the more my mind is fixed on love.

I am happy whenever I can find a chance
to go, undetected, to my lover,
to confide in him and talk.
And when I go, I want never to leave again;
and when I cannot go, I send
my heart, at least; nothing can stop my heart
from going where my love is.
The more my jealous husband beats and hounds me,
the more my mind is fixed on love.

No one should reproach or blame me
if I have a lover, for I can give my word
that no one could find in my husband
any trait to make a woman love him.
He watches me closely, but he wastes his time
more than if he tried to plant seed in gravel,
for however tightly I am held, he will be a cuckold.
The more my jealous husband beats and hounds me,
the more my mind is fixed on love.

All the virtues one could list
are in the man to whom I give myself freely;
he knows how to hide his heart from others
but to me he reveals it gladly.
No more than one could part or uncouple
Tristan and blonde Yseut from their love
could one uncouple us from ours.
The more my jealous husband beats and hounds me,
the more my mind is fixed on love.

Dame, ains ke je voise en ma contree (L 185-7)
Chanson avec des refrains

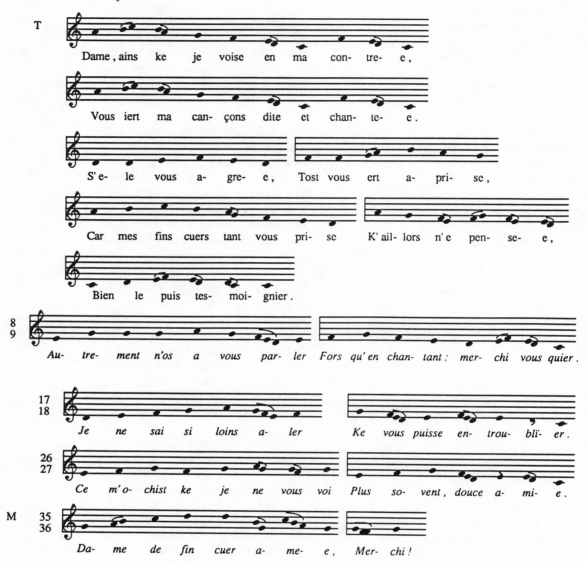

Dame, ains ke je voise en ma contree,
Vous iert ma cançons dite et chantee.
        S'ele vous agree,
            Tost vous ert aprise,   1.4
        Car mes fins cuers tant vous prise
            K'aillors n'a pensee,
        Bien le puis tesmoignier.
    Autrement n'os a vous parler
    Fors qu'en chantant: merchi vous quier.   1.9

My lady, before I leave for my country,
my song will be performed for you.
If you like it,
it won't take you long to learn it,
for my true heart values you so much
that it has no thought for anyone else;
I can testify to that.
The only way I dare to speak to you
is by singing: I seek your mercy.

Dame, en chantant vous iert demandee
Vostre amors, ke j'ai tant desiree.
   S'or ne m'est donee
    Ou au mains pramise,   2.4
   Jamais n'ert ens mon cuer mise
    Joie ne trovee,
  K'autre ke vous ne voil amer.
   Je ne sai si loins aler
    Ke vous puisse entroublïer. 2.9

Dame, lonc tans vos avrai celee
Ceste amor, mais or vos ert mostree.
   Dieus, ki vous fist nee,
    Mete en vous franchise,   3.4
   Si ke l'amors ki m'atise
    Soit ens vos doblee;
  Lors ert ma dolors garie.
  Ce m'ochist ke je ne vous voi
   Plus sovent, douce amie.   3.9

Dame, proi vos ne soiés iree
De çou k'amie vos ai clamee,
   Car la renomee
    De vo vaillandise,   4.4
   Ke Dieus en vous a asise,
    M'a fait que nomee
   Vous ai ensi.
  Dame de fin cuer amee,
    Merchi!   4.9

Dame, a droit porriés estre blasmee
Se en vous n'estoit merchi trovee.
   Ore iert esprovee
    Vostre gentelise,   5.4
   Car, se l'amors ke j'ai quise
    M'aviés refusee,
  Saichiés ke pour vous morroie.
   Dame, amer ne porroie
   Nule autre ke je voie.   5.9

My lady, my song will ask you
for your love, which I have long desired.
If it isn't granted to me now
or at least promised,
joy will never come into my heart
or be found there,
for I wish to love no one but you.
I cannot go so far away
as to be able to forget you.

My lady, I have long kept my love
a secret, but it will now be revealed to you.
May God, who gave you life,
grant you such generosity
that the love that glows in me
will be mirrored in you;
then my pain will be relieved.
It kills me that I don't see you
more often, my sweet belovèd.

My lady, I beg you not to be angered
that I have called you my belovèd,
for the fame
of the virtue
that God has placed in you
is what has made me
give you that name.
Lady loved wholeheartedly,
mercy!

My lady, you could rightfully be blamed
if mercy were not found in you.
Now your nobility
will be put to the test,
for if the love that I have sought
were denied me,
you may be sure I would die.
My lady, I could not love
any other woman that I see.

GUILLAUME LE VINIER

Guillaume le Vinier came from a bourgeois family of Arras and had a brother, Gilles, who was also a trouvère. A cleric of low rank, he was married. He was active in the literary life of his city from about 1220 to his death in 1245. About forty lyric compositions of various types are attributed to him.

EDITIONS: Ménard 1970 (1983).

● "Sire, ne me celez mie": L 97-1, RS 1185, MW 1159. Sources: ms. O, also AKMNTVXab; one melody in OKMX, another in A, a third in V; no music in NTab. Attribution to Guillaume in KTX. RT 320-323/548-553; Wallensköld 1925, 139-144; Långfors 1926, 1:19-23; Ménard 1970, 193-199. Performed on Anthology CD.

The only notable dialectal forms are Burgundian *nuns* = Central Fr. *nus; saichiez = sachiez.*

Lines 7 and 8 of each stanza form a single metric unit of eleven syllables: 7 + *e* + 3 (beginning with a consonant) or + 4 (beginning with a vowel, in which case *e* is elided).

Guillaume's partner in this *jeu-parti* is Thibaut de Champagne, who is asked to state whether he would rather make love at night in total darkness or enjoy the company of his mistress in daylight without making love. Thibaut chooses the first alternative. *Gilon* and *Jehan* are asked to judge the debate.

The melody of ms. O, presented here, is in the scale of *d* (Dorian), with an opening on *f.* Its scheme is of the *pedes cum cauda* type: ABAB A′CDEFG. Unlike the other manuscripts in its group, O writes the melody in mensural notation (first rhythmic mode).

● "Bien doit chanter la qui chançon set plaire": L 102-3, RS 169, MW 2371, B 1567. Sources: ms. M, also RT; music in all. Attribution to Guillaume in MT. RT 326-329/558-563; Ménard 1970, 124-128.

The poem shows a number of varied exceptions to the normal 4 + 6 decasyllabic meter; see, for example, 1.6, 2.6, 2.7, 3.5.

1.5-6: Cf. the proverb *Qui sert et ne parsert son loier pert* ('He who serves but does not serve thoroughly, forgoes his reward')(Morawski, no. 2138).

4.1-2: The ruby, which appears in a number of *chansons d'amour,* is credited in medieval lapidaries with sovereign mystical or wondrous properties.

The *sire freres* of the envoy is perhaps Guillaume's brother Gilles, who apparently composed very few love songs.

The melody presented, that of ms. M, is built on *g,* which provides the cadence at the *diesis* (end of line 4) and at the end of the stanza. The refrain, from *f* to the final *g,* recapitulates the entire scale. The melody is through-composed: ABCDEFGH/refrain I.

Sire, ne me celez mie   (L 97-1)

Jeu-parti

Si- re ne me ce- lez mi- e

Li quelx vos iert plus a gré :

S' il a- vient que vostre a- mi- e

Vos ait par- le- ment man- dé

Nu a nu lez son cos- té

Par nuit, que n' an ver- roiz mi- e,

Ou de jor vos bait et ri- e

En un beau pré

Et en- braz, mais ne di mi- e

Qu' il i ait de plus par- lé ?

Sire, ne me celez mie	My lord, don't hide from me
Li quelx vos iert plus a gré:	which situation you would prefer:
S'il avient que vostre amie	your lady-friend invites you
Vos ait parlement mandé	to a tête-à-tête
Nu a nu lez son costé 1.5	naked, side by side,
Par nuit, que n'an verroiz mie,	but at night, so you won't see a thing,
Ou de jor vos bait et rie	or else, by day, in a lovely meadow,
En un beau pré	she kisses you and smiles
Et enbraz, mais ne di mie	and puts her arms around you, but I can't say
Qu'il i ait de plus parlé? 1.10	there's any more to it than that.

— Guillaume, c'est grant folie
Quant ensi avez chanté;
Li bergiers d'une abbaïe
Eüst assez mieuz parlé.
Quant j'avrai lez mon costé   2.5
Mon cuer, ma dame, m'amie,
Que j'avrai toute ma vie
     Desirré,
Lors vos quit la drüerie
Et le parlement dou pré.   2.10

    William, what a foolish thing
    you've just sung to me!
    The shepherd at a monastery
    would have spoken better.
    If I can have lying beside me
    my lady, my heart, my sweetheart,
    whom I have all my life
    desired,
    I'll do without all the cooing
    and the love-talk in your meadow.

— Sire, je di qu'en s'enfance
Doit on aprendre d'amors;
Mais mout faites mal semblance
Que vos sentez les dolors:
Pou prisiez esté ne flors,   3.5
Gent cors ne douce acointance,
Beaus resgarz ne contenance
     Ne colors;
En vos n'a point d'astenance;
Ce deüst prendre uns priors.   3.10

    My lord, it's as a youth, I tell you,
    that a man is bound to learn about love,
    but you hardly give the impression
    of feeling its sting:
    you don't care about summer's flowers,
    a shapely body or a sweet encounter,
    lovely glances or comportment
    or complexion;
    you have no thought for abstinence;
    a prior might have made your choice!

— Guillaume, qui ce comance
Bien le demoinne folors,
Et mout a pou conoissance
Qui n'en va au lit le cors,
Que desoz beaus covertors   4.5
Prent on tele seürtance
Dont l'on s'oste de doutance
     Et de freors;
Tant comme soie en balance,
N'iert ja mes cuers sanz paors.   4.10

    William, anyone who gets into this
    is led on by passion,
    and there is very little understanding
    in the man who doesn't run straight to bed,
    for under fine covers is where
    you find the confidence
    to put aside hesitation
    and alarm;
    as long as I remain uncertain,
    my heart cannot be free of fear.

— Sire, por rien ne voudroie
Que nuns m'eüst a ce mis.
Quant celi cui j'ameroie
Et qui tout m'avroit conquis
Puis veoir en mi le vis   5.5
Et baisier a si grant joie
Et embracier toute voie
     A mon devis,
Saichiez, se l'autre prenoie,
Ne seroie pas amis.   5.10

    My lord, not for anything would I want
    to be led to that point.
    If I can see the woman I love,
    the woman who has won my heart,
    and can gaze at her face
    and enjoy her kisses
    and go on holding her in my arms
    as long as I like,
    you may be sure, if I chose the other side,
    I would not be a lover.

— Guillaume, se Deus me voie,
Folie avez entrepris,
Que, se nue la tenoie,
N'en prendroie paradis.
Ja por esgarder son vis   6.5
A paiez ne m'en tendroie
S'autre chose n'en avoie.
     J'ai mieuz pris,
Qu'au partir se vos convoie,
N'en porteroiz c'un faus ris.   6.10

    William, so help me God,
    you've been speaking foolishly,
    for if I could hold her naked,
    I wouldn't give her up for heaven!
    For all the gazing at her face,
    I wouldn't consider myself satisfied
    if I had nothing else.
    I have made the better choice,
    for if she walks you to the gate,
    you'll carry away only a faithless smile.

— Sire, Amors m'a si sopris
Que siens sui, ou que je soie,
Et sor Gilon m'en metroie
    A son devis,
Li quelx va plus droite voie
Ne li quelx maintient le pis.   E1.6 (10)

My lord, love has so caught hold of me
that I am his wherever I may be.
I leave it to Giles
to decide
which of us has chosen the right way
and which the wrong.

— Guillaume, fous et pensis
I remaindroiz tote voie,
Et cil qui ensi donoie
    Est mout chaitis.
Bien vuil que Gilon en croie,
Et sor Jehan m'en sui mis.   E2.6 (10)

William, you will always be
foolish and dreamy,
and a man who makes love like that
is a sad case.
I am willing to take Giles's word,
but I have asked John to decide.

Bien doit chanter la qui chançon set plaire   (L 102-3)

Chanson d'amour

Bien doit chan- ter la qui chan- çon set plai- re

En ma- nie- re d'a- mour et de bon- té.

Je.1 di pour moi qui tel fois ai chan- té

Que au- si bien u mieuz me ve- nist tai- re.

Maiz qui sert sanz son ser- vi- ce par fai- re,

Vis m'est qu'en fo- lour ait son tanz u- sé.

Pour ce, et pluz pour ma grant vo- len- té,

Ser- vi- rai tant que je sa- vrai par- ti- e

Quel joie est d'a- voir a- mi- e.

Bien doit chanter la qui chançon set plaire
En maniere d'amour et de bonté.
Je.l di pour moi qui tel fois ai chanté
Que ausi bien u mieuz me venist taire. 1.4
Maiz qui sert sanz son service parfaire,
Vis m'est qu'en folour ait son tanz usé.
Pour ce, et pluz pour ma grant volenté,
Servirai tant que je savrai partie
   Quel joie est d'avoir amie. 1.9

De bien amer avrai joie u contraire,
Qu'ensi l'ai pieç'a pramis et vöé,
Si com firent nostre ancissour ainsné
En qui cuers ot fine Amors son repaire. 2.4
Or voi chascun l'amourous contrefaire
Sanz cuer de desirrier entalenté,
Dont trop se tendroient pour engané,
S'il avoient seü une foïe
   Quel joie est d'avoir amie. 2.9

La vïele et amours par essamplaire
Doivent estre d'un samblant comparé,
Car la vïele et amours sunt paré
De joie et de soulaz qui l'en set traire. 3.4
Mais cil qui ne set vïeler fait raire
La vïele, si li tolt sa bonté;
Ausi fait l'en amours par fausseté:
A soi la tolt ne ne set, que qu'il die,
   Quel joie est d'avoir amie. 3.9

Li rubis a tesmoins del lapidaire
Est des pierres sires en dignité,
Et amours dame de joliveté,
Resjoïssanz en fin cuer debonaire. 4.4
Mes cuers en li s'esjoïst et resclaire.
Pieç'a l'a de moi parti et sevré,
Et s'il li plaist qu'ait le cors de bonté
Pour savourer cuer et cors sanz partie —
   Quel joie est d'avoir amie! 4.9

Com de celui qui l'or de son aumaire
A si maumis, despendu et gasté
Qu'il ne parose savoir la purté
A comfait chief li remanans puet traire 5.4
Est il de moi, quant voi cors et viaire
Furni de sens, de valour, de bonté.
La n'os savoir ma mort ne ma santé,
Quar, qui bon espoir pert, il ne set mie
   Quel joie est d'avoir amie. 5.9

Sire freres, trop vous voi demoré,
Si cuit qu'aiez seü et savouré
   Quel joie est d'avoir amie. E.3 (9)

He needs to sing, whose song can please
as love and virtue would have it do.
I speak for myself, who have sometimes sung
when silence would have done as well or better.
But the servant of love who falls short of his goal
seems to me to have foolishly wasted his time.
Therefore, and even more because of my keen desire,
I will serve until I somewhat know
what joy it is to have a lover.

Loving well will bring me joy or disappointment,
for so I vowed and swore some time ago,
just as our early forebears did
who had opened their hearts to true love.
Now I see everyone pretending to be in love
with a heart untouched by desire;
they would surely deem themselves deluded
if just once they had known
what joy it is to have a lover.

The fiddle and love, in terms of an image,
are in one respect to be compared:
the fiddle and love afford joy and pleasure
to the man who knows how to draw them forth;
but he who knows not how to play makes
the instrument grate and robs it of its virtue.
Just so with love, when the lover is untrue:
whatever he says, he robs himself and knows not
what joy it is to have a lover.

The ruby, as the lapidary states,
is in its station the lord of gems,
and love is the lady of delight,
rejoicing in the pure and noble heart.
My heart finds its joy in her and glows.
Some time ago, love disjoined and parted it from me,
and if love cares, in its goodness, to have my body too
and savor heart and body undivided —
Oh, what joy to have a lover!

Just like a man who has so misused and wasted
and fooled away the gold in his chest
that he dares not face the truth
about how little remains,
just so am I when I see her, see her face
filled with intelligence, virtue, and goodness;
then I dare not consider health or my mortality,
because no one who loses confidence can know
what joy it is to have a lover.

Brother, sir, I see that you are very quiet,
yet I do believe that you have known and tasted
what joy it is to have a lover.

THIBAUT DE CHAMPAGNE

The most illustrious of the trouvères and one of the most prolific, Thibaut IV, count of Champagne and king of Navarre, born an orphan in 1201, grandson of the great patroness of poets Marie de Champagne, was also an important political figure. After several years' education at the royal court of Philip II Augustus, young Thibaut began his life as a ruler under the regency of his mother, Blanche de Navarre. He later took part in the war of the newly-crowned King Louis VIII against the English, appearing at the siege of La Rochelle in 1224, and continued to serve the king, his overlord, thereafter. In 1226, however, he withdrew his support during the royal siege of Avignon and returned home in secret. Upon the king's death a few months later, Thibaut was accused of having poisoned him, but nothing came of this apparently groundless charge. The following year, he allied himself with other feudal powers in an attempt to dethrone Blanche de Castille, widow of Louis VIII and regent for their son Louis IX, but the queen succeeded in detaching him from the rebellious group and making him her defender. Attacked by his erstwhile allies, Thibaut was saved by the royal army. Relations with the Crown, however, were extremely unsteady, particularly after 1234, when Thibaut succeeded his uncle Sancho the Strong as king of Navarre, and it was not until 1236 that a final peace was achieved, based on the vassal's submission. Three years later, he left for the Holy Land as head of the Crusade of 1239; the undertaking was marked from the start by discord among the Christian leaders and by Saracen military superiority, the result of which was Thibaut's decision in 1240 to withdraw from his charge and return to France. There, various armed struggles engaged his attention through the following years, and in 1248 he made a penitent's pilgrimage to Rome. He died in Pamplona in 1253. He had been betrothed twice, married three times, divorced once, widowed once, and had fathered several children. The rumor has persisted since his day that the great love of his life was none other than Blanche de Castille, but apart from offering a tempting key to his political shifts, it seems to have no merit.

As a trouvère, Thibaut was immediately successful, seen as equaled only by his great predecessor, Gace Brulé. Dante was to consider him one of the "illustrious" poets in the vernacular, and the medieval songbooks that group their contents by composer place his works before all others. The more than sixty pieces ascribed to him with reasonable certainty, almost all preserved with music, show a majority of courtly *chansons,* none anti-conventional in theme or form but most marked by a rather unusual development of imagery, especially allegorical, use of refrains,

or self-confident lightness of tone. The other works, revealing a style similarly characteristic of Thibaut, are *jeux-partis* (which are among the earliest known), debates, devotional songs (including one in the form of a *lai*), crusade songs, *pastourelles,* and a *serventois.* Note that we present one of Thibaut's *jeux-partis* with songs by Guillaume le Vinier.

STUDY: Bellenger-Quéruel 1987.

EDITIONS: Wallensköld 1925; van der Werf 1979, 3-311; Brahney 1989.

- "Ausi conme unicorne sui": L 240-3, RS 2075, MW 2437. Sources: ms. X, also ABCFKMORSTUVZa; music in KMORVXZa. Attribution to Thibaut in KRTXa; to Pierre de Gand in C. RT 339-343/578-583; Wallensköld 1925, 111-116; van der Werf 1979, 290-298; Brahney 1989, 102-105, Switten 1988, 140-141.

Johannes de Grocheio, whose treatise *De musica* dates from ca. 1300, cites this composition as a *cantus coronatus,* thus recognized as representative of the highest achievement in secular monophonic song.

The allegorical style of this poem derives from the *Roman de la Rose* of Guillaume de Lorris. For a discussion of it, see Dragonetti 1960, 246-248.

1.1-6: It was a widespread belief that the only way to capture a unicorn was to expose it to a virgin; the animal would be irresistibly drawn to her and swoon in her lap. For the best-known Old French presentation of the legend, with allegorical interpretation, see the *Bestiaire* of the twelfth-century writer Philippe de Thaon.

4.3: Roland is the hero of the great *chanson de geste* bearing his name; Oliver is his companion and one of the major characters of the tale.

The eight readings of the music are much the same, the several differences representing only slight changes in line openings or in cadential ornamentation. The melody is syllabic and could elegantly support a metrical rhythm. However, ms. O, which usually shows semi-mensural notation, does not do so in this instance.

The melodic scheme in all readings is through-composed: ABCDEFGHI. This repetitionless type has no apparent formal tie to the two-part rhyme scheme, *abba ccbdd,* yet it is possible to detect a melodic division, too, at the juncture of lines 4 and 5. In lines 1-4, the scale of g and its prolongation, the tone of c, prevail, whereas the following lines tend toward f (line 6) before reverting to the initial scale of g. Note, though, for vocal performance, that mss. OZ flat the b from line 5 on, emphasizing the move toward f in the second half of the stanza, while mss. Va take a different stance, flatting occurrences of b throughout the song, and the other sources (KMRX) offer no guidance on this point. We can only observe that the use of *musica ficta* was left to the discretion of singers, which leads us right back to the melodic mobility of medieval lyric: every realization of the song must be considered a new creation.

- "Tout autresi con l'ente fait venir": L 240-53, RS 1479, MW 1468. Sources: ms. X, also BKMORSTUV; music in all mss. except STU. R presents the song twice, once with a melody different from that of the other redactions. Attribution to Thibaut in KX. RT 343-347/582-587; Wallensköld 1925, 68-72; van der Werf 1979, 220-229; Brahney 1989, 96-101.

2.2: The love of Pyramus and Thisbe is recounted in the fourth book of Ovid's *Metamorphoses*; it was also known to the medieval public through at least one French adaptation of the tale.

4.1-2: According to Wallensköld 1925, these lines allude to the ultimate defection of the faithful, as formulated in I Timothy 4:1, "Now the Spirit expressly says that in later times some will depart from the faith by giving heed to deceitful spirits . . .". The reference to I Timothy seems to us gratuitously specific; it is at least as likely that Thibaut's allusion is to one of the "prophecies" of Merlin, as expressed in Geoffrey of Monmouth's *Historia regum Britanniae* or related French works, or to one of the thirteenth century's biblically inspired apocalytic works.

5.1: The vocative *Aygles,* repeated in the envoy, is a *senhal* (Occitan term to denote a device borrowed from troubadour poetry), or code-name, intended to conceal the identity of the poet's real or fictive lady.

The main version of this melody, represented here by X, is largely cadenced on *d.* In the opening of lines 1 and 3, we find a transposition to *b* of a formula in *e,* a formula often used in pieces meant for dancing. The melodic scheme is of the regular, classic trouvère type: ABAB CDEFG.

- "Chançon ferai, car talent m'en est pris": L 240-6, RS 1596, MW 2062, B 1127/1225/583/1217/1692/530. Sources: ms. N, also KMORSTVXza; music in KMNORVX. Attribution in KNTX. RT 352-355/590-595; Wallensköld 1925, 76-82; van der Werf 1979, 242-246; Brahney 1989, 38-43; Switten 1988, 142-144.

It is unusual to find variable refrains, generally borrowed from popular sources, incorporated into the aristocratic *chanson d'amour,* turning the work into a *chanson avec des refrains.* The deliberateness of this hybridization is underscored by the poet's choice of particularly familiar refrains; indeed, the fourth is found in one other context, the fifth in two others, and the first in as many as five other works.

2.9 and 11: Note that *joie* and *delaie* rhyme in Old French.

4.3: Tristan was widely regarded as the perfect lover.

All sources transmit essentially the same melody. It is tonally quite homogeneous, with a *d* cadence occurring six times and the subfinal *c* three times. The reading of O, presented here, is, as usual, the only one in mensural notation; it shows the third rhythmic mode (long-short-short). The melodic scheme blends the *pedes cum cauda* type with a refrain: ABAB CDEF/refrain GH.

- "J'aloie l'autrier errant": L 240-27, RS 342, MW 847. Sources: ms. K, also MNOSTVX; music in KMNOVX. Attribution to Thibaut in MOSTV. RT 362-365/604-609; Bartsch 1870, 231-232; Wallensköld 1925, 176-179; van der Werf 1979, 58-63; Paden 1987 (1) 132-135; Brahney 1989, 150-153. Performed on Anthology CD.

This is one of only two *pastourelles* attributed to Thibaut; the other follows.

3.9-11: The tradition that allows imperfect rhymes in *pastourelles* and similar compositions is manifested in these verses: only here is the *c* rhyme, which appears in all stanzas, interpreted as *-is* rather than *-i,* but note that in this stanza it is *-is* exclusively.

All sources transmit the same melody, built on *c,* with only a few transpositional variants. We present that of ms. K. The O reading is measured, in the sixth rhythmic mode (short-short-short). The melodic scheme is regular, with *pedes* developed over four lines: ABCD ABCD EFGH.

- "L'autrier par la matinee": L 240-33, RS 529, MW 1762. Sources: ms. X, also BKMTV; music in all except T. Attribution to Thibaut in KTX. RT 365-368/608-613; Bartsch 1870, 232-234; Wallensköld 1925, 180-183; van der Werf 1979, 88-92; Paden 1987 (1) 134-137; Brahney 1989, 154-157.

The only notable dialectal form is Picard *trichie* = Central Fr. *trichiee.*

This is one of only two *pastourelles* attributed to Thibaut; the other precedes.

1.6: This is a variant of a known refrain (B 534). The final line of the poem may also be a refrain, but it has not been found elsewhere and is not listed in Boogaard 1969.

4.6: Here as in numerous other medieval works, Ganelon, the traitor of the *Chanson de Roland,* provides the standard by which all treachery may be measured.

The melody, which we present in the reading of ms. X, is a very simple syllabic one. The first half is built on the alternation of two formulas. The first (lines 1, 3) concludes on *d,* while the second (lines 2, 4) states the fourth *g-c* (also stated in line 9). Lines 7-8 lead the melody toward *f,* while the refrain ends on *a* and thus brings a certain tonal instability to the composition. The scheme is classic in its regularity: ABAB' CDEFG/refrain D'.

Ausi conme unicorne sui (L 240-3)

Chanson d'amour

Ausi conme unicorne sui	I am like the unicorn
Qui s'esbahit en regardant	whom contemplation stuns
Quant la pucele va mirant.	as he gazes at the maiden.
Tant est liee de son ennui, 1.4	He is so elated and unnerved
Pasmee chiet en son giron;	that he falls fainting in her lap;
Lors l'ocit on en traïson.	then he is traitorously slain.
Et moi ont mort d'autel senblant	I have been killed in the same way,
Amors et ma dame, por voir;	truly, by love and my lady;
Mon cuer ont, n'en puis point ravoir. 1.9	they have my heart, and I can't have it back.

Dame, quant je devant vos fui
Et je vos vi premierement,
Mes cuers aloit si tresaillant
Qu'il vos remest quant je m'en mui.   2.4
Lors fu menés sanz raençon
En la douce chartre en prison,
Dont li piler sont de talent
Et li huis sont de biau veoir
Et li anel de bon espoir.   2.9

De la chartre a la clef Amors,
Et si i a mis trois portiers:
Biau Semblant a non li premiers,
Et Biautez ceus en fait seignors;   3.4
Dangier a mis a l'uis devant,
Un ort felon, vilain puant,
Qui mult est maus et pautoniers.
Cist troi sont et viste et hardi;
Mult ont tost un home saisi.   3.9

Qui porroit souffrir la tristors
Et les assaus de ces huissiers?
Onques Rollans ne Oliviers
Ne vainquirent si fors estors;   4.4
Il vainquirent en conbatant,
Mais ceus vaint on humiliant.
Soufrirs en est gonfanoniers;
En cest estor dont je vos di,
N'a nul secors que de merci.   4.9

Dame, je ne dout mes riens plus
Fors tant que faille a vos amer.
Tant ai apris a endurer
Que je sui vostres tout par us;   5.4
Et se il vos en pesoit bien,
Ne m'en puis je partir por rien
Que je n'aie le remenbrer
Et que mes cuers ne soit adés
En la prison et de moi pres.   5.9

Dame, quant je ne sai guiler,
Merciz seroit de saison mes
De soustenir si grevain fes.   E.3 (9)

My lady, when I stood before you
and saw you for the first time,
my heart went leaping so
that it stayed with you when I took my leave.
Then it was led, an unransomed
captive, into the precious prison
whose columns are made of desire,
whose gates are of beautiful sight,
and whose chains, of good hope.

Love holds the key to this prison
and has posted three wardens there:
Attraction is the name of the first;
Beauty is master of the others;
and posted at the front gate is Rejection,
a filthy scoundrel, a stinking knave,
a thoroughly wicked wretch.
All three are fast and bold;
it takes no time for them to seize a man.

Who could endure the beatings
and assaults of such wardens?
Never did Roland or Oliver
win such ruthless battles;
they won by fighting,
but only humility can defeat these foes.
Suffering is the standard-bearer
in the battle that I am speaking of,
and only mercy can bring deliverance.

My lady, I now fear nothing more
than failing in my love for you.
I have learned to endure so much
that habit has made me wholly yours;
and even if you should find this vexing,
nothing can make me go away
without remembering it all
and leaving my heart forever
in your prison, and yet close to me.

My lady, since I cannot lie,
it is surely time for mercy to reward me
for bearing such a heavy burden.

Tout autresi con l'ente fait venir   (L 240-53)

Chanson d'amour

Tout au- tre- si con l'en- te fait ve- nir

Li ar- ro- sers de l'e- ve qui chiet jus,

Fait bone a- mor nestre et croistre et flo- rir

Li re- mem- brers par cos- tume et par us.

D'a- mors loi- al n'iert ja nus au des- sus,

Ainz li co- vient au de- souz main- te- nir.

Por c'est ma do- ce do- lor   Plai- ne de si grant pa- or,

Da- me, si fas grant vi- gor   De chan- ter quant de cuer plor.

Tout autresi con l'ente fait venir	Just as the graft is made to grow
Li arrosers de l'eve qui chiet jus,	by the water that rains down on it,
Fait bone amor nestre et croistre et florir	good love is born and grows and thrives
Li remembrers par costume et par us.	through the habit and work of memory.
D'amors loial n'iert ja nus au dessus, 1.5	A man can never be master of faithful love
Ainz li covient au desouz maintenir.	but must rather let himself be mastered;
Por c' est ma doce dolor	my sweet pain is therefore
Plaine de si grant paor,	full of great fear,
Dame, si fas grant vigor	my lady, and it takes a great effort
De chanter quant de cuer plor. 1.10	to sing when my heart is in tears.
Pleüst a Dieu, por ma dolor garir,	Would to God, to relieve my pain,
Qu'el fust Tisbé, car je sui Piramus;	that she were Thisbe, since I am Pyramus!
Mais je voi bien ce ne puet avenir;	But I see that it cannot be,
Ensi morrai que ja n'en avrai plus.	and so I'll die, for I can have nothing more.
Ahi, bele! tant sui por vos confus! 2.5	Ah, my beauty, I am undone by you!
Que d'un quarrel me venistes ferir,	You struck me with an arrow,
Espris d'ardant feu d'amor,	blazing with the fire of love,
Quant vos vi le premier jor;	when I saw you that first day;
Li ars ne fu pas d'aubor	it was no sapwood bow
Qui se traist par grant douçor. 2.10	that was drawn with such tenderness.

Dame, se je servise Dieu autant
Et priasse de verai cuer entier
Con je fas vos, je sai certainement
Qu'en paradis n'eüst autel loier;
Mais je ne puis ne servir ne proier   3.5
Nului fors vos, a qui mes cuers s'atent;
    Si ne puis aparcevoir
    Que ja joie en doie avoir,
    Ne je ne vos puis veoir
    Fors d'euz clos et de cuer noir.   3.10

La prophete dit voir, qui pas ne ment,
Que en la fin faudront li droiturier;
Et la fins est venue voirement,
Que cruautés vaint merci et prier,
Ne servises ne peut avoir mestier,   4.5
Ne bone amor n'atendre longuement;
    Ainz a plus orgueils, pooir
    Et beubanz que douz voloir,
    N'encontre amor n'a savoir
    Qu'atendue sans espoir.   4.10

Aygles, sans vos ne puis merci trover.
Bien sai et voi qu'a toz biens ai failli
Se vos ensi me volés eschiver
Que vos n'aiés de moi quelque merci.
Ja n'avrez mais nul si loial ami,   5.5
Ne ne porrois a nul jor recovrer,
    Et je me morrai chaitis.
    Ma vie sera mais pis
    Loing de vostre biau cler vis,
    Ou naist la rose et li lis.   5.10

    Aygles, j'ai touz jors apris
    A estre loiaus amis,
    Si me vaudroit melz un ris
    De vos qu'estre en paradis.   E.4 (10)

My lady, if I served God as well
as I do you, and prayed with a heart
as sincere, I know for certain
that such would not be my reward in heaven;
but I can neither serve nor entreat
anyone but you, for whom my heart yearns;
    yet I cannot foresee
    that it will ever bring me joy,
    and you I can only see
    with my eyes closed and darkness in my heart.

The prophet who does not lie says truly
that in the end the righteous will fall away;
now the end has truly come,
when cruelty triumphs over mercy and prayer,
when service has no purpose,
nor faithful love nor patient waiting;
    pride and arrogance, indeed, have
    greater force than tender longing,
    and there is no remedy for love
    but hopeless expectation.

Eagle, without you I can find no mercy.
I clearly see that I have lost every good
if you want to avoid me
and show me no mercy at all.
Never again will you have, never be able
to find, so faithful a lover,
    and I shall die wretched;
    my life will now decline,
    far from your lovely, radiant face
    where the rose and lily bloom.

    Eagle, I have always endeavored
    to be a faithful lover,
    and I would rather have a smile
    from you than be in heaven.

Chançon ferai, car talent m'en est pris (L 240-6)

Chanson d'amour, avec des refrains

Chan- çon fe- rai, car ta- lent m'en est pris,

De la meil- lor qui soit en tout le mont.

De la meil- lor? Je cuit que j'ai mes- pris.

S' e- le fust tels -- se Deus joi- e me dont --

De moi li fust au- cu- ne pi- tiez pri- se,

Qui sui touz siens et sui a sa de- vi- se.

Pi- tiez de cuer, Deus! que ne s'est as- si- se

En sa biau- té? Da- me, qui mer- ci proi,

Je sent les maus d'a- mor pour vous,

Sen- tez les vous pour moi?

Chançon ferai, car talent m'en est pris,	I will compose a song, since desire has taken hold of me,
De la meillor qui soit en tout le mont.	about the finest woman in the whole world.
De la meillor? Je cuit que j'ai mespris.	The finest? I think I have made a mistake.
S'ele fust tels — se Deus joie me dont — 1.4	If she were (God grant me that joy!),
De moi li fust aucune pitiez prise,	some slight pity would have taken hold of her,
Qui sui touz siens et sui a sa devise.	for I am all hers and at her command.
Pitiez de cuer, Deus! que ne s'est assise	Why, God, is no heartfelt pity to be found
En sa biauté? Dame qui merci proi, 1.8	in her beauty? Lady whom I beg for mercy,
Je sent les maus d'amor pour vous,	*I feel the pangs of love for you;*
Sentez les vous pour moi?	*do you feel them for me?*

Douce dame, sanz amour fui jadis,
Quant je choisi vostre gente façon;
Et quant je vi vostre tres biau cler vis,
Si me raprist mes cuers autre reson: 2.4
De vous amer me semont et justise,
A vos en est a vostre conmandise.
Li cors remaint, qui sent felon juïse,
Se n'en avez merci de vostre gré.   2.8
Li douz mal dont j'atent joie
M'ont si grevé
Mors sui s'ele mi delaie.

Mult a Amours grant force et grant pouoir,
Qui sanz reson fet choisir a son gré.
Sanz reson? Deus! je ne di pas savoir,
Car a mes euz en set mes cuers bon gré,   3.4
Qui choisirent sa tres bele senblance
Dont jamés jor ne ferai desevrance;
Ainz sousfrerai por li grief penitance
Tant que pitiez et mercis l'en prendra.   3.8
Dirai vous qui mon cuer enblé m'a?
Li douz ris et li bel oeil qu'ele a!

Douce dame, s'il vous plesoit un soir,
M'avrïez vous plus de joie doné
C'onques Tristans, qui en fist son pouoir,
N'en pout avoir nul jor de son aé.   4.4
La moie joie est tornee a pesance.
Hé, cors sanz cuer! De vous fet grant venjance
Cele qui m'a navré sanz defiance,
Et neporquant je ne la lerai ja.   4.8
L'en doit bien bele dame amer
Et s'amor garder, cil qui l'a.

Dame, pour vous vueil aler foloiant,
Que je en aim mes maus et ma dolor;
Qu'aprés les maus ma grant joie en atent
Que g'en avrai, se Dieu plest, a brief jor.   5.4
Amors, merci! Ne soiez oublïee!
S'or me failliez, s'iert traïson doublee,
Que mes granz maus por vos si fort m'agree.
Ne me metez longuement en oubli!   5.8
Se la bele n'a de moi merci,
Je ne vivrai mie longuement ensi.

Sa grant biautez, qui m'esprent et agree,
Qui seur toutes est la plus desirree,
M'a si lacié mon cuer en sa prison.   E.3 (8)
Deus! je ne pens s'a li non.
A moi que ne pense ele donc?

Dear lady, I was once without love,
but then I discovered your gracious self;
and when I saw your lovely, radiant face,
my heart taught me a new language:
it urges me and drives me to love you,
and it is yours and obeys you.
My body stands back, cruelly punished
unless you care to grant it mercy.
The sweet pains that promise me bliss
have so hurt me
that I'll die if she makes me wait.

Love has great strength and great power
and there is no reason in the discovery it leads us to.
No reason? God! What a stupid thing to say,
when my heart is so grateful to my eyes
for discovering a creature of such beauty
that I will never take leave of her;
I will rather do penance and suffer
until pity and mercy take hold of her.
Shall I tell you who has stolen my heart?
Her sweet smile and her beautiful eyes!

Dear lady, if you wished, one evening,
you would give me more joy
than Tristan, who did whatever he could,
ever had any day of his life;
but my joy has turned to grief.
Ah, body stripped of its heart, victim of vengeance!
She has wounded me by stealth,
and yet I will never leave her.
You have to love a lovely lady
and, once you have it, keep her love.

My lady, on your account I will persist in folly,
for I love the pains and sorrow it brings me:
after the pains I expect the joyous fulfillment
that, please God, I shall have before long.
Love, have mercy! Don't forget me!
If you fail me now, it will be a double betrayal,
for it's on your account that I welcome my torment.
Let me not remain forgotten for long!
If my sweetheart shows me no mercy,
I can't go on like this for long.

Her great beauty, which enflames me and charms me
and is more longed for than any other,
has bound up my heart in her prison.
God! I think of nothing but her.
Why doesn't she think of me?

J'aloie l'autrier errant (L 240-27)
Pastourelle

J'a- loi- e l'au- trier er- rant Sanz com- pai- gnon

Seur mon pa- le- froi pen- sant A fere u- ne chan- çon,

quant j'o- ï, ne sai con- ment, Lez un buis- son

La voiz du plus bel en- fant C'on- ques ve- ïst nus hon;

Et n'es- toit pas en- fes, si N'e- üst quinze anz et de- mi,

N'on- ques nu- le riens ne vi De si gen- te fa- çon.

J'aloie l'autrier errant
    Sanz compaignon
Seur mon palefroi pensant
    A fere une chançon,   1.4
Quant j'oï, ne sai conment,
    Lez un buisson
La voiz du plus bel enfant
    C'onques veïst nus hon;   1.8
Et n'estoit pas enfes, si
N'eüst quinze anz et demi,
N'onques nule riens ne vi
    De si gente façon.   1.12

Vers li m'en vois maintenant,
    Mis l' a reson:
"Bele, dites moi conment,
    Pour Dieu, vous avez non."   2.4
Et ele saut tout errant
    A son baston:
"Se vous venez plus avant,
    Ja avroiz la tençon.   2.8
Sire, fuiez vous de ci!
N'ai cure de tel ami,
Car j'ai mult plus biau choisi,
    Qu'en claime Robeçon."   2.12

Quant je la vi esfreer
    Si durement
Qu'el ne mi daigne esgarder
    Ne fere autre senblant,   3.4
Lors conmençai a penser
    Confaitement
Ele me porroit amer
    Et changier son talent.   3.8
A terre lez li m'assis;
Quant plus regart son cler vis,
Tant est plus mes cuers espris,
    Qui double mon talent.   3.12

Lors li pris a demander
    Mult belement
Que me daignast esgarder
    Et fere autre senblant.   4.4
Ele conmence a plorer
    Et dist itant:
"Je ne vos puis esgarder,
    Ne sai qu'alez querant."   4.8
Vers li me trais, si li di:
"Ma bele, pour Dieu, merci!"
Ele rist, si respondi:
    "Nou faites pour la gent."   4.12

As I was out riding on my palfrey
all alone
the other day, thinking
of composing a song,
I heard near a hedge
(I can't say how)
the voice of the loveliest child
a man could ever have seen,
though she was not really a child
and must have been fifteen and a half;
never before had I seen a creature
of so pleasing a stamp.

I went up to her right away
and started to speak:
"Do please tell me, dear girl,
what your name is."
And she jumped right up,
staff in hand:
"If you take another step,
you're in for trouble!
Go away from here, my lord!
I've no interest in your kind of friend;
my eye is on a much handsomer one,
a fellow named Robin."

When I saw her so thoroughly
perturbed
that she disdained to look at me
or show any other response,
I began to wonder
in what way
she could come to love me
and feel a change of heart.
I sat down on the ground beside her;
the more I looked at her fair face,
the more my heart burned
and doubled my desire.

Then I decided to ask her,
very properly,
to deign to look at me
and show me some other response.
She started to weep
and then said,
"I can't look at you;
I don't know what you want."
I drew up close and said,
"Mercy, dear girl, in God's name!"
She laughed and replied,
"Don't! There are people around!"

Devant moi lors la montai	Right away, I set her in the saddle
De maintenant	in front of me
Et trestout droit m'en alai	and rode straight off
Vers un bois verdoiant. 5.4	to a green-leafed wood.
Aval les prez regardai,	I looked across the fields
S'oï criant	and heard two shepherds
Deus pastors parmi un blé	shouting as they came
Qui venoient huiant 5.8	through the wheat,
Et leverent un haut cri.	raising a hue and cry.
Assez fis plus que ne di;	I did rather more than I'm saying;
Je la les, si m'en foï:	I left her behind and took flight:
N'oi cure de tel gent. 5.12	I had no interest in such people.

L'autrier par la matinee   (L 240-33)
Pastourelle

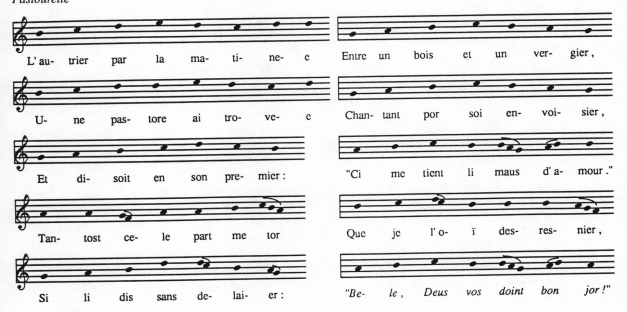

L'autrier par la matinee	The other day in the morning,
Entre un bois et un vergier,	between the woods and an orchard,
Une pastore ai trovee	I came across a shepherdess
Chantant por soi envoisier,	singing for her pleasure;
Et disoit en son premier: 1.5	her first song went,
"Ci me tient li maus d'amours."	"I'm overcome by the pain of love."
Tantost cele part me tor	At once I turned toward
Que je l'oï desresnier,	where I heard her trilling,
Si li dis sans delaier:	and didn't wait to say,
"Bele, Deus vos doint bon jor!" 1.10	"God give you a good day, dear girl!"

Mon salu sanz demoree
Me rendi et sanz targier;
Mult ert fresche, coloree,
Si mi plot a acointier.
"Bele, vostre amor vos quier,   2.5
S'avrez de moi riche ator."
Ele respont: "Tricheor
Sont mes trop li chevalier;
Melz aim Perrin mon bergier
Que riche honme menteor."   2.10

"Bele, ce ne dites mie.
Chevalier sont trop vaillant.
Qui set donc avoir amie
Ne servir a son talent
Fors chevalier et tel gent?   3.5
Mais l'amor d'un bergeron
Certes ne vaut un bouton.
Partez vos en a itant
Et m'amez; je vous creant,
De moi avrés riche don."   3.10

"Sire, par sainte Marie,
Vos en parlés por noient.
Mainte dame avront trichie
Cil chevalier soudoiant;
Trop sont faus et mal pensant,   4.5
Pis valent que Guenelon.
Je m'en revois en maison,
Car Perrinés qui m'atent
M'aime de cuer loiaument.
Abaissiés vostre raison."   4.10

G'entendi bien la bergiere,
Qu'ele me veut eschaper;
Mult li fis longue priere,
Mais n'i poi riens conquester.
Lors la pris a acoler   5.5
Et ele gete un haut cri:
"Perrinet, traï! traï!"
Dou bois prenent a huper.
Je la lez sans demorer,
Seur mon cheval m'en parti.   5.10

Quant ele m'en vit aler,
Ele dist par ranponer:
"Chevalier sont trop hardi!"   E.3 (10)

She returned my greeting
right away, without a pause;
she was hearty and glowing,
and I was pleased to meet her.
"Dear girl, I ask for your love,
and I'll give you something precious to wear."
She answered, "Knights these days
are awful tricksters;
I'd rather have my shepherd Pete
than a rich man who's a liar."

"Don't say that, dear girl.
Knights are awfully vigorous.
Who can offer his sweetheart
all the service she wants,
except a knight or his like?
The love of a shepherd-boy, though,
isn't worth a button.
Leave the fellow, then,
and love me; I promise you
you'll have a precious gift from me."

"By holy Mary, my lord,
you're wasting your words.
Many a lady has been tricked
by those knights out for hire;
they're false and evil-minded,
far worse than Ganelon.
I'm going back home;
my Pete, who is there waiting,
loves me with all his heart.
There's no need for any more words."

I realized that the shepherdess
wanted to get away from me;
I went on at length
but failed to make headway.
Then I put my arms around her,
and she let out a cry:
"Pete, help! help!"
Shouts came from the woods.
I left her at once
and rode away on my horse.

When she saw me go,
she threw me a rebuke:
"Knights are awfully bold!"

RICHARD DE FOURNIVAL

Son of the king's physician, Richard de Fournival, born in Amiens in 1201, acquired probably in Paris the basis of the vast, encyclopedic learning for which he came to be widely respected. He was, inter alia, a surgeon, canon of Rouen, chancellor of the cathedral of Amiens, and the creator of an exceptional library. He died in 1259 or 1260. Apart from a score of lyric pieces, mainly courtly love songs, Richard de Fournival was the author of several didactic works in Latin and in French, especially the latter, including three arts of love and his best-known work, the *Bestiaire d'amours.*

EDITIONS: Zarifopol 1904; Lepage 1981.

- "Quant chante oisiauz tant seri": L 223-14, RS 1080, MW 538. Sources: ms. M, also Ta; music in all. Attribution to Richard in all mss. RT 376-378/626-629; Zarifopol 1904, 32-33; Lepage 1981, 85-88.

This poem is especially noteworthy for the way in which the stanzas are linked through rhyme. The *a* and *b* rhymes are identical in stanzas 1, 3, and 5, and are reversed in stanzas 2 and 4 (*coblas retrogradadas*), the first rhyme of each stanza being the same as the last of the preceding stanza (*coblas capcaudadas*). The *c* rhyme occurs only once in each stanza (*rim estramp*) but is carried throughout the poem by the single word *esperance.*

The melody is not built upon a well-defined scale; it is instead made up of composite material, as shown by the cadences of the lines: *c, a, g, f.* This is true not only of the reading in ms. M but of the others as well; thus, T, in comparison, shows partial transpositions of the melodic material in lines 1, 3, 4, and 5. Along with these heterogeneous transpositions, the through-composed scheme of the piece—ABCDEFG—suggests the work of a singer performing inventively.

Quant chante oisiauz tant seri (L 223-14)
Chanson d'amour

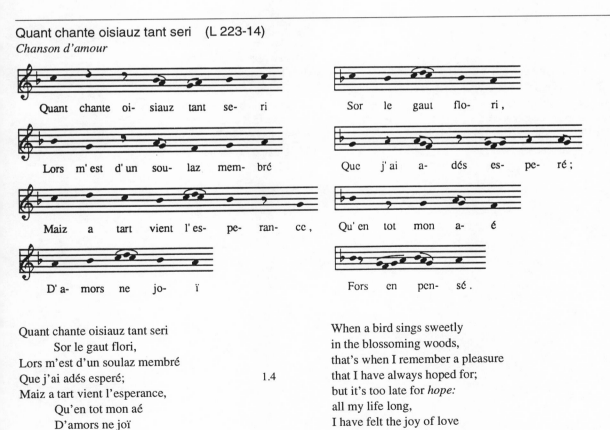

Quant chante oisiauz tant seri
    Sor le gaut flori,
Lors m'est d'un soulaz membré
Que j'ai adés esperé;   1.4
Maiz a tart vient l'esperance,
    Qu'en tot mon aé
    D'amors ne joï
        Fors en pensé.   1.8

When a bird sings sweetly
in the blossoming woods,
that's when I remember a pleasure
that I have always hoped for;
but it's too late for *hope:*
all my life long,
I have felt the joy of love
only in my imagination.

Tant m'a Amors honoré
    Et tant m'a doné,
Por quant que j'ai desservi,
Qu'ele m'en a fait hardi   2.4
Et m'a de bone esperance
    Mon fin cuer guarni
    Et asseüré
          D'avoir merci.   2.8

Quar, se je mesfis vers li
    Et je l'en perdi,
Je l'ai trop chier comperé,
Se j'ai puis adés celé   3.4
Mon anui, en esperance
    Qu'el ne m'ait grevé
    Fors por son ami
          Avoir prové.   3.8

Et se pluz l'ai eschivé
    Qu'il n'i ot dehé,
Por ce que trop la cremi,
Ja si tart ne m'iert meri   4.4
Que bien ne quit m'esperance
    Avoir acompli,
    Car tot preing en gré
          Et l'en merci.   4.8

Chançon, va t'en, si li di
    Que quant j'entendi
Qu'ele m'ot congié doné,
Se ne m'eüst conforté   5.4
Haute emprise et esperance,
    J'eüsse adiré
    Gai cuer et joli,
          Que j'ai gardé.   5.8

Love has honored me this much,
has granted me this much
(for whatever I deserve):
she has made me bold
and with good *hope*
filled my pure heart
and made me confident
of finding mercy.

If I misbehaved toward her
and thereby lost her,
I have paid all too dear a price
by always hiding my pain
ever since, in the *hope*
that she hurt me
only as a test
of my love.

And even if I have avoided her
more than her dislike warranted
(avoided her out of fear),
my reward will come, and not so late
that I won't deem my *hope*
thereby fulfilled,
for I accept whatever comes
and thank her for it.

Song, go now and tell her this:
when I heard
that she'd given me my leave,
if I had not had the comfort
of a noble task and *hope,*
I would have lost
my light and joyful heart;
but I have kept it.

JEAN ERART

The name Jean Erart is thought to designate two different trouvères, probably father and son, both belonging to the same literary milieu of Arras and both dying in 1258 or 1259. There is no clear distinction between the lyric compositions of one and the other. More than a score of pieces, half of them *pastourelles*, are attributed to Jean Erart.

EDITIONS: Newcombe 1972; Newcombe 1975.

● "Nus chanters mais le mien cuer ne leeche": L 154-18, RS 485, MW 1477. Single source: ms. T; music. Attribution to Jean Erart. RT 429-431/726-729; Newcombe 1972, 129-132; Newcombe 1975, 21. Performed on Anthology CD.

Dialectal features: Picard, including *saiges* = Central Fr. *sages, usaige = usage, teche = tache; aus = eus, ceaus = ceus; boin = bon; pule = pueple; leeche = leece, chil = cil, piech'a = pieç'a; departis = departiz, grans = granz, mors = morz, tos = to(u)z; jou = je, çou = ce; le = la, me = ma; men = mon; avera = avra; mece = mete, endece = endete, demece = demete, promece = promete*. Note, too, in 5.2, *mes as = m'as*.

Of the few lyric *plaintes funèbres,* or death-laments, in Old French, all concern a belovèd except this one, which mourns the passing of Jean's protector, a certain *Gherart,* and concludes with an appeal for new sources of support.

5.5-6ff: Henri and Robert Crespin belonged to one of the richest and most powerful families of thirteenth-century Arras. Pierre and Vaugon Guion, named in the envoy, were brothers in a family of financiers in the same city; Pierre died in 1268 and Vaugon in 1272-1273.

6.1: The word *serventois* is a very imprecise term applied in Old French to various songs of a polemical character touching on contemporary moral or political questions but also to some pieces of a more personal stamp; sometimes it is used to refer somewhat dismissively to any poem. The term comes from the Occitan *sirventes,* which is a more meaningful lyric genre designation but which has etymologically the sense of 'servant's song'.

Homogeneous in *g,* with an *f#* which we suggest although it is not indicated in the manuscript, the melody lends itself, with its syllabic style and its regular scheme (ABAB′B″CD), to a metrical rhythm and even dancing.

Nus chanters mais le mien cuer ne leeche   (L 154-18)
Serventois, plainte funèbre

Nus   chan- ters   mais   le   mien   cuer   ne   le- e- che

Des   ke   chil   est   del   sie-   cle   de-   par-   tis

Ki   des   ho-   nors   iert   la   voie   et   l'a-   dre-   che,

Lar-   ges,   cor-   tois,   sai-   ges,   nes   de   mes-   dis.

Grans   do-   lors   est   ke   si   tost   est   fe-   nis ;

A   oés   tos   ceaus   a   cui   es-   toit   a-   mis,

D'aus   ho-   no-   rer   et   ai-   dier   n'ot   pe-   re-   ce.

Nus chanters mais le mien cuer ne leeche		No more can any singing gladden my heart
Des ke chil est del siecle departis		now that from this world the man has departed
Ki des honors iert la voie et l'adreche,		who was the route and road of honor,
Larges, cortois, saiges, nes de mesdis.	1.4	generous, courteous, wise, a stranger to gossip.
Grans dolors est ke si tost est fenis;		It is a great sorrow that he is gone so soon;
A oés tos ceaus a cui estoit amis,		to benefit any of those to whom he was a friend
D'aus honorer et aidier n'ot perece.	1.7	he was never slow to offer honor or help.
Gherart, amis, la toie mors me blece,		Gerard, my friend, your death pains me
Quant me sosvient des biens ke me fesis.		when I recall how good you were to me.
Dieus, ki en crois soffri mort et destreche		May God, who suffered death and torment
Pour son pule jeter des andecris,	2.4	to save his people from the antichrists,
Le vos rengë ensi com jou devis;		reward you for it, as I wish;
K'il vous otroit le sien saint paradis:		may He admit you to his holy heaven:
Bien avés deservi c'om vos i mece.	2.7	you have well deserved a place there.
Mors, villaine iés, en toi n'a gentillece,		Death, you are base, with no nobility,
Car tu as trop villainement mespris;		for you have made a base mistake;
Bien deüssiés esparnier le jonece,		you should spare the youthful man,
Et le cortois, le large, au siecle mis.	3.4	the courteous, the generous set down in this world.
Mais tel usaige as de piech'a apris		But long ago you learned a behavior
Ke nus n'en iert tensés ne garandis,		from which no one can be protected or secured,
Ne haus ne bas, jonece ne viellece.	3.7	neither high-born nor low, neither young nor old.

N'i puet valoir ne avoirs ne richesse
Contre la mort; de çou soit chascuns fis.
Pour çou se fait boin garder c'on n'endece
L'armë en tant ke on n'i soit sospris.   4.4
Ki en honor et em bien faire iert pris
Et avra Dieu par ses biens fais conquis,
Il avera faite boine pröeche.   4.7

Mors, tolu m'as et men blé et me veche
Et mes cortieus; tos les mes as ravis.
Bien est raisons ke me joie demece
Puis ke tu m'as tolu et jeu et ris.   5.4
Bien mi deüst reconforter Henris,
Robers Crespins, ou j'ai mon espoir mis:
En ceaus ne sai nule mauvaise teche.   5.7

Des serventois va t'en tos aatis;
Signeur Pieron Wyon et Wagon dis
Ke petit truis ki me doinst ne promece.   E.3 (7)

Nothing avails, neither power nor wealth,
against death; everyone can be certain of that,
and so it is good to avoid indebting
one's soul, lest one be taken without warning.
A man of honor taken while doing good works,
a man whose good works have won him God's favor,
will have accomplished a deed of great prowess.

Death, you have stripped me of my wheat and vetch
and my garden; you have robbed me of all.
It is only right that I should put aside joy
now that you have stripped me of cheer and laughter.
Comfort ought to come to me from Henry
and Robert Crespin, in whom I have placed my hope:
I see no bad trait in them.

Go now, most eager of servers' songs;
tell Sir Peter Guyon and Vaugon that I find
few men who will give or promise me anything.

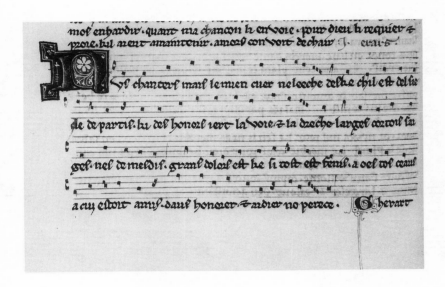

Jean Erart, "Nvs chanters mais le mien cuer ne leeche" (p. 320). Ms. T, 130v, bottom.
Cliché Bibliothèque Nationale de France - Paris.

PHILIPPE DE REMY

Philippe de Remy, sire de Beaumanoir, was a royal administrator and a writer of romances and lyric poetry, born ca. 1205-1210 in the Beauvaisis and probably deceased by 1265. He was part of the literary world of Arras. Since he was the father of the well-known jurist of the same name, scholars tended until recently to confuse his career with that of the younger man. Philippe the elder is now generally acknowledged to be the composer of ten lyric pieces, along with better known works, especially the romances *La Manekine* and *Jehan et Blonde*.

EDITION: Jeanroy 1897.

● "Or me respondez, Amours": L 199-6, RS 2029, MW 1494. Single source: ms. V; music. Attribution to Philippe. RT 530-532/682-685; Jeanroy 1897, 535-536.

This *tenson* is one of only four Old French lyric dialogues with the allegorical figure of Love.

4.7-8: The unusual imperfection of the rhyme *mout : clamours* leads us to think that *finz mout* may be a scribal error for *amours*, in which case these verses would mean 'for through false claims it (=what he is expressing) resembles love'.

The music of the last three syllables of line 2 is missing; a singer may fill in with the cadence of either line 4 or 6. The first half of the melody is in the Lydian, or *f*, scale, while the *cauda* concludes on *d*. The melodic scheme is irregular, though the pattern of its cadences (*f f f f / c a d a d*) provides it with a *diesis:* ABAC DC'EFG.

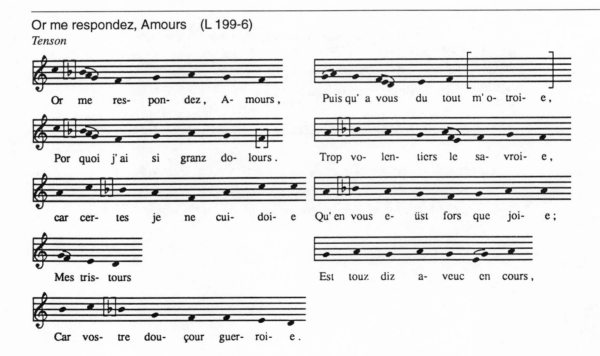

Or me respondez, Amours,
Puis qu'a vous du tout m'otroie,
Por quoi j'ai si granz dolours.
Trop volentiers le savroie,   1.4
Car certes je ne cuidoie
Qu'en vous eüst fors que joie;
    Mes tristours
Est touz diz aveuc en cours,
Car vostre douçour guerroie.   1.9

Now answer me, love,
since I grant myself wholly to you:
Why do I have such great sorrows?
I would very gladly know,
for I certainly never thought
that there was anything in you but joy;
but pain
is always in competition,
at war with your gentleness.

— Ge.l vous dirai, amis douz:
Se chascun confort donnoie
Si tost c'on fet l'amourous,
Trop mainz prisiee en seroie;　　　2.4
Por ce m'esteut qu'aspre soie
Por oster hors de ma voie
　　　　Tricheours,
Car c'est ma plus granz paours
Que mauvés de moi n'ait joie.　　　2.9

— De ce m'acort bien a vous,
A tort vous en blameroie;
Mes de ce sui mout irous
Que j'esgart, quant faux cuers proie　　3.4
Il set mieus trouver la voie
De vous trere a sa corroie
　　　　Que tretouz
Ceus qui se tienent a vous,
Car qui mieus aime pis proie.　　　3.9

— Biaus amis, c'est la dolours
Dont mes finz mestiers s'effroie;
Mes il i a tant priours,
Por rienz touz ne.s connistroie.　　　4.4
Compere fausse monnoie
A celui qui ainsi proie,
　　　　Car finz mout
Semble par fausses clamours;
Par ce mon senz me desvoie.　　　4.9

— Or vous pardoing mon corrous,
Amours, et a vous m'otroie;
Quant vous haez traïtours,
A tort aussi vous harroie.　　　5.4
Mes de la simple, la coie,
M'aidiez que ele soit moie,
　　　　Car si douz
Sont si maintieng savourous
Que sienz sui, ou que je soie.　　　5.9

I will tell you, good friend:
If I gave comfort to everyone
as soon as he started playing the lover,
I would be far less appreciated;
and so I must be harsh
to clear my path
of tricksters,
for my greatest fear
is that a scoundrel will find joy in me.

On that I agree with you
and would be wrong to blame you;
but what disturbs me so much
is to see that a mere pretender at love
is more successful
in leashing you and pulling you along
than all
those who are truly yours,
for he who loves best is worst at wooing.

Dear friend, that is the pain
that my pure work fears;
but there are so many suitors
that I could never know them all.
A man who woos like that
is like counterfeit money,
for with false claims
he closely resembles a true lover;
it makes me lose my mind!

Now forgive me my anger,
love, and I yield to you;
since you hate traitors,
I would be wrong to hate you.
But that modest, quiet woman now —
help me to make her mine,
for her charming ways
are so sweet
that I am hers, wherever I may be.

PERRIN D'ANGICOURT

Probably born in the Beauvaisis, Perrin d'Angicourt was active in the literary circles of Arras and the court of Brabant mainly between 1245 and 1250. Later, he may have been part of the entourage of Charles d'Anjou in Italy. Some thirty lyric compositions are attributed to him, chiefly *chansons d'amour.*

EDITION: Steffens 1905.

● "Quant partiz sui de Prouvence": L 192-23, RS 625, MW 2285. Sources: ms. N, also KRVXZ; one melody in KNXZ, a second in R, a third in V. Attribution to Perrin in KNX. RT 411-414/698-703; Steffens 1905, 214-218.

The only notable dialectal form is Picard *envoïe* = Central Fr. *envoiee.*

In addition to authorship, the rubric in ms. X indicates that this song was "crowned" (*coronee*) with a prize. It seems to have been composed ca. 1250.

2.3: *France* here designates the north, in contrast to *Prouvence* in 1.1.

The melody, given here in the N reading, is focused on *c,* the tone of instrument-playing jongleurs. The scheme is of the *pedes cum cauda* type (ABAB CDC′D′ EFGH), with a well-developed cauda (lines 5-12).

● "Quant je voi l'erbe amatir": L 192-19, RS 1390, MW 1246, B 1133/426/1638/289. Sources: ms. K, also NOVX; one melody in KNOX, another in V. Attribution to Perrin in KNX. RT 420-422/714-717; Steffens 1905, 241-242.

All four stanzas of this *chanson avec des refrains* are linked not only by a constant *b* rhyme but also through the device of *coblas capfinidas,* which here serves too to integrate the refrains into the main text. The device entails beginning each stanza with the word or phrase that ended the preceding stanza.

1.8: The term *motet,* here as in 2.8, refers to the brief refrain, the 'little word', that follows, rather than the entire song.

The melody of O, presented here, is written a fifth higher than the music in KNX. It is syllabic and is built on *g* with tenor on *c* (lines 1, 2, 3, 4) and on *d* (lines 5, 6, 7, 8), thereby fluctuating between a plagal configuration of the scale and an authentic. Subfinal *f* is stated in lines 1, 3, 8. Note the ornamental triolet occurring three times in the refrain. The melodic scheme is the classic *pedes cum cauda:* ABAB CDEF/refrain G.

Quant partiz sui de Prouvence   (L 192-23)

Chanson d'amour

Quant partiz sui de Prouvence		Having left Provence		
Et du tens felon,		and the cruel season,		
Ai voloir que je conmence		I wish to begin		
Nouvele chançon	1.4	a gay		
Jolie		new song		
Et qu'en chantant prie		and in singing ask		
Bone Amour		true love		
Que tant de douçor	1.8	to put so much tenderness		
Mete a mon chant conmencier		into the beginning of my song		
Qu'ele me face cuidier		that I'll be led to think		
Que ma douce dame daigne vouloir		my dear lady deigns to want		
Que ja la puisse a son gré revooir.	1.12	me to please her with a visit.		
Atorné m'est a enfance		It is considered childish of me		
Et a mesprison		and a mistake,		
Li desirs d'aler en France		this reasonable desire of mine		
Que j'ai par reson.	2.4	to go to France.		
Folie		It is foolish		
Fet qui me chastie		for anyone to rebuke me		
Se j'ator		if I ready		
Mon cuer au retor,	2.8	my heart for the return,		
Quant je ne le puis lessier;		since I cannot leave it behind;		
Car tout autre desirrier		for I am made indifferent		
Me fet metre du tout en nonchaloir		to every other desire by the lady		
Cele sanz qui riens ne me puet valoir.	2.12	without whom nothing is worthwhile.		

De biauté et de vaillance
A si grant foison,
Lués que g'en oi conoissance,
Mis en sa prison   3.4
Ma vie.
Je ne mesfaz mie
Se j'aor
Et aim la meillor,   3.8
Car pour ce m'aim j' et tien chier
Que je sui en son dangier.
Deus! Quant g'i pens, je ne m'ai dont doloir,
Et mes pensers i est sanz ja mouvoir.   3.12

Sousfrir loial penitance
Me senble plus bon
Que avoir par decevance
Ne par traïson   4.4
Amie.
Fausse drüerie
Sanz savor
Ont li tricheor,   4.8
Q'il conquierent par pledier.
Tel joie ne m'a mestier;
Dou porchacier n'aie je ja pouoir!
J'aim melz languir que fausse joie avoir.   4.12

Onques n'oi cuer ne vueillance
Ne entencion
Que je feïsse senblance
D'amer s'a droit non.   5.4
Polie
Langue apareillie
A folor
En set bien le tor;   5.8
Mes ce n'i puet riens aidier,
Qu'a la parole afetier
Puet on choisir qui bee a decevoir;
Et Deus en lest ma dame apercevoir!   5.12

Fenie,
Chançon, envoïe
Sanz demor
Seras a la flor   E.4 (8)
Des dames, a droit jugier;
Et par pitié li reqier,
S'eürs te fet devant li aparoir,
Q'il li plese que je vive en espoir.   E.8 (12)

She has beauty and virtue
in such abundance
that as soon as I met her
I put my life
into her prison.
I am not making a mistake
to love
and adore the finest woman,
for it makes me love and value myself
to be held in her power. God!
when I think of it, I have no cause for grief,
and my thoughts never waver.

Suffering penance with fidelity
seems better to me
than winning your lady
with deception
and betrayal.
The affection of tricksters
is false
and insipid,
gained through clever pleading.
Such joy is worthless to me;
may I never be able to seek it!
I'd rather pine away than have false joy.

I have never had the heart or will
or the intention
to pretend
to be in love.
A polished
tongue, trained
in lechery,
knows how to go about it;
but it can't really help,
for by his turn of phrase
you can spot the would-be hypocrite.
May God let my lady realize it!

Finished,
song, you will be sent
with no delay
to the very flower (no doubt of it!)
of womanhood;
and if luck brings you to her attention,
I ask that she be moved
to grant that I live in hope.

Quant je voi l'erbe amatir   (L 192-19)
Chanson d'amour, avec des refrains

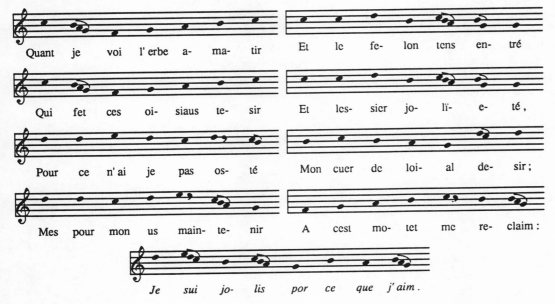

Quant je voi l'erbe amatir	Though I see the grass stop growing
Et le felon tens entré	and the cruel season come
Qui fet ces oisiaus tesir	that makes the birds keep still
Et lessier jolïeté, 1.4	and grow less cheerful,
Pour ce n'ai je pas osté	I have not relieved
Mon cuer de loial desir;	my heart of faithful longing;
Mes pour mon us maintenir	but to stay true to my wont
A cest motet me reclaim:	I turn to this brief word:
Je sui jolis por ce que j'aim. 1.9	*I am cheerful because I'm in love.*
J'aim loiaument sanz traïr,	I love faithfully, with no deceit,
Sanz faindre et sanz fausseté	with no second thoughts or falsity,
Cele qui me fet languir	the woman who makes me languish
Sanz avoir de moi pité 2.4	and takes no pity on me
Et bien set de verité	though she well knows for a truth
Que je sui siens sanz guenchir,	that I am inescapably hers;
Mes en espoir de joïr	but in the hope of succeeding
Li ert cest motet chantez:	I'll sing her this brief word:
Dame, merci! Vos m'ocïez. 2.9	*My lady, mercy! You are killing me.*
Vous m'ocïez sanz reson,	You are killing me for no reason,
Dame sanz humilité.	lady with no humility!
Ne pert pas a vo façon	It is not obvious, to look at you,
Qu'en vo cuer ait cruauté, 3.4	that your heart is cruel,
Mes grant debonereté;	but only gracious;
Pour ce sui g' en soupeçon;	that is why I am apprehensive;
Simple vis et cuer felon	an unassuming face and wicked heart
M'ont mis en grant desconfort.	have brought me great discomfort.
Sa biauté m'a mort. 3.9	*Her beauty has slain me.*

Mort m'a sanz point d'acheson
Cele en qui j'ai atorné
Mon sens et m'entencion
Pour fere sa volenté.   4.4
S'or le daignoit prendre en gré,
Pour tout autre guerredon
Mis m'avroit fors de friçon,
Si diroie sanz esmai:
Bone amor que j'ai mi tient gai.   4.9

Slain me without the slightest grounds
she has, though I have concentrated
my mind and my attention
on accomplishing her will.
If she deigned to accept that,
that more than any other reward
would relieve me of anxiety,
and I would have no trouble saying:
The true love I feel keeps me joyful.

JEAN BRETEL

Born ca. 1200, Jean Bretel belonged to the rich bourgeoisie of Arras, in whose literary world he seems to have become active around 1245. It was not long before his fellow-trouvères chose him to be *prince du Puy*, or head of the poets' circle, and he remained in that position until his death in 1272. About one hundred lyric pieces are attributed to Jean Bretel, almost all of them *jeux-partis* which he composed above all with Jean de Grieviler, Lambert Ferri, and Adam de la Halle.

EDITION: Långfors 1926 (1).

• "Grieviler, vostre ensïent": L 133-45, RS 668, MW 2191. Sources: ms. a, also AGZb; music in AZa. Attribution to Jean Bretel in b. RT 478-482/800-805; Långfors 1926 (1), 98-102.

Dialectal features: Picard, including *faus* = Central Fr. *fous; ju = gieu; raisnaulement = raisnablement; çou = ce; chele = cele, coisi = choisi, kaï = chaï.*

Jean Bretel's partner in this *jeu-parti* is Jean de Grieviler, who is asked to state whether he would prefer ordinary beauty and great intelligence in his mistress, or ordinary intelligence and great beauty. Grieviler chooses the first combination. *Dragon* and *Demoiselle Oede* are asked to judge the debate.

5.3-4: These lines, referring to the great trouvère Thibaut de Champagne, king of Navarre, himself a participant in a number of *jeux-partis*, have been interpreted in various ways, largely because both *grant sens* and *desfendi* are ambiguous terms. The verb may mean either 'defended' or 'rejected', and the noun may either have the same reference as it has had in the poem up to this point or mean the 'intelligent, reasonable opinion', i.e., that beauty is more to be prized than intelligence. It is worth noting that the single surviving *jeu-parti* in which Thibaut confronts this issue (or, rather, one that is very similar) shows him defending the case of beauty. What strikes us as more compelling, however, is that in his reply (st. 6) to these verses, Jean Bretel obviously takes them to mean that Thibaut preferred beauty. Our translation reflects this interpretation.

The three melodies preserved are all different. Nevertheless, ms. a, which we present, and A have points in common both in their *pedes cum cauda* scheme (ABAB CDEFGH) and in their melodic development; often at line openings, A is a fourth or a fifth higher than a. Lines 4, 8, and 10 in A are hypermetric and show irregularities of copying; ms. a is more precise, which is true of tonality as well. In a, the scale of *g* is clearly affirmed. We suggest the subtonic *f#* in lines 9-10, but a singer should feel free to disregard the two *f#* in favor of tritones, whose modal coloring is remarkable.

Grieviler, vostre ensïent   (L 133-45)
Jeu-parti

Grie-vi-ler, vostre en-si-ent   Me di-tes d'un ju par-ti:

Se vous a-més loi-au-ment   Et on vous aime au-tre-si,

Li qieus se-ra mieus vos grés,   U che-le qui vous a-més

Se-ra be-le par rai-son   Et sage a tres grant fui-son,

U sa-ge rais-nau-le-ment   Et tres bele ou-tre-e-ment?

Grieviler, vostre ensïent		Grieviler, give me your opinion
Me dites d'un ju parti:		in this dilemma.
Se vous amés loiaument		If you love faithfully
Et on vous aime autresi,		and are loved in return,
Li qieus sera mieus vos grés,	1.5	which will you prefer:
U chele qui vous amés		that the woman you love
Sera bele par raison		be reasonably attractive
Et sage a tres grant fuison,		and exceptionally intelligent,
U sage raisnaulement		or reasonably intelligent
Et tres bele outreement?	1.10	and extraordinarily beautiful?
— Sire Jehan, bel present		My lord John, that's a fine proposal
M'offrés et j'ai bien coisi.		you offer me, and I've made my choice.
Pour plus vivre longuement		In order to live longer
Sans estre jalous de li,		and not grow jealous of her,
Veil que ses cuers soit fondés	2.5	I want her heart to be grounded
En sens, puis que bele assés		in intelligence (assuming she's attractive);
Est; sens est sans soupechon.		a good mind doesn't provoke suspicion.
Biautés a plus cuer felon:		Beauty has a more deceitful heart:
Orgeus i maint, qui souvent		pride dwells there, which often
Muet grant joie en grant tourment.	2.10	turns great joy into torment.
— Grieviler, biautés n'entent		Grieviler, beauty doesn't listen
Ne n'ot ne voit, je vous di,		or hear or see, I tell you,
Ne n'a nul apensement		and it has no intention
De griété faire a ami;		of causing a lover any pain;
Mais tres grant sens est fondés	3.5	but great intelligence is grounded
De felounie et retés		in deceit and readily accused
D'orguel et de traïson,		of pride and betrayal,
Et par si fait cas pert on;		and you can lose that way;
Et biautés doune talent		beauty, though, always spurs you on
Toutans d'amer asprement.	3.10	to ardent love.

— Sire, sachiés vraiement	My lord, know for a fact
Grant biautés enorgeilli	that great beauty was the cause
Lucifer, qui trop vilment	of Lucifer's pride, which led
Dedens infer en kaï;	to his base fall into hell;
Par grant sens n'est pas dampnés.　4.5	it wasn't a great mind that damned him.
Par sens est deduis menés.	Intelligence lets you feel pleasure.
Puis que ma dame a le non	Assuming my lady is with all reasonableness
Que bele est par grant raison,	acknowledged to be beautiful,
Del sens ait abondamment	let her have a keen mind,
Pour mieus amer fermement.　4.10	all the better to love.

— Grieviler, mauvaisement	Grieviler, that's a poor
Respondés, je vous afi.	response, I assure you.
Li rois u Navare apent	The king who rules Navarre
Le tres grant sens desfendi	defended the sensible opinion,
Qu'en aucun point est sieunés,　5.5	which in some quarters is rejected;
Mais tres grant fine biautés	but great, true beauty
Est tout adés en saison.	is always the right choice.
Pour tres grant biauté aim' on	Great beauty is a hundred times
Plus ferm et plus taillaument	stronger and sharper a spur
Que pour grant sens contre un cent.　5.10	to love than great intelligence.

— Sire, si sauvagement	My lord, I have never before
Ains mais parler ne vous vi.	heard you speak so thoughtlessly.
S'uns rois parla folement	Just because a king spoke foolishly,
Volés vous faire autresi?	must you do the same?
Bons sens n'ert ja refusés　6.5	A good mind will never be scorned
Se çou n'est de faus dervés.	except by foolish madmen.
Amours vous done tel don	Love gives you the power
K'adés bele amie a on	to see beauty in your lover
Puis c'on aime corelment.	as soon as you're in love.
Al grant sens pour çou m'asent.　6.10	That's why I choose intelligence.

— Dragon, vous nous jugerés,	Dragon, you shall be our judge.
Je di, et s'est verités,	I say, and it's the truth,
Que pour le sens Salemon	that a man loves Marion
N'aime on pas tant Marion	less for her Solomonic intelligence
C'on fait pour son bel jouvent,	than for her beautiful youth,
C'on n'aime pas sagement.　E1.6 (10)	for we do not love with the mind.

— Demisele Oede, entendés.	My lady Oda, hear me.
Je di qu'il est faus prouvés	I say that whoever thinks like that
Qui a tele entencion.	is a proven fool.
Bons sens dure duq'en son,	A good mind lasts to the end,
Mais n'est, a droit jugement,	while beauty, to judge aright,
Biautés c'un trespas de vent.　E2.6 (10)	is just a passing breeze.

ADAM DE LA HALLE

Adam de la Halle, also known as Adam le Bossu, was the foremost musician, poet, and playwright of Arras, where he was born sometime between 1240 and 1250 and where, before and after the studies in Paris that earned him the title of *maître ès arts,* he spent much of his life. Around 1280 he entered the service of Robert II, count of Artois, with whom he traveled to Italy to join the French court of Naples. It is probable that he died in Italy in 1288. Adam composed about one hundred lyric pieces of divers genres, polyphonic (*rondeaux,* motets) as well as monophonic. The most notable of his various other works are two comic plays, the *Jeu de la Feuillée* and the *Jeu de Robin et Marion,* the second of which is a kind of dramatization of *pastourelle* material.

STUDY: Maillard 1982.

EDITIONS: Coussemaker 1872; Berger 1900; Nicod 1917; Wilkins 1967; Marshall 1971; van der Werf 1979; Nelson 1985.

● *"A Dieu commant amouretes":* MW 919; B rond. 73, refr. 12. Single source: ms. W; music. Attribution to Adam. RT 483-484/838-841; Gennrich 1921, 60-61; Wilkins 1967, 60-61; Boogaard 1969, 52-53; Maillard 1982, 125.

Like the next piece, this is one of Adam's sixteen polyphonic *rondeaux.* For a discussion of this type and the simpler *rondet de carole,* see Bec 1977, chapter 16.

The three-part rondeau-conductus is meant for dancing. The melodies of the quite ornate upper voice and of the tenor are in *f,* with the middle voice in *c.* The textual and melodic cyclicity is normal for a rondeau with a three-line refrain:

Line	1 2 3 / 4 5 / 6 7 / 8 9 10/ 11 12 13
Text: rhyme scheme	a b c / a b / a b / a b c / a b c
statement	a b c / d e / a b / f g h / a b c
Melody	A B C / A B / A B / A B C / A B C

● *"Hé, Dieus, quant verrai":* MW 282; B rond. 79, refr. 823. Single source: ms. W; music. Attribution to Adam. RT 484-485/842-843; Gennrich 1921, 65; Wilkins 1967, 56; Boogaard 1969, 55; Maillard 1982, 130-131.

Note the Picard form *vir* = Central Fr. *veoir.*

The melody represents an adaptation of the three-part conductus style to the rondeau meant for dancing. The tenor and middle voice are in *f,* while the the upper voice is in *c.* The textual and melodic cyclicity is normal for a rondeau with a two-line refrain:

Line	1 2 / 3 / 4 / 5 6 / 7 8
Text: rhyme scheme	a b / a / a / a b / a b
statement	a b / c / a / d e / a b
Melody	A B / A / A / A B / A B

● *"Jou senc en moi l'amor renouveler":* L 2-18, RS 888, MW 1718. Sources: ms. P, also QRTW; ms. W presents the song twice. Music in all mss. except T. Attribution to Adam in PTW. RT 489-491/850-855; Coussemaker 1872, 31-35; Berger 1900, 135-150; Wilkins 1967, 8; Marshall 1971, 51-53; van der Werf 1979, 558-561; Nelson 1985, 30-33.

Dialectal features: Picard, including *renouviele* = Central Fr. *renouvele, biele = bele, desiert = desert, viers = vers; ju = jeu, mius = mieuz; boine = bone, boins = bons; merchi = merci, chi = ci, largeche = largece; doc = douz; jou = je, chou = ce; le = la; vo = vostre; senc = (je) sent, vienc = (je) vien.*

1.6: Understand word-play here: *ju* as in *jeu d'amour* and as in *jeu-parti* (whence our translation).

2.8: Proverb cited in Morawski (no. 2138).

The melody is the same in all readings, with variants of little significance; we present the second melody of W. A focus on *g* is affirmed by the principal cadences, those of lines 2, 4, and 8; the subtonic *f#* is twice noted by the scribe. The scheme is the very classic ABAB CDEA′.

● *"Dame, vos hom vous estrine":* L 2-5, RS 1383, MW 2397. Sources: ms. W, also PRTa; music in PRW. Attribution to Adam in all mss. RT 494-497/858-863; Coussemaker 1872, 88-92; Berger 1900, 368-415; Wilkins 1967, 23; Marshall 1971, 92-94; van der Werf 1979, 592-596; Nelson 1985, 100-103.

Dialectal features: Picard, including *canchon* = Central Fr. *chançon, capel = chapel, enrachine = enracine, boichon = boiçon; got = joït, sourgon = sourjon; portés = portez, avés = avez, sanlés = semblez; se = sa, me = ma; vos, vo = vostre; chieus = cil; perc = (je) pert; arai = avrai.*

1.2: The song may well be *nouvele* not only in the sense of 'newly composed' but also in that of 'belonging to a new or different type'. As a musical composition, it has the distinction of being Adam's only refrainless *chanson* that is through-composed. As a text, it is much more a personal reprimand than a conventional expression of love.

3.8: Here as in numerous other medieval works, Ganelon, the traitor of the *Chanson de Roland,* provides the standard by which all treachery may be measured.

5.1-4: The point of this somewhat confusing comparison is that the lady is doing the opposite of what is reasonable.

The music in P and R is very similar to that of W, which is the melody presented. Built on the scale of *f* with *b*-flat indicated by the scribe (principal cadence on *f* at the line 4 *diesis* and at the end of the stanza), the melody reveals a through-composed scheme somewhat unusual for the trouvères: ABCDEFGHI. Nevertheless, the melodic features of the song (the melodic movement and the cadences [*c, a, f*]) display a kind of precision quite removed from the tonal indeterminacy of various other trouvère pieces. This is perhaps a style peculiar to Adam de la Halle.

A Dieu commant amouretes
Rondeau

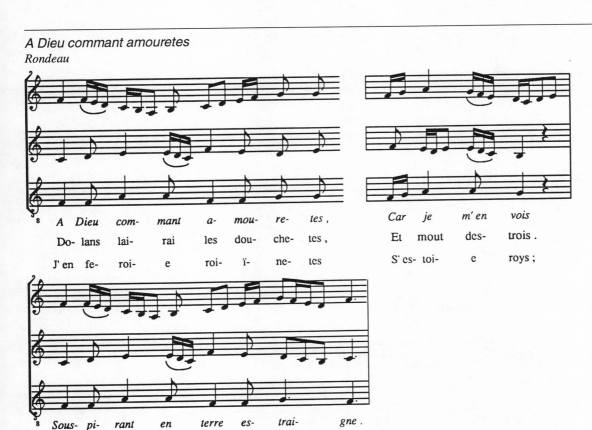

A Dieu com- mant a- mou- re- tes,   Car je m'en vois
Do- lans lai- rai les dou- che- tes,   Et mout des- trois.
J'en fe- roi- e roi- ï- ne- tes   S'es- toi- e roys;

Sous- pi- rant en terre es- trai- gne.
Com- ment que la chose em- prai- gne,

A Dieu commant amouretes,	I commend my loves to God,
Car je m'en vois	for I am leaving
Souspirant en terre estraigne.	with a sigh for foreign lands.
Dolans lairai les douchetes, 4	I'll be sad and very sorry
Et mout destrois.	to leave those sweet young things.
A Dieu commant amouretes,	I commend my loves to God,
Car je m'en vois.	for I am leaving.
J'en feroie roïnetes 8	I would make them little queens
S'estoie roys;	if I were king;
Comment que la chose empraigne,	however I go about it,
A Dieu commant amouretes,	I commend my loves to God,
Car je m'en vois 12	for I am leaving
Souspirant en terre estraigne.	with a sigh for foreign lands.

Hé, Dieus, quant verrai
Rondeau

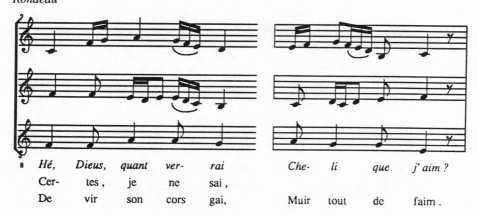

8 Hé,   Dieus,   quant   ver-   rai   Che-   li   que   j'aim?
Cer-   tes,   je   ne   sai,
De   vir   son   cors   gai,   Muir   tout   de   faim.

Hé, Dieus, quant verrai
   Cheli que j'aim?
Certes, je ne sai,
Hé, Dieus, quant verrai.
De vir son cors gai,
   Muir tout de faim.
Hé, Dieus, quant verrai
   Cheli que j'aim?

4

8

Oh, God, when will I see
the woman I love?
I really don't know.
Oh, God, when will I see.
I am dying of hunger
to see her lovely self.
Oh, God, when will I see
the woman I love?

Jou senc en moi l'amor renouveler   (L 2-18)
Chanson d'amour

Jou   senc   en   moi   l'a-   mor   re-   nou-   ve-   ler,

Ki   au-   tre   fois   m'a   fait   le   doç   mal   trai-   re

Dont   je   so-   loie   en   de-   si-   rant   chan-   ter,

Par   koy   mes   chans   re-   nou-   viele   et   re-   pai-   re.

C'est   bons   maus   ki   cuer   es-   clai-   re,

Mais   A-   mors   m'a   le   ju   trop   mal   par-   ti,

Car   j'es-   poir   et   pens   par   li   Trop   haut,   s'est   drois   k'il   i   pai-   re.

Jou senc en moi l'amor renouveler,
Ki autre fois m'a fait le doç mal traire
Dont je soloie en desirant chanter,
Par koy mes chans renouviele et repaire.   1.4
          C'est bons maus ki cuer esclaire,
Mais Amors m'a le ju trop mal parti,
          Car j'espoir et pens par li
          Trop haut, s'est drois k'il i paire.   1.8

Et nepourquant bien fait a pardouner,
Car quant dame est noble et de haut afaire
Et biele et boine et gent set honorer,
Tant desiert mius c'on l'aint par essemplaire;   2.4
          Et doit estre deboinaire
Enviers povre home en otriant merchi,
          Sauve s'ounor, car jou di:
          Ki de boins est, souëf flaire.   2.8

Et par mi chou le m'estuet comparer:
Mes cuers me laist, ma dame m'est contraire,
Et vous, Amors, ki de ma dame amer
Dounés talent autrui por moi mal faire.   3.4
          Les gens ne se poeënt taire,
Et nis pitiés s'est repunse pour mi;
          Asés de meschiés a chi,
          Ains c'on en puist joie estraire.   3.8

Dame, vo oeil me font joie esperer,
Mais vo bouce se paine de retraire
Le largeche k'il font en resgarder;
Par leur douçour vienc en espoir de plaire,   4.4
          Car il sont en un viaire
Si amoureus, si doç et si poli
          C'onkes courous n'en issi
          Fors ris et samblans d'atraire.   4.8

Pour si dous ieus doit on bien lonc aler
Et moult i a pressïeus saintuaire;
Mais on n'i laist baisier ni adeser,
Ne on ne doit penser si haut salaire.   5.4
          Drois est c'on se fraingne et maire
Viers tel joiel et c'on soit bien nouri,
          Sans faire le fol hardi
          De parole u de pres traire.   5.8

I feel in me the renewal of love,
which once before made me bear the sweet pain
that I would sing of in my desire;
that's what renews and brings back my song.
It is a good pain that brightens the heart;
but love has given me a hard part to sing,
making me set my hopes and thoughts
too high — and it is right it should be apparent.

Nevertheless, it is quite forgivable,
for when a lady is noble and high-born,
beautiful and good and respectful of people,
she all the more deserves exemplary love;
and she should be gracious
to a poor man by granting mercy
(with no disrespect to herself), for I say:
A person of good quality smells sweet.

Still, I must pay the price:
my heart leaves me, my lady is unkind,
and so are you, love, who in order to hurt me
make another man desire my lady.
People cannot be silent,
and even pity has shunned me;
there are many setbacks to suffer
before one can draw forth some joy.

My lady, your eyes make me hope for joy,
but your mouth makes a point of denying
the generosity that their glance expresses;
their gentleness leads me to hope I can please you,
for they are in a face
so lovable, so sweet, so smooth
that it has never shown anger
but only smiles and appealing glances.

For such gentle eyes one must go far,
and there is a very precious reliquary there;
but no kiss or touch is permitted,
nor any thought of such a great reward.
It is proper to restrain and control oneself
before such a treasure and show good breeding,
not behave like a brash fool
either in speech or by drawing near.

Dame, vos hom vous estrine (L 2-5)
Chanson courtoise

Da- me, vos hom vous es- tri- ne   D'u- ne nou- ve- le can- chon.

Or ver- rai a vos- tre don   Se cour- toi- sie i est fi- ne.

Je vous aim sans tra- ï- son: A tort m'en por- tés cue- ri- ne,

Car con plus a- vés fui- son   De biau- té sans mes- pri- son,

Plus fort cuers s'i en- ra- chi- ne.

Dame, vos hom vous estrine	My lady, your liegeman presents you
D'une nouvele canchon.	with a new song.
Or verrai a vostre don	Now, by your gift, I shall see
Se courtoisie i est fine. 1.4	whether its courtliness is pure.
Je vous aim sans traïson:	I love you beyond betrayal:
A tort m'en portés cuerine,	you are wrong to scorn me,
Car con plus avés fuison	for the more bounteous
De biauté sans mesprison,	your flawless beauty is,
Plus fort cuers s'i enrachine. 1.9	the more firmly a heart takes root in it.
Tel fait doit une roïne	A queen should certainly forgive
Pardonner a un garchon,	a common fellow for such an act,
Qu'en cuer n'a point de raison	for there is no reason in a heart
Ou Amours met se saisine. 2.4	where love has taken over.
Ja si tost n'ameroit on	Never would one be so quick to love
Une caitive meschine	a girl of no account,
Maigre et de male boichon	skinny and ill-tempered,
C'une de clere fachon,	as a woman bright-faced and smiling,
Blanche, riant et rosine. 2.9	white and pink in color.
En vous ai mis de ravine	To you I have rushed to dedicate
Cuer et cors, vie et renon,	my heart and body, life and reputation,
Coi que soit de guerredon;	regardless of the possible reward;
Je n'ai mais qui pour moi fine. 3.4	I no longer have anyone to pay my way.
Tout ai mis en abandon,	I have abandoned everything,
Et s'estes aillours encline;	and yet you incline toward someone else;
Car je truis samblant felon	I see treachery there
Et oevre de Guennelon:	and the behavior of a Ganelon:
Autres got dont j'ai famine. 3.9	another man is enjoying what I hunger for.

Hé! las, j'ai a bonne estrine
Le cunquiiet dou baston,
Quant je vous di a bandon
De mon cuer tout le couvine   4.4
Pour venir a garison.
Vo bouche a dire ne fine
Que ja n'arai se mal non
Et que tout perc mon sermon:
Bien sanlés estre devine.   4.9

Vous faites capel d'espine,
S'ostés le vermeil bouton
Qui mieus vaut, esgardés mon,
Comme chieus qui l'or afine   5.4
Laist l'ort et retient le bon.
Je ne.l di pas pour haïne
Ne pour nule soupechon,
Mais gaitiés vous dou sourgon
Que vous n'i quaés souvine.   5.9

Jalousie est me voisine,
Par coi en vostre occoison
Me fait dire desraison,
Si m'en donnés decepline.   E.4 (9)

Alas, the fine gift I receive
is the dirty end of the stick,
when I tell you freely
what it will take for my heart
to be healed.
Your lips keep saying
that I will never have anything but pain
and that I am wasting my words.
You sound just like a seer.

You make a chaplet of thorns
and throw away the red buds
(which, I assure you, are more valuable),
just as the refiner of gold
rejects the dross and retains what is pure.
I don't say this out of hate
or any suspicion,
but watch out for runners on the ground
lest you trip and fall on your back.

Jealousy is my neighbor
who, when it comes to you,
makes me say foolish things;
but you administer my correction.

GILLEBERT DE BERNEVILLE

A native of the region of Arras, Gillebert de Berneville was associated from about 1255 with the literary circles of that city and the ducal court of Brabant. He is credited with approximately thirty lyric pieces of various types, chiefly *chansons d'amour courtoises*; almost all texts survive with music.

EDITIONS: Waitz 1899; Fresco 1988.

● "J'ai souvent d'Amors chanté": L 84-16, RS 414, MW 1218, B 1911. Sources: ms. K, also CNOUVX; music in KNOX and V. Attribution to Gillebert in CKNX. RT 432-435/730-735; Scheler 1876, 92-95; Waitz 1899, 72-74; Fresco 1988 109-115.

The person whose name occurs as a refrain in this song is in all likelihood Béatrice de Brabant, sister of Henri III, duke of Brabant from 1248 to 1261. She was the protectress of several trouvères and is referred to in more than one poem by Gillebert. There is no reason to believe that the love expressed for *Bietriz* is anything but fictive.

The music in V is distinct from that of the other sources. The melody in O, which we present, differs from that of KNX only in a few transpositions of melodic formulas (beginning of line 5 and all of lines 9, 10, 11) and to some extent in its ornamentation. It is built essentially on *c*, with principal cadences on *g* and *c*. The scheme includes an extensively developed *cauda:* ABAB CDADEFGF.

● "De moi dolereus vos chant": L 84-10, RS 317, MW 312, B 915. Sources: ms. M, also T (twice); music in all sources. Attribution to Gillebert in T; to Guiot de Dijon in M. RT 448-449/750-753; Scheler 1876, 74; Waitz 1899, 82; Nissen 1928, 14-15; Fresco 1988, 257-260.

Authorship by Gillebert is by no means certain, and this song might almost as readily have been presented above, under Guiot de Dijon.

This composition has been viewed both as a *ballette* without initial statement of the refrain (see BALLETTES) and as a *rotrouenge* (see note to "Chanter m'estuet de recomens" by Gontier de Soignies).

The very simple, syllabic, two-step melody is built on *a* and *g*. Its scheme recalls that of the *chansons de toile:* AABC/refrain D.

J'ai souvent d'Amors chanté   (L 84-16)
Chanson d'amour

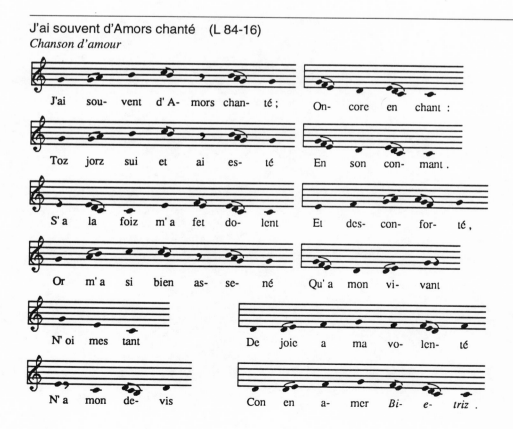

J'ai sou- vent d'A- mors chan- té ;   On- core en chant :

Toz jorz sui et ai es- té   En son con- mant .

S'a la foiz m'a fet do- lent   Et des- con- for- té ,

Or m'a si bien as- se- né   Qu'a mon vi- vant

N'oi mes tant   De joie a ma vo- len- té

N'a mon de- vis   Con en a- mer *Bi- e- triz* .

J'ai souvent d'Amors chanté;
    Oncore en chant:
Toz jorz sui et ai esté
    En son conmant.   1.4
S'a la foiz m'a fet dolent
    Et desconforté,
Or m'a si bien assené
    Qu'a mon vivant   1.8
      N'oi mes tant
De joie a ma volenté
    N'a mon devis
Con en amer *Bietriz*.   1.12

Cil qui sont espoanté
    Et esmaiant
Par fame sont tost maté
    Et recreant;   2.4
Or ferai plus que devant
    De joliveté.
Pour ce, s'on m'a marié,
    N'ai je talent,   2.8
      Poi ne grant,
Que ja soient mi pensé
    Ailleurs assis
Qu'a la bele *Bietriz*.   2.12

Toutes dames ont bonté,
    Mien encïent,
Mes sachiez, pour verité
    Le vous creant,   3.4
Que la lune tost luisant
    Soleil en esté
Passe de fine clarté;
    N'a son senblant   3.8
      Ne se prent,
N'a la tres grande biauté
    Ne au doz ris
De la bele *Bietriz*.   3.12

Clers soleus sanz tenebror
    Enluminez
Passe toute autre luor,
    Bien le savez;   4.4
Autresi a sormontez
    Toz cuers de valor
Cele qui de tout honor
    Est dame et clés.   4.8
      Ja mes grez
N'iert que j'aie bien nul jor
    Nes paradis
Sanz la bele *Biatriz*.   4.12

I have often sung of love;
I still sing of it:
I am and have always been
at its command.
If it has sometimes left me dejected
and disappointed,
this time it has treated me so well
that in my whole life
I have never had so much
joy — as much as I could
wish or want —
as I have in loving *Beatrice*.

Those who are frightened
and troubled
by women are soon defeated
and give up,
but I will be more jovial
than ever.
And so, even if married,
I have no desire,
great or small,
to let my thoughts
settle elsewhere
than on fair *Beatrice*.

There is goodness in all ladies,
to my mind,
but the truth is,
I assure you,
that with its bright light
the summer sun surpasses
the most gleaming moon;
yet it does not compare
to the appearance,
to the great beauty,
to the sweet smile
of fair *Beatrice*.

The bright sun, radiant
and untouched by darkness,
surpasses all other light,
as you well know;
in like fashion, the lady who is
the key to every honor
has risen above
all other hearts in virtue.
Never will I one day
be glad to have
even a place in heaven
without fair *Beatrice*.

Bele dame qui j'aor,		Fair lady whom I adore	
Qui tant valez,		and who are so worthy,	
Je me tieng a grant seignor		I consider myself a great lord	
Quant mes pensez	5.4	now that my every thought	
Est en vos servir tournez;		is bent on serving you;	
Et pour vostre amor		and for love of you	
Sui de mon cuer sanz retor		I am forever dispossessed	
Desheritez:	5.8	of my own heart:	
Vous l'avez,		you have it,	
Si que n'ai mal ne dolor,		yet I feel no hurt or pain,	
Tant m'esjoïs,		so much do I delight	
Quant j'oi nonmer *Bietriz*.	5.12	in hearing the name *Beatrice*.	

De moi dolereus vos chant   (L 84-10)

Ballette? rotrouenge?

De moi dolereus vos chant.		I sing to you of my doleful self.	
Je fui nez en descroissant,		I was born under the waning moon	
N'onques n'eu en mon vivant		and have never in my life had	
Deux bons jors.		two good days.	
J'ai a nom Mescheans d'Amors.	1.5	*My name is Luckless in Love.*	
Adés vois merci criant:		I always go crying for mercy:	
Amors, aidiez vo servant!		Love, help your servant!	
N'ainc n'i peu trover noiant		Yet never have I been able to find	
De secors.		any aid.	
J'ai a nom Mescheans d'Amors.	2.5	*My name is Luckless in Love.*	
Hé! trahitor mesdisant,		Ah! slanderous traitors,	
Con vos estes mal parlant!		what terrible things you say!	
Tolu avez maint amant		You have stripped many a lover	
Lor honors.		of his honor.	
J'ai a nom Mescheans d'Amors.	3.5	*My name is Luckless in Love.*	
Certes, pierre d'aÿmant		The lodestone, to be sure,	
Ne desirre pas fer tant		does not desire iron so much	
Con je sui d'un douz semblant		as I yearn	
Covoitoz.		for a smiling face.	
J'ai a nom Mescheans d'Amors.	4.5	*My name is Luckless in Love.*	

COLIN MUSET

A trouvère-jongleur of the second half of the thirteenth century, Colin Muset has been credited with a score of lyrics, varied in genre and unusually reflective of the poet's life; about half survive with music. He was from Lorraine, of humble condition, and made his living as an itinerant entertainer. Colin was inventive in compositional form and original in substance, less concerned with the constraints of *fin' amors* than with the delights, real or imagined, of a freer sensuality. Apart from love, his themes include the pleasures of the table, spring and revery, the satisfactions as well as difficulties of a minstrel's calling, the avarice of some patrons, the animation of tournaments. Along with more usual lyric types, his corpus contains such rare ones as the *lai-descort* and the *reverdie*.

EDITIONS: Bédier 1938; van der Werf 1979, 435-445.

● "Ancontre le tens novel": L 44-1, RS 582, MW 443, B 1897. Single source: ms. C; no music. Attribution to Colin. RT 452-454/756-759; Bédier 1938, 18-20.

Dialectal features: Lorraine, including *a* = Central Fr. *au; bernaige = barnage, chaistel = chastel, lai = la, mairs = mars, jai = ja, per = par, amesce = amasse; soneir = soner, teils = tels, esteit = esté; broiche = broche; brut = bruit; boen = bon; escut = escu; oixels = oisels, pouxons = poussons, plux = plus, frexe = fraische; jeu = je, ceu = ce; lou = le; seux = sui*. Note the verb form *ait = a*.

This song offers a jongleur's view of castle life in spring. Note the unusual placement of the refrain within the body of the stanza rather than at the end.

1.4-5: The words *triboudel* and *tribu martel* are not attested elsewhere. The first, like *triboudaine* in 1.10, seems to designate a kind of playful, exuberant song; the sense of *tribu martel* is readily inferred from 1.6, whence our translation, 'great party'.

3.4: The precise meaning of this line is not clear.

4.7-8: The phrase *mon mantel despandre* is ambiguous, meaning either 'hang up my cloak' or 'spend (i.e., trade in) my cloak'; a pun is no doubt intended.

5.10-11: It is doubtful whether these verses belong in the stanza, which does not repeat the earlier pattern, *aabaabaabAab*, but shows the unique structure, *aabaabaababAab*. Without them, the sentence begun with three parallel subordinate clauses (lines 1-9) would conclude—after the syntactically independent refrain in line 10—with *Plus ain . . .* as its main clause.

● "Sospris sui d'une amorette": L 44-14, RS 972, MW4,16. Sources: ms. U, also C; no music. Attribution to Colin in C. RT 457-460/764-767; Bartsch 1870, 355-357; Jeanroy 1901, 9-11; Bédier 1938, 15-17.

The only notable dialectal form is Lorraine *lo = le*.

This song is in content a *reverdie* (see REVERDIES) and in form a *lai* (see ARTHURIAN LAIS and note to "La douce pensee" by Gautier de Dargies). Note the structural symmetry that emerges from the remarkable correspondences of its ten full stanzas:

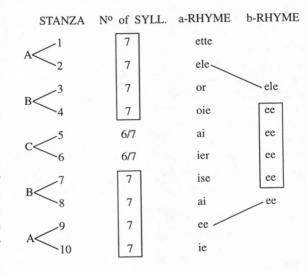

STANZA	№ of SYLL.	a-RHYME	b-RHYME
A 1	7	ette	
2	7	ele	
B 3	7	or	ele
4	7	oie	ee
C 5	6/7	ai	ee
6	6/7	ier	ee
B 7	7	ise	ee
8	7	ai	ee
A 9	7	ee	
10	7	ie	

2.2: Tudela, in Navarre, is often named in Old French works in association with ideas of wealth and power.

10.4: 'Syria' designates the Holy Land.

● "Quant voi lo douz tens repairier": L 44-12, RS 1302, MW 902,17. Sources: ms. U, also C; no music. Attribution to Colin in C. RT 460-463/768-773; Jeanroy 1901, 11-13; Bédier 1938, 13-15.

Dialectal features: Lorraine, including *lais* = Central Fr. *las; s'abasse = s'abaisse, lassiez = laissiez; loieir = loier; prosier = proisier; boen = bon; meux/meuz = mieuz; faudrat = faudra; ceu = ce; lo = le*.

In st. 8, this *descort*, like others, identifies itself as such. (See note to "La douce pensee" by Gautier de Dargies.)

The recipient of the song, called *La bone duchesse* in st. 8 and *Dame* in st. 9, is no doubt different from the personage addressed as *Bele* in stanza 7.

Ancontre le tens novel   (L 44-1)
Chanson de jongleur

Ancontre le tens novel
Ai le cuer gai et inel
A termine de Pascor;
Lors veul faire un triboudel,   1.4
Car j'ain moult tribu martel,
Brut et bernaige et baudor;
Et quant je suis en chaistel
Plain de joie et de rivel,   1.8
Lai veul estre et nuit et jor.
Triboudaine et triboudel!
Deus confonde le musel
Ki n'aime joie et baudor!   1.12

De toute joie m'est bel,
Et quant j'oi lou flaihutel
Soneir aveuc la tabor;
Damoiselles et donzel   2.4
Chantent et font grant rivel;
Chascuns ait chaipel de flor;
Et verdurë et brondelz
Et li douls chans des oixels   2.8
Me remet en grant baudor.
Triboudaine, triboudel!
Plus seux liés, per saint Marcel,
Ke teils ait chaistel ou tor.   2.12

Ki bien broiche lou poutrel
Et tient l'escut en chantel
A comencier de l'estor
Et met la lance en estel,   3.4
Por muelz vancre lou sembel
Vait asembleir a millor;
Cil doit bien avoir jüel
De belle dame et anel —   3.8
Per drüerie, s'amor.
Triboudainne, triboudel!
Por la belle a chief blondel
Ki ait frexe la color.   3.12

Teilz amesce en un moncel
Mil mairs et fait grant fardel
Ki vit a grant deshonor;
Jai n'en avra boen morcel,   4.4
Et diauble en ont la pel,
Cors et aime sens retor.
Por ceu veul jeu mon mantel
Despandre tost et inel   4.8
En bone ville a sejor.
Triboudainne, triboudel!
K'i valt avoirs en fardel,
S'on ne.l despent a honor?   4.12

When the new season begins,
my heart is gay and buoyant
at the time of Easter;
then I want to sing a triboudel,
for I love a great party
and lordly clamor and revelry;
and once I am in a castle
full of joy and high spirits,
I want to stay there night and day.
Triboudaine and triboudel!
God confound the sluggard
who dislikes revelry and joy!

I enjoy all joy,
especially when I hear the reed pipe
played with the drum
and young ladies and lords
sing and have a good time;
each one wears a garland of flowers;
and green boughs and branches
and the sweet song of the birds
make me feel all alive again.
Triboudaine and triboudel!
I am happier, by Saint Marcel,
than a castle lord or tower owner.

He who spurs his young horse forward,
holding his shield up for defense
at the start of the skirmish
and pointing his lance toward the goal,
in order to win the prize more impressively
looks to the best fighter for his match;
he is bound to have the gift
of a fair lady and her ring —
have, through gallantry, her love.
Triboudaine and triboudel!
for the blond-haired beauty
with glowing skin!

A man may well pile up
a thousand marks and make a bundle
and live disgracefully;
he'll never get any good out of it,
and his hide will go to the devil —
body and soul gone forever.
That's why I'm in a hurry
to hang up my cloak
and enjoy myself in town.
Triboudaine and triboudel!
What's the use of a bundle of money
if you don't spend it honorably?

Quant je la tieng ou praiel
Tout entor clos d'airbrexelz
En esteit a la verdor
Et j'ai oies et gaistel,　5.4
Pouxons, tairtes et porcel,
Buef a la verde savor,
Et j'ai lou vin en tonel,
Froit et fort et friandel,　5.8
Por boivre a la grant chalor,
Muels m'i ain k'en un baitel
En la meir en grant poor.
Triboudainne, triboudel!　5.12
Pluz ain le jeu de praiel
Ke faire malvaix sejor.

When I hold her in the meadow
hedged all around with shrubs
in the greenness of summer,
and I have geese and biscuits,
fish, tarts, and piglet,
beef with green sauce,
and I have my barrel of wine,
cold and strong and tasty,
to drink in the summer's heat,
I am happier than I'd be in a boat
on the sea, quaking with fear.
Triboudaine and triboudel!
I'm happier to play games in the meadow
than to have a boring rest on the road.

Sospris sui d'une amorette　(L 44-14)
Reverdie, lai

Sospris sui d'une amorette
D'une jone pucelette.
Belle est et blonde et blanchette
Plus que n'est une erminette,　1.4
S'a la color vermeillette
Ensi com une rosette.

I've been suddenly smitten
by a young maiden.
She is pretty and blond and whiter
than a little ermine,
and she has a reddish blush
just like a little rose.

Itels estoit la pucele,
La fille au roi de Tudele;
D'un drap d'or qui reflambele
Ot robe fresche et novele;　2.4
Mantel, sorcot et gonele
Mout sist bien a la donzelle.

Such was the maiden,
daughter to the king of Tudela;
she wore a fine new dress
of shimmering golden cloth;
cloak, surcoat, and tunic
suited the damsel very well.

En son chief ot chapel d'or
Ki reluist et estancele;
Saphirs, rubiz ot encor
Et mainte esmeraude bele.　3.4
Biaus Deus, cor fusse je or
Amis a tel damoisele!

On her head a golden garland
gleamed and sparkled;
there were sapphires too, rubies
and many a fine emerald.
Dear God, if only I could be
the lover of such a damsel!

Sa ceinture fut de soie,
D'or et de pierres ovree;
Toz li cors li reflamboie,
Ensi fut enluminee.　4.4
Or me doinst Deus de li joie,
K'aillors nen ai ma pansee.

Her sash was made of silk,
of gold and gems;
her whole body shone,
she was so full of light.
God grant me joy of her,
for she is in my every thought!

G'esgardai son cors gai,
Qui tant me plaist et agree.
Je morrai, bien lo sai,
Tant l'ai de cuer enamee.　5.4
Se Deu plaist, non ferai,
Ainçois m'iert s'amors donee.

I gazed at her lively body,
so pleasing and appealing.
I'll die, I know,
so wholeheartedly am I in love with her.
God willing, I won't,
and her love will instead be mine.

En un trop bel vergier
La vi cele matinee
　Jüer et solacier;
Ja par moi n'iert oblïee,　　　　　6.4
　Car bien sai, senz cuidier,
Ja si bele n'iert trovee.

In a beautiful orchard
I saw her that morning
frolicking and enjoying herself;
I won't ever forget her,
for well I know, with no illusions,
that another so lovely will never be found.

Lez un rosier s'est assise
La tres bele et la sennee;
Ele resplant a devise
Com estoile a l'anjornee.　　　　7.4
S'amors m'esprent et atise,
Qui enz el cuer m'est entree.

She has sat down beside a rosebush,
the lovely, sharp-witted girl;
she shines as brightly as I could want,
like a star at daybreak.
Love for her has entered my heart
and sets me on fire.

El regarder m'obliai
Tant qu'ele s'en fu alee.
Deus! tant mar la resgardai,
Quant si tost m'est eschapee,　　8.4
Que ja mais joie n'avrai
Se par li ne m'est donee.

Gazing at her, I forgot all else,
until she went away.
God! what a pity that I looked at her,
since she escaped from me so soon!
I'll never have joy anymore
unless it comes to me from her.

Tantost com l'oi regardee,
Bien cuidai qu'ele fust fee.
Ne lairoie por riens nee
Q'encor n'aille en sa contree,　　9.4
Tant que j'aie demandee
S'amor, ou mes fins cuers bee.

As soon as I looked at her,
I realized she was a fairy.
Nothing at all could stop me
from going back to her land
and asking for her love,
which my true heart longs for.

Et s'ele devient m'amie,
Ma granz joie iert acomplie,
Ne je n'en prendroie mie
Lo roialme de Surie,　　　　　10.4
Car trop meine bone vie
Qui aime en tel seignorie.

And if she becomes my lover,
my great joy will be a reality
and I wouldn't trade it
for the kingdom of Syria,
for whoever is ruled by such love
leads a wonderful life.

Deu pri qu'il me face aïe,
Que d'autre nen ai envie.　　　E.2 (6)

I pray God that He help me,
for she is the only one I want.

Quant voi lo douz tens repairier　(L 44-12)
Descort

　Quant voi lo douz tens repairier,
　Que li rosignols chante en mai,
　Et je cuiz que doie alegier
　Li mals et la dolors que j'ai,　　1.4
　Adonc m'ocïent li delai
　D'amors, qui les font engregnier.
　Lais! mar vi onques son cors gai
　S'a ma vie ne lo conquier.　　　1.8

When I see the mild season come back
and the nightingale sings in May
and I expect my pain and woe
to grow less weighty,
just then love kills me with delays
that make them heavier.
Alas that I ever saw her lively body
if I never win her!

Amors de moi ne cuide avoir pechiez
Por ceu que sui ses hom liges sosgiez.
Douce dame, pregne vos en pitiez!
Qui plus s'abasse, plus est essauciez.　　2.4

Love does not think he has wronged me
because I am his submissive liegeman.
Dear lady, take pity on me! The more
a man humbles himself, the more exalted he is.

Et qant si grant chose empris ai
Con de vostre amor chalengier,
Toz tens en pardons servirai
Se tout n'en ai altre loier.   3.4
Ma tres douce dame honoree,
    Je ne vos os nes proier:
Cil est mout fols qui si haut bee
    Ou il nen ose aprochier.   3.8

      Mais tote voie
    Tres bien revoudroie
    Vostre amors fust moie
    Por moi ensengnier,   4.4
      Car a grant joie
    Vit et s'esbanoie
    Cui Amors maistroie;
    Meux s'en doit prosier.   4.8

Qui bien vuet d'amors joïr
    Si doit soffrir
    Et endurer
Qan k'ele li vuet merir;   5.4
    Au repentir
    Ne doit panser,
C'om puet bien tot a loisir
    Son boen desir   5.8
    A point mener.
Endroit de moi, criem morir
    Meuz que garir
    Par bien amer.   5.12

Se je n'ai la joie grant
Que mes fins cuers va chacent,
Deffenir m'estuet briément.
Douce riens por cui je chant,   6.4
En mon descort vos demant
Un ris debonairement,
S'en vivrai plus longemant;
Moins en avrai de torment.   6.8

Bele, j'ai si grant envie
D'embracier vostre cors gent,
S'Amors ne m'en fait aïe,
J'en morrai coiteusement.   7.4
Amors ne m'en faudrat mie,
Car je l'ai trop bien servie
Et ferai tote ma vie
Senz nule fause pansee.   7.8
Preuz de tote gent löee
Plus que nule qui soit nee,
Se vostre amors m'est donee,
Bien iert ma joie doublee.   7.12

Since I have undertaken so great a task
as to contend for your love,
I shall always be serving in vain
unless I receive a quite different reward.
Dear honored lady,
I dare not even voice my desire:
The man is mad who aspires to a height
that he dares not approach.

But still
I would very much want
your love to be mine
and be a guide to me,
for he who is governed by love
lives and delights
in great joy;
he is bound to value himself more highly.

Whoever wants to enjoy love
must suffer
and bear
whatever reward love wants to give him;
he must not think
of changing his mind,
for a man can, if he wishes,
bring his desire
to fulfillment.
But in my case, I am more afraid
of dying than of being cured
through loving well.

Unless I attain the great joy
that my true heart is seeking,
I must soon die.
Dear creature for whom I sing,
I ask you in my descort
for a generous smile;
it will lengthen my life
and I shall have less torment.

My dear, I have such a great urge
to embrace your lovely body
that, if love brings no aid,
I shall die right away.
But love will not fail me,
for I have served him too well
and will always do so,
without any false thought.
O worthy one, more greatly praised
by all than any other woman,
if you grant me your love,
my joy will be doubled.

Mon descort ma dame aport,
La bone duchesse, por chanter.
De toz biens a li m'acort,
K'ele aime deport, rire et jüer.   8.4

Dame, or voil bien mostrer
Que je ne sai vostre per
De bone vie mener
Et de leialment amer.   9.4
Adés vos voi enmender
En vaillance et en doner:
Ne.l lassiez ja por jangler,
Que ceu ne vos puet grever.   9.8

I bring my descort to my lady,
the good duchess, for a performance.
I agree with her in all good things,
for she loves laughter, gaiety, and games.

My lady, I want to show you now
that I do not know your equal
for enjoying life
and loving loyally.
I see you constantly growing
in virtue and generosity:
do not let idle gossip stop you,
for it cannot harm you.

MONIOT DE PARIS

Moniot de Paris, a Parisian, was apparently a monk before becoming a trouvère; his poetic activity occurred during the third quarter of the thirteenth century. Nine lyric compositions are attributed to him.

EDITION: Dyggve 1938; van der Werf 1979.

- "Je chevauchoie l'autrier": L 186-3, RS 1255, MW 934, B 961. Sources: ms. P, also KN; same music in all. Attribution to Moniot in KN. RT 513-515/824-827; Bartsch 1870, 87-88; Dygvve 1938, 197-200; van der Werf 1979, 420-421; Paden 1987 (2), 386-389.

This *chanson de rencontre* is an urban transplant of a *pastourelle,* with a willing *malmariée* of the bourgeoisie substituted for the shepherdess.

3.3: The *Grand Pont* connected the Ile-de-la-Cité and the right bank of the Seine. Houses and shops lined the bridge.

4.6: The allusion to Winchester, in England, is to be taken as simply indicating a great distance.

5.7-8: Two mss. have plural *Dames* instead of *Dame* and all three have plural *Vos maris* instead of our emended *Vostre mari.* Such readings argue in favor of interpreting these lines as an exhortation by the woman—or by the knight—to all the ladies of Paris, and previous editors have in fact so interpreted them, attributing them to the woman. In the context of the entire poem, however, we have to question such generalization of the woman's sentiments; moreover, the phrase *venez o moi jöer* appears intended as a reply by the knight to the lady's earlier phrase, *vueil avec vos aler jöer* (3.8). It is true, of course, that neither interpretation stops the other from being implied.

The melody, in *g* with a major third in the first six lines, calls for a dance rhythm. Often in French folkloric traditions, a single composition may be played partly in a major tone and then continued in a minor tone, which is a way of re-energizing the piece or giving special emphasis to a spirited text. This is what we have attempted by flatting the *b* as of line 7; it creates a different modal effect (*d* scale transposed to *g*) in the music of the refrain. The melodic scheme combines the litany and rondel-with-refrain types: ABABABCC/refrain CC.

- "Quant je oi chanter l'alöete": L 186-8, RS 969, MW 591. Sources: ms. K, also NP; music in all. Attribution to Moniot de Paris in KN and to Jean Moniot in the text. RT 515-518/828-833; Dyggve 1938, 211-214; van der Werf 1979, 509-410.

Dialectal features: Picard, including *renvoisie* = Central Fr. *renvoisiee; mi = moi; deveroie = devroie.*

This song offers an interesting, post-"classical" channeling of *fin' amors* away from the "lady" and toward a mere *pucelete.* The form, which entails the repetition of the middle section of each stanza at the end, is unique in the corpus of Old French lyrics and may have been inspired by contemporary Latin poetry.

Melodically, K, whose reading is presented here, is identical to N and P. The first part (lines 1-4) is built on *d* transposed to *g,* the second (lines 5-12, which also constitute the refrain) on *f* and *c,* and the third (lines 13-16) on *d.* The melodic scheme blends systematic repetition of the lai-sequence type with a refrain: ABAB CDCD′ CDCD′ EFEF CDCD′ CDCD′.

Je chevauchoie l'autrier   (L 186-3)

Chanson de rencontre

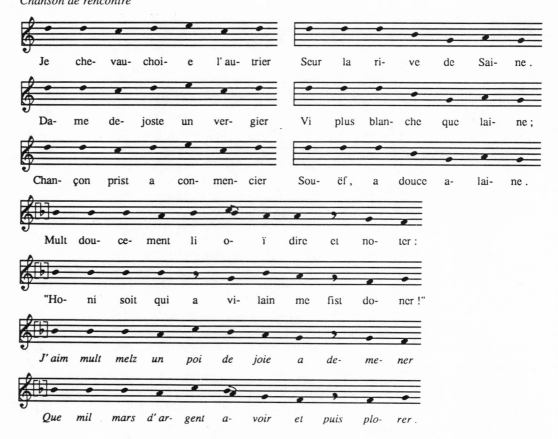

Je che- vau- choi- e l'au- trier   Sour la ri- ve de Sai- ne.

Da- me de- joste un ver- gier   Vi plus blan- che que lai- ne;

Chan- çon prist a con- men- cier   Sou- ëf, a douce a- lai- ne.

Mult dou- ce- ment li o- ï dire et no- ter:

"Ho- ni soit qui a vi- lain me fist do- ner!"

J'aim mult melz un poi de joie a de- me- ner

Que mil mars d'ar- gent a- voir et puis plo- rer.

Je chevauchoie l'autrier	I was out riding the other day
Seur la rive de Saine.	along the banks of the Seine.
Dame dejoste un vergier	Beside an orchard I noticed
Vi plus blanche que laine;	a lady whiter than wool;
Chançon prist a conmencier 1.5	she began to sing
Souëf, a douce alaine.	softly and sweetly.
Mult doucement li oï dire et noter:	Very softly I heard her singing these words:
"Honi soit qui a vilain me fist doner!	"Shame to the one who wed me to a boor!
J'aim mult melz un poi de joie a demener	*I would much rather have a little joy*
Que mil mars d'argent avoir et puis plorer." 1.10	*than get a thousand silver marks and then weep."*
Hautement la saluai	I greeted her out loud
De Dieu le filz Marie.	in the name of God, the son of Mary.
El respondi sanz delai:	She was quick to respond:
"Jhesu vos beneïe!"	"Jesus bless you!"
Mult doucement li proié 2.5	Very gently I asked her
Q'el devenist m'amie.	to become my belovèd.
Tot errant me conmençoit a raconter	Right away she began to tell me
Conme ses maris la bat por bien amer.	how her husband beat her for being in love.
J'aim mult melz un poi de joie a demener	*I would much rather have a little joy*
Que mil mars d'argent avoir et puis plorer. 2.10	*than get a thousand silver marks and then weep.*

"Dame, estes vos de Paris?"
    "Oïl, certes, biau sire;
Seur Grant-Pont maint mes maris,
    Des mauvés tot le pire.
Or puet il estre marris: 3.5
    Jamés de moi n'iert sire!
Trop est fel et rioteus, trop puet parler,
Car je m'en vueil avec vous aler jöer."
J'aim mult melz un poi de joie a demener
Que mil mars d'argent avoir et puis plorer.   3.10

    "Mal ait qui me maria!
    Tant en ait or le prestre,
Qu'a un vilain me dona
    Felon et de put estre.
Je croi bien que poior n'a   4.5
    De ci tresqu'a Vincestre.
Je ne pris tot son avoir pas mon souler,
Quant il me bat et ledenge por amer."
J'aim mult melz un poi de joie a demener
Que mil mars d'argent avoir et puis plorer.   4.10

    "Enondieu, je amerai
    Et si serai amee
Et si me renvoiserai
    El bois soz la ramee
Et mon mari maudirai   5.5
    Et soir et matinee."
"Dame de Paris, amez, lessiez ester
Vostre mari, si venez o moi jöer!"
J'aim mult melz un poi de joie a demener
Que mil mars d'argent avoir et puis plorer.   5.10

"My lady, are you from Paris?"
    "Yes, indeed, dear sir;
my husband lives on the Great Bridge;
    he is the worst of the bad.
Now he has grounds to be angry:
    he'll never be my master!
He is cruel and quick-tempered and can say what he likes:
I want to go have a good time with you."
I would much rather have a little joy
than get a thousand silver marks and then weep.

"Curse the one who married me off!
    Same for the priest,
for he wed me to a boor
    who is cruel and base-born.
I am sure there is no worse a man
    between here and Winchester.
I wouldn't give my shoe for all his wealth,
since he beats and insults me for being in love."
I would much rather have a little joy
than get a thousand silver marks and then weep.

"By God, I will love
    and I'll be loved, too,
and I'll go frolicking
    under the trees in the woods
and I'll curse my husband
    night and day."
"Lady of Paris, let yourself love, forget
your husband, and come have a good time with me!"
I would much rather have a little joy
than get a thousand silver marks and then weep.

Quant je oi chanter l'alöete   (L 186-8)
Chanson d'amour

Quant je oi chan- ter l'a- lö- e- te

Pour la ve- nu- e du tens cler,

Lors mi se- mont une a- mo- re- te

De chan- çon fere et de chan- ter.

D'u- ne pu- ce- le- te   Fe- rai chan- ço- ne- te

Qui mult est sa- de- te.   Je l'aim sanz faus- ser.

Bele a la bou- che- te,   Co- lor ver- meil- le- te;

Tant la voi sa- de- te   Que n'i puis du- rer.

Or voi je bien que sanz mo- rir

Ne por- rai ces maus en- du- rer;

S'e- le mi let en- si fe- nir,

Tout li mons l'en de- vroit blas- mer.

D'u- ne pu- ce- le- te	Fe- rai chan- ço- ne- te
Qui mult est sa- de- te .	Je l'aim sanz faus- ser .
Bele a la bou- che- te ,	Co- lor ver- meil- le- te ;
Tant la voi sa- de- te	Que n'i puis du- rer .

Quant je oi chanter l'alöete		When I hear the meadowlark sing
Pour la venue du tens cler,		because the bright season has come,
Lors mi semont une amorete		an *affaire de coeur* urges me
De chançon fere et de chanter.	1.4	to compose a song and sing.
D'une pucelete		I'll compose a little song
Ferai chançonete		about a young girl
Qui mult est sadete.		who is very charming.
Je l'aim sanz fausser.	1.8	I love her sincerely.
Bele a la bouchete,		She has a lovely little mouth,
Color vermeillete;		bright rose in color;
Tant la voi sadete		I find her so charming
Que n'i puis durer.	1.12	that I can't resist her.
Or voi je bien que sanz morir		I see now that, unless I die,
Ne porrai ces maus endurer;		I won't be able to to bear this torment;
S'ele mi let ensi fenir,		if she lets me reach my end like this,
Tout li mons l'en devroit blasmer.	1.16	everyone should condemn her.
D'une pucelete		*I'll compose a little song*
Ferai chançonete		*about a young girl*
Qui mult est sadete.		*who is very charming.*
Je l'aim sanz fausser.	1.20	*I love her sincerely.*
Bele a la bouchete,		*She has a lovely little mouth,*
Color vermeillete;		*bright rose in color;*
Tant la voi sadete		*I find her so charming*
Que n'i puis durer.	1.24	*that I can't resist her.*

A dolor userai ma vie   I'll wear away my life in pain
Se cele n'a merci de mi   unless she takes pity on me,
Que je ai si lonc tens servie,   for I have served her so long
Qu'ele mi tiengne pour ami.   2.4   that she should consider me her lover.
   Je ne vivrai mie   I cannot live
   S'ele n'est m'amie,   if she doesn't return my love,
   Mes a grant haschie   but will die instead
   Me morrai ensi.   2.8   in agony.
   Se muir por s'aïe,   If I die for want of her help,
   Jamés n'iert qui die   there will never be anyone to sing
   Chançon renvoisie   a lively song
   Pour l'amor de li.   2.12   for love of her.
Or voi bien que mar acointai   I see now that I should never have
Son cors, s'el n'a merci de mi.   met her, if she takes no pity on me.
Sa grant biauté mar remirai;   I should never have gazed at her beauty;
Je m'en tieng bien a maubailli.   2.16   I consider myself ruined.
   Je ne vivrai mie   *I cannot live*
   S'ele n'est m'amie,   *if she doesn't return my love,*
   Mes a grant haschie   *but will die instead*
   Me morrai ensi.   2.20   *in agony.*
   Se muir por s'aïe,   *If I die for want of her help,*
   Jamés n'iert qui die   *there will newver be anyone to sing*
   Chançon renvoisie   *a lively song*
   Pour l'amor de li.   2.24   *for love of her.*

Oncor tenir ne mi porroie   Yet I cannot refrain
De chanter com loiaus amis.   from singing as a faithful lover.
Je chant et plorer deveroie   I sing though I should weep
Conme dolenz et esbahiz.   3.4   in sorrow and distress.
   Se cele n'est moie   If she to whom I give my heart
   Laou mes cuers s'otroie,   will not be mine,
   Faillie est ma joie   my joy is vanished
   Et touz mes deliz;   3.8   along with all my pleasures;
   Et Deus, qui g'en proie,   I pray God
   Dont qu'ele soit moie   to grant that she be mine,
   Si c'oncore en soie   so I may again be
   Joianz et jolis.   3.12   joyous and gay.
Jehan Moniot dit ensi   Jean Moniot thus says
Q'il a en tel lieu son cuer mis   that he addressed his heart
Laou il a bien du tout failli.   to a place where all has been lost.
Gardez que ne faciez ausi!   3.16   Beware lest you do likewise!
   Se cele n'est moie   *If she to whom I give my heart*
   Laou mes cuers s'otroie,   *will not be mine,*
   Faillie est ma joie   *my joy is vanished*
   Et touz mes deliz;   3.20   *along with all my pleasures;*
   Et Deus, qui g'en proie,   *I pray God*
   Dont qu'ele soit moie   *to grant that she be mine,*
   Si c'oncore en soie   *so I may again be*
   Joianz et jolis.   3.24   *joyous and gay.*

RUTEBEUF

Rutebeuf, a native of Champagne but the first great poet of Paris, received a cleric's education and remained tied to the ecclesiastical and academic milieu of the city. His literary activity extended from the middle of the thirteenth century to ca. 1285. Aside from his two lyric pieces, more than fifty non-musical poetic texts, some apparently personal in character, attest a deep concern with the religious, moral, and political issues and quarrels of his time. Rutebeuf is perhaps most widely known for his play, *Le Miracle de Théophile*.

STUDY: Regalado 1970.

EDITIONS: Faral 1959-60; Dufournet 1986; Zink 1989-90.

● "Chanson m'estuet chanteir de la meilleur": L 245-1, RS 1998, MW 1968. Sources: Paris, B.N. fr. 1635, also Paris, B.N. fr. 1593; no music. Attribution to Rutebeuf. RT 548-549/890-893; Faral 1959-60 (2), 245-246; Dufournet 1986, 124-129; Zink 1989-90 (2), 292-295.

Dialectal features: Lorraine, including *chanteir* = Central Fr. *chanter, bontei = bonté, teile = tele; boen = bon*.

This devotional song is introduced in the ms. by the phrase *C'est de Notre Dame*.

Chanson m'estuet chanteir de la meilleur   (L 245-1)
Chanson pieuse

Chanson m'estuet chanteir de la meilleur		I must sing a song about the best woman
Qui onques fust ne qui jamais sera.		who ever was or ever will be.
Li siens douz chanz garit toute douleur;		Her sweet song cures every ill;
Bien iert gariz cui ele garira.		anyone she cures will be cured for good.
Mainte arme a garie;	1.5	She has cured many a soul;
Huimais ne dot mie		henceforth I am not afraid
Que n'aie boen jour,		of not having a good day,
Car sa grant dosour		for her great sweetness
N'est nuns qui vous die.	1.9	is greater than anyone can say.
Mout a en li cortoizie et valour;		She is filled with courteousness and virtue,
Bien et bontei et charitei i a.		with goodness and kindness and charity.
Con folz li cri merci de ma folour;		A fool, I beg her mercy for my folly;
Foloié ai s'onques nuns foloia.		I have been a greater fool than other fools.
Si pleur ma folie	2.5	So I lament my folly
Et ma fole vie,		and my foolish life,
Et mon fol senz plour		and lament my foolish mind
Et ma fole errour		and the foolish ways
Ou trop m'entroblie.	2.9	into which I lapse too often.
Quant son doulz non reclainment picheour		When sinners invoke her sweet name
Et il dïent son Ave Maria,		and recite her Hail Mary,
N'ont puis doute dou maufei tricheour		they no longer fear the evil trickster
Qui mout doute le bien qu'en Marie a,		who fears the virtue that Mary embodies,
Car qui se marie	3.5	for anyone who marries himself
En teile Marie,		to such a Mary
Boen mariage a.		has a good marriage.
Marions nos la,		Let us marry her,
Si avrons s'aïe.	3.9	and we shall have her help.

Mout l'ama cil qui, de si haute tour
Com li ciel sunt, descendi juque ça.
Mere et fille porta son creatour,
Qui de noiant li et autres cria.
    Qui de cuer s'escrie   4.5
    Et merci li crie
    Merci trovera;
    Jamais n'i faudra
    Qui de cuer la prie.   4.9

Si com hom voit le soloil toute jour
Qu'en la verriere entre et ist et s'en va,
Ne l'enpire tant i fiere a sejour,
Ausi vos di que onques n'empira
    La vierge Marie: 5.5
    Vierge fu norrie,
    Vierge Dieu porta,
    Vierge l'aleta,
    Vierge fu sa vie.   5.9

She was well loved by the One who from
his heaven-high tower came down to earth.
She was mother and daughter to her creator,
who created her, like others, out of nothing.
Whoever cries out in his heart
and cries to her for mercy
will receive mercy;
whoever prays to her with his heart
will never fail.

Just as we see sunlight every day
pass through the window and disappear
and the glass, however struck, remain intact,
so too, I tell you, the Virgin Mary
remained intact:
she was raised as a virgin;
she bore God as a virgin;
she nursed him as a virgin;
a virgin she was all her life long.

The DUCHESS OF LORRAINE

It is not clear which Duchess of Lorraine is intended by this title that appears in only one manuscript. Several identifications are possible, including the daughter of the great trouvère Thibaut de Champagne, Marguerite, who was married in 1255 to Ferri III, duke of Lorraine. Two songs are attributed to her.

● "Par maintes fois avrai esteit requise": L 57-1, RS 1640, MW 2344. Sources: ms. U, also C; no music. Attribution to the Duchesse de Lorraine in C. RT 503-504/808-811.

Dialectal features: Lorraine, including *jai* = Central Fr. *ja; esteit = esté, iteil = itel; poinne = peine; antreprise = entreprise, jant = gent, rante = rente; amins = amis;* *Afelisse = Afelise, justice = justise; at = a, tolut = tolu; jeu = je, ceu = ce; lou = le; seu = sui.* Note in particular the verb form *rait = ra (re + a).*

As becomes gradually apparent, this song is a *plainte funèbre*. It is one of the very few lyric death-laments in Old French, where the thematic type never developed into a distinct genre, as was the case in Occitan. It is also the only one composed by, or in the voice of, a woman.

3.1: The reference is to Fouque and Anfelise, hero and heroine of Herbert le Duc de Dammartin's epic poem, *Fouque de Candie*. The characters appear as well in Old French romance literature.

Par maintes fois avrai esteit requise   (L 57-1)
Chanson courtoise, plainte funèbre

Par maintes fois avrai esteit requise		Many a time I have been asked
C'ains ne chantai ansi con je soloie;		why I no longer sing as I used to;
Car je suix si aloingnie de joie		the truth is, I am so removed from joy
Que j'en devroie estre plus antreprise,	1.4	that I ought to be even further deterred,
Et a mien voil moroie an iteil guise		and, if I could, I would die in the same way
Con celle fist cui je sanbler voroie:		as the woman I would like to resemble:
Didol, qui fut por Eneas ocise.	1.7	Dido, who slew herself because of Aeneas.
Ahi, amins! Tout a vostre devise		Ah, my love, why didn't I do
Que ne fis jeu tant con je vos veoie?		as you wished when I could still see you?
Jant vilainne cui je tant redotoie		Foul people whom I greatly feared
M'ont si greveit et si ariere mise	2.4	so troubled me and held me back
C'ains ne vos pou merir vostre servise.		that I could never reward your service.
S'estre poioit, plus m'an repantiroie		If it were possible, I would repent more
C'Adans ne fist de la pome c'ot prise.	2.7	than Adam did for the apple that he ate.
Ains por Forcon ne fist tant Afelisse		Never did Anfelise do as much for Fouque
Con je por vos, amins, s'or vos ravoie;		as I would do for you, my love, if I had you back;
Mais ce n'iert jai, se premiers ne moroie.		but that will never be, unless I die.
Mais je ne puis morir an iteil guise,	3.4	But I cannot die this way,
C'ancor me rait Amors joie promise.		for love has yet promised me joy;
Si vuel doloir an leu de mener joie:		I wish, though, not for joy, but sorrow:
Poinne et travail, ceu est ma rante assise.	3.7	pain and torment are the tribute I must pay.
Par Deu, amins, en grant dolour m'a mise		By God, my love, I have been plunged into sorrow
Mors vilainne, qui tout lou mont gerroie.		by foul death, which wars against the entire world.
Vos m'at tolut, la riens que tant amoie!		It has robbed me of you, you whom I loved so much!
Or seu Fenis, lasse, soule et eschise,	4.4	Now bereft, alone, deprived, I am a Phoenix,
Dont il n'est c'uns, si con an le devise.		although they say there is only one such.
Mais a poinnes m'en reconfortiroie		But I might yet find some comfort
Se por ceu non, c'Amors m'at an justice.	4.7	were it not that love has me in its power.

JACQUES DE CAMBRAI

Nothing is known of Jacques de Cambrai except that he was no doubt from the North and was active sometime between 1260 and 1290. A dozen lyric compositions are attributed to him, including seven *chansons pieuses*.

EDITION: Rivière 1978.

• "Retrowange novelle": L 121-12, RS 602, MW 47. Single source: ms. C; no music (see below). Attribution to Jacques. RT 540-541/880-883; Järnström 1910, 93-94; Rivière 1978, 87-89.

This is the only devotional song of Jacques de Cambrai with no secular model specified in the ms. It is widely agreed, however, that the composition is a contrafactum of an anonymous song, "Quant voi la flour novele" (L 265-1493), and we therefore present it with that music (as preserved in ms. K).

The first verse identifies this song as a *rotrouenge,* a term used in self-identification by several other trouvère compositions. See our note to "Chanter m'estuet de recomens" by Gontier de Soignies. The uncertainty of description of the type is reinforced by the present example, which lacks a refrain, normally regarded as a defining feature. It is possible, however, that this very difference is what the poet is alluding to when he describes his *rotrouenge* as *novelle*—not new, then, so much as novel.

2.2: The reference is to Isaiah 7:14 and 11:1-10.

The melody is in the scale of *d.* Opening with the classic intonation *d-a,* it concludes with the low tetrachord of *d.* The scheme, ABAB CDC'F, is slightly irregular in the second half, in that line 6 (D) ends with an ouvert on *c* and line 8 (F) with a clos on *d;* this suggests a dance-song.

Retrowange novelle   (L 121-12)
Chanson pieuse, rotrouenge?

Retrowange novelle	I will sing a new rotrouenge,
Dirai et bone et belle	fair and good,
De la virge pucelle	about the virgin girl
Ke meire est et ancelle 1.4	who is mother and servant
Celui ki de sa chair belle	of the One who redeemed us
Nos ait raicheteit	with his fair flesh
Et ki trestous nos apelle	and who beckons us all
A sa grant clairteit. 1.8	to his great light.

Ce nos dist Isaïe
En une profesie:
D'une verge delgie,
De Jessé espanie, 2.4
Istroit flors per signorie
De tres grant biaulteit.
Or est bien la profesie
Torneie a verteit. 2.8

Celle verge delgie
Est la virge Marie;
La flor nos senefie,
De ceu ne douteis mie, 3.4
Jhesu Crist, ki la haschie
En la croix sousfri;
Fut por randre ceaus en vie
Ki ierent peri. 3.8

Isaiah told us
in a prophecy
that from a delicate branch
growing out of Jesse
would bloom a noble flower
of very great beauty.
Indeed, the prophecy has now
come true.

The delicate branch
is the Virgin Mary;
the flower speaks to us
(don't doubt this!)
of Jesus Christ, who suffered
torture on the cross;
the purpose was to give new life
to those who had perished.

REFERENCES

MANUSCRIPT SOURCES

Identified below are the troubadour and trouvère manuscripts relevant to the compositions included in the present anthology. They are listed in alphabetical order of their conventional sigla; an initial black dot (•) indicates the presence of music.

Troubadour Manuscripts

A   Rome, Biblioteca Apostolica Vaticana, lat. 5232.

B   Paris, Bibliothèque Nationale, fr. 1592.

C   Paris, Bibliothèque Nationale, fr. 856.

D   Modena, Biblioteca Nazionale Estense, Estero 45 (Alpha R.4.4).
D^a = Ibid., ff. 153-211
D^b = Ibid., ff. 232-43
D^c = Ibid., ff.243-60

E   Paris, Bibliothèque Nationale, fr. 1749.

F   Rome, Biblioteca Apostolica Vaticana, Chigiani L.IV.106.

•G   Milan, Biblioteca Ambrosiana, R 71 superiore.

H   Rome, Biblioteca Apostolica Vaticana, lat. 3207.

I   Paris, Bibliothèque Nationale, fr. 854.

J   Florence, Biblioteca Nazionale Centrale, Conventi soppressi F.IV.776.

K   Paris, Bibliothèque Nationale, fr. 12473.

L   Rome, Biblioteca Apostolica Vaticana, lat. 3206.

M   Paris, Bibliothèque Nationale, fr. 12474.

Mc   Rome, Biblioteca Apostolica Vaticana, lat. 4796.

N   New York, Pierpont Morgan Library, 819.

N^2 Berlin, Staatsbibliothek, Phillipps 1910.

O   Rome, Biblioteca Apostolica Vaticana, latini 3208.

P   Florence, Biblioteca Medicea Laurenziana, Plut. 41.42.

Q   Florence, Biblioteca Riccardiana, 2909.

•R   Paris, Bibliothèque Nationale, fr. 22543.

S   Oxford, Bodleian Library, Douce 269.

Sg   Barcelona, Biblioteca de Cataluña, 146.

T   Paris, Bibliothèque Nationale, fr. 15211.

U   Florence, Biblioteca Medicea Laurenziana, Plut. 41.43.

V   Venice, Biblioteca Nazionale Marciana, 278 (fr. App. cod. XI).

Ve. Ag. I.   Barcelona, Biblioteca de l'Institut d'Estudis Catalans.

•W   Paris, Bibliothèque Nationale, fr. 844 (=trouvère ms. M).

•X   Paris, Bibliothèque Nationale, fr. 20050 (=trouvère ms. U).

a   *The lost ms. compiled by Bernart Amoros, represented by two copies:*
Pillet-Carstens a (or a^2): Florence, Biblioteca Riccardiana, 2814.
Pillet-Carstens a^1: Modena, Biblioteca Nazionale Estense, Càmpori Appendice 426, 427, 494 (formerly Gamma.N.8.11-13).

b   *The lost ms. compiled by Miquel de la Tor, represented by two copies:*
Pillet-Carstens b (bI and bII): Rome, Biblioteca Apostolica Vaticana, Barberiniani 4087.
Pillet-Carstens e: Rome, Biblioteca Apostolica Vaticana, Barberiniani 3965.

c   Florence, Biblioteca Medicea Laurenziana, Plut. XC inferiore 26.

d   Modena, Biblioteca Estense, Appendix to D.

e   *See above,* b.

f   Paris, Bibliothèque Nationale, fr. 12472.

g^1 Rome, Biblioteca Apostolica Vaticana, ms. 3205.

g^2 Bologna, Biblioteca Universitaria, ms. 1290.

•η   Rome, Biblioteca Apostolica Vaticana, Reg. 1659.

Extracts:

α   Matfre Ermengaud, *Le Breviari d'Amor*

$β^1$ Raimon Vidal, *So fo el temps c'om era gays*

ι   Francesco da Barberino, *Documenti d'Amore*

χ   G.M. Barberi, *Dell'origine della poesia rimata*

μ   Terramagnino of Pisa, *Doctrina de cort*

Trouvère Manuscripts

•A   Arras, Bibliothèque Municipale, 657.

•B   Bern, Stadtbibliothek, 231.

C   Bern, Stadtbibliothek, 389.

•F   London, British Library, Egerton 274.

H   Modena, Biblioteca Estense, R 4, 4.

I   Oxford, Bodleian Library, Douce 308.

•K   Paris, Bibliothèque de l'Arsenal, 5198.

•L   Paris, Bibliothèque Nationale, fr. 765.

•M	Paris, Bibliothèque Nationale, fr. 844 (=troubadour ms. W).
•N	Paris, Bibliothèque Nationale, fr. 845.
•O	Paris, Bibliothèque Nationale, fr. 846.
•P	Paris, Bibliothèque Nationale, fr. 847.
•Q	Paris, Bibliothèque Nationale, fr. 1109.
•R	Paris, Bibliothèque Nationale, fr. 1591.
S	Paris, Bibliothèque Nationale, fr. 12581.
•T	Paris, Bibliothèque Nationale, fr. 12615.
•U	Paris, Bibliothèque Nationale, fr. 20050 (=troubadour ms. X).
•V	Paris, Bibliothèque Nationale, fr. 24406.
•W	Paris, Bibliothèque Nationale, fr. 25566.
•X	Paris, Bibliothèque Nationale, nouv. acq. fr. 1050.
•Z	Siena, Biblioteca Comunale, H. X. 36.
•a	Rome, Biblioteca Vaticana, Reg. 1490.
b	Rome, Biblioteca Vaticana, Reg. 1522.
e	*Lost ms.; see:* Wallensköld, A. "Un fragment de chansonnier, actuellement introuvable, du XIIIe siècle," *Neuphil. Mitteil.* 18 (1917), 2-17.
•i	Paris, Bibliothèque Nationale, fr. 12483.
za	Zagreb, University Library, Agram.
•	Bamberg, Staatliche Bibliothek, Lit. 115 (*formerly* Ed. IV.6) (motets).
•	Montpellier, Faculté de Médecine, H 196 (motets).
•	Paris, Bibliothèque Nationale, nouv. acq. fr. 13521 (motets).

WORKS CITED

The following list makes no claim to completeness. It includes only the published works that are cited in abbreviated form through the pages of this volume. For more extensive bibliographical data—and for data classified by topic—readers should consult Spanke 1955, Mölk-Wolfzettel 1972, Bec 1977, Taylor 1977, Linker 1979, Hughes 1980, *New Grove* 1980, Doss-Quinby 1994, Switten 1995, or, in the broader context of French medieval literature in general, Hasenohr-Zink 1992 or Robert Bossuat's *Manuel bibliographique de la Littérature française du moyen âge* (1951) and its various supplements.

Abbreviations are used below for the titles of a few major collections. These are: CFMA = Les Classiques Français du Moyen Age, SATF = Société des Anciens Textes Français, TLF = Textes Littéraires Français.

Through the volume, we use abbreviations for several works of frequent reference. These are: B = Boogaard 1969, L= Linker 1979, MW = Mölk-Wolfzettel 1972, PC = Pillet-Carstens, RS = Spanke 1955, RT = Rosenberg-Tischler 1981/95. See below for complete bibliographical data.

Anglade, Joseph. 1905. *Le Troubadour Guiraut Riquier: Etude sur la décadence de l'ancienne poésie provençale.* Bordeaux-Paris.

Anglade, Joseph. 1923. *Les Poésies de Peire Vidal.* 2nd ed. CFMA, 11. Paris: Champion. [lst ed. 1913]

Anglés, Higinio. 1926. "Les Mélodies del trobador Guiraut Riquier." *Estudis Universitaris Catalans* 2: 1-78.

Appel, Carl. 1915. *Bernart von Ventadorn, Seine Lieder.* Halle: Niemeyer.

Appel, Carl. 1932. *Die Lieder Bertrans von Born.* Halle.

Appel, Carl. 1934. "Die Singweisen Bernarts von Ventadorn nach dem Handschriften mitgeteilt." *Beihefte zur Zeitschrift für romanische Philologie,* 81. Halle: Niemeyer.

Arlt, Wulf. 1988. "Musica e testo nel canto francese: dai primi trovatori al mutamento stilistico intorno al 1300." *La Musica nel tempo di Dante.* Ed. Luigi Pestalozza. Milan: Unicopli. 175-197 and 306-321.

Arlt, Wulf. 1989. "Secular Monophony." *Performance Practice: Music Before 1600.* Ed. H.M. Brown and S. Sadie. New York-London: Norton/Grove. 55-78.

Aston, S.C. 1953. *Peirol, Troubadour of Auvergne.* Cambridge: Cambridge UP.

Aubrey, Elizabeth. 1982. *A Study of the Origins, History and Notation of the Troubadour Chansonnier Paris, Bibliothèque Nationale, F.Fr. 22543.* Diss. U of Maryland.

Aubrey, Elizabeth. 1989. "References to Music in Old Occitan Literature." *Acta Musicologica* 61: 110-149.

Aubrey, Elizabeth. 1996. *The Music of the Troubadours.* Bloomington: Indiana UP.

Audiau, Jean. 1922. *Les Poésies des quatre troubadours d'Ussel.* Paris: Delagrave.

Avalle, D'Arco S. 1960. *Peire Vidal, Poesie.* 2 vols. Milan: Napoli.

Bahat, Avner and Gérard Le Vot. 1996. *L'Oeuvre lyrique de Blondel de Nesle: Mélodies.* Paris: Champion.

Barolini, Teodolinda. 1984. *Dante's Poets: Textuality and Truth in the* Comedy. Princeton: Princeton UP.

Bartsch, Karl. 1870. *Romances et pastourelles françaises des XIIe et XIIIe siècles. Altfranzösische Romanzen und Pastourellen.* Leipzig. Rpt. Darmstadt: Wissenschaftliche Buchges., 1967, and Geneva: Slatkine, 1973.

Bec, Pierre. 1973. "L'aube française 'Gaite de la tor': pièce de ballet ou poème lyrique?" *Cahiers de civilisation médiévale* 16: 17-33.

Bec, Pierre. 1977-78. *La Lyrique française au moyen âge (XIIe et XIIIe siècles). Contribution à une typologie des genres poétiques médiévaux.* Vol. 1: Etudes. Vol. 2: Textes. Paris: Picard.

Bec, Pierre. 1979. " 'Trobairitz' et chansons de femme. Contribution à la connaissance du lyrisme féminin au moyen âge." *Cahiers de civilisation médiévale* 22: 235-262.

Bec, Pierre. 1982. "Le problème des genres chez les premiers troubadours." *Cahiers de civilisation médiévale* 25: 30-47.

Bec, Pierre. 1984. *Burlesque et obscénité chez les troubadours: le contre-texte au Moyen Age*. Paris: Stock.

Bec, Pierre. 1995. *Chants d'amour des femmes-troubadours*. Paris: Stock.

Bédier, Joseph and Pierre Aubry. 1909. *Les Chansons de croisade avec leurs mélodies*. Paris: Champion. Rpt. New York: Burt Franklin, 1971, and Geneva: Slatkine, 1974.

Bédier, Joseph. 1938. *Les chansons de Colin Muset*. CFMA. 2nd ed. Paris: Champion.

Bellenger, Yvonne and Danielle Quéruel. 1987. *Thibaut de Champagne. Prince et poète au XIIIe siècle*. Lyon: La Manufacture.

Berger, Rudolf. 1900. *Canchons und Partures des altfranzösischen Trouvere Adan de le Hale le Bochu d'Arras*. Vol. I: Canchons. Romanische Bibliothek. Halle a. S.: Niemeyer. Rpt. Geneva: Slatkine, 1978.

Bertolucci [Pizzorusso], Valeria. 1978. "Il canzoniere di un trovatore: il 'libro' di Guiraut Riquier." *Medioevo romanzo* 5: 216-259. Rpt. *Morfologie del testo medievale*, Bologna: Mulino, 1989.

Billy, Dominique. 1987. "Les Empreintes métriques de la musique dans l'estampie lyrique." *Romania* 108: 207-229.

Bond, Gerald A. 1982. *The Poetry of William VII, Count of Poitiers, IX Duke of Aquitaine*. New York: Garland.

Boogaard, Nico H.J. van den. 1969. *Rondeaux et refrains du 12e siècle au début du 14e*. Paris: Klincksieck.

Bossy, Michel-André. 1991. "Cyclical Composition in Guiraut Riquier's Book of Poems." *Speculum* 66: 277-293.

Boutière, Jean and A.-H. Schutz. 1964. *Biographies des troubadours*. 2nd ed. Paris: Nizet.

Brahney, Kathleen. 1989. *The Lyrics of Thibaut de Champagne*. New York: Garland.

Bruckner, Matilda Tomaryn. 1992. "Fictions of the Female Voice: The Women Troubadours." *Speculum* 67: 865-891.

Bruckner, Matilda Tomaryn, Laurie Shepard, and Sarah White. 1995. *The Songs of the Women Troubadours*. New York: Garland.

Brunel, Clovis. 1973. *Les plus anciennes chartes en langue provençale*. 2 vols. Geneva: Slatkine. [Rpt. of 1926 ed.]

Butterfield, Ardis. 1991. "Repetition and Variation in the Thirteenth-Century Refrain." *Journal of the Royal Musical Association* 116: 1-23.

Butterfield, Ardis. 1993. "The Language of Medieval Music: Two Thirteenth-Century Motets." *Plainsong and Medieval Music* 2: 1-16.

Chailley, Jacques. 1955. "Les premiers troubadours et les *versus* de l'école d'Aquitaine." *Romania* 76: 212-239.

Chambers, Frank M. 1952-3. "Imitation of Form in the Old Provençal Lyric." *Romance Philology* 6: 104-120.

Chambers, Frank M. 1971. *Proper Names in the Lyrics of the Troubadours*. U of North Carolina Studies in the Romance Languages and Literatures, 113. Chapel Hill: U of N. Carolina P.

Chambers, Frank M. 1985. *An Introduction to Old Provençal Versification*. Philadelphia: American Philosophical Society.

Cheyette, Fredric. "Women, Poets, and Politics in Occitania." Unpublished ms.

Chiarini, Georgio. c1985. *Il canzoniere di Jaufre Rudel*. L'Aquila: Lapadre.

Cohen, Joel. 1990. "Peirol's Vielle: Instrumental Participation in the Troubadour Repertory." *Historical Performance* 3: 73-77.

Coldwell, Maria V. 1986. " 'Jongleresses' and 'Trobaritz': Secular Musicians in Medieval France." *Women Making Music: The Western Art Tradition, 1105-1950*. Ed. Jane Bowers and Judith Tick. Urbana: U of Illinois P. 39-61.

Corbin, Solange. 1972. "La musique des troubadours." *Nouvelle anthologie de la lyrique occitane*. Ed. Pierre Bec. 2nd ed. Avignon: Aubanel. 72-77.

Coussemaker, Edmond de. 1872. *Oeuvres complètes du trouvère Adam de la Halle*. Paris: Société des Sciences, des Lettres et des Arts de Lille. A. Durand & Pédone-Lauriel. Rpt. Ridgewood, New Jersey: Gregg P, 1965, and Geneva: Slatkine, 1970.

Crocker, Richard. 1990. "French Polyphony of the Thirteenth Century." *The New Oxford History of Music, Vol. II: The Early Middle Ages to 1300*. Ed. Richard Crocker and David Hiley. Oxford: Oxford UP. 636-662.

Cropp, Glynnis M. 1975. *Le Vocabulaire courtois des troubadours de l'époque classique*. Geneva: Droz.

Cullmann, Arthur. 1914. *Die Lieder und Romanzen des Audefroi le Bastard*. Halle a. S.: Niemeyer. Rpt. Geneva: Slatkine, 1974.

Cummins, Patricia W. 1982. "Le Problème de la musique et de la poésie dans l'estampie." *Romania* 103: 259-277.

Dante Alighieri. *De vulgari eloquentia*. Editions include: 1) Ed. and trans. W. Welliver, Ravenna: Longo, 1981 [Latin and English]. 2) Trans. M. Shapiro, *q.v.* [English only].

Davenson: *See* Marrou

Dejeanne, J.M.L. 1909. *Poésies complètes du troubadour Marcabru*. Toulouse: Privat. Rpt: New York: Johnson, 1971.

Del Monte, Alberto. 1955. *Peire d'Alvernha: Liriche; testo, traduzione, e note*. Turin: Loescher-Chiantore.

Dijkstra, Cathrynke Th.J. 1995. *La Chanson de croisade: Etude thématique d'un genre hybride*. Amsterdam: Brinkman.

Doss-Quinby, Eglal. 1984. *Les Refrains chez les trouvères du XIIe siècle au début du XIVe*. New York: Peter Lang.

Doss-Quinby, Eglal. 1994. *The Lyrics of the Trouvères, A Research Guide (1970-1990)*. New York-London: Garland.

Dragonetti, Roger. 1960. *La Technique poétique des trouvères dans la chanson courtoise*. Bruges: "De Tempel".

Dronke, Peter. 1968. *The Medieval Lyric*. London: Hutchinson. [2nd ed. Cambridge UP, 1977]. *See* Dronke 1996.

Dronke, Peter. 1984a. "The Provençal Trobairitz: Casteloza." *Medieval Women Writers*. Ed. Katherine M. Wilson. Athens: U of Georgia P. 131-152.

Dronke, Peter. 1984b. *Women Writers of the Middle Ages*. Cambridge: Cambridge UP.

Dronke, Peter. 1996. *The Medieval Lyric*. 3rd ed. Cambridge: D. S. Brewer.

Dufournet, Jean. 1986. *Rutebeuf. Poèmes de l'infortune et autres poèmes*. Poésie, 209. Paris: Gallimard.

Dyggve, Holger Petersen. 1938. "Moniot d'Arras et Moniot de Paris." *Mémoires de la Société Néo-Philologique de Helsinki* 13, 1-252.

Dyggve, Holger Petersen. 1951. *Gace Brulé, trouvère champenois*. Mémoires de la Soc. Néophil. de Helsinki (Helsingfors), 16. Helsinki.

Eusebi, Mario. 1984. *Arnaut Daniel: Il sirventese e le canzoni*. Milan: Vanni Scheiwiller.

Everist, Mark. 1994. *French Motets in the Thirteenth Century: Music, Poetry and Genre*. Cambridge: Cambridge UP.

Faral, Edmond and Julia Bastin. 1959-60. *Oeuvres complètes de Rutebeuf*. 2 vols. Rpt. 1977. Paris: Picard.

Field, W.H.W. 1971. *Raimon Vidal: Poetry and Prose*. Vol. 2: *Abril issia*. Chapel Hill: U of N. Carolina P.

Formisano, Luciano. 1980. *Gontier de Soignies. Il canzoniere*. Documenti di filologia, 23. Milan: Riccardo Ricciardi.

Fotitch, Tatiana and Ruth Steiner. 1974. *Les Lais du roman de Tristan en prose*. Münchener Romanistische Arbeiten, 38. Munich: Fink.

Foulon, Charles. 1958. *L'Oeuvre de Jehan Bodel*. Travaux de la Fac. des Lettres et Sci. Hum. de Rennes, sér. 1, vol. 2. Paris: PU de France.

Frank, István. 1953, 1957. *Répertoire métrique de la poésie des troubadours*. 2 vols. Paris: Champion.

Fresco, Karen. 1988. *Gillebert de Berneville. Les poésies*. TLF. Geneva: Droz.

Gaunt, Simon B. 1989. *Troubadours and Irony*. Cambridge: Cambridge UP.

Gennrich, Friedrich. 1921, 1927. *Rondeaux, Virelais und Balladen aus das Ende des XIII. und dem ersten Drittel des XIV. Jahrhunderts*. Vol. I: Texte. Gesellschaft für romanische Literatur, 43. Dresden. Vol. II: Materialen, Literaturnachweise, Refrainverzeichnis. Gesell. für rom. Lit., 47. Göttingen.

Gennrich, Friedrich. 1932. *Grundriss einer Formenlehre des mittelalterlichen Liedes als Grundlage einer musikalischen Formenlehre des Liedes*. Halle: Niemeyer.

Gennrich, Friedrich. 1951. "Simon d'Authie, ein pikardischer Sänger." *Zeit. für romanische Philologie* 67: 49-104.

Gennrich, Friedrich. 1957. *Bibliographie der ältesten französischen und lateinischen Motetten*. Summa Musicae Medii Aevi, 2. Darmstadt.

Gonfroy, Gerard. 1982. "Le Reflet de la *canso* dans le *De Vulgari Eloquentia* et dans les *Leys d'Amors*." *Cahiers de civilisation médiévale* 25: 187-196.

Gossen, Nicoletta. 1988. "Musik und Text in Liedern des Trobadors Bernart de Ventadorn." *Schweizer Jahrbuch fur Musikwissenschaft* 4-5: 9-40.

Gouiran, Gérard. 1985. *L'Amour et la Guerre: l'oeuvre de Bertran de Born*. 2 vols. Aix-en-Provence: U de Provence.

Gouiran, Gérard. 1987. *Le Seigneur-Troubadour d'Hautefort: l'oeuvre de Bertran de Born*. 2nd edition. Aix-en-Provence: U de Provence.

Grassano, N. S. 1975. "Per un' edizione del sirventese: 'Pos Peire d'Alverng'a chantat.' " *Mélanges G. Favati*. Genoa. 193-213.

Gruber, Jörn. 1983. *Die Dialektik des Trobar*. Tübingen: Niemeyer.

Hamlin, Frank R., Peter T. Ricketts, and John Hathaway. 1985. *Introduction a l'étude de l'ancien provençal*: Textes d'étude. 2nd ed. Geneva: Droz. [lst ed. 1967]

A Handbook of the Troubadours. 1995. Ed. F.R.P. Akehurst and Judith M. Davis. Berkeley: U. of California P.

Harvey, Ruth E. and Simon Gaunt. 1988. "Bibliographie commentée du troubadour Marcabru (mise à jour)." *Le Moyen Age* 94: 425-455.

Harvey, Ruth E. 1989. *The Troubadour Marcabru and Love*. London: Westfield Publications in Medieval Studies.

Hasenohr, Geneviève and Michel Zink. 1992. *Dictionnaire des Lettres françaises, Le Moyen âge*. Paris: Fayard.

Hatto, Arthur T. 1965. *Eos: An Enquiry into the Theme of Lovers' Meetings and Partings at Dawn in Poetry.* The Hague: Mouton.

Hoppin, Richard H. 1978. *Medieval Music.* Accompanied by an Anthology of Medieval Music. New York: Norton.

Huet, Gédéon. 1912. *Chansons et descorts de Gautier de Dargies.* SATF. Paris: Firmin-Didot.

Hughes, Andrew. 1980. *Medieval Music: The Sixth Liberal Art.* Rev. ed. Toronto: Toronto UP. [lst ed. 1974]

Huot, Sylvia. 1987. *From Song to Book: The Poetics of Writing in Old French Lyric and Lyrical Narrative Poetry.* Ithaca-London: Cornell UP.

Huot, Sylvia. 1989. "Voices and Instruments in Medieval French Secular Music: On the Use of Literary Texts as Evidence for Performance Practice." *Musica Disciplina* 43: 63-113.

Huot, Sylvia. 1992. "Visualization and Memory: The Illustration of Troubadour Lyric in a Thirteenth-Century Manuscript." *Gesta* 31: 3-14.

Huot, Sylvia. 1994. "Languages of Love: Vernacular Motets on the Tenor FLOS FILIUS EJUS." *Conjunctures: Medieval Studies in Honor of Douglas Kelly.* Ed. K. Busby and N. Lacy. Amsterdam: Rodopi. 169-180.

Huot, Sylvia. 1997. *Allegorical Play in the Old French Motet: The Sacred and the Profane in Thirteenth-Century Polyphony.* Stanford: Stanford UP.

Järnström, Edw. 1910. *Recueil de chansons pieuses du 13e siècle,* I. Suomalaisen Tiedeakatemian Toimituksia (Annales Academiae Scientiarum Fennicae), sér. B, 3. Helsinki.

Järnström, Edw. and A. Långfors. 1927. *Recueil de chansons pieuses du 13e siècle,* II. Suomalaisen Tiedeakatemian Toimituksia (Annales Academiae Scientiarum Fennicae), sér. B, 20. Helsinki.

Jeanroy, Alfred. 1889. *Les Origines de la poésie lyrique en France au moyen âge.* Paris: Champion. Rpt. 1965.

Jeanroy, Alfred. 1897. "Les Chansons de Philippe de Beaumanoir." *Romania* 26: 517-536.

Jeanroy, Alfred, Louis Brandin and Pierre Aubry. 1901. *Lais et descorts français du XIIIe siècle. Texte et musique.* Mélanges de Musicologie Critique, 3. Paris: H. Welter. Rpt. Geneva: Slatkine, 1975.

Jeanroy, Alfred. 1924. *Les Chansons de Jaufre Rudel.* 2nd ed. rev. CFMA, 15. Paris: Champion. Rpt. 1965. [lst ed. 1915]

Jeanroy, Alfred. 1927. *Les Chansons de Guillaume IX, duc d'Aquitaine (1071-1127).* 2nd ed. rev. CFMA, 9. Paris: Champion. Rpt. 1972. [1st ed. 1913]

Le Jeu de Sainte Agnès: Drame provençal du XIVe siècle. Ed. Alfred Jeanroy. 1931. Paris: Champion.

Johnson, Susan. 1992. *The Lyrics of Richard de Semilli. A Critical Edition and Musical Transcription.* Binghamton: Center for Medieval and Early Renaissance Studies.

Karp, Theodore. 1964. "The Trouvère Manuscript Tradition." *The Department of Music Queens College of the City University of New York: Twenty-fifth Anniversary Festschrift (1937-1962).* Ed. Albert Mell. New York: Queens College P. 25-52.

Kay, Sarah. 1985. "La Notion de personnalité chez les troubadours: encore la question de la sincérité." *Mittelalterbilder aus neuer Perspektive.* Ed. E. Ruhe and R. Behrens. Munich: Wilhelm Fink. 166-182.

Kay, Sarah. 1987. "Rhetoric and Subjectivity in the Troubadour Lyric." *The Troubadours and the Epic.* Ed. L.M. Paterson and S.B. Gaunt. Coventry: U of Warwick. 102-142.

Kay, Sarah. 1989. "Derivation, Derived Rhyme, and the Trobairitz." *The Voice of the Trobairitz.* Ed. William D. Paden. Philadelphia: U of Pennsylvania P. 157-182.

Kay, Sarah. 1990. *Subjectivity in Troubadour Poetry.* Cambridge: Cambridge UP.

Klein, Otto. 1885. *Die Dichtungen des Mönchs von Montaudon.* Marburg.

Kolsen, Adolf. 1910, 1935. *Sämtlichte Lieder des Trobadors Giraut de Bornelh.* 2 vols. Halle.

Kussler-Ratyé, Gabrielle. 1917. "Les Chansons de la comtesse Béatrix de Dia." *Archivum Romanicum* 1: 161-182.

Långfors, Arthur. 1926. *Recueil général des jeux-partis français.* 2 vols. Paris: Champion.

Långfors, Arthur. 1945. *Deux recueils de sottes chansons.* Suomalaisen Tiedeakatemian Toimituksia (Annales Academiae Scientiarum Fennicae), sér. B, 53. Helsinki. Rpt. Geneva: Slatkine, 1977.

Lavaud, René. 1910. In Félix de la Salle de Rochemaure, *Les Troubadours cantaliens.* Aurillac.

Lavaud, René. 1957. *Poésies complètes du troubadour Peire Cardenal (1180-1278).* Toulouse: Privat.

Lazar, Moshé. 1966. *Bernard de Ventadorn, troubadour du XIIe siècle: Chansons d'amour.* Paris: Klincksieck.

Le Vot, Gérard, Pierre Lusson and Jacques Roubaud. 1979. "La Chanson de 'l'amour de loin' de Jaufre Rudel: Essai de lecture rythmique." *Mesura* 3: 1-92.

Le Vot, Gérard, Pierre Lusson and Jacques Roubaud. 1980. "La Sextine d'Arnaut Daniel: Essai de lecture rythmique." *Musique, Littérature et Société au Moyen Age.* Ed. Danielle Buschinger and André Crépin. Paris: Champion. 123-157.

Lecoy, Félix. 1956. Review of *Peirol, Troubadour of Auvergne,* ed. S.C. Aston. *Romania* 77: 522-523.

Lejeune, Rita. 1959. "La chanson de l''amour de loin' de Jaufre Rudel." *Studi in onore di Angelo Monteverdi*. 2 vols. Modena: S.T.E.M. 1: 403-443.

Lepage, Yvan. 1981. *L'Oeuvre lyrique de Richard de Fournival*. Publ. Médiévales de l'U d'Ottawa, 7. Ottawa: Editions de l'U d'Ottawa.

Lepage, Yvan. 1994. *L'Oeuvre lyrique de Blondel de Nesle*. Paris: Champion.

Lerond, Alain. 1964. *Chansons attribuées au Chastelain de Couci*. Paris: PU de France.

Levy, Emile. 1909. *Petit dictionnaire provençal-français*. Heidelberg: Winter. 5th rpt. 1973.

Leys d'amors. (Molinier, Guilhem). 1) 1841-43. *Las flors del Gay Saber, estiers dichas Las Leys d'Amors*. Trans. d'Aguilar and d'Escouloubre, revised and completed by Adolphe-F. Gatien-Arnoult. Monumens de la littérature romane, 1-3. Toulouse. Rpt. Geneva: Slatkine, 1977. 2) 1919-20. *Las Leys d'amors*. Ed. Joseph Anglade. 3 vols. Toulouse: Privat. Rpt. New York: Johnson, 1971.

Linker, Robert W. 1979. *A Bibliography of Old French Lyrics*. University, MS: Romance Monographs.

Linskill, Joseph. 1964. *The Poems of the Troubadour Raimbaut de Vaqueiras*. The Hague: Mouton. Rpt. 1983.

Longobardi, Monica. 1982-3. "I vers del trovatore Guiraut Riquier." *Studi mediolatini e volgari* 29: 17-163.

Lote, Georges. 1949-55. *Histoire du vers français*. 3 vols. Paris: Boivin.

Maillard, Jean. 1982. *Adam de la Halle. Perspective musicale*. Paris: Champion.

Marrou, Henri-Irenee. 1971. *Les Troubadours*. 2nd ed. Paris: Seuil. [1st ed. under the name of Henri Davenson, Paris, 1961]

Marshall, John H. 1971. *The Chansons of Adam de la Halle*. Manchester: Manchester UP.

Marshall, John H. 1975. *The Transmission of Troubadour Poetry*. Inaugural Lecture at Westfield College. London.

Marshall, John H. 1978-79. "Imitation of Metrical Form in Peire Cardenal." *Romance Philology* 32: 18-48.

Marshall, John H. 1980. "Pour l'étude des contrafacta dans la poésie des troubadours." *Romania* 403: 289-335.

McGee, Timothy J. 1989. "Medieval Dances: Matching the Repertory with Grocheio's Descriptions." *Journal of Musicology* 7: 498-517.

McGee, Timothy J. 1996. *Singing Early Music: The Pronunciation of European Languages in the Late Middle Ages and Renaissance*. Bloomington: Indiana UP.

Ménard, Philippe. 1970. *Les Poésies de Guillaume le Vinier*. TLF. Geneva: Droz; Paris: Minard. 2nd ed. Geneva: Droz, 1983.

Meneghetti, Maria Luisa. 1984. *Il pubblico dei trovatori*. Modena: Mucchi.

Mölk, Ulrich and Friedrich Wolfzettel. 1972. *Répertoire métrique de la poésie lyrique française des origines à 1350*. Munich: Fink.

Mölk, Ulrich. 1962. *Guiraut Riquier. Las Cansos*. Heidelberg: Winter.

Monson, Don Alfred. 1985. "Jaufre Rudel et l'amour lointain: les origines d'une légende." *Romania* 106: 36-56.

Morawski, Joseph. 1925. *Proverbes français antérieurs au XVe siècle*. CFMA. Paris: Champion.

Mouzat, Jean. 1965. *Les Poèmes de Gaucelm Faidit*. Paris: Nizet.

Nelson, Deborah and Hendrik van der Werf. 1985. *The Lyrics and Melodies of Adam de la Halle*. New York: Garland.

The New Grove Dictionary of Music and Musicians. 1980. Ed. Stanley Sadie. 20 vols. London: Macmillan. "Sources": III, Secular monophony; V, Early motet. David Fallows (III), Ernest H. Sanders (V). "Troubadours and trouvères": I, Troubadour poetry; II, Trouvère poetry; III, Music. John Stevens (I, II), Theodore Karp (III).

The New Oxford History of Music. II: The Early Middle Ages to 1300. 1990. Rev. edition. Ed. Richard Crocker and David Hiley. Oxford: Oxford UP. *See* Crocker 1990 *and* Stevens 1990.

Newcombe, Terence. 1972. *Les Poésies du trouvère Jehan Erart*. TLF. Geneva: Droz—Paris: Minard.

Newcombe, Terence. 1975. *The Songs of Jehan Erart, 13th Century Trouvère*. Corpus Mensurabilis Musicae, 67. American Inst. of Musicology.

Newcombe, Terence H. 1978. *Les Poésies de Thibaut de Blaison*. Geneva: Droz.

Nichols, Stephen G. Jr. et al. 1965. *The Songs of Bernart de Ventadorn*. U of North Carolina Studies in the Romance Languages and Literatures, 39. Chapel Hill: U of N. Carolina P.

Nichols, Stephen G. Jr. 1976. "Toward an Aesthetic of the Provencal Lyric II: Marcabru's Dire vos vuoill ses doptansa (BdT 293, 18)." *Italian Literature, Roots and Branches*. Ed. Giose Rimanelli and Kenneth John Atchity. New Haven: Yale UP. 15-37.

Nicod, Lucie. 1917. *Les Jeux partis d'Adam de la Halle*. Paris: Champion. Rpt. Geneva: Slatkine, 1974.

Nissen, Elisabeth. 1928. *Les Chansons attribuées à Guiot de Dijon et Jocelin*. CFMA, 59. Paris: Champion.

Paden, William D. Jr., et al. 1981-2. "The Poems of the Trobairitz Na Castelloza," *Romance Philology* 35: 158-182.

Paden, William D. Jr., Tilde Sankovitch and Patricia H. Stablein. 1986. *The Poems of the Troubadour Bertran de Born*. Berkeley: U of California P.

Paden, William. 1987. *The Medieval Pastourelle*. 2 vols. New York: Garland.

Page, Christopher. 1986. *Voices and Instruments of the Middle Ages. Instrumental Practice and Songs in France, 1100-1300*. Berkeley: U of California P. [London: Dent, 1987]

Page, Christopher. 1989. *The Owl and the Nightingale: Musical Life and Ideas in France 1100-1300*. London. [Berkeley: U of California P, 1990.]

Page, Christopher. 1993a. *Discarding Images: Reflections on Music and Culture in Medieval France*. Oxford: Clarendon P.

Page, Christopher. 1993b. "Johannes de Grocheio on Secular Music: A Corrected Text and a New Translation." *Plainsong and Medieval Music* 2: 17-41.

Page, Christopher, ed. 1995. *Songs of the Trouvères*. Devon: Antico Editions.

Parker, Ian R. 1977. "Troubadour and Trouvère Songs: Problems in Modal Analysis." *Revue Belge de Musicologie* 31: 20-37.

Parker, Ian R. 1978. "A propos de la tradition manuscrite des chansons de trouvères." *Revue de Musicologie* 64: 181-202.

Pasero, Nicolò. 1973. *Guglielmo IX d'Aquitania: Poesie*. Modena: Mucchi.

Pasero, Nicolò. 1980. "Sulla collocazione socioletteraria della 'pastorela' de Marcabruno." *L'Immagine riflessa* 4: 347-364.

Pasero, Nicolò. 1983. "Pastora contro cavaliere, Marcabruno contro Guglielmo IX - Fenomeni di intertestualità in *L'autrier jost'una sebissa* (BdT 293,30)." *Cultura Neolatina* 43: 9-25.

Paterson, Linda. 1975. *Troubadours and Eloquence*. Oxford: Oxford UP.

Pattison, Walter T. 1952. *The Life and Works of the Troubadour Raimbaut d'Orange*. Minneapolis: U of Minnesota P.

Perrin, R.H. 1956. "Some Notes on Troubadour Melodic Types." *Journal of the American Musicological Society* 9: 12-18.

Perugi, Maurizio. 1978. *Le canzoni di Arnaut Daniel*. 2 vols. Milan-Naples: Ricciardi.

Pesce, Dolores. 1987. *The Affinities and Medieval Transposition*. Bloomington: Indiana UP.

Pfaff, S.L.H. 1853. *Guiraut Riquier*. Vol. 4 of C. A. F. Mahn's *Werke der Troubadours*. Berlin-Paris.

Phan, Chantal. 1987. "Le Style poético-musical de Guiraut Riquier." *Romania* 108: 66-78.

Philippson, Emil. 1873. *Der Mönch von Montaudon*. Halle.

Pickens, Rupert T. 1978. *The Songs of Jaufre Rudel*. Toronto: Pontifical Institute.

Pillet, Alfred and Henry Carstens. 1933. *Bibliographie der Troubadours*. Halle: Niemeyer.

Pinguet, A. 1930. *Les Chansons et pastourelles de Thibaut de Blaison*. Angers: Société des Amis du Livre Angevin.

Pirot, François. 1973. "'A la fontana del vergier' du troubadour Marcabru (PC, 293,1): Edition, traduction et notes." *Mélanges . . . offerts à Monsieur Paul Imbs*. Strasbourg: Klincksieck. 621-642.

Poe, Elizabeth Wilson. 1984a. *From Poetry to Prose in old Provençal. The Emergence of the* Vidas, *the* Razos, *and the* Razos de trobar. Birmingham, AL: Summa Publications.

Poe, Elizabeth Wilson. 1984b. "New Light on the Alba: A Genre Redefined." *Viator* 15: 139-150.

Poe, Elizabeth Wilson. 1984c. "The Three Modalities of the Old Provençal Dawn Song." *Romance Philology* 37: 259-272.

Poe, Elizabeth Wilson. 1985. "The Lighter Side of the Alba: Ab la genser que sia." *Romanistisches Jahrbuch* 36: 87-103.

Pollina, Vincent. 1988. "Melodic Continuity and Discontinuity in *A chantar m'er* of the Comtessa de Dia." *Miscellanea di studi romanzi offerta a Giuliano Gasca-Quierazza* . 2 vols. Alessandria: Edizioni dell' Orso. 2: 887-896.

Pollina, Vincent. 1989. "Word/Music Relations in the Work of the Troubadour Gaucelm Faidit: Some Preliminary Observations on the Planh." *Miscellanea di studi in onore di Aurelio Roncaglia*. 2 vols. Modena: Mucchi. 2: 1075-1090. [First published in *Cultura Neolatina* 47 (1987).]

Pollina, Vincent. 1991. *Si cum Marcabrus declina: Studies in the Poetics of the Troubadour Marcabru*. Modena: Mucchi.

Pollina, Vincent. 1992. "Structure verbale et expression mélodique dans *Mon cor e mi* du troubadour Gaucelm Faidit." *Contacts de langues, de civilisations et intertextualités, Actes du IIIème Congrès International de l'Association d'Etudes Occitanes*. Ed. Gérard Gouiran. Montpellier: U Paul Valéry. 2: 669-678.

Pollina, Vincent. 1993. "Les Mélodies du troubadour Marcabru: Questions de style et de genre." *Atti del Secondo Congresso Internazionale della "Association Internationale d'Etudes occitanes."* Torino, 31 agosto-5 settembre 1987. Ed. Giuliano Gasca-Queirazza. 2 vols. Turin: AIEO/Dipartimento di Scienze Letterarie e Filologiche, U di Torino. 1: 289-306.

Randel, Don Michael, ed. 1986. *The New Harvard Dictionary of Music*. Cambridge: Harvard UP.

Raugei, Anna Maria. 1981. *Gautier de Dargies: Poesie*. Pubbl. della Fac. di Lett. e Filologia dell'U di Milano, 90. Florence: La Nuova Italia.

Raynaud, Gaston. 1881-1883. *Recueil de Motets français des XIIe et XIIIe siècles*. 2 vols. Paris: Vieweg. Rpt. Hildesheim-New York: Georg Olms, 1972.

Regalado, Nancy F. 1970. *Poetic Patterns in Rutebeuf: A Study in Noncourtly Poetic Modes of the Thirteenth Century*. New Haven: Yale UP.

Ricketts, Peter and E. J. Hathaway. 1966. "Le 'Vers del lavador' de Marcabrun: édition critique, traduction et commentaire." *Revue des langues romanes* 77: 1-11.

Rieger, Angelica. 1985. " 'Ins e.l cor port, dona, vostra faisso': Image et imaginaire de la femme à travers l'enluminure dans les chansonniers de troubadours." *Cahiers de civilisation médiévale* 28: 385-415.

Rieger, Angelica. 1991. *Trobairitz: Der Beitrag der Frau in der altokzitanischen höfischen Lyrik*. Edition des Gesamtkorpus. *Beihefte zur Zeitschrift für romanische Philologie*, 233. Tübingen: Niemeyer.

Rieger, Dietmar. 1983. "Audition et lecture dans le domaine de la poésie troubadouresque." *Revue des langues romanes* 87: 69-85.

Rieger, Dietmar. 1987. " 'Senes breu de parguamina'? Zum Problem des 'gelesenen Lieds' im Mittelalter." *Romanische Forschungen* 99: 1-18.

Riquer, Martín de. 1983. *Los trovadores: historia literaria y textos*. 3 vols. Barcelona. [First published 1975]

Rivière, Jean-Claude. 1974, 1975, 1976. *Pastourelles*. 3 vols. TLF. Geneva: Droz.

Rivière, Jean-Claude. 1978. *Les Poésies du trouvère Jacques de Cambrai*. TLF. Geneva: Droz.

Rohloff, Ernst. 1967. *Die Quellenhandschriften zum Musiktraktat des Johannes de Grocheio*. Leipzig: Deutscher Verlag für Musik.

Roques, Mario. 1949. *Etudes de littérature française*. Geneva: Droz.

Rosenberg, Samuel N. and Hans Tischler. 1981. *Chanter m'estuet: Songs of the Trouvères*. Bloomington: Indiana UP—London: Faber and Faber.

Rosenberg, Samuel N., Samuel Danon, and Hendrik van der Werf. 1985. *The Lyrics and Melodies of Gace Brulé*. New York: Garland.

Rosenberg, Samuel N., Hans Tischler, and Marie-Geneviève Grossel. 1995. *Chansons des trouvères*. Lettres gothiques. Paris: Librairie Générale Française.

Rosenstein, Roy. 1990. "New Perspectives on Distant Love: Jaufre Rudel, Uc Bru, and Sarrazina." *Modern Philology* 87: 225-238.

Routledge, Michael J. 1969. "Essai d'établissement du texte du sirventes: 'Pos Peire d'Alvernhe a chantat.' " *Revue des langues romanes* 78: 103-127.

Routledge, Michael J. 1977. *Les Poésies du Moine de Montaudon*. Montpellier: Centre d'Etudes Occitanes.

Sachs, Curt. 1961. *The Wellsprings of Music*. Ed. Jaap Kunst. The Hague.

Sakari, Aimo. 1949. "Azalais de Porcairagues, le Joglar de Raimbaut d'Orange." *Neuphilologische Mitteilungen* 50: 23-43, 56-87, 174-198.

Saville, Jonathan. 1972. *The Medieval Erotic Alba*. New York: Columbia UP.

Scheler, Aug. 1876. *Trouvères belges du XIIe au XIVe siècle*. Brussels: Closson. Rpt. Geneva: Slatkine, 1977.

Scheler, Aug. 1879. *Trouvères belges (nouvelle série)*. Louvain: Lefever. Rpt. Geneva: Slatkine, 1977.

Schlager, Karlheinz. 1984. "Annaherung an ein Troubadour-Lied. 'Tant m'abellis l'amoros pessamens' von Folquet de Marseille." *Analysen: Beitrage zu einer Problemgeschichte des Komponierens. Festschrift für Hans Heinrich Eggebrecht zum 65. Geburtstag*. Ed. Werner Breig, Reinhold Brinkmann and Elmar Budde. Stuttgart: Steiner. 1-13.

Schultz[-Gora], Oskar. 1888. *Die provenzalischen Dichterinnen*. Leipzig. Rpt. Geneva: Slatkine, 1975.

Schulze-Busacker, Elisabeth. 1988. "L'Influence littéraire du 'Vers del lavador.' " *Miscellanea de studi romanzi offerta a Giuliano Gasca Queirazza*. Ed. Anna Cornagliotti et al. Turin: Edizioni dell'Orso. 977-988.

Schwan, Eduard. 1886. *Die altfranzösischen Liederhandschriften, ihre Verhältnis, ihre Entstehung une ihre Bestimmung*. Berlin: Weidmann.

Seay, Albert, trans. 1974. Johannes de Grocheo, *De Musica*. Colorado Springs: Colorado Coll. Music P.

Sesini, Ugo. "Le Melodie trobadoriche nel canzoniere provenzale della Biblioteca Ambrosiana R71 Sup." *Studi medievali*, n.s. 12 (1939): 1-101; 13 (1940): 1-107; 14 (1941): 31-105; 15 (1942): 189-190, plus 24 pp. of facsimiles. [Also Turin, 1942.]

Shapiro, Marianne. 1990. *De vulgari eloquentia: Dante's Book of Exile*. Lincoln: U of Nebraska P.

Sharman, Ruth Verity. 1989. *The 'Cansos' and 'Sirventes' of the Troubadour Giraut de Borneil: A Critical Edition*. Cambridge: Cambridge UP.

Smith, Nathaniel and Thomas G. Bergin. 1984. *An Old Provençal Primer*. New York: Garland.

Spanke, Hans. 1925. *Eine altfranzösische Liedersammlung*. Halle a. S.: Niemeyer.

Spanke, Hans. 1955. *G. Raynauds Bibliographie des altfranzösischen Liedes*. Leyden: Brill. Rpt. 1980.

Steffens, Georg. 1902. "Der kritische Text der Gedichte von Richart de Semilli." *Beiträge zur rom. und engl. Philologie. Festgabe für Wendelin Foerster*. Halle a. S.: Niemeyer. 331-362. Rpt. Geneva: Slatkine, 1977.

Steffens, Georg. 1905. *Die Lieder des Troveors Perrin von Angincourt*. Romanische Bibliothek. Halle a. S.: Niemeyer.

Stevens, John. 1986. *Words and Music in the Middle Ages: Song, Narrative, Dance and Drama, 1050-1350.* Cambridge: Cambridge UP.

Stevens, John. 1990. "Medieval Song." *The New Oxford History of Music, Vol. II: The Early Middle Ages to 1300.* Ed. Richard Crocker and David Hiley. Oxford: Oxford UP. 357-451.

Stimming, Albert. 1913. *Bertran von Born.* Halle, Niemeyer. [1st ed. 1879]

Stronski, Stanislaw. 1910. *Le Troubadour Folquet de Marseille.* Cracow: Spolka Widawnicza Polska.

The Study of Chivalry. 1988. Ed. Howell Chickering and Thomas H. Seiler. Kalamazoo: Medieval Inst. Publications.

Switten, Margaret. 1985. *The* Cansos *of Raimon de Miraval: A Study of Poems and Melodies.* Cambridge, MA: Medieval Academy.

Switten, Margaret and Howell Chickering. 1988. *The Medieval Lyric: Anthologies and Cassettes for Teaching.* A Project Supported by the National Endowment for the Humanities and Mount Holyoke College. 3 Anthologies; Commentary volume; 5 audio cassettes. South Hadley, MA: Mount Holyoke College.

Switten, Margaret. 1991. "De la Sextine: amour et musique chez Arnaut Daniel." *Mélanges de langue et de littérature occitanes en hommage à Pierre Bec.* Poitiers: U de Poitiers C.E.S.C.M. 549-565.

Switten, Margaret. 1992a. "Modèle et variations: Saint Martial de Limoges et les troubadours." *Contacts de langues, de civilisations et intertextualité, Actes du IIIeme Congrès International de l'Association Internationale d'Etudes occitanes.* Ed. Gérard Gouiran. 2 vols. Montpellier: U Paul Valéry. 2: 679-696.

Switten, Margaret. 1992b. "Singing the Second Crusade." *The Second Crusade and the Cistercians.* Ed. Michael Gervers. New York: St. Martin's P. 67-76.

Switten, Margaret. 1993. "The Voice and the Letter: On Singing in the Vernacular." *Acta 17: Words and Music.* Ed. Paul R. Laird. Binghamton: CEMERS. 51-73.

Switten, Margaret. 1995. *Music and Poetry in the Middle Ages. A Guide to Research on French and Occitan Song, 1100-1400.* New York-London: Garland.

Taylor, Robert A. 1977. *La Littérature occitane du moyen âge: Bibliographie sélective et critique.* Toronto: U of Toronto P. [Updates of this bibliography are published in the *Bulletins de l'Association Internationale d'Etudes occitanes.* U of London, 1990, and following yrs.]

Tischler, Hans. 1978. *The Montpellier Codex.* 4 vols. Madison: A-R Editions.

Toja, Gianluigi. 1960. *Arnaut Daniel: Canzoni.* Florence: Sansoni.

Topsfield, L.T. 1975. *Troubadours and Love.* Cambridge: Cambridge UP.

Topsfield, Leslie. 1971. *Les Poésies du Troubadour Raimon de Miraval.* Paris: Nizet.

Treitler, Leo. 1965-66. "Musical Syntax in the Middle Ages: Background to an Aesthetic Problem." *Perspectives of New Music* 4: 75-85.

Treitler, Leo. 1981. "Oral, Written, and Literate Process in the Transmission of Medieval Music." *Speculum* 56: 471-491.

Treitler, Leo and Ritva Jonsson. 1983. "Medieval Music and Language: A Reconsideration of the Relationship." *Studies in the History of Music*, Vol. 1: *Music and Language*, 1-23. New York: Broude Brothers.

Treitler, Leo. 1991. "The Troubadours Singing Their Poems." *The Union of Words and Music in Medieval Poetry.* Ed. Rebecca A. Baltzer, Thomas Cable and James I. Wimsatt. Austin: U of Texas P. 15-48.

Treitler, Leo. 1992. "Medieval Lyric." *Models of Musical Analysis: Music before 1600.* Ed. Mark Everist. Oxford: Blackwell. 1-19.

van der Werf, Hendrik. 1972. *The Chansons of the Troubadours and Trouvères. A Study of the melodies and their Relation to the Poems.* Utrecht: Oosthoek.

van der Werf, Hendrik. 1977, 1979. *Trouvères-Melodien I-II.* Monumenta Monodica Medii Aevi, 11-12. Cassel-Basle-Tours-London: Bärenreiter.

van der Werf, Hendrik. 1983. *The Emergence of Gregorian Chant.* Rochester: published by the author.

van der Werf, Hendrik. 1984. *The Extant Troubadour Melodies.* Rochester: published by the author. Texts edited by Gerald A. Bond.

Van Vleck, Amelia E. 1991. *Memory and Re-Creation in Troubadour Lyric.* Berkeley: U of California P.

Vatteroni, S. 1990. "Peire Cardenal e 'l'estribot' nella poesia provenzale." *Medioevo Romanzo* 15: 61-91.

Waitz, Hugo. 1899. "Der kritische Text der Gedichte von Gillebert de Berneville mit Angabe sämtlicher Lesarten nach den Parisen Handschriften." *Beiträge zur rom. Phil., Festgabe für Gustav Gröber.* Halle a. S. 39-118. Rpt. Geneva: Slatkine, 1975.

Wallensköld, Axel. 1921. *Les Chansons de Conon de Béthune.* CFMA. Paris: Champion.

Wallensköld, Axel. 1925. *Les Chansons de Thibaut de Champagne, roi de Navarre.* SATF. Paris: Champion.

Wiese, Leo. 1904. *Die Lieder des Blondel de Nesle.* Gesellschaft für romanishe Literatur, 5. Dresden.

Wilhelm, James J. 1981. *The Poetry of Arnaut Daniel.* New York: Garland.

Wilkins, Nigel. 1967. *The Lyric Works of Adam de la Hale.* Corpus Mensurabilis Musicae, 44. [Dallas:] American Inst. of Musicology.

Wilkins, Nigel. 1988. *The Lyric Art of Medieval France.* Fulbourn: New Press.

Wilson, David Fenwick. 1990. *Music of the Middle Ages: Style and Structure.* With *An Anthology for Performance and Study*, trans. of Latin and Italian texts by Robert Crouse and of French and Provençal by Hans T. Runte, and *Recording to Accompany Music of the Middle Ages* by the Hilliard Ensemble and the Western Wind, Paul Hillier, dir. New York: Schirmer.

Woledge, Brian. 1965. "Old Provençal and Old French." *Eos: An Enquiry into the Theme of Lovers' Meetings and Partings at Dawn in Poetry.* Ed. Arthur T. Hatto. The Hague: Mouton. 344-389.

Wolf, George and Roy Rosenstein. 1983. *The Poetry of Cercamon and Jaufre Rudel.* New York: Garland. Melodies transcribed by Hendrik van der Werf.

Yudkin, Jeremy. 1989. *Music in Medieval Europe.* Englewood Cliffs: Prentice Hall.

Zarifopol, P. 1904. *Kritischer Text der Lieder Richards de Fournival.* Diss. Halle a. S. 1904. Halle a. S.: Karras.

Zenker, Rudolf. 1900. *Die Lieder Peires von Auvergne.* Erlangen: Junge. Rpt. Geneva: Slatkine 1977.

Zink, Michel. 1972. *La Pastourelle. Poésie et folklore au moyen âge.* Paris-Montreal: Bordas.

Zink, Michel. 1978. *Belle. Essai sur les Chansons de toile.* Paris: Champion. Melodies transcribed by Gérard Le Vot.

Zink, Michel. 1989-90. *Rutebeuf. Oeuvres complètes.* 2 vols. Classiques Garnier. Paris: Bordas.

Zink, Michel. 1990. *Le Moyen Age: Littérature française.* Nancy: PU de Nancy. [Translation: *Medieval French Literature: An Introduction*, trans. Jeff Rider. Binghamton: Medieval and Renaissance Texts and Studies, 1994.]

Zink, Michel. 1992. *Littérature française du Moyen Age.* Paris: PU de France.

Zufferey, François. 1987. *Recherches linguistiques sur les chansonniers provençaux.* Geneva: Droz.

Zumthor, Paul. 1963. *Langue et techniques poétiques à l'époque romane (Xie - XIIIe siècles).* Paris: Klincksieck.

Zumthor, Paul. 1972. *Essai de poétique médiévale.* Paris: Seuil. [Translation: *Toward a Medieval Poetics*, trans. Ph. Bennett. Minneapolis: U of Minnesota P, 1992.]

Zumthor, Paul. 1987. *La Lettre et la voix.* Paris: Seuil.

Zumthor, Paul. 1993. "L'absente, ou de la poésie des troubadours." *Omaggio a Gianfranco Folena.* Ed. P.V. Mengaldo. 3 vols. Padua: Editoriale Programma. 1: 109-117.

SELECTIVE DISCOGRAPHY

The compact disc accompanying this Anthology is entitled *SONGS OF THE TROUBADOURS AND TROUVÈRES: MUSIC AND POETRY FROM MEDIEVAL FRANCE*, Peter Becker, baritone, and Robert Eisenstein, medieval fiddle. Songs performed are indicated in the Table of Contents of the Anthology and are not included in this discography. The CD [Bard BDCD 1-9711] is also available separately from the Folger Shakespeare Library, 201 East Capitol Street SE, Washington, DC 20003; from Albany Music Distributors Inc., Albany, New York; or from record stores nationwide.

1. *"A chantar": Lieder der Frauen-Minne im Mittelalter.* ESTAMPIE: MÜNCHNER ENSEMBLE FÜR FRÜHE MUSIK. CD, Christophorus 74583, 1990.

2. *Bella Domna. The Medieval Woman: Lover, Poet, Patroness and Saint.* SINFONYE, Stevie Wishart, director. CD Hyperion CDA66283, 1988.

3. *Camino de Santiago: Musik auf dem Pilgerweg zum Hl. Jacobus.* ENSEMBLE FÜR FRÜHE MUSIK AUGSBURG. LP, Christophorus SCGLX 74032, recorded 1986.

4. *Cansós de Trobairitz (Lyrik der Trobairitz um 1200).* HESPÈRION XX. CD ADD Reflexe EMI CBM 7 63417 2, 1990. [First issued 1978.]

5. *La Chambre des Dames: Chansons et polyphonies de trouvères (XIIe & XIIIe siècles).* ENSEMBLE DIABOLUS IN MUSICA, Antoine Guerber, director. CD Studio SM D2604, recorded 1994.

6. *La Chanson d'ami: Chansons de femme-XIIe et XIIIe siècles.* Katia Karé, chant; ENSEMBLE PERCEVAL, Guy Robert, director. CD Arion ARN68290, 1994.

7. *Chansons des Rois et des Princes du Moyen Age.* ENSEMBLE PERCEVAL, Guy Robert, director. CD Arion ARN 68031, 1987.

8. *Chansons des Troubadours & Trouvères.* Gérard Le Vot. CD AAD Studio SM 12 21.75 [SM 62], 1993. [Reissue of troubadour pieces from LP 30 1043, SM 37, 1981, and trouvère pieces from LP 3011.51, SM 37, 1982.]

9. *Chansons de Toile au temps du Roman de la rose.* Esther Lamandier. CD ADD, AL 1011, 1987. [First issued 1983.]

10. *Chansons de Trouvères.* Paul Hillier, voice; Andrew Lawrence-King, harp, psaltery, portative organ. CD Harmonia Mundi HMU 907184, 1997.

11. *Chanterai por mon coraige.* STUDIO DER FRÜHEN MUSIC, Thomas Binkley, director. CD ADD Teldec 4509-95073-2, 1994. [First issued 1970, 1974.]

12. *The Courts of Love: Music from the Time of Eleanor of Aquitaine.* SINFONYE, Stevie Wishart, director. CD Hyperion CDA66367, 1990.

13. *Crusades in nomine Domini.* ESTAMPIE: MÜNCHNER ENSEMBLE FÜR FRÜHE MUSIK. CD Christophorus CHR 77183, 1996.

14. *Dante and the Troubadours.* SEQUENTIA. CD Deutsche Harmonia Mundi DM 05472-77227-2, 1995.

15. *Les Escholiers de Paris: Motets, Chansons et Estampies du XIIIe siecle.* ENSEMBLE GILLES BINCHOIS, Dominique Vellard, director. CD Harmonic Records H/CD9245, 1992. [Excellent introduction to the motet.]

16. *Forgotten Provence: Music-Making in the South of France, 1150-1550.* THE MARTIN BEST CONSORT. CD Nimbus Records NI5445, 1995.

17. *Le Fou sur le pont. Bernatz de Ventadorn: Troubadour Songs.* CAMERATA MEDITERRANEA, Joel Cohen, director. CD Erato 4509-94825-2, 1994.

18. *Lo Gai Saber: Troubadours et jongleurs 1100-1300.* CAMERATA MEDITERRANEA, Joel Cohen, director. CD Erato 2292-45647-2, 1991.

19. *Love's Illusion. Music from the Montpellier Codex, 13th-Century.* ANONYMOUS 4. CD, Harmonia Mundi HMU 907109, 1994.

20. *Le Manuscrit du Roi (vers 1250). Trouvères & Troubadours.* ENSEMBLE PERCEVAL, Guy Robert, director. CD Arion ARN 68225, 1993.

21. *The Marriage of Heaven and Hell. Motets and Songs from Thirteenth-Century France.* GOTHIC VOICES. Christopher Page, director. CD Hyperion, CDA66423, 1990. [Excellent introduction to the motet.]

22. *The Medieval Lyric.* Five audio cassettes. Recorded 1987 and 1988, Stereo/Dolby. Margaret Switten, director, Mount Holyoke College, South Hadley, MA 01075.

23. *Music for the Lion-Hearted King.* GOTHIC VOICES, Christopher Page, director. CD Hyperion CDA66336, 1989.

24. *Music of the Crusades.* THE EARLY MUSIC CONSORT OF LONDON, David Munrow, director. CD ADD, London 430 264-2, 1991. [First issued 1971.]

25. *Musique en Aquitaine au temps d'Alienor (XIIe s.): Chants de troubadours et versus aquitains.* ENSEMBLE DIABOLUS IN MUSICA, Dominique Touron, director. CD Editions Plein Jeu DMP 9105 C, recorded 1990.

26. *Proensa.* THEATRE OF VOICES, Paul Hillier, director. CD ECM 1368 (837 360-2[Y]), 1989.

27. *The Spirits of England and France 2: Songs of the Trouvères.* GOTHIC VOICES, Christopher Page, director. CD Hyperion CDA66773, 1995.

28. *"The sweet look and the loving manner." Trobairitz Love Lyrics and Chansons de Femme from Medieval France.* SINFONYE, Stevie Wishart, director. CD Hyperion CDA66625, 1993.

29. *The Testament of Tristan: Songs of Bernart de Bentadorn (1125-1195).* Martin Best. CD Hyperion CDA66211, 1987.

30. *Le Troubadour Guiraut Riquier.* Katia Caré and Gérard Zuchetto, chant; PERCEVAL, Guy Robert, director. CD Arion ARN68315, 1995.

31. *Troubadour Songs and Medieval Lyrics*. Paul Hillier, baritone, medieval harp; Stephen Stubbs, medieval lute; Lena-Liis Kiesel, portative organ. CD, Hyperion CDA66094, issued 1990. [First issued 1984.]

32. *Troubadours*. CLEMENCIC CONSORT, Rene Clemencic, director. CD Harmonia Mundi HMX 2901524-7, 1995. [Coffret with *Cantigas de Santa María*; first issued in 1977.]

33. *Troubadours and Trouvères*. Russell Oberlin, counter-tenor; Seymour Barab, viol. CD, Lyrichord Early Music Series LEMS 8001, 1994. [First issued c. 1958.]

34. *Trouvères: Courtly Love Songs from Northern France c. 1175-1300*. SEQUENTIA. CD Harmonia Mundi 7715-2-RC, 2 disks, recorded 1984, issued 1990.

35. *Trouvères à la cour de Champagne*. ENSEMBLE VENANCE FORTUNAT, Anne-Marie Deschamps, director. CD Harmonia Mundi ED 13045, 1995.

36. *Trouvères, Troubadours, et Gregorien*. L'ARCHE: Chanterelle del Vasto, voice; Yves Tessier, voice; Mildred Clary, lute. LP, SM 30M - 419T, recorded c.1956.

37. *I Trovatori nei castelli e nelle corti d'Europa: Canzoniere provenzale Ambrosiano R71*. Grazielle Benini, voce; Walter Benvenuti, liuto. CD ADD Sarx Records SXAM 2035-2, issued 1995. [First issued 1979.]

38. *The Unicorn: Anne Azéma. Medieval French Songs*. Anne Azéma, voice; Cheryl Ann Fulton, harps; Shira Kammen, vielle, rebec, harp; Jesse Lepkoff, flute. CD, Erato 4509-94830-2, 1994.

ANTHOLOGY SONGS RECORDED
(numbers refer to discography list)

Occitan

A chantar m'er de so qu'ieu non volria 1, 2, 4, 16 (3 stanzas), 22, 32 (with *vida*)

Ab joi et ab joven m'apais 4 (melody Bernart de Ventadorn), 18 (melody borrowed, 4 stanzas)

Ab la dolchor del temps novel 18 (melody borrowed, 5 stanzas)

Aissi cum es genser pascors 22, 26

Amics Bernartz de Ventadorn 22

Anc no mori per amor ni per al 37 (2 stanzas)

Ar em el freg temps vengut 32 (melody borrowed)

Ar me puesc ieu lauzar d'Amor 18 (4 stanzas)

Baron, de mon dan covit 11, 32

Be.m degra de chantar tener 18 (melody Benart de Ventadorn, 4 stanzas)

Bel m'es q'ieu chant e coindei 8 (2 stanzas)

Bel m'es, quan vei chamjar lo senhoratge 18 (melody borrowed, 3 stanzas)

Can vei la lauzeta mover 17 (6 stanzas), 21 (3 stanzas & tornada), 22, 26, 31 (6 stanzas & tornada), 32, 33, 36 (2 stanzas)

Cantarai d'aqestz trobadors 17 (melody Gautier de Coincy, 2 stanzas)

Chansson do.ill mot son plan e prim 14, 33

Deiosta.ls breus iorns e.ls loncs sers 14

Dirai vos senes duptansa 18 (6 stanzas), 22, 25 (8 stanzas)

Eissamen ai gerreiat ab amor 22

En chantan m'aven a membrar 37 (2 stanzas)

Fortz chausa es que tot lo major dan 22, 24 (1 stanza & tornada), 37 (2 stanzas)

Humils, forfaitz, repres e penedens 36 (2 stanzas)

Kalenda maia 12, 32 (with *razo*)

L'autrier jost'una sebissa 22, 26, 32, 36 (2 stanzas)

Lanquand li jorn son lonc en mai 16 (5 stanzas), 20, 22 (with *vida*), 32 (with *vida*), 36 (2 stanzas)

Lo ferm voler q'el cor m'intra 14, 22

Non es meravelha s'eu chan 17 (4 stanzas), 29 (5 stanzas), 37 (2 stanzas)

Pax in nomine Domini! 24 (3 stanzas), 36 (2 stanzas)

Per dan que d'amor mi veigna 37 (2 stanzas)

Pois preyatz me, senhor 17 (3 stanzas), 29

Pos de chantar m'es pres talentz 3 (6 stanzas & tornada), 7 (5 stanzas), 22, 25 (6 stanzas & tornada)

Pus astres no m'es donatz 8 (3 stanzas), 30

Pus tornatz sui em Proensa 18 (1 stanza), 22, 26, 37 (2 stanzas)

Reis glorios, verais lums e clartatz 16, 22, 26, 31, 33, 36 (2 stanzas)

S'ie.us quer conselh, bel'ami'Alamanda 4, 12

Sitot me soi a tart aperceubutz 32

Tant m'abellis l'amoros pessamens 14, 37 (2 stanzas)

Vos que.m semblatz dels corals amadors 4 (melody Gaucelm Faidit)

French

A Dieu commant amouretes 5, 34

A la douçor de la bele seson 10, 23 (4 stanzas & envoi)

Ahi, Amours! come dure departie 13 (3 stanzas), 24 (3 stanzas & envoi), 35 (4 stanzas)

Ausi conme unicorne sui 10, 22, 38

Bele Doette as fenestres se siet 9, 22, 28, 34, 38

Bele Yolanz en ses chambres seoit 8 (4 stanzas), 9, 34, 35

Bele Ysabiauz, pucele bien aprise 1 (9 stanzas), 9

Bien m'ont Amours entrepris 35

Cant voi l'aube dou jor venir 6 (melody R1604a)

Chançon ferai, car talent m'en est pris 10, 22

Chanterai por mon corage 11, 13 (4 stanzas), 20, 24 (3 stanzas)

De moi dolereus vos chant 11

Hé, Dieus, quant verrai 5

J'aloie l'autrier errant 7 (5 stanzas)

Je chevauchoie l'autrier 38

Jherusalem grant damage me fais 6

L'on dit qu'amors est dolce chose 6

La douce pensee 27

Lasse, pour quoi refusai 2, 6, 11

Les oxelés de mon païx 5 (2 stanzas), 10, 35 (2 stanzas)

Li nouviaz tanz et mais et violete 23 (4 stanzas), 24 (3 stanzas)

Por coi me bait mes maris? 1, 6, 28

Retrowange novelle 11

Volez vous que je vous chant 10, 22

INDEX OF FIRST LINES

GENERAL INDEX

N.B. Boldface type indicates pages where definitions or other basic data are given.

stanza, 9, 11-12, 15, 16, **17** *et passim; see also*
    heterometric, isometric
subfinal, **19**, 26 *et passim*
syllabic style, 8, 9, 10, **20**, 23 *et passim*
syllable, 8, 17
syntax, 12, 17, 20, 22, 24, 26; melodic, 19 *et passim*

tenor (polyphonic voice), 234
tenor (reciting tone), **19**, 20 *et passim*
tenso, 59, 76, 81, 151, 164, 227
tenson, 227, 322
tessitura, 7, **22**, 26 *et passim*
tetrachord, 20, 23 *et passim*
Thèbes, Roman de, 277
Thibaut de Blaison, 197, 283
Thibaut de Champagne, 3, 10, 227, 256, 283, 300, 305,
    329, 355
third chain, 10, **20**, 26 *et passim; see also* intervallic
    chains
through-composed, *see* oda continua
tonality, 9, 10, 19, 22 *et passim*
tones, hierarchy of, 19; *see also* psalm tone, reciting tone
tornada, 2, **18** *et passim*
Toulouse, 3, 143, 165; counts of, 36, 59, 95, 164
transcription, 7, 8
transformation, *see* melodic transformation
transposition, *see* melodic transposition
Tristan, 61, 70, 230, 306
tritone, 76

trobairitz, 2, 81, 95, 96, 210
trobar clus, **3**, 42, 70, 76, 80, 87
trobar leu, **3**, 59, 60, 70, 80, 96, 118, 135
trobar ric, **3**, 87, 88
Troie, Roman de, 277

Uc de Baux, 165
Uc de Saint Circ, 151
Uc IX of Lusignan, 127

variants, melodic, 7, 8, 9, 10, 24, 25, 26 *et passim*;
    textual, 16
Vaugon Guion, 319
vers, **35**, 43, 54, 59, 76, 169; vers entiers, 76
verse, 8, 15, **17** *et passim; see also* decasyllabic,
    octosyllabic
versification, 17
versus, 19, **35**
vida, 3, 59, 76, 80, 87, 95, 100, 102, 108, 126, 135, 151,
    162
Villon, François, 95
Violette, Roman de la, 295
virelai, 11
voice, 12, 14

William IX, *see* Guilhem IX
William X, 36, 42, 44, 54
women's songs, *see* chanson de femme

INDEX OF GENRES REPRESENTED IN THE ANTHOLOGY

Occitan

alba, 83
canso, 36, 56, 57, 62, 64, 66, 68, 78, 81, 89, 91, 93, 96,
    98, 100, 110, 112, 115, 120, 122, 124, 130, 132, 136,
    137, 145, 147, 149, 156, 160, 162, 166, 176
coblas, 164
crusade song, 51
descort, 155
devinaill, 38
estampida, 156
gap, 112
no-sai-que-s'es, 74
pastorela, 49
planh, 39, 106, 128
razo, 87, 152, 156
retroencha, 174
sestina, 93
sirventes, 47, 77, 103, 104, 141, 167
sirventes-canso, 45, 114
tenso, 61, 71, 84, 139, 152
vers, 37, 38, 39, 40, 47, 57, 72, 78, 137, 141, 172, 173
vida, 54

French

Arthurian lai, 231, 233
aube, 191, 193, 194
ballette, 181, 182, 208, 340
chanson avec des refrains, 298, 311, 327
chanson courtoise, 336, 355
chanson d'amour, 223, 225, 239, 242, 244, 250, 252, 254,
    258, 260, 262, 275, 282, 296, 303, 307, 309, 311,
    317, 325, 327, 334, 338, 350
chanson de croisade, 214, 242, 250, 290
chanson de femme, 181, 182, 193, 194, 211, 213, 214,
    290, 296
chanson de jongleur, 342
chanson de rencontre, 207, 208, 348
chanson de toile, 185 (2), 186, 188, 286
chanson pieuse, 182, 219, 220, 353, 356
débat, 228, 246
descort, 278, 344
jeu-parti, 301, 330
lai, 343
motet, 235, 236, 237